Teach Yourself VISUALLY™

Macromedia® Web Collection

Flash™ • Dreamweaver® • Fireworks®

by Sherry Willard Kinkoph, Mike Wooldridge, and Sue Plumley
Compiled by Michael Toot

Visual

From

maranGraphics®

&

Hungry Minds™

Best-Selling Books • Digital Downloads • e-Books • Answer Networks • e-Newsletters
Branded Web Sites • e-Learning
New York, NY • Cleveland, OH • Indianapolis, IN

Teach Yourself VISUALLY™ Macromedia Web Collection

Published by
Hungry Minds, Inc.
909 Third Avenue
New York, NY 10022

maranGraphics, Inc.
5755 Coopers Avenue
Mississauga, Ontario, Canada
L4Z 1R9

Library of Congress Control Number: 2001093693

ISBN: 0-7645-3648-6 Printed in the United States of America

10 9 8 7 6 5 4 3 2 1

1K/RR/QZ/QR/IN

Distributed in the United States by Hungry Minds, Inc.

Distributed by CDG Books Canada Inc. for Canada; by Transworld Publishers Limited in the United Kingdom; by IDG Norge Books for Norway; by IDG Sweden Books for Sweden; by IDG Books Australia Publishing Corporation Pty. Ltd. for Australia and New Zealand; by TransQuest Publishers Pte Ltd. for Singapore, Malaysia, Thailand, Indonesia, and Hong Kong; by Gotop Information Inc. for Taiwan; by ICG Muse, Inc. for Japan; by Intersoft for South Africa; by Eyrolles for France; by International Thomson Publishing for Germany, Austria and Switzerland; by Distribuidora Cuspide for Argentina; by LR International for Brazil; by Galileo Libros for Chile; by Ediciones ZETA S.C.R. Ltda. for Peru; by WS Computer Publishing Corporation, Inc., for the Philippines; by Contemporanea de Ediciones for Venezuela; by Express Computer Distributors for the Caribbean and West Indies; by Micronesia Media Distributor, Inc. for Micronesia; by Chips Computadoras S.A. de C.V. for Mexico; by Editorial Norma de Panama S.A. for Panama; by American Bookshops for Finland.

For corporate orders, please call maranGraphics at 800-469-6616 or

fax 905-890-9434.

For general information on Hungry Minds' products and services, please contact our Customer Care Department within the U.S. at 800-762-2974, outside the U.S. at 317-572-3993, or fax 317-572-4002.

For sales inquiries and reseller information, including discounts, premium and bulk quantity sales, and foreign-language translations, please contact our Customer Care Department at 800-434-3422, fax 317-572-4002, or write to Hungry Minds, Inc., Attn: Customer Care Department, 10475 Crosspoint Boulevard, Indianapolis, IN 46256.

For information on licensing foreign or domestic rights, please contact our Sub-Rights Customer Care Department at 212-884-5000.

For information on using Hungry Minds' products and services in the classroom or for ordering examination copies, please contact our Educational Sales Department at 800-434-2086, or fax 317-572-4005.

For press review copies, author interviews, or other publicity information, please contact our Public Relations department at 317-572-3168, or fax 317-572-4168.

For authorization to photocopy items for corporate, personal, or educational use, please contact Copyright Clearance Center, 222 Rosewood Drive, Danvers, MA 01923, or fax 978-750-4470.

Screen shots displayed in this book are based on pre-released software and are subject to change.

Trademark Acknowledgments

Permissions

maranGraphics: Certain text and illustrations by maranGraphics, Inc., used with maranGraphics' permission.

U.S. Corporate Sales

Contact maranGraphics
at (800) 469-6616 or
Fax (905) 890-9434.

U.S. Trade Sales

Contact Hungry Minds
at (800) 434-3422 or
fax (317) 572-4002.

Some comments from our readers...

"I have to praise you and your company on the fine products you turn out. I have twelve of the *Teach Yourself VISUALLY* and *Simplified* books in my house. They were instrumental in helping me pass a difficult computer course. Thank you for creating books that are easy to follow."

–Gordon Justin (Brielle, NJ)

"I commend your efforts and your success. I teach in an outreach program for the Dr. Eugene Clark Library in Lockhart, TX. Your *Teach Yourself VISUALLY* books are incredible and I use them in my computer classes. All my students love them!"

–Michele Schalin (Lockhart, TX)

"Thank you so much for helping people like me learn about computers. The Maran family is just what the doctor ordered. Thank you, thank you, thank you."

–Carol Moten (New Kensington, PA)

"I would like to take this time to compliment maranGraphics on creating such great books. Thank you for making it clear. Keep up the good work."

–Kirk Santoro (Burbank, CA)

"I write to extend my thanks and appreciation for your books. They are clear, easy to follow, and straight to the point. Keep up the good work!

–Seward Kollie (Dakar, Senegal)

"What fantastic teaching books you have produced! Congratulations to you and your staff. You deserve the Nobel prize in Education in the Software category. Thanks for helping me to understand computers."

–Bruno Tonon (Melbourne, Australia)

"Over time, I have bought a number of your 'Read Less, Learn More' books. For me, they are THE way to learn anything easily.

–José A. Mazón (Cuba, NY)

"I was introduced to maranGraphics about four years ago and YOU ARE THE GREATEST THING THAT EVER HAPPENED TO INTRODUCTORY COMPUTER BOOKS!"

–Glenn Nettleton (Huntsville, AL)

"Compliments To The Chef!! Your books are extraordinary! Or, simply put, Extra-Ordinary, meaning way above the rest! THANK YOU THANK YOU THANK YOU! for creating these.

–Christine J. Manfrin (Castle Rock, CO)

"I'm a grandma who was pushed by an 11-year-old grandson to join the computer age. I found myself hopelessly confused and frustrated until I discovered the Visual series. I'm no expert by any means now, but I'm a lot further along than I would have been otherwise. Thank you!"

–Carol Louthain (Logansport, IN)

"Thank you, thank you, thank you....for making it so easy for me to break into this high-tech world. I now own four of your books. I recommend them to anyone who is a beginner like myself. Now....if you could just do one for programming VCR's, it would make my day!"

–Gay O'Donnell (Calgary, Alberta, Canada)

"You're marvelous! I am greatly in your debt."

–Patrick Baird (Lacey, WA)

maranGraphics is a family-run business located near Toronto, Canada.

At **maranGraphics**, we believe in producing great computer books — one book at a time.

maranGraphics has been producing high-technology products for over 25 years, which enables us to offer the computer book community a unique communication process.

Our computer books use an integrated communication process, which is very different from the approach used in other computer books. Each spread is, in essence, a flow chart — the text and screen shots are totally incorporated into the layout of the spread. Introductory text and helpful tips complete the learning experience.

maranGraphics' approach encourages the left and right sides of the brain to work together — resulting in faster orientation and greater memory retention.

Above all, we are very proud of the handcrafted nature of our books. Our carefully-chosen writers are experts in their fields, and spend countless hours researching and organizing the content for each topic. Our artists rebuild every screen shot to provide the best clarity possible, making our screen shots the most precise and easiest to read in the industry. We strive for perfection, and believe that the time spent handcrafting each element results in the best computer books money can buy.

Thank you for purchasing this book. We hope you enjoy it!

Sincerely,

Robert Maran
President
maranGraphics
Rob@maran.com
www.maran.com
www.hungryminds.com/visual

CREDITS

Authors
Sherry Willard Kinkoph, Mike Wooldridge, Sue Plumley
Compiling Editor
Michael Toot
Acquisitions Editor
Jennifer Dorsey
Product Development Supervisor
Lindsay Sandman
Copy Editor
Timothy Borek
Technical Editors
Kyle Bowen, Yolanda Burrell, Paul Vachier
Editorial Manager
Rev Mengle
Media Development Manager
Laura Carpenter
Editorial Assistant
Amanda Foxworth

Book Design
maranGraphics®
Production Coordinator
Ryan Steffen
Layout
LeAndra Johnson, Kristin Pickett, Kathie Schutte
Illustrators
Ronda David-Burroughs, David E. Gregory, Mark Harris, Sean Johannesen, Russ Marini, Suzana G. Miokovic, Jill A. Proll, Steven Schaerer, Dave Thronhill, Natalie Tweedie
Proofreaders
John Bitter, Joel K. Draper
Indexer:
Sherry Massey
Special Help
Macromedia, Inc., Jennifer Amaral, Martine Edwards, Maridee Ennis, Leslie Kersey, Treena Lees, Dana Rhodes Lesh, Judy Maran, Nancee Reeves, Maureen Spears, Jade L. Williams

ACKNOWLEDGMENTS

General and Administrative

Hungry Minds, Inc.: John Kilcullen, CEO; Bill Barry, President and COO; John Ball, Executive VP, Operations & Administration; John Harris, Executive VP and CFO

Hungry Minds Technology Publishing Group: Richard Swadley, Senior Vice President and Publisher; Mary Bednarek, Vice President and Publisher, Networking; Walter R. Bruce III, Vice President and Publisher; Joseph Wikert, Vice President and Publisher, Web Development Group; Mary C. Corder, Editorial Director, Dummies Technology; Andy Cummings, Publishing Director, Dummies Technology; Barry Pruett, Publishing Director, Visual/Graphic Design

Hungry Minds Manufacturing: Ivor Parker, Vice President, Manufacturing

Hungry Minds Marketing: John Helmus, Assistant Vice President, Director of Marketing

Hungry Minds Production for Branded Press: Debbie Stailey, Production Director

Hungry Minds Sales: Michael Violano, Vice President, International Sales and Sub Rights

The publisher would like to give special thanks to Patrick J. McGovern, without whom this book would not have been possible.

ABOUT THE AUTHORS

Michael Toot

Michael Toot is an author and software program manager in the Seattle area. He is an MCSE and MCP+I and has been involved with Microsoft operating systems since 1992. He has written a book on Windows 2000 Server and enjoys learning new programs and operating systems, even those not from Microsoft. When not working or writing books, he is reading, sailing, writing movie reviews, fiction, and nonfiction, and conducting adventures in home renovation and repair on his ninety-three year old home.

Sherry Willard Kinkoph

Sherry Willard Kinkoph has written more than 40 books over the past nine years, covering a variety of computer topics ranging from software to hardware, from Microsoft Office programs to the Internet. Sherry's ongoing quest is to help users of all levels master the ever-changing computer technologies. No matter how many times they — the software giants and hardware conglomerates — throw out a new version or upgrade, Sherry vows to be there to make sense of it all and help computer users get the most out of their machines.

Mike Wooldridge

Mike Wooldridge is a technology writer and Web designer in the San Francisco Bay Area. He has a day job at Namesecure, which registers domain names. He is the author of several other books in the Visual series, including *Teach Yourself VISUALLY Photoshop 6*. For more information about using Dreamweaver, visit his site, www.mediacosm.com

Sue Plumley

Sue Plumley has a B.A. in education and taught in public school before starting her own business, Humble Opinions, in 1988. Humble Opinions is a firm that specializes in computer consulting and training. In the years since she started Humble Opinions, Sue has trained staff and employees of local companies, large corporations, and federal agencies in the use of various applications, including FrontPage and Fireworks. She also offers support for the use of different products. In addition, Sue has taught Internet classes at the College of West Virginia and Glenville College. Finally, Sue has written and contributed to over seventy books about computer software for various publishers, including Hungry Minds (formerly IDG Books), John Wiley and Sons, Que Corporation, and DDC.

TABLE OF CONTENTS

USING FLASH

1) Flash Basics

Tour the Flash Window 4
Open a Flash File 6
Start a New Flash File 7
Save a Flash File 8
Close a Flash File 9

2) Drawing and Painting Objects

Draw Line Segments .10
Format Line Segments 12
Edit Line Segments .14
Edit Fills 16
Draw Curves with the Pen Tool 18
Smooth or Straighten Line Segments 20
Draw Oval and Rectangle Shapes 22
Fill Objects with the Paint Bucket Tool 24

3) Enhancing and Editing Objects

Select Objects 26
Move and Copy Objects 30
Rotate and Flip Objects 32
Group and Ungroup Objects 34
Work with Stacked Objects 36
Align Objects 38

4) Creating Text Effects

Add Text with the Text Tool 40
Format Text 42
Change Text Alignment 44

5) Working with Layers

Add and Delete Layers 46
Set Layer Properties 48
Change the Layer Stacking Order 50

6) Working with Symbols and Instances

Create Symbols 52
Insert a Symbol Instance 54
Modify a Symbol Instance 56
Edit Symbols 58
Import Graphics 60

7) Animation Techniques

Set Movie Dimensions and Speed 62
Add Regular Frames or Keyframes 64
Move and Copy Frames 68
Delete Frames 70
Create Frame-by-Frame Animation 72
Modify Frame Properties 76
Preview a Flash Animation 77

8) Animating with Tweening Effects

Create a Motion Tween 78
Set Tween Speed 82
Create a Shape Tween 84

9) Creating Interactive Buttons

Create a Button Symbol 88
Create an Animated Button 92
Assign Button Actions 96

10) Adding Sounds

Import a Sound File .100
Add a Sound Layer .102
Assign Sounds to Frames 104
Assign Sounds to Buttons 106
Assign Streaming Sounds 108

11) Adding Flash Actions

Add Actions to Frames 110
Assign Stop and Play Actions 112
Assign Stop and Play Actions 114
Load a New Movie .116

12) Distributing Flash Movies

Play a Flash Movie in Flash 118
Play a Flash Movie in a Browser 120
Test Movie Bandwidth 122
Publish a Movie 126
Publish a Movie in HTML Format 128

TABLE OF CONTENTS

USING DREAMWEAVER

13) Dreamweaver Basics

Start Dreamweaver on a PC 134
Start Dreamweaver on a Macintosh 135
Show or Hide a Panel 136
Add Objects with the Objects Panel 137
Correct Errors with the History Panel 138
Exit Dreamweaver 139

14) Setting Up Your Web Site

Set Up a Local Site 140
Open a Web Page 142
Create a New Web Page 144
Add a Web Page Title 145
Save a Web Page 146

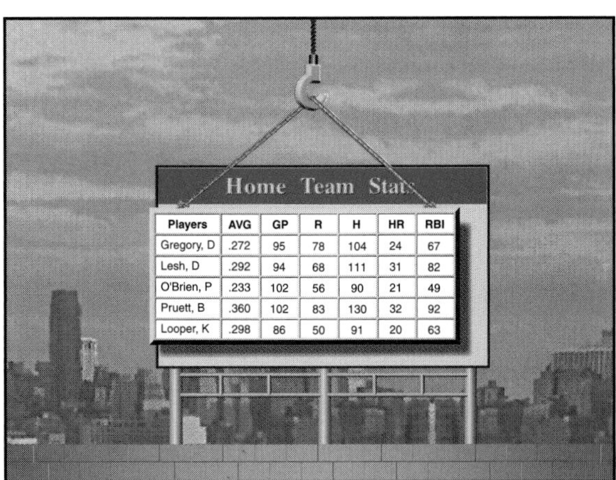

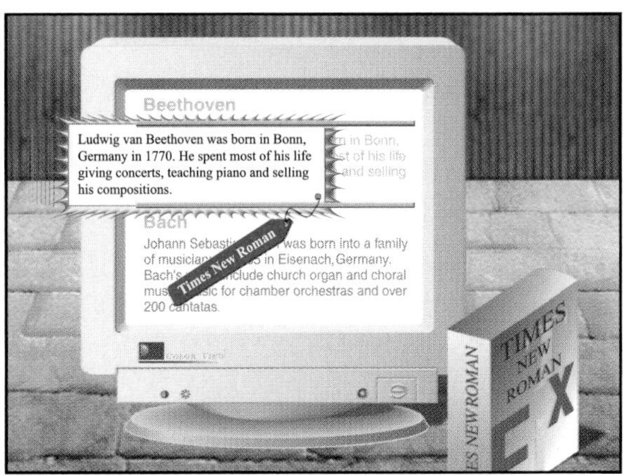

15) Working with Web Page Text

Explore Structural Tags 148
Explore Text-Formatting Tags 149
View and Edit the Source Code 150
Create and align Paragraphs 152
Create a New Heading 154
Create Line Breaks 156
Indent Paragraphs 157
Change Font style 158
Create Bold or Italic Text 160

16) Working with Images and Graphics

Insert an Image into a Web Page 162
Wrap Text Around an Image 164
Change the Size of an Image 166
Add a Background Image 168
Insert Multimedia 170

17) Creating Hyperlinks

Create Hyperlinks to Other Pages on Your Web Site 172

Create Hyperlinks to Another Web Site 174

Create Image Hyperlinks 176

Create Hyperlinks to Content on the Same Web Page 178

Create Hyperlinks to Other Files 180

18) Creating Tables

Insert a Table into Your Web Page 182

Insert Content into a Table 184

Change the Table Background 186

Insert or Delete a Row or Column 188

Create a Layout Table 190

Rearrange a Layout Table 192

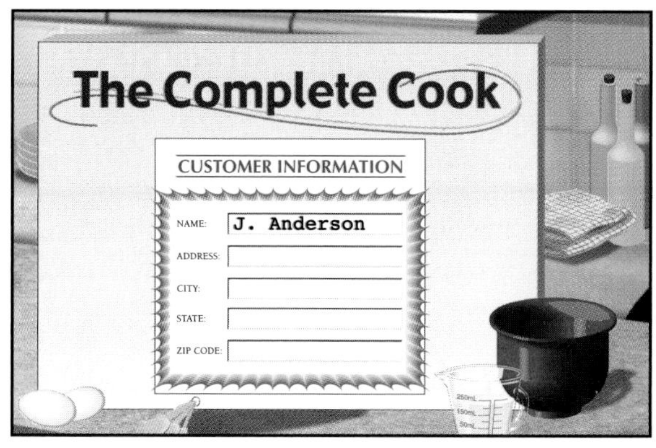

19) Working with Forms

Set Up a Form 194

Add a Text Field to a Form 195

Add Check Boxes to a Form 196

Add Radio Buttons to a Form 198

Add a Menu to a Form 200

Add a List to a Form 202

Validate a Form 204

20) Designing with Frames

Divide a Page into Frames 206

Insert a Predefined Frameset 207

Name a Frame 208

Delete a Frame 209

Add Content to a Frame 210

Change Frame Dimensions 212

Hyperlink to a Frame 214

Save a Framed Site .216

TABLE OF CONTENTS

21) Using Library Items and Templates

Create a Library Item 218

Insert a Library Item 220

Edit a Library Item and Update Your Web Site 222

Create a Template 224

Edit a Template and Update Your Web Site 226

22) Implementing Style Sheets and Layers

Create a New HTML Style 228

Apply HTML Styles .229

Customize an HTML Tag 230

Create a Class 232

Apply a Class 234

Edit a Style Sheet Class 236

Create a Layer 238

Resize and Reposition Layers 240

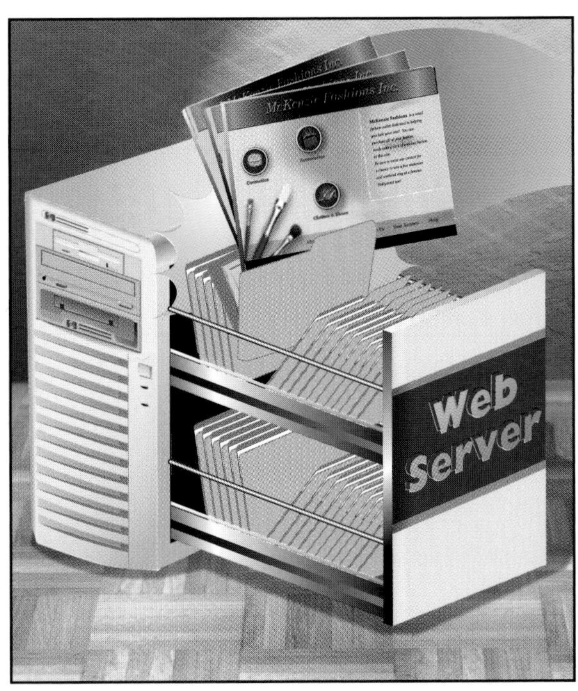

23) Implementing Timelines

Create a Straight-Line Animation 242

Create an Animation by Dragging a Path 244

Create a Flashing Animation 246

Change Animation Speed 248

24) Publishing a Web Site

Set Up a Remote Site 250

Connect to a Remote Site 252

Upload Files 254

Download Files 256

USING FIREWORKS

25) Fireworks Basics

Start Fireworks 260
View Previews 261
Create a New Document 262
Modify Canvas Size .264
Change Canvas Color 266
Save a Document 268
Open an Existing Document 270
Close a Document .272
Undo and Redo a Change 273

26) Working with Text

Enter and Edit Text 274
Select Text and Change the Font Size 276
Change the Font Style 278
Change Text Color and Text Attributes 280
Change Text Orientation and Alignment 282
Move or Copy Text .284
Import Text 286

27) Working with Objects

Draw Lines and Curves 288
Edit a Path 292
Draw a Shape 294
Apply a Fill 296
Work with Color 298
Arrange Objects 302
Group Objects 304
Import an Object 306

28) Working with Images

Modify an Image 308
Crop an Image 312
Select and Move Pixels 314
Erase Pixels 318
Adjust Brightness and Contrast 320
Blur an Image 322
Sharpen an Image .324

TABLE OF CONTENTS

29) Applying Effects

Bevel and Emboss Edges 326

Blur and Sharpen Edges 328

Apply a Shadow 330

Apply a Glow 332

Set Default Effects 334

Save and Use Styles 336

Create Masks 338

Edit Masks 340

30) Creating Buttons and Navigation Bars

Create a Button 342

Convert an Object to a Button 344

Copy and Edit a Button 346

Assign a URL to a Button 348

Import and Update a Button 352

Create a Navigation Bar 354

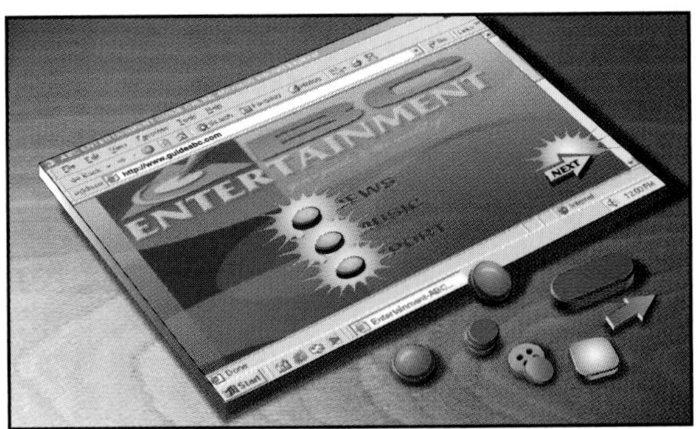

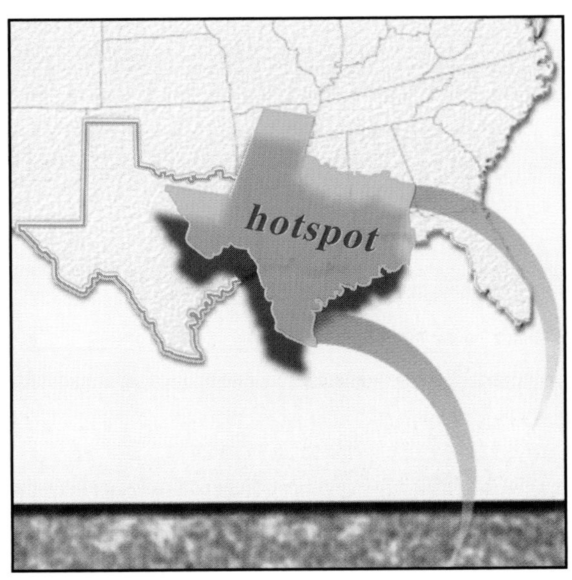

31) Creating Hotspots and Image Maps

Create or Insert a Hotspot 358

Edit Hotspots 360

Create an Image Map 364

32) Slicing Images

Using the Slice Tools 366

Hide or Show a Slice 370

Name a Slice 371

Create a Text Slice 372

Assign a URL Link to an Image Slice 374

Update and Export a Slice 376

33) Creating Rollovers

Create a Simple Rollover 378
Assign a Behavior 380
Swap an Image 382

34) Optimizing Graphics

Select a Graphic File Format 386
Optimize PNGs and GIFs 388
Optimize JPEGs 392

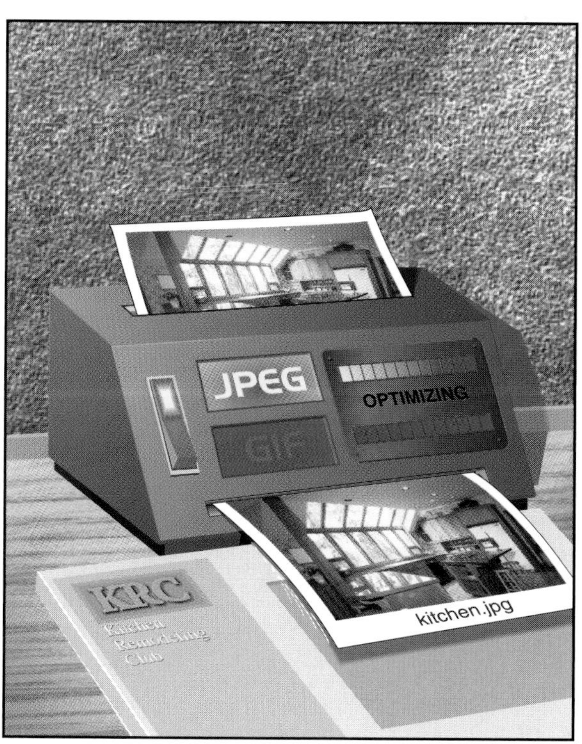

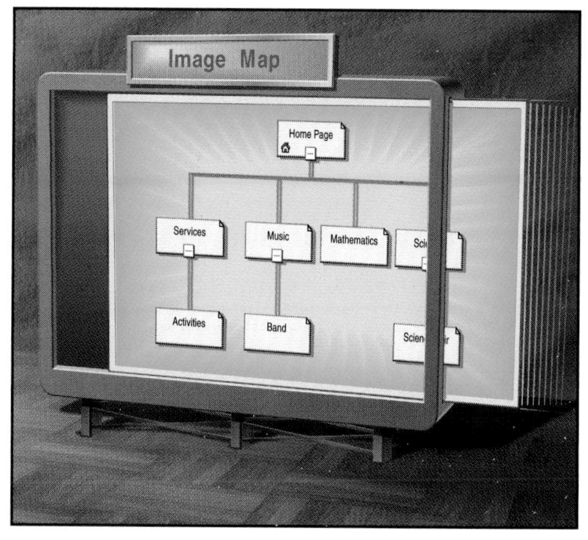

35) Exporting Objects and Slices

Export an Area or an Entire Graphic Image . . .394
Export a Slice 396
Export Layers or Frames 398
Export an Image Map 400

36) Integrating Graphics with HTML Editors

Copy and Paste HTML 402
Copy HTML for Sliced Objects 406
Copy JavaScript 408

Index 410

HOW
TO GET
HELP
Flash
Scene 1

PART 1

Using Flash

1 Flash Basics
Pages 4-9

2 Drawing and Painting Objects
Pages 10-25

3 Enhancing and Editing Objects
Pages 26-39

4 Creating Text Effects
Pages 40-45

5 Working with Layers
Pages 46-51

6 Working with Symbols and Instances
Pages 52-61

7 Animation Techniques
Pages 62-77

8 Animating with Tweening Effects
Pages 78-87

9 Creating Interactive Buttons
Pages 88-99

10 Adding Sounds
Pages 100-109

11 Ading Flash Actions
Pages 110-117

12 Distributing Flash Movies
Pages 118-131

TOUR THE FLASH WINDOW

Macromedia Flash is used to create Web page animations that you can deploy using Dreamweaver. The Flash program window has several components for working with graphics and movies. Take time to familiarize yourself with the on-screen elements.

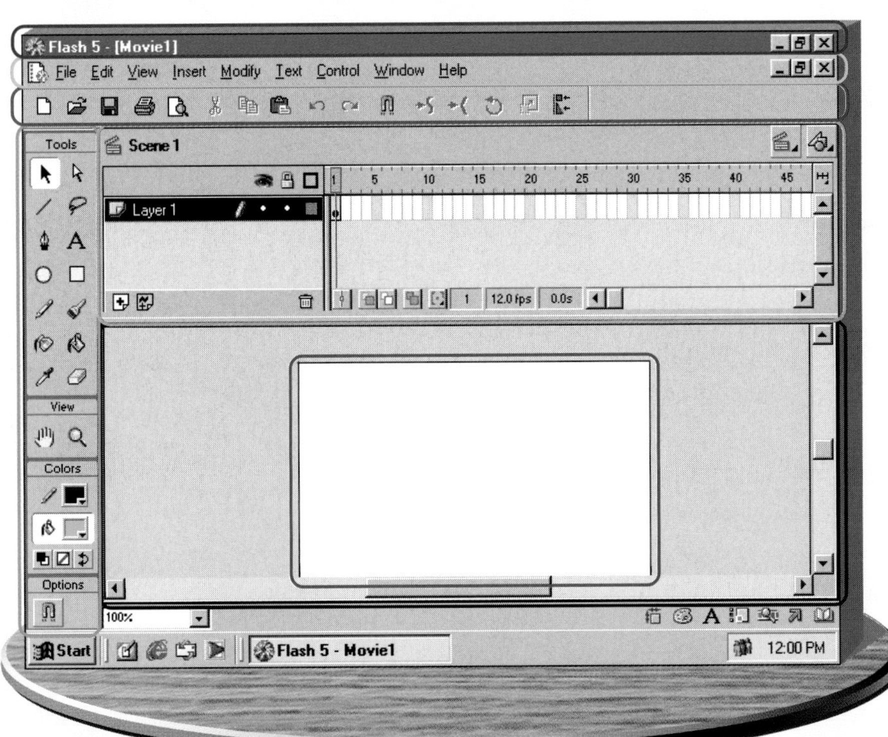

Title Bar

Displays the name of the open file.

Menu Bar

Displays Flash menus which, when clicked, reveal commands.

Main Toolbar

The Main, or Standard, toolbar contains shortcut buttons for common commands, such as creating a new file.

Timeline

Contains all the frames, layers, and scenes that make up a movie.

Drawing Toolbar

Contains the basic tools needed to create vector graphics.

Stage or Movie Area

The area where a movie or graphic displays. This area is also called the *Flash Editor*.

Work Area

The area surrounding the Stage. Anything placed on the work area does not appear in the movie.

NAVIGATE WITH THE MOUSE

Use the mouse to move around the Flash window, select tools and activate menus. To activate a button or menu, move the mouse pointer over the item and click it.

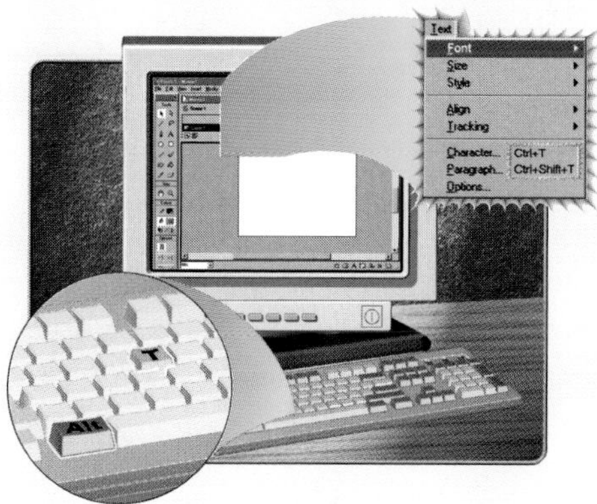

NAVIGATE WITH THE KEYBOARD

You can also use the keyboard to select commands. For example, Windows users can display the Text menu by pressing and holding the Alt key and then pressing the letter T. To activate a command, press the corresponding underlined character. You can find keyboard shortcut commands scattered throughout the menus.

NAVIGATE COMPONENT WINDOWS

Many of the Flash features open into separate mini-windows onscreen, like the Library window shown here. To close an open feature, simply click the feature's ☒ button. Mac users can click the Mac Close box (□).

OPEN A FLASH FILE

Flash files are called *documents* or *movies*. When you save a file, you can open it and work on it again. Use the Open dialog box to access Flash files you have saved.

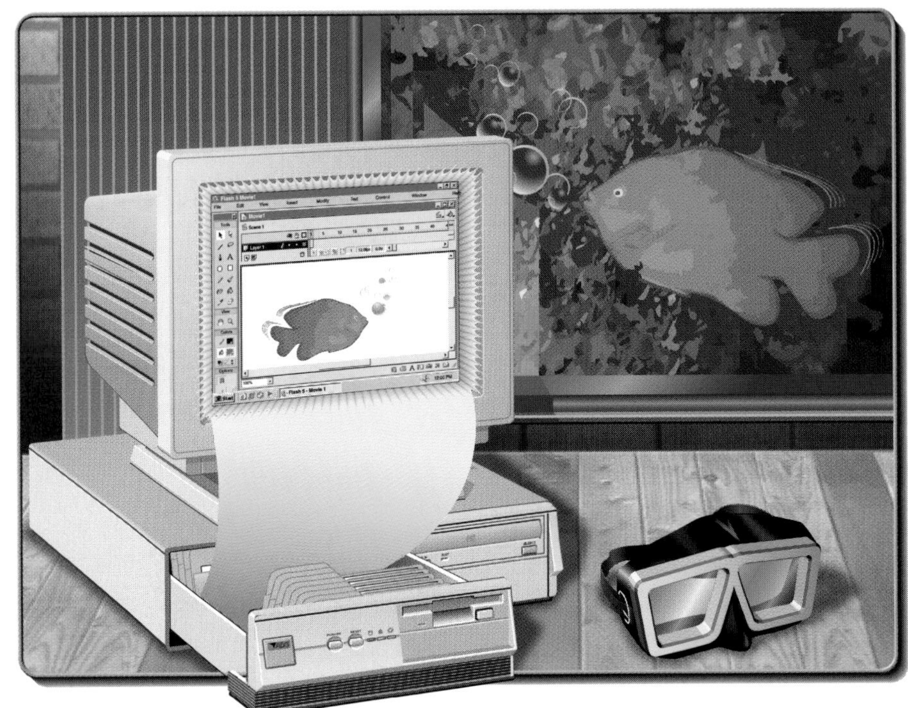

OPEN A FLASH FILE

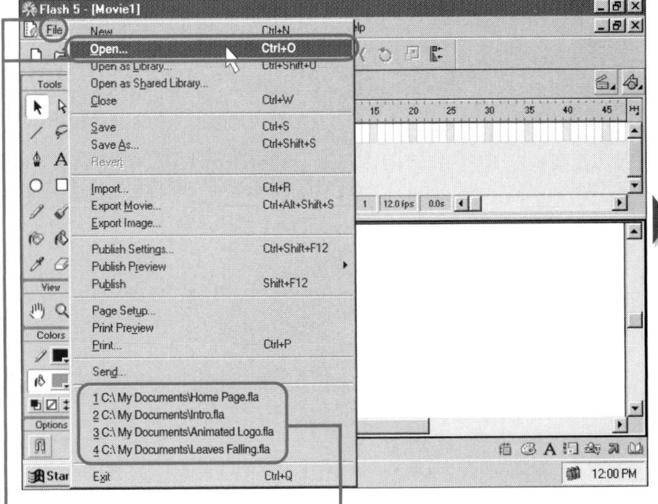

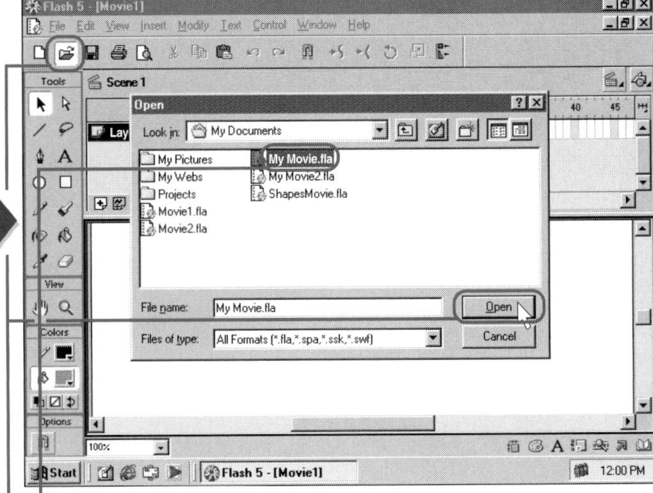

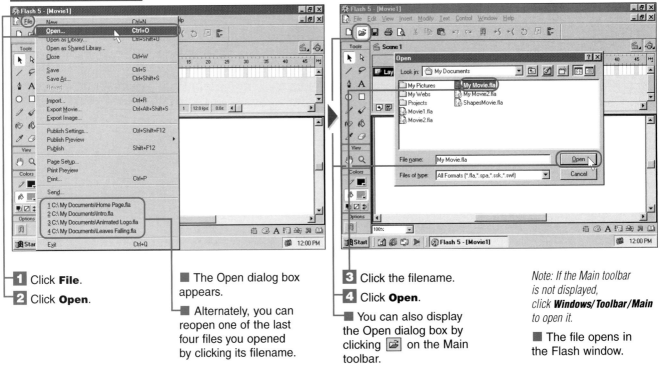

1 Click **File**.

2 Click **Open**.

■ The Open dialog box appears.

■ Alternately, you can reopen one of the last four files you opened by clicking its filename.

3 Click the filename.

4 Click **Open**.

■ You can also display the Open dialog box by clicking [open icon] on the Main toolbar.

Note: If the Main toolbar is not displayed, click ***Windows/Toolbar/Main*** *to open it.*

■ The file opens in the Flash window.

START A NEW FLASH FILE

You can start a new Flash file at any time, even if you are currently working on another file.

START A NEW FLASH FILE

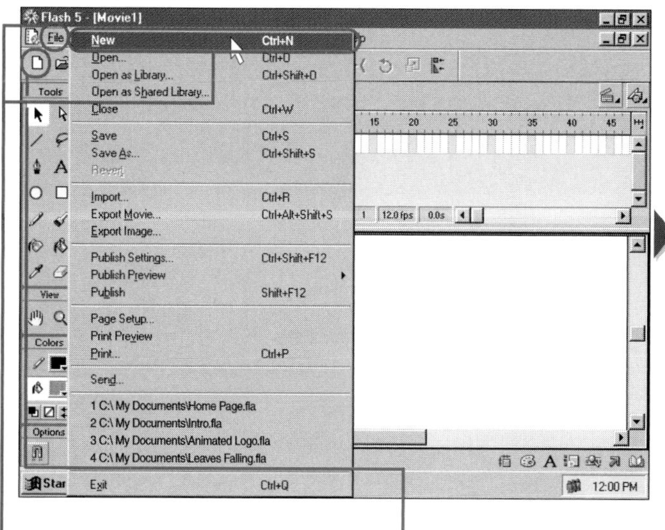

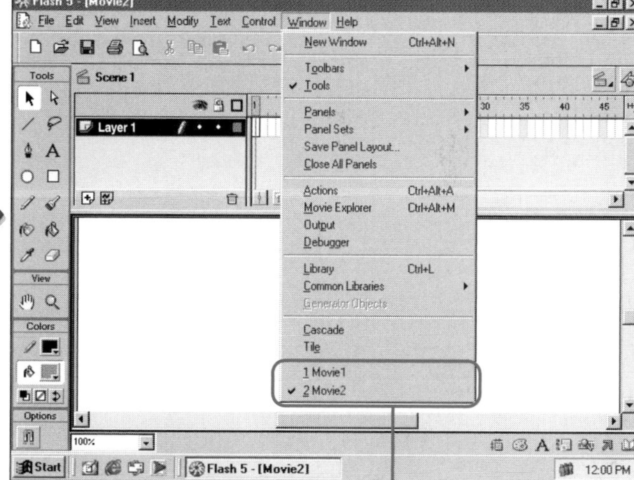

1. Click **File**.
2. Click **New**.

■ Alternately, you can open a new file by clicking 🗋.

■ A blank document appears in the Flash window.

■ You can have several Flash files open and switch between them via the Window menu.

SAVE A FLASH FILE

As you create movies in Flash, you need to save them in order to work on them again, or to use them in a Dreamweaver Web site. FLA is the default file format for Flash movies.

Saving graphics, called symbols, to the Flash Library works a bit differently than saving a file. See Chapter 6 for more information about symbols.

SAVE A FLASH FILE

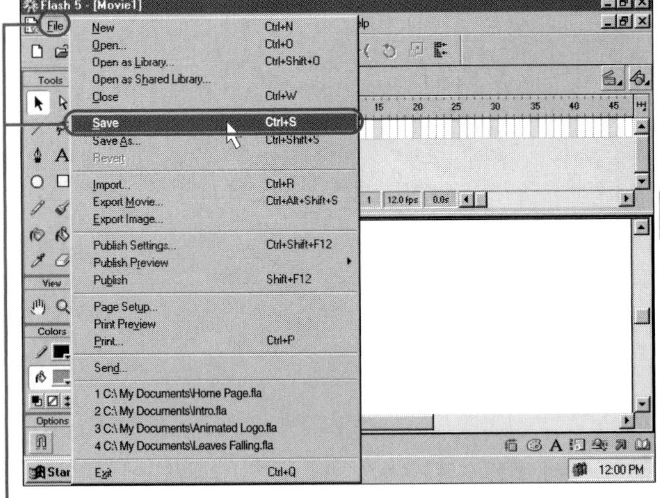

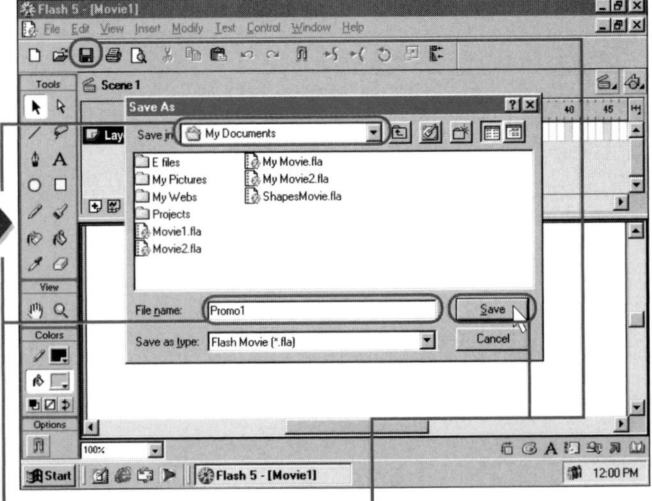

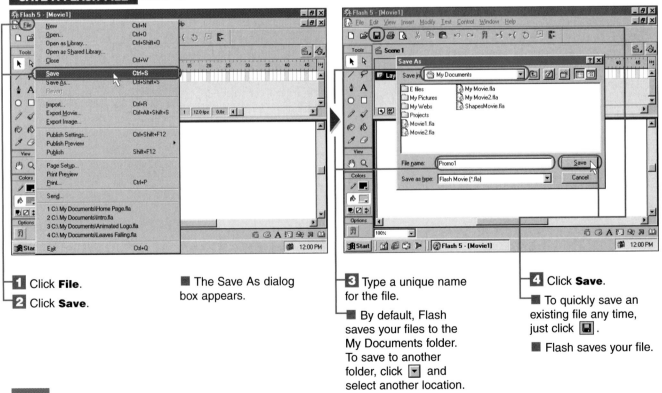

1 Click **File**.

2 Click **Save**.

■ The Save As dialog box appears.

3 Type a unique name for the file.

■ By default, Flash saves your files to the My Documents folder. To save to another folder, click ▾ and select another location.

4 Click **Save**.

■ To quickly save an existing file any time, just click 💾.

■ Flash saves your file.

CLOSE A FLASH FILE

You can close Flash files that you are no longer using to free up memory on your computer. Be sure to save your changes before closing a file.

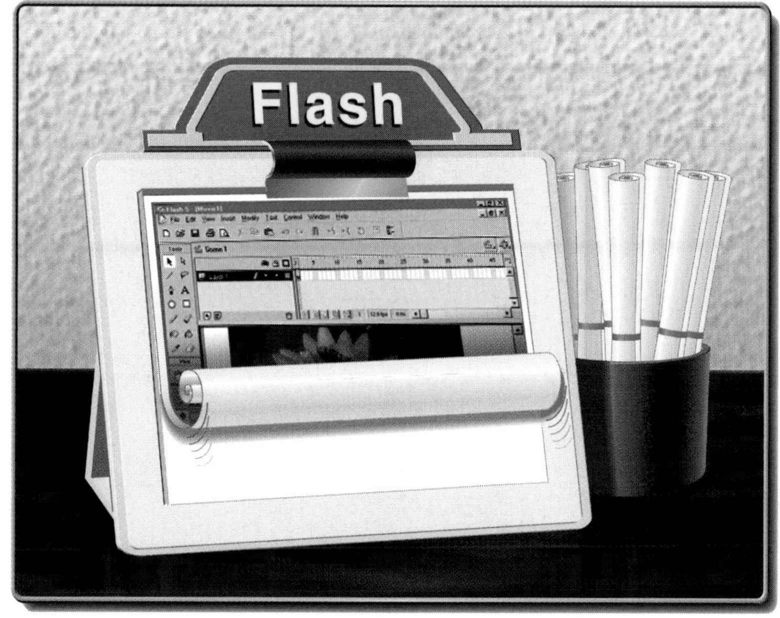

CLOSE A FLASH FILE

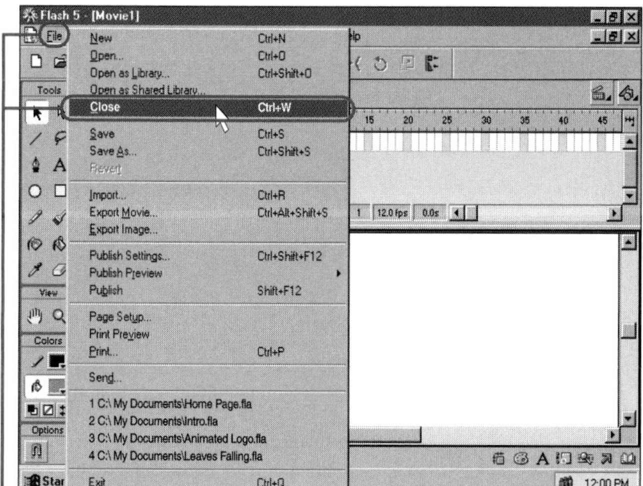

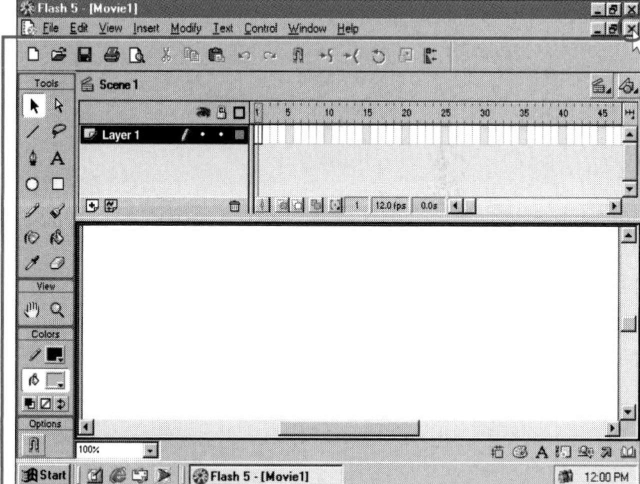

USE THE MENU BAR

1 Save your file (see the Section "Save a Flash File").

2 Click **File**.

3 Click **Close**.

■ Flash closes the file you were working on, but the program window remains open.

Note: If you have not saved your changes, Flash prompts you to do so before closing a file.

USE THE CLOSE BUTTON

1 Save your file (see the Section "Save a Flash File").

2 Click ☒.

Note: Clicking the program window's ☒ button closes the Flash application entirely and might result in lost files.

Note: If you have not saved your changes, Flash prompts you to do so before closing a file.

DRAW LINE SEGMENTS

You can draw all sorts of objects with lines, also called *strokes* in Flash. The easiest way to draw straight lines in Flash is to use the Line tool. To draw a freeform line, use the Pencil tool.

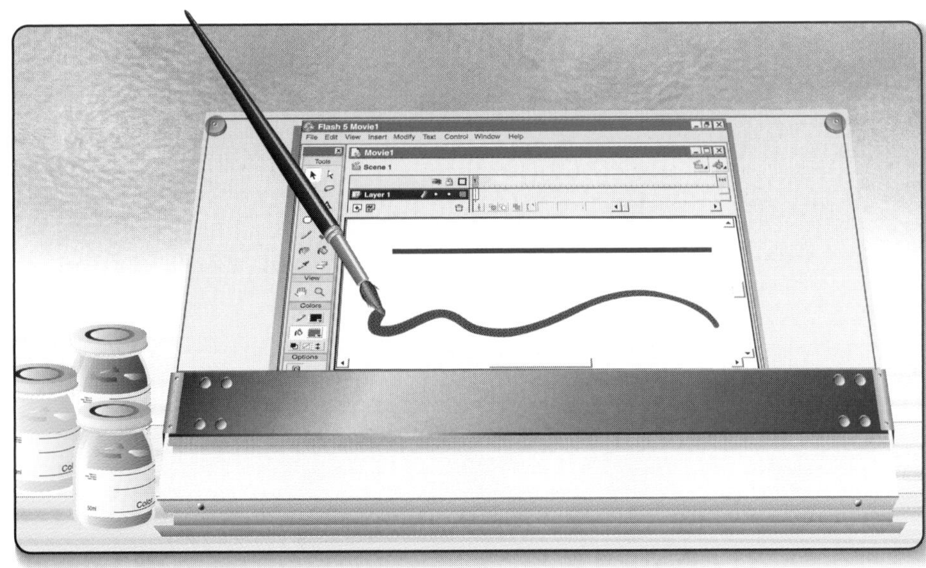

DRAW LINE SEGMENTS

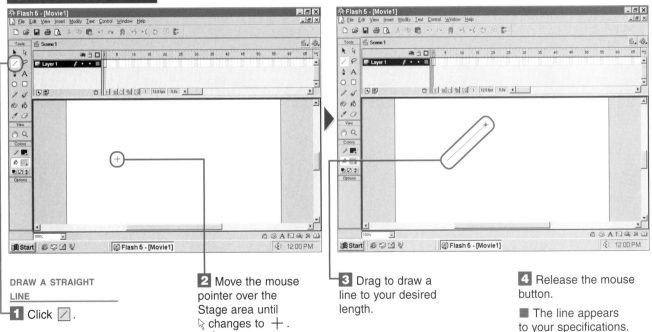

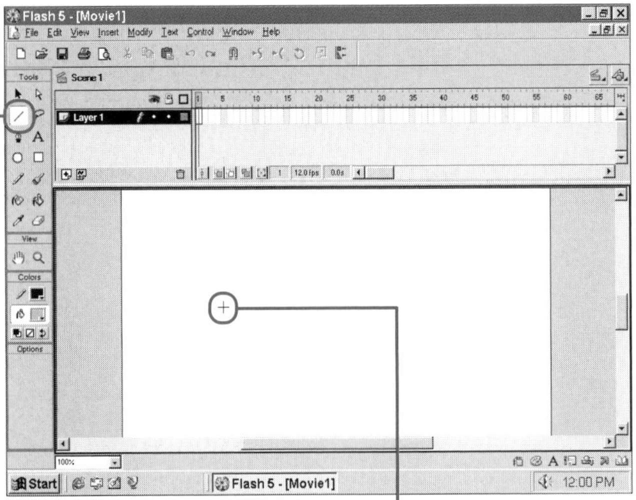

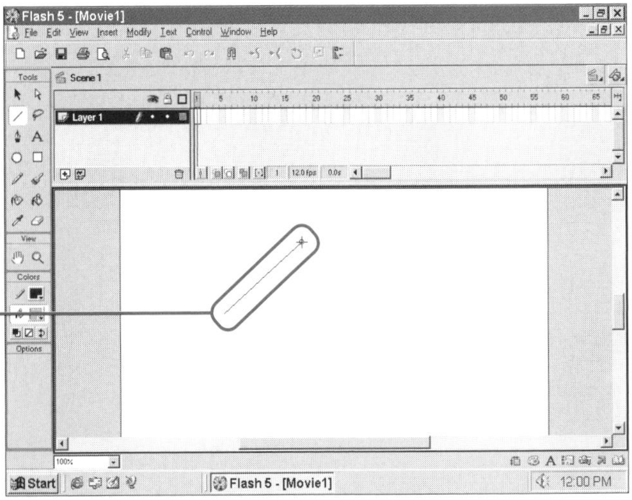

DRAW A STRAIGHT LINE

1 Click ⁄.

2 Move the mouse pointer over the Stage area until ↖ changes to +.

3 Drag to draw a line to your desired length.

4 Release the mouse button.

■ The line appears to your specifications.

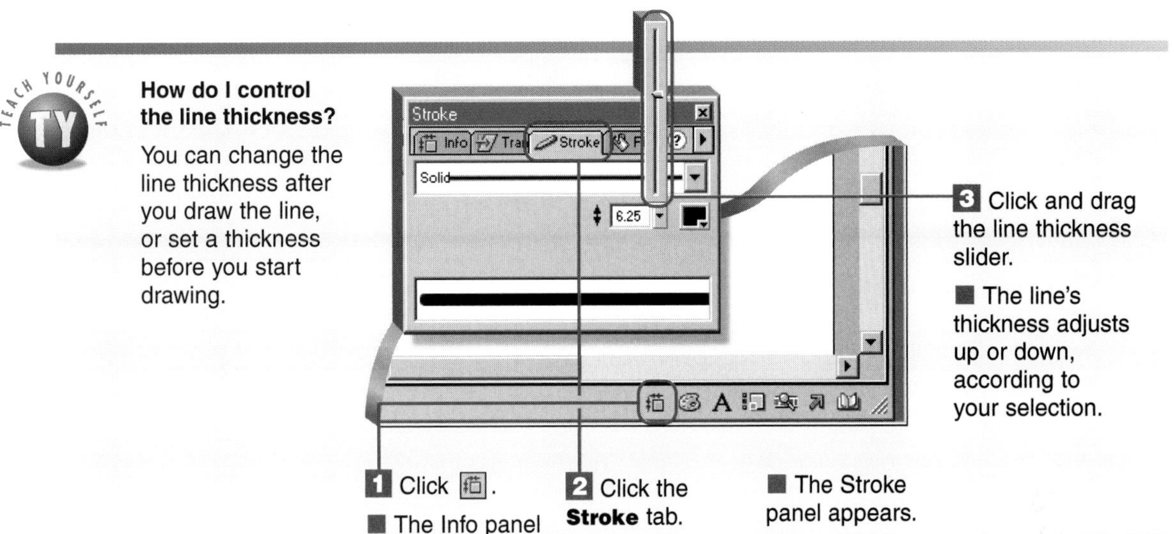

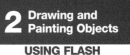

How do I control the line thickness?

You can change the line thickness after you draw the line, or set a thickness before you start drawing.

1 Click .

■ The Info panel opens.

2 Click the **Stroke** tab.

■ The Stroke panel appears.

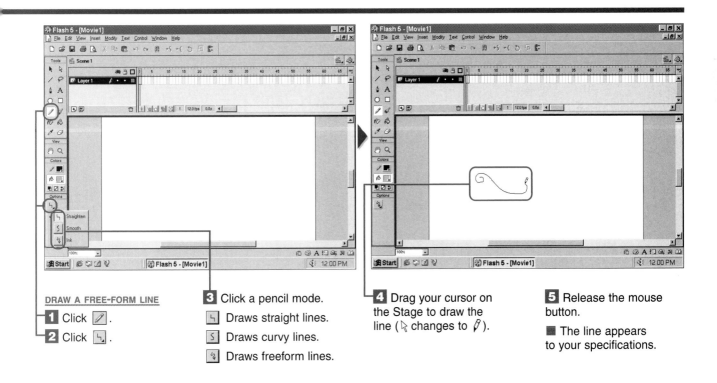

3 Click and drag the line thickness slider.

■ The line's thickness adjusts up or down, according to your selection.

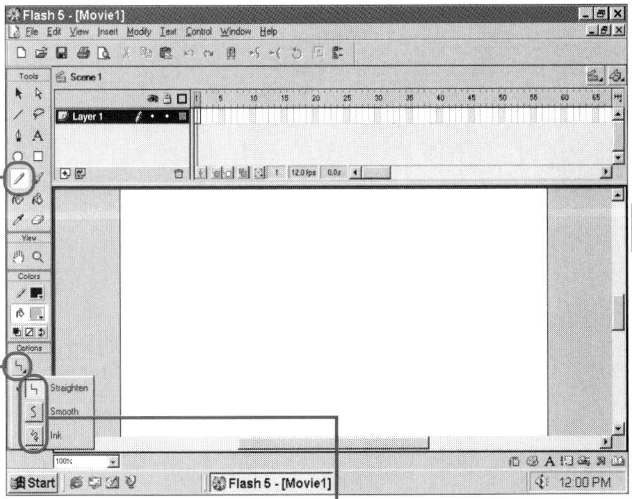

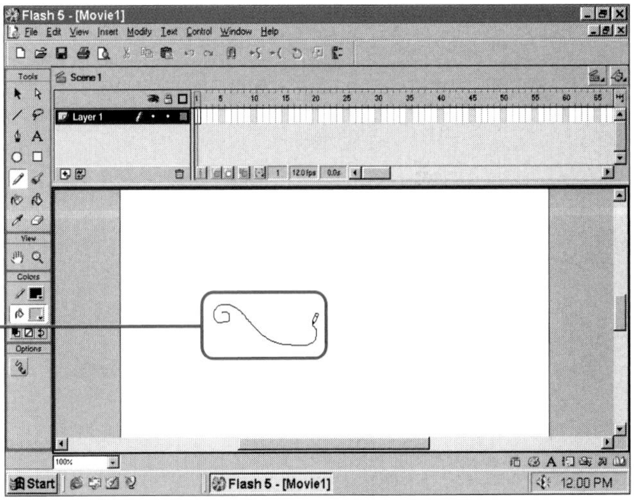

DRAW A FREE-FORM LINE

1 Click .

2 Click .

3 Click a pencil mode.

- Draws straight lines.
- Draws curvy lines.
- Draws freeform lines.

4 Drag your cursor on the Stage to draw the line (changes to).

5 Release the mouse button.

■ The line appears to your specifications.

FORMAT LINE SEGMENTS

By default, lines you draw on the Stage are solid black lines, 1-point thick. You can control a line's thickness, style, and color using the formatting controls found in the panel window.

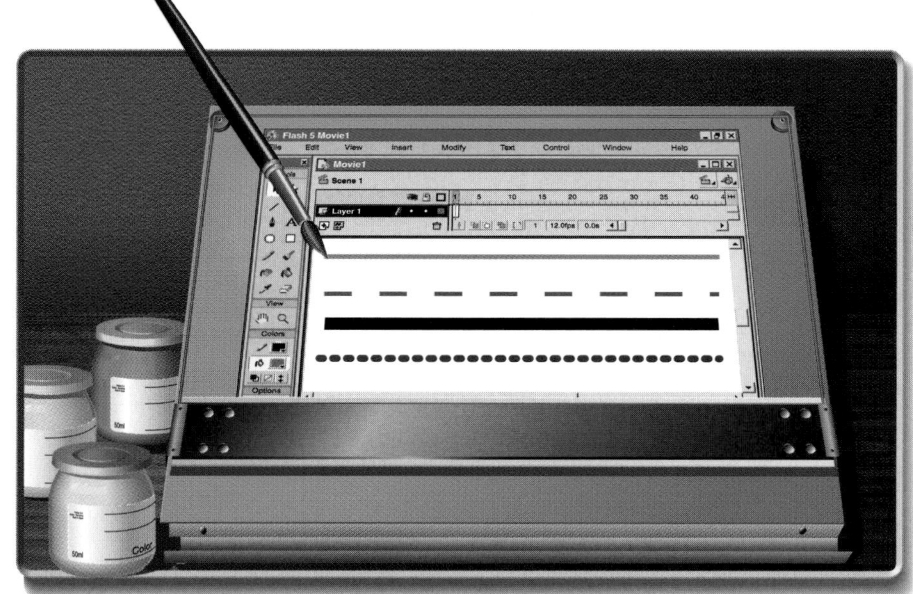

FORMAT A LINE SEGMENT

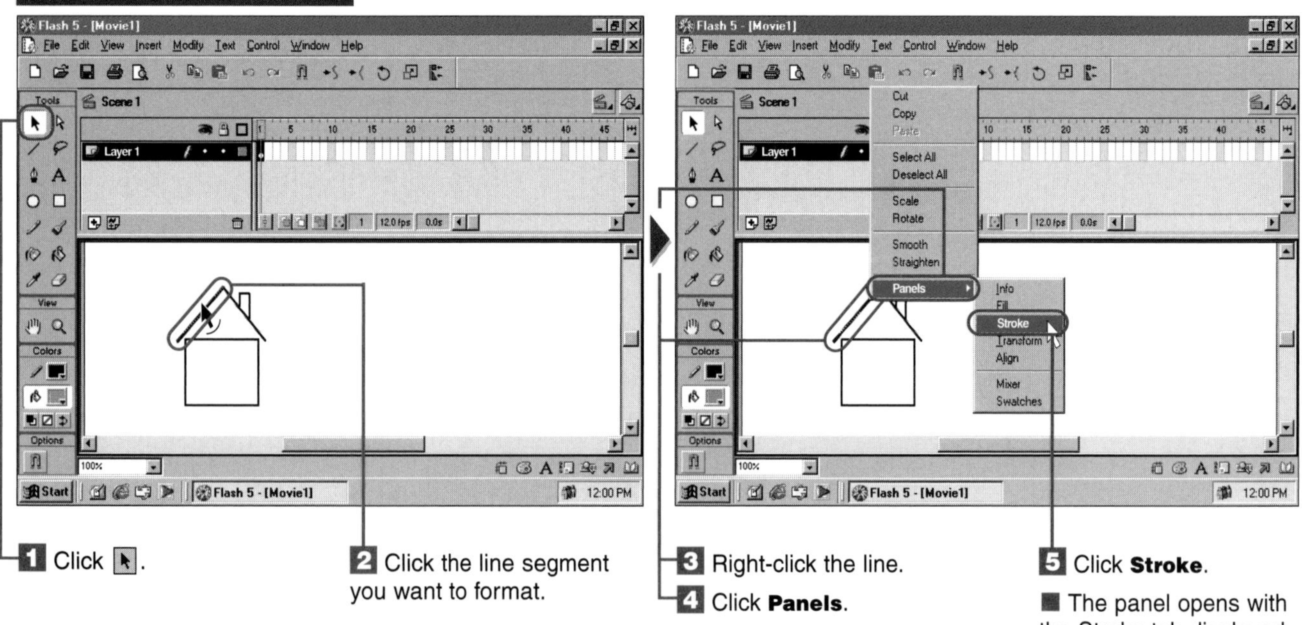

1 Click ![select tool].

2 Click the line segment you want to format.

3 Right-click the line.

4 Click **Panels**.

5 Click **Stroke**.

■ The panel opens with the Stroke tab displayed.

How do I change the line color?

From the Stroke tab of the panel, click the Line Color box (▢) to display a palette of color choices. Then click the color you want to assign.

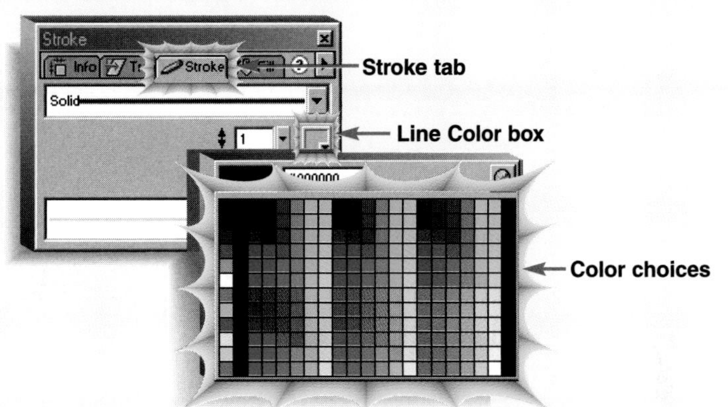

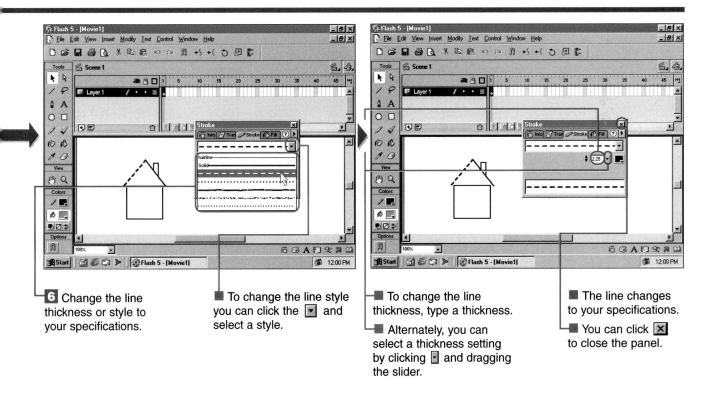

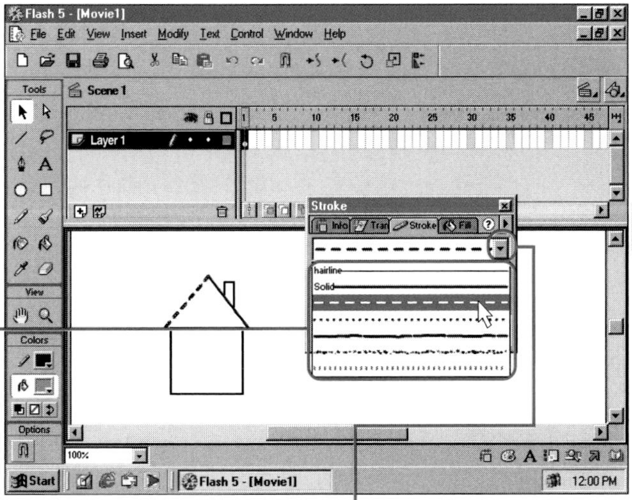

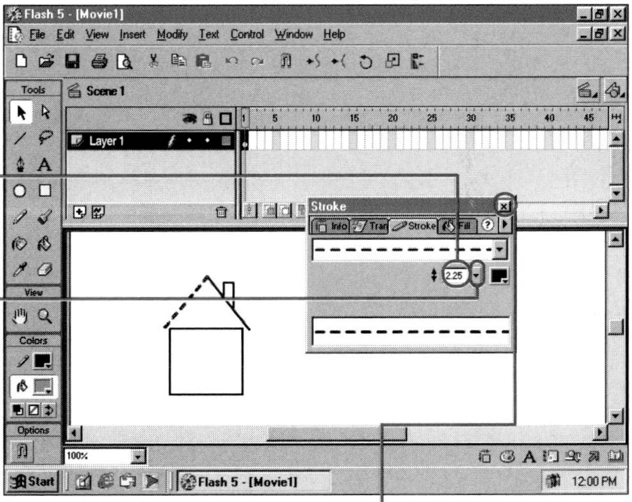

6 Change the line thickness or style to your specifications.

■ To change the line style you can click the ▾ and select a style.

■ To change the line thickness, type a thickness.

■ Alternately, you can select a thickness setting by clicking ▾ and dragging the slider.

■ The line changes to your specifications.

■ You can click ☒ to close the panel.

EDIT LINE SEGMENTS

You can change a line by adjusting its length or reshaping its curve. For example, you may want to change a line's angle, extend a curved line to make it appear longer, or simply make the curve more curvy.

CHANGE A LINE SEGMENT LENGTH

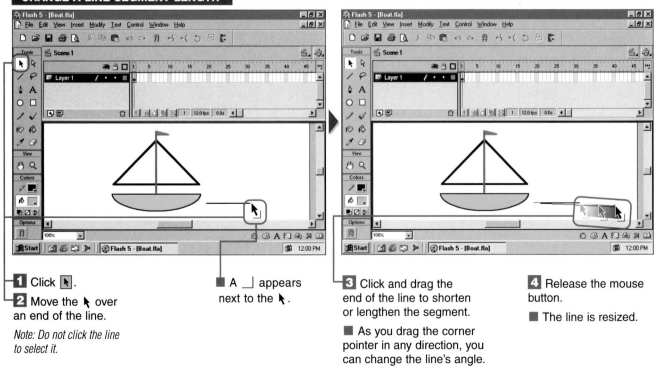

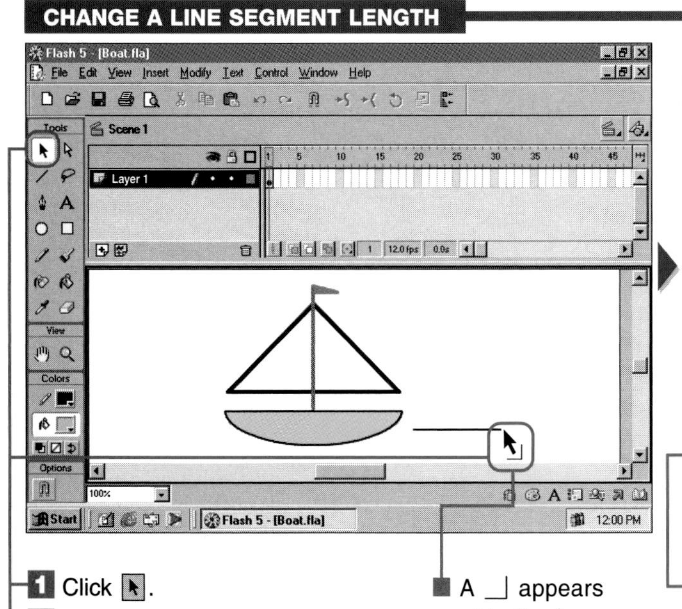

1 Click [selection tool].

2 Move the [arrow] over an end of the line.

Note: Do not click the line to select it.

■ A ⌟ appears next to the [arrow].

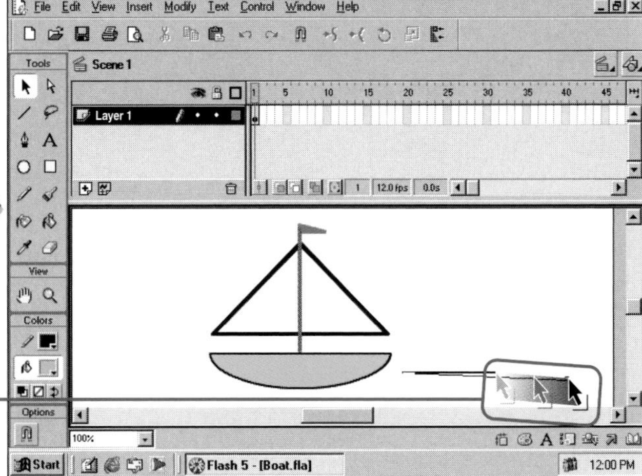

3 Click and drag the end of the line to shorten or lengthen the segment.

■ As you drag the corner pointer in any direction, you can change the line's angle.

4 Release the mouse button.

■ The line is resized.

How do I draw perfect vertical and horizontal lines?

It can be difficult to have a steady hand while drawing a line on the Stage. You can draw perfectly straight horizontal and vertical lines if you hold the Shift key down while dragging the Line tool across the Stage.

CHANGE A LINE SHAPE

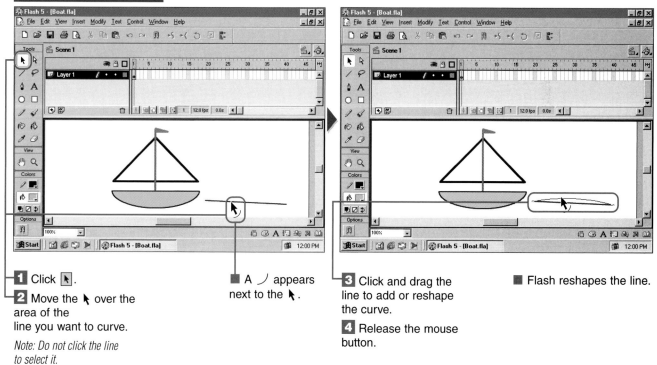

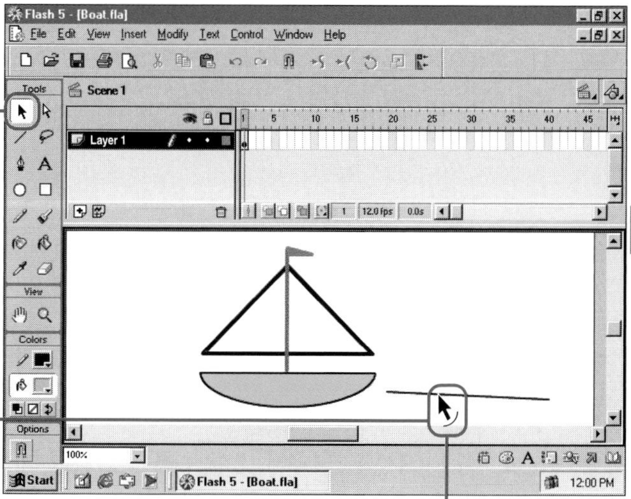

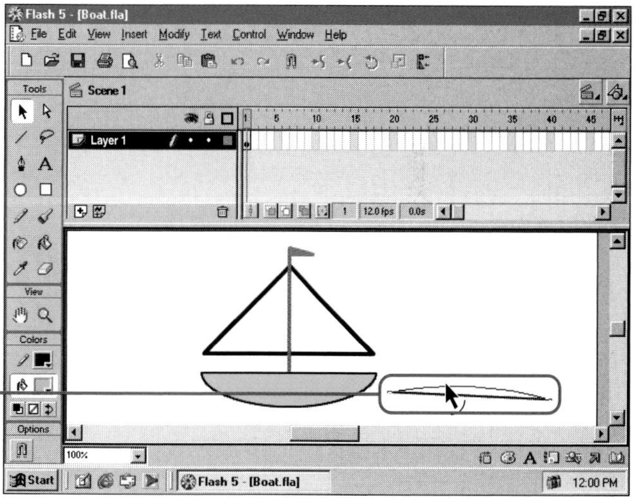

1. Click the arrow tool.
2. Move the arrow over the area of the line you want to curve.

Note: Do not click the line to select it.

- A curve symbol appears next to the arrow.

3. Click and drag the line to add or reshape the curve.
4. Release the mouse button.

- Flash reshapes the line.

EDIT FILLS

You can edit fills just as you can edit line segments. For example, you can change a fill shape by adjusting the sides of the fill, and you can change the fill color at any time.

EDIT FILLS

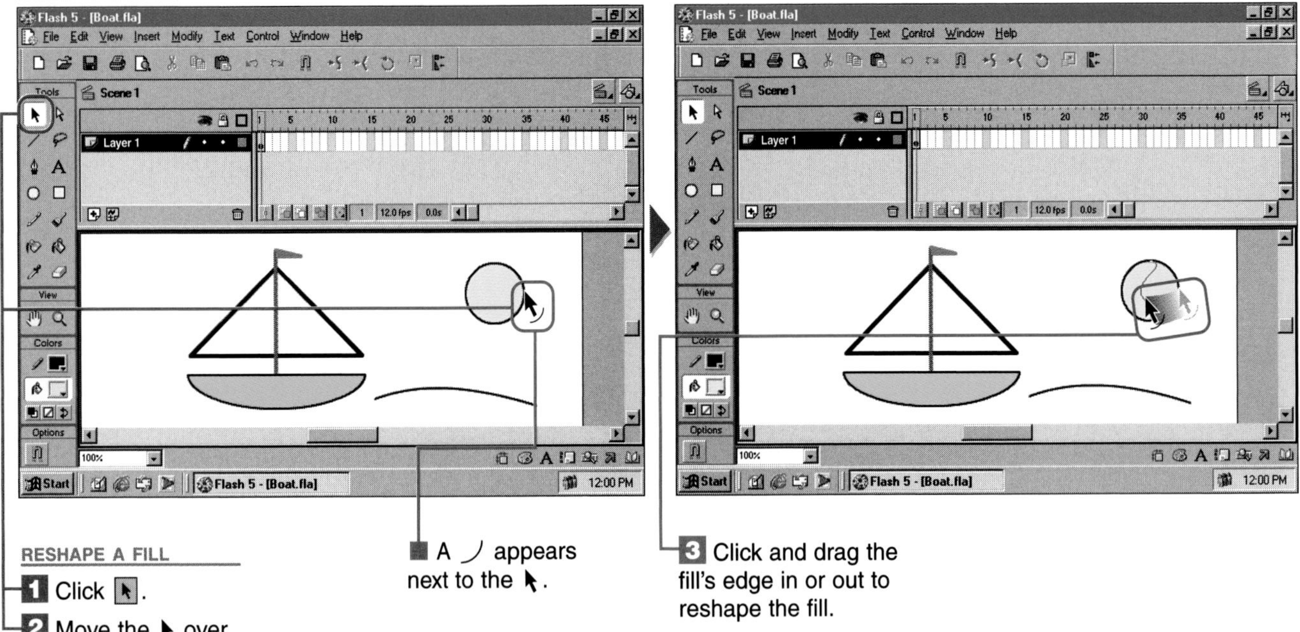

RESHAPE A FILL

1. Click the Arrow tool.
2. Move the arrow pointer over the edge of the fill.

Note: Do not select the fill.

■ A curve icon appears next to the arrow pointer.

3. Click and drag the fill's edge in or out to reshape the fill.

Can I use other ways to edit fill shapes?

You can find additional Shape commands on the Modify menu that can help you edit fills. For example, to soften a fill's edges, perform the following steps:

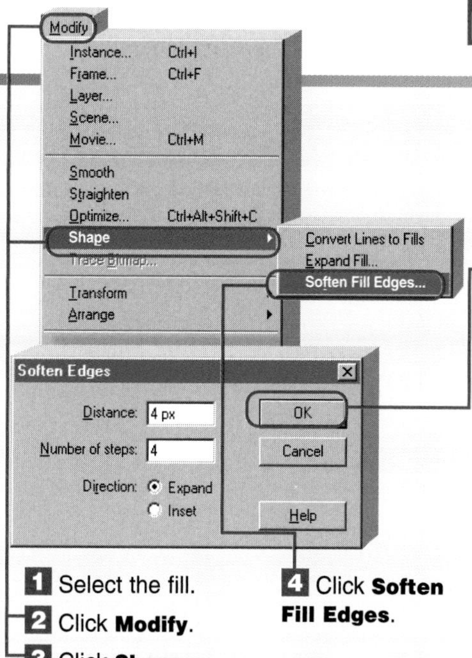

1 Select the fill.

2 Click **Modify**.

3 Click **Shape**.

4 Click **Soften Fill Edges**.

5 From the Soften Edges dialog box, adjust the settings and click **OK**.

■ Experiment with the settings to see what sort of effects you can create.

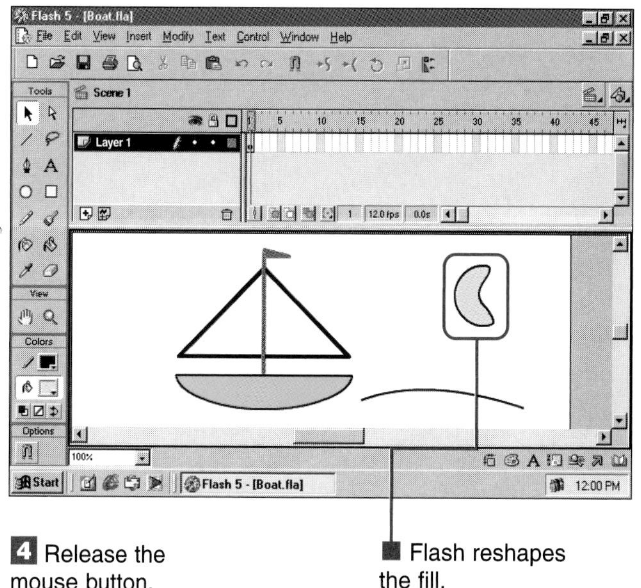

4 Release the mouse button.

■ Flash reshapes the fill.

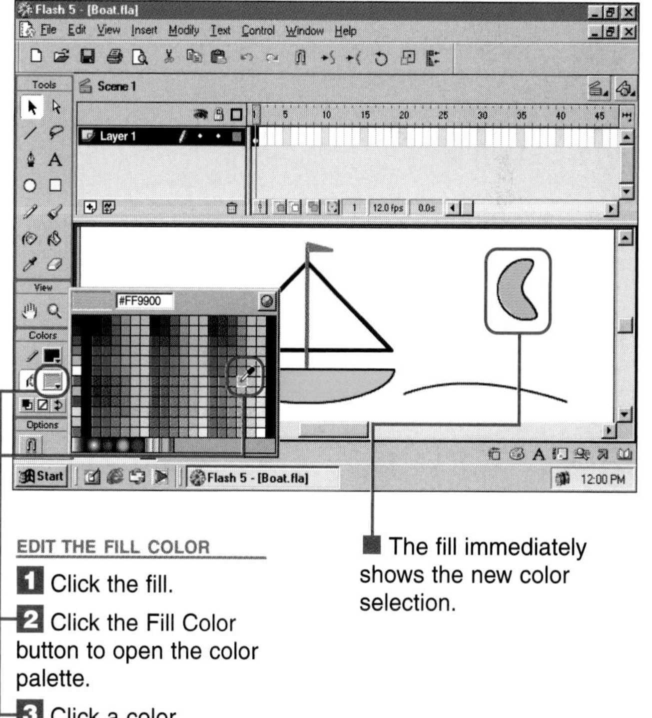

EDIT THE FILL COLOR

1 Click the fill.

2 Click the Fill Color button to open the color palette.

3 Click a color.

■ The fill immediately shows the new color selection.

DRAW CURVES WITH THE PEN TOOL

You can draw precise lines and curves using the Pen tool. Using this tool takes some getting used to, but with a little practice, you can draw curves easily.

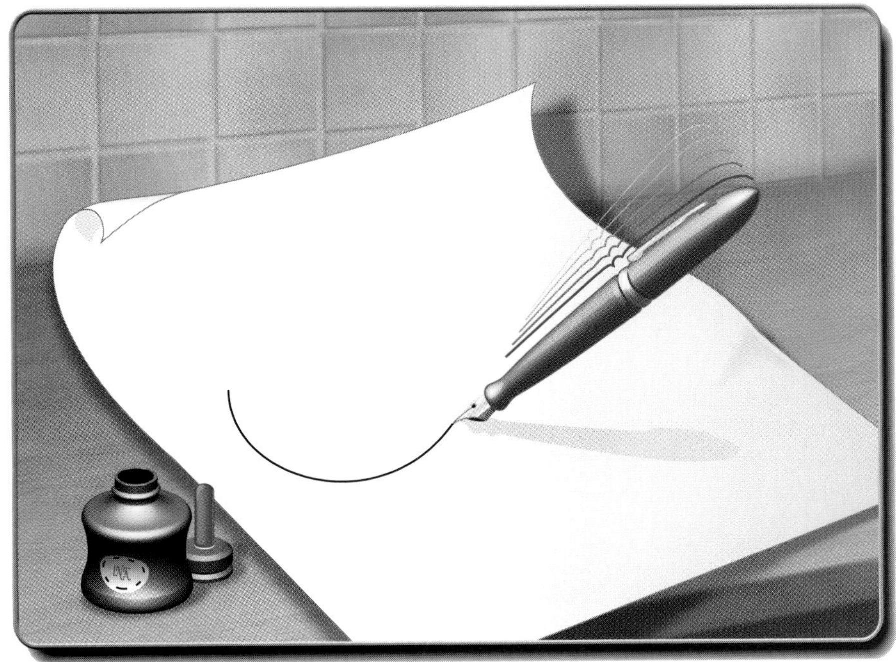

DRAW CURVES WITH THE PEN TOOL

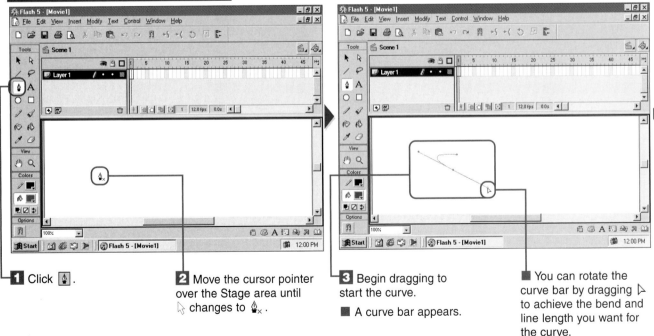

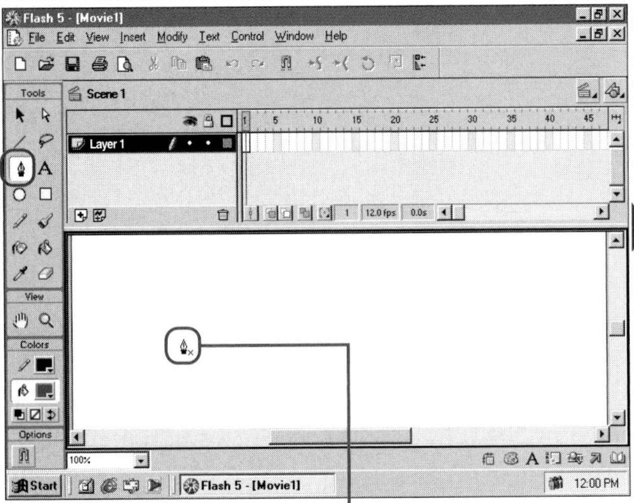

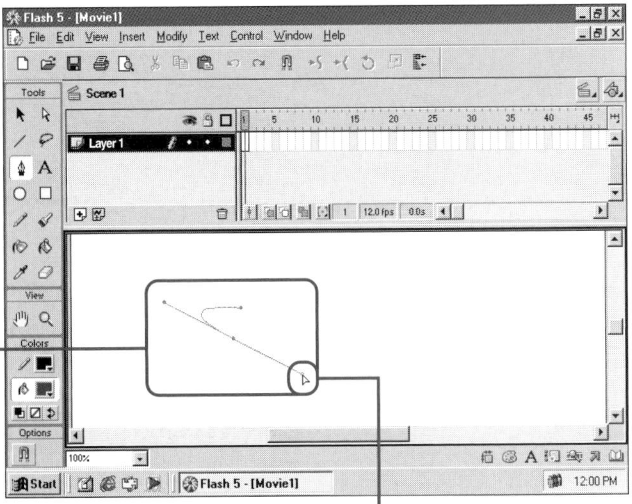

1 Click [pen tool icon].

2 Move the cursor pointer over the Stage area until [arrow pointer] changes to [pen pointer].

3 Begin dragging to start the curve.

■ A curve bar appears.

■ You can rotate the curve bar by dragging [arrow pointer] to achieve the bend and line length you want for the curve.

How can I reshape a curved line?

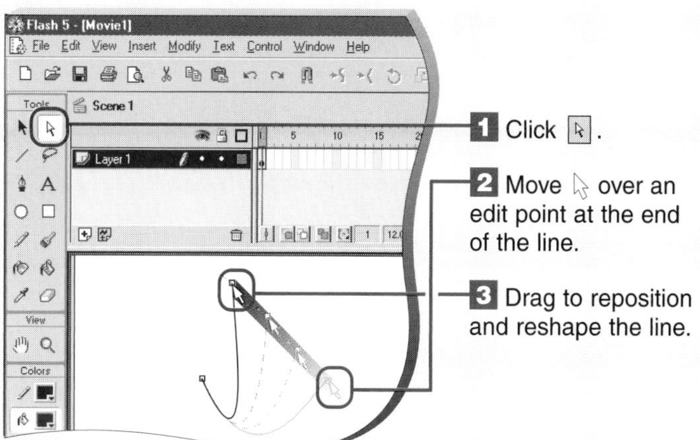

1 Click .

2 Move over an edit point at the end of the line.

3 Drag to reposition and reshape the line.

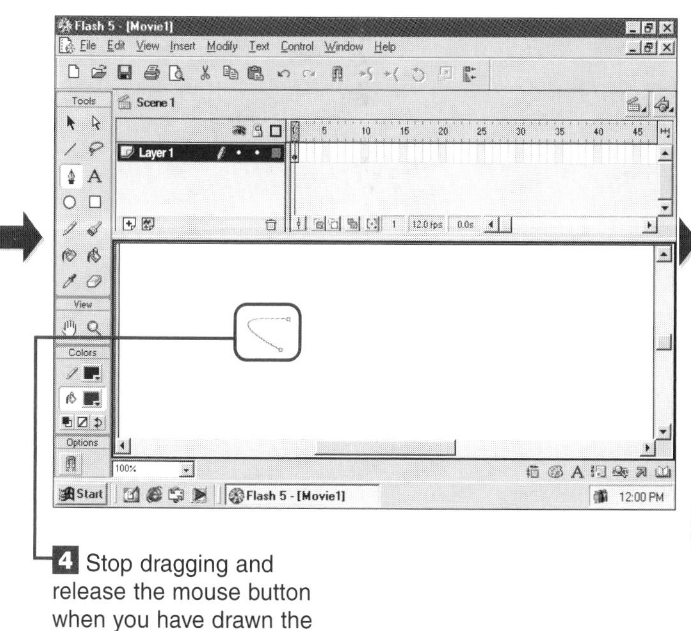

4 Stop dragging and release the mouse button when you have drawn the curve you want.

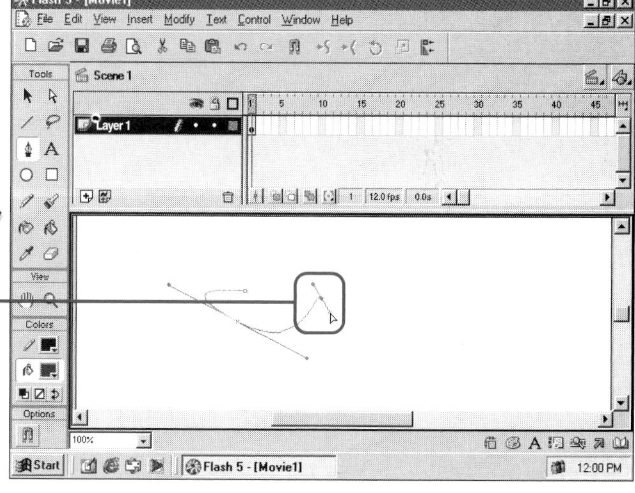

■ You can add more curves to an existing curved line as long as the Pen tool is still active. Simply drag another line segment.

■ Flash automatically attaches the second line segment to the first curved line.

SMOOTH OR STRAIGHTEN LINE SEGMENTS

Flash has two controls for modifying the appearance of lines you draw. You can smooth or straighten them to create subtle or dramatic changes to your drawing.

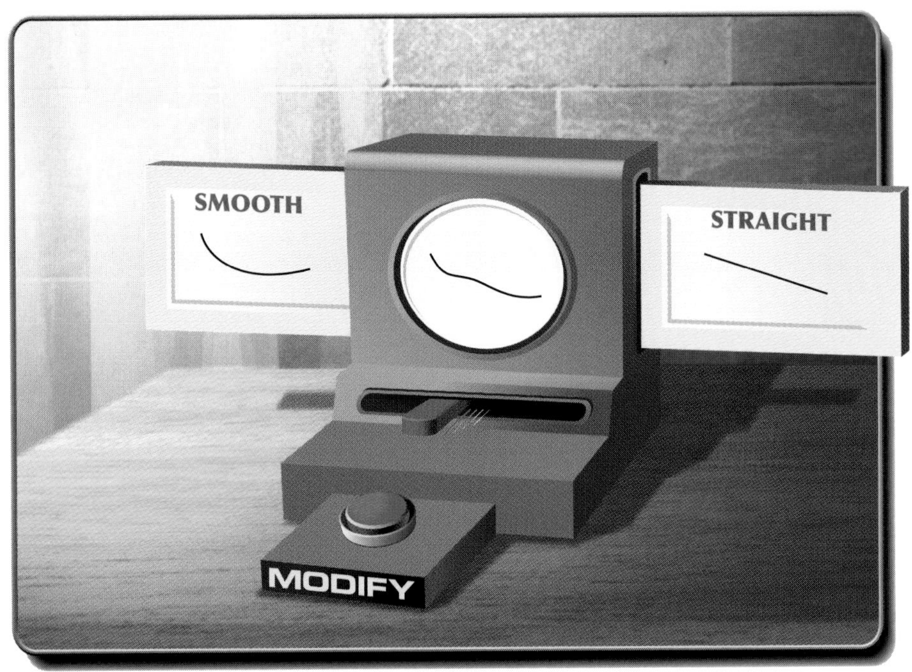

SMOOTH A LINE SEGMENT

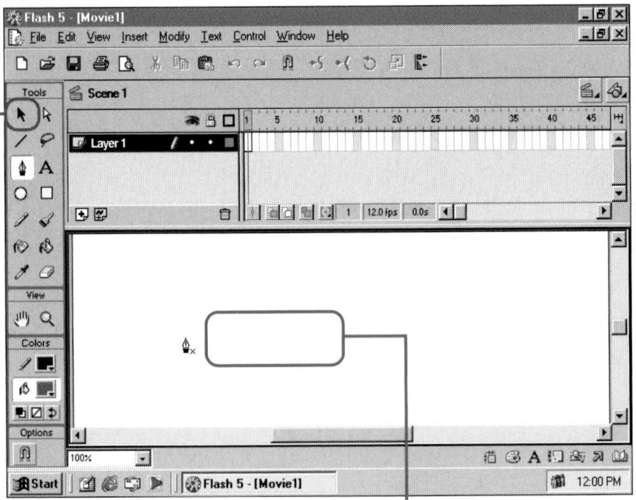

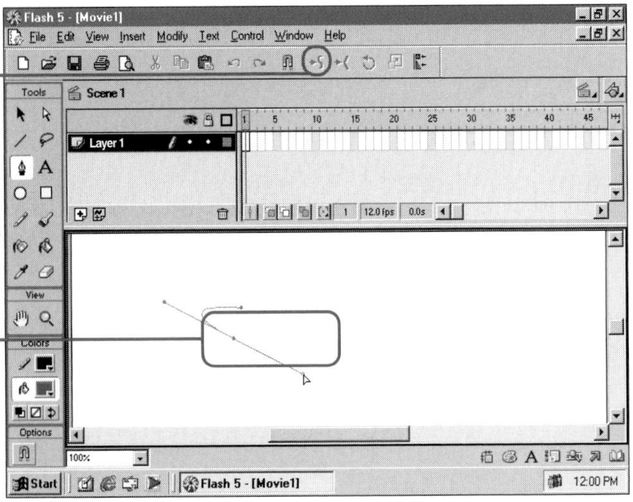

1 Click ![select].

2 Click the line segment you want to smooth.

3 Click ![smooth].

■ The line is altered slightly.

■ You can keep clicking ![smooth] until you achieve the desired effect.

Can I draw in Smooth or Straighten mode?

Flash can help you with your line-drawing skills. When you click , appears in the Options tray at the bottom of the Drawing toolbar. Click and select a mode (, or) before you begin drawing lines. When you finish drawing a line, Flash smooths or straightens it for you.

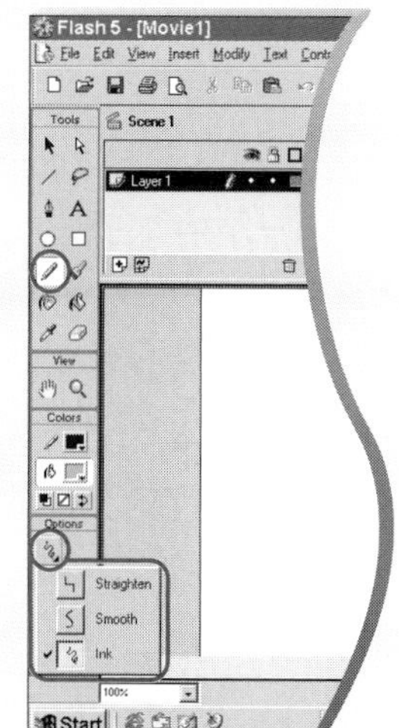

STRAIGHTEN A LINE SEGMENT

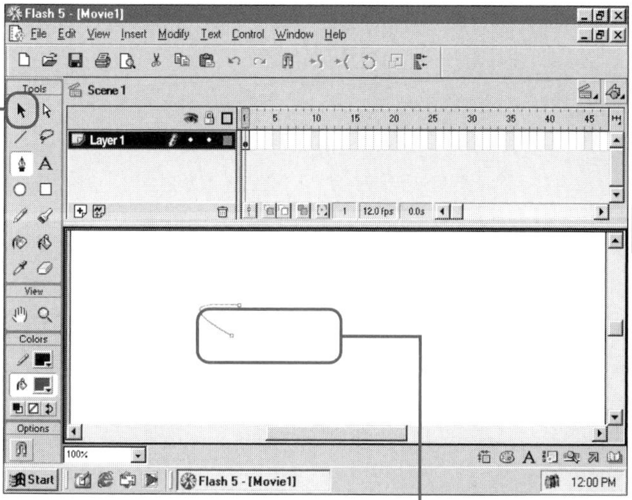

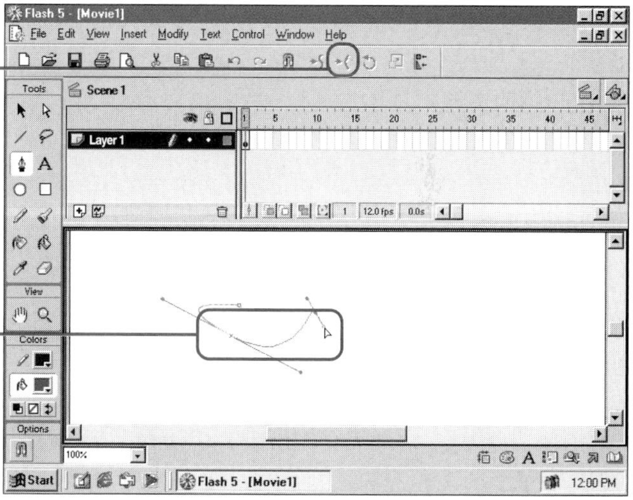

1 Click .

2 Click the line segment you want to straighten.

3 Click .

■ The line is altered slightly.

■ You can keep clicking until you achieve the desired effect.

DRAW OVAL AND RECTANGLE SHAPES

You can create simple shapes in Flash and then fill them with a color or pattern, or use them as part of a drawing.

DRAW OVAL AND RECTANGLE SHAPES

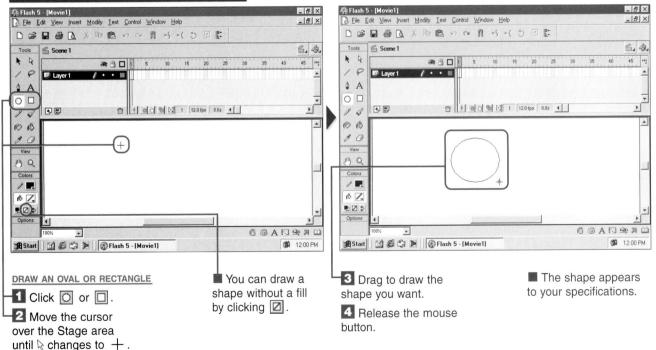

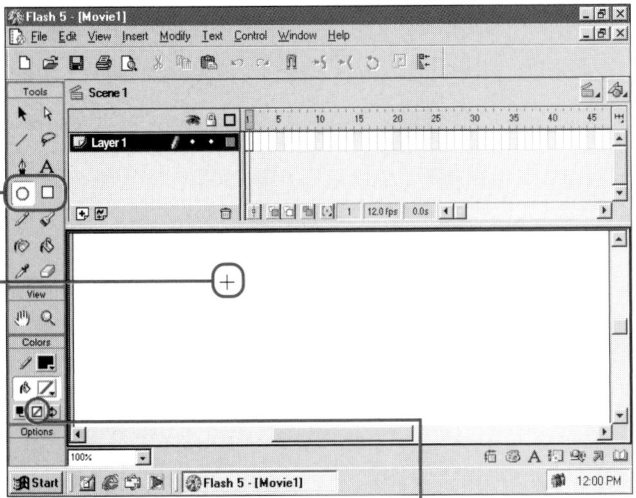

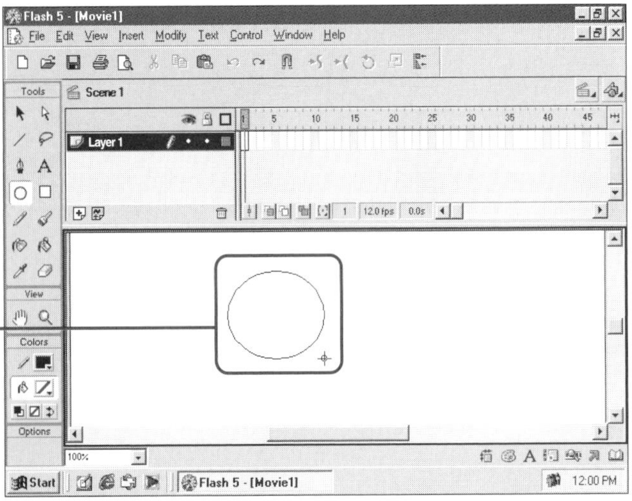

DRAW AN OVAL OR RECTANGLE

1 Click ○ or □.

2 Move the cursor over the Stage area until ↖ changes to +.

■ You can draw a shape without a fill by clicking ☒.

3 Drag to draw the shape you want.

4 Release the mouse button.

■ The shape appears to your specifications.

How do I draw a rectangle with rounded corners?

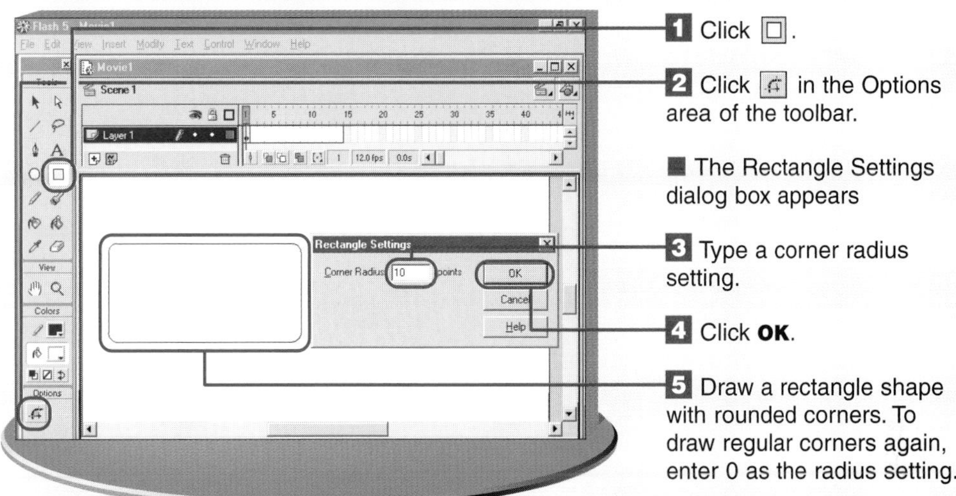

1 Click ▢.

2 Click ⌗ in the Options area of the toolbar.

■ The Rectangle Settings dialog box appears

3 Type a corner radius setting.

4 Click **OK**.

5 Draw a rectangle shape with rounded corners. To draw regular corners again, enter 0 as the radius setting.

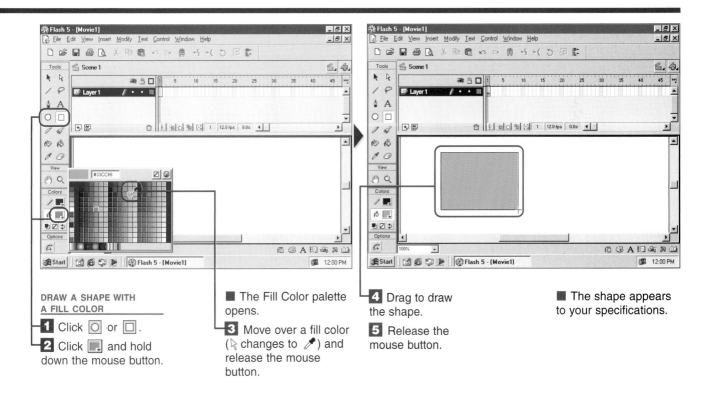

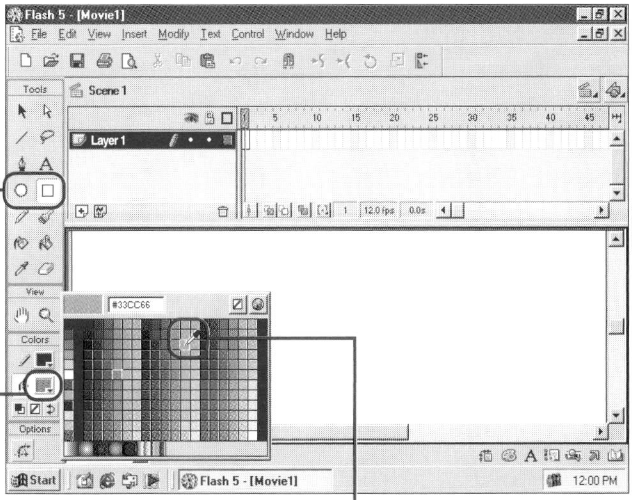

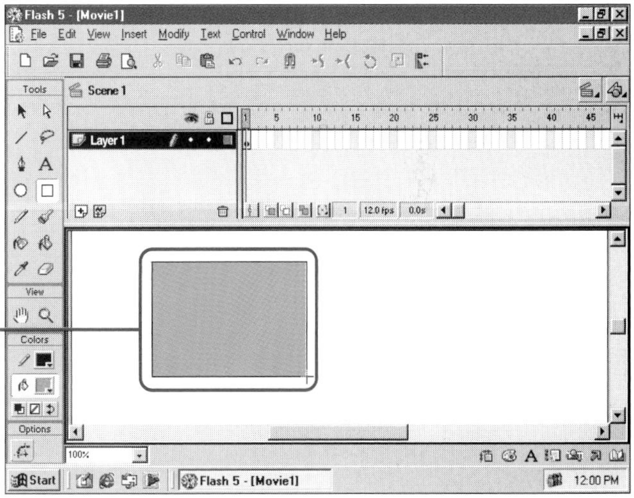

DRAW A SHAPE WITH A FILL COLOR

1 Click ○ or ▢.

2 Click ▣ and hold down the mouse button.

■ The Fill Color palette opens.

3 Move over a fill color (↖ changes to ✎) and release the mouse button.

4 Drag to draw the shape.

5 Release the mouse button.

■ The shape appears to your specifications.

FILL OBJECTS WITH THE PAINT BUCKET TOOL

You can use the Paint Bucket tool to quickly fill in objects, such as shapes. You can fill objects with a color, a gradient effect, or even a picture. The Flash color palette comes with numerous colors and shades, as well as several pre-made gradient effects.

FILL OBJECTS WITH THE PAINT BUCKET TOOL

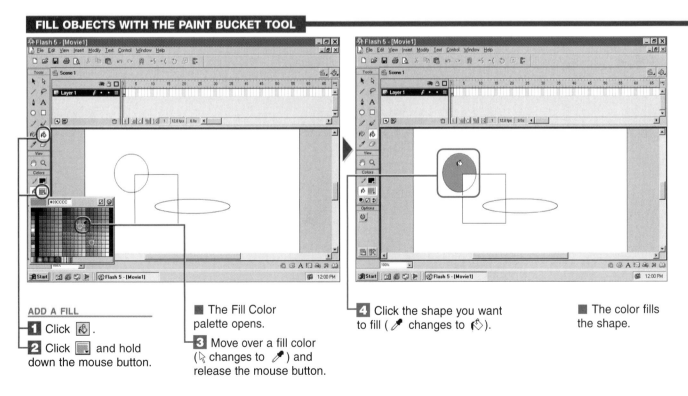

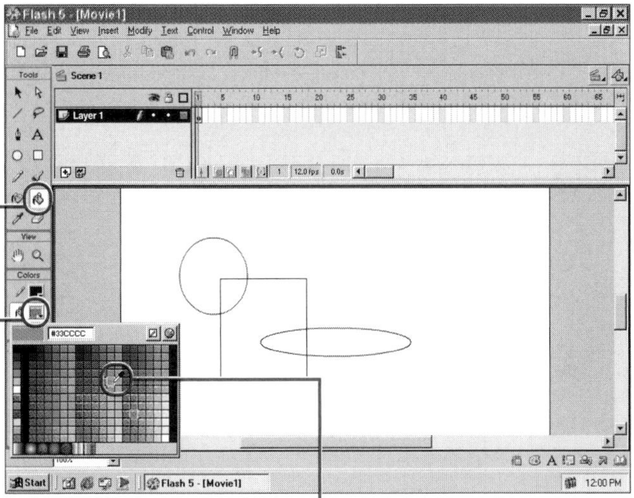

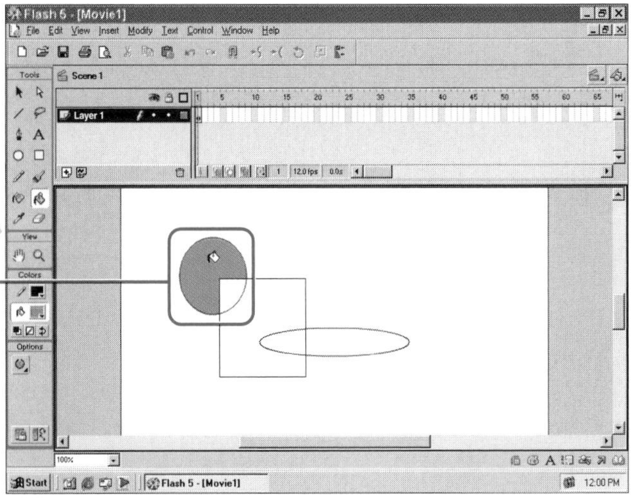

ADD A FILL

1 Click [paint bucket icon].

2 Click [fill color icon] and hold down the mouse button.

■ The Fill Color palette opens.

3 Move over a fill color ([arrow] changes to [dropper]) and release the mouse button.

4 Click the shape you want to fill ([dropper] changes to [paint bucket]).

■ The color fills the shape.

What is a gradient effect?

A *gradient effect* shows one or several colors of different intensities, creating a three-dimensional effect. With Flash, you can create a linear gradient effect that intensifies color shading from left to right or top to bottom, or create a radial gradient effect that intensifies color shading from the middle to the outer edges or vice versa.

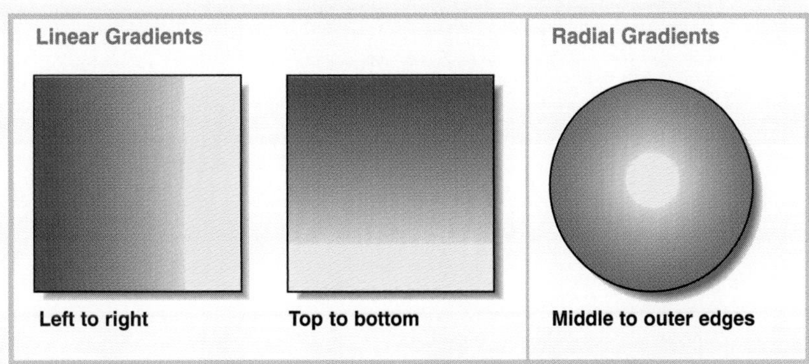

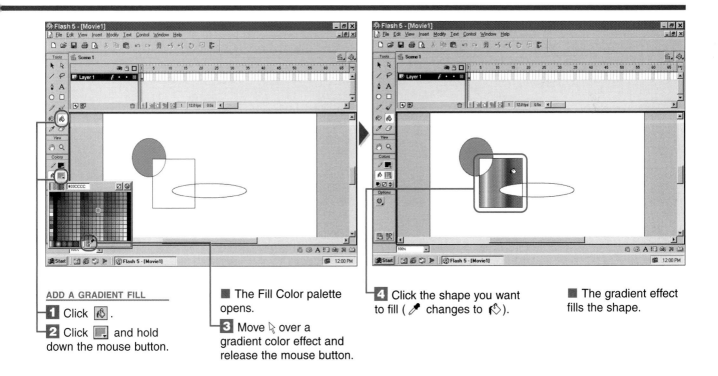

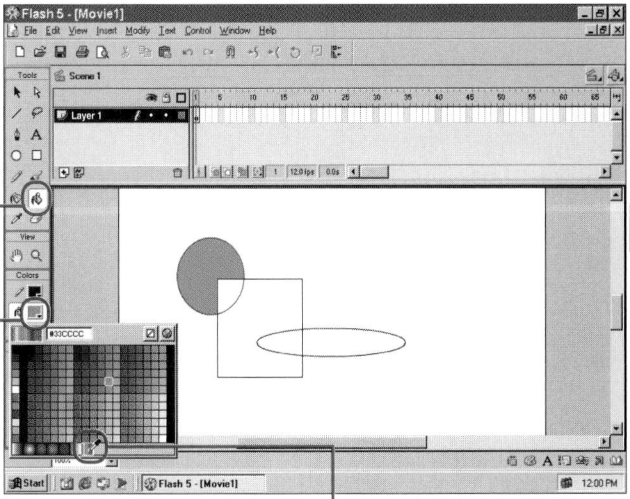

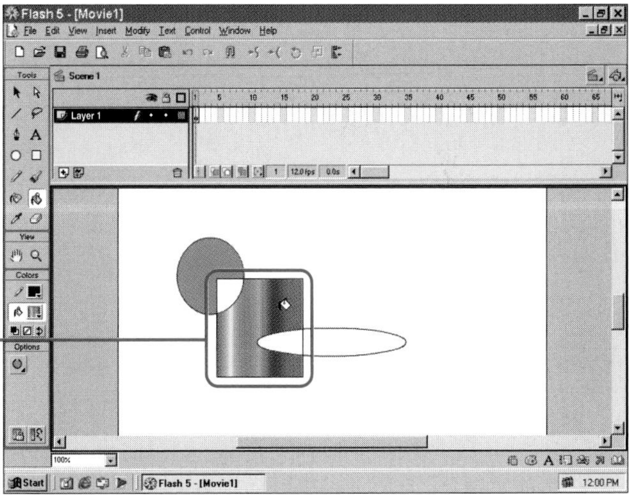

ADD A GRADIENT FILL

1 Click .

2 Click and hold down the mouse button.

■ The Fill Color palette opens.

3 Move over a gradient color effect and release the mouse button.

4 Click the shape you want to fill (changes to).

■ The gradient effect fills the shape.

SELECT OBJECTS

To work with objects you draw or place on the Flash stage, you must first select them. The more lines and shapes you place on the Stage, the trickier it is to select only the ones you want. Flash gives you four ways to select objects: clicking, dragging, lassoing, and selecting parts of an object.

SELECT OBJECTS

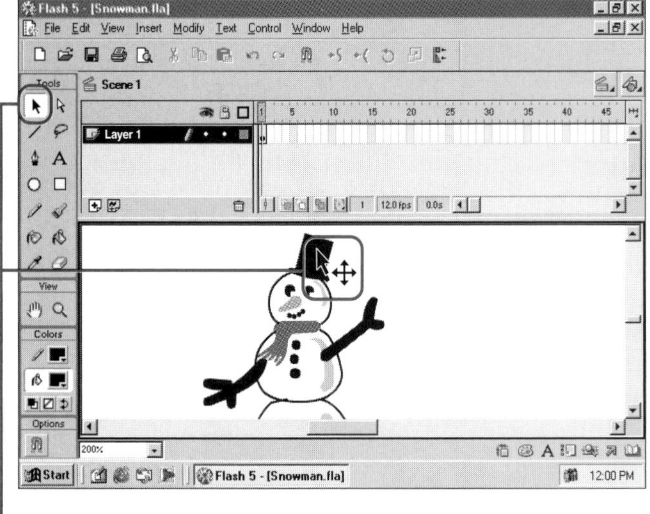

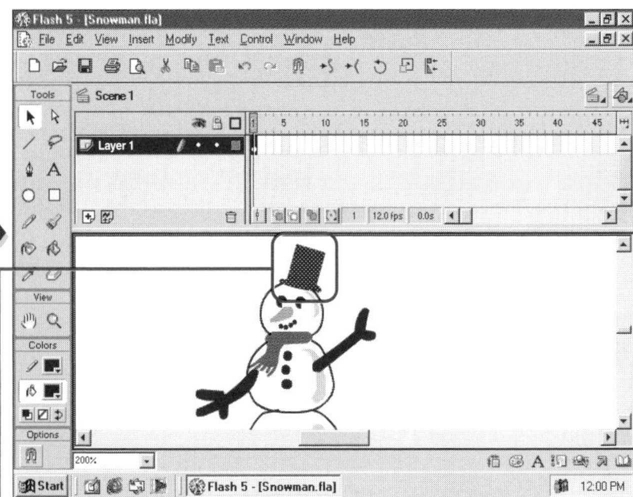

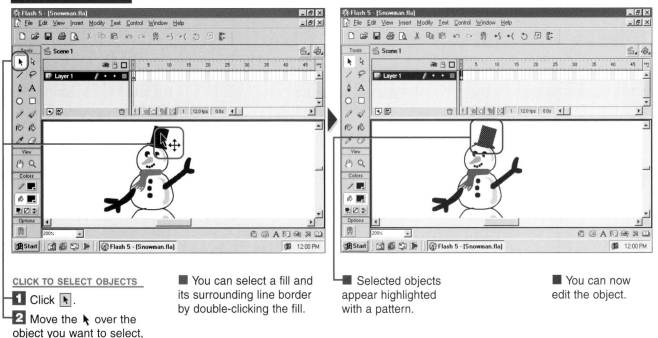

CLICK TO SELECT OBJECTS

1 Click [selection tool icon].

2 Move the [pointer icon] over the object you want to select, and then click.

■ You can select a fill and its surrounding line border by double-clicking the fill.

■ Selected objects appear highlighted with a pattern.

■ You can now edit the object.

How do I select multiple objects?

Hold down the Shift key while clicking objects when you want to select more than one at a time. For example, if a line is composed of several segments, you can select all of them for editing. Click [selection arrow]; then hold the Shift key and click each line segment you want to select.

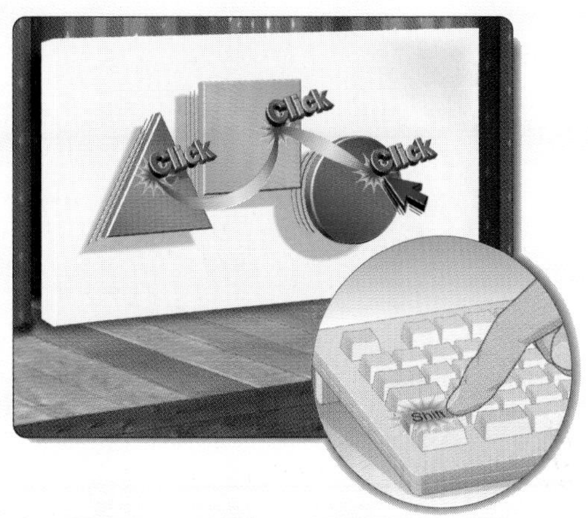

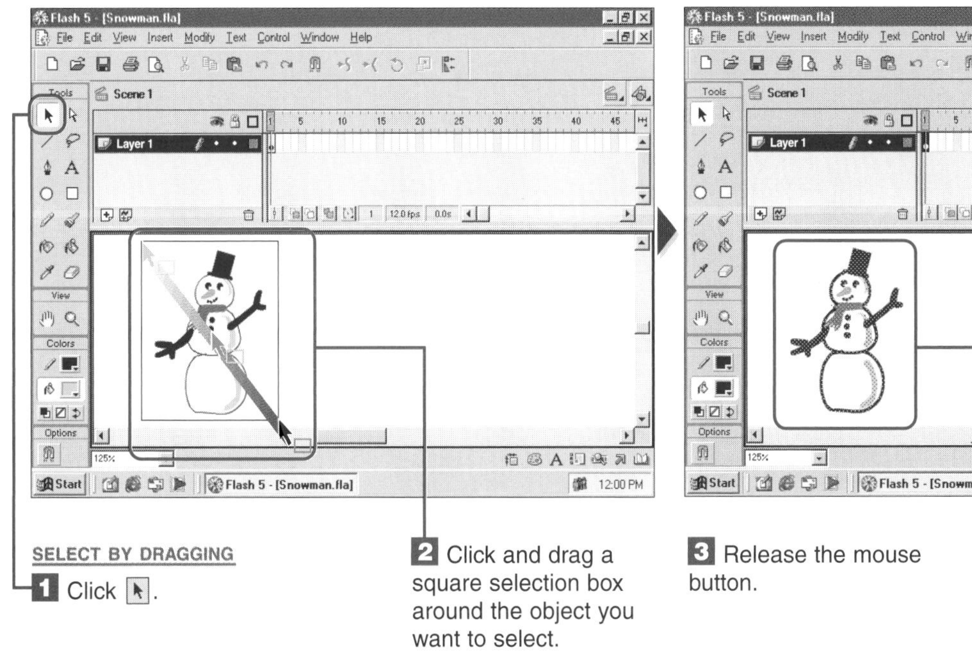

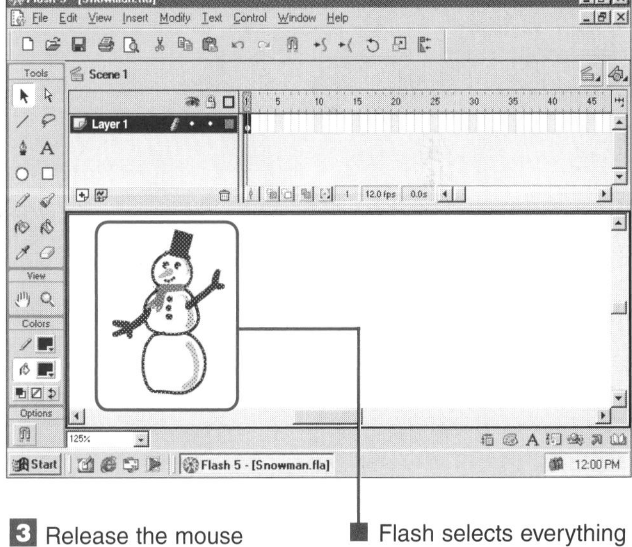

SELECT BY DRAGGING

1 Click [selection arrow].

2 Click and drag a square selection box around the object you want to select.

3 Release the mouse button.

■ Flash selects everything inside selection box.

CONTINUED

SELECT OBJECTS

You can use the Lasso tool to select irregular objects. The Lasso tool draws a freehand "rope" around the item you want to select. This allows you to select an oddly-shaped object or just a small portion of an object.

SELECT OBJECTS (CONTINUED)

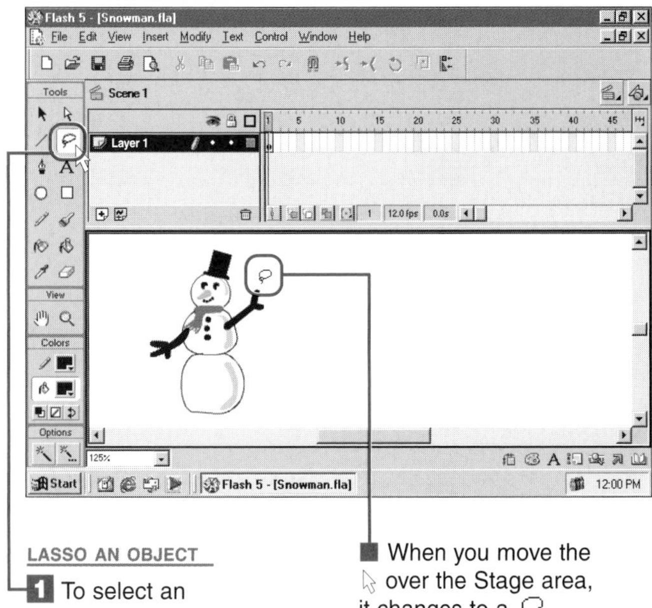

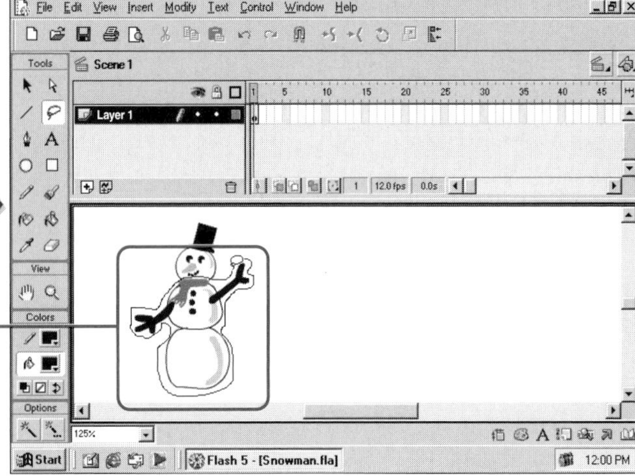

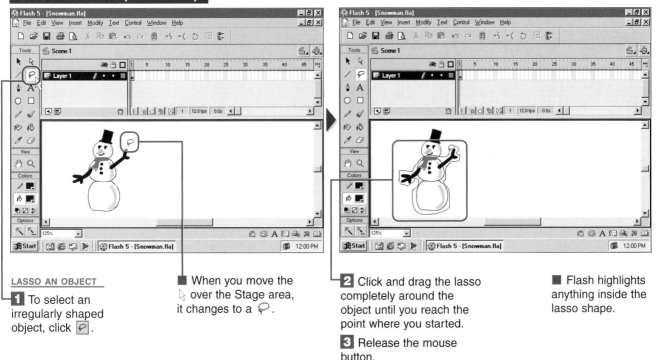

LASSO AN OBJECT

1 To select an irregularly shaped object, click the lasso tool.

■ When you move the pointer over the Stage area, it changes to a lasso.

2 Click and drag the lasso completely around the object until you reach the point where you started.

3 Release the mouse button.

■ Flash highlights anything inside the lasso shape.

How can I select complex shapes?

Drawing around irregular items with the lasso can be difficult. For additional help, use the Lasso tool's Polygon Mode modifier. Click [lasso icon] and then click [polygon icon] in the Modifier Tray. Now click your way around the object you want to select. Every click creates a connected line to the last click. To turn off the Polygon Mode, double-click.

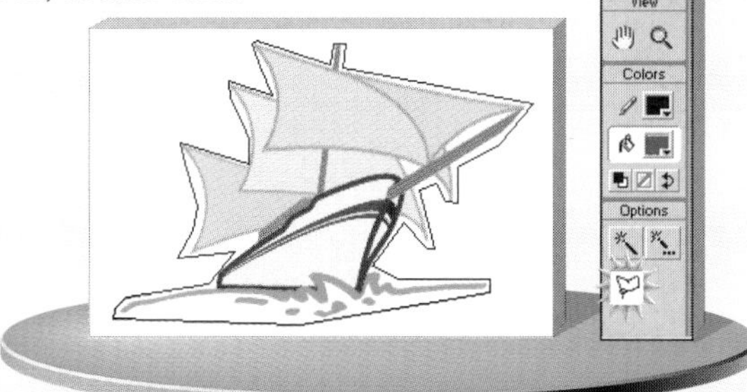

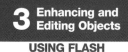

How do I select just a fill and not its border?

Simply click the fill to select it. To select both the fill and the fill's border, double-click the fill.

Fill **Fill and border**

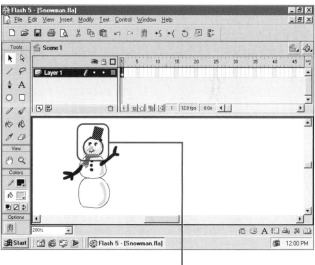

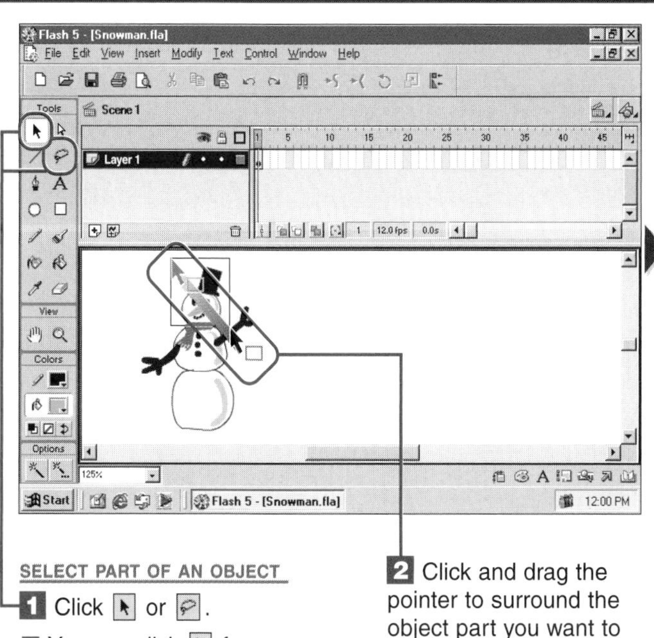

SELECT PART OF AN OBJECT

1 Click [arrow icon] or [lasso icon].

■ You can click [arrow icon] for simple shapes or lines.

■ You can click [lasso icon] for irregularly shaped objects.

2 Click and drag the pointer to surround the object part you want to select.

3 Release the mouse button.

■ Everything inside the area you dragged over is selected.

MOVE AND COPY OBJECTS

You can easily reposition objects on the Flash stage. Flash lets you quickly move an object from one area to another, and you can make copies of the original object.

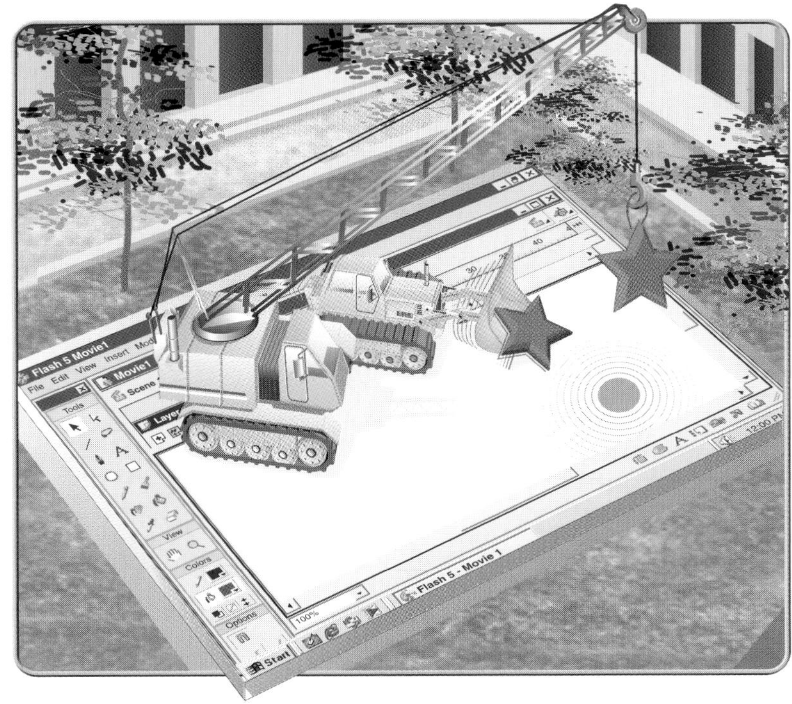

MOVE AN OBJECT

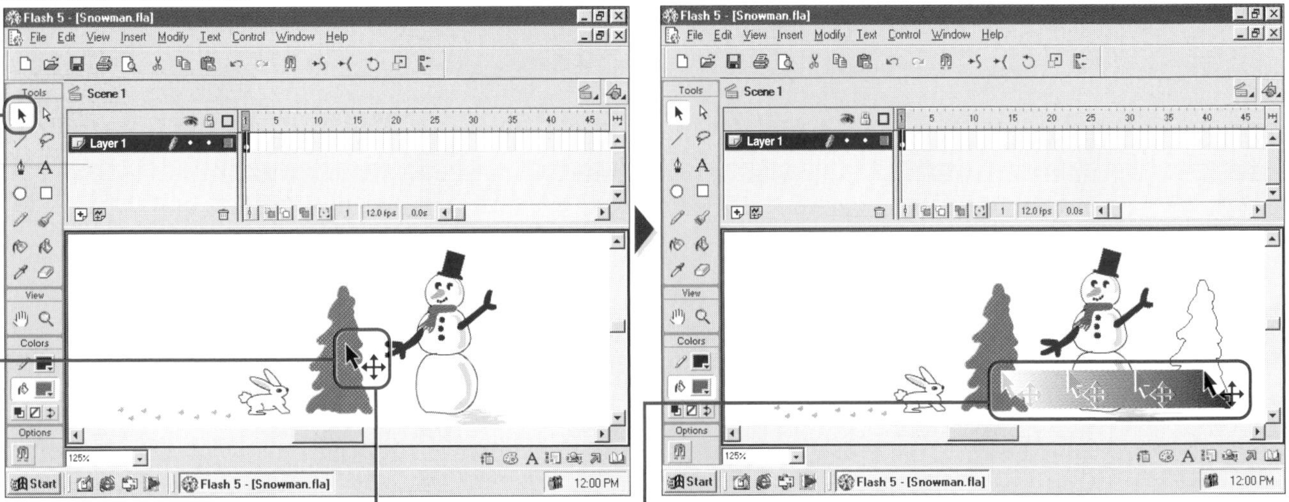

1 Click .

2 Click the object you want to move.

■ A appears next to the .

3 Click and drag the object to a new position.

4 Release the mouse button.

■ Your object moves to the location you selected.

Can I precisely control where an object is positioned?

For more precise positioning controls, open the Align panel. Press Ctrl + K (Windows) or ⌘ + K (Mac), or click to open the Align panel where you will find a variety of controls for positioning an object precisely on the Stage. To learn more about using the alignment controls, see the section "Align Objects."

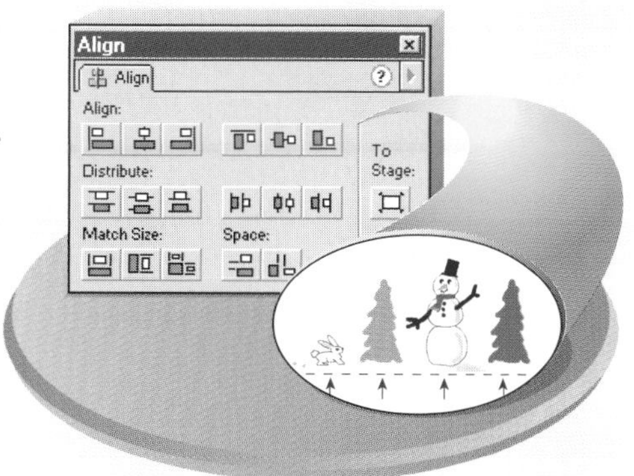

COPY AN OBJECT

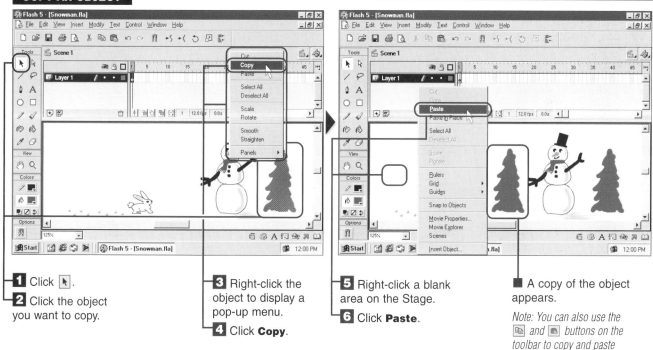

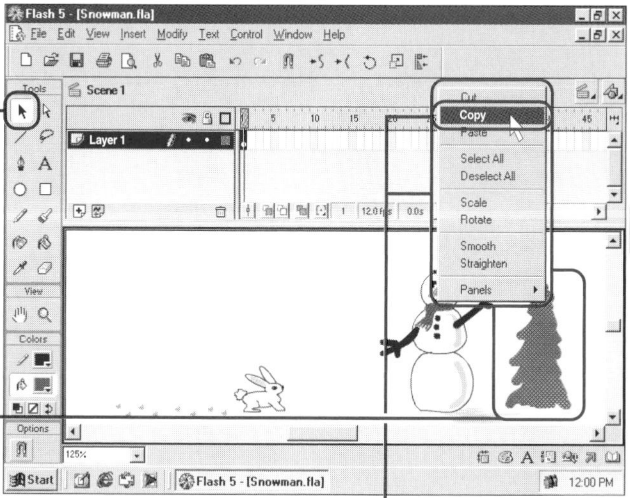

1 Click .

2 Click the object you want to copy.

3 Right-click the object to display a pop-up menu.

4 Click **Copy**.

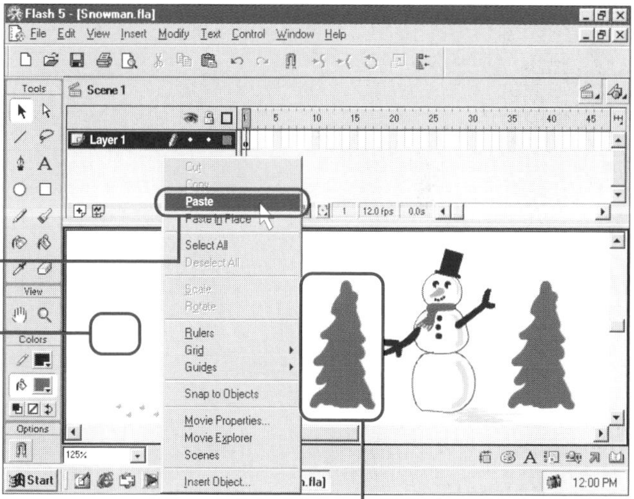

5 Right-click a blank area on the Stage.

6 Click **Paste**.

■ A copy of the object appears.

Note: You can also use the and buttons on the toolbar to copy and paste an object.

ROTATE AND FLIP OBJECTS

You can spin an object based on its center point, or you can flip an object vertically or horizontally. Both actions enable you to quickly change an object's position in a drawing.

ROTATE AN OBJECT

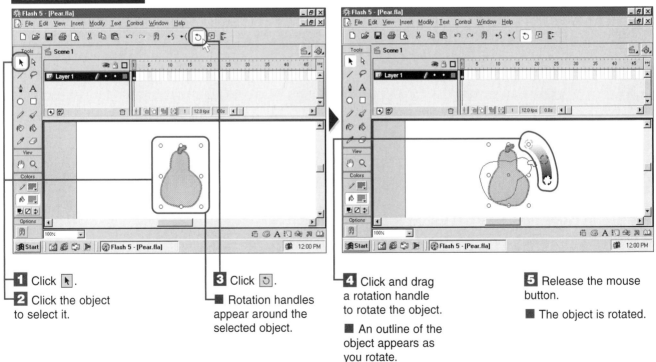

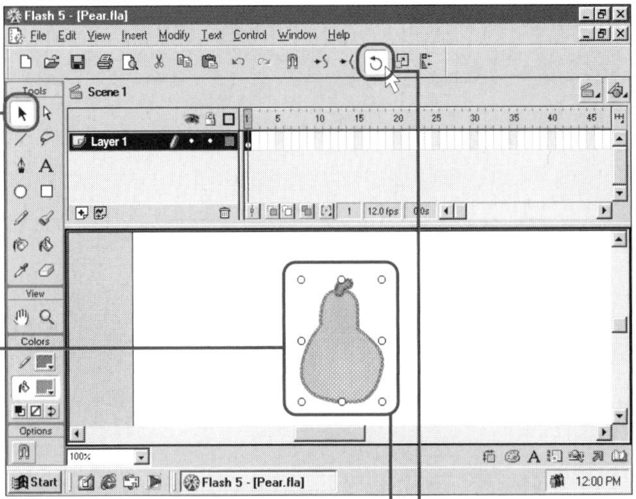

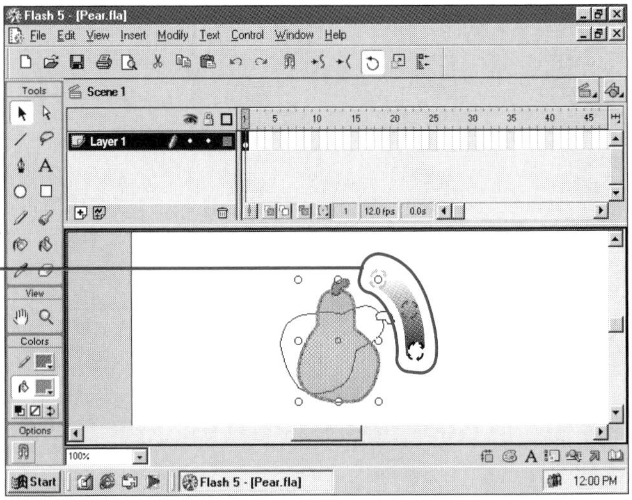

1 Click .

2 Click the object to select it.

3 Click .

■ Rotation handles appear around the selected object.

4 Click and drag a rotation handle to rotate the object.

■ An outline of the object appears as you rotate.

5 Release the mouse button.

■ The object is rotated.

TEACH YOURSELF

Can I change an object's center point?

For most objects you draw, the center point is truly at the center of the object. But there are times when you want the center point to reference another part of the object. To change an object's center point perform the following steps:

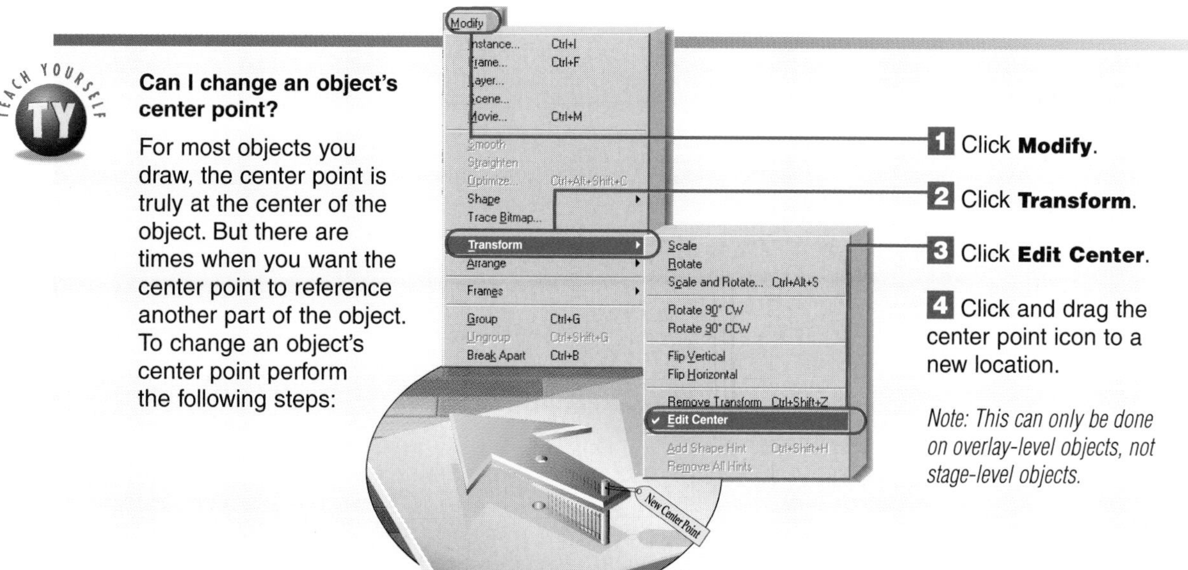

1 Click **Modify**.

2 Click **Transform**.

3 Click **Edit Center**.

4 Click and drag the center point icon to a new location.

Note: This can only be done on overlay-level objects, not stage-level objects.

FLIP AN OBJECT

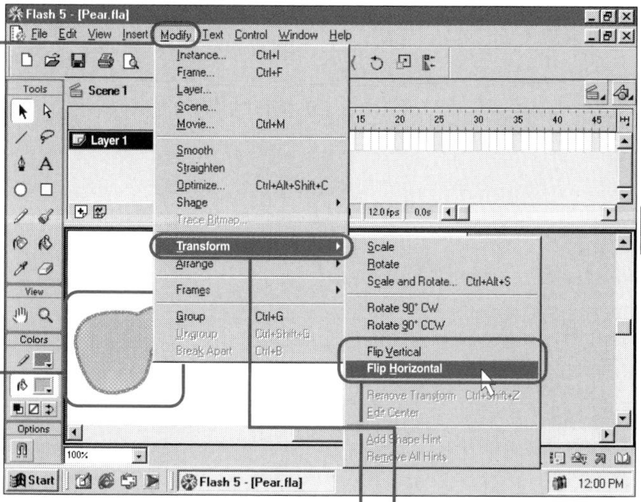

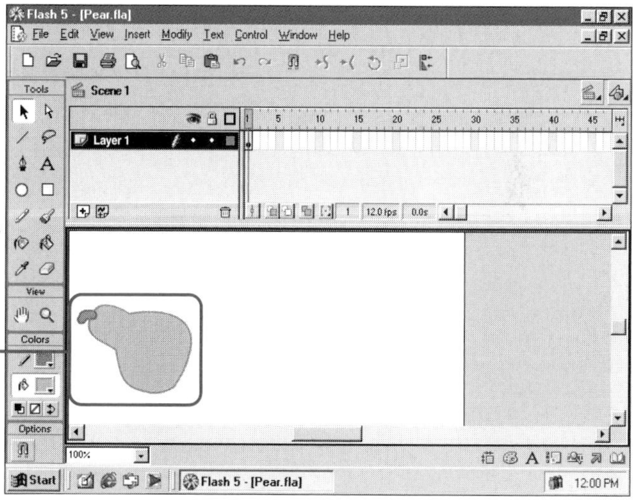

1 Click the object to select it.

Note: To learn more about selecting objects, see the section "Select Objects."

2 Click **Modify**.

3 Click **Transform**.

4 Click **Flip Vertical** or **Flip Horizontal**.

■ The object flips on the Stage.

GROUP AND UNGROUP OBJECTS

To work on multiple items at the same time, place them in a group. A group enables you to treat the items as a single unit. Any edits you make affect any items in the group.

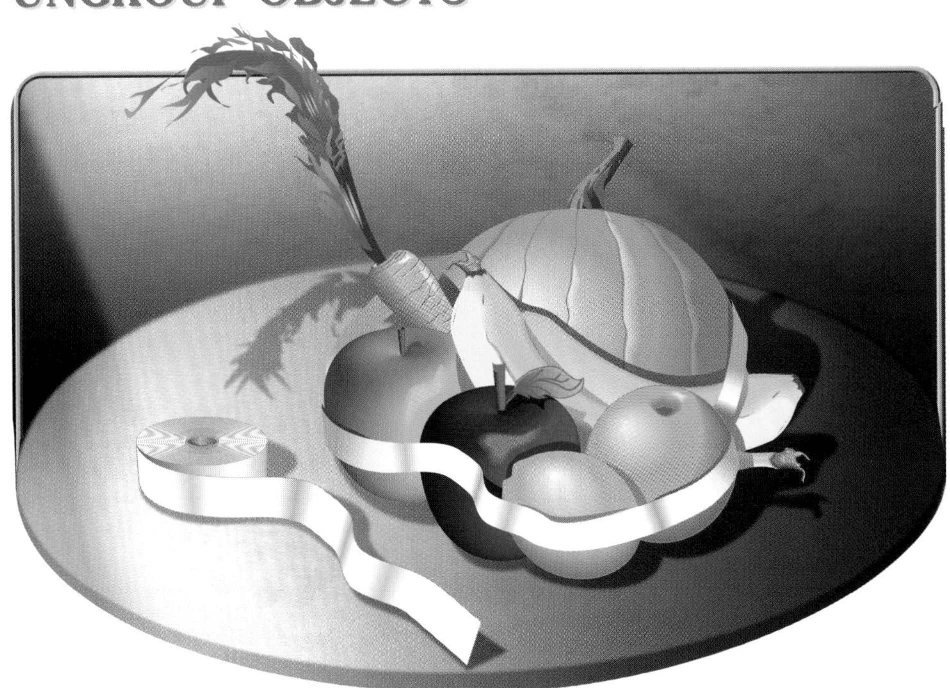

GROUP OBJECTS

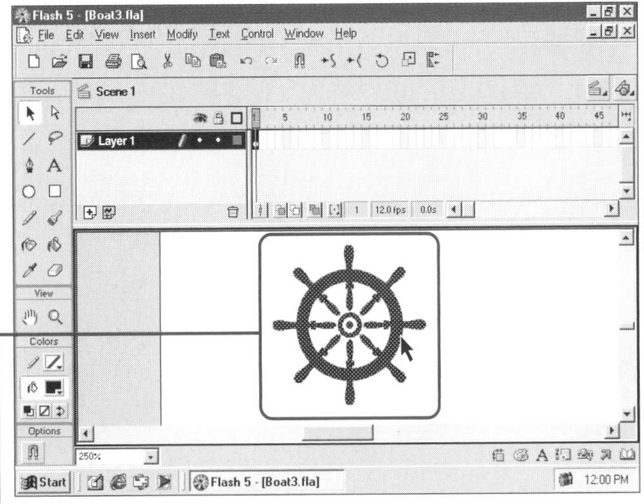

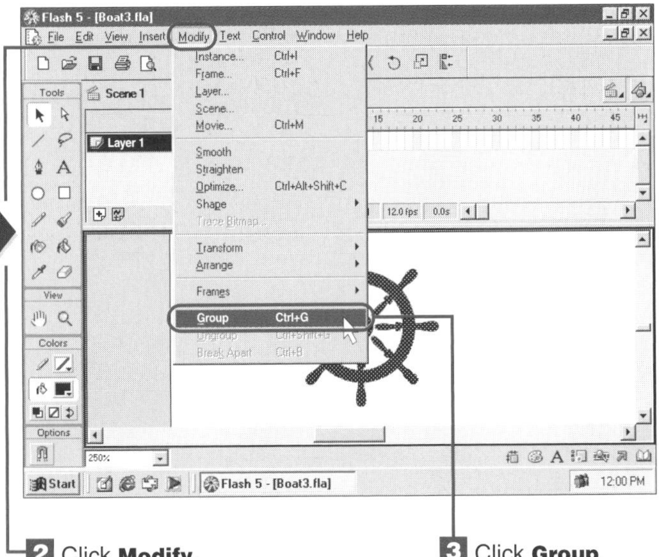

CREATE A GROUP

1 Select all the objects to be included in a group.

■ *To select multiple items, press and hold the Shift key down while clicking each item.*

Note: See the section "Select Objects" to learn more about selecting items on the Flash Stage.

2 Click **Modify**.

3 Click **Group**.

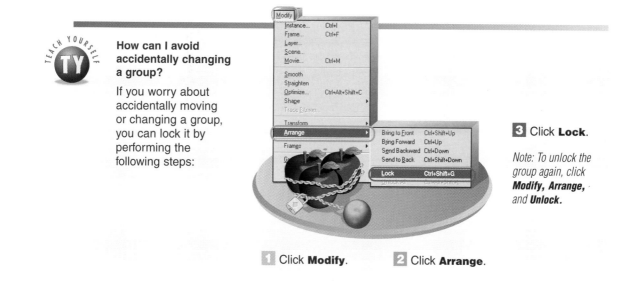

How can I avoid accidentally changing a group?

If you worry about accidentally moving or changing a group, you can lock it by performing the following steps:

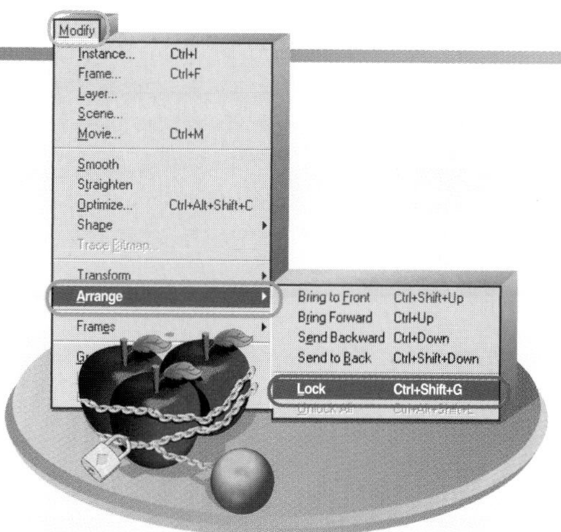

1 Click **Modify**.

2 Click **Arrange**.

3 Click **Lock**.

Note: To unlock the group again, click ***Modify, Arrange,*** *and* ***Unlock.***

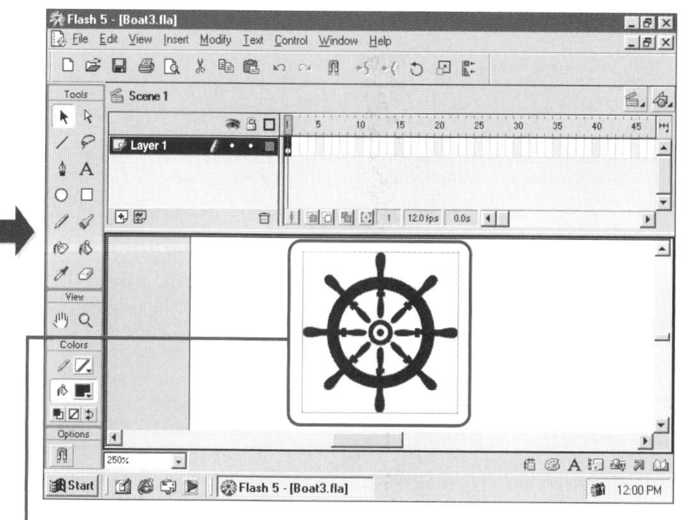

■ Flash groups the objects together and surrounds them with a blue box.

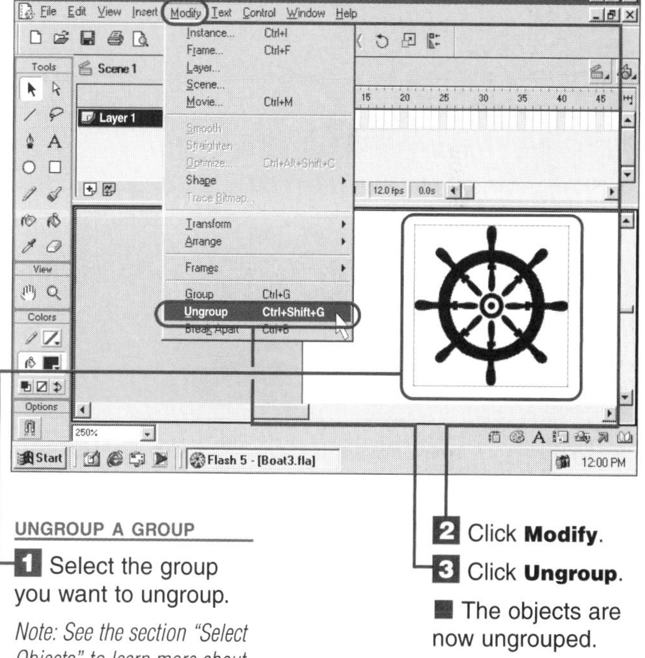

UNGROUP A GROUP

1 Select the group you want to ungroup.

Note: See the section "Select Objects" to learn more about selecting items on the Flash Stage.

2 Click **Modify**.

3 Click **Ungroup**.

■ The objects are now ungrouped.

WORK WITH STACKED OBJECTS

When you move an object on top of another object, it creates a *stacked* object. With stacked objects you can control exactly where an object appears in the stack. You can place an object at the very back of a stack, at the very front, or somewhere in-between.

WORK WITH STACKED OBJECTS

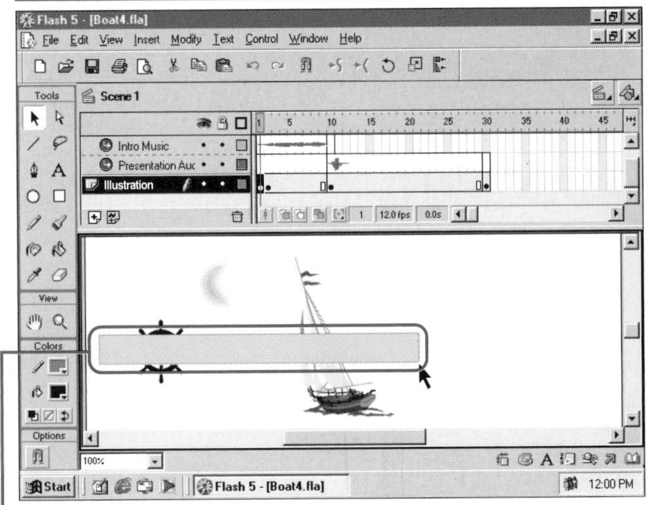

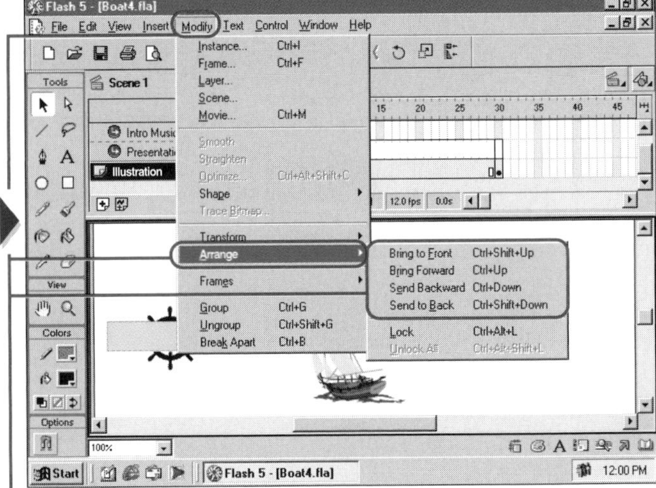

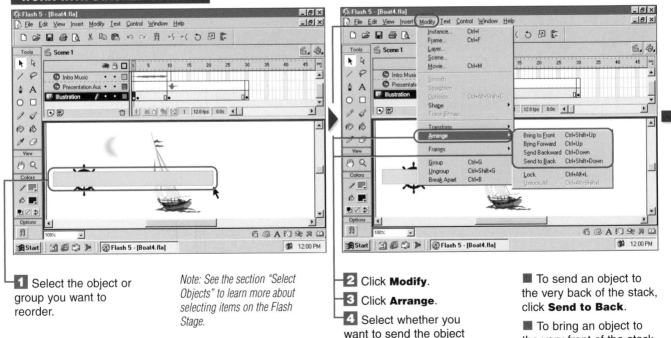

1 Select the object or group you want to reorder.

Note: See the section "Select Objects" to learn more about selecting items on the Flash Stage.

2 Click **Modify**.

3 Click **Arrange**.

4 Select whether you want to send the object to the front or back of the stack.

■ To send an object to the very back of the stack, click **Send to Back**.

■ To bring an object to the very front of the stack, click **Bring to Front**.

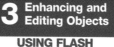

How do I move an object in a stack using the keyboard?

Move the object up one layer	Press Ctrl + ↑ (Windows) Press ⌘ + ↑ (Mac)
Move the object directly to the top of the stack	Press Ctrl + Shift + ↑ (Windows) Press ⌘ + Shift + ↑ (Mac)
Move the object back a layer	Press Ctrl + ↓ (Windows) Press ⌘ + ↓ (Mac)
Move the object directly to the back of the stack	Press Ctrl + Shift + ↓ (Windows) Press ⌘ + Shift + ↓ (Mac)

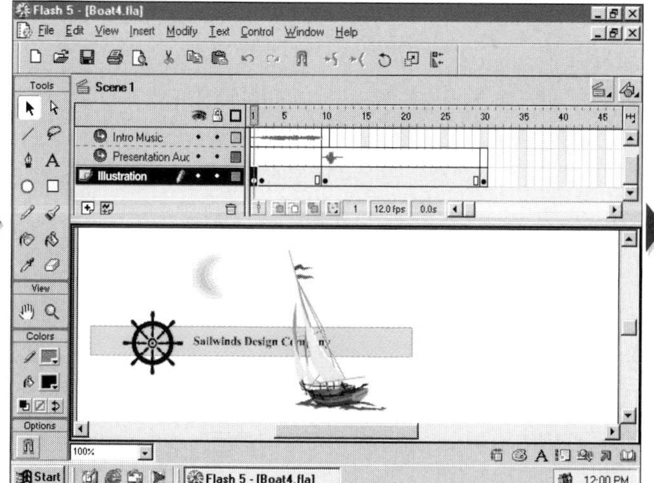

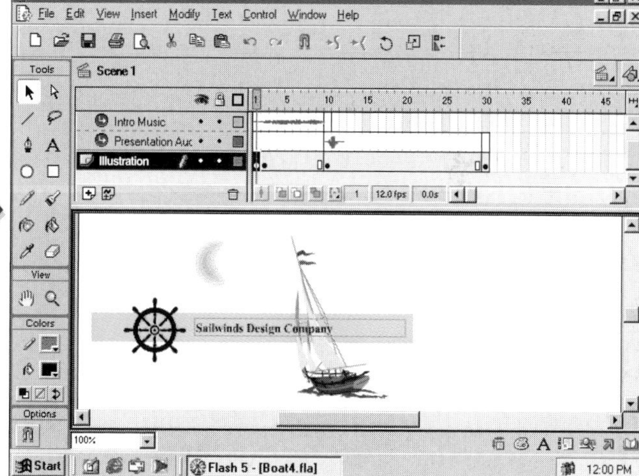

■ The object now relocates in the stacking order as directed.

■ In this example, the blue bar moved to the back of the stack.

■ In this example, the text block moves in front of the sail boat.

ALIGN OBJECTS

The Align panel has tools for controlling precisely where an object sits on the Stage. You can align objects vertically and horizontally by their edges or centers. You can align objects with other objects, with the edges of the Stage, or even control the amount of space between the objects.

ALIGN OBJECTS

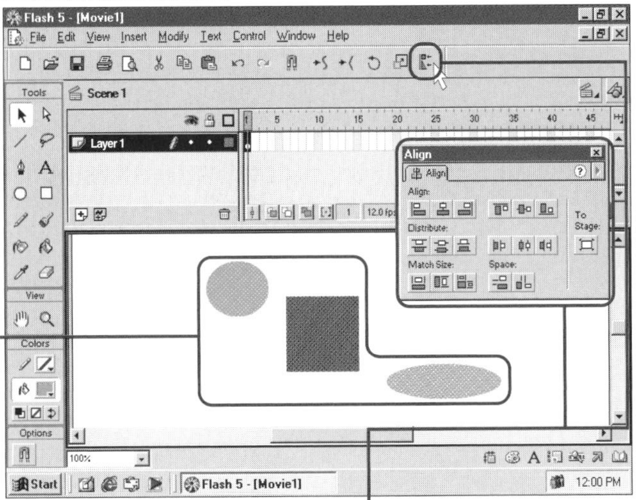

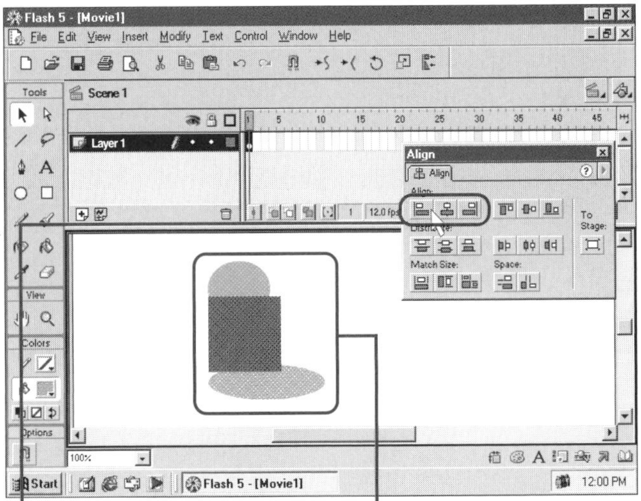

ALIGN OBJECTS WITH OTHER OBJECTS

1 Select the objects you want to align.

Note: See the section "Select Objects" to learn more about selecting items on the Flash Stage.

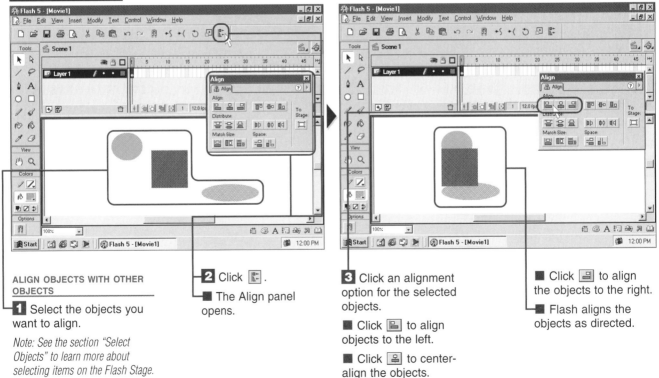

2 Click .

■ The Align panel opens.

3 Click an alignment option for the selected objects.

■ Click to align objects to the left.

■ Click to center-align the objects.

■ Click to align the objects to the right.

■ Flash aligns the objects as directed.

How can I align objects vertically?

The Align panel has buttons for setting vertical alignments along with horizontal alignments. Each button in the Align panel has an image that shows how the objects will align when that button is selected. You can use the three vertical alignment buttons to align objects vertically with each other or align them vertically with the Flash Stage. To align objects with the Stage, be sure to click the button first before clicking an alignment button.

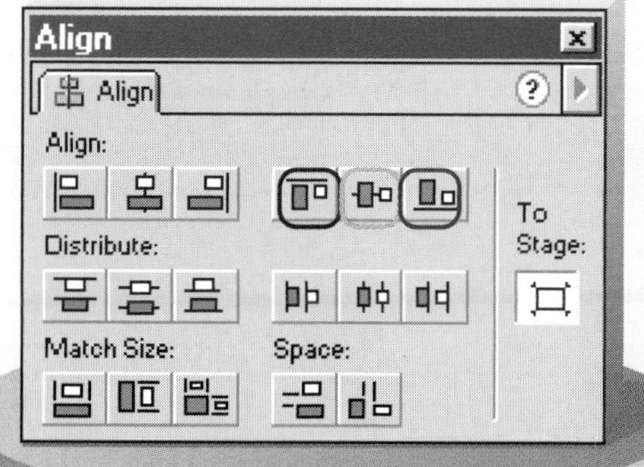

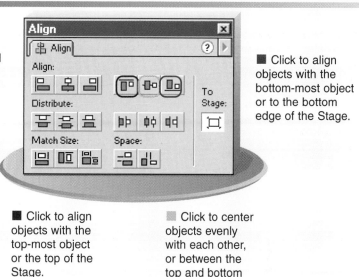

■ Click to align objects with the bottom-most object or to the bottom edge of the Stage.

■ Click to align objects with the top-most object or the top of the Stage.

■ Click to center objects evenly with each other, or between the top and bottom of the Stage.

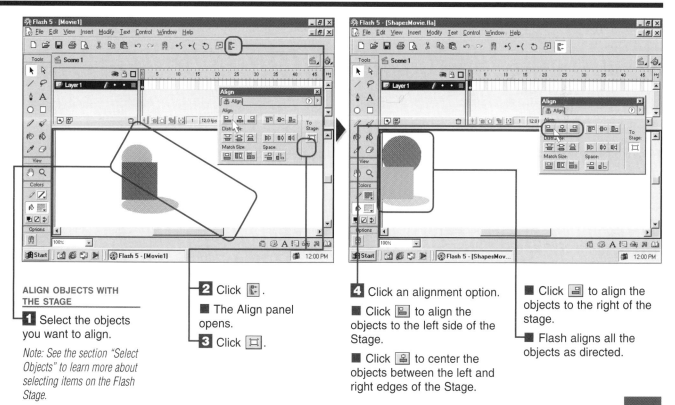

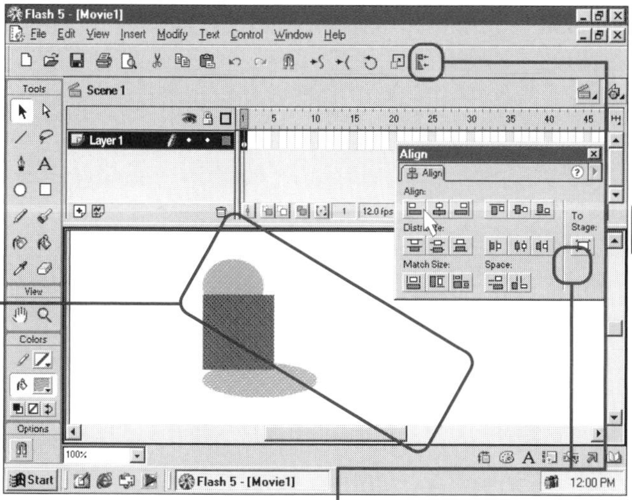

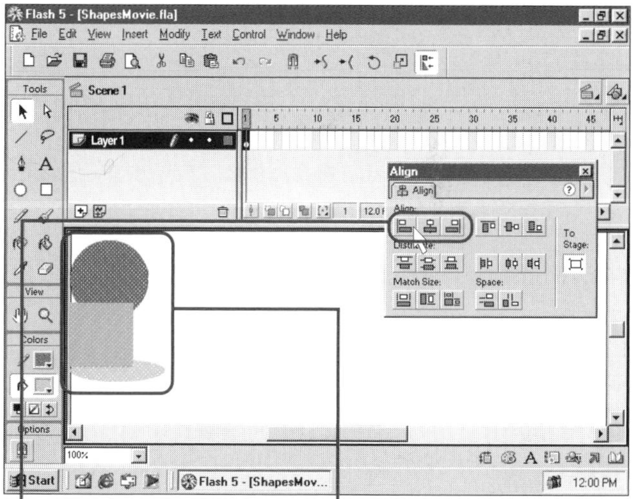

ALIGN OBJECTS WITH THE STAGE

1 Select the objects you want to align.

Note: See the section "Select Objects" to learn more about selecting items on the Flash Stage.

2 Click .

■ The Align panel opens.

3 Click .

4 Click an alignment option.

■ Click to align the objects to the left side of the Stage.

■ Click to center the objects between the left and right edges of the Stage.

■ Click to align the objects to the right of the stage.

■ Flash aligns all the objects as directed.

ADD TEXT WITH THE TEXT TOOL

Use the Text tool to add text to a movie or graphic. You can insert label or block text boxes on the Stage area. With a label text box, you can click where you want the text to appear and start typing. With block text, you define the box size first.

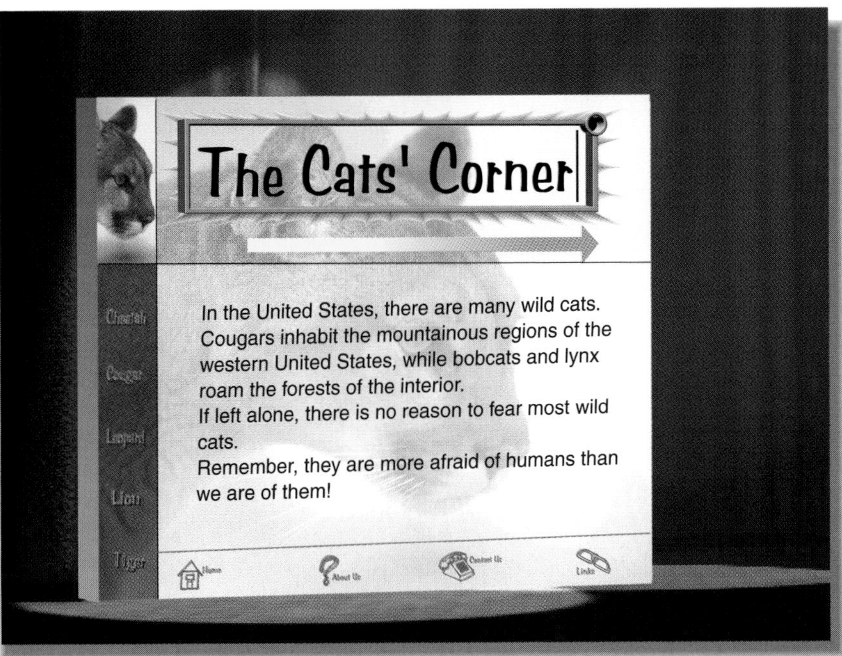

ADD TEXT WITH THE TEXT TOOL

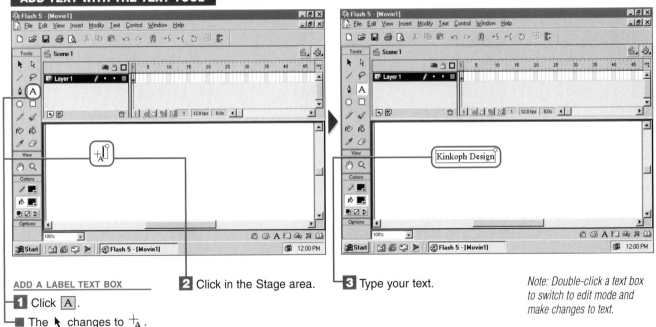

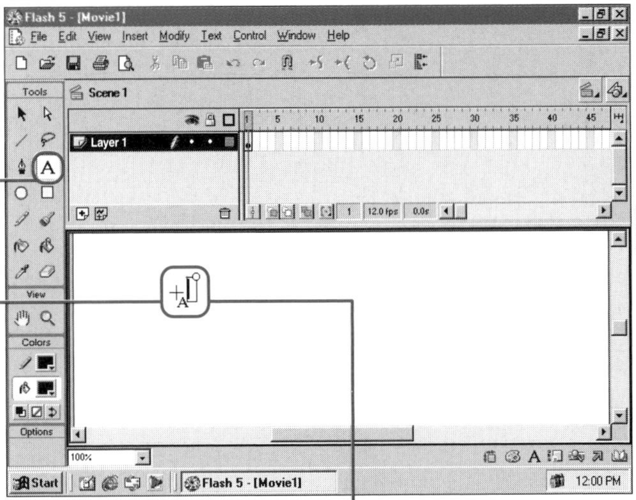

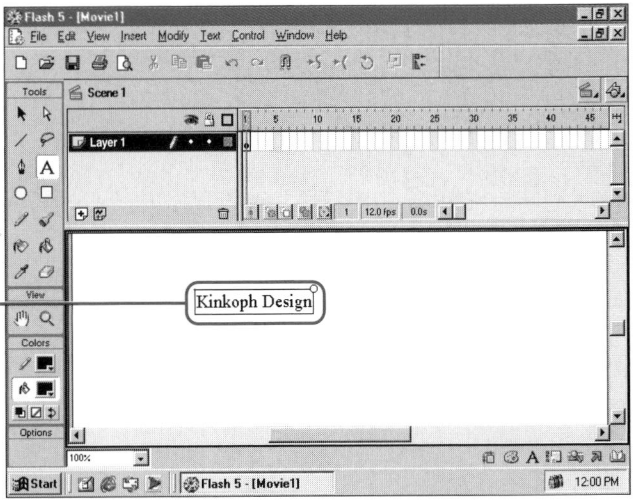

ADD A LABEL TEXT BOX

1 Click A.

■ The pointer changes to the Text tool pointer ($+_A$).

2 Click in the Stage area.

3 Type your text.

Note: Double-click a text box to switch to edit mode and make changes to text.

What is the difference between labels and blocks?

When you type text into a label text box, text does not wrap. The width of the text box keeps expanding as you type characters. With a block text box, you specify a width, and when the text you are typing reaches the end of the block, it wraps to start a new line, increasing the depth of the text box.

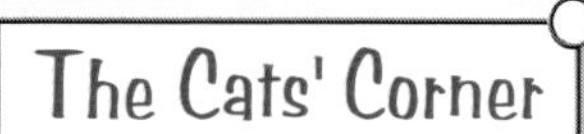

Label text box

Block text box

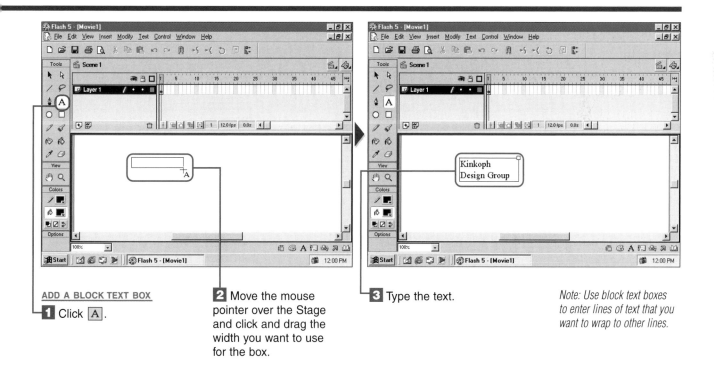

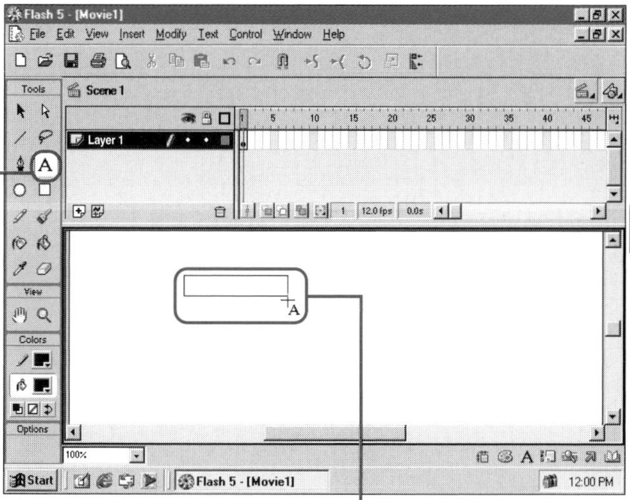

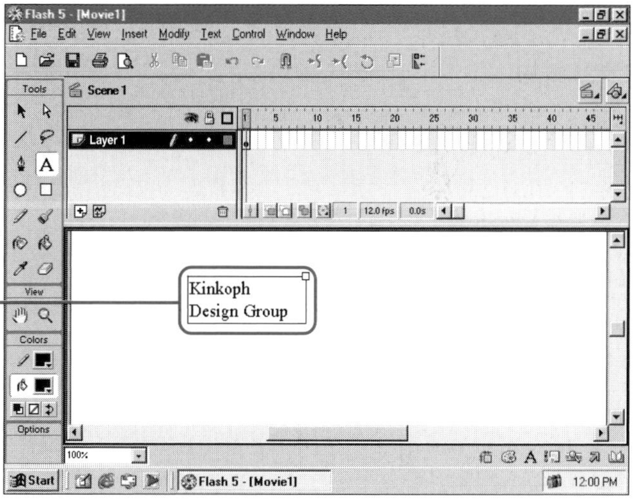

ADD A BLOCK TEXT BOX

1 Click [A].

2 Move the mouse pointer over the Stage and click and drag the width you want to use for the box.

3 Type the text.

Note: Use block text boxes to enter lines of text that you want to wrap to other lines.

FORMAT TEXT

You can easily format text by using the Character panel. It has all the controls for formatting text located in one convenient mini-window.

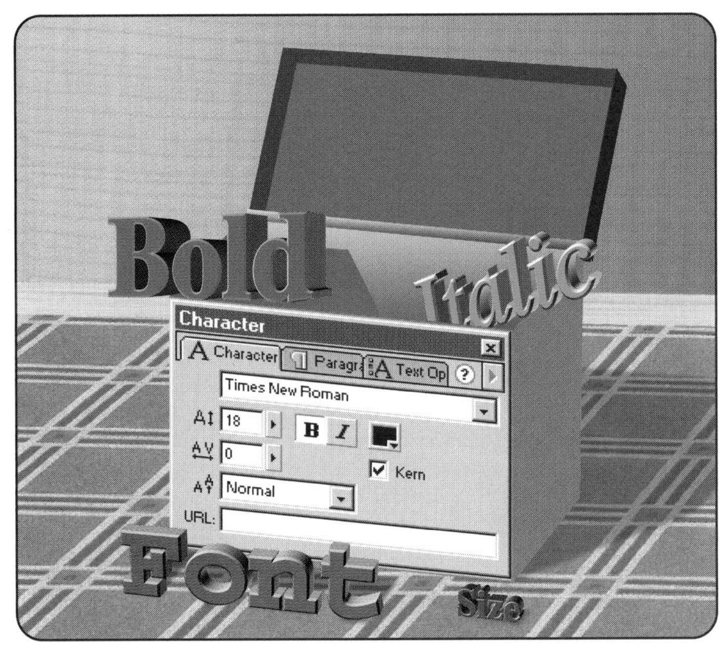

APPLY BOLD AND ITALICS

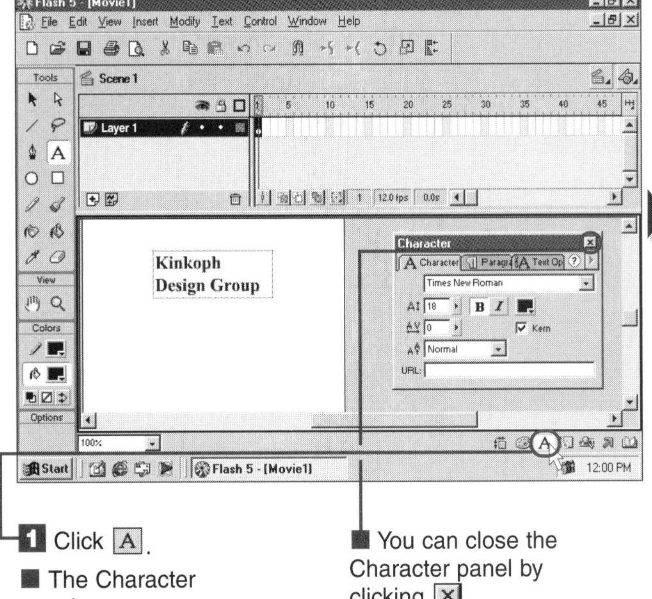

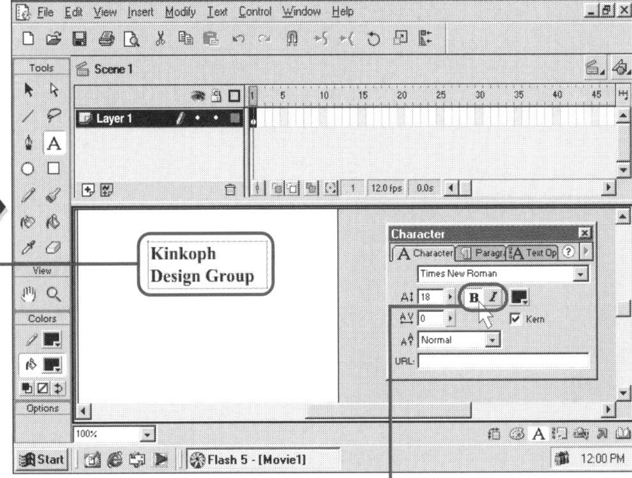

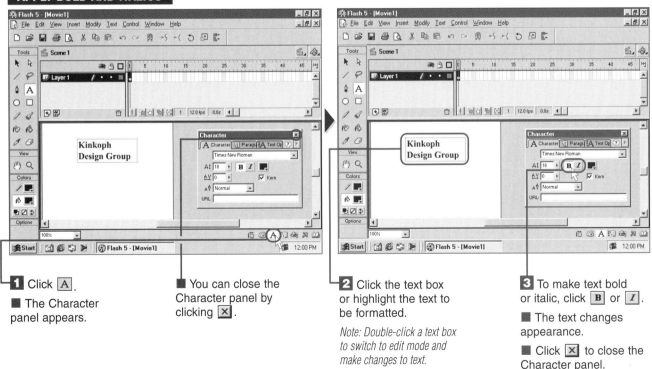

1 Click A.

■ The Character panel appears.

■ You can close the Character panel by clicking ☒.

2 Click the text box or highlight the text to be formatted.

Note: Double-click a text box to switch to edit mode and make changes to text.

3 To make text bold or italic, click **B** or *I*.

■ The text changes appearance.

■ Click ☒ to close the Character panel.

Do I have to use the Character panel to format text?

You can also find text formatting controls in the Text menu. For example, to change the font:

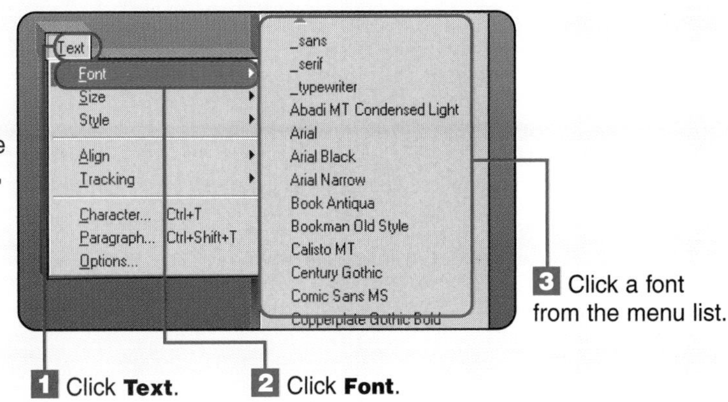

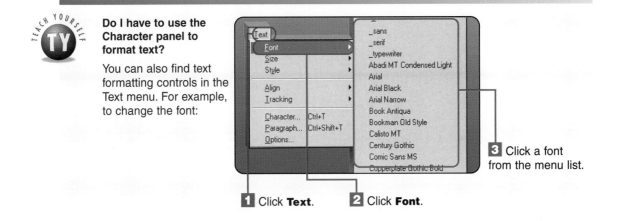

1 Click **Text**.

2 Click **Font**.

3 Click a font from the menu list.

CHANGE FONT STYLE AND SIZE

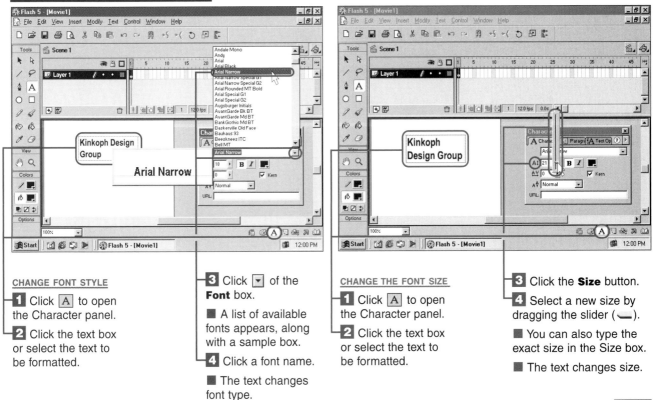

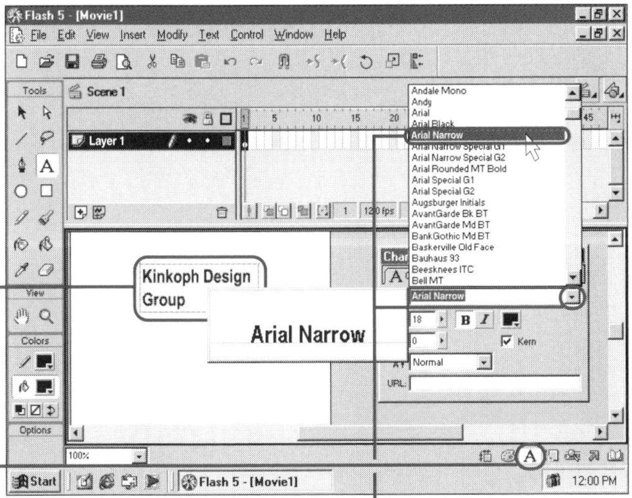

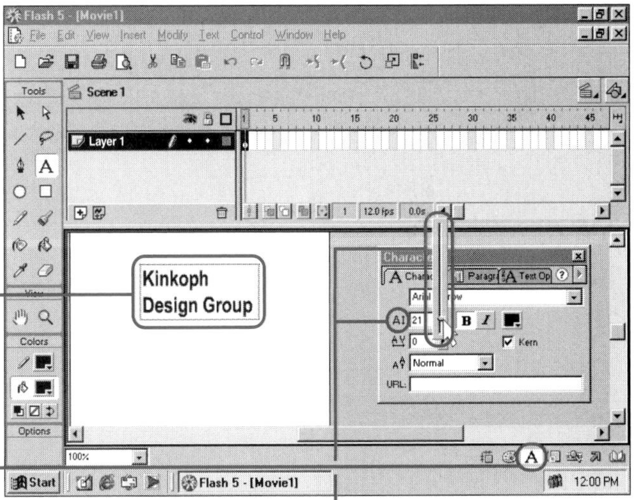

CHANGE FONT STYLE

1 Click A to open the Character panel.

2 Click the text box or select the text to be formatted.

3 Click ▾ of the **Font** box.

■ A list of available fonts appears, along with a sample box.

4 Click a font name.

■ The text changes font type.

CHANGE THE FONT SIZE

1 Click A to open the Character panel.

2 Click the text box or select the text to be formatted.

3 Click the **Size** button.

4 Select a new size by dragging the slider ( ).

■ You can also type the exact size in the Size box.

■ The text changes size.

CHANGE TEXT ALIGNMENT

You can change the way text appears within a text box using the options found in the Paragraph panel or on the Text menu. When you change kerning, you adjust the amount of space between individual letters.

ALIGN TEXT

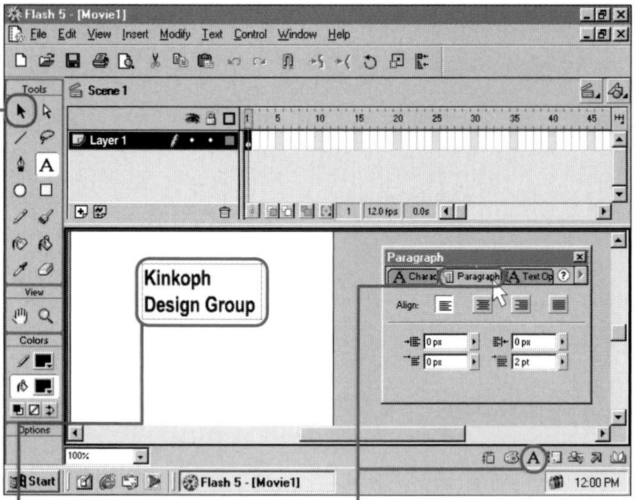

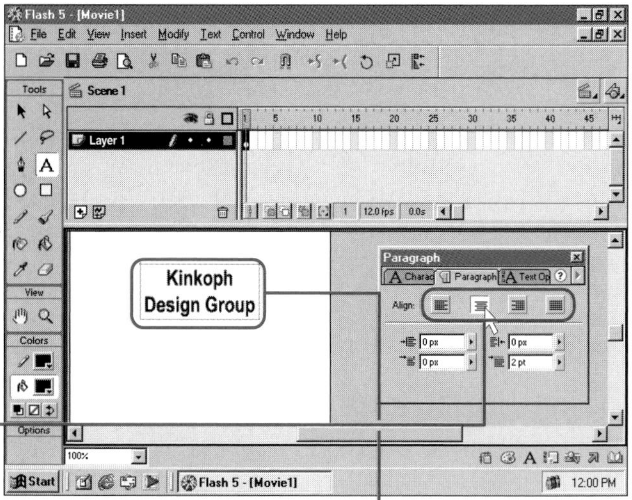

1 Click the text box.

■ You can use the [selection arrow] to select items on the Stage.

2 Click [A] to open the Character panel.

3 Click the **Paragraph** tab.

4 Click an alignment button.

■ The text aligns immediately in the text box.

What is kerning?

Kerning refers to the spacing of characters. By changing the kerning setting, you can create text effects such as word characters squished together or pulled apart.

CHANGE KERNING

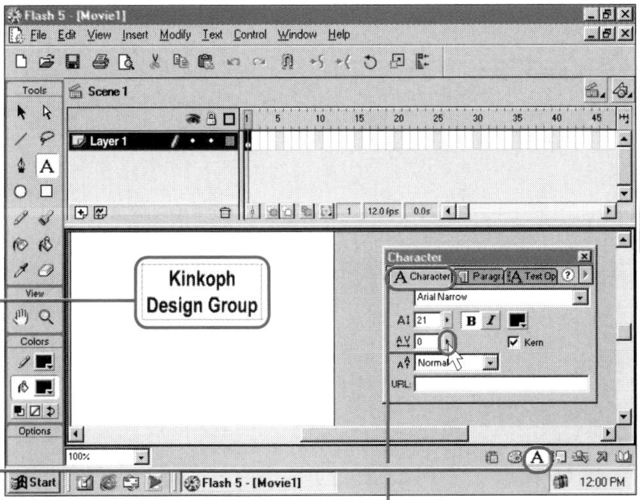

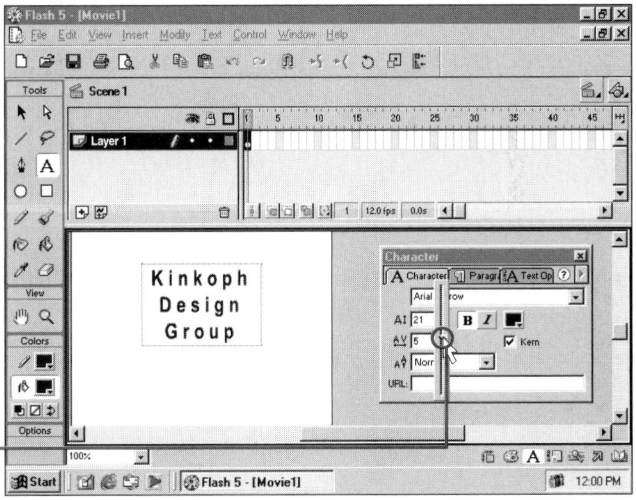

1 Click the text box.

2 Click [A] to open the Character panel.

3 Click the **Character** tab.

4 Click the **Kerning** button.

5 Click and drag the slider (▭) up to add space between characters or down to remove space.

ADD AND DELETE LAYERS

When you create a new movie or scene, Flash starts you out with a single layer and a Timeline. You can add layers to the Timeline, or delete layers you no longer need. Additional layers do not affect the file size, so you can add and delete as many layers as your project requires.

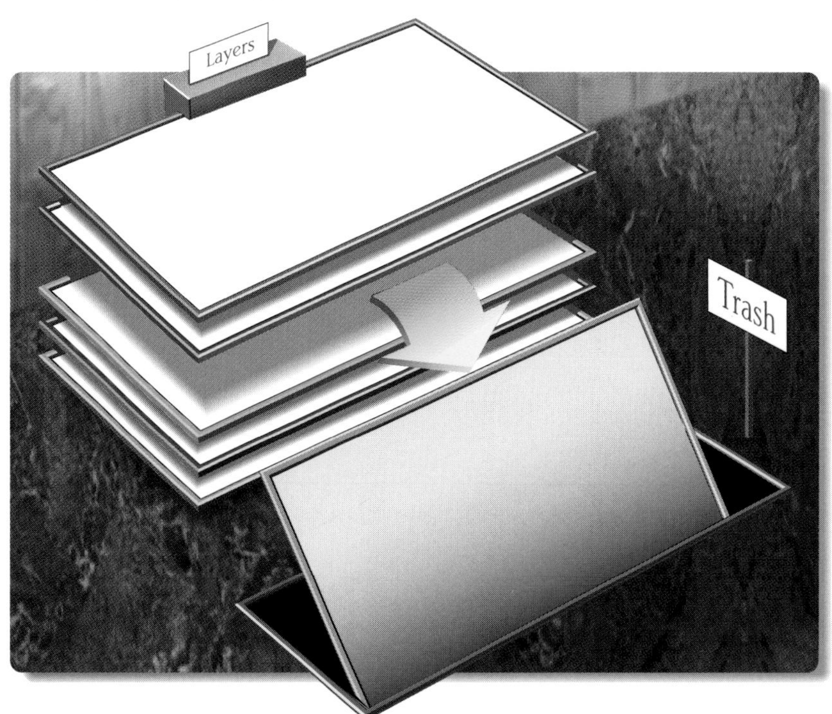

ADD A LAYER

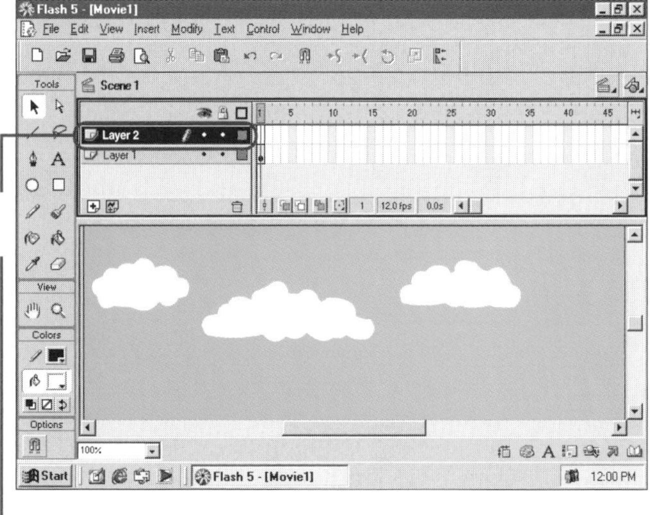

1 Click the layer that will appear below the new layer.

2 Click [icon].

■ A new layer immediately appears.

■ Flash adds the same amount of frames to the new layer to match the layer with the longest frame sequence.

Note: See Chapter 7 to learn more about frames.

Can I delete several layers at once?

You can delete more than one layer at a time. Click the first layer to remove, then press Ctrl (Windows) or ⌘ (Mac) while clicking other layers to remove. Click 🗑 to remove them all at once.

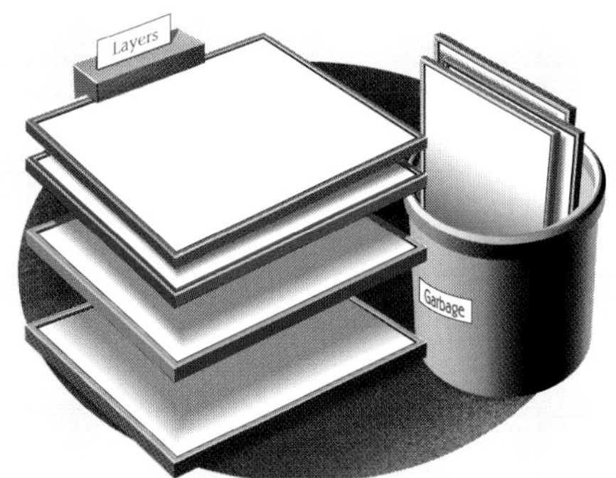

DELETE A LAYER

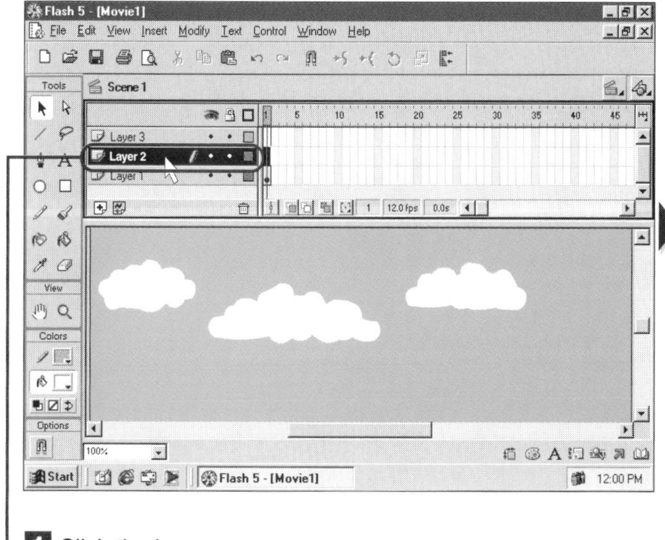

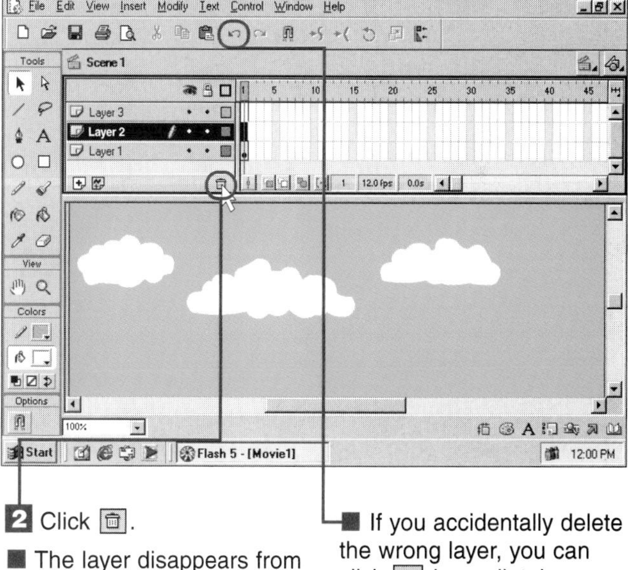

1 Click the layer you want to delete.

2 Click 🗑.

■ The layer disappears from the Timeline.

■ If you accidentally delete the wrong layer, you can click ↶ immediately.

SET LAYER PROPERTIES

You can change any aspect of a given layer through the Layer Properties dialog, a one-stop shop for controlling a layer's name, function, and appearance.

To create a layer, see the section "Add and Delete Layers."

SET LAYER PROPERTIES

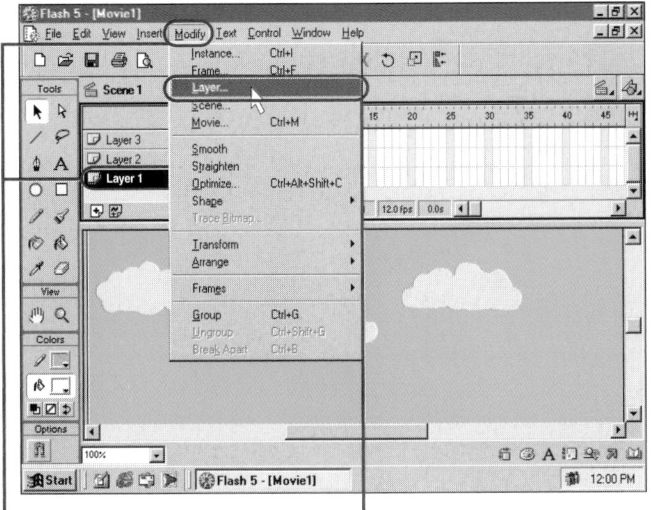

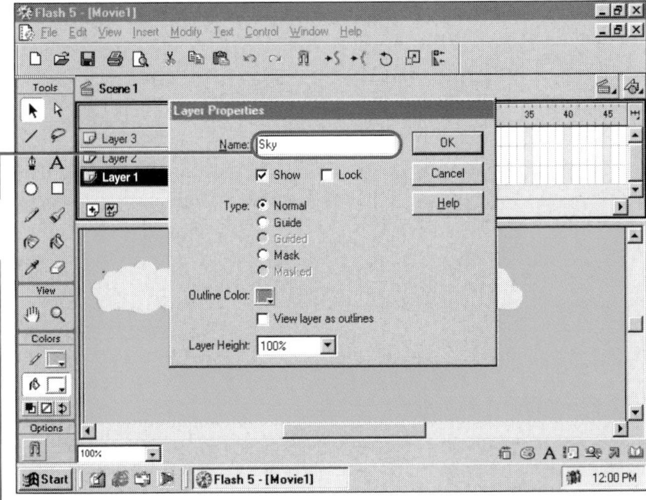

1 Click the layer for which you want to set controls.

2 Click **Modify**.

3 Click **Layer**.

■ The Layer Properties dialog box opens.

4 Type a distinctive name for the layer in the Name text box.

What are layer types?

By default, all layers you add to the Timeline are *normal*, which means all the objects on the layer appear in the movie. Objects you place on guide layers do not appear in the movie. A regular *guide* layer can be used for reference points and alignment. A *guided* layer is a layer linked to a regular guide layer. A *mask* layer hides any layers linked to it. To change the layer type, click a type in the Layer Properties dialog box (○ changes to ⊙).

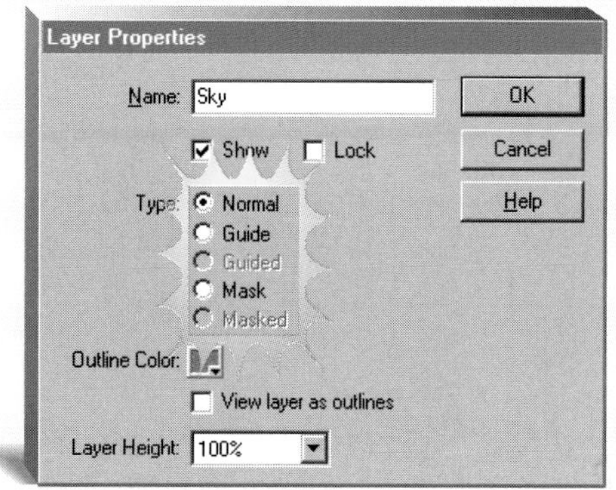

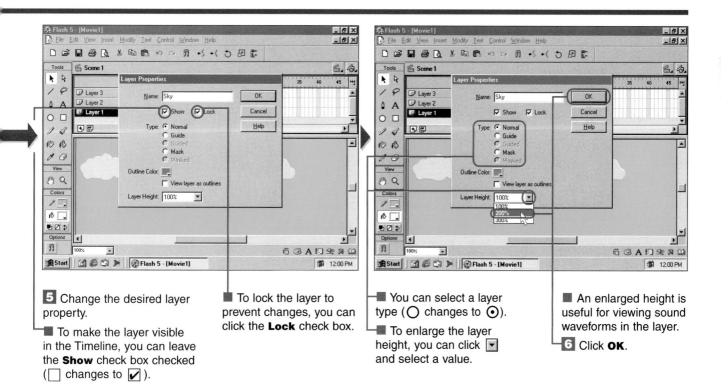

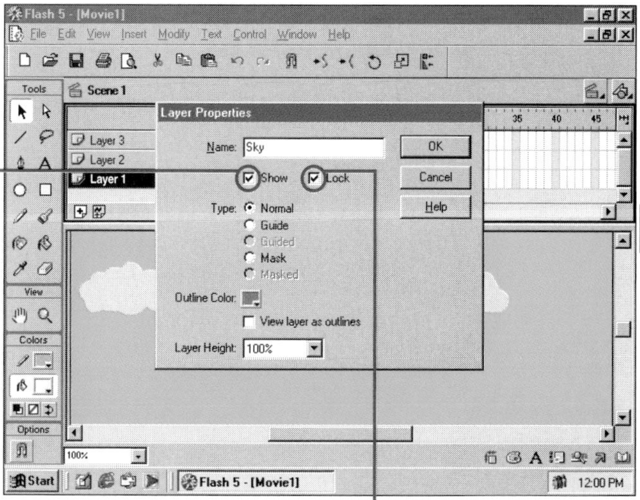

5 Change the desired layer property.

■ To make the layer visible in the Timeline, you can leave the **Show** check box checked (☐ changes to ☑).

■ To lock the layer to prevent changes, you can click the **Lock** check box.

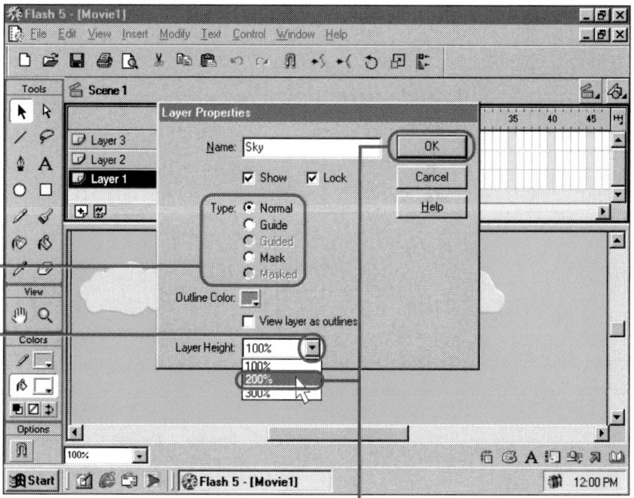

■ You can select a layer type (○ changes to ⊙).

■ To enlarge the layer height, you can click ▼ and select a value.

■ An enlarged height is useful for viewing sound waveforms in the layer.

6 Click **OK**.

CHANGE THE LAYER STACKING ORDER

To rearrange how objects appear in the movie, you can stack Flash layers in a manner similar to how you stack objects in a drawing. For example, if you have a layer containing background elements, you can move it to the back of the layer stack.

To create a layer, see the section "Add and Delete Layers."

CHANGE THE STACKING ORDER

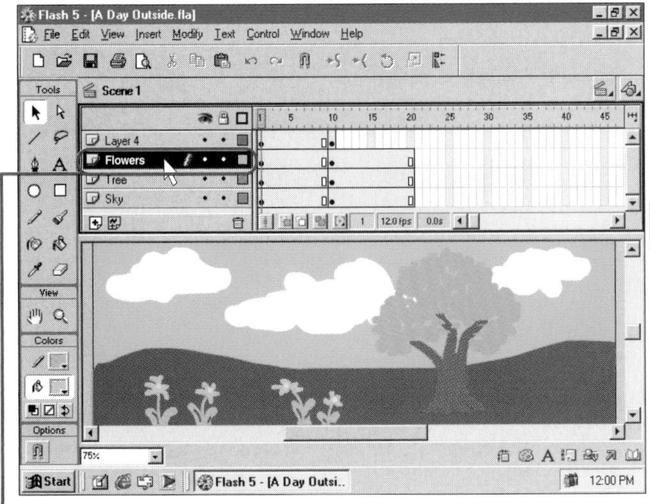

1 Click the layer you want to move.

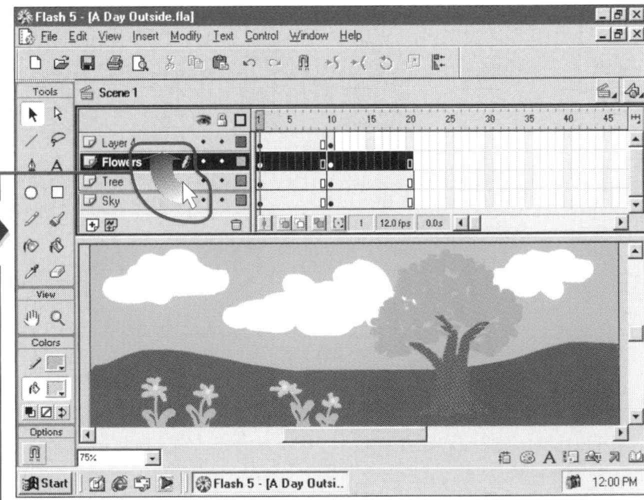

2 Drag the layer up or down to its new location in the stack.

■ An insertion point appears, showing where the dragged layer will rest.

Can I copy a layer?

First create a new layer (see the section "Add and Delete Layers"), then click the layer you want to copy. Click [copy icon] on the toolbar. Click the new layer, then click [paste icon] on the toolbar. Flash copies the contents of the first layer and places them on the second layer, slightly offset.

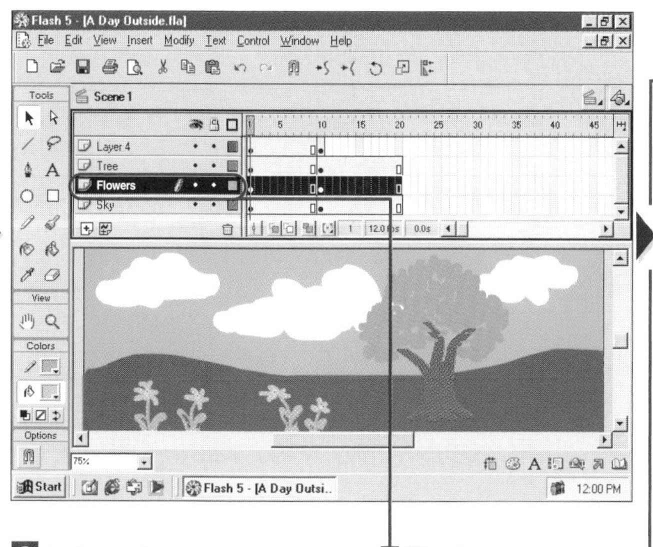

3 Release the mouse button.

■ The layer assumes its new position.

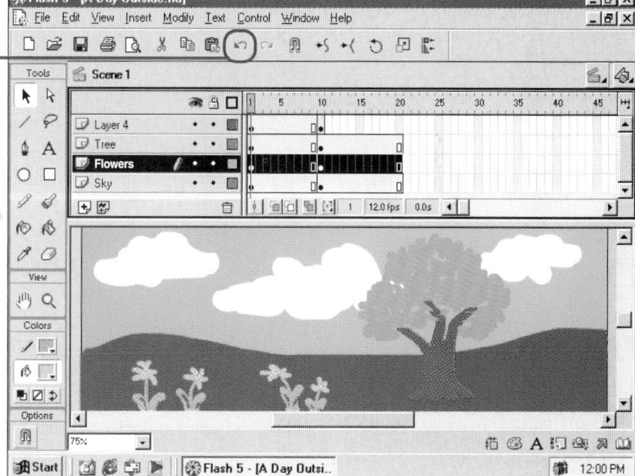

■ To move the layer back to its original position, click [undo icon].

CREATE SYMBOLS

You can easily turn any object you draw on the Flash Stage into a symbol you can reuse throughout your project.

CREATE SYMBOLS

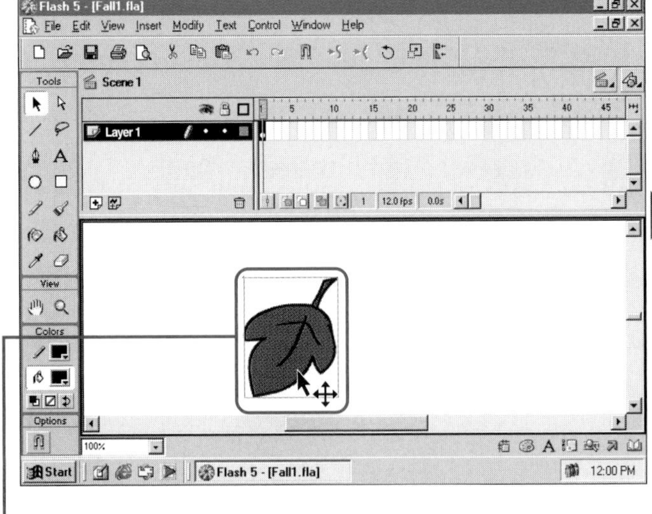

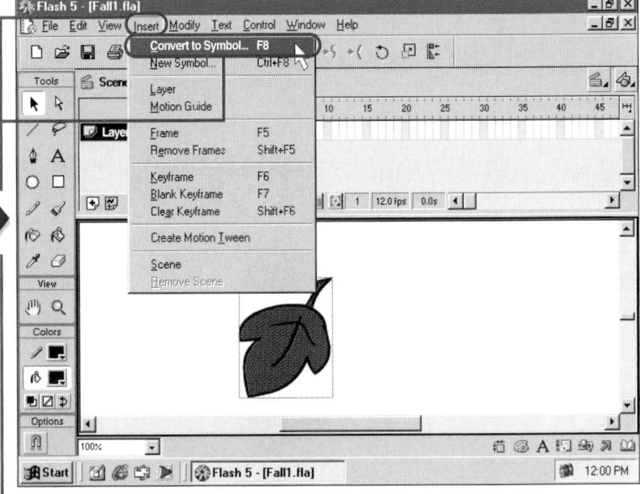

CONVERT OBJECTS TO SYMBOLS

1 Click all the objects on the stage you want to convert into a symbol.

■ To select multiple objects, hold down Shift while clicking on each object.

2 Click **Insert**.

3 Click **Convert to Symbol**.

■ The Symbol Properties dialog box opens.

TEACH YOURSELF **TY**

Can I create a duplicate symbol?

You may want to copy a symbol and change it slightly.

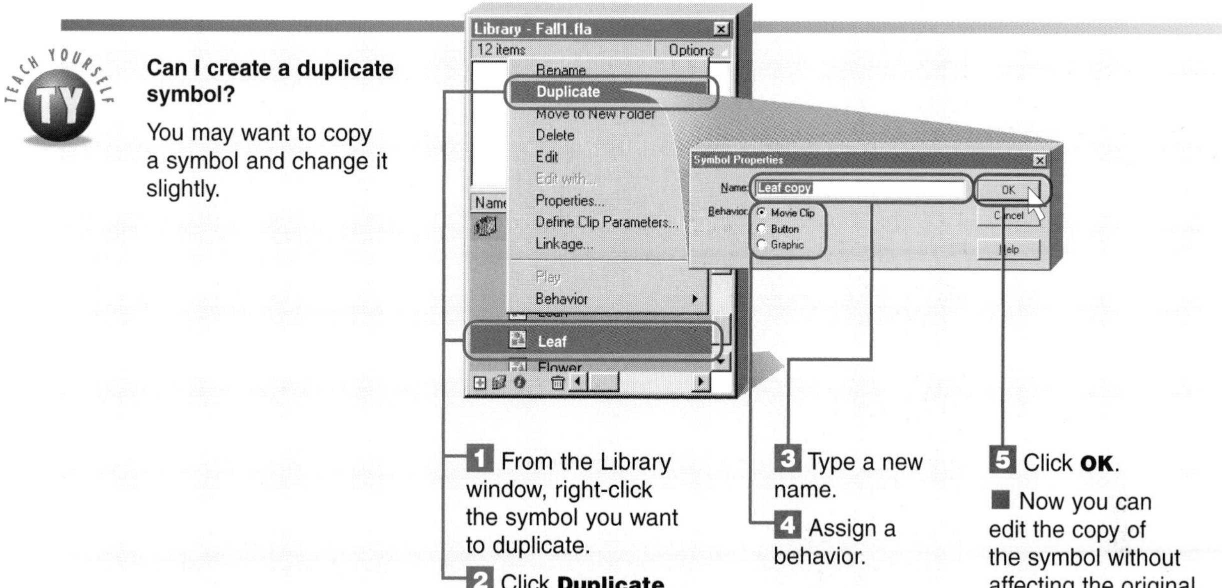

1 From the Library window, right-click the symbol you want to duplicate.

2 Click **Duplicate**.

3 Type a new name.

4 Assign a behavior.

5 Click **OK**.

■ Now you can edit the copy of the symbol without affecting the original.

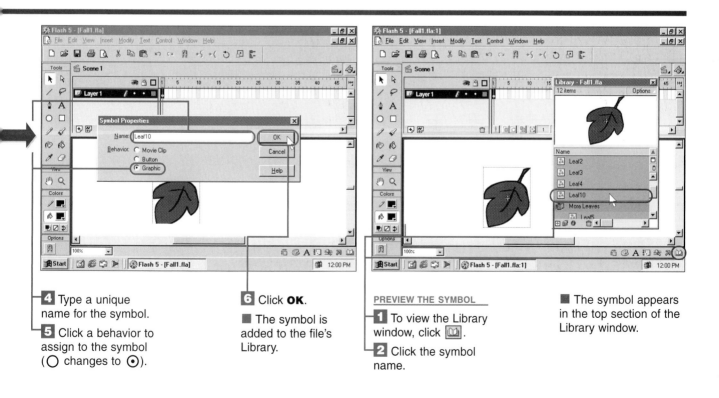

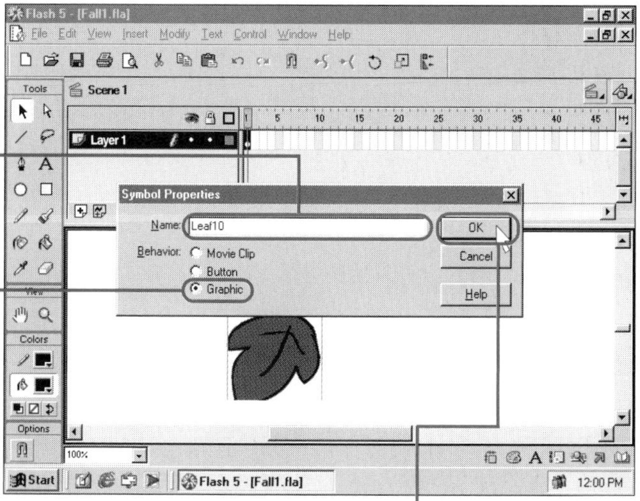

4 Type a unique name for the symbol.

5 Click a behavior to assign to the symbol (○ changes to ⊙).

6 Click **OK**.

■ The symbol is added to the file's Library.

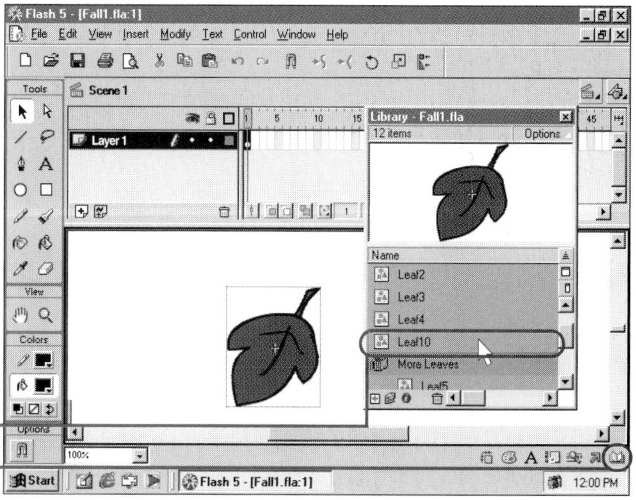

PREVIEW THE SYMBOL

1 To view the Library window, click 📖.

2 Click the symbol name.

■ The symbol appears in the top section of the Library window.

INSERT A SYMBOL INSTANCE

To reuse a symbol in your Flash project, you can place an *instance* of it on the Stage. The instance references the original instead of duplicating it all over again, which decreases the movie's file size.

INSERT A SYMBOL INSTANCE

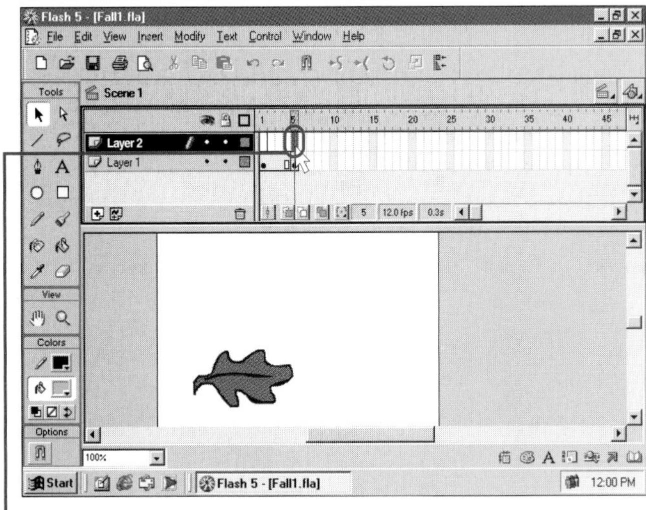

1 Open the frame and layer where you want to insert the instance.

Note: To learn more about frames, see Chapter 7. To learn more about layers, turn to Chapter 5.

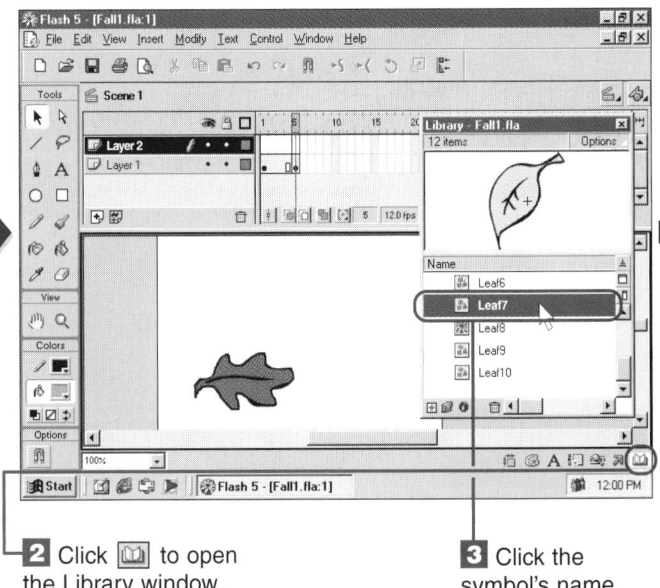

2 Click 📖 to open the Library window.

3 Click the symbol's name.

Can I replace one instance with another?

To replace an existing symbol in your project with another from the library:

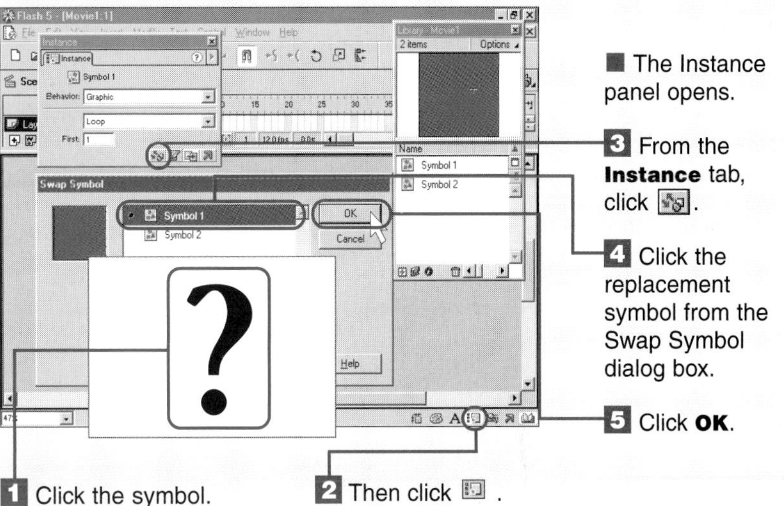

1 Click the symbol.

2 Then click .

■ The Instance panel opens.

3 From the **Instance** tab, click .

4 Click the replacement symbol from the Swap Symbol dialog box.

5 Click **OK**.

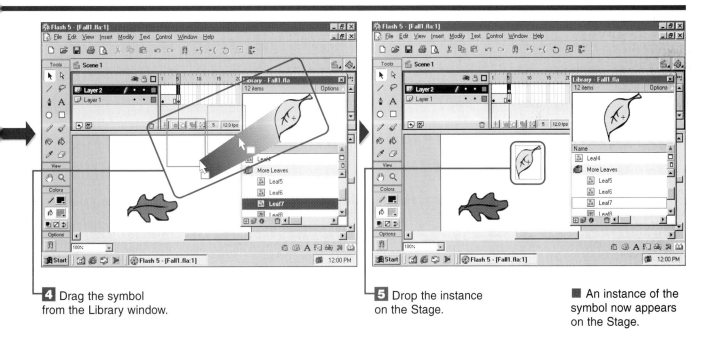

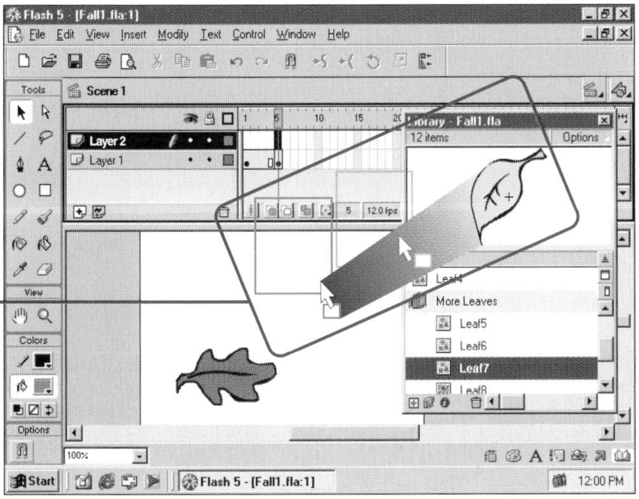

4 Drag the symbol from the Library window.

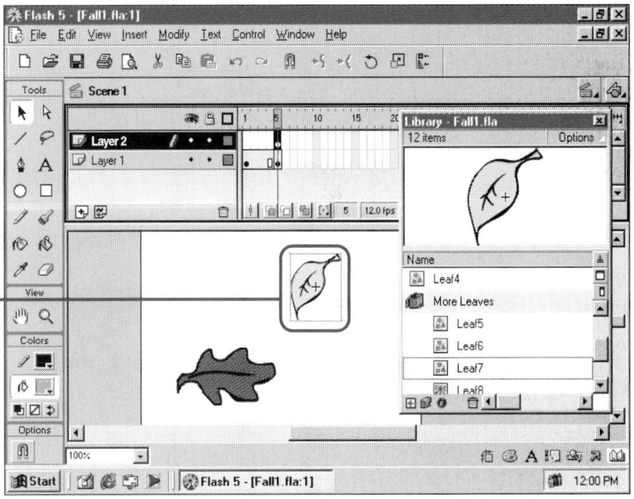

5 Drop the instance on the Stage.

■ An instance of the symbol now appears on the Stage.

MODIFY A SYMBOL INSTANCE

After you place a symbol instance on the Stage, you can change the way it appears without changing the original symbol. For example, you can change its color or make it appear transparent.

MODIFY AN INSTANCE'S COLOR EFFECTS

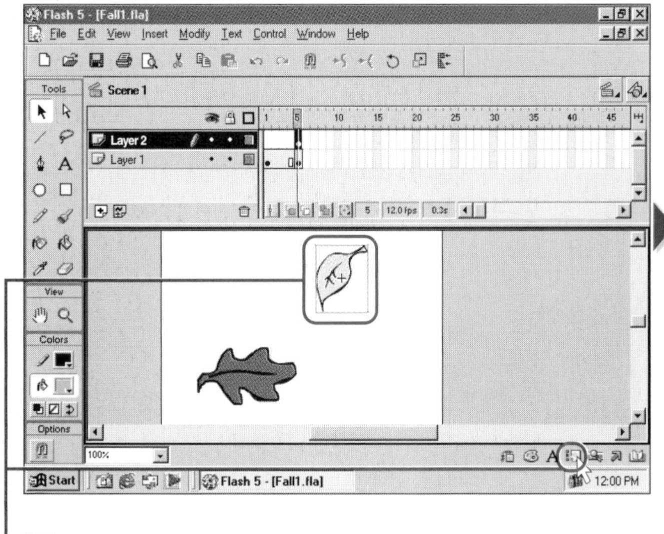

1 Click the instance you want to modify.

2 Click .

■ The Instance panel opens.

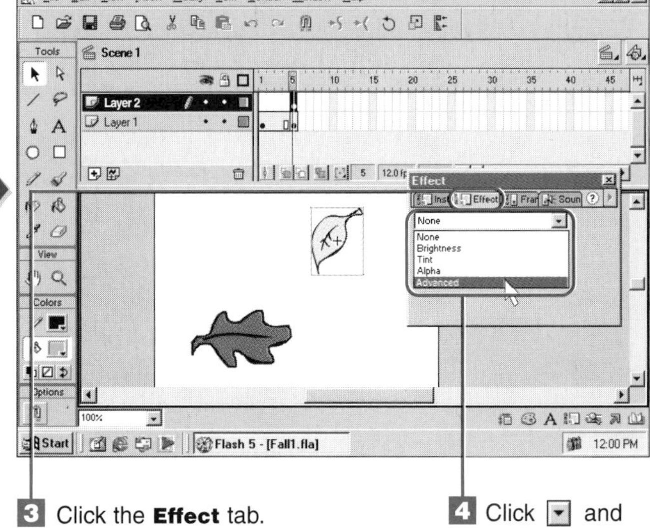

3 Click the **Effect** tab.

4 Click and select **Advanced**.

TEACH YOURSELF

How do I make the instance transparent?

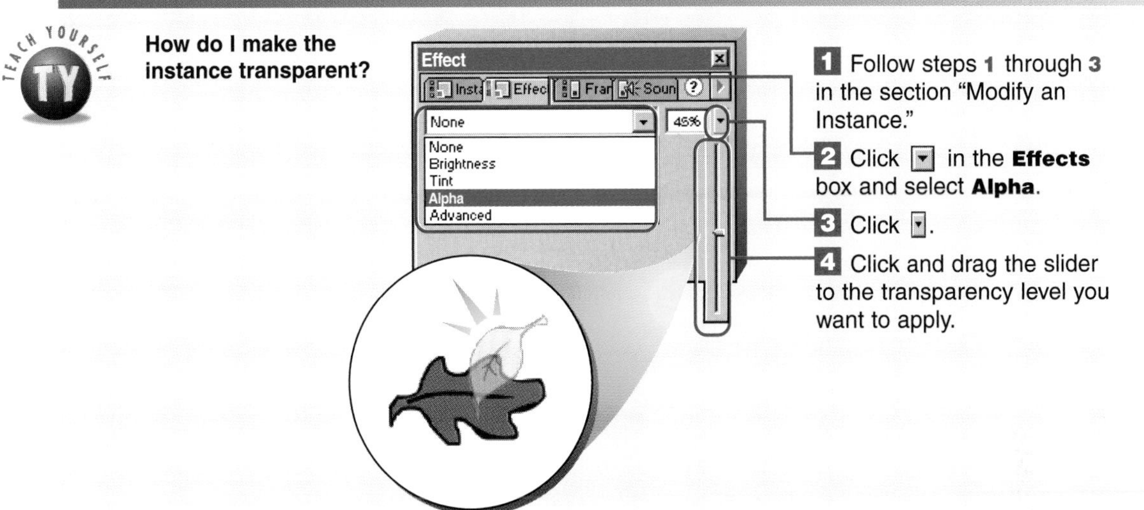

1 Follow steps 1 through 3 in the section "Modify an Instance."

2 Click ▼ in the **Effects** box and select **Alpha**.

3 Click ▼.

4 Click and drag the slider to the transparency level you want to apply.

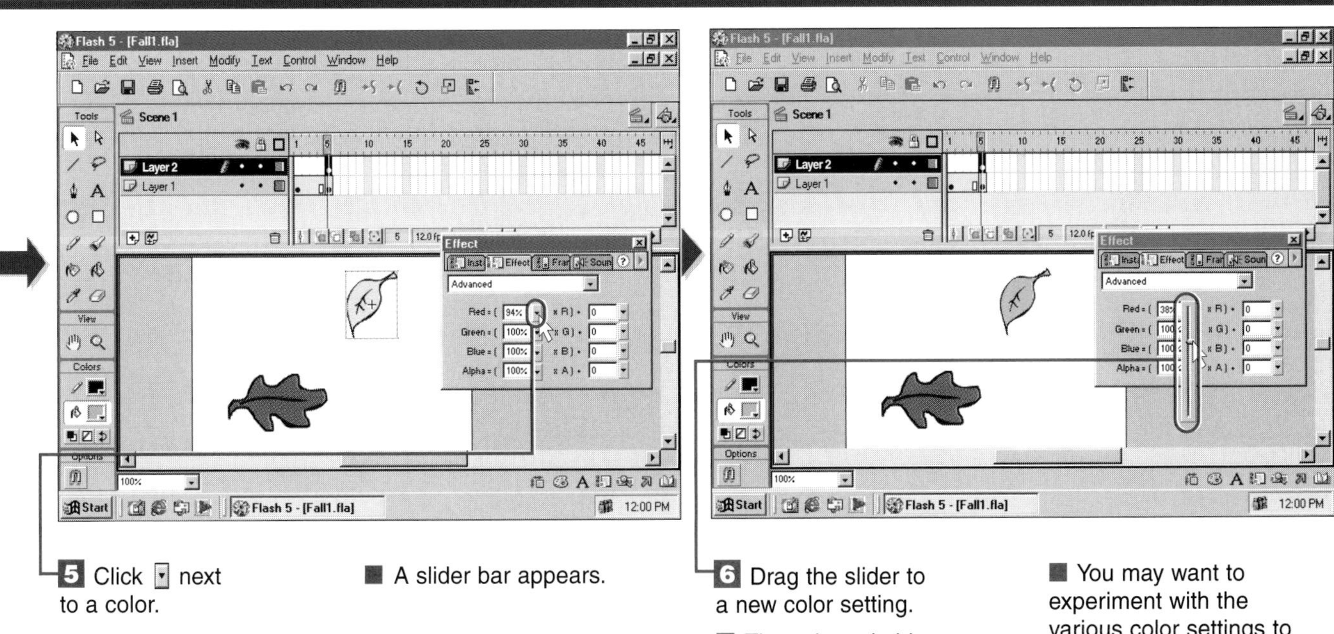

5 Click ▼ next to a color.

■ A slider bar appears.

6 Drag the slider to a new color setting.

■ The selected object changes color as you drag the slider.

■ You may want to experiment with the various color settings to achieve the color effect you want.

You can make changes to the original symbol and Flash will automatically update all instances of it in your movie.

See the sections "Create Symbols" and "Insert an Instance" to learn more about creating and using Flash symbols.

EDIT SYMBOLS

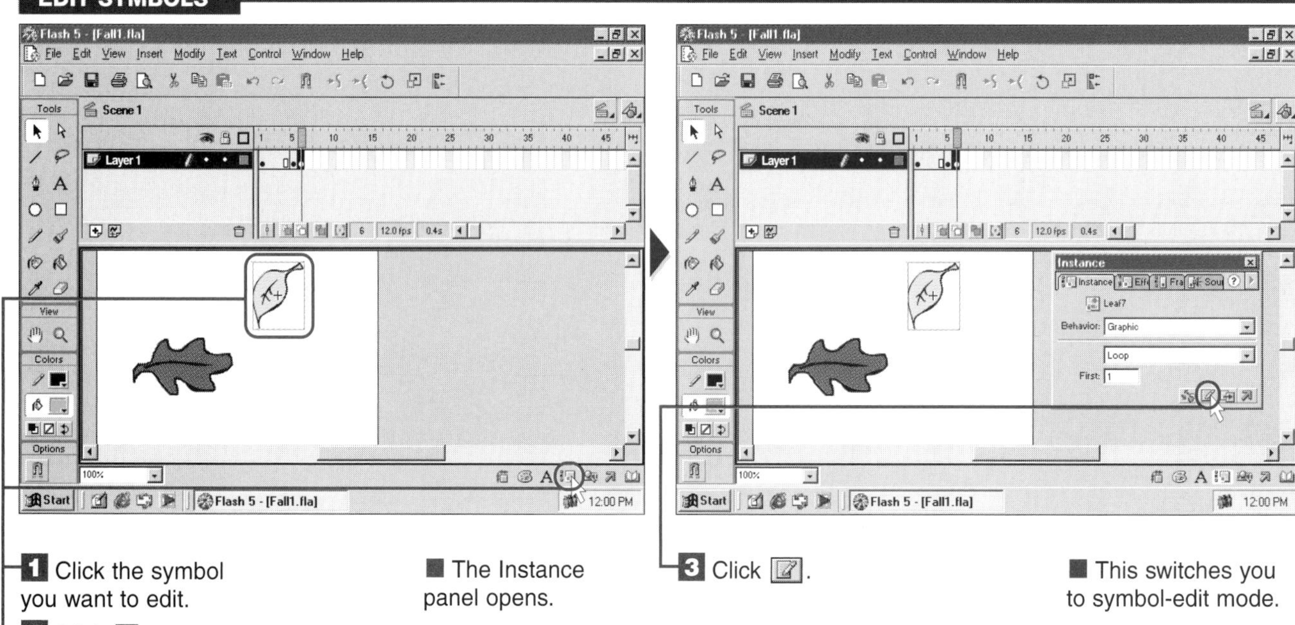

1 Click the symbol you want to edit.

2 Click [icon].

■ The Instance panel opens.

3 Click [icon].

■ This switches you to symbol-edit mode.

Can I test how my edits affect the movie?

As you edit a symbol, you might want to see the results of your edits before exiting symbol-edit mode. Click **Control**, **Test Movie** to run the movie and check the symbol's appearance.

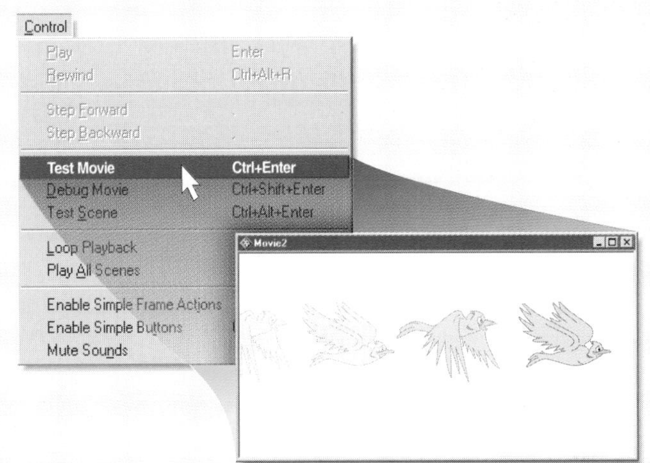

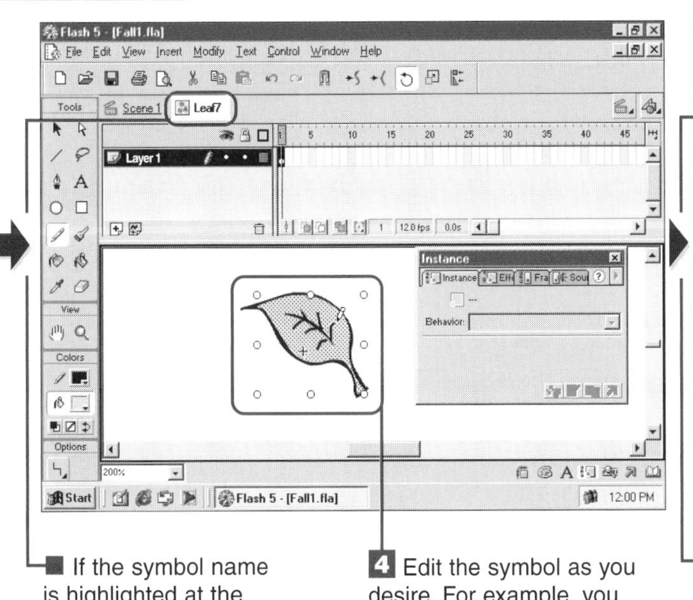

■ If the symbol name is highlighted at the top of the Timeline, you know you are in symbol-edit mode.

4 Edit the symbol as you desire. For example, you can use the Flash drawing tools to make changes to the object, such as changing the fill color, or adjusting a line segment.

Note: See Chapter 3 to learn more about editing objects.

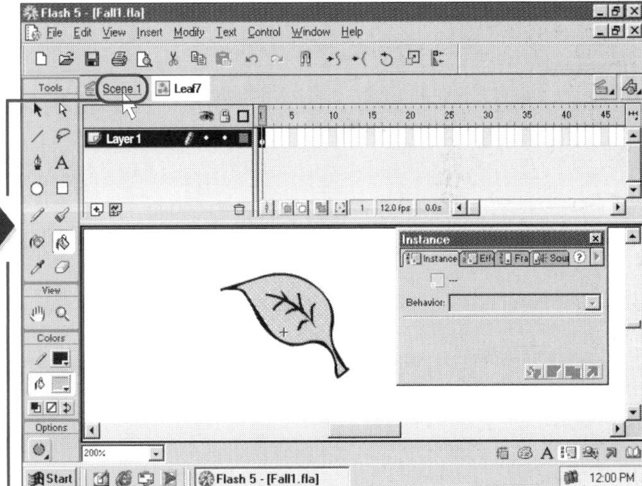

5 After editing the symbol, click the **Scene** button.

■ You are no longer in symbol-edit mode.

IMPORT GRAPHICS

You can import graphics, including vector or bitmap graphics, from other sources to use in Flash. For example, you can import an illustration or company logo created using Fireworks in order to animate it.

IMPORT GRAPHICS

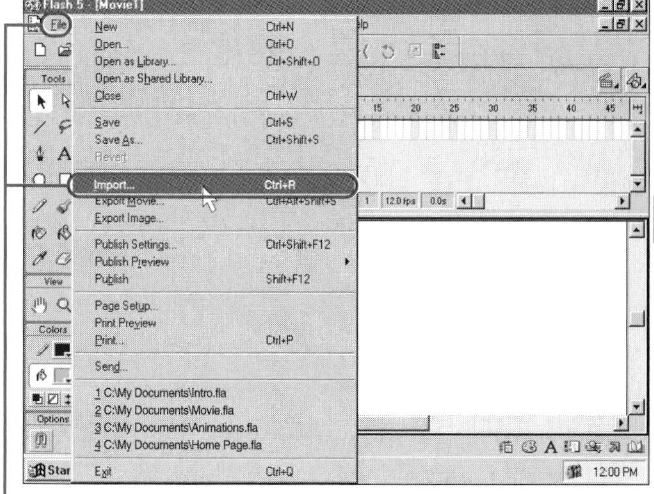

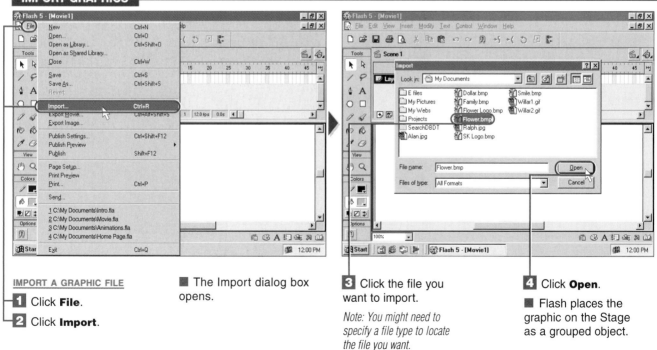

IMPORT A GRAPHIC FILE

1 Click **File**.

2 Click **Import**.

■ The Import dialog box opens.

3 Click the file you want to import.

Note: You might need to specify a file type to locate the file you want.

4 Click **Open**.

■ Flash places the graphic on the Stage as a grouped object.

Can I reuse the bitmap graphic?

When you import a bitmap graphic, it is immediately added to the Flash library for use in other frames in your movie. To view the Library, click [icon].

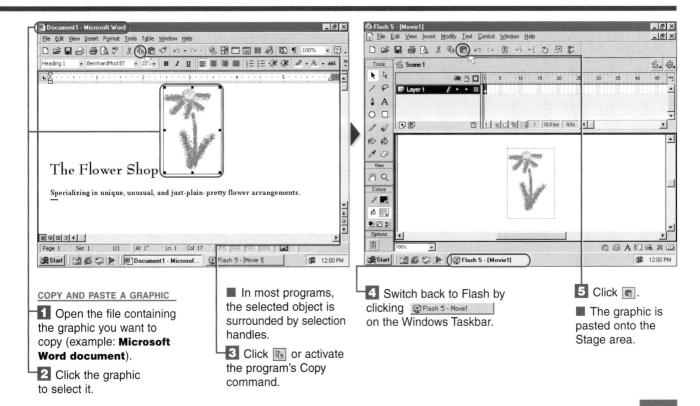

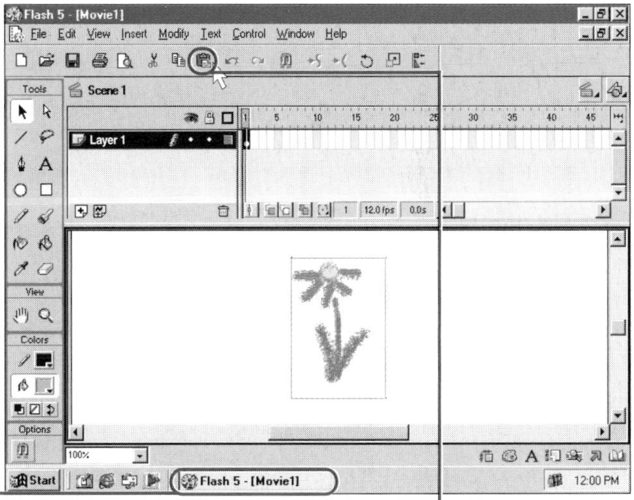

COPY AND PASTE A GRAPHIC

1 Open the file containing the graphic you want to copy (example: **Microsoft Word document**).

2 Click the graphic to select it.

■ In most programs, the selected object is surrounded by selection handles.

3 Click [icon] or activate the program's Copy command.

4 Switch back to Flash by clicking [Flash 5 - Movie1] on the Windows Taskbar.

5 Click [icon].

■ The graphic is pasted onto the Stage area.

SET MOVIE DIMENSIONS AND SPEED

Before you begin an animation project, take time to set up the size of your movie and the speed at which you want it to play. A movie's dimensions refer to its vertical and horizontal size on the Flash Stage. The movie's play speed determines the number of frames per second, or fps, that the animation occurs. Planning out your project in advance saves you time and headaches later.

For more helpful definitions, see the Appendix "Web Graphic and Animation Terms."

SET MOVIE DIMENSIONS AND SPEED

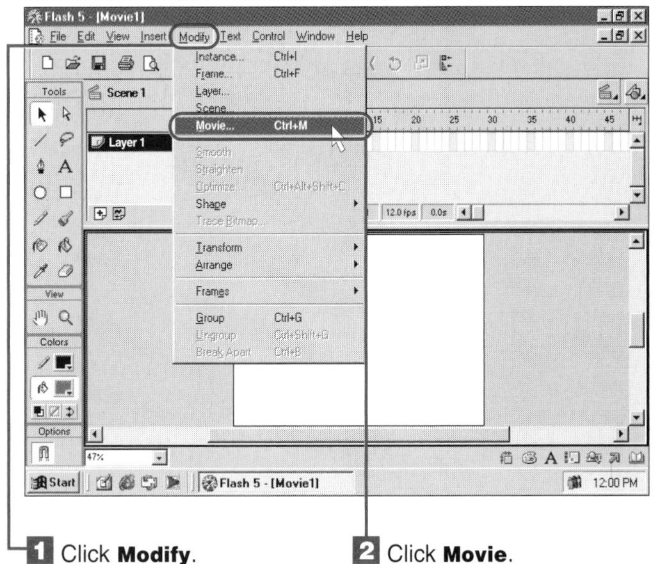

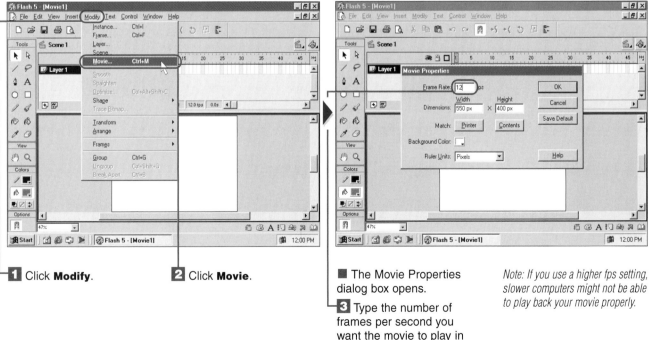

1 Click **Modify**.

2 Click **Movie**.

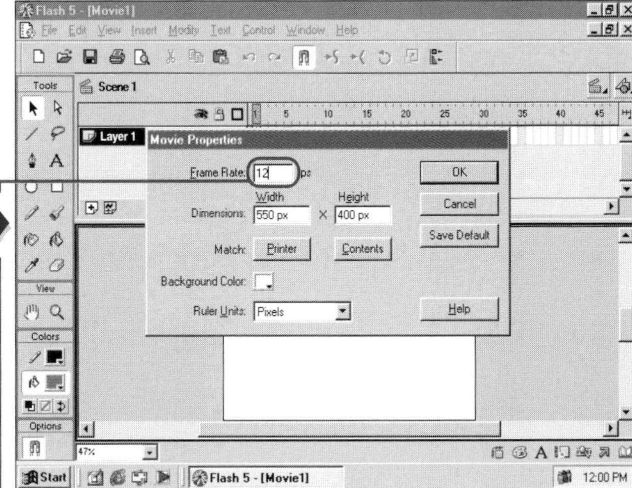

■ The Movie Properties dialog box opens.

3 Type the number of frames per second you want the movie to play in the **Frame Rate** text box.

Note: If you use a higher fps setting, slower computers might not be able to play back your movie properly.

What is a good frame rate for my movie?

The default frame rate of 12 fps works well for most projects. The maximum rate you should set is 24 fps, unless you are exporting your movie as a QuickTime or Windows AVI video file (which can handle higher rates without consuming computer processor power). If you set a higher frame rate, slower computers struggle to play at such speeds. Most simply cannot, and a very high fps rate slows all but a supercomputer down.

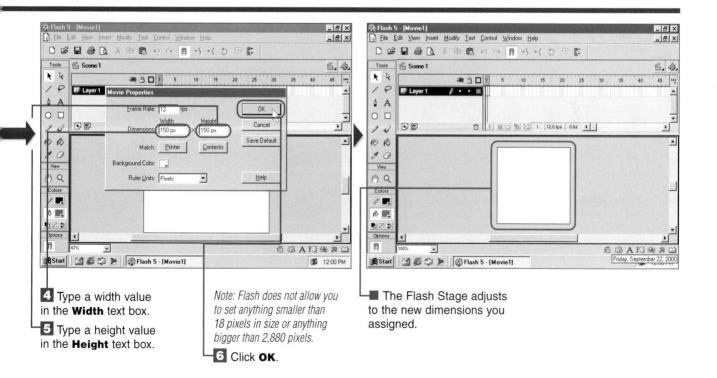

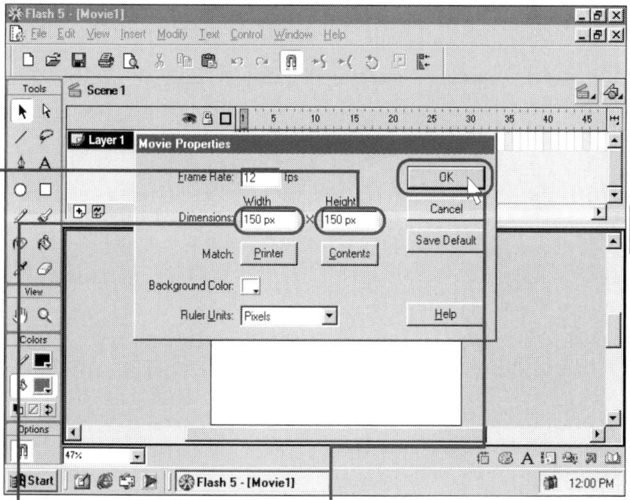

4 Type a width value in the **Width** text box.

5 Type a height value in the **Height** text box.

Note: Flash does not allow you to set anything smaller than 18 pixels in size or anything bigger than 2,880 pixels.

6 Click **OK**.

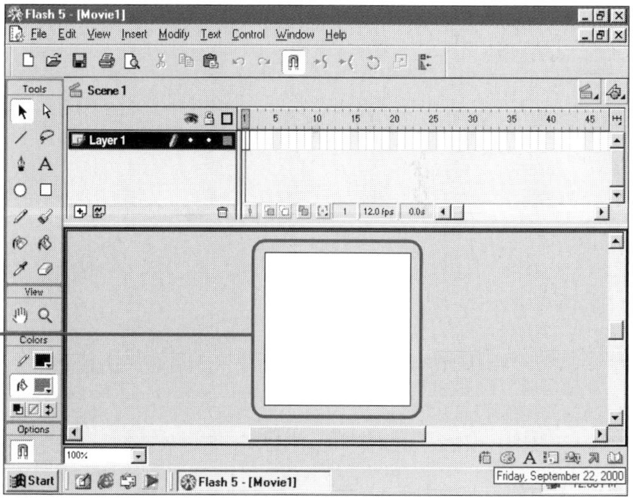

■ The Flash Stage adjusts to the new dimensions you assigned.

ADD REGULAR FRAMES OR KEYFRAMES

When you add a new layer or start a new file, Flash starts you out with one keyframe in the Timeline and lots of placeholder frames. To add content to your movie, you must add frames to the Timeline. You can add keyframes to define changes in the animation's appearance, or add regular frames to repeat keyframe content.

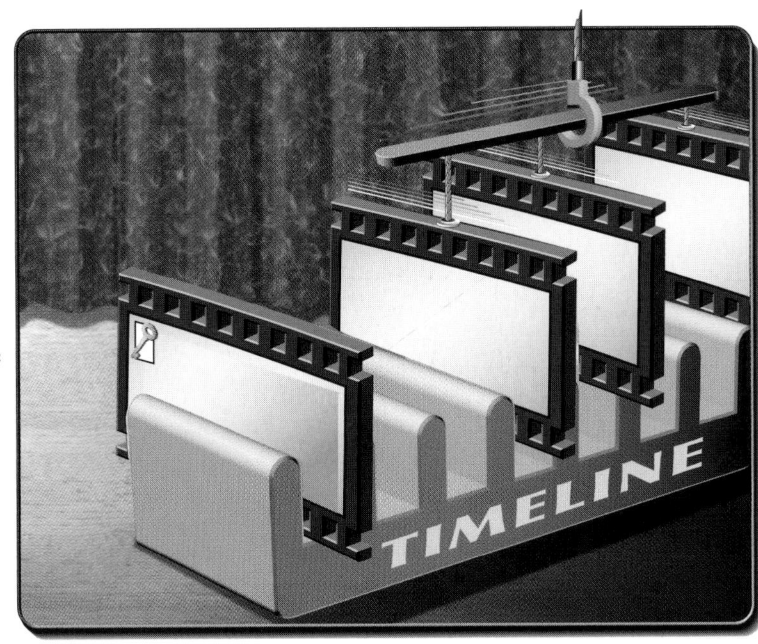

See Chapter 8 to learn more about working with tweened frames.

ADD REGULAR FRAMES OR KEYFRAMES

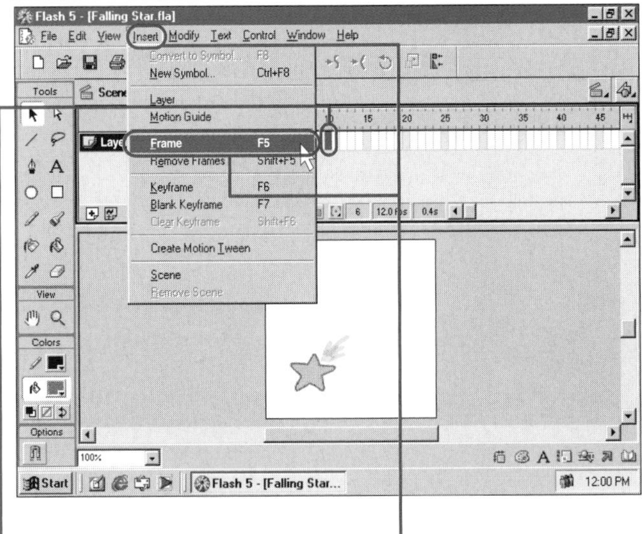

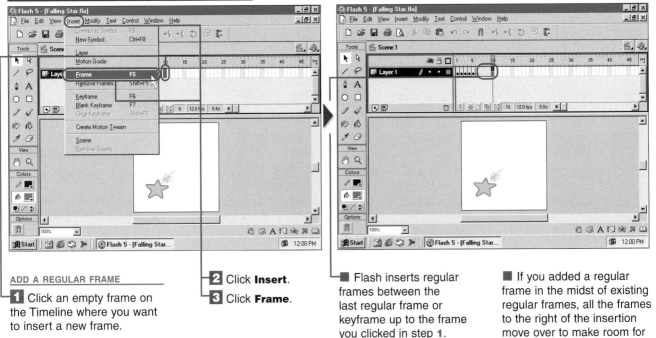

ADD A REGULAR FRAME

1 Click an empty frame on the Timeline where you want to insert a new frame.

2 Click **Insert**.

3 Click **Frame**.

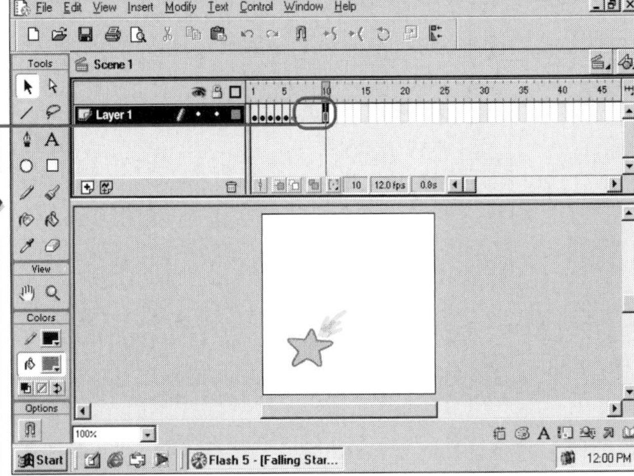

■ Flash inserts regular frames between the last regular frame or keyframe up to the frame you clicked in step **1**.

■ If you added a regular frame in the midst of existing regular frames, all the frames to the right of the insertion move over to make room for the new frame.

How can I tell which frames are which in the Timeline?

You can identify Flash frames by the following characteristics:

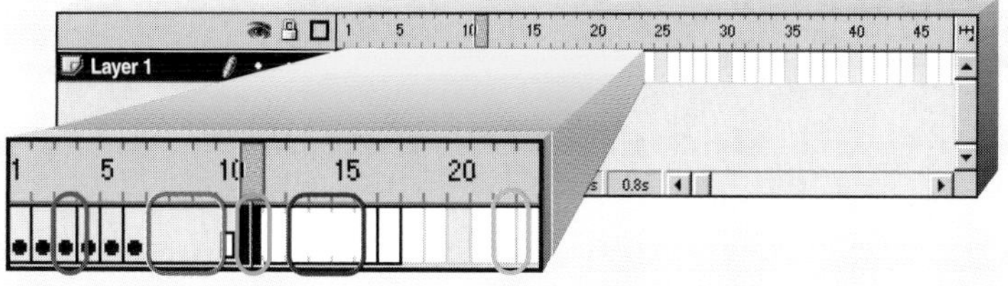

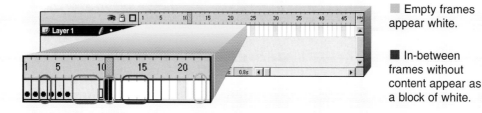

■ Empty frames appear white.

■ In-between frames without content appear as a block of white.

■ Keyframes with content appear with a solid bullet in the Timeline.

■ In-between frames that contain content appear tinted or grayed on the Timeline.

■ When you insert a blank keyframe, which has no content added yet, Flash places a hollow box in the preceding frame.

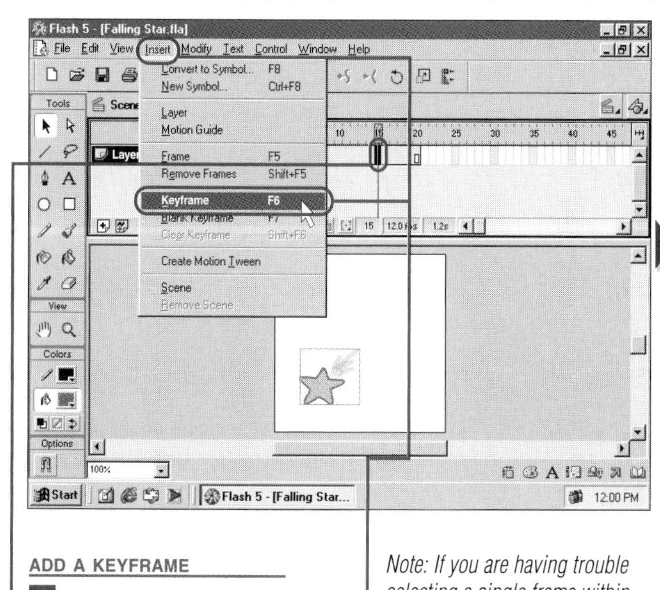

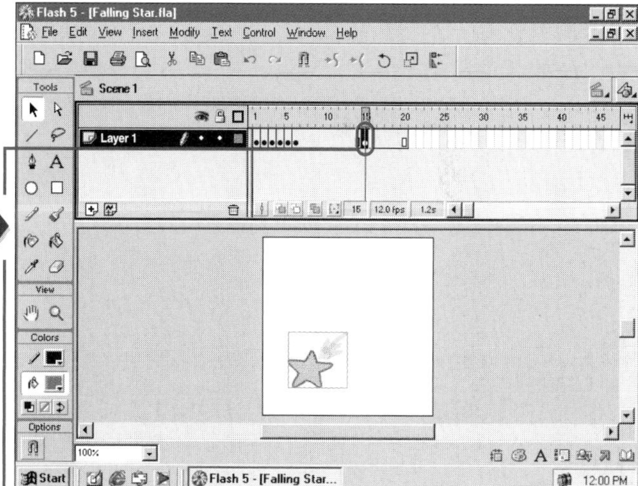

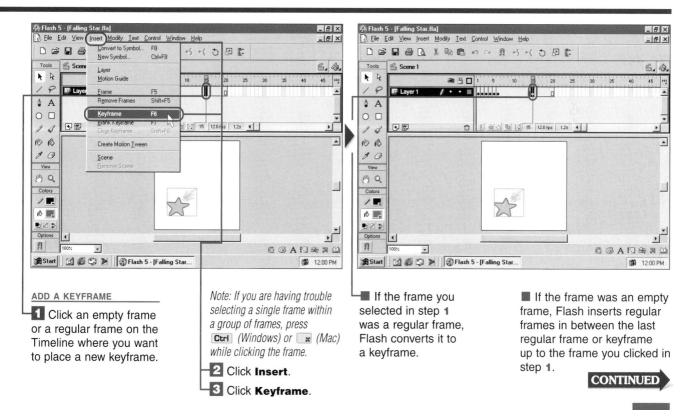

ADD A KEYFRAME

1 Click an empty frame or a regular frame on the Timeline where you want to place a new keyframe.

Note: If you are having trouble selecting a single frame within a group of frames, press Ctrl *(Windows) or* ⌘ *(Mac) while clicking the frame.*

2 Click **Insert**.

3 Click **Keyframe**.

■ If the frame you selected in step **1** was a regular frame, Flash converts it to a keyframe.

■ If the frame was an empty frame, Flash inserts regular frames in between the last regular frame or keyframe up to the frame you clicked in step **1**.

CONTINUED

ADD REGULAR FRAMES OR KEYFRAMES

You can choose between adding a blank keyframe or adding a default keyframe. If you add a default keyframe, Flash copies the contents of the previous keyframe and you can quickly edit the content on the Stage to create a change in your animation sequence. If you add a blank keyframe, the frame is completely empty and ready for brand-new content to be placed on the Stage.

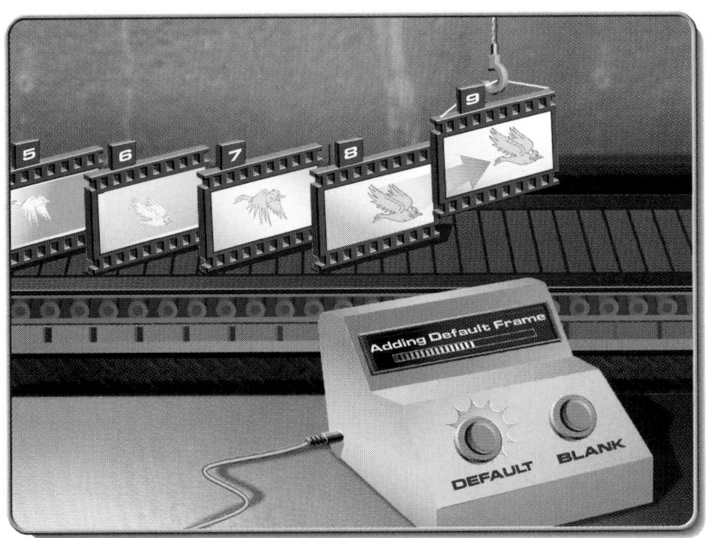

See the section "Understanding Frames" to find out more about Flash frame types.

ADD REGULAR FRAMES OR KEYFRAMES (CONTINUED)

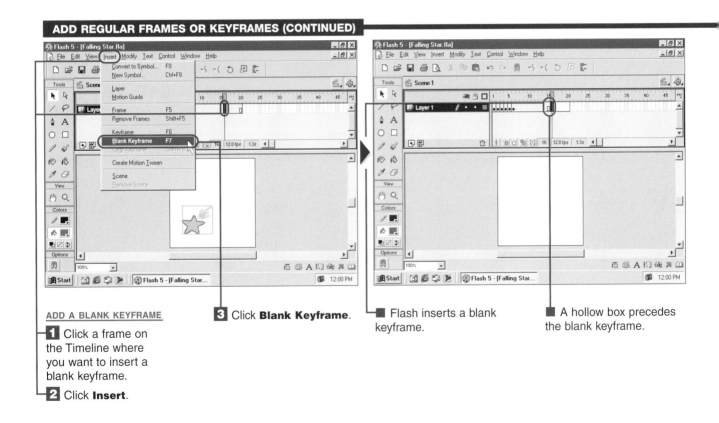

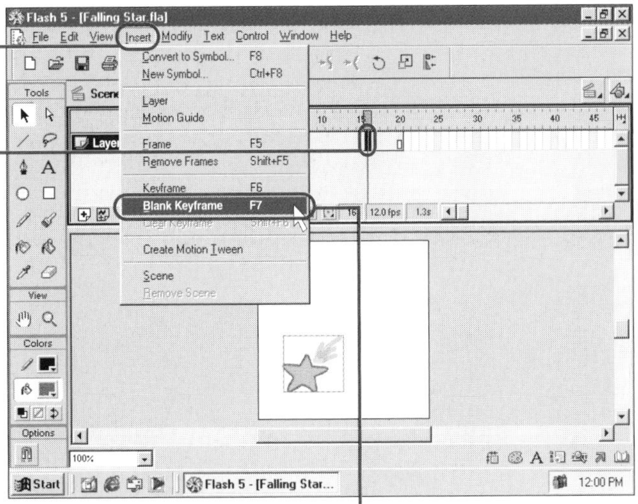

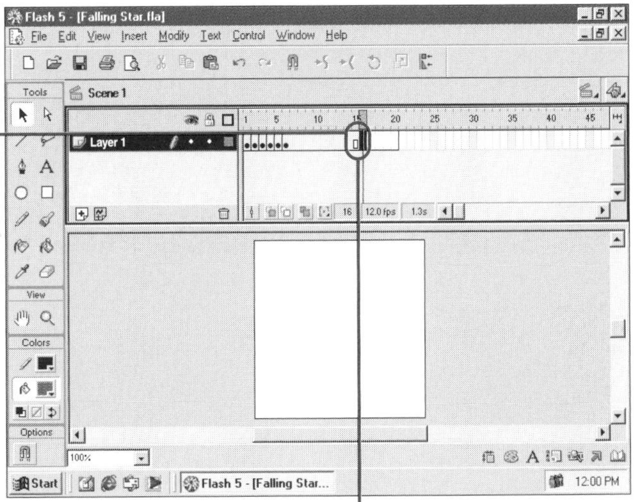

ADD A BLANK KEYFRAME

1 Click a frame on the Timeline where you want to insert a blank keyframe.

2 Click **Insert**.

3 Click **Blank Keyframe**.

■ Flash inserts a blank keyframe.

■ A hollow box precedes the blank keyframe.

Can I change the size of the Timeline frames?

You can change the size of the frames in the Timeline using the Timeline menu. By default, the frames appear in Normal size. You can change them to Tiny or Small to fit more frames in the Timeline view, or try Medium or Large to make the frames easier to see.

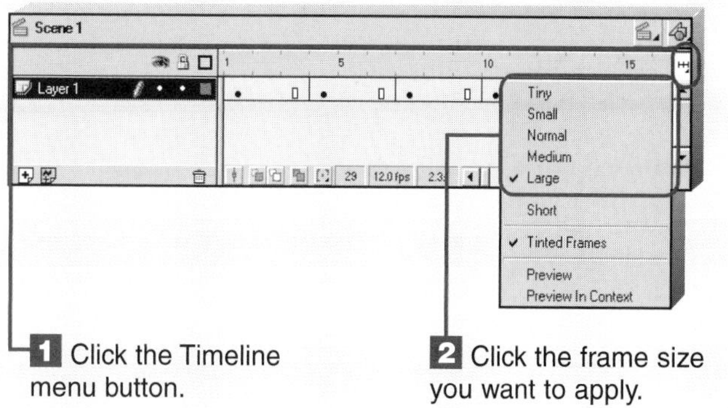

1 Click the Timeline menu button.

2 Click the frame size you want to apply.

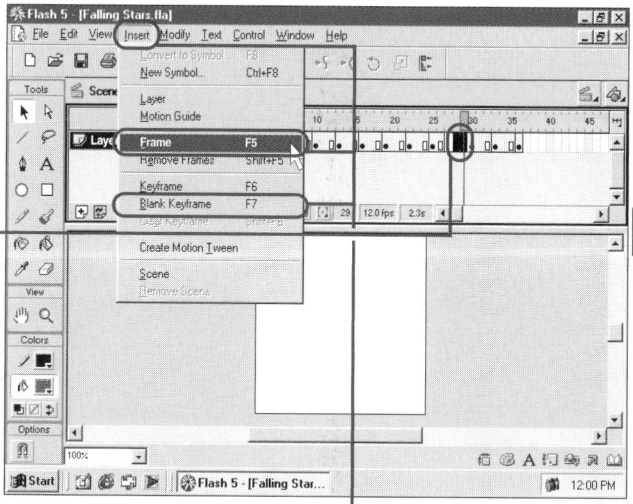

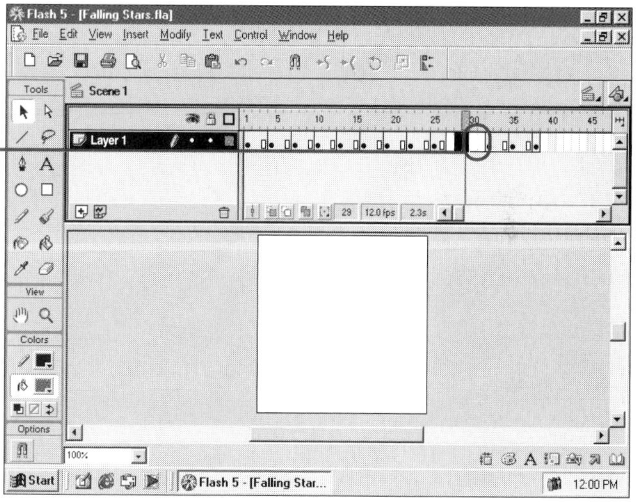

ADD MULTIPLE FRAMES

1 Select two or more frames by clicking them.

■ To select multiple frames, click the first frame in the range, press the Shift key and click the last frame in the range.

Note: See the section "Select Frames" to find out more about selecting frames.

2 Click **Insert**.

3 Click **Frame** to insert regular frames, or click **Blank Keyframe** to make the new frames all keyframes.

■ Flash inserts the same number of new frames and lengthens the movie.

MOVE AND COPY FRAMES

One way you can edit your Flash movie is to move or copy frames in the animation sequence. For example, you might want to move a keyframe up or back in the Timeline, or copy multiple regular frames to place between two keyframes. You cannot copy frames like you copy other objects in Flash; you must use the Copy Frames and Paste Frames commands found in the Edit menu.

See the sections "Add Frames" and "Delete Frames" to find out more about adding and deleting frames from the Timeline.

MOVE AND COPY FRAMES

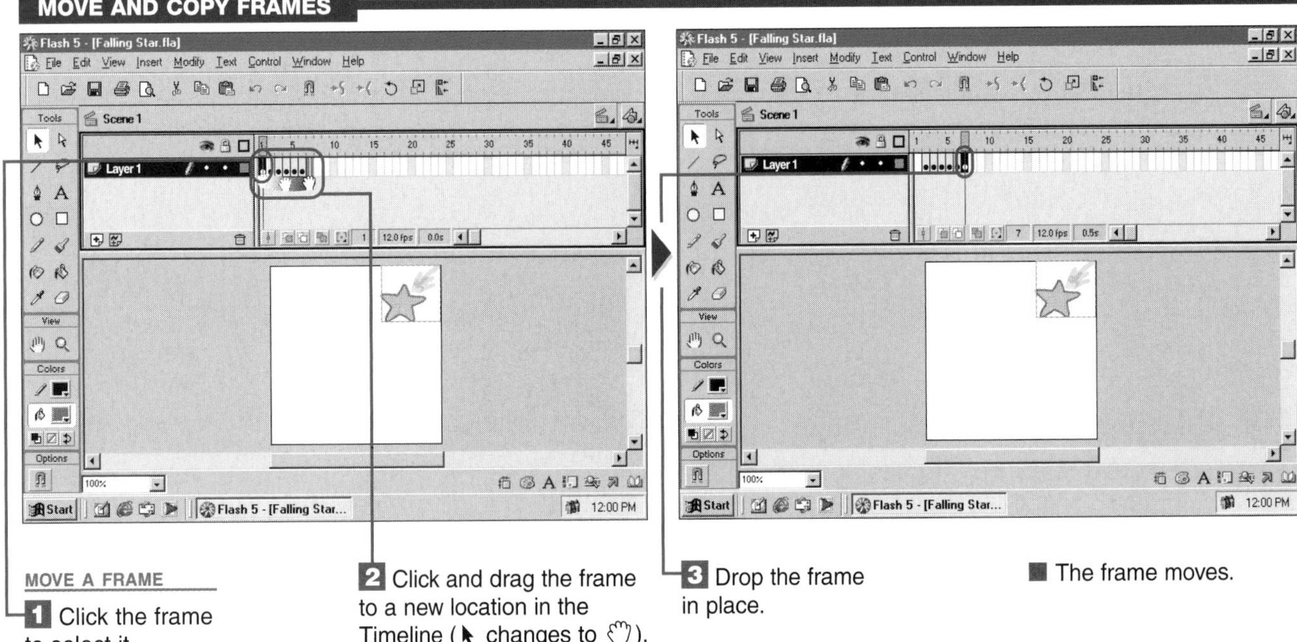

MOVE A FRAME

1 Click the frame to select it.

■ Flash highlights the frame in the Timeline.

2 Click and drag the frame to a new location in the Timeline (↖ changes to ✋).

3 Drop the frame in place.

■ The frame moves.

I pasted a copy in the wrong place, what do I do?

Anytime you make a mistake in Flash, click [undo button] to undo your last action. This command only works if you click the button immediately after performing the action. If you perform another action before clicking [undo button], Flash undoes the most recent action and the previous action is lost.

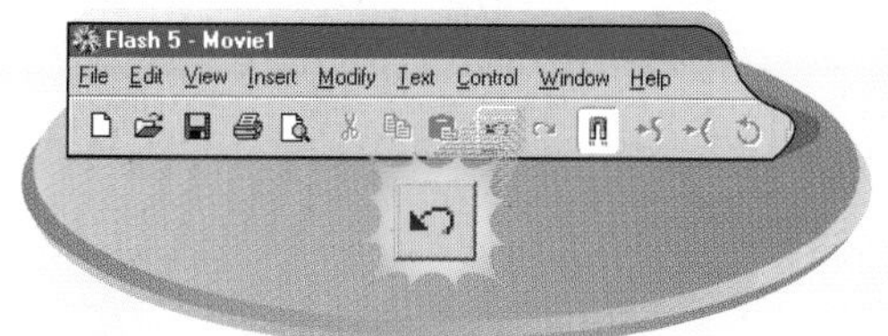

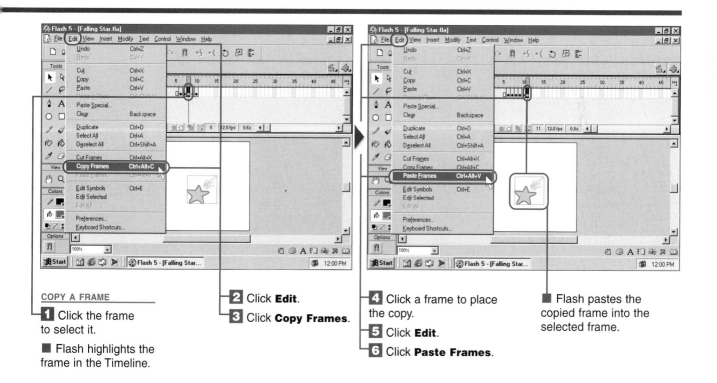

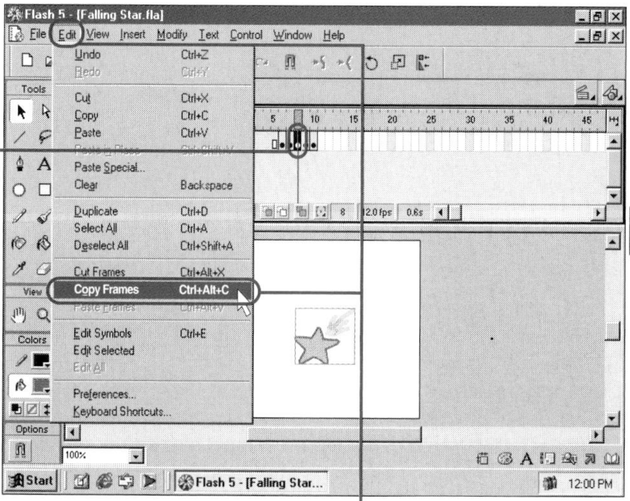

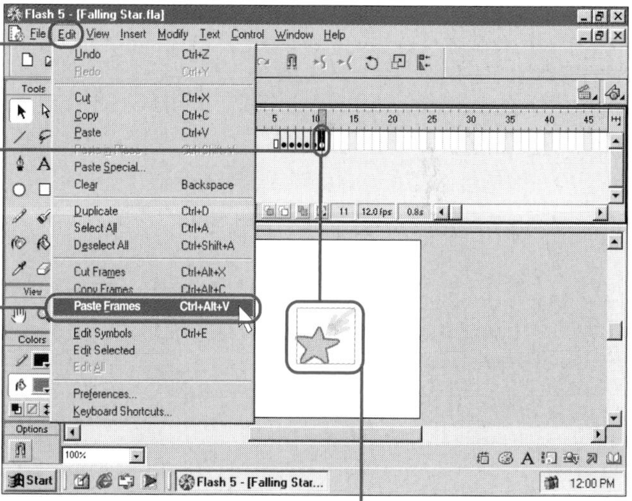

COPY A FRAME

1 Click the frame to select it.

■ Flash highlights the frame in the Timeline.

2 Click **Edit**.

3 Click **Copy Frames**.

4 Click a frame to place the copy.

5 Click **Edit**.

6 Click **Paste Frames**.

■ Flash pastes the copied frame into the selected frame.

DELETE FRAMES

You can remove frames you no longer need. If you want to remove a frame, or several frames, completely from the Timeline, use the Remove Frames command. To turn a keyframe into a regular frame, you can remove the frame's keyframe status and demote it to a regular frame. If you change a keyframe's status, all in-between frames are altered as well.

DELETE FRAMES

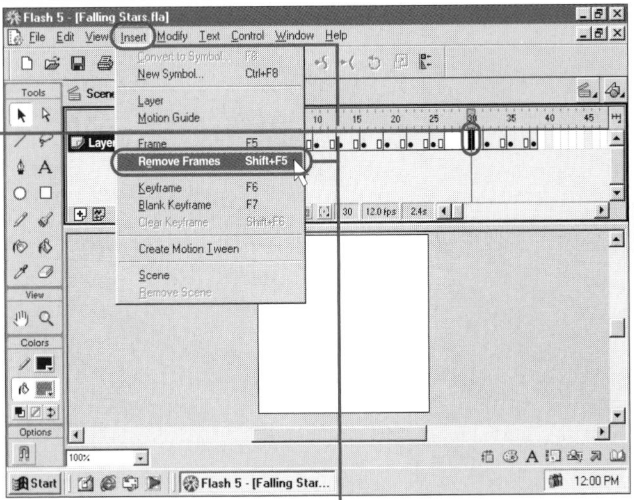

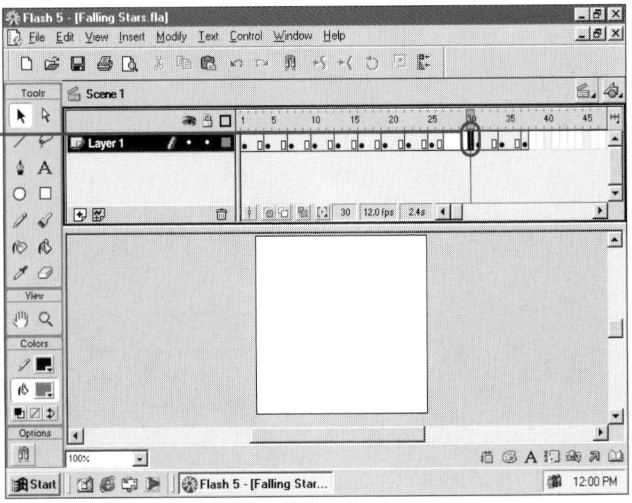

DELETE A FRAME

1 Click the frame, or range of frames, you want to delete.

■ To delete a range of frames, select the range first. See the section "Select Frames" to find out more about selecting frames.

2 Click **Insert**.

3 Click **Remove Frames**.

■ Flash removes the frame and any existing frames to the right move over to fill the void.

Can I delete a keyframe?

To remove a keyframe completely from the Timeline, you must select both the keyframe and all the in-between frames associated with it; otherwise, the **Remove Frames** command does not work properly to remove the keyframe.

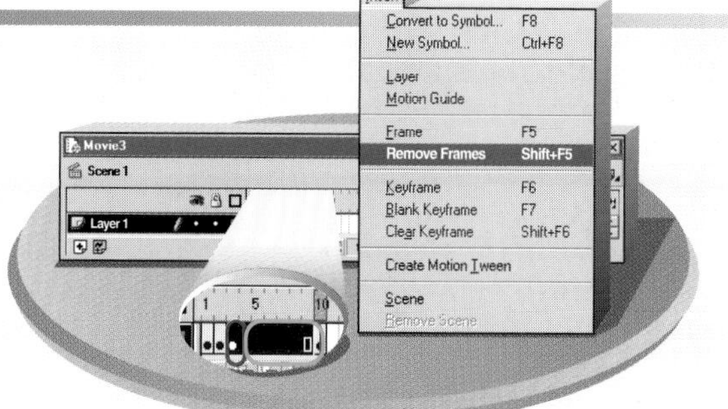

■ Keyframe ■ In-between frames

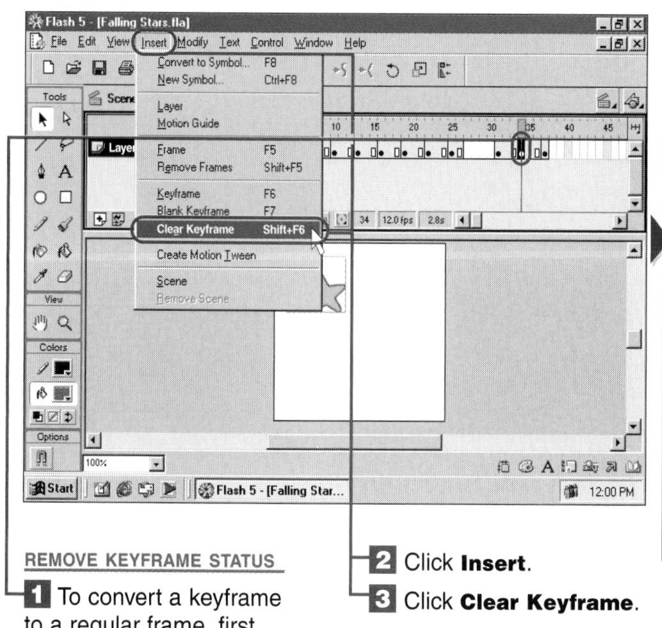

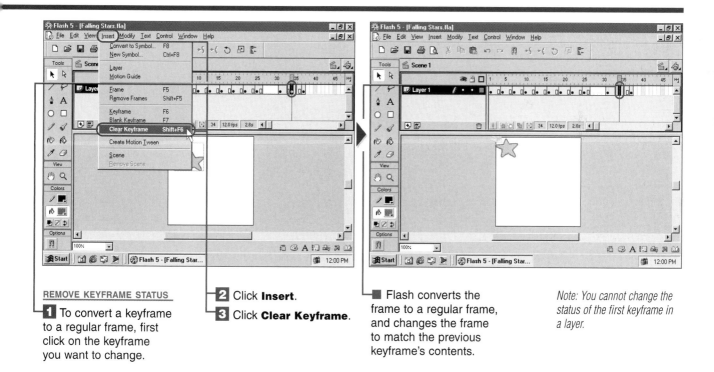

REMOVE KEYFRAME STATUS

1 To convert a keyframe to a regular frame, first click on the keyframe you want to change.

2 Click **Insert**.

3 Click **Clear Keyframe**.

■ Flash converts the frame to a regular frame, and changes the frame to match the previous keyframe's contents.

Note: You cannot change the status of the first keyframe in a layer.

CREATE FRAME-BY-FRAME ANIMATION

You can create the illusion of movement in a Flash movie by changing the placement or appearance of the Stage content from keyframe to keyframe in the Flash Timeline. This type of animation is called, appropriately, *frame-by-frame animation.*

CREATE FRAME-BY-FRAME ANIMATION

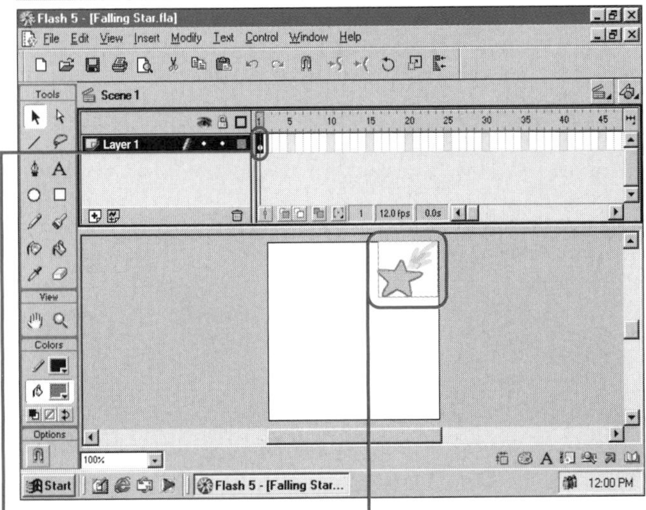

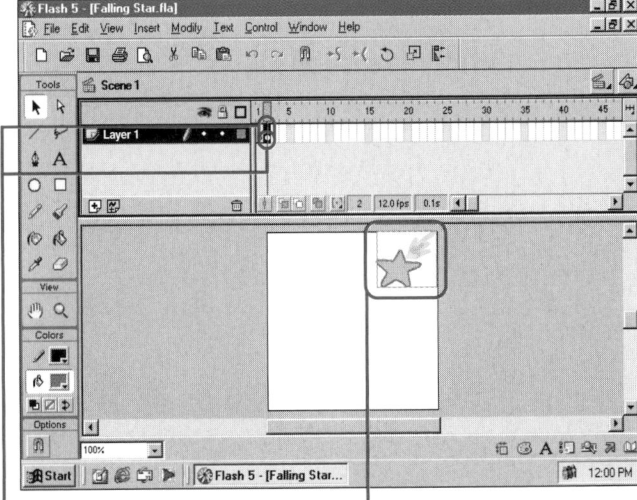

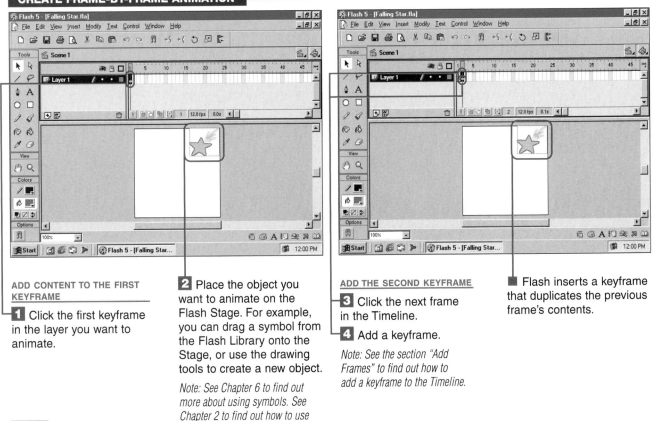

ADD CONTENT TO THE FIRST KEYFRAME

1 Click the first keyframe in the layer you want to animate.

2 Place the object you want to animate on the Flash Stage. For example, you can drag a symbol from the Flash Library onto the Stage, or use the drawing tools to create a new object.

Note: See Chapter 6 to find out more about using symbols. See Chapter 2 to find out how to use the Flash drawing tools.

ADD THE SECOND KEYFRAME

3 Click the next frame in the Timeline.

4 Add a keyframe.

Note: See the section "Add Frames" to find out how to add a keyframe to the Timeline.

■ Flash inserts a keyframe that duplicates the previous frame's contents.

Can I add in-between frames to the animation?

To slow down the animation sequence, especially if the changes between keyframes are happening too fast to see very well, just add regular frames between keyframes in your frame-by-frame animation.

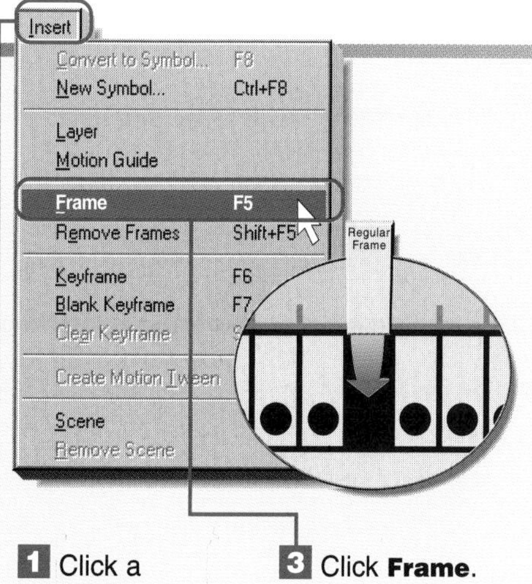

1 Click a keyframe.

2 Click **Insert**.

3 Click **Frame**.

■ Flash adds a regular frame behind the keyframe.

You can keep adding more regular frames to achieve the effect you want. When you play back the movie, the animation appears to slow down a bit in its movement.

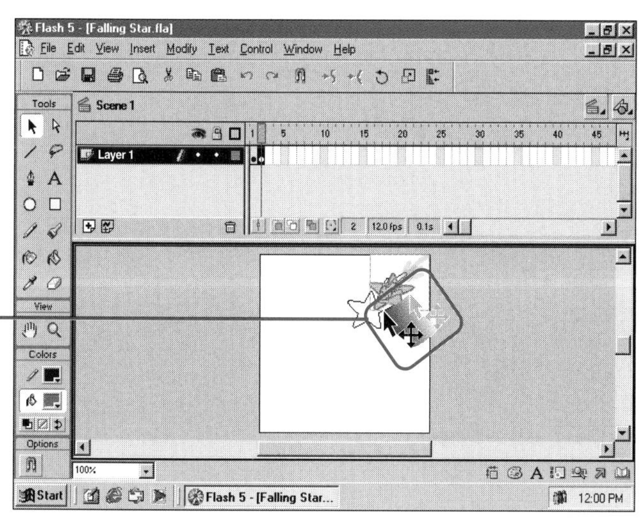

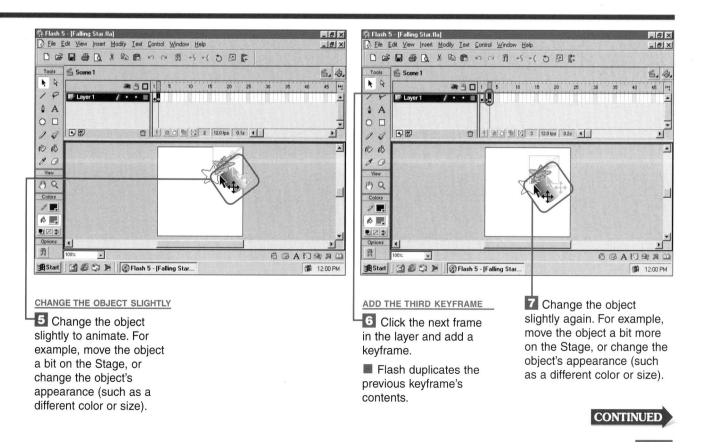

CHANGE THE OBJECT SLIGHTLY

5 Change the object slightly to animate. For example, move the object a bit on the Stage, or change the object's appearance (such as a different color or size).

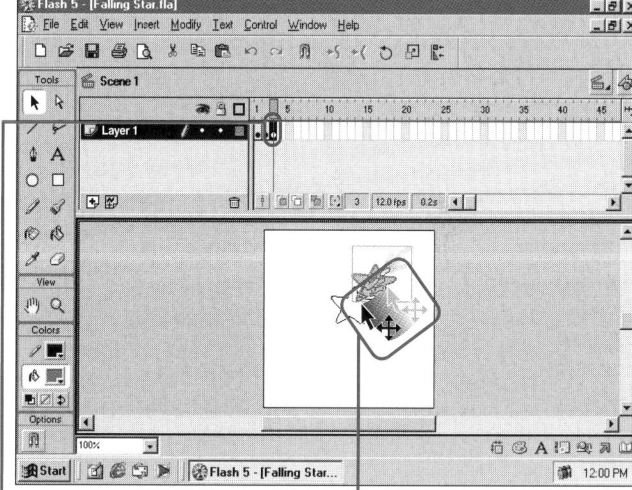

ADD THE THIRD KEYFRAME

6 Click the next frame in the layer and add a keyframe.

■ Flash duplicates the previous keyframe's contents.

7 Change the object slightly again. For example, move the object a bit more on the Stage, or change the object's appearance (such as a different color or size).

CONTINUED

CREATE FRAME-BY-FRAME ANIMATION

You can learn the principles of frame-by-frame animation by creating a simple animation sequence, such as making an object move across the Flash Stage. The illustrations in this section show how to create the illusion of a falling star by moving the star ever so slightly down the Stage in each keyframe. By the last keyframe, the star has reached the bottom. When the animation is played back, the star appears to drop from the top-right corner to the bottom-left corner.

CREATE FRAME-BY-FRAME ANIMATION (CONTINUED)

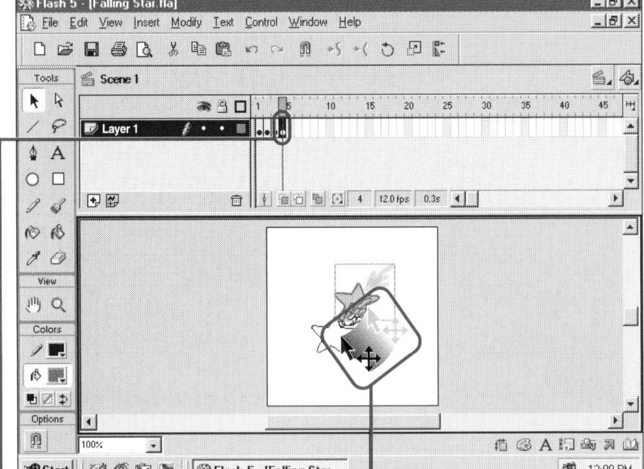

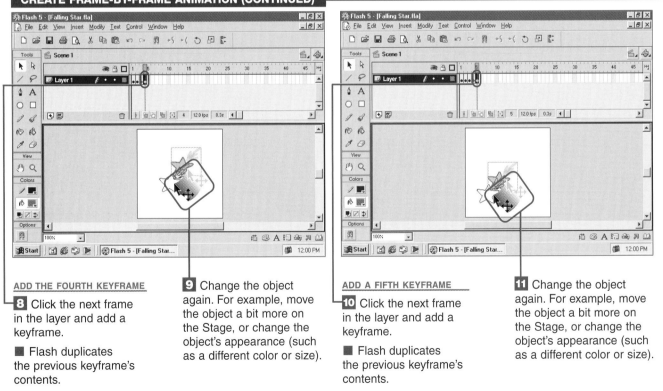

ADD THE FOURTH KEYFRAME

8 Click the next frame in the layer and add a keyframe.

■ Flash duplicates the previous keyframe's contents.

9 Change the object again. For example, move the object a bit more on the Stage, or change the object's appearance (such as a different color or size).

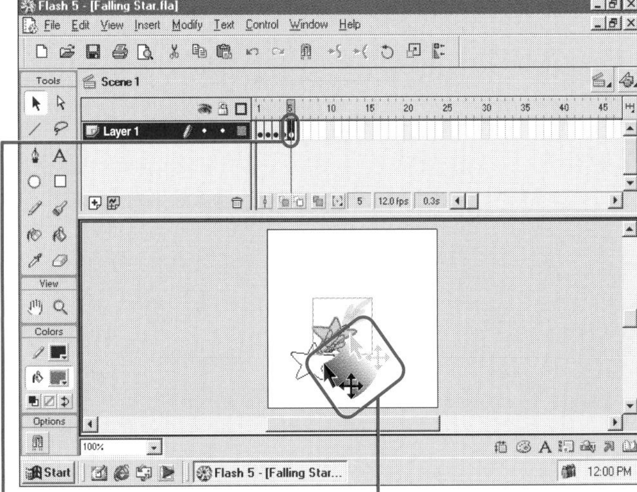

ADD A FIFTH KEYFRAME

10 Click the next frame in the layer and add a keyframe.

■ Flash duplicates the previous keyframe's contents.

11 Change the object again. For example, move the object a bit more on the Stage, or change the object's appearance (such as a different color or size).

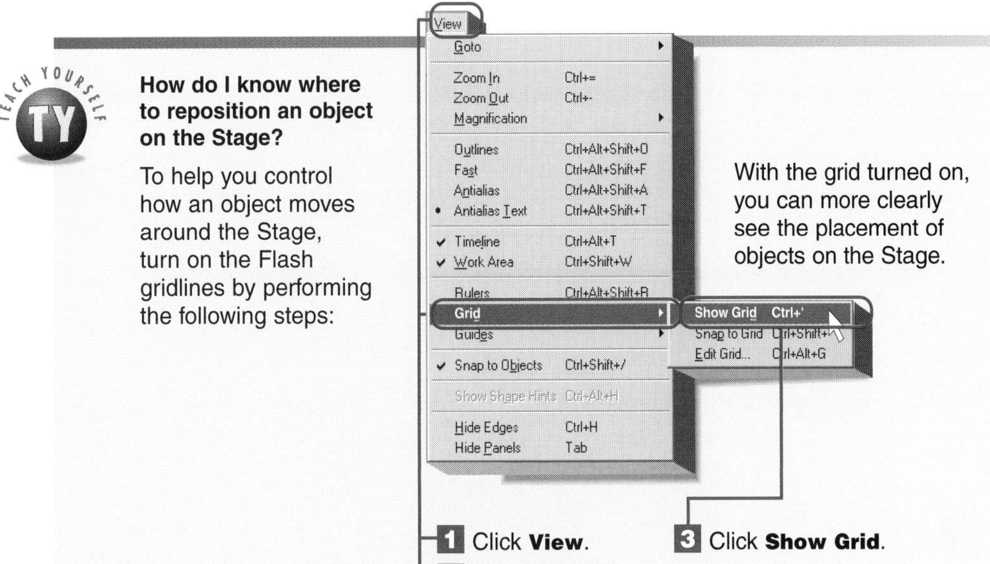

How do I know where to reposition an object on the Stage?

To help you control how an object moves around the Stage, turn on the Flash gridlines by performing the following steps:

1 Click **View**.

2 Click **Grid**.

3 Click **Show Grid**.

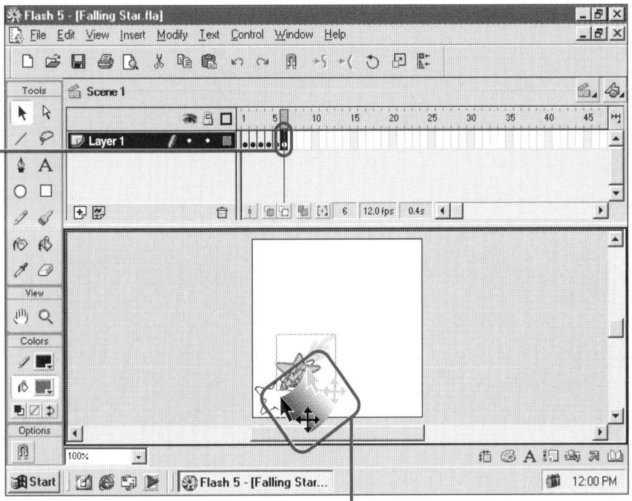

With the grid turned on, you can more clearly see the placement of objects on the Stage.

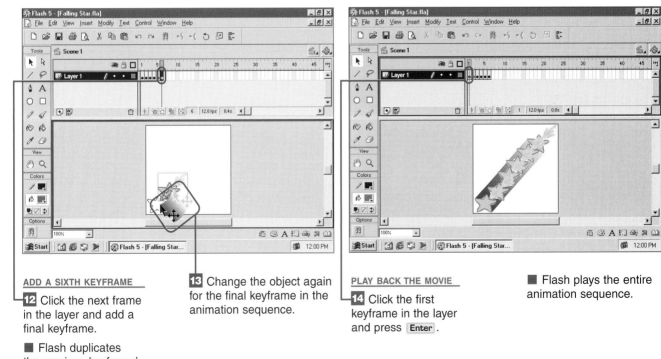

ADD A SIXTH KEYFRAME

12 Click the next frame in the layer and add a final keyframe.

■ Flash duplicates the previous keyframe's contents.

13 Change the object again for the final keyframe in the animation sequence.

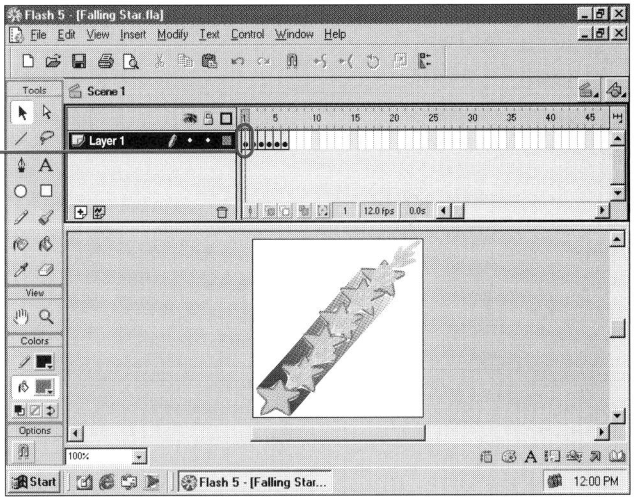

PLAY BACK THE MOVIE

14 Click the first keyframe in the layer and press Enter.

■ Flash plays the entire animation sequence.

MODIFY FRAME PROPERTIES

You can use the Frame panel to help organize frames with labels, assign actions, or even add sound clips.

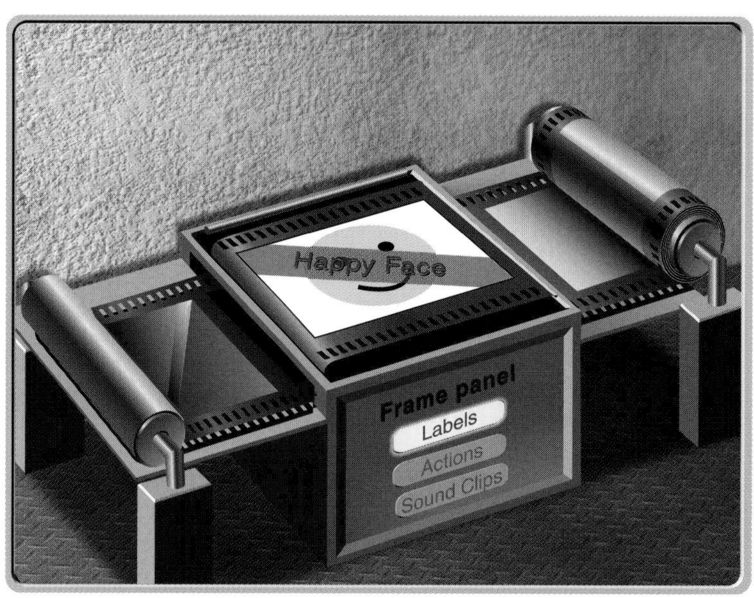

MODIFY FRAME PROPERTIES

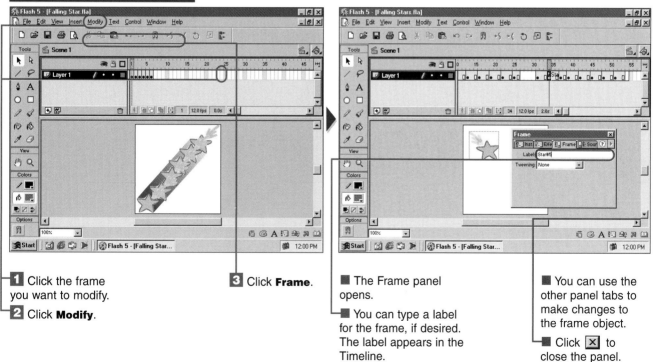

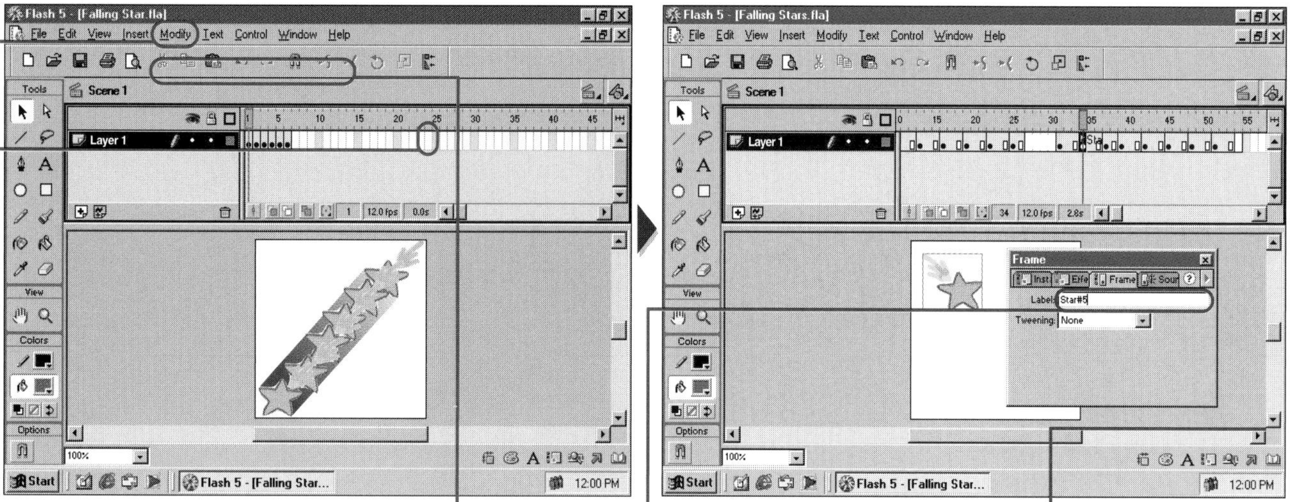

1 Click the frame you want to modify.

2 Click **Modify**.

3 Click **Frame**.

■ The Frame panel opens.

■ You can type a label for the frame, if desired. The label appears in the Timeline.

■ You can use the other panel tabs to make changes to the frame object.

■ Click ☒ to close the panel.

PREVIEW A FLASH ANIMATION

You can click on an animation sequence one frame at a time to see each frame's contents, but a faster way to check the sequence is to play the movie. One way to play a movie is to use the Test Movie command and preview the animation in the Flash Player window.

PREVIEW A FLASH ANIMATION

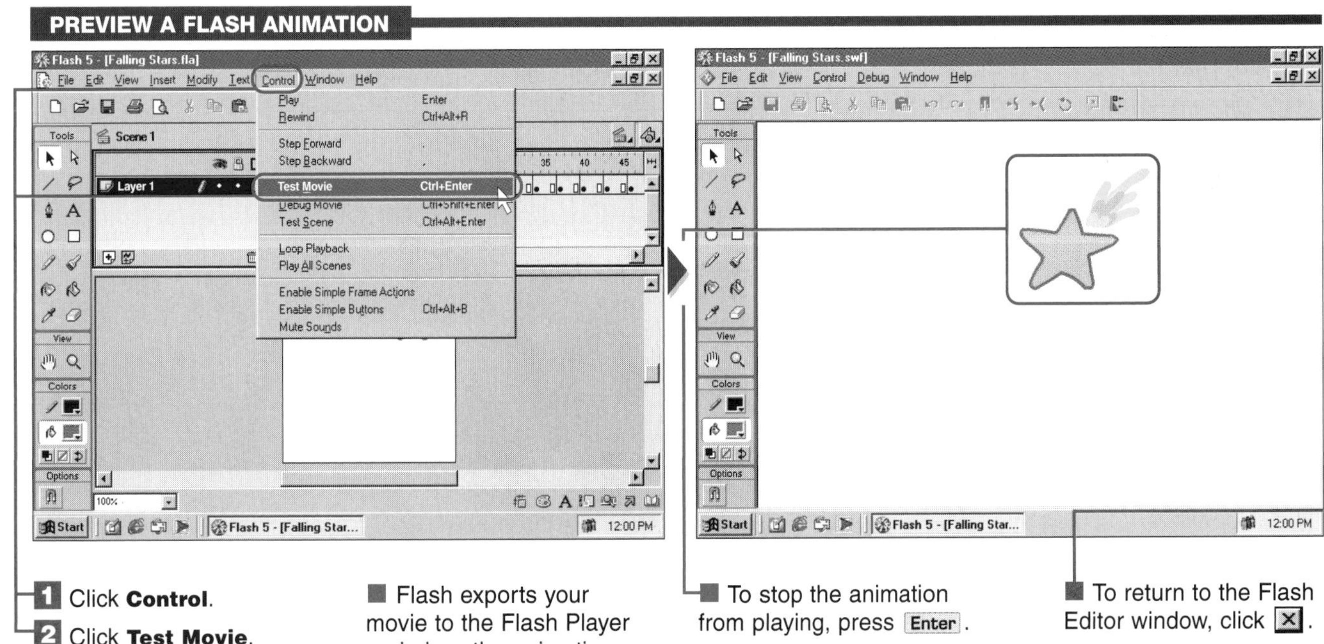

1 Click **Control**.

2 Click **Test Movie**.

■ Flash exports your movie to the Flash Player and plays the animation.

■ To stop the animation from playing, press Enter.

■ To return to the Flash Editor window, click ☒.

CREATE A MOTION TWEEN

You can animate moving symbols with a *motion* tween. A motion tween is when you define two points of movement in the Timeline with two keyframes, then let Flash calculate all the in-between frames necessary to get from point A to point B. You can only motion tween symbols or grouped objects and you can only tween one symbol per layer.

For more helpful definitions, see the Appendix "Web Graphic and Animation Terms."

CREATE A MOTION TWEEN

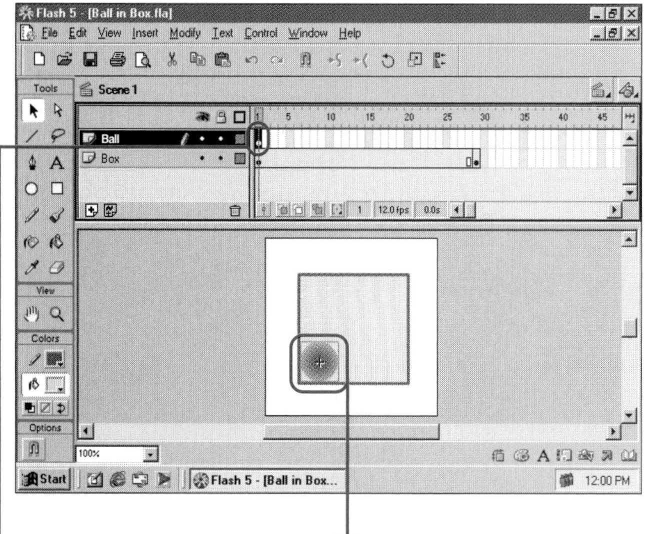

SELECT KEYFRAMES AND SYMBOL

1 Insert a keyframe where you want to start the motion tween.

Note: See Chapter 7 to find out more about adding frames to the Timeline.

2 Place the symbol you want to animate on the Stage.

■ The symbol's position should be the starting point of the animation effect, such as a corner or side of the movie area.

Note: See Chapter 6 to find out more about working with symbols.

3 Click the last frame you want to include in the motion tween.

4 Insert a keyframe.

What is the difference between a motion tween and a frame-by-frame animation?

When you create a frame-by-frame animation, you manually input the changes made to each frame in the sequence. When you use a motion tween, you specify the first frame and the last frame and tell Flash to calculate all the in-between frames. By having Flash calculate the in-between frames, the resulting file size is much smaller than the same sequence created manually frame-by-frame.

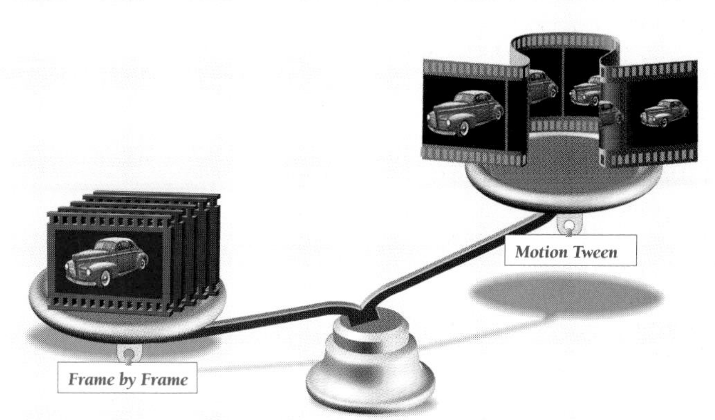

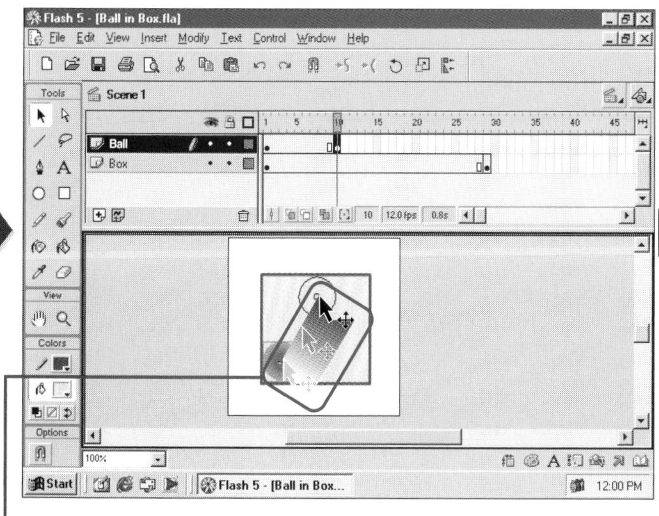

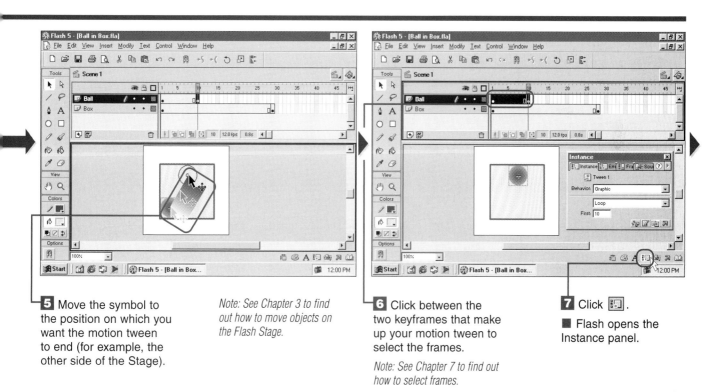

5 Move the symbol to the position on which you want the motion tween to end (for example, the other side of the Stage).

Note: See Chapter 3 to find out how to move objects on the Flash Stage.

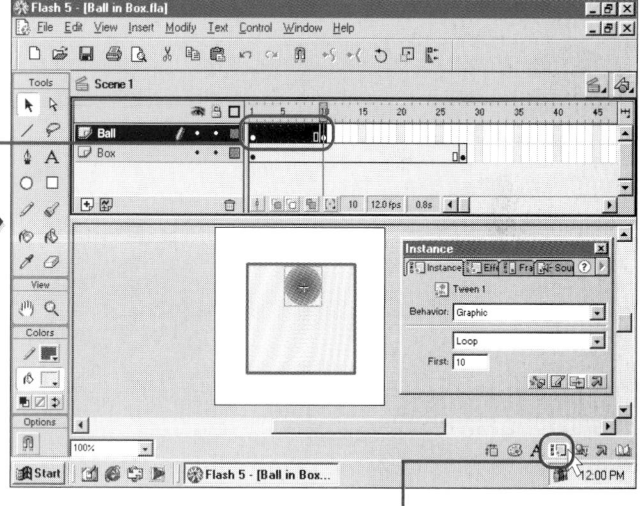

6 Click between the two keyframes that make up your motion tween to select the frames.

Note: See Chapter 7 to find out how to select frames.

7 Click the Instance button.

■ Flash opens the Instance panel.

CONTINUED

CREATE A MOTION TWEEN

You can assign as many motion tween segments as you like throughout your movie, or you can make your animation one long motion tween.

CREATE A MOTION TWEEN (CONTINUED)

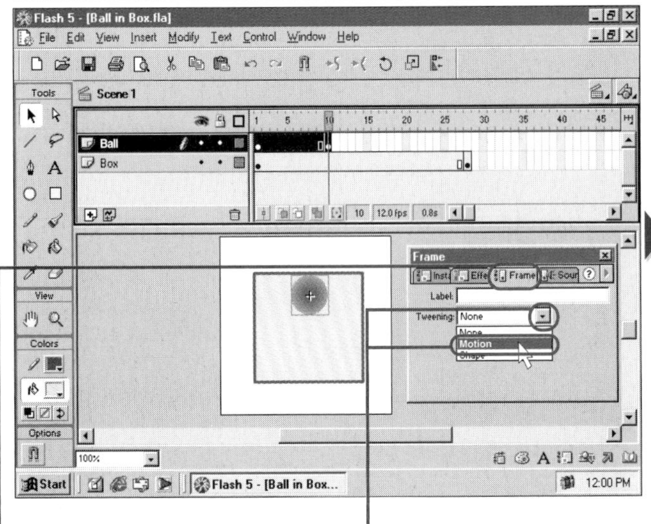

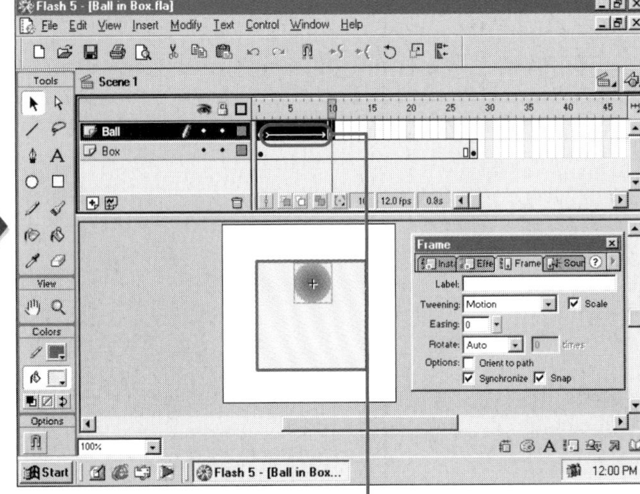

CREATE TWEEN EFFECT

8 Click the **Frame** tab.

■ Flash displays the Frame tab and its related options.

9 Click ▾ in the **Tweening** box.

10 Click **Motion**.

■ Flash calculates the in-between changes the symbol must undergo to move from the first keyframe to the next keyframe.

■ Flash adds a motion tween arrow ⟶ from the first keyframe in the tween effect to the last keyframe in the tween effect.

Can I create a motion tween as I go?

You can start a motion tween without defining the end keyframe in the sequence. To do so, perform the following steps:

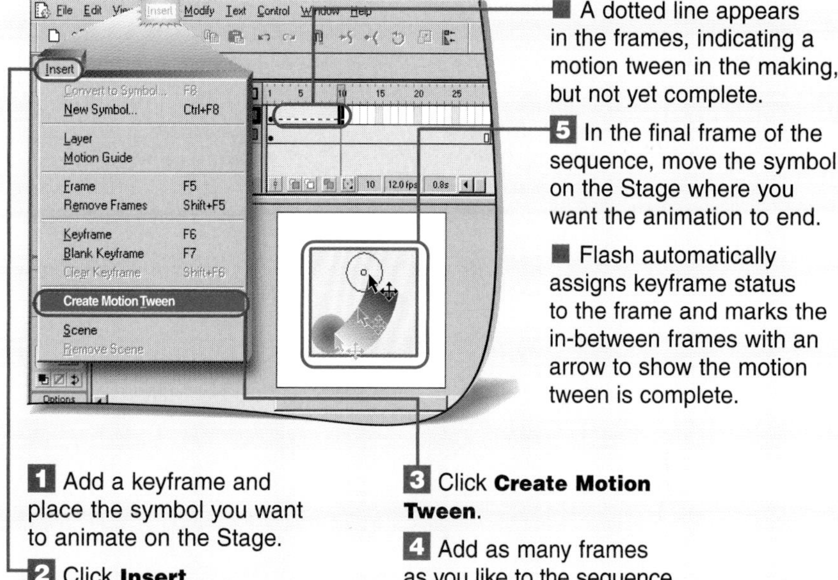

■ A dotted line appears in the frames, indicating a motion tween in the making, but not yet complete.

5 In the final frame of the sequence, move the symbol on the Stage where you want the animation to end.

■ Flash automatically assigns keyframe status to the frame and marks the in-between frames with an arrow to show the motion tween is complete.

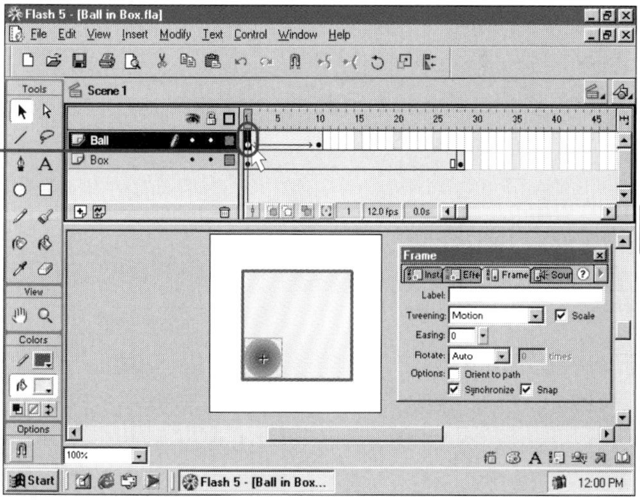

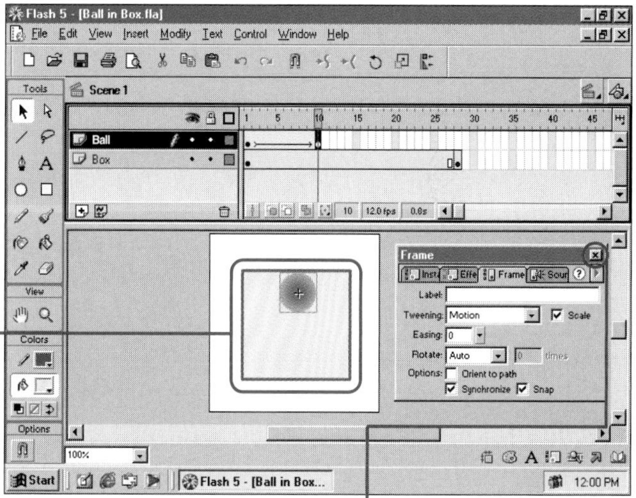

1 Add a keyframe and place the symbol you want to animate on the Stage.

2 Click **Insert**.

3 Click **Create Motion Tween**.

4 Add as many frames as you like to the sequence.

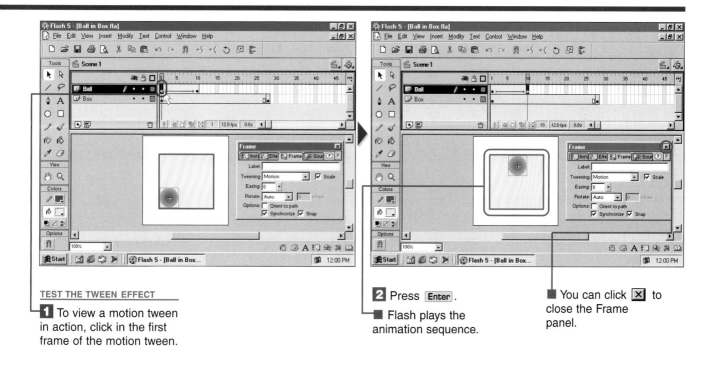

TEST THE TWEEN EFFECT

1 To view a motion tween in action, click in the first frame of the motion tween.

2 Press Enter.

■ Flash plays the animation sequence.

■ You can click ☒ to close the Frame panel.

SET TWEEN SPEED

You can control a tweened animation's speed by using the Ease control. The Ease control is found in the Frame panel and enables you to speed up or slow down the tween effect.

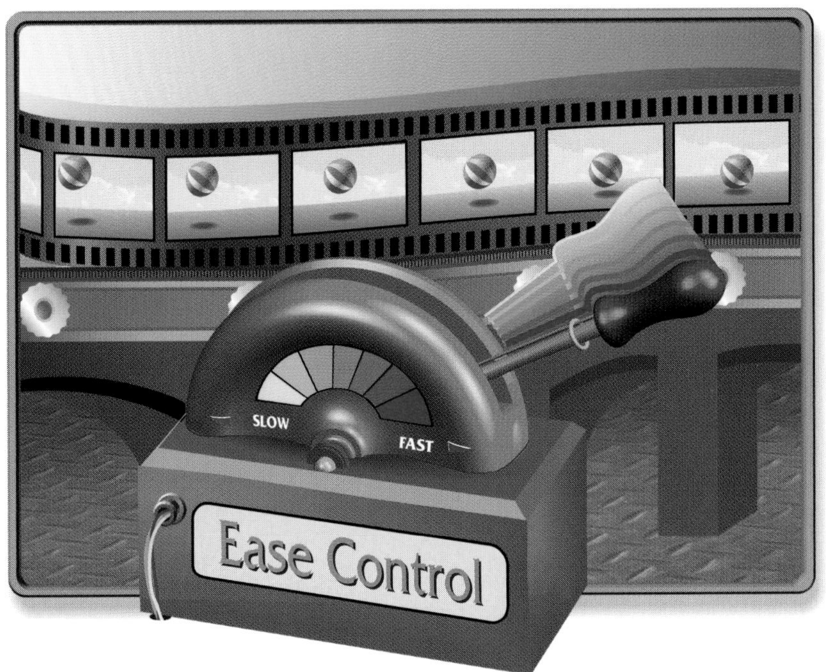

See the section "Create a Motion Tween" to learn more about the motion tween effect.

SET TWEEN SPEED

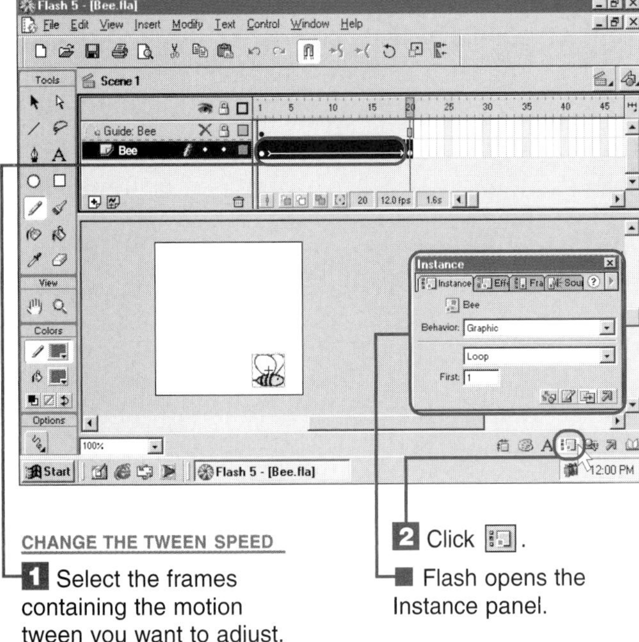

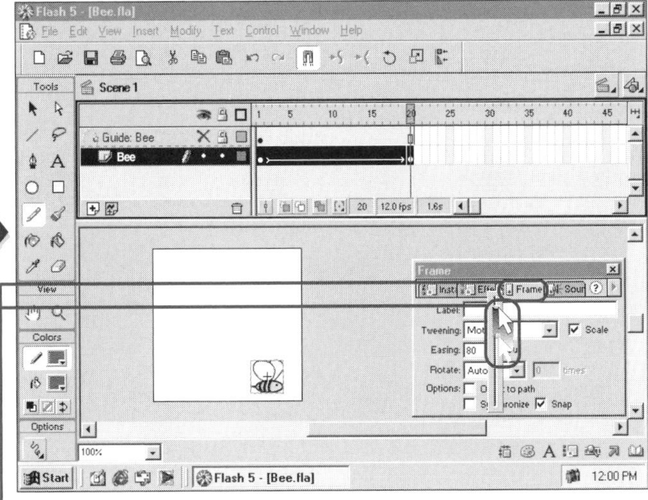

CHANGE THE TWEEN SPEED

1 Select the frames containing the motion tween you want to adjust.

2 Click .

■ Flash opens the Instance panel.

3 Click the **Frame** tab.

4 Click and drag the Easing slider to a new setting.

■ Drag the slider up to accelerate the tween speed.

■ Drag the slider down to decelerate the tween speed.

■ A zero value indicates a constant rate of speed.

Does tween speed affect fps?

Tweening distributes the animation evenly between the two keyframes. When you adjust the Ease control to a setting other than the default 0, it merely accelerates or decelerates the beginning or end of the tween. It does not affect the movie's frames per second rate.

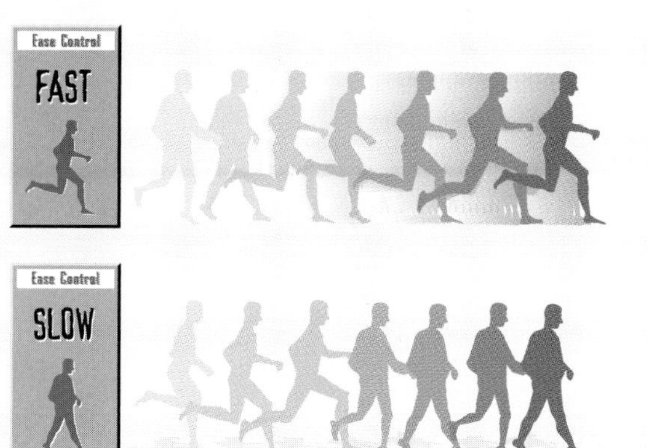

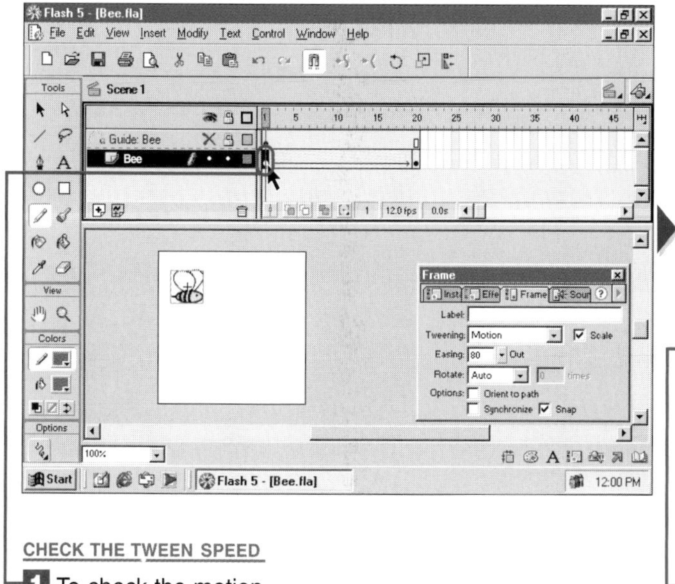

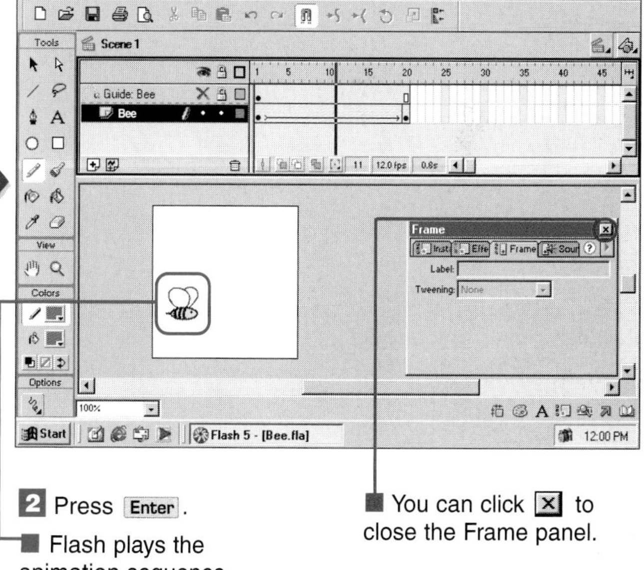

CHECK THE TWEEN SPEED

1 To check the motion tween speed, click in the first frame of the motion tween.

2 Press Enter.

■ Flash plays the animation sequence.

■ You can click ☒ to close the Frame panel.

CREATE A SHAPE TWEEN

You can create a shape tween to morph objects you draw on the Stage. For example, you may morph a circle shape into an oval. Shape tweening does not require the use of symbols or groups. You can animate any object you draw with the Drawing tools with the shape tween effect.

See the section "Create a Motion Tween" to learn more about the motion tween effect.

CREATE A SHAPE TWEEN

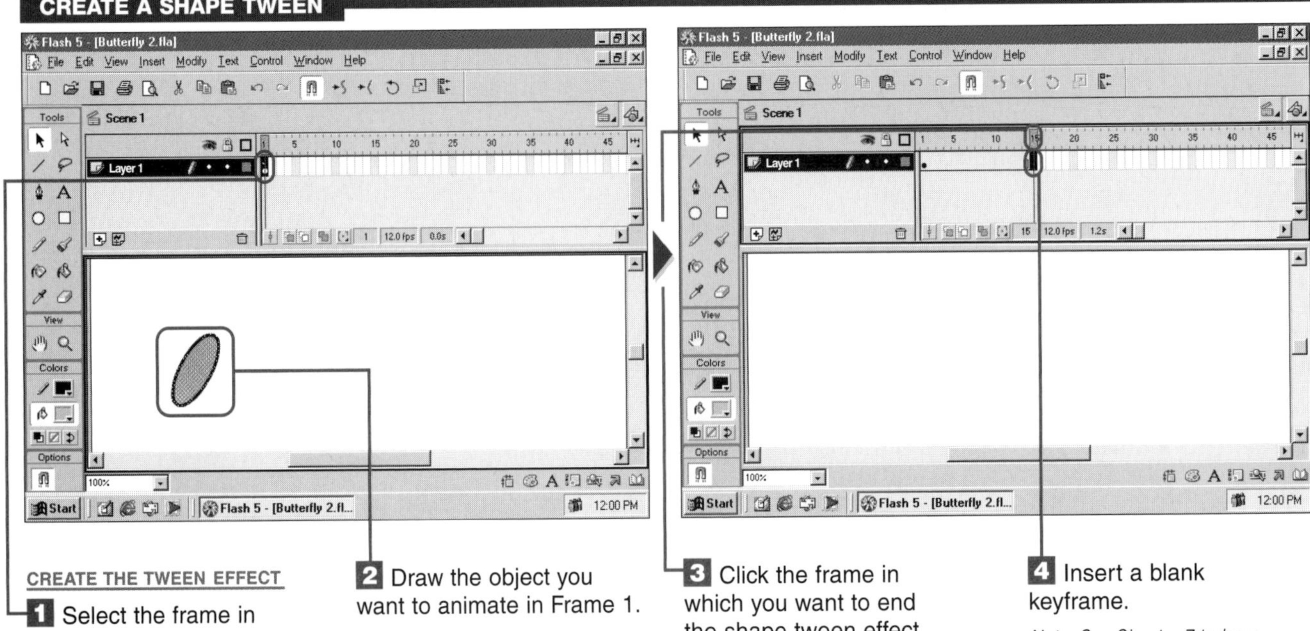

CREATE THE TWEEN EFFECT

1 Select the frame in which you want to start a shape tween.

2 Draw the object you want to animate in Frame 1.

Note: See Chapter 2 to learn how to use the Flash Drawing tools.

3 Click the frame in which you want to end the shape tween effect.

4 Insert a blank keyframe.

Note: See Chapter 7 to learn how to use Flash frames.

How is a shape tween different from a motion tween?

With a motion tween, you can only animate symbols, grouped objects, or text blocks. With a shape tween, you can animate any object you draw on the Stage. You do not have to save it as a symbol first, or group it in order for Flash to create in-between frames. You cannot shape tween a symbol or group. While a motion tween is good for moving objects from one point to another, a shape tween is the tool to use when you want to morph the object into another object entirely.

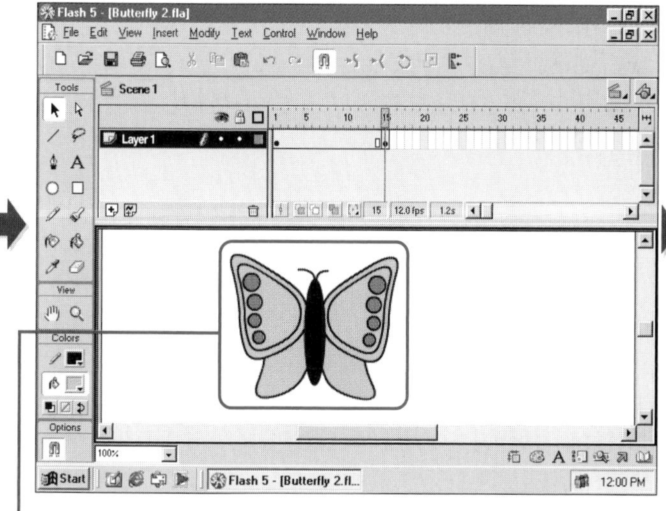

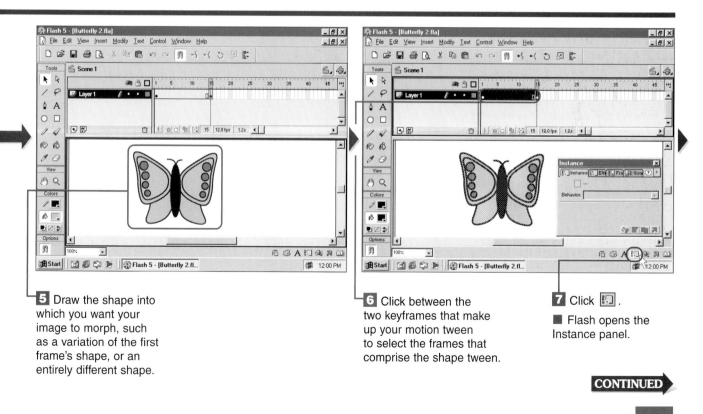

5 Draw the shape into which you want your image to morph, such as a variation of the first frame's shape, or an entirely different shape.

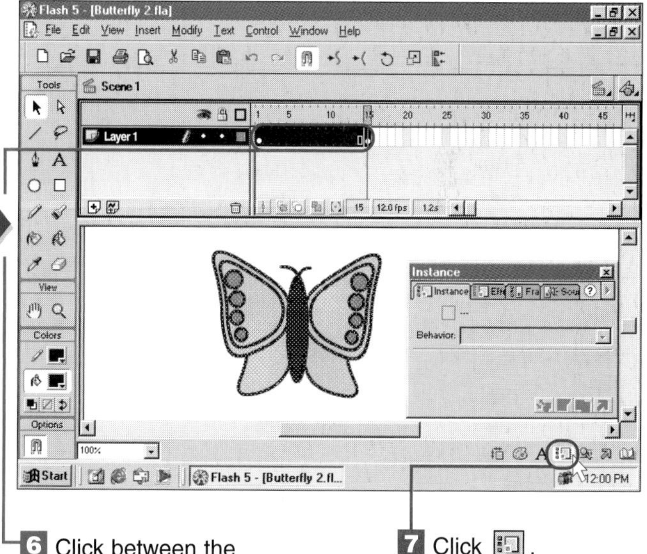

6 Click between the two keyframes that make up your motion tween to select the frames that comprise the shape tween.

7 Click .

■ Flash opens the Instance panel.

CONTINUED

CREATE A SHAPE TWEEN

You can use shape tweens to morph between all kinds of objects you draw, including text that you turn into an object. You can use as many shape tweens as you like in an animation, and you can start one right after the other in the Timeline.

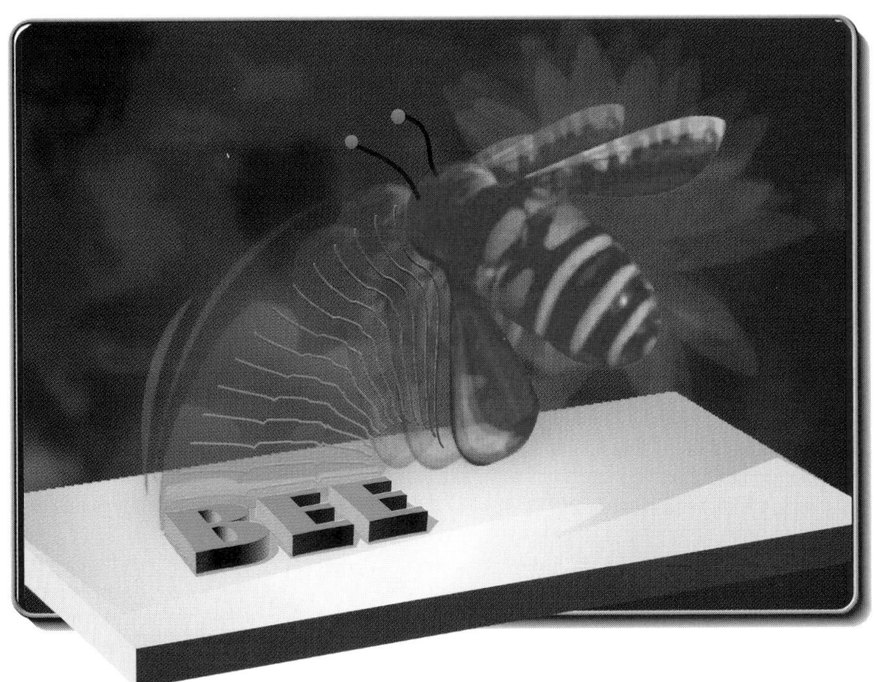

CREATE A SHAPE TWEEN (CONTINUED)

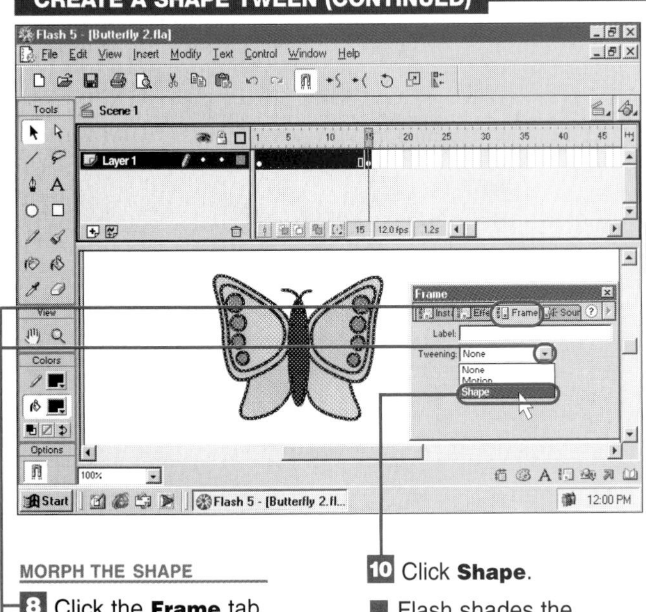

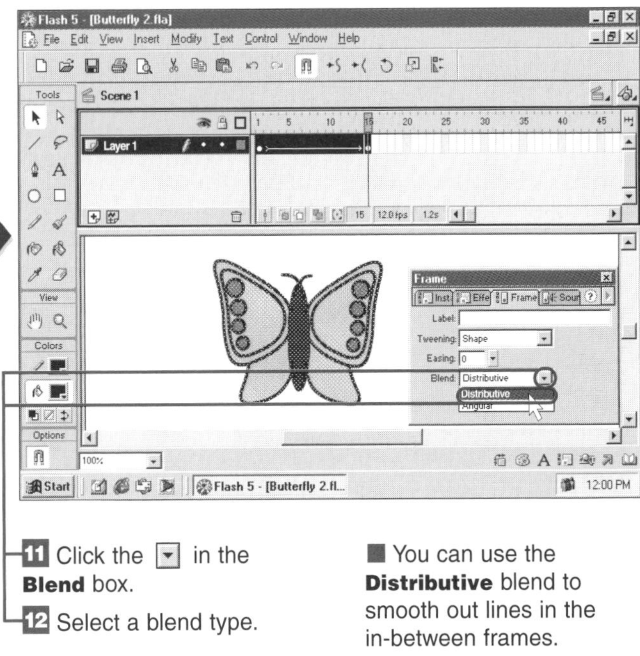

MORPH THE SHAPE

8 Click the **Frame** tab.

9 Click the ▼ in the **Tweening** box.

10 Click **Shape**.

■ Flash shades the selected frames green in the Timeline and adds a tween arrow from the first keyframe to the last.

11 Click the ▼ in the **Blend** box.

12 Select a blend type.

■ You can use the **Distributive** blend to smooth out lines in the in-between frames.

■ You can use the **Angular** blend to keep the sharp corners and straight lines that occur during the morph effect.

Can I use a symbol from my movie's Library?

You cannot shape tween symbols, but you can take a symbol and break it apart into objects which the shape tween effect can morph. To turn a symbol into an object, perform the following steps:

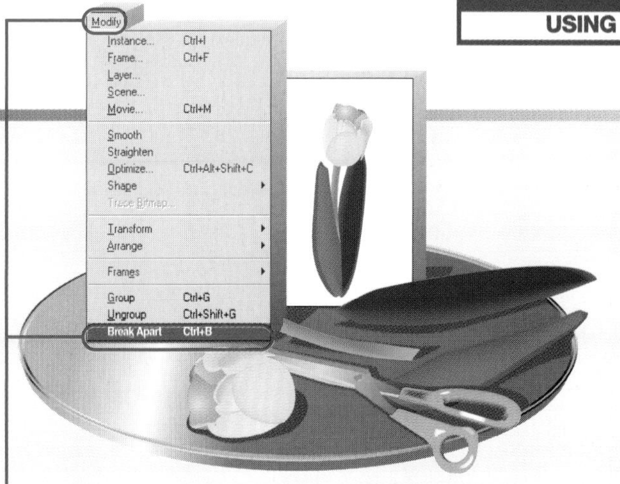

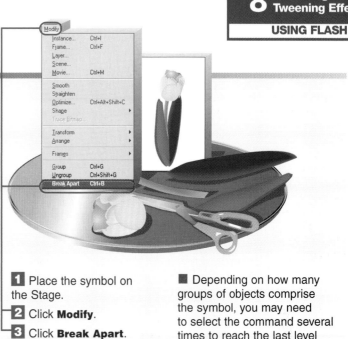

1 Place the symbol on the Stage.

2 Click **Modify**.

3 Click **Break Apart**.

■ Depending on how many groups of objects comprise the symbol, you may need to select the command several times to reach the last level of ungrouped objects.

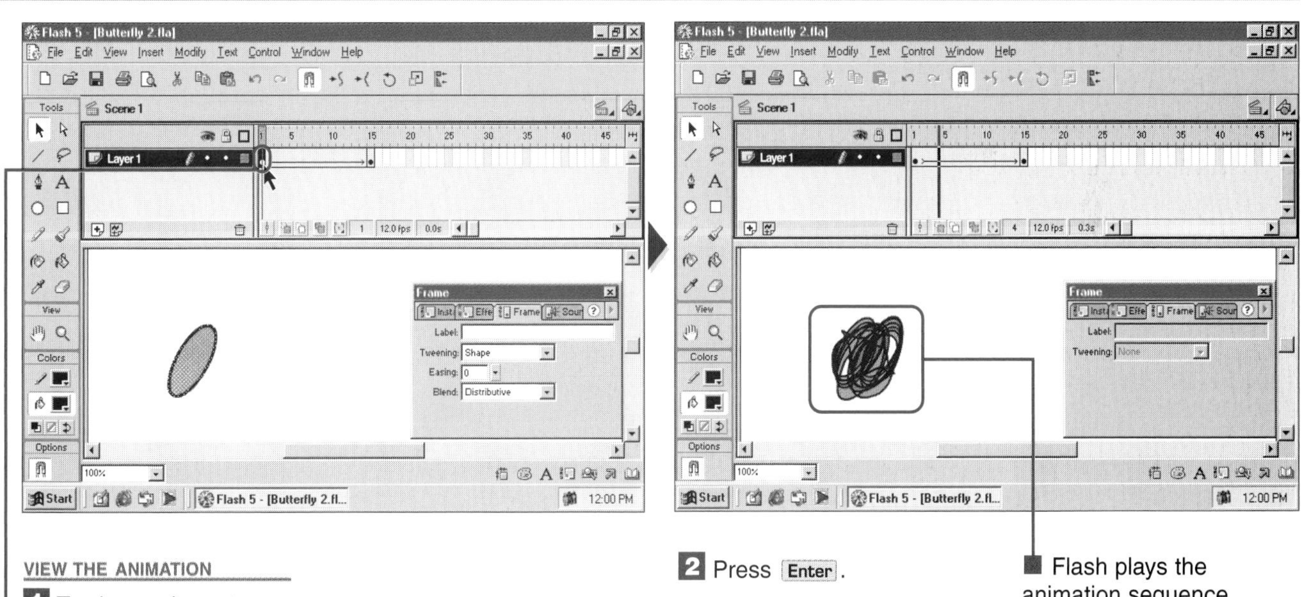

VIEW THE ANIMATION

1 To view a shape tween in action, click in the first frame of the shape tween.

2 Press Enter.

■ Flash plays the animation sequence.

CREATE A BUTTON SYMBOL

A button can be any object or drawing, such as a simple geometric shape. You can draw a new object with the Flash drawing tools, or you can use an imported graphic as a button. A button includes a Timeline with four frames: Up, Over, Down, and Hit. You must assign an image or action to each of the four button states.

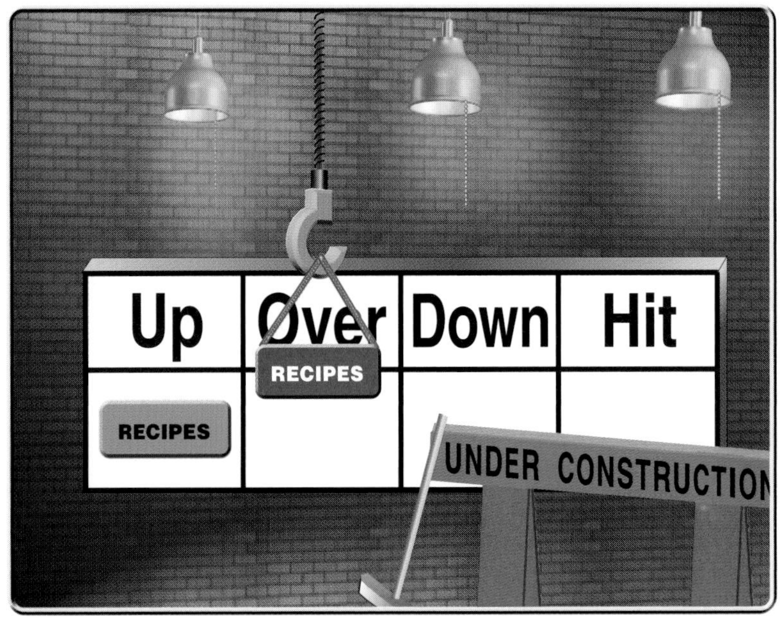

CREATE A BUTTON SYMBOL

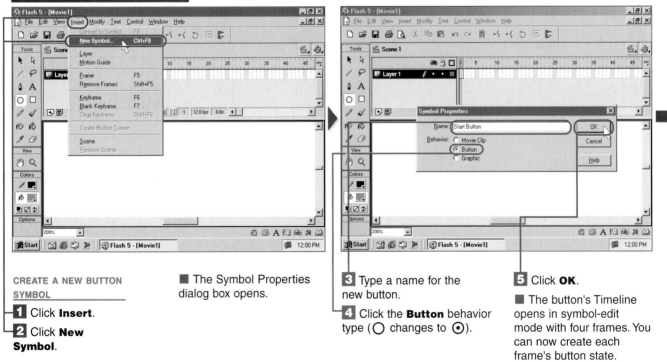

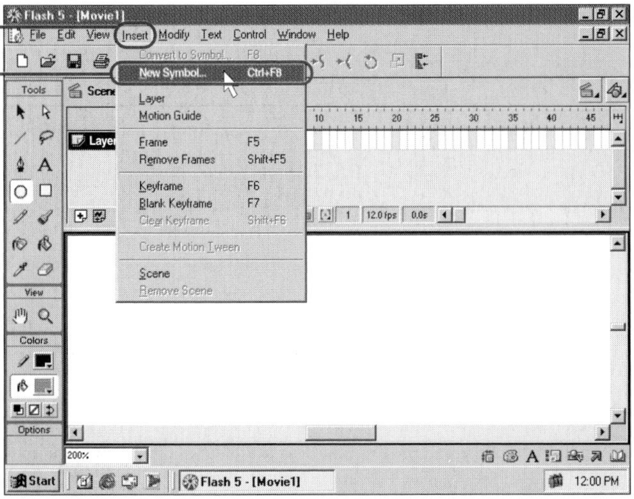

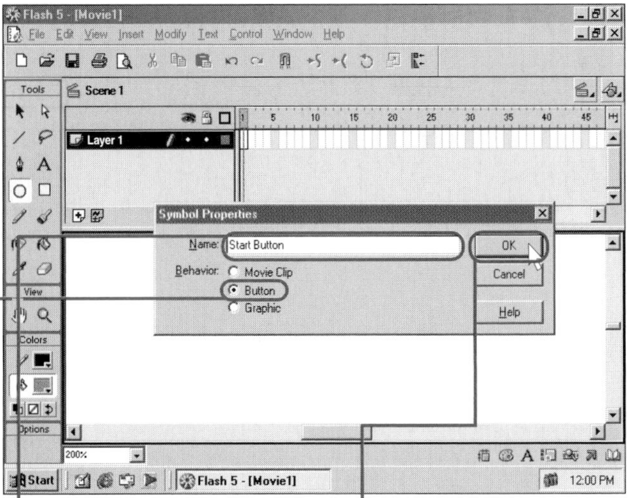

CREATE A NEW BUTTON SYMBOL

1 Click **Insert**.

2 Click **New Symbol**.

■ The Symbol Properties dialog box opens.

3 Type a name for the new button.

4 Click the **Button** behavior type (○ changes to ⊙).

5 Click **OK**.

■ The button's Timeline opens in symbol-edit mode with four frames. You can now create each frame's button state.

Does Flash have premade buttons I can use?

Flash has two common libraries, one with buttons, the other with sounds. To display the button library:

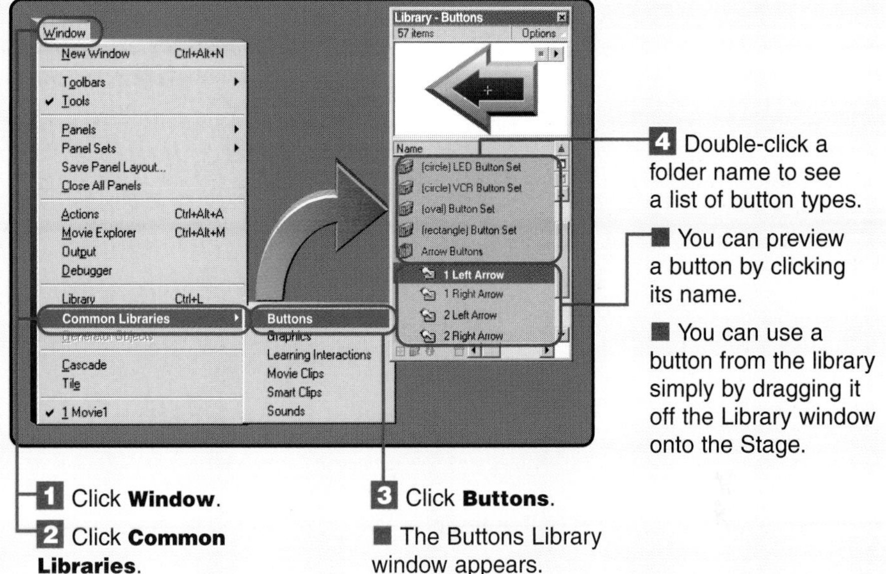

1 Click **Window**.

2 Click **Common Libraries**.

3 Click **Buttons**.

■ The Buttons Library window appears.

4 Double-click a folder name to see a list of button types.

■ You can preview a button by clicking its name.

■ You can use a button from the library simply by dragging it off the Library window onto the Stage.

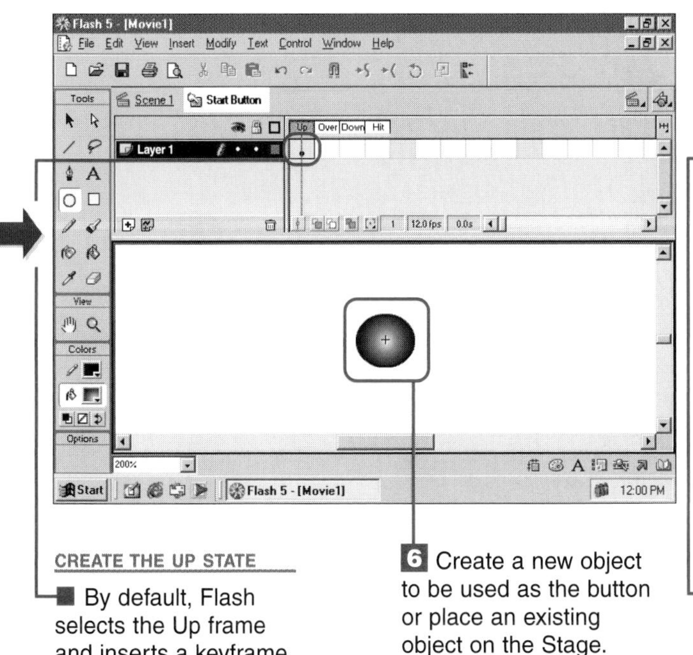

CREATE THE UP STATE

■ By default, Flash selects the Up frame and inserts a keyframe.

6 Create a new object to be used as the button or place an existing object on the Stage.

Note: See Chapter 2 to learn more about using the Flash drawing tools.

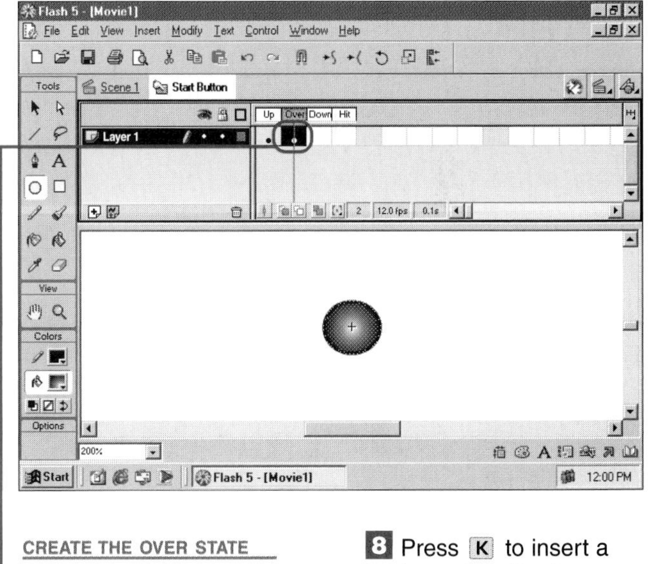

CREATE THE OVER STATE

7 Click the **Over** frame.

8 Press K to insert a keyframe into the frame.

Note: See Chapter 7 to learn more about frames.

CONTINUED

CREATE A BUTTON SYMBOL

You can draw a new object with the Flash drawing tools, or you can import a graphic created in Fireworks as a button. If you duplicate the same object in each button frame, you can make minor changes to make the button differ in each state. For example, you can change the color, scale, or shape for each keyframe.

See Chapter 2 to learn more about drawing with the Flash tools or see Chapter 6 to learn more about importing graphics.

CREATE A BUTTON SYMBOL (CONTINUED)

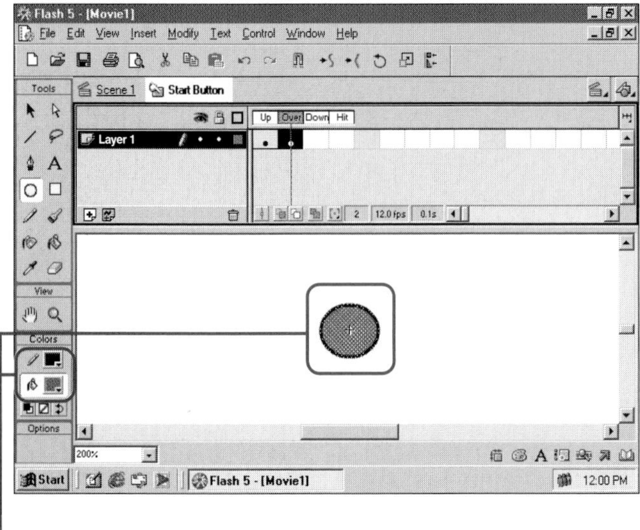

■ Flash duplicates the object you placed in the Up keyframe.

■ You can make minor changes to the object.

■ In this example, the object's fill color changes to alert the user that the button is active.

Note: See Chapter 3 to learn more about editing objects.

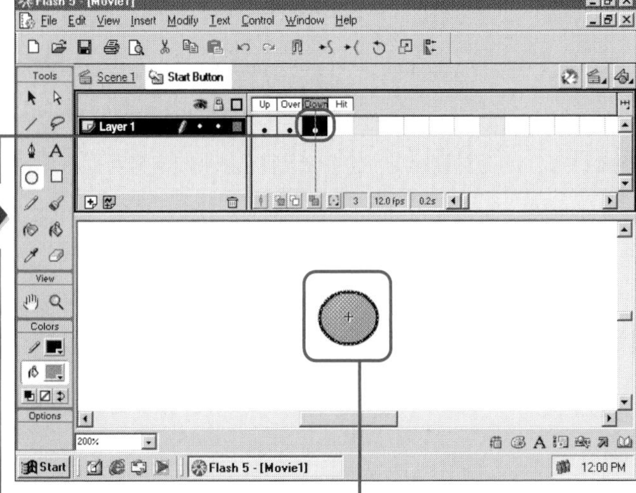

CREATE THE DOWN STATE

9 Click the **Down** frame.

10 Press K to insert a keyframe into the frame.

■ Flash duplicates the object you placed in the Over keyframe.

■ You can edit the object, if desired. For example, you might add a sound to the frame, or a short animation.

How do I preview a button?

In symbol-edit mode, click the button's Up frame, then press Enter. Watch the Stage as Flash plays through the four button frames. Any changes made to frames appear during playback.

You can preview the button in movie-edit mode. Press Ctrl + E (Windows) or ⌘ + E (Mac) to return to movie-edit mode. Press Ctrl + Alt + B to activate the button on the Stage and move the mouse pointer over the button and click it to see the rollover capabilities.

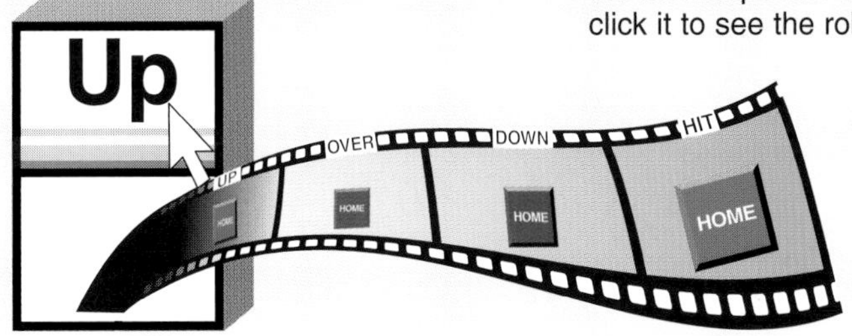

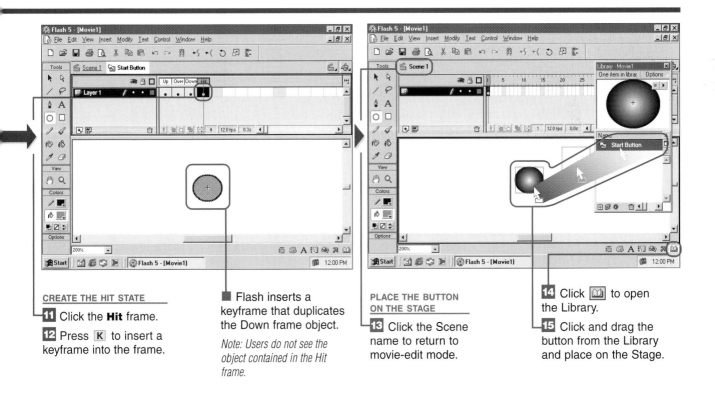

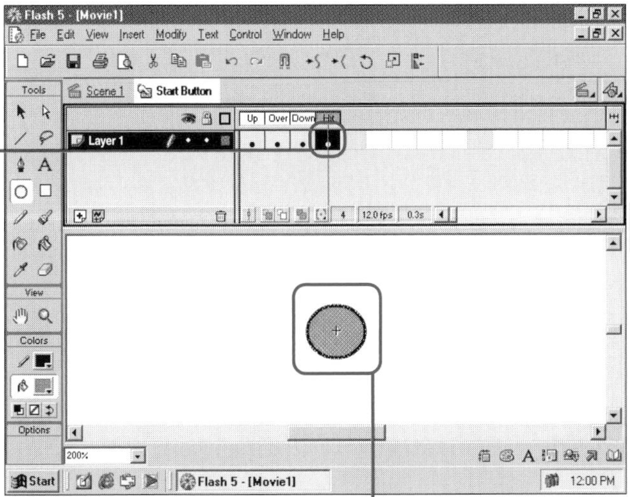

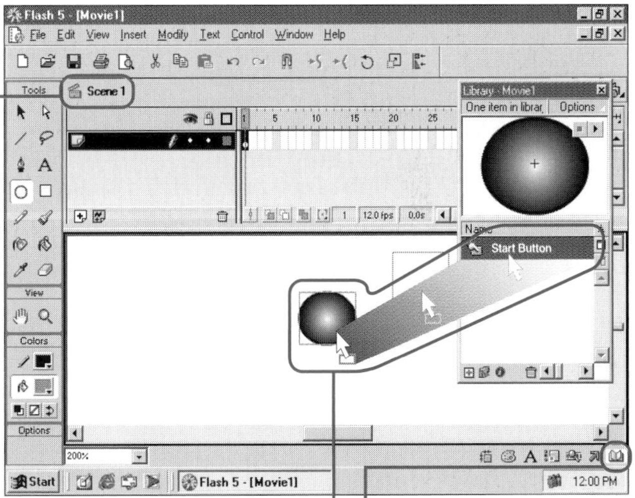

CREATE THE HIT STATE

11 Click the **Hit** frame.

12 Press K to insert a keyframe into the frame.

■ Flash inserts a keyframe that duplicates the Down frame object.

Note: Users do not see the object contained in the Hit frame.

PLACE THE BUTTON ON THE STAGE

13 Click the Scene name to return to movie-edit mode.

14 Click [Library] to open the Library.

15 Click and drag the button from the Library and place on the Stage.

CREATE AN ANIMATED BUTTON

You can create impressive animation effects for buttons. For example, you might make a button glow when the mouse pointer hovers over it, or animate the button with a cartoon that includes sound. Flash makes it easy to place movie clips into your button frames.

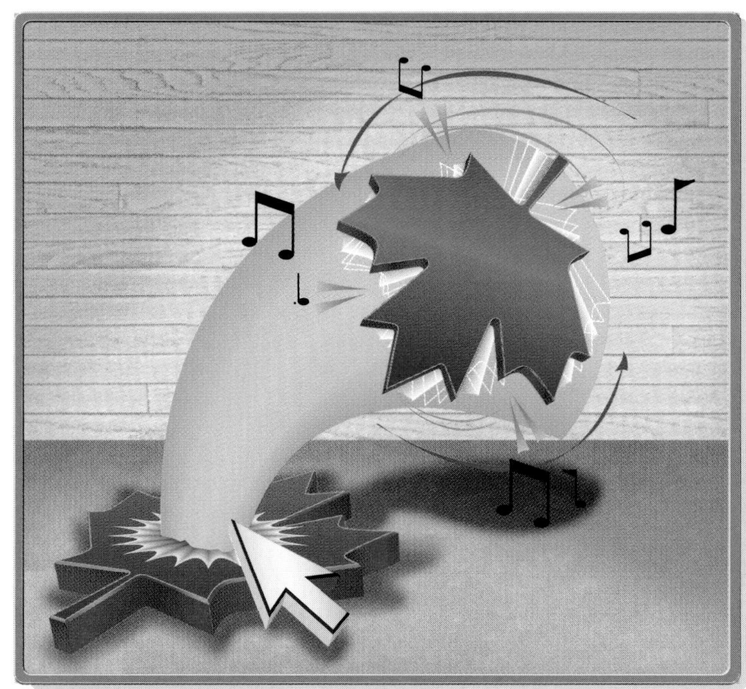

See Chapter 7 to learn how to create animations in Flash.

CREATE AN ANIMATED BUTTON

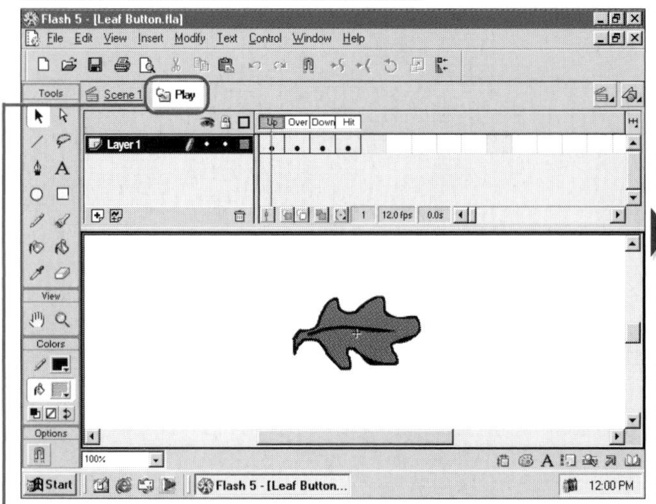

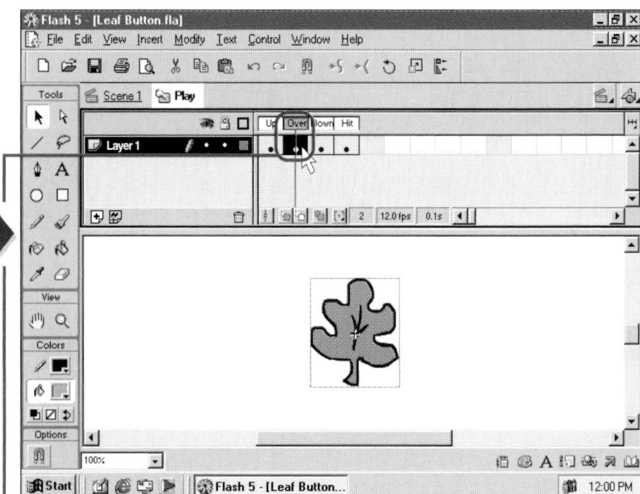

SELECT A BUTTON FRAME

1 Double-click the button to which you want to assign an animation.

■ The button's name appears above the Timeline, indicating you are in symbol=edit mode.

Note: See the section "Create a Button Symbol" to learn how to create a button.

2 Click the frame to which you want to add an animation, such as the Up, Over, or Down frame.

Note: The Hit frame is not seen by the user, so it is not useful to animate the frame.

Can I add sounds to button frames?

You can add sound clips to button frames the same way you add movie clips. Try adding a sound from Flash's Sound Library:

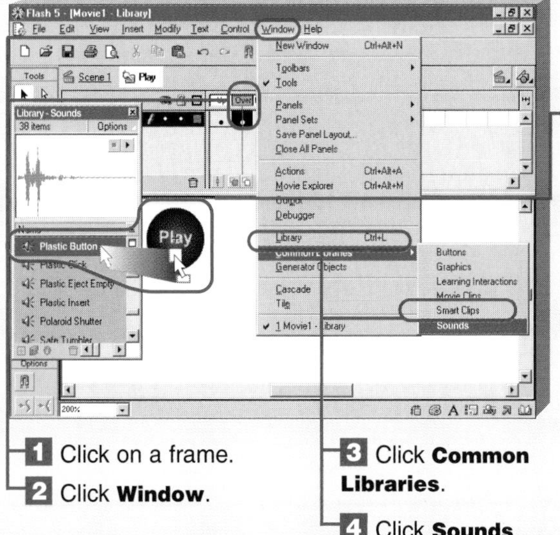

1 Click on a frame.

2 Click **Window**.

3 Click **Common Libraries**.

4 Click **Sounds**.

5 In the Sounds Library, click the sound clip and drag it out to the button area on the Stage. A sound wave appears in the frame.

■ You can press Enter to test the button sequence. See Chapter 11 to learn more about adding sounds to frames.

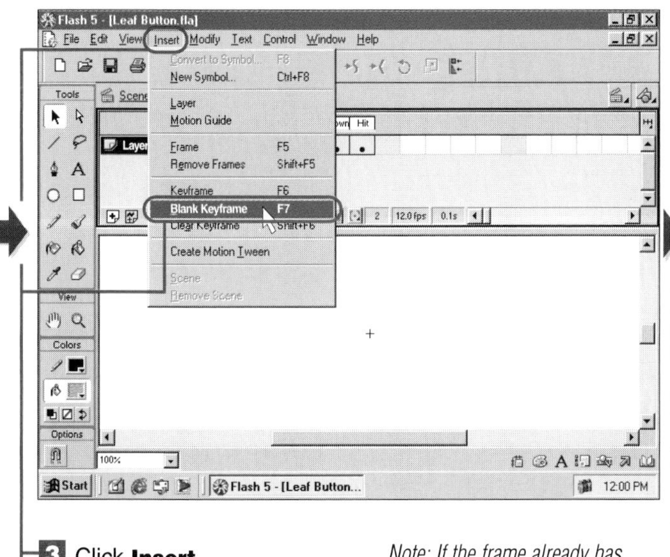

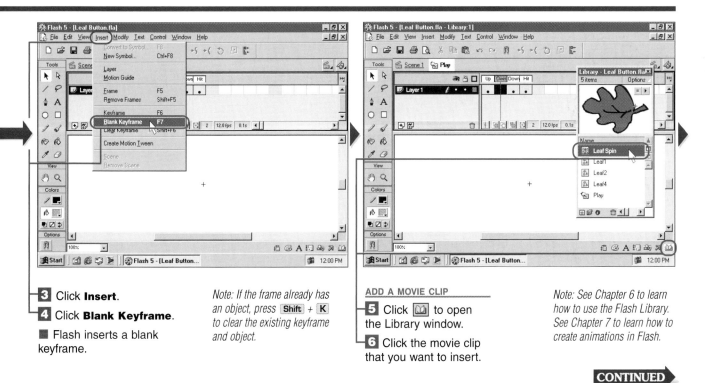

3 Click **Insert**.

4 Click **Blank Keyframe**.

■ Flash inserts a blank keyframe.

Note: If the frame already has an object, press Shift + K to clear the existing keyframe and object.

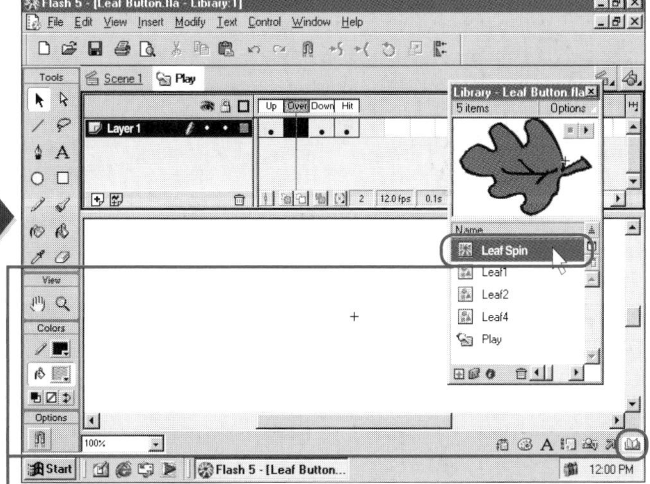

ADD A MOVIE CLIP

5 Click 📖 to open the Library window.

6 Click the movie clip that you want to insert.

Note: See Chapter 6 to learn how to use the Flash Library. See Chapter 7 to learn how to create animations in Flash.

CONTINUED

CREATE AN ANIMATED BUTTON

You can add an animation frame to any button state. For example, you might want the user to see a spinning leaf when the button is inactive, or you might want the leaf object to spin only when the user rolls over the button with the mouse. You can play the animation when the user actually clicks the mouse button.

CREATE AN ANIMATED BUTTON (CONTINUED)

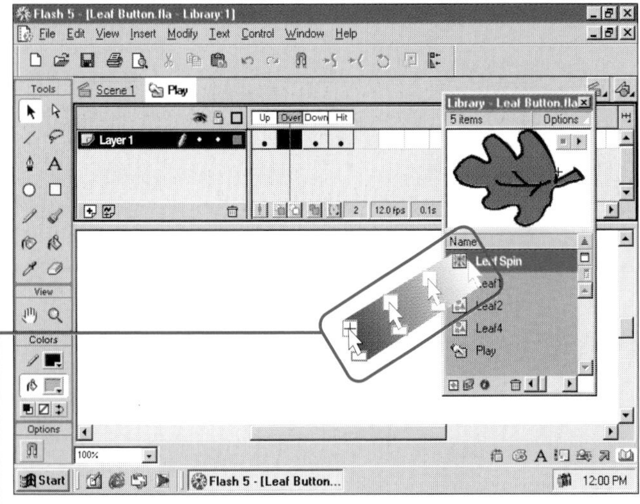

7 Click and drag the movie clip from the Library window and place it on the Stage where the button appears.

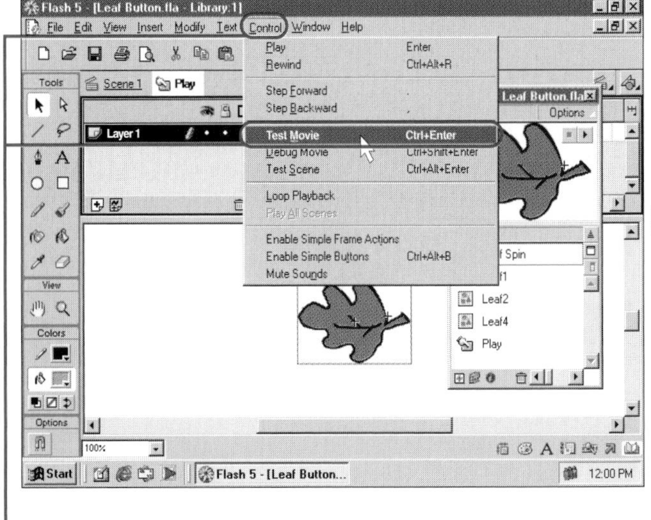

TEST THE MOVIE CLIP

1 Click **Control**.

2 Click **Test Movie**.

■ The Flash Player window opens.

How do I preview the animated button in movie-edit mode?

When you press Ctrl + Alt + B to preview a button's rollover capabilities in movie-edit mode, any movie clips you added to button frames do not run. Instead, you see the first frame of the movie clip. To see the fully animated button, click **Control** and then click **Test Movie**.

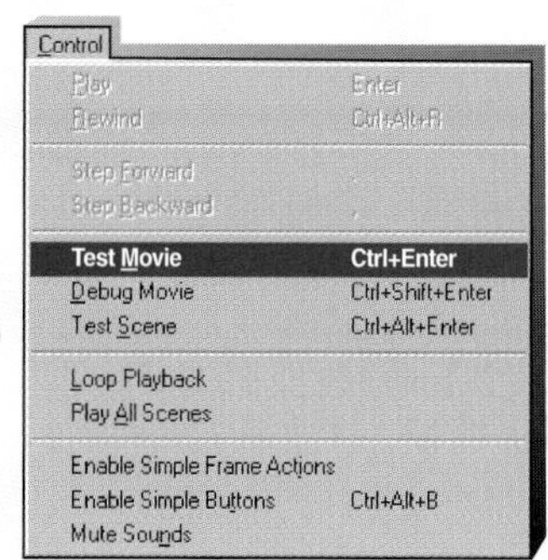

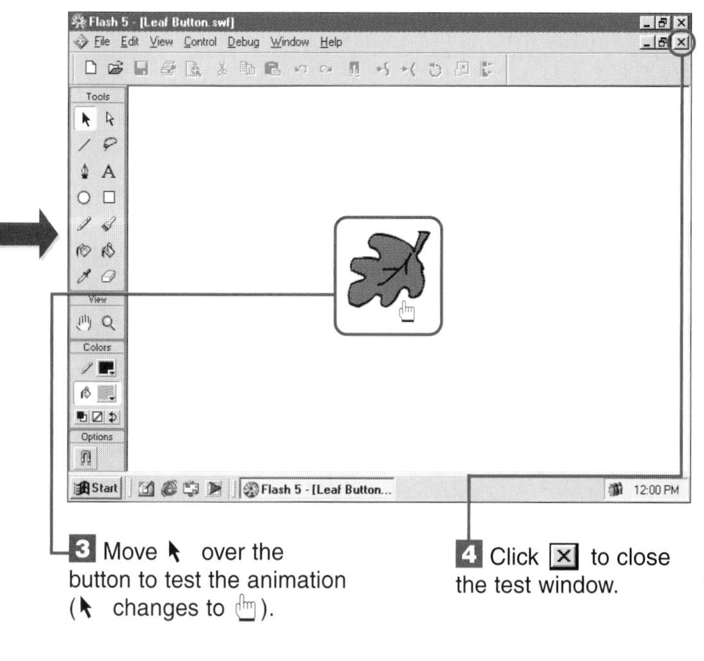

3 Move ↖ over the button to test the animation (↖ changes to ☝).

4 Click ☒ to close the test window.

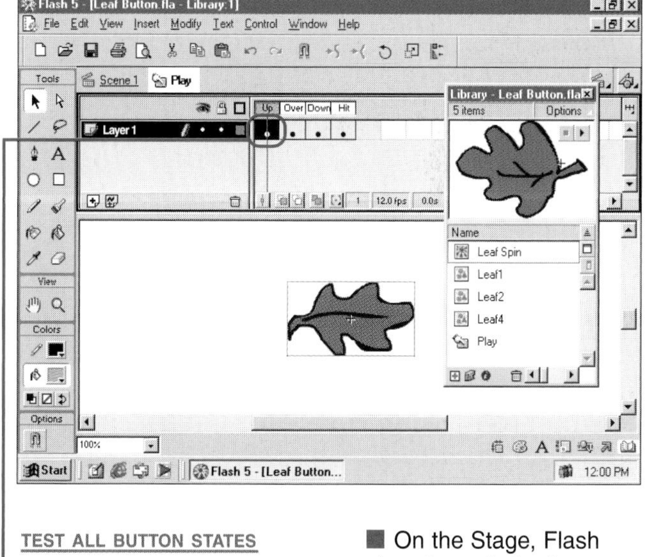

TEST ALL BUTTON STATES

1 Click the **Up** frame to select it.

2 Press Enter.

■ On the Stage, Flash plays through the four button frames including the animation effect.

ASSIGN BUTTON ACTIONS

Buttons already utilize built-in actions, such as moving immediately to the Down frame when a user clicks the button. You can add other Flash actions to your buttons. For example, you can add a Play action to a button so that a movie clip starts playing when the user clicks the button, or a Stop action that enables the user to stop the movie.

See Chapter 11 to learn more about assigning actions.

ASSIGN BUTTON ACTIONS

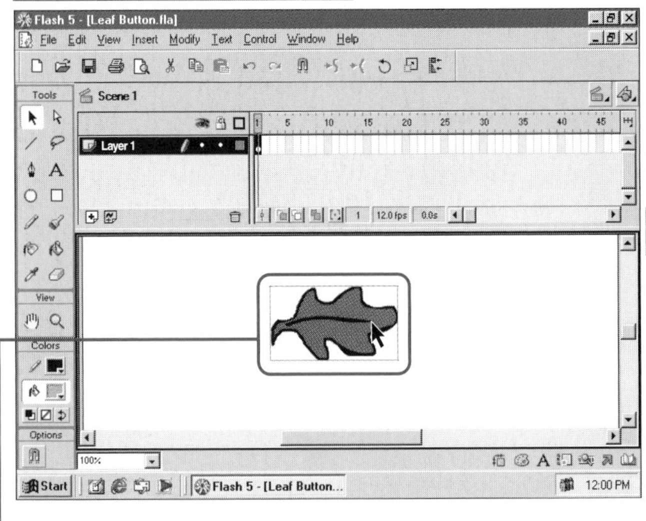

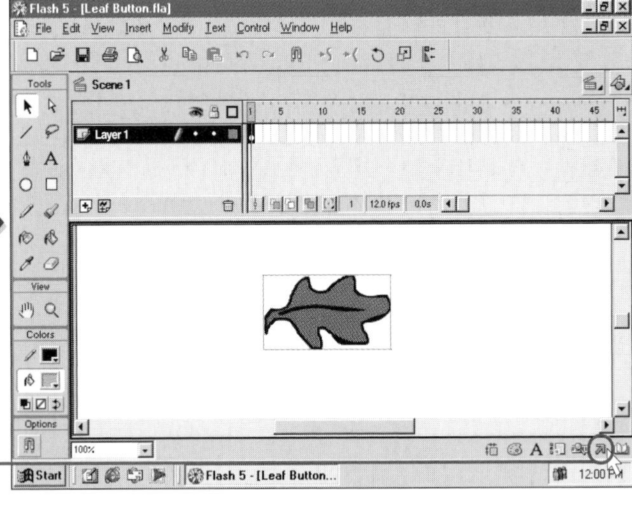

ADD AN ACTION TO A BUTTON

1 Click the button to switch to symbol-edit mode.

Note: See the section "Create a Button Symbol" to learn how to create a button.

2 Click [icon].

■ The Object Actions dialog box opens.

Why am I unable to select my button on the Flash Stage?

If Flash displays the button animation sequence when you move your mouse pointer over the button on the Stage, this means that you have left the Enable Simple Buttons feature active. Press Ctrl + Alt + B to disable the feature. Now you can click the button to select it.

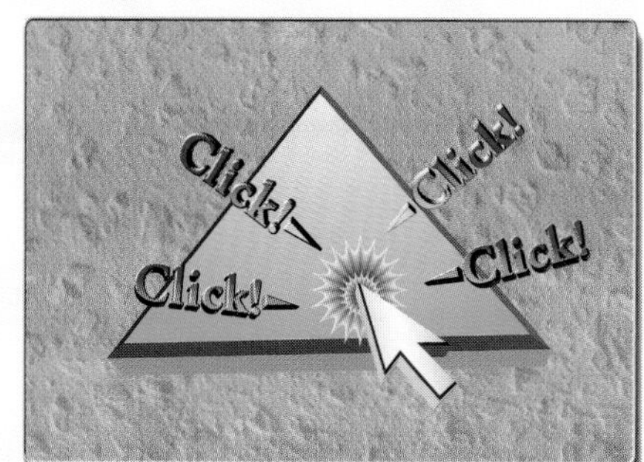

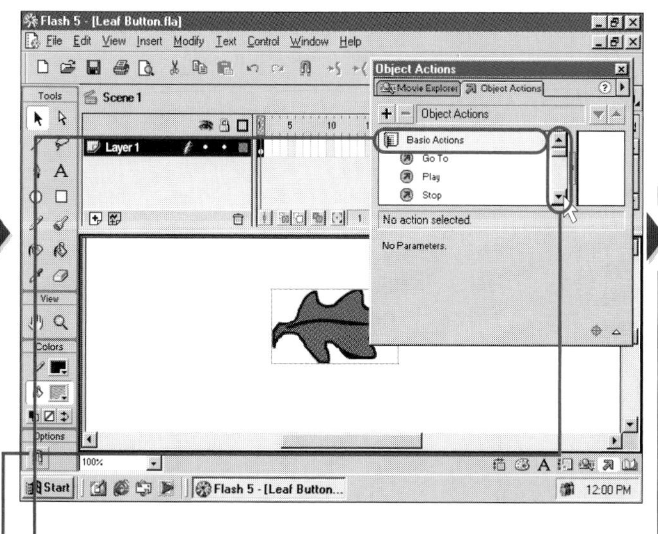

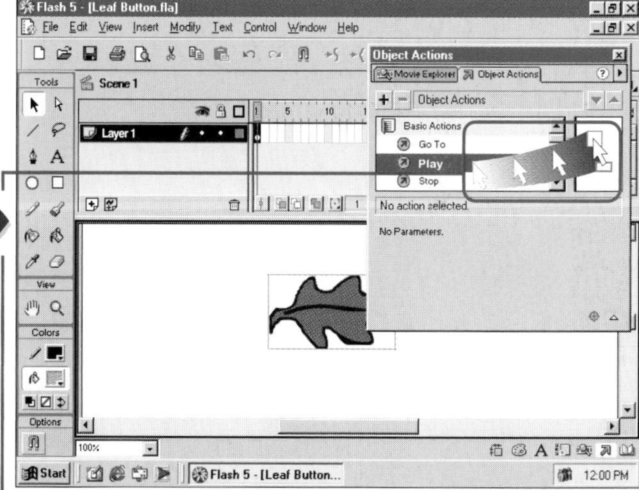

3 From the Object Actions Toolbox list, click **Basic Actions**.

4 Scroll through the list of actions and locate the one you want to apply.

5 Click and drag the action from the list and drop it in the Actions list box.

■ You can also double-click the action name to immediately place it in the Actions list box.

CONTINUED

ASSIGN BUTTON ACTIONS

Flash actions are simplified programming scripts that instruct Flash how to perform a certain task, such as loading a movie or stopping a sound clip. Actions include command strings to spell out exactly what action Flash must perform. Most button actions require input from the user, such as moving the mouse over the button, or clicking the button. You don't have to know programming in order to use Flash actions.

See Chapter 11 to learn more about Flash actions and how you can put them to use.

ASSIGN BUTTON ACTIONS (CONTINUED)

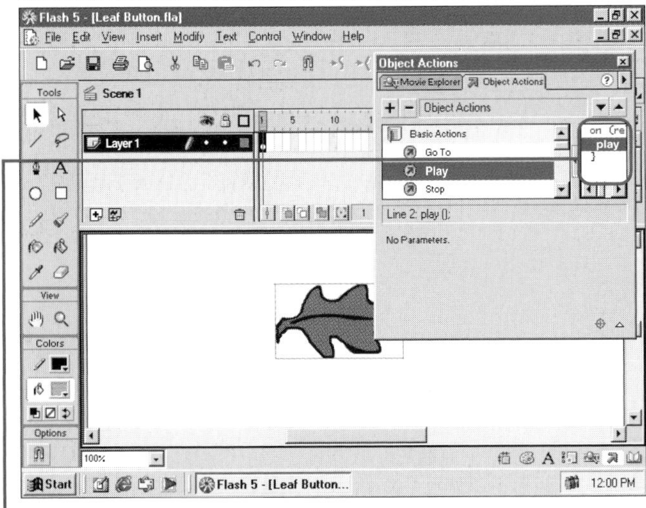

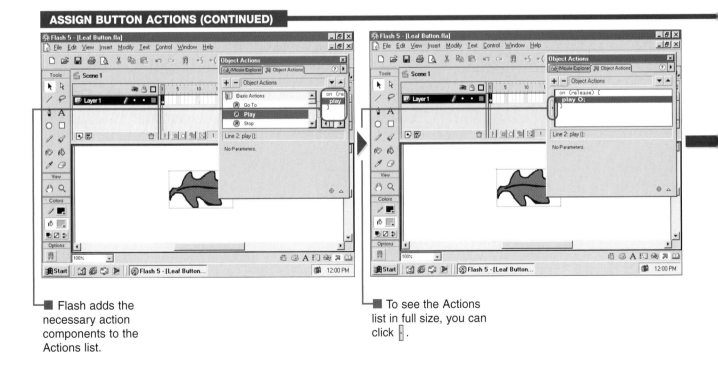

■ Flash adds the necessary action components to the Actions list.

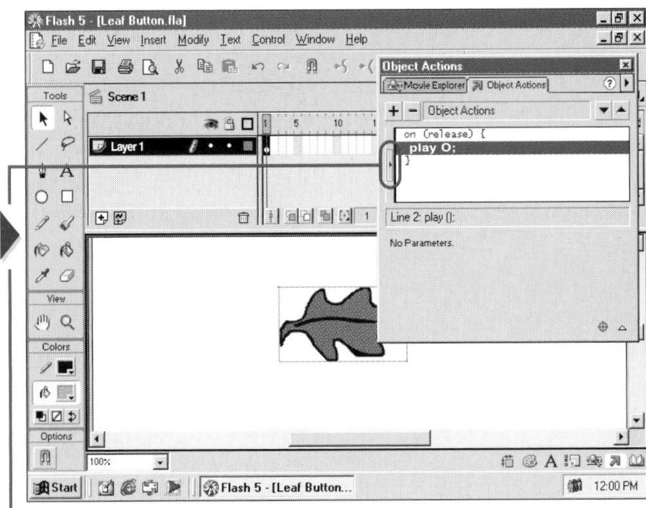

■ To see the Actions list in full size, you can click .

How do I edit an action assigned to a button?

You can perform edits to your button actions in the Object Actions box. Click the line you want to edit in the Actions list. Depending on the action, a variety of parameters appear at the bottom of the box. You can make changes to those parameters, if necessary. To remove an action component from the Actions list, click the line you want to delete and then click [-]. To add an action, click [+] and then click another action.

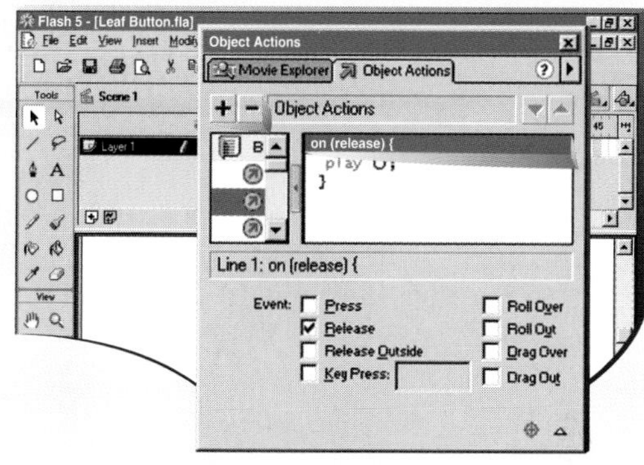

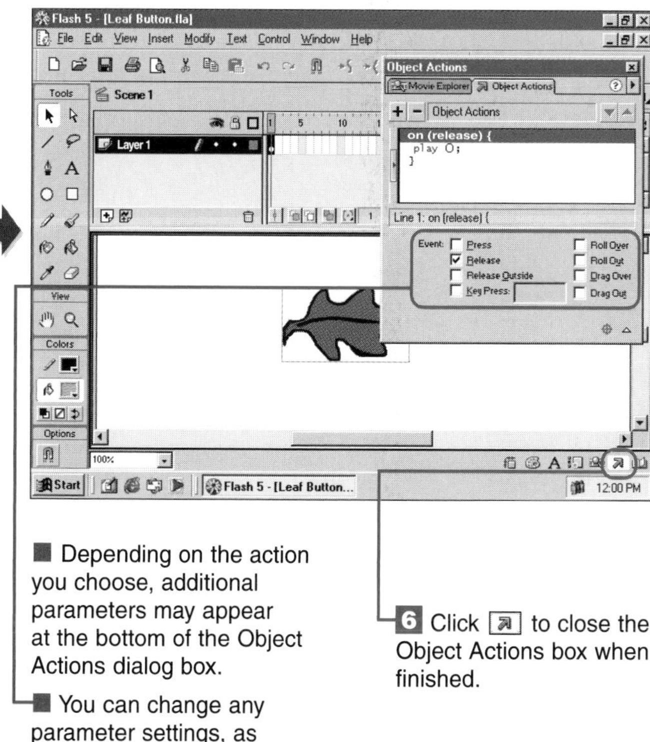

■ Depending on the action you choose, additional parameters may appear at the bottom of the Object Actions dialog box.

■ You can change any parameter settings, as necessary.

6 Click [close] to close the Object Actions box when finished.

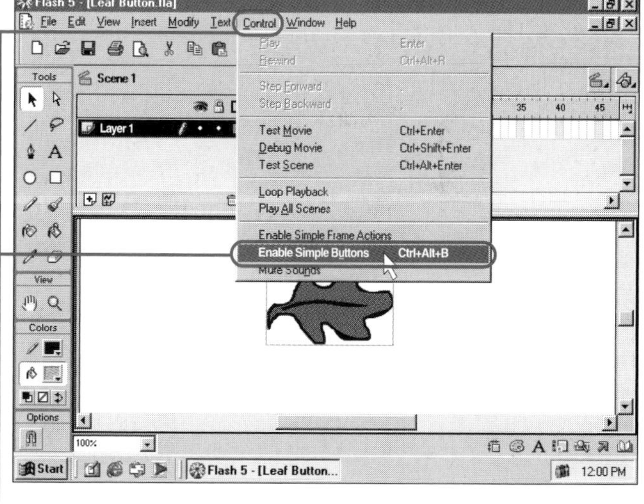

TEST A BUTTON ACTION

1 Click **Control**.

2 Click **Enable Simple Buttons**.

■ You can now move the pointer over the button and click to see the associated action.

IMPORT A SOUND FILE

Although you cannot record sounds in Flash, you can import sounds from other sources for use with movies and other projects. For example, you can download an MP3 file off the Internet and add it to a movie, or import a saved recording to play with a Flash button. Flash supports popular sound file formats, such as WAV and AIF.

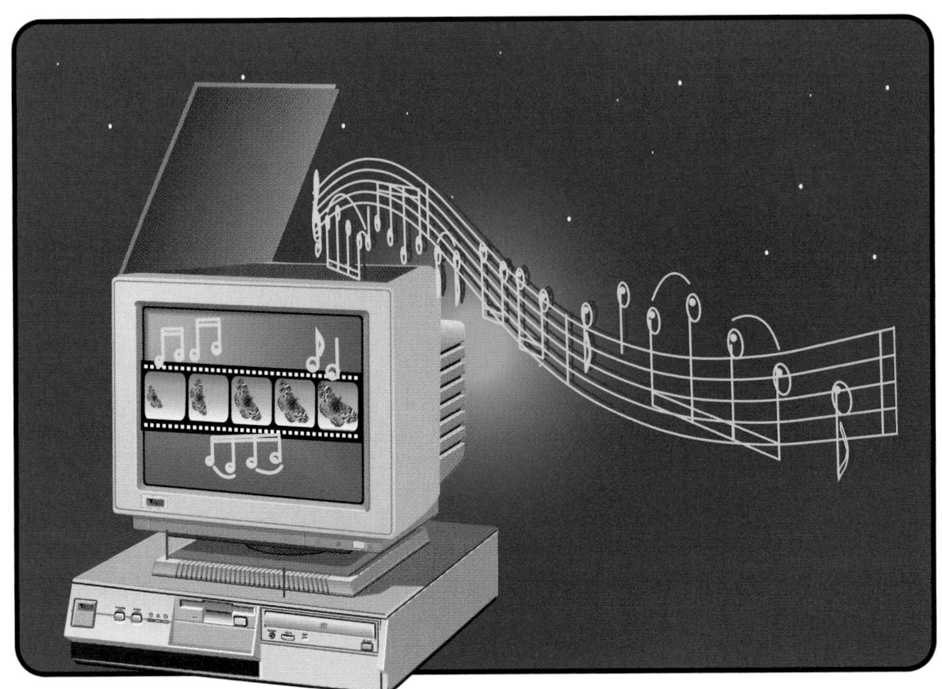

IMPORT A SOUND FILE

1 Click **File**.

2 Click **Import**.

■ The Import dialog box opens.

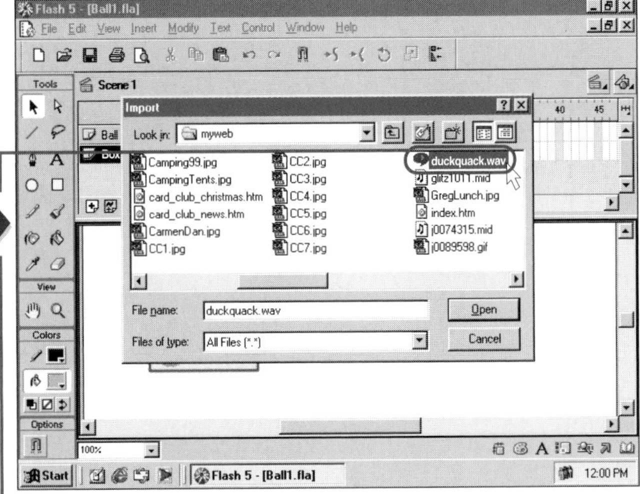

3 Click the sound file you want to import.

Does Flash have any sounds I can use?

Flash has several common libraries from which you can borrow items: one includes sounds. To display the sound library:

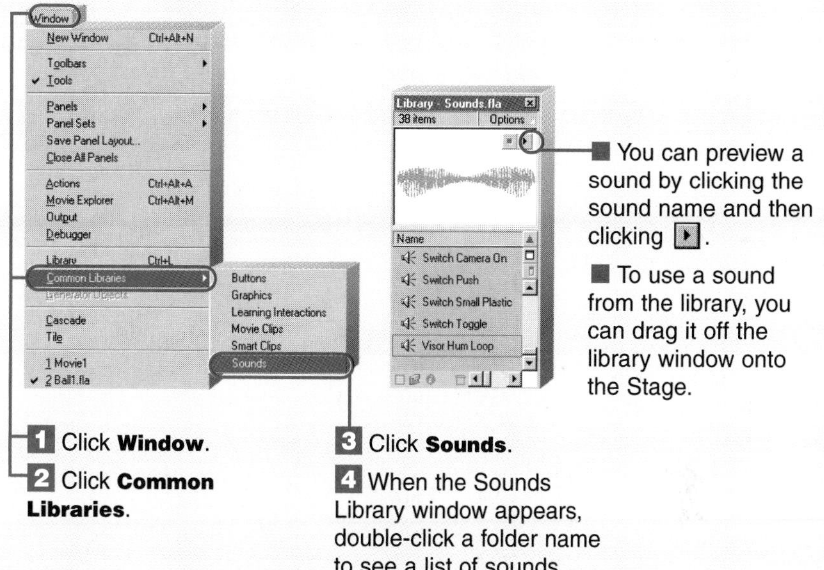

1 Click **Window**.

2 Click **Common Libraries**.

3 Click **Sounds**.

4 When the Sounds Library window appears, double-click a folder name to see a list of sounds.

■ You can preview a sound by clicking the sound name and then clicking ▶.

■ To use a sound from the library, you can drag it off the library window onto the Stage.

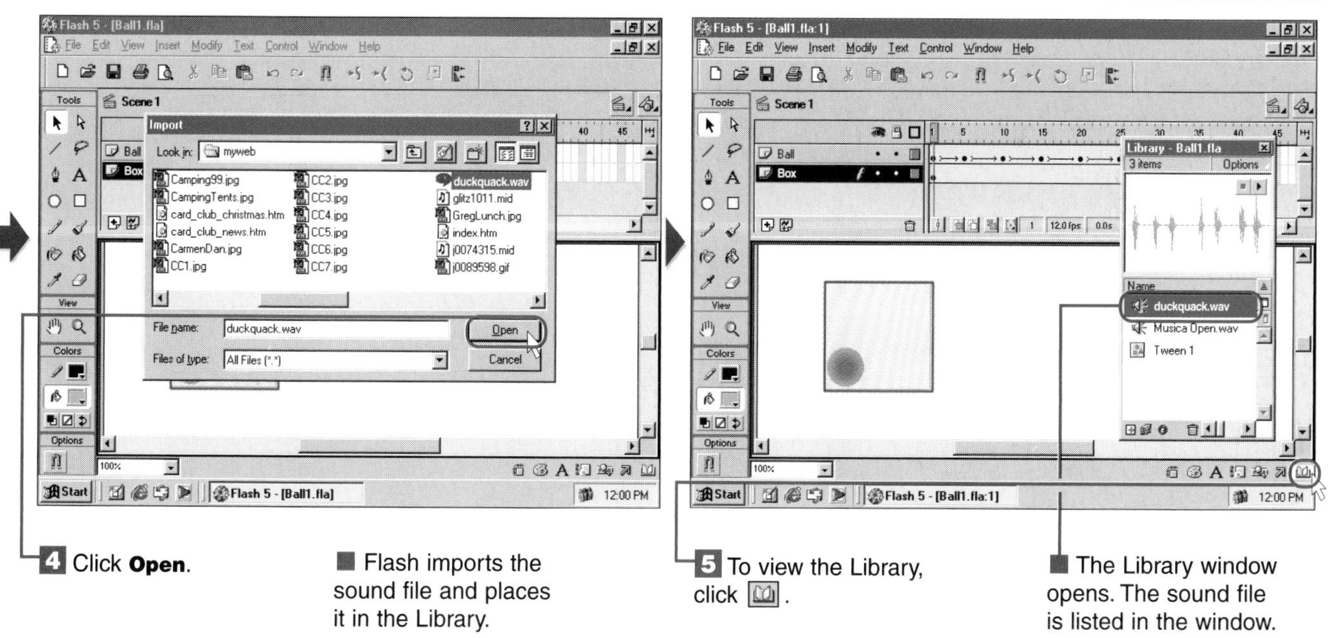

4 Click **Open**.

■ Flash imports the sound file and places it in the Library.

5 To view the Library, click 📖.

■ The Library window opens. The sound file is listed in the window.

ADD A SOUND LAYER

Flash helps organize your movie by allowing you to place sound clips in another layer. This makes it easier to find sound files quickly and edit them as needed. Flash allows for multiple sound layers in your movie.

See Chapter 5 to learn more about working with Flash layers.

ADD A SOUND LAYER

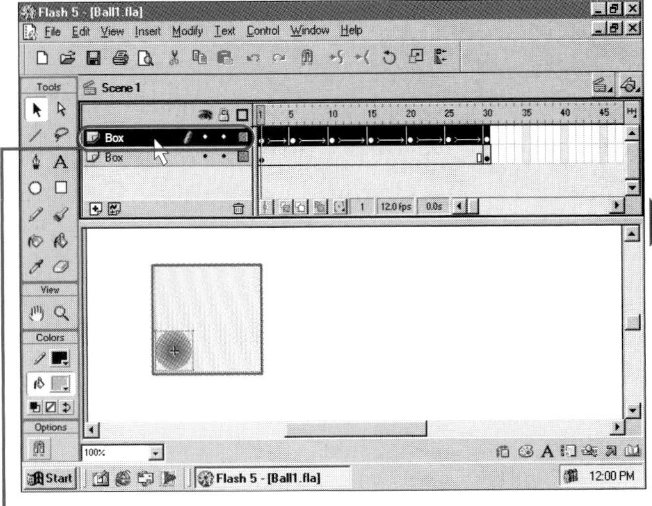

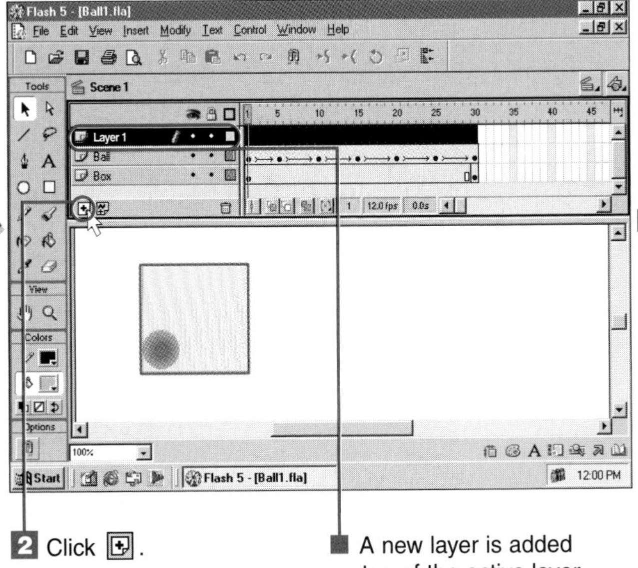

1 Click the layer you want to appear beneath the added layer.

■ Flash always adds a new layer to the Timeline directly above the active layer.

2 Click ⊞.

■ A new layer is added on top of the active layer.

Can I make a soundtrack layer?

There is no such thing as a soundtrack layer in Flash, but you can organize multiple sound layers and place them visually under a mask layer and name the mask layer Sound track. By placing all of your sound layers beneath a labeled mask layer, you can quickly see the organization of sound files in your Flash movie.

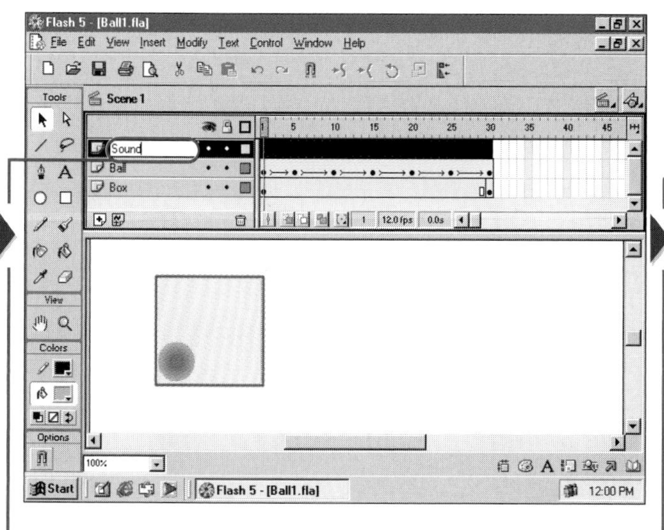

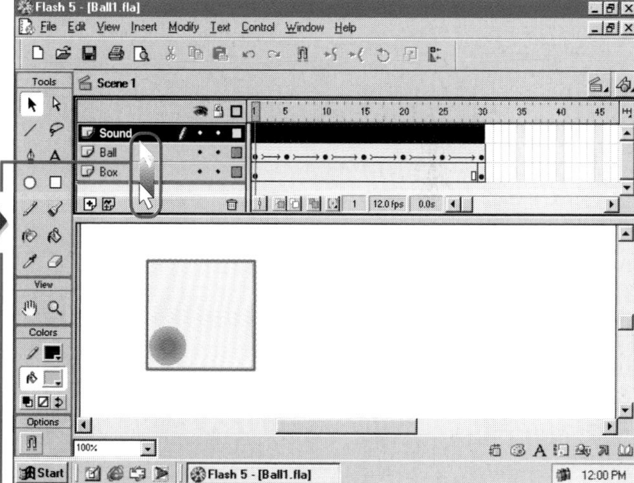

3 Double-click the default layer name to give the layer a distinct name.

4 Type a name that identifies this layer as a sound layer.

■ In this example, the layer is labeled "Sound."

5 Press Enter.

■ Flash saves the new name of the layer.

■ To make the sound layer easy to find, you can drag the layer to the top or bottom of the Timeline layer stack.

ASSIGN SOUNDS TO FRAMES

You can enliven any animation sequence with a sound clip whether you add a single sound effect or an entire sound track. Like graphics, sound files are saved as instances that can be inserted into frames on the Timeline and used throughout your movie. Sounds are represented as waveforms in Flash frames.

See Chapter 7 to learn more about frames.

ASSIGN A SOUND TO A FRAME

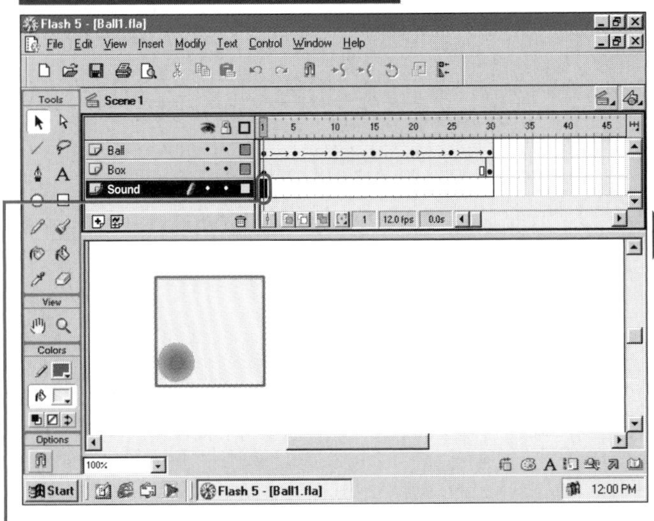

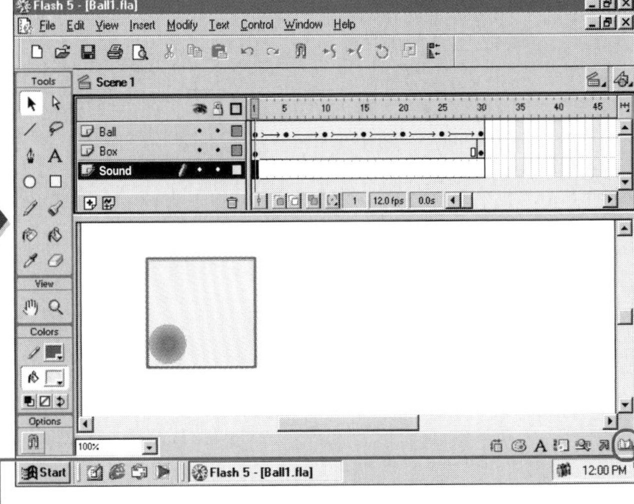

1 Click the frame to which you want to add a sound.

■ It is a good idea to add your sound to a sound layer.

Note: See the previous section "Add a Sound Layer" to learn more about sound layers.

2 Press F6 to insert a keyframe.

3 Click .

■ The Library window opens.

What is a waveform?

When you drag a sound from the Library onto the Stage, there is no visual representation of the sound. Instead, a waveform image of vertical lines representing the digital sampling of the sound appears in the Timeline frame.

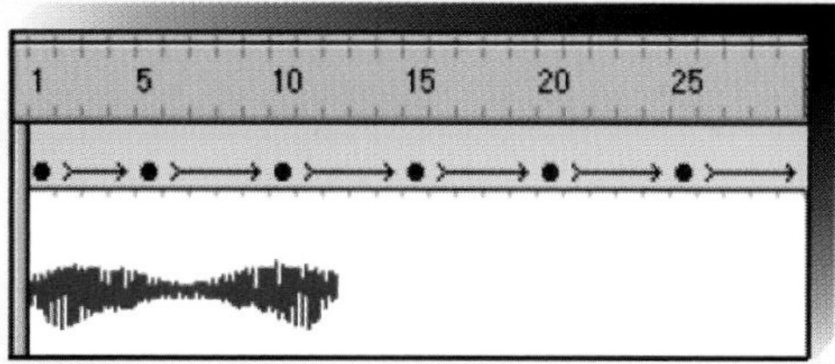

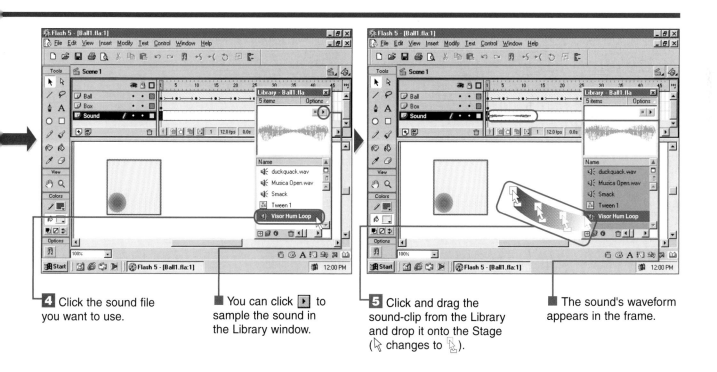

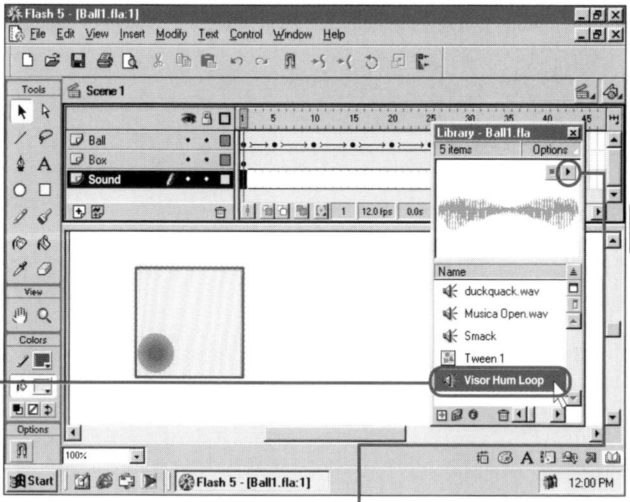

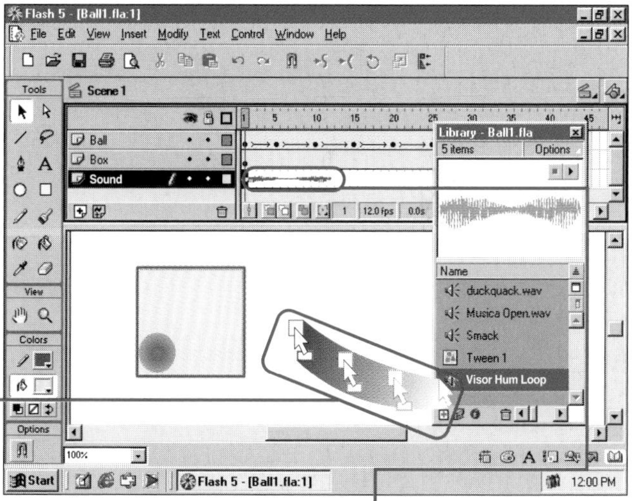

4 Click the sound file you want to use.

■ You can click ▶ to sample the sound in the Library window.

5 Click and drag the sound-clip from the Library and drop it onto the Stage (↖ changes to ↖).

■ The sound's waveform appears in the frame.

ASSIGN SOUNDS TO BUTTONS

You can apply sounds to page buttons to help people know how to interact with the buttons or just to give the buttons added flair. For example, you might add a clicking sound that the user hears when he or she clicks a button.

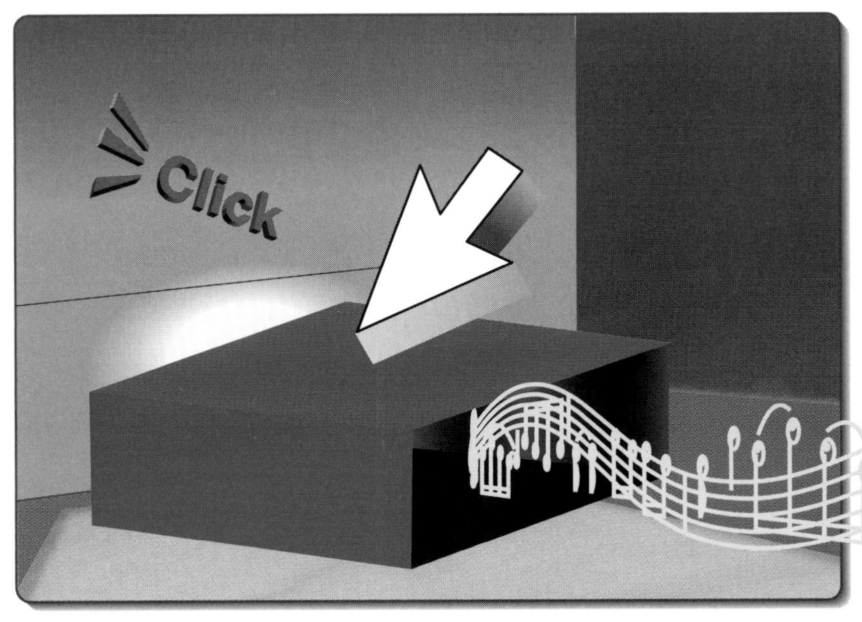

See Chapter 9 to learn more about creating interactive buttons.

ASSIGN SOUNDS TO BUTTONS

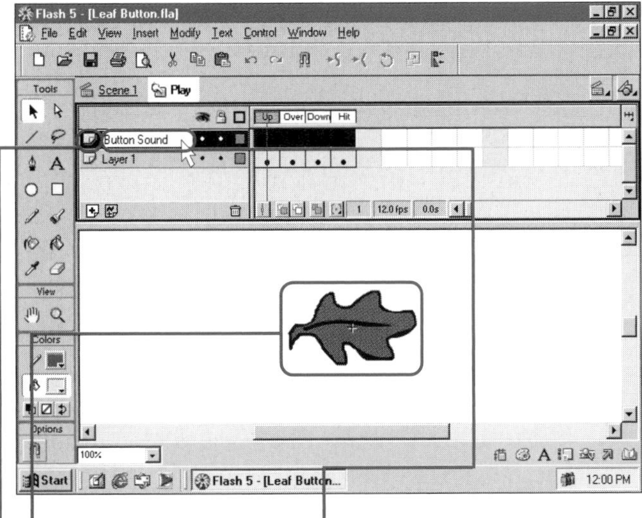

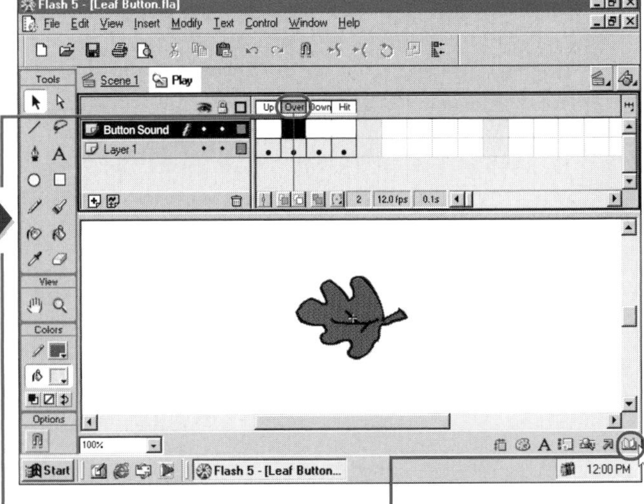

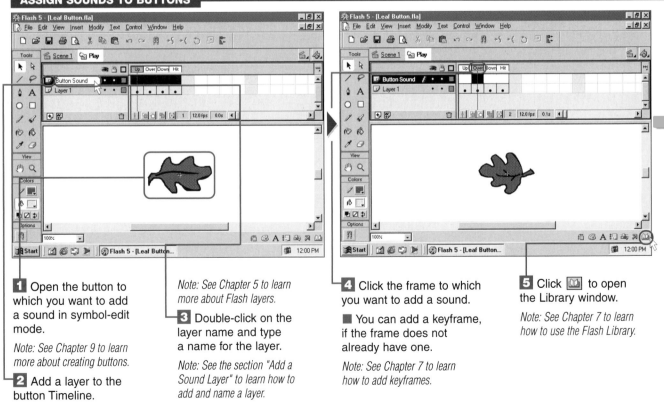

1 Open the button to which you want to add a sound in symbol-edit mode.

Note: See Chapter 9 to learn more about creating buttons.

2 Add a layer to the button Timeline.

Note: See Chapter 5 to learn more about Flash layers.

3 Double-click on the layer name and type a name for the layer.

Note: See the section "Add a Sound Layer" to learn how to add and name a layer.

4 Click the frame to which you want to add a sound.

■ You can add a keyframe, if the frame does not already have one.

Note: See Chapter 7 to learn how to add keyframes.

5 Click [Library icon] to open the Library window.

Note: See Chapter 7 to learn how to use the Flash Library.

To which button frame should I assign a sound?

The most practical frames to use when assigning sounds are the Over and Down frames, but you can assign sounds to any button frame. For example, you might want the button to beep when the user rolls over the button with the mouse pointer. This alerts the users to the button. To do this, assign a sound to the Over frame. You might also want the button to make another type of sound when the user actually clicks it; assign a sound to the Down frame.

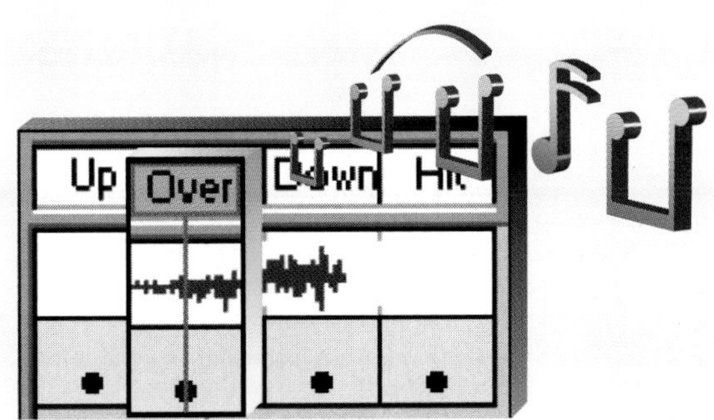

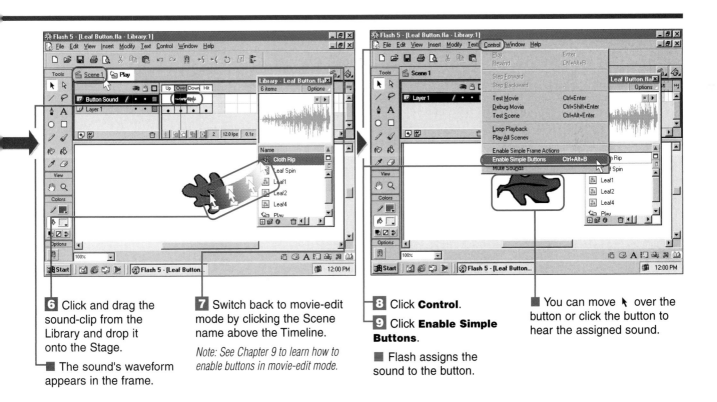

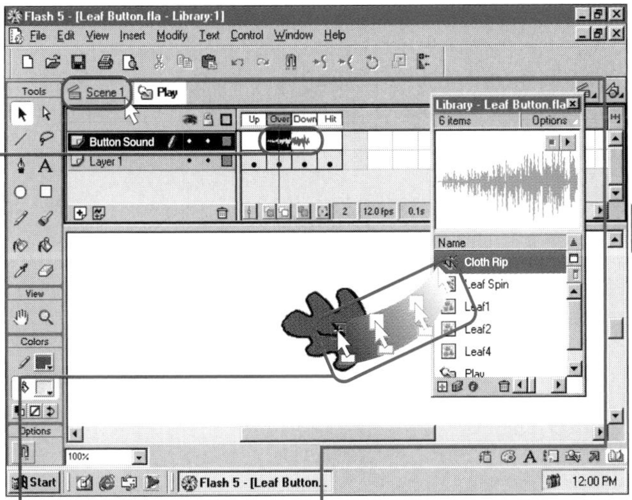

6 Click and drag the sound-clip from the Library and drop it onto the Stage.

■ The sound's waveform appears in the frame.

7 Switch back to movie-edit mode by clicking the Scene name above the Timeline.

Note: See Chapter 9 to learn how to enable buttons in movie-edit mode.

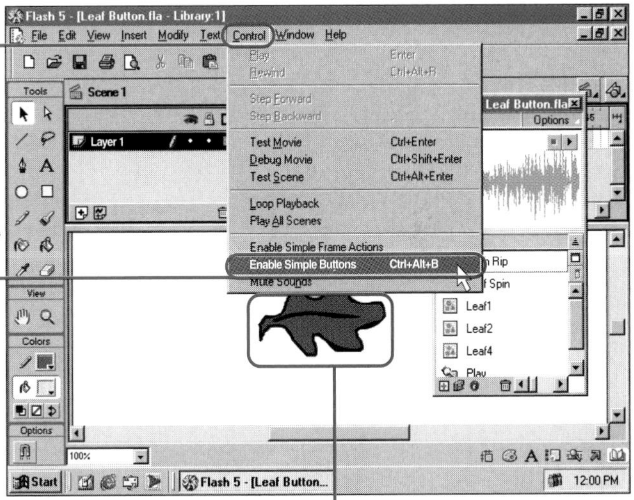

8 Click **Control**.

9 Click **Enable Simple Buttons**.

■ Flash assigns the sound to the button.

■ You can move the pointer over the button or click the button to hear the assigned sound.

ASSIGN STREAMING SOUNDS

You can use Streaming sounds for Flash movies you place on Dreamweaver Web pages. The sound starts streaming as the page downloads, so the user does not have to wait for the entire file to finish downloading. The frames are synchronized with the sound, so if the sound is a bit slow downloading, the frames slow down as well. Streaming sounds are good for long sound files, such as a musical sound track.

See Chapter 11 to learn more about assigning actions.

ASSIGN STREAMING SOUNDS

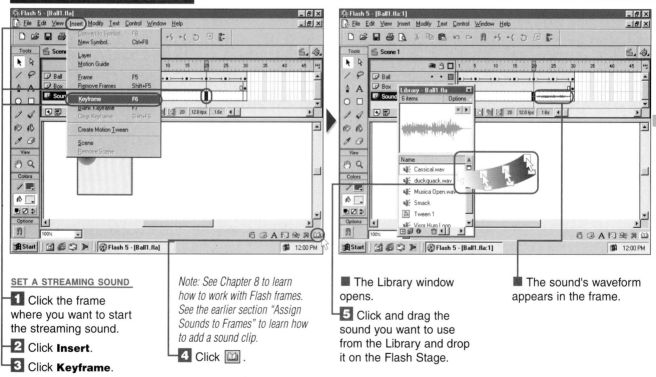

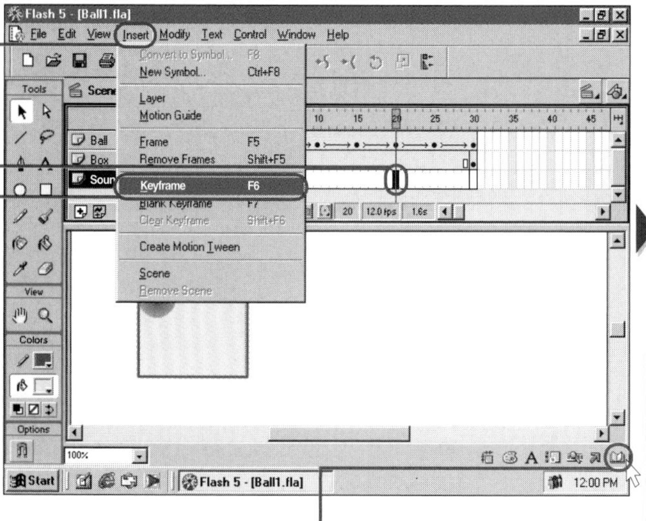

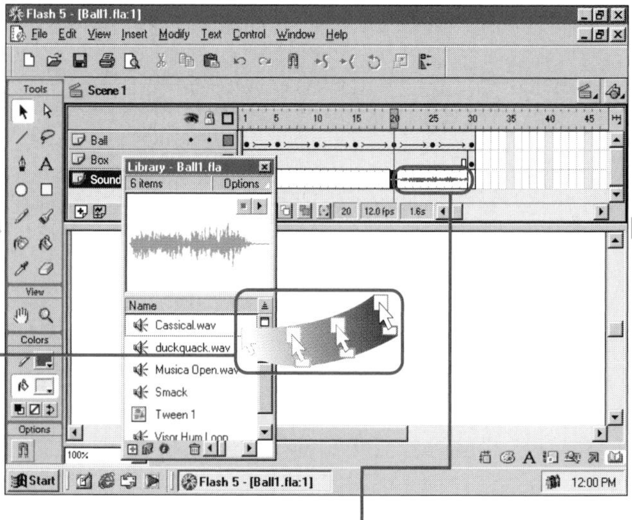

SET A STREAMING SOUND

1 Click the frame where you want to start the streaming sound.

2 Click **Insert**.

3 Click **Keyframe**.

Note: See Chapter 8 to learn how to work with Flash frames. See the earlier section "Assign Sounds to Frames" to learn how to add a sound clip.

4 Click .

■ The Library window opens.

5 Click and drag the sound you want to use from the Library and drop it on the Flash Stage.

■ The sound's waveform appears in the frame.

What do I do if my streaming sound gets cut off too soon?

Try switching the units from seconds to frames:

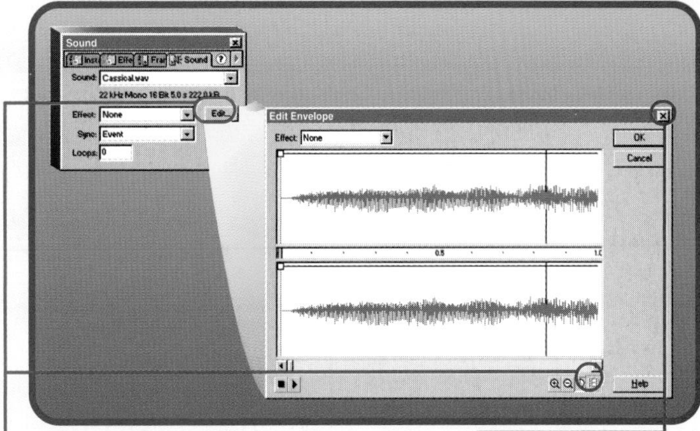

1 In the Sound panel, click **Edit**.

■ This opens the Edit Envelope dialog box for the sound file.

2 Click [icon] to set the unit scale to frames.

3 Click [X] to close the dialog box.

4 Play the movie again to test it.

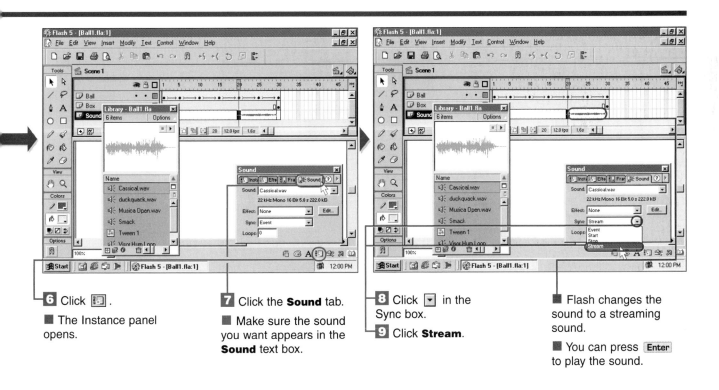

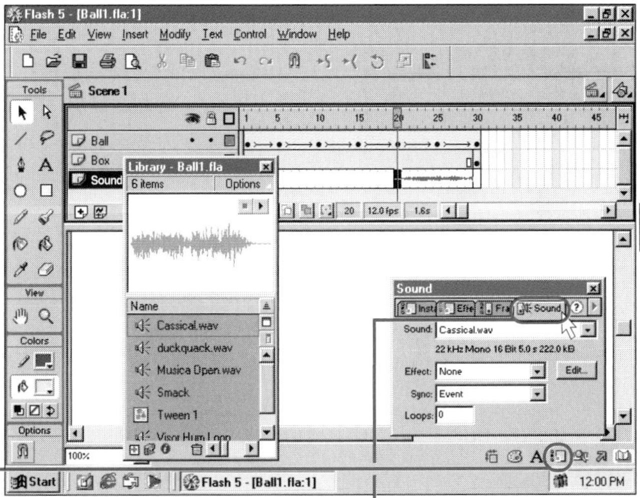

6 Click [icon].

■ The Instance panel opens.

7 Click the **Sound** tab.

■ Make sure the sound you want appears in the **Sound** text box.

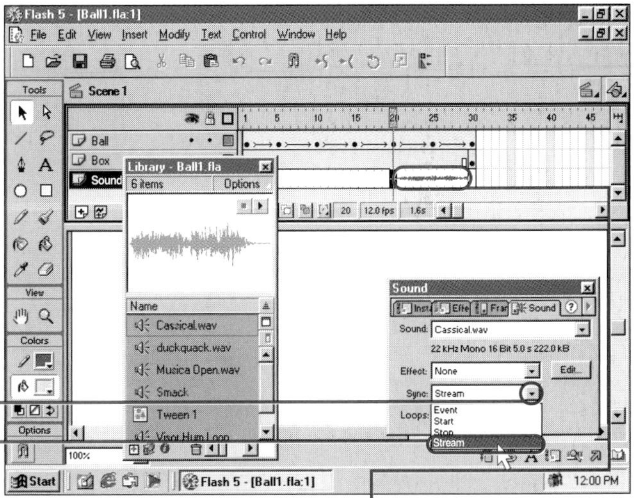

8 Click [▼] in the Sync box.

9 Click **Stream**.

■ Flash changes the sound to a streaming sound.

■ You can press Enter to play the sound.

You can add actions to your movie using Frame Actions. Frame Actions trigger events that happen at certain points in your movie. Frames can include multiple actions, but you can only assign an action one frame at a time. Flash performs the actions in the order they appear in the list.

See Chapter 5 to find out more about Flash layers.

ADD ACTIONS TO FRAMES

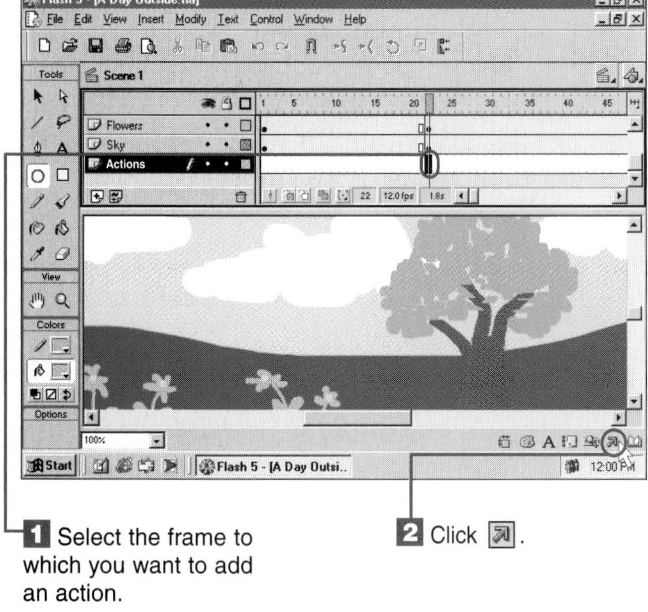

1 Select the frame to which you want to add an action.

Note: You can only insert actions into keyframes.

2 Click .

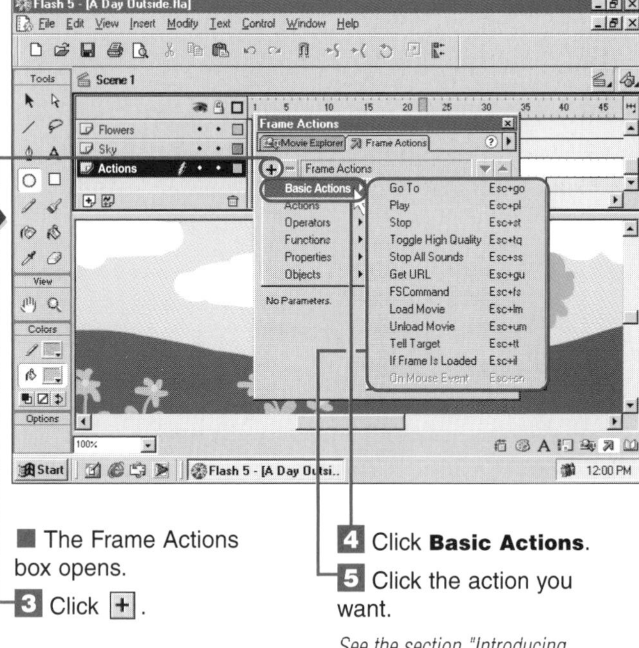

■ The Frame Actions box opens.

3 Click +.

4 Click **Basic Actions**.

5 Click the action you want.

See the section "Introducing Flash Actions" to find out more about actions.

How do I organize actions in my movie?

To help you clearly identify actions you assign to frames, consider creating a layer specifically for actions in your movie. This technique makes finding the action you want to edit easier. To add a layer to the Timeline, click [icon]. A new layer appears above the current layer. You can rename the layer, or move it to another position in the layer stack. See Chapter 5 to find out more about moving and positioning Flash layers.

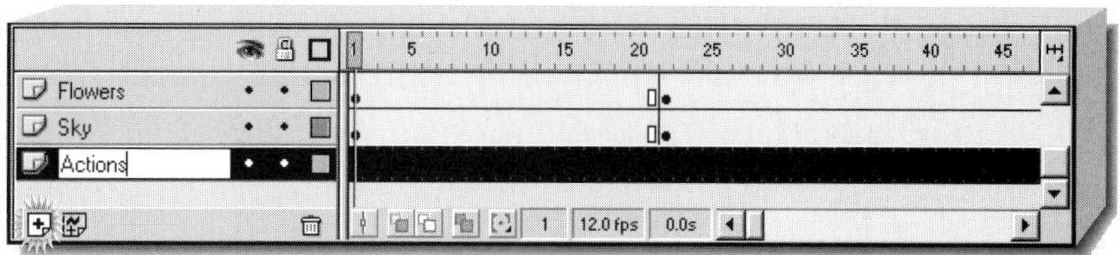

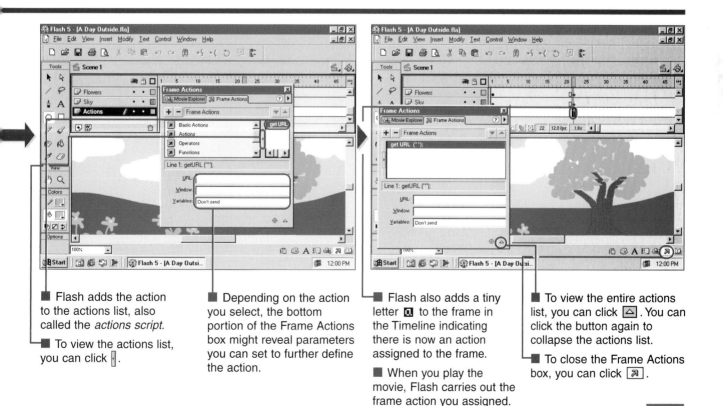

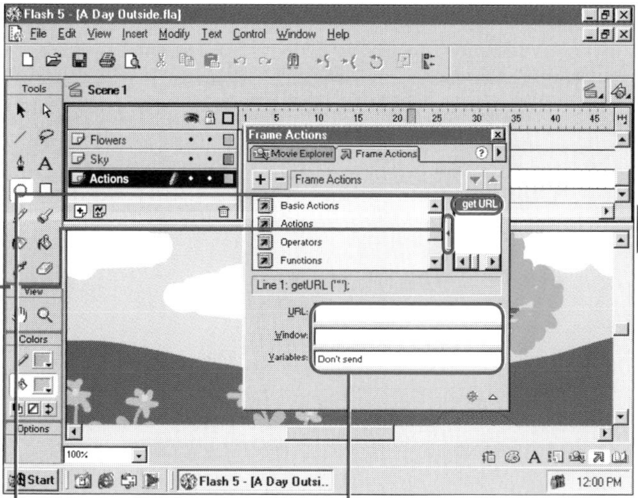

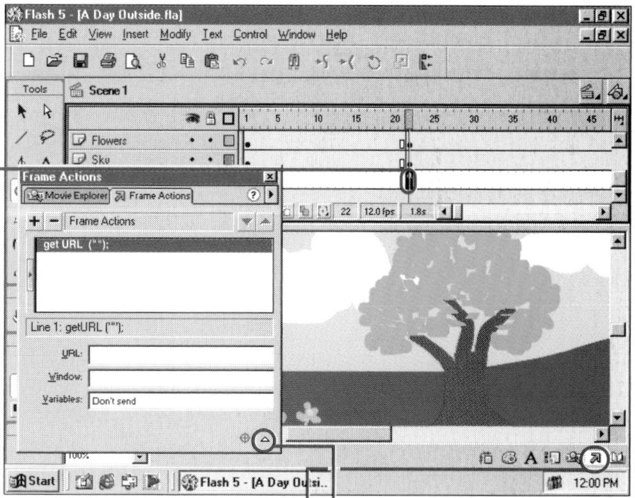

■ Flash adds the action to the actions list, also called the *actions script*.

■ To view the actions list, you can click [icon].

■ Depending on the action you select, the bottom portion of the Frame Actions box might reveal parameters you can set to further define the action.

■ Flash also adds a tiny letter [icon] to the frame in the Timeline indicating there is now an action assigned to the frame.

■ When you play the movie, Flash carries out the frame action you assigned.

■ To view the entire actions list, you can click [icon]. You can click the button again to collapse the actions list.

■ To close the Frame Actions box, you can click [icon].

ASSIGN STOP AND PLAY ACTIONS

You can assign a Stop action to stop a movie from playing, or you can assign a Play action to play it again. For example, perhaps one of the keyframes in your movie is text heavy and you want to allow the user to read the text. When you are ready to play the movie again, insert a keyframe and add the Play action.

ASSIGN STOP AND PLAY ACTIONS

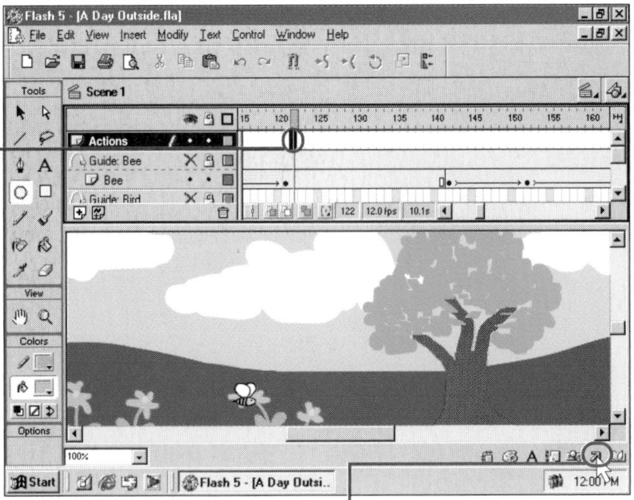

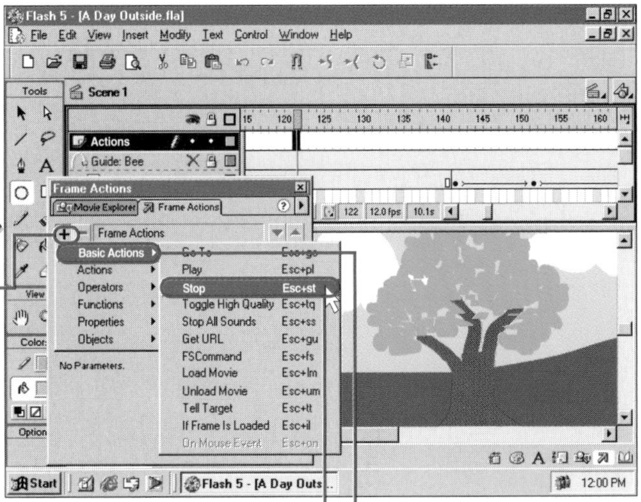

ADD A STOP ACTION

1 Select the keyframe to which you want to insert a Stop action.

2 Click ↗.

■ The Frame Actions dialog box opens.

3 Click +.

4 Click **Basic Actions**.

5 Click **Stop**.

What is the difference between frame actions and object actions?

Actions can be applied to frames or buttons. Frame actions are assigned to frames and control how a movie plays. Button actions, as demonstrated in the steps in this section, are assigned to buttons and require input from the user. For example, a Stop action assigned to a button enables the user to stop a movie by clicking on the button to which the action is assigned. You can assign Stop and Play actions to frames or buttons, but remember that button actions require user input in order to carry out the action. To assign a Stop action to a frame rather than a button, simply click the frame to which you want the action assigned and follow steps **2** through **5** in this section. To assign a Play action to a frame, follow steps 1 through 4 on the next page.

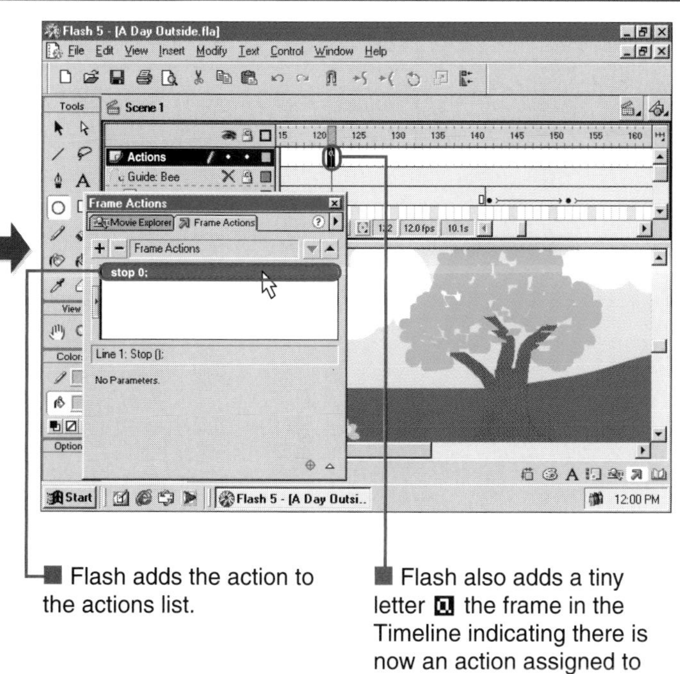

■ Flash adds the action to the actions list.

■ Flash also adds a tiny letter **a** the frame in the Timeline indicating there is now an action assigned to the frame.

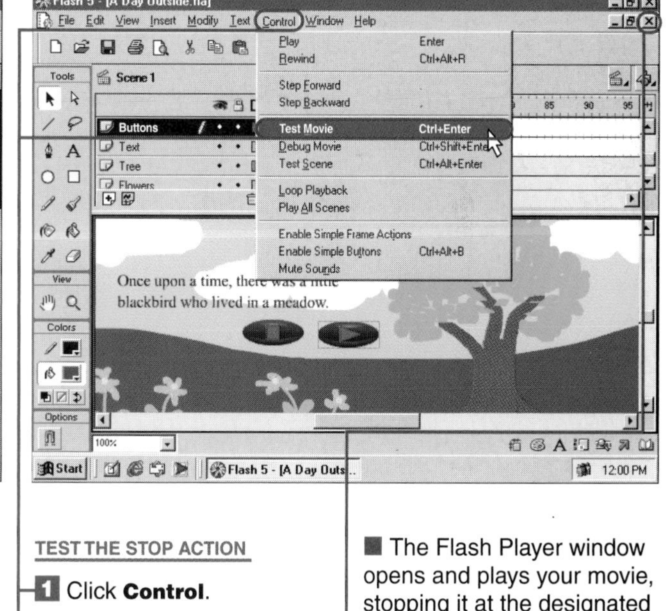

TEST THE STOP ACTION

1 Click **Control**.

2 Click **Test Movie**.

■ The Flash Player window opens and plays your movie, stopping it at the designated frame.

■ You can click ☒ to exit the Player window.

CONTINUED

ASSIGN STOP AND PLAY ACTIONS

Stop and Play are two of the most commonly used actions, and are used for both button actions and frame actions. They act much like the controls found on a VCR or CD player. You can use the Play action to start a movie you have previously stopped with the Stop action.

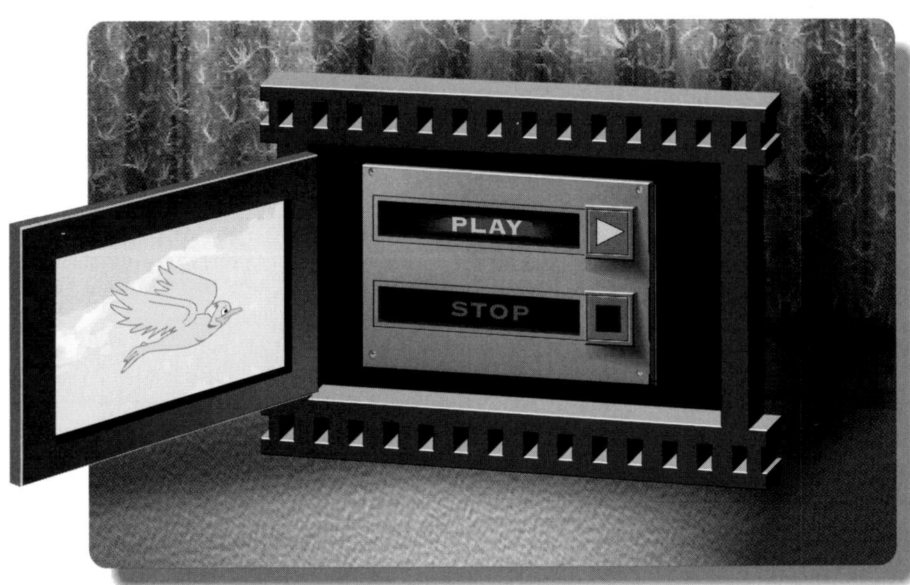

ASSIGN STOP AND PLAY ACTIONS (CONTINUED)

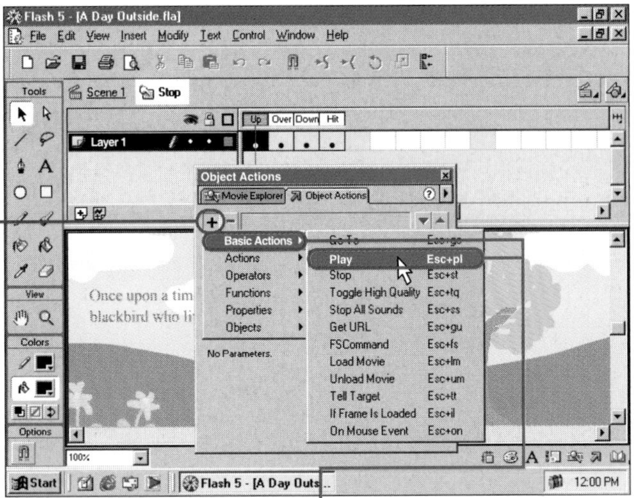

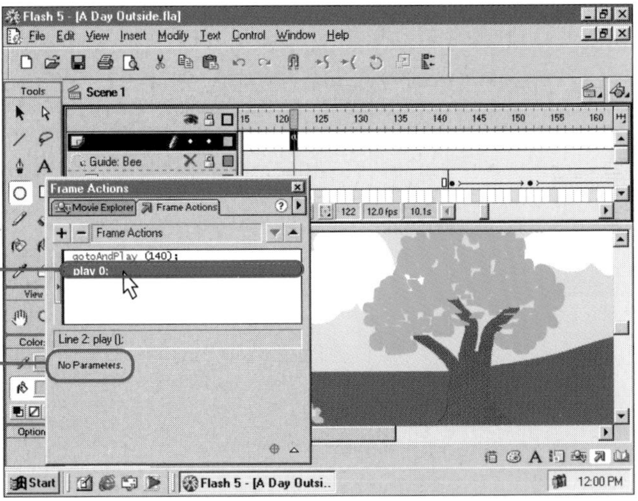

ADD A PLAY ACTION

1. Click the keyframe where you want to start the movie again.
2. Click +.
3. Click **Basic Actions**.
4. Click **Play**.

■ Flash adds the action to the actions list.

■ No parameters are available for the Play action.

■ Flash adds a tiny letter a to the Timeline, indicating an action is now assigned to the frame.

Can I resize the type in the actions list?

If you have trouble reading the small type in the actions list, you can resize it. To do so, perform these steps:

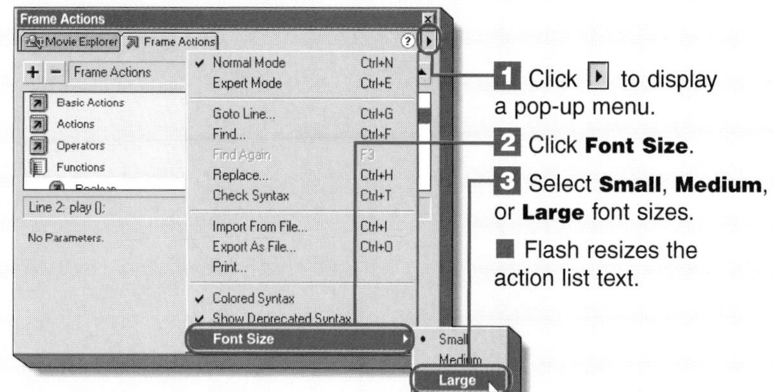

1 Click ▶ to display a pop-up menu.

2 Click **Font Size**.

3 Select **Small**, **Medium**, or **Large** font sizes.

■ Flash resizes the action list text.

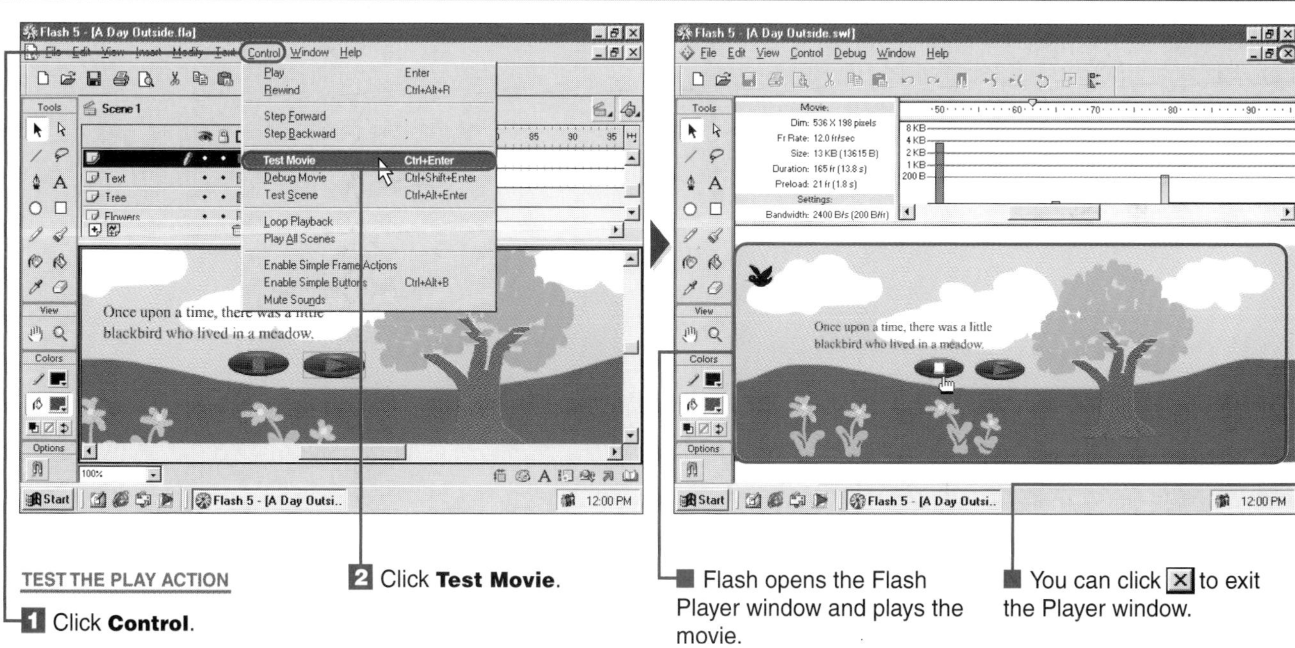

TEST THE PLAY ACTION

1 Click **Control**.

2 Click **Test Movie**.

■ Flash opens the Flash Player window and plays the movie.

■ You can click ☒ to exit the Player window.

LOAD A NEW MOVIE

You can use the Load Movie action to start a movie file within your current movie. The Load Movie action can replace the current movie with another you have previously created, or play the loaded movie on top of the current movie as if it were another layer.

LOAD A NEW MOVIE

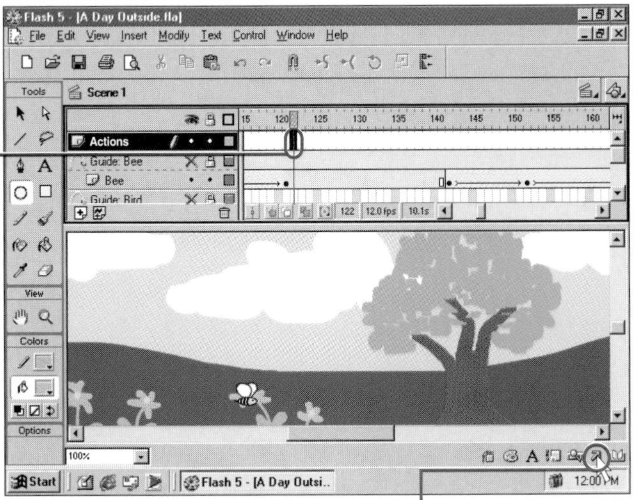

1 Select the keyframe to which you want to add the action.

2 Click [icon].

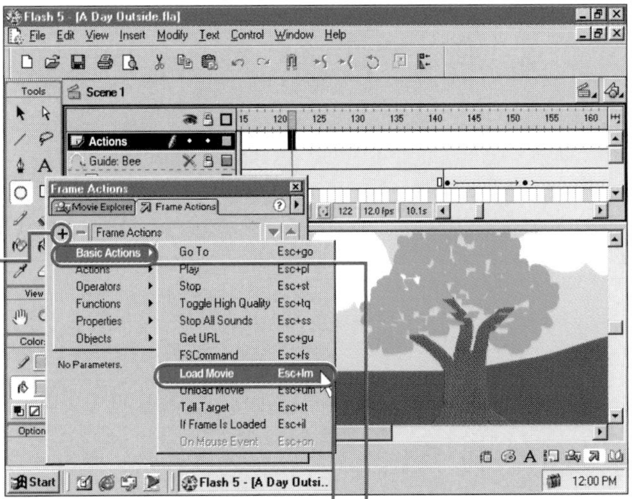

■ The Frame Actions box opens.

3 Click [+].

4 Click **Basic Actions**.

5 Click **Load Movie**.

Can I open the movie in a separate browser window?

Another way you can load a new movie file to play is to use the Get URL action. This action opens the new movie in a separate browser window. Follow the same steps shown in this section, but select the Get URL action instead of the Load Movie action. In the parameters, type the following:

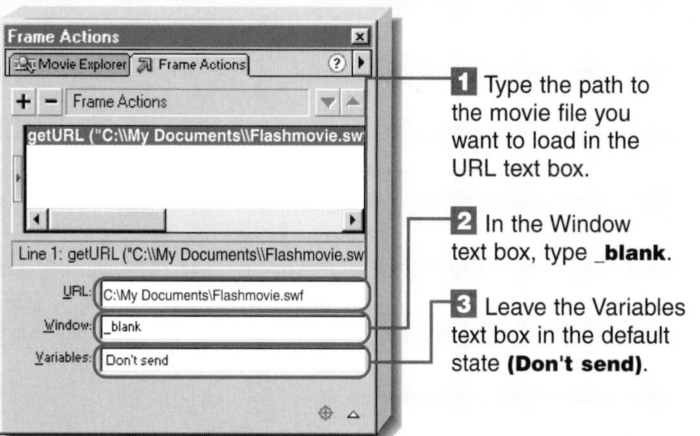

1 Type the path to the movie file you want to load in the URL text box.

2 In the Window text box, type **_blank**.

3 Leave the Variables text box in the default state **(Don't send)**.

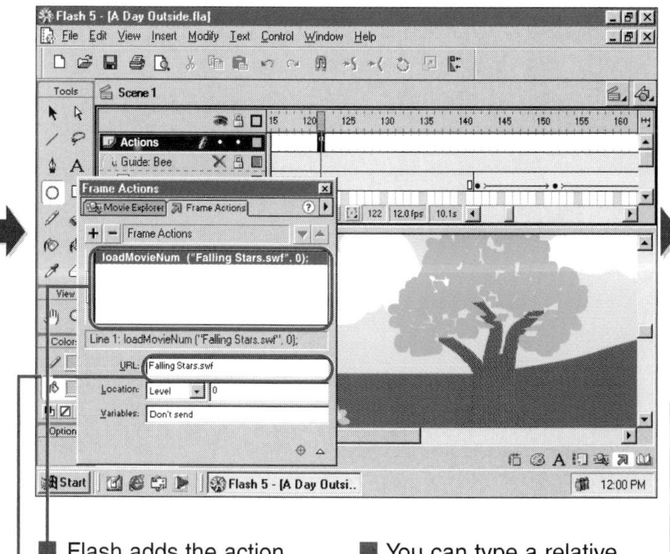

■ Flash adds the action to the actions list.

6 Click in the URL text box and type the name of the movie file you want to load.

■ You can type a relative path, which includes just the filename and extension, or you can enter an absolute path to the movie. An absolute path includes the drive and folder where the file is located.

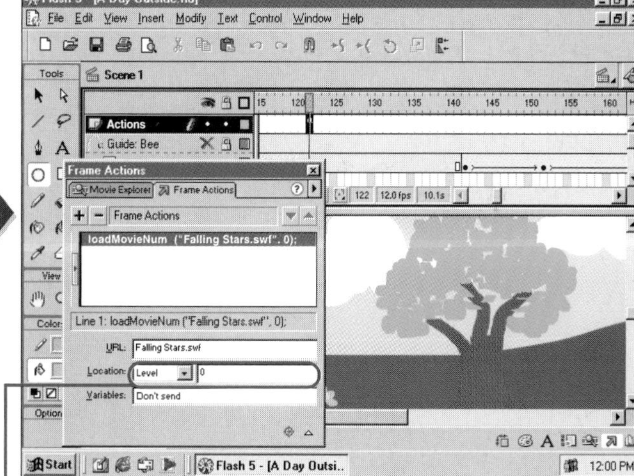

■ Select a location parameter for your movie.

■ Leave the Location level set to 0 if you want the new movie to replace the current movie.

■ To make the new movie play on top of the current movie, type 1 or higher in the Location level text box.

■ You can test the action by playing the movie in the Flash Player window.

PLAY A FLASH MOVIE IN FLASH

You can use the Flash Player to play your Flash movies. You can play movies from within Flash 5, or outside the confines of the Flash 5 program window by using the Flash Player window. The Flash Player is installed when you install Flash 5 onto your computer.

PLAY A FLASH MOVIE IN FLASH

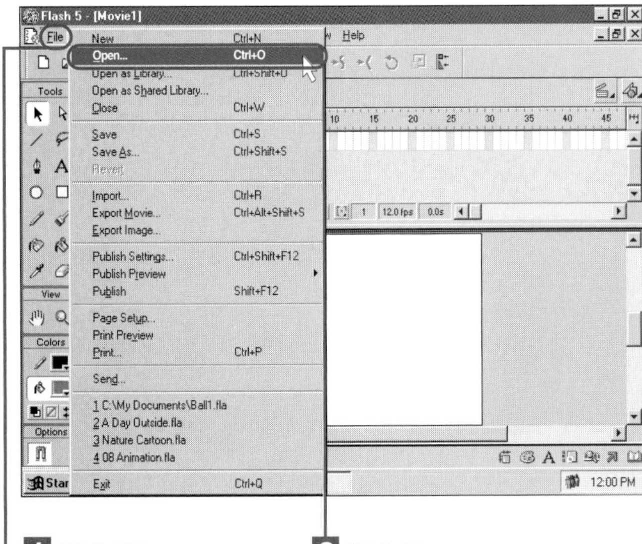

1 Click **File**.

2 Click **Open**.

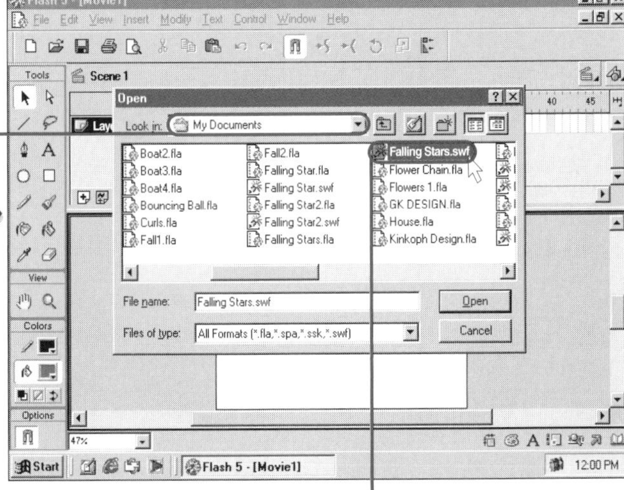

■ The Open dialog box appears.

3 Navigate to the folder containing the Flash movie file you want to play.

4 Double-click the Flash movie file you want to play.

Can I control how the movie plays?

The Flash Player window has a few tools you can use to control how the movie plays. Click the **Control** menu to see the available commands. For example, by default, the Loop command is turned on. To deactivate the command, click **Loop**.

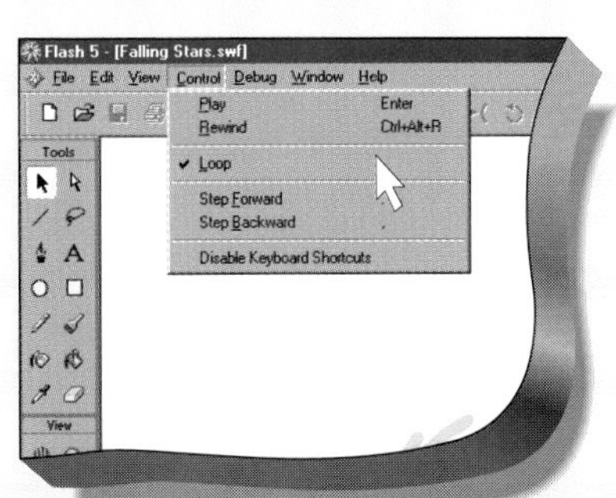

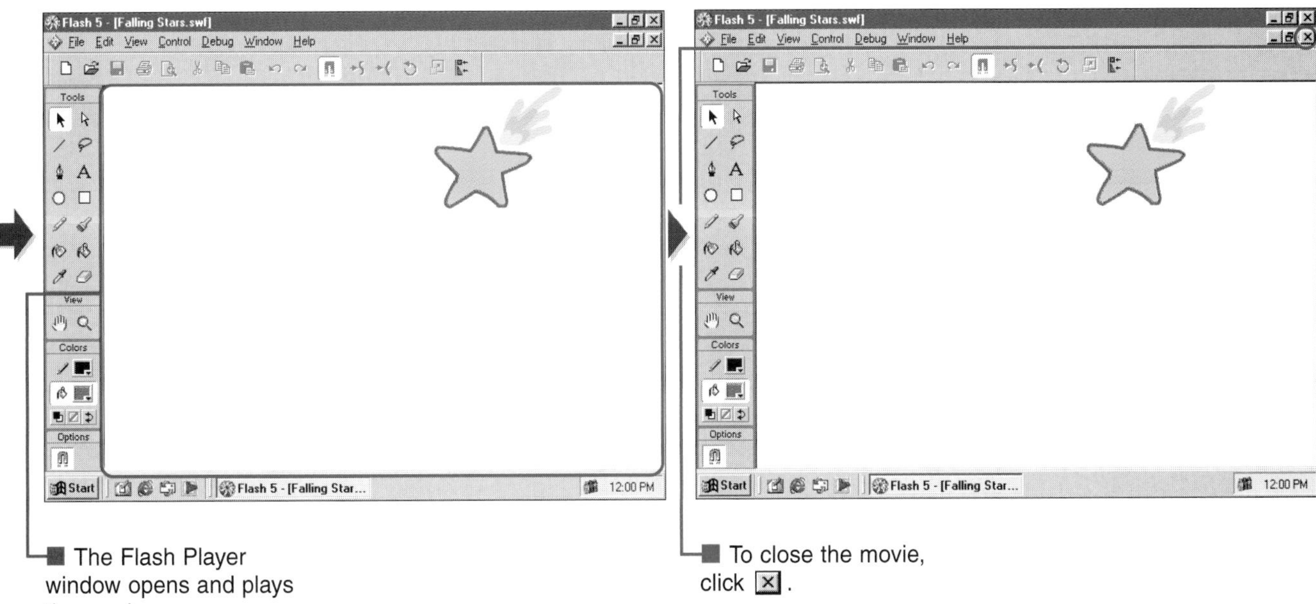

■ The Flash Player window opens and plays the movie.

■ To close the movie, click ☒.

PLAY A FLASH MOVIE IN A BROWSER

You can play a Flash movie using the browser's Flash plug-in. Most browsers, such as Microsoft Internet Explorer and Netscape Navigator, include the Flash Player plug-in program for playing SWF files. This way you can incorporate Flash movies into your Dreamweaver Web pages and have visitors view your movie without requiring the full Flash program on a computer.

PLAY A FLASH MOVIE IN A BROWSER

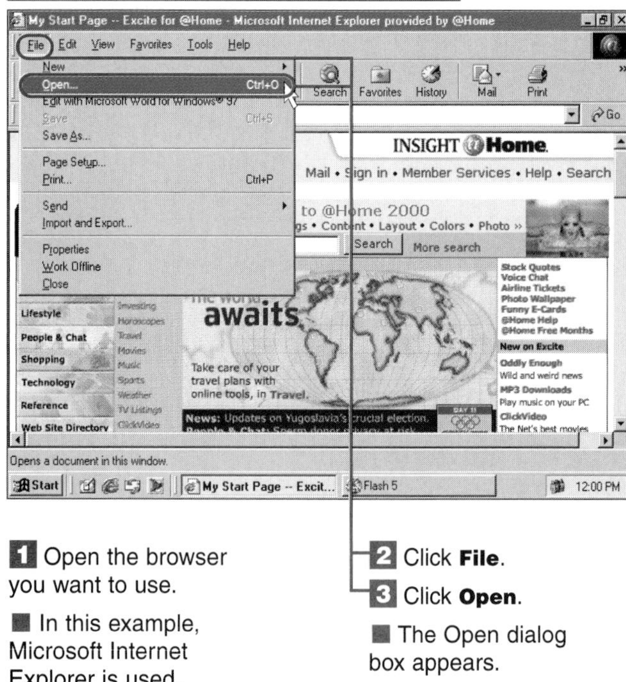

1 Open the browser you want to use.

■ In this example, Microsoft Internet Explorer is used.

2 Click **File**.

3 Click **Open**.

■ The Open dialog box appears.

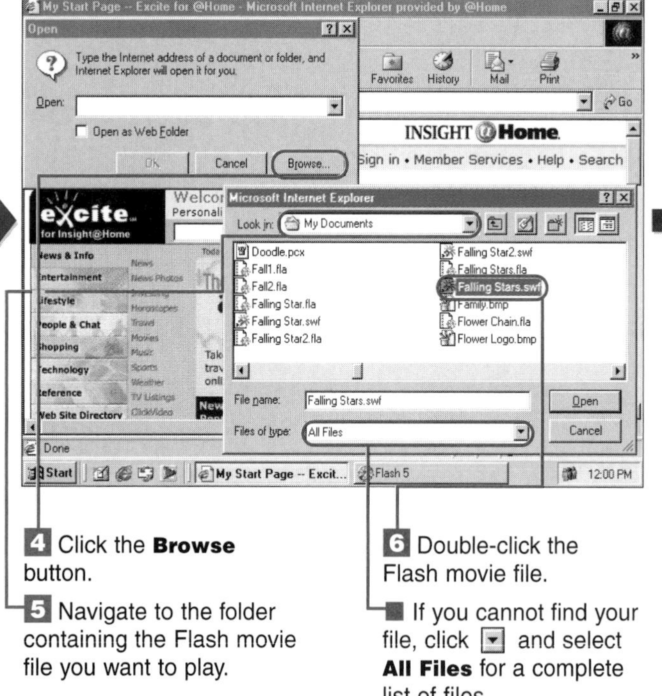

4 Click the **Browse** button.

5 Navigate to the folder containing the Flash movie file you want to play.

6 Double-click the Flash movie file.

■ If you cannot find your file, click ▼ and select **All Files** for a complete list of files.

How do I open another movie to play in the Flash Player window?

As long as you have the Flash Player window open, you can view other Flash movies as well. To view another movie, perform the following steps:

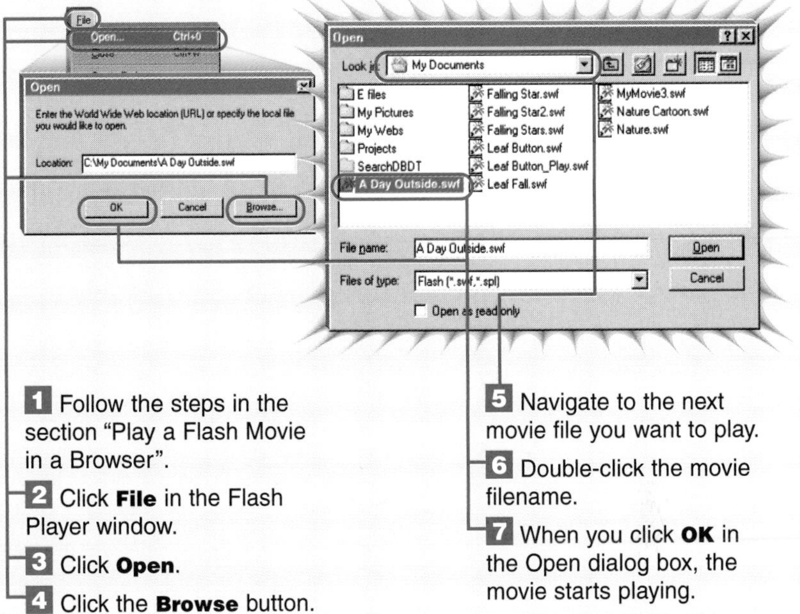

1 Follow the steps in the section "Play a Flash Movie in a Browser".

2 Click **File** in the Flash Player window.

3 Click **Open**.

4 Click the **Browse** button.

5 Navigate to the next movie file you want to play.

6 Double-click the movie filename.

7 When you click **OK** in the Open dialog box, the movie starts playing.

7 Click **OK**.

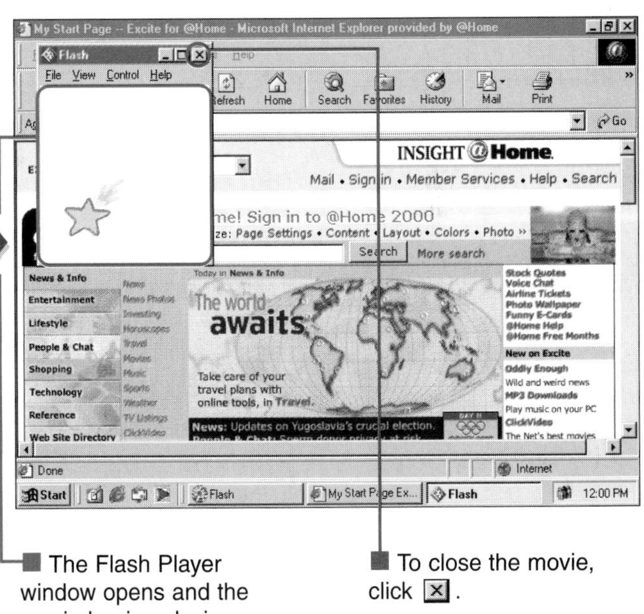

■ The Flash Player window opens and the movie begins playing.

■ To close the movie, click ☒.

TEST MOVIE BANDWIDTH

You can use the Bandwidth Profiler to help you determine which movie frames might cause problems during playback from your Dreamweaver Web site. File size and the user's data-transfer rate determines how smoothly and quickly your movie downloads and plays. You can test six different modem speeds, and gauge which frames use the most bytes to see exactly where your movie might slow down during playback.

TEST MOVIE BANDWIDTH

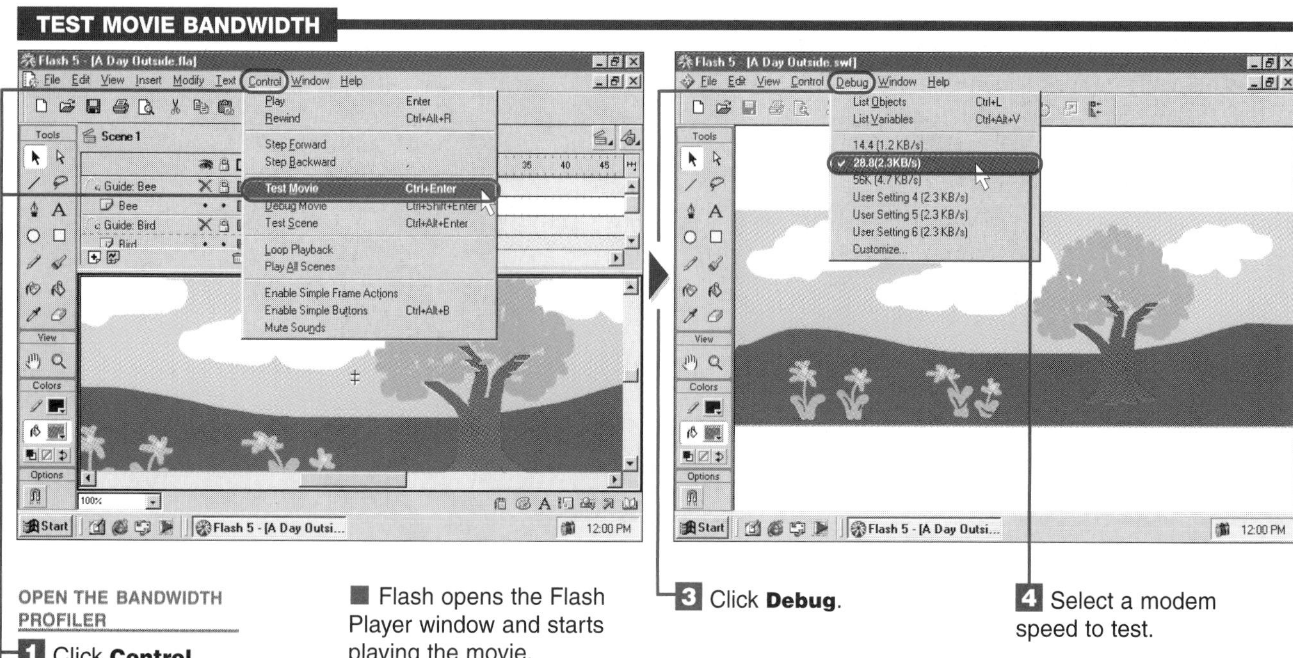

OPEN THE BANDWIDTH PROFILER

1. Click **Control**.
2. Click **Test Movie**.

■ Flash opens the Flash Player window and starts playing the movie.

3. Click **Debug**.
4. Select a modem speed to test.

Can I customize the download speed I want to test?

To customize the modem speed, perform the following steps:

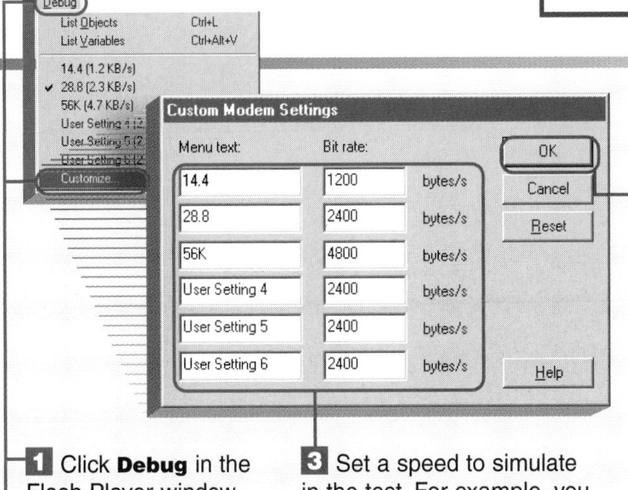

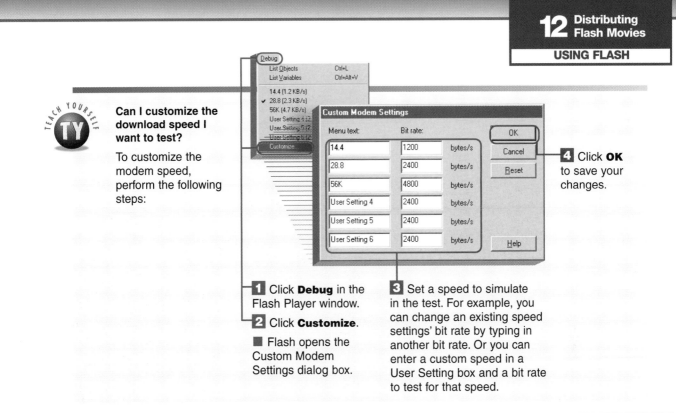

1 Click **Debug** in the Flash Player window.

2 Click **Customize**.

■ Flash opens the Custom Modem Settings dialog box.

3 Set a speed to simulate in the test. For example, you can change an existing speed settings' bit rate by typing in another bit rate. Or you can enter a custom speed in a User Setting box and a bit rate to test for that speed.

4 Click **OK** to save your changes.

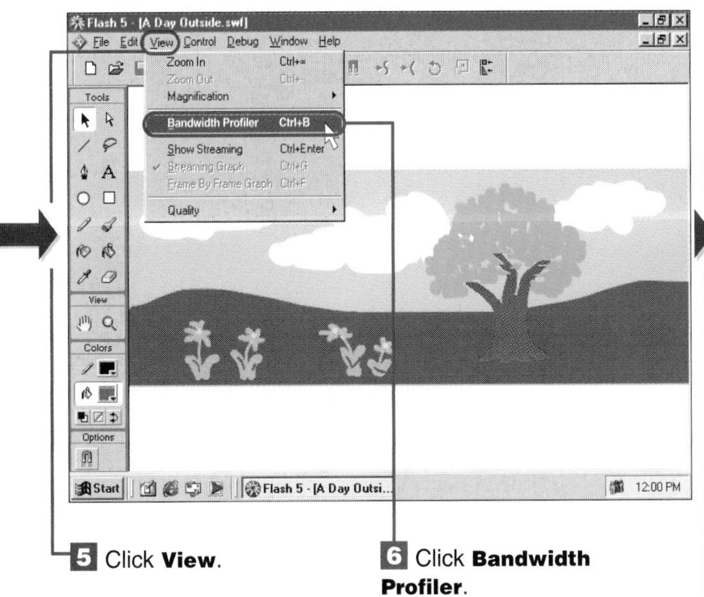

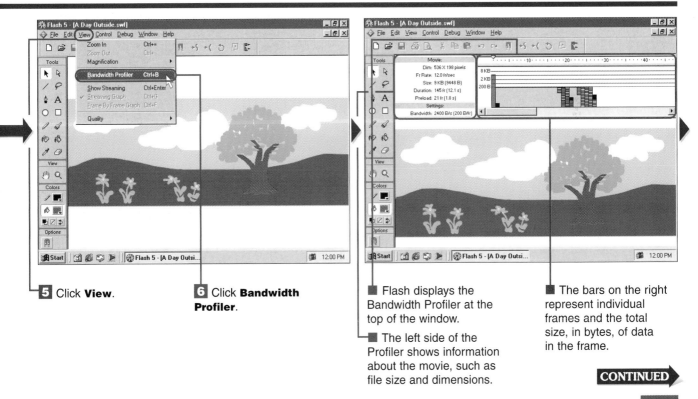

5 Click **View**.

6 Click **Bandwidth Profiler**.

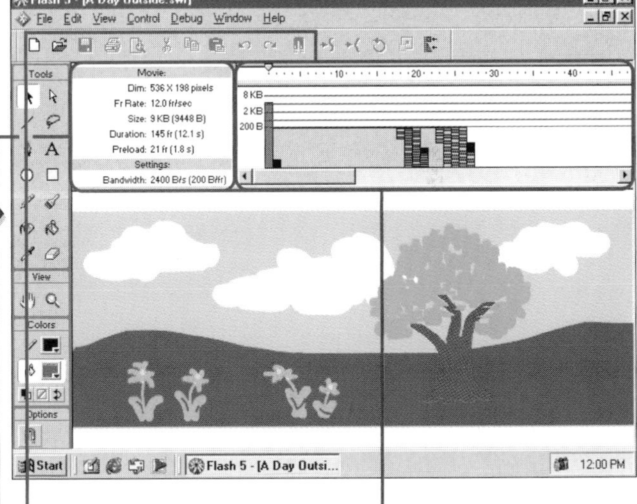

■ Flash displays the Bandwidth Profiler at the top of the window.

■ The left side of the Profiler shows information about the movie, such as file size and dimensions.

■ The bars on the right represent individual frames and the total size, in bytes, of data in the frame.

CONTINUED

TEST MOVIE BANDWIDTH

You can use two different views in the Flash Bandwidth Profiler to see how the frames play. A bar on the graph represents a frame. In Streaming Graph mode, the width of each bar shows how long it takes the frame to download. The default view is Streaming Graph mode. In Frame by Frame Graph mode, if the bar extends above the bottom red line of the graph, the Flash movie pauses to download the frame's data.

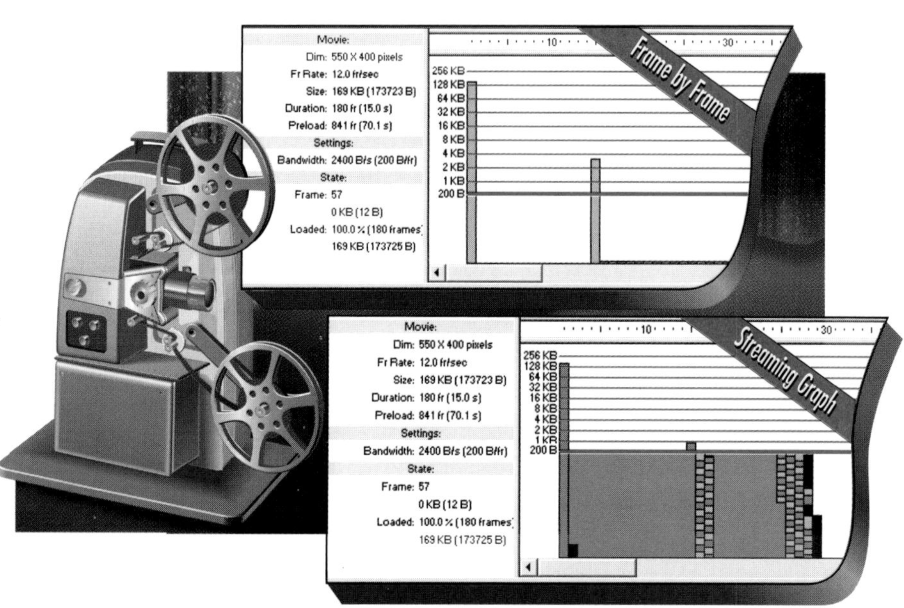

TEST MOVIE BANDWIDTH (CONTINUED)

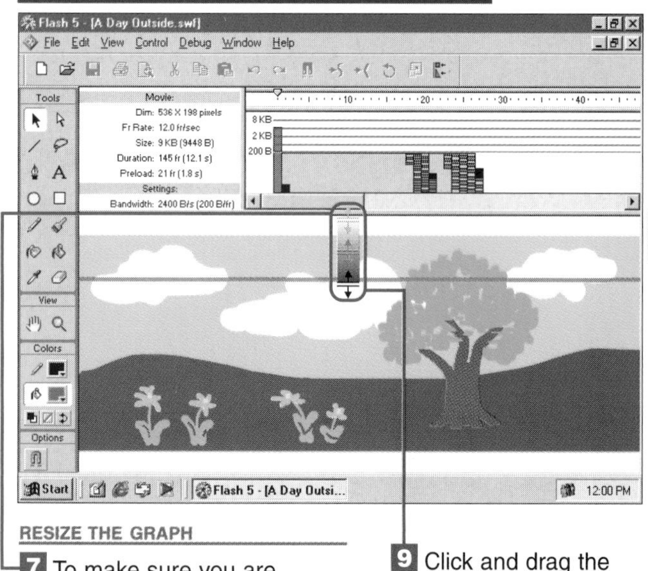

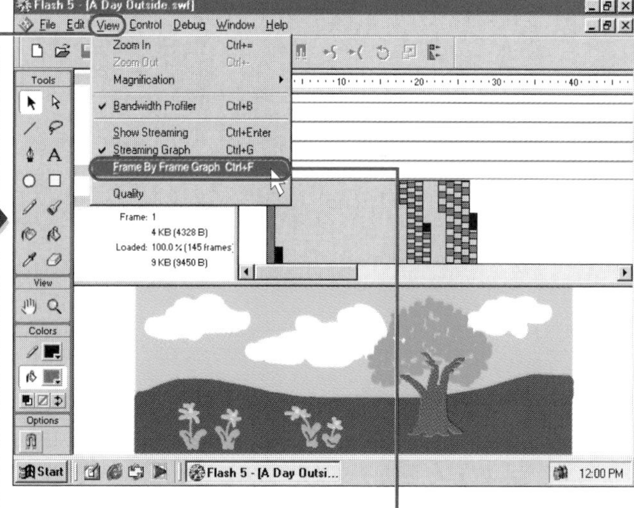

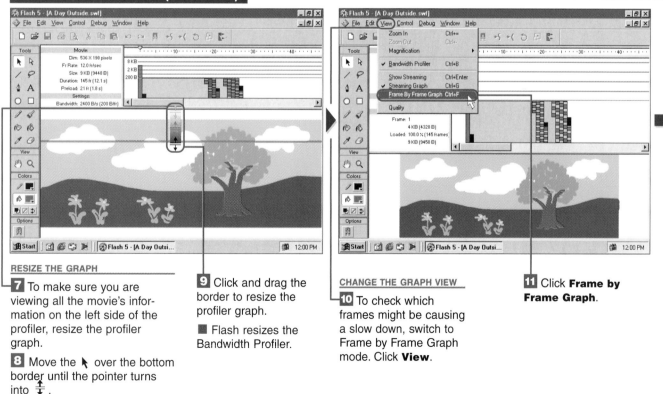

RESIZE THE GRAPH

7 To make sure you are viewing all the movie's information on the left side of the profiler, resize the profiler graph.

8 Move the pointer over the bottom border until the pointer turns into a resize pointer.

9 Click and drag the border to resize the profiler graph.

■ Flash resizes the Bandwidth Profiler.

CHANGE THE GRAPH VIEW

10 To check which frames might be causing a slow down, switch to Frame by Frame Graph mode. Click **View**.

11 Click **Frame by Frame Graph**.

How do I view a specific frame in the profiler?

Use the scroll bar arrows ▽ to move left or right in the Profiler Timeline at the top of the Profiler graph. To view a specific frame, drag the playhead to the frame, or click the playhead where you want it to go.

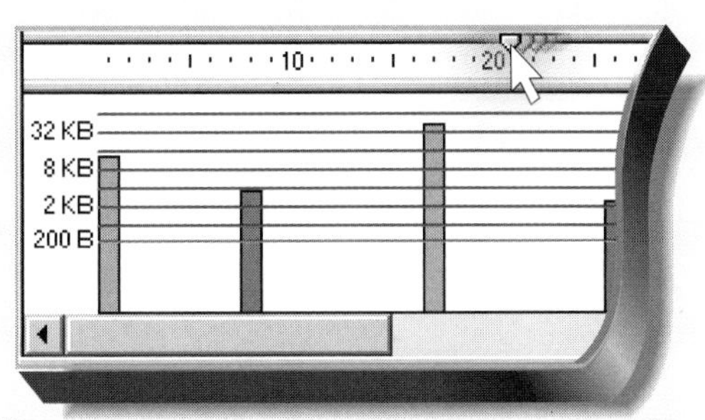

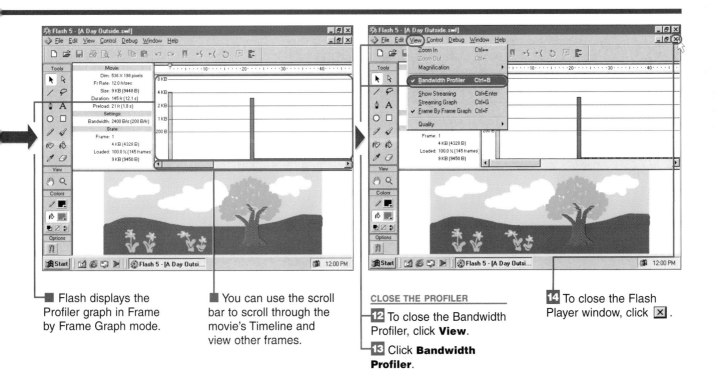

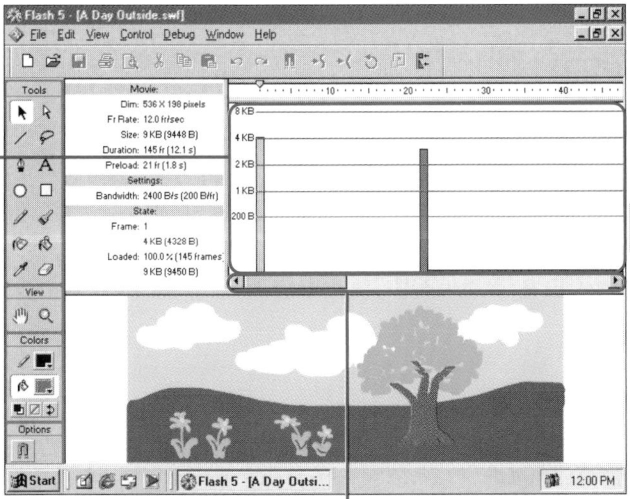

■ Flash displays the Profiler graph in Frame by Frame Graph mode.

■ You can use the scroll bar to scroll through the movie's Timeline and view other frames.

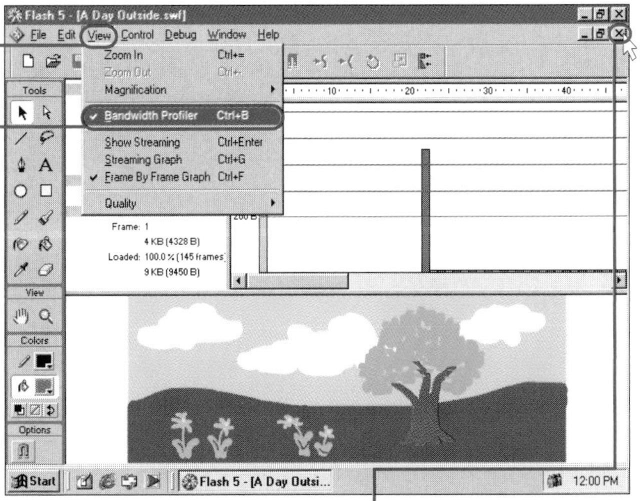

CLOSE THE PROFILER

12 To close the Bandwidth Profiler, click **View**.

13 Click **Bandwidth Profiler**.

14 To close the Flash Player window, click ☒.

PUBLISH A MOVIE

You can use two phases to publish your Flash movie. First you prepare the files for publishing using the Publish Settings dialog box, and then publish the movie using the Flash Publish command. By default, Flash is set up to publish your movie as an SWF file for the Web. This makes it easy to deploy your movie to the Web site using Dreamweaver.

PUBLISH A MOVIE

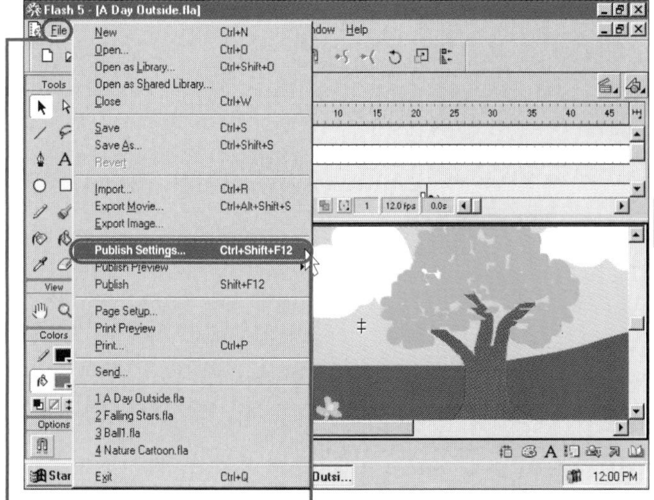

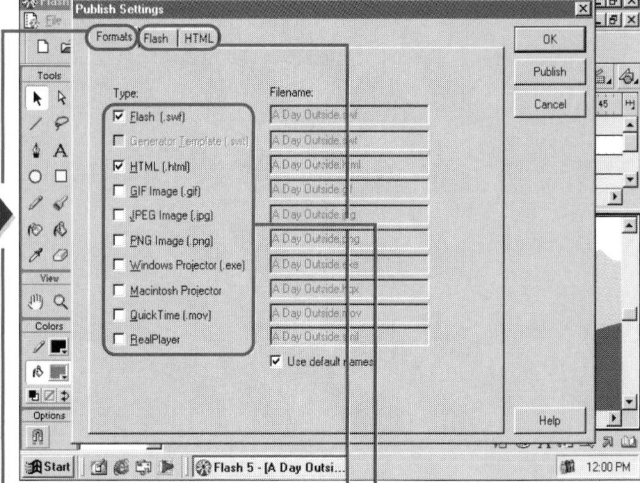

PREPARE FILES FOR PUBLISHING

1 Click **File**.

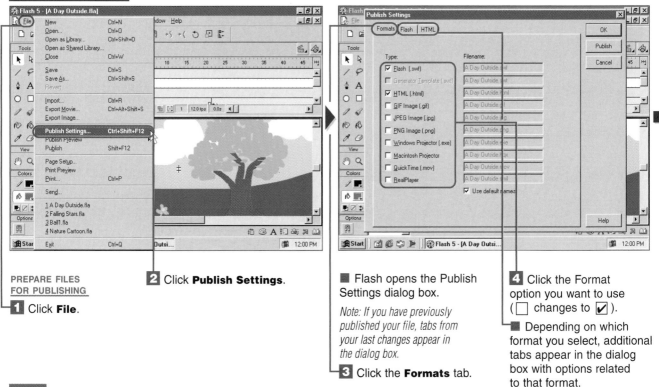

2 Click **Publish Settings**.

■ Flash opens the Publish Settings dialog box.

Note: If you have previously published your file, tabs from your last changes appear in the dialog box.

3 Click the **Formats** tab.

4 Click the Format option you want to use (☐ changes to ☑).

■ Depending on which format you select, additional tabs appear in the dialog box with options related to that format.

Can I preview a movie before I publish it?

Testing your movie often is a good idea, especially in a browser, to check how it plays. Flash has a feature that lets you preview a movie in a browser window before you publish the movie.

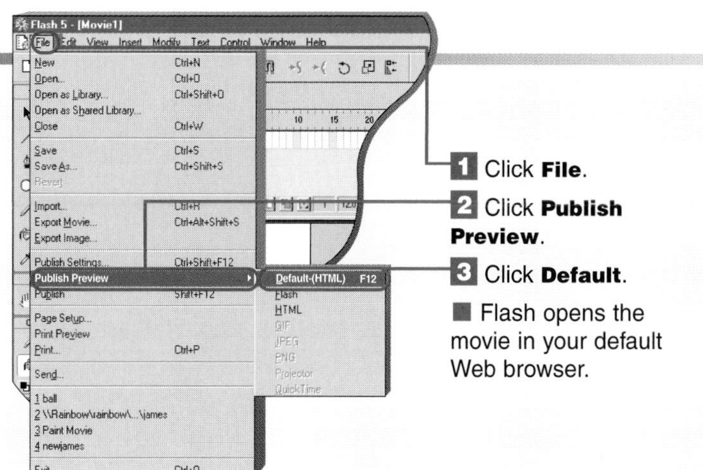

1 Click **File**.

2 Click **Publish Preview**.

3 Click **Default**.

■ Flash opens the movie in your default Web browser.

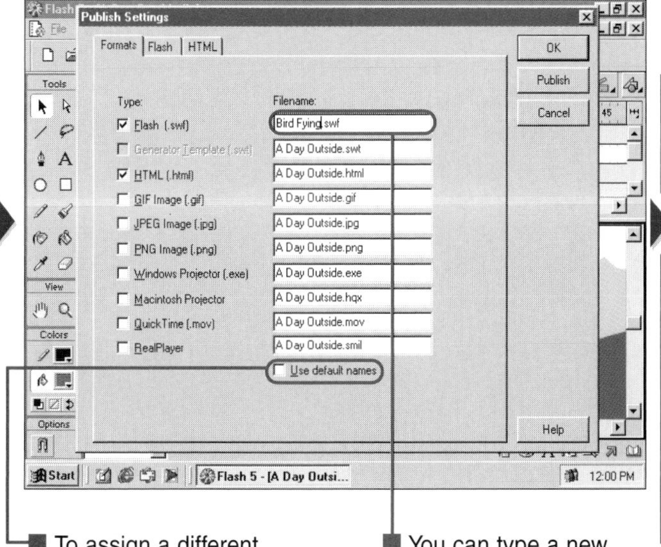

■ To assign a different filename other than the default supplied by Flash, you can click the **Use default names** option (☑ changes to ☐).

■ You can type a new filename in the format's text box.

■ Flash publishes your files to the My Documents folder unless you specify another folder and file name path in the file name text box.

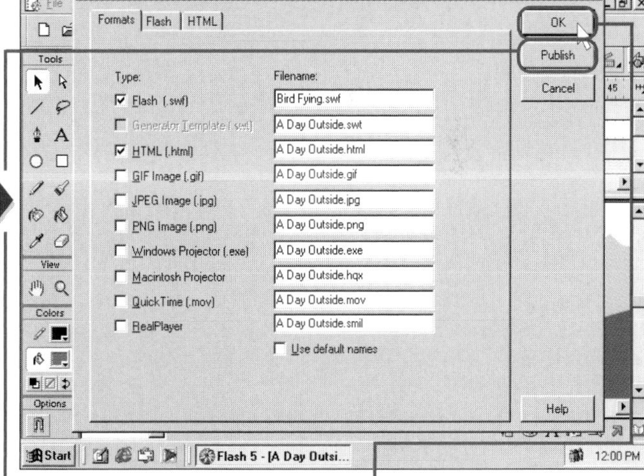

5 Click **Publish** when you are ready to publish the movie using the settings you selected.

■ Flash generates the necessary files for the movie.

6 Click **OK** to save the settings and close the Publish Settings dialog box.

PUBLISH A MOVIE IN HTML FORMAT

You can save a movie in HTML format. Flash creates an HTML page that displays your movie along with the SWF movie file. Flash generates all the necessary HTML code for you, including the tags needed to view your page in both Microsoft Internet Explorer and Netscape Navigator. You can then upload the HTML document to your Web server using Dreamweaver.

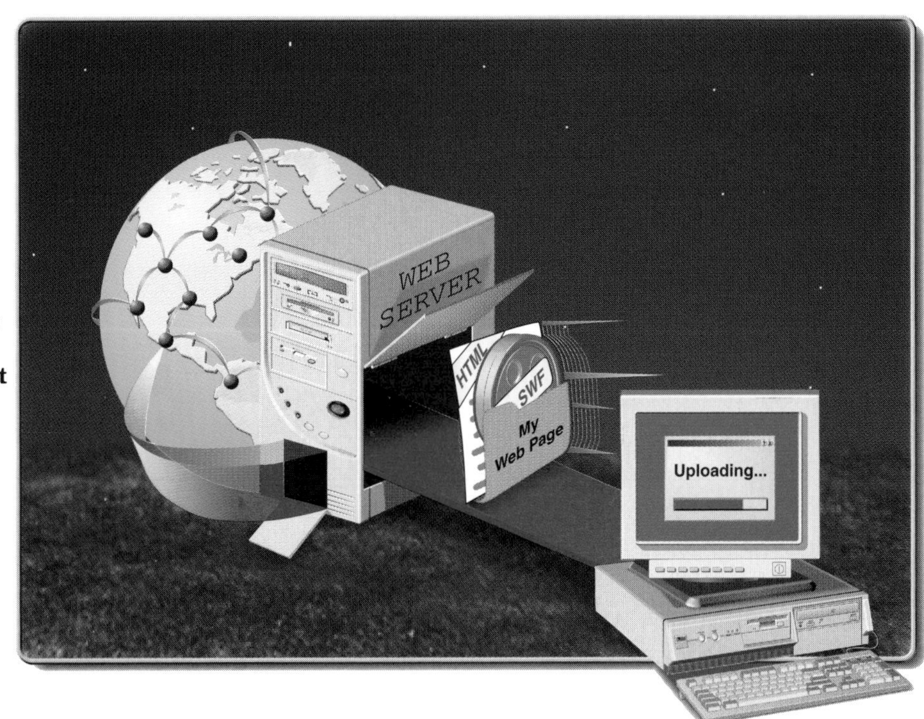

PUBLISH A MOVIE IN HTML FORMAT

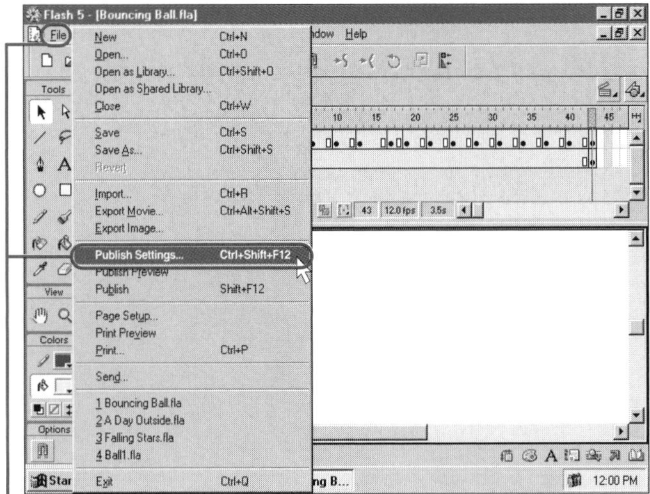

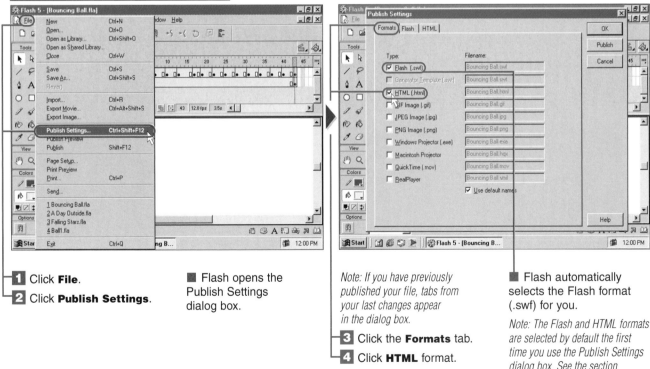

1 Click **File**.

2 Click **Publish Settings**.

■ Flash opens the Publish Settings dialog box.

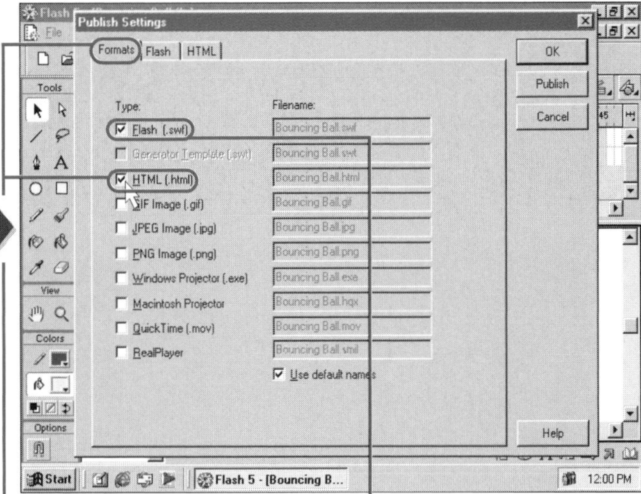

Note: If you have previously published your file, tabs from your last changes appear in the dialog box.

3 Click the **Formats** tab.

4 Click **HTML** format.

■ Flash automatically selects the Flash format (.swf) for you.

Note: The Flash and HTML formats are selected by default the first time you use the Publish Settings dialog box. See the section "Publish a Movie" to find out more about publishing Flash movies.

What HTML tags does Flash insert into the HTML document?

The Publish feature inserts the tags necessary for playing a Flash movie file in the browser window, including the `OBJECT` tag needed for Microsoft's Internet Explorer browser and the `EMBED` tag needed for Netscape's Navigator browser. Flash also inserts the `IMG` tag for displaying the movie file in another format, such as animated GIF or JPEG. The `OBJECT`, `EMBED`, and `IMG` tags create the movie display window used to play the Flash movie.

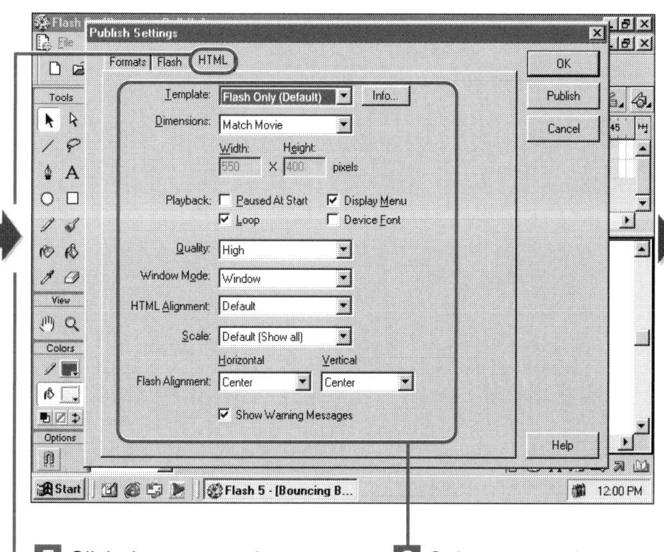

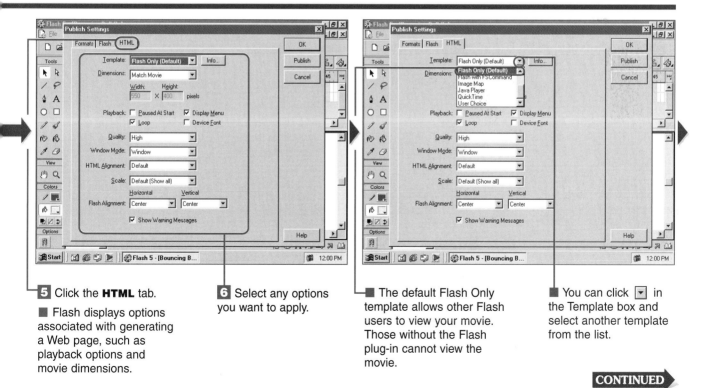

5 Click the **HTML** tab.

■ Flash displays options associated with generating a Web page, such as playback options and movie dimensions.

6 Select any options you want to apply.

■ The default Flash Only template allows other Flash users to view your movie. Those without the Flash plug-in cannot view the movie.

■ You can click ▼ in the Template box and select another template from the list.

CONTINUED

PUBLISH A MOVIE IN HTML FORMAT

The Publish Settings dialog box specifies exactly how you want your movie to appear in the browser window. You can set alignment, dimensions, and even playback options. Any changes you make to the settings override any previous settings for the file.

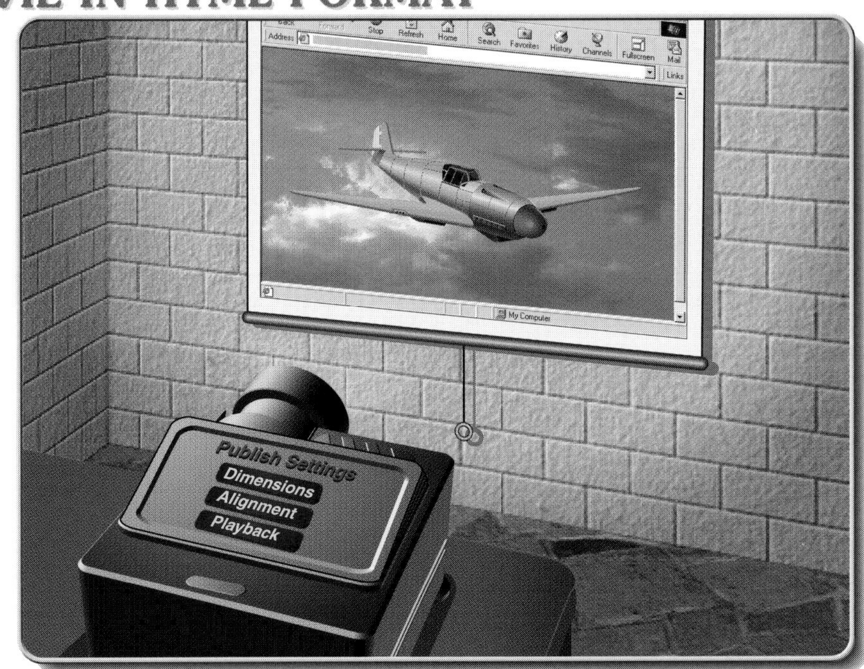

PUBLISH A MOVIE IN HTML FORMAT (CONTINUED)

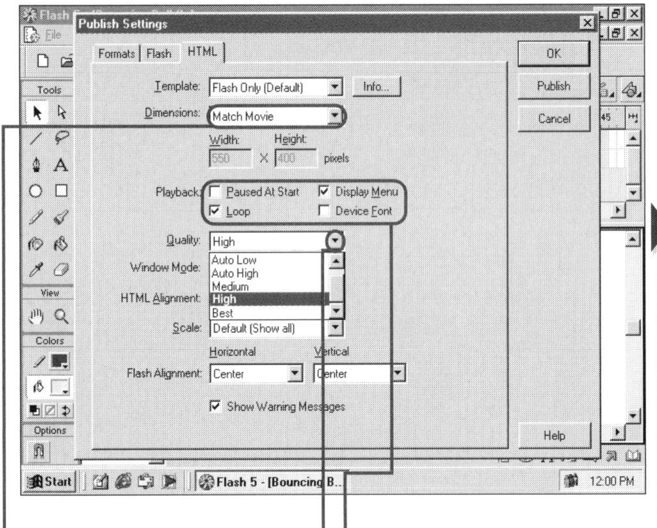

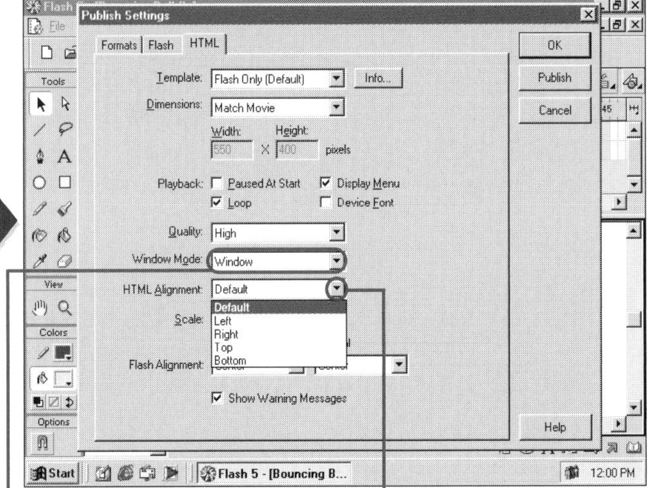

■ You can click the ▼ in the Dimensions box to set width and height attribute values for the movie-display window—the area where the Flash plug-in plays the movie.

■ You can click the **Playback** options to control how the movie plays on the Web page (☐ changes to ☑).

■ You can click the ▼ in the Quality box to view options for controlling the image quality during playback.

■ You can click the ▼ in the Window Mode box and select options for playing your movie on a regular, opaque, or transparent background (Windows browsers only).

■ You can click the ▼ in the HTML Alignment box and change the alignment of your movie as it relates to other Web page elements.

How do I make my movie full-size in the browser window?

To make your Flash movie appear full-screen size in the browser window, perform the following steps:

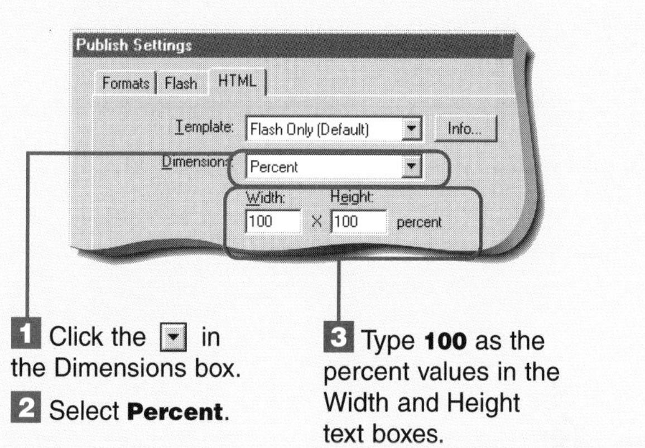

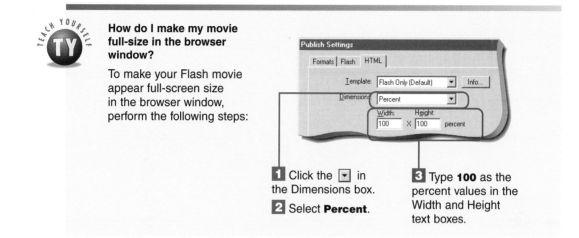

1 Click the ▾ in the Dimensions box.

2 Select **Percent**.

3 Type **100** as the percent values in the Width and Height text boxes.

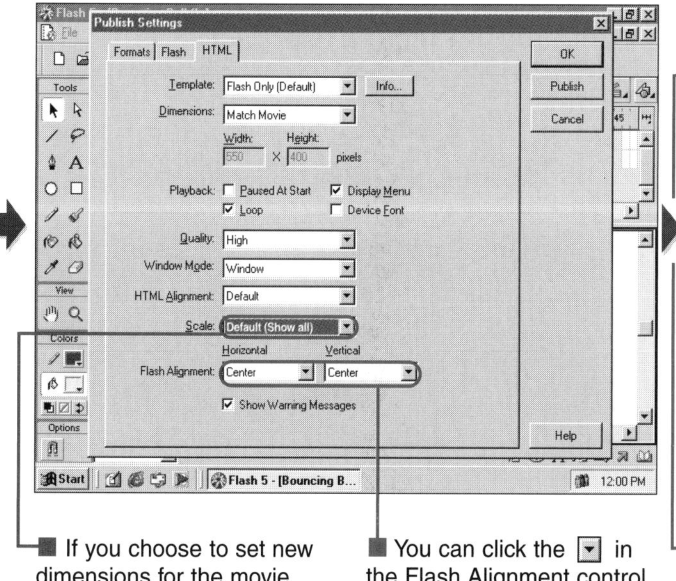

■ If you choose to set new dimensions for the movie, you can click the ▾ in the Scale box to rescale movie elements to fit the new size.

■ You can click the ▾ in the Flash Alignment control boxes and designate how the movie aligns in the movie window area.

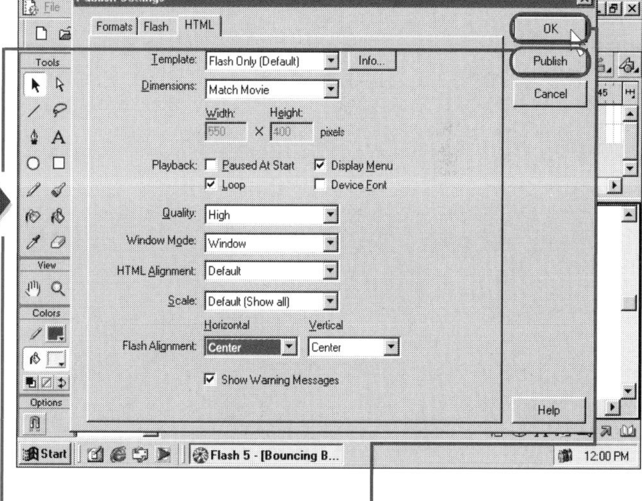

7 Click the **Publish** button when you are ready to publish the movie using the settings you selected.

■ Flash generates the necessary files for the HTML document.

8 Click **OK** to save the settings and close the Publish Settings dialog box.

BIRD WATCHERS'
HOME PAGE
The page dedicated to people who love to watch birds!

NATURE
Wildlife
Rainforests
Memberships

Steve's
TOTALLY AMAZING WORLD OF
GAMES

EXOTIC
Automobiles

Travel the World

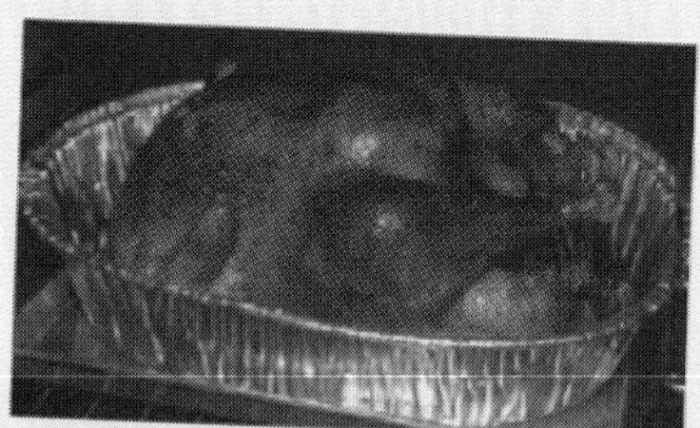
Home
Recipes
Cooking Tips
Vegetarian Specials
Healthy Snacks
E-Mail the Chef
Country Kitchen Template
Your Internet source for recipes, cooking tips and more!
Site maintained by: Jane Wilson

New Releases
Top Ten
Concerts

BCG
music store
About BCG

PART 2

Using Dreamweaver

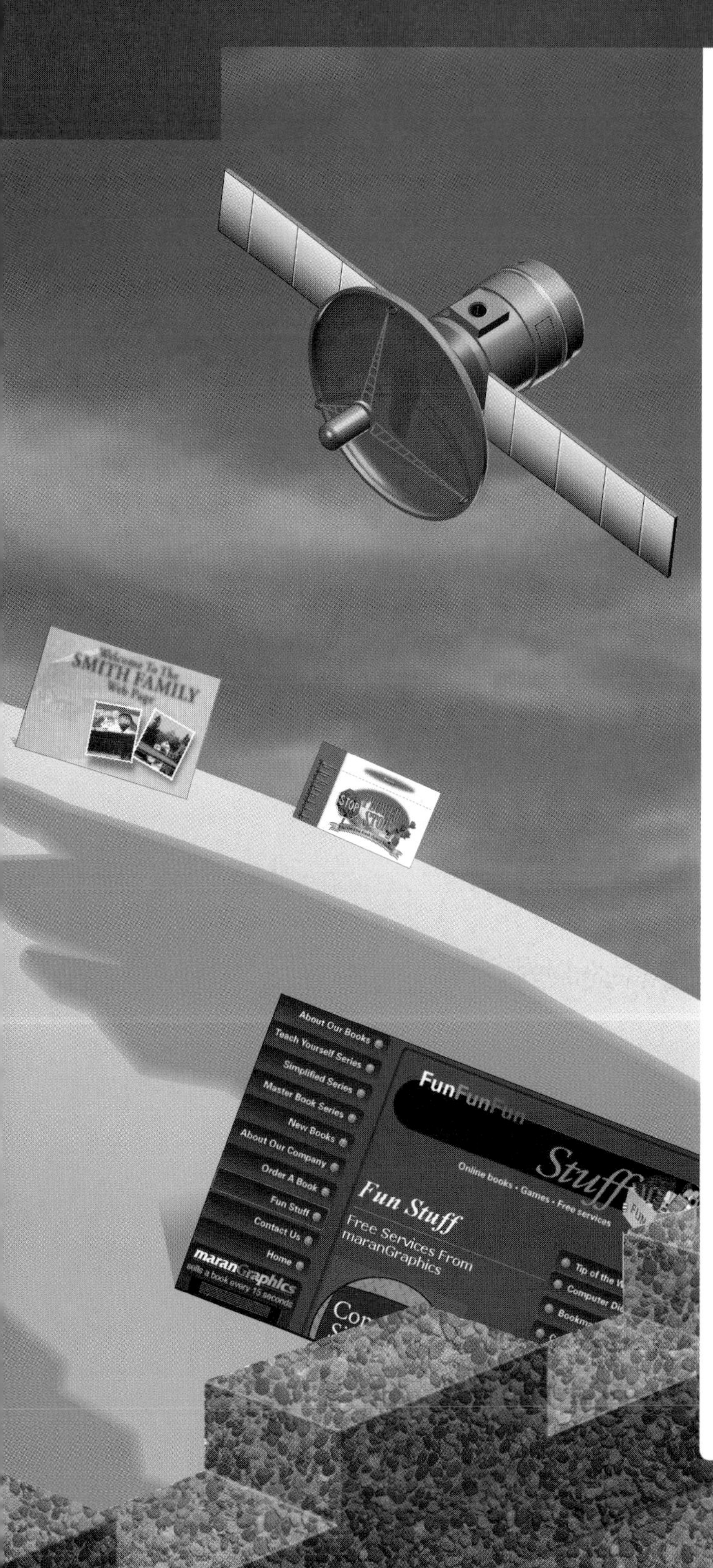

13 Dreamweaver Basics
Pages 134-139

14 Setting Up Your Web Site
Pages 140-147

15 Working with Web Page Text
Pages 148-161

16 Working with Images and Graphics
Pages 162-171

17 Creating Hyperlinks
Pages 172-181

18 Creating Tables
Pages 182-193

19 Working with Forms
Pages 194-205

20 Designing with Frames
Pages 206-217

21 Using Library Items and Templates
Pages 218-227

22 Implementing Style Sheets and Layers
Pages 228-241

23 Implementing Timelines
Pages 242-249

24 Publishing a Web Site
Pages 250-257

START DREAMWEAVER ON A PC

You can start Dreamweaver on a PC and begin building pages that you can publish on the Web.

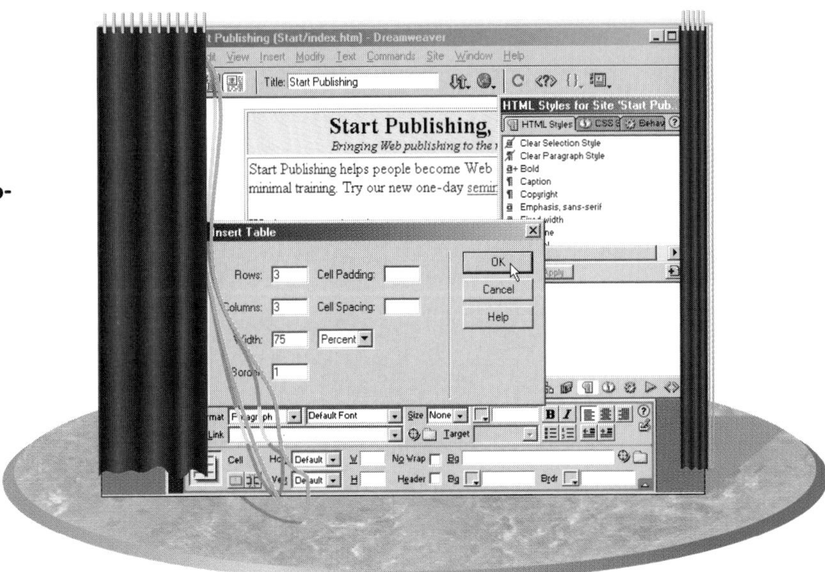

START DREAMWEAVER ON A PC

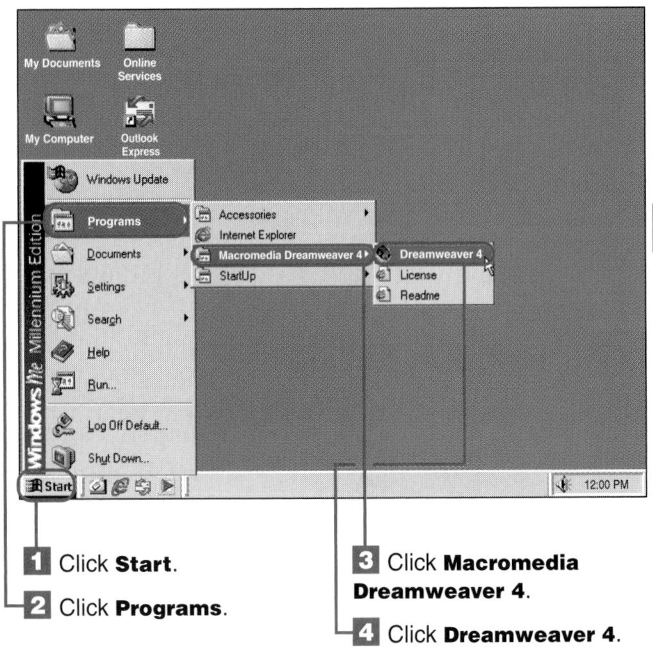

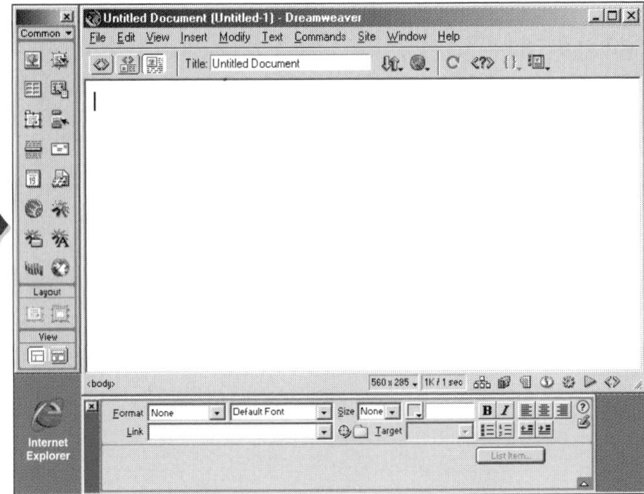

1 Click **Start**.

2 Click **Programs**.

3 Click **Macromedia Dreamweaver 4**.

4 Click **Dreamweaver 4**.

Note: Your path to the Dreamweaver application may be different, depending on how you installed your software.

■ An untitled Web page appears in a Document window.

START DREAMWEAVER ON A MACINTOSH

You can start Dreamweaver on a Macintosh and begin building pages that you can publish on the Web.

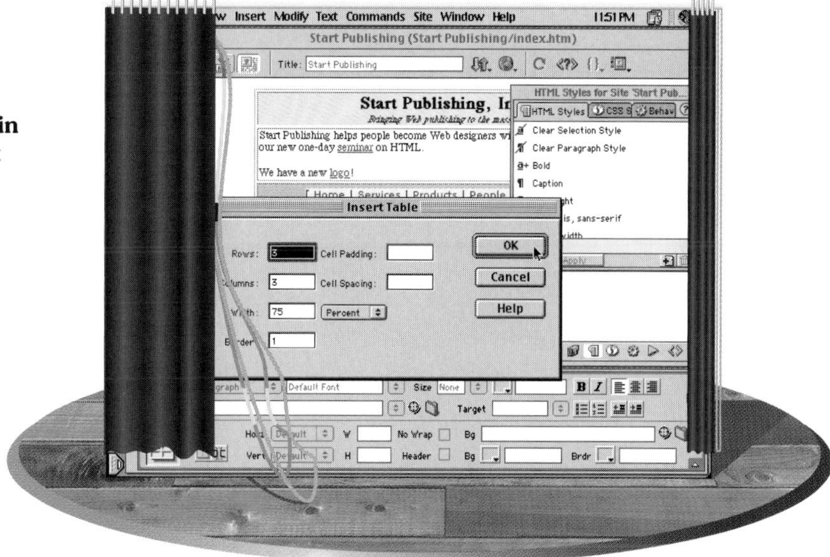

START DREAMWEAVER ON A MACINTOSH

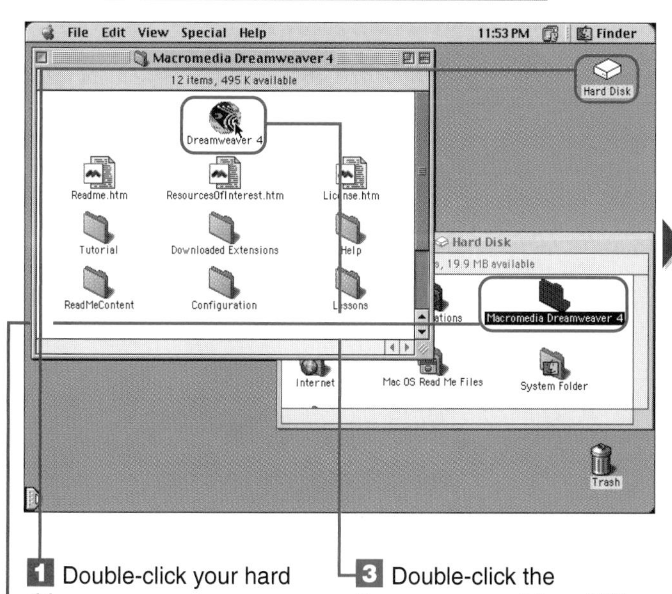

1 Double-click your hard drive.

2 Double-click the **Macromedia Dreamweaver 4** folder.

3 Double-click the **Dreamweaver 4** icon.

Note: The exact location of the Dreamweaver folder will depend on how you installed your software.

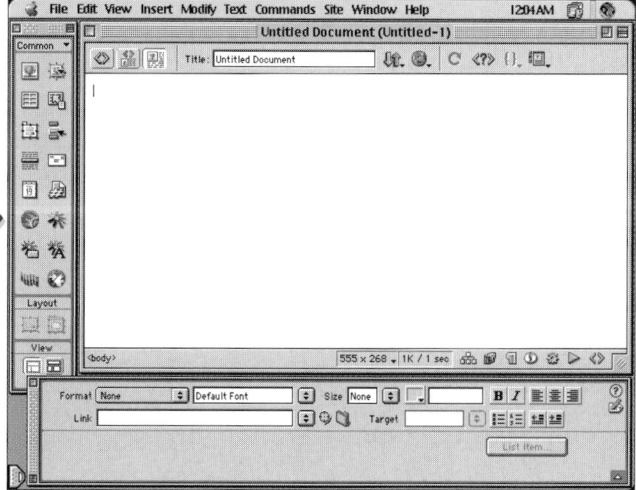

■ An untitled Web page appears in a Document window.

SHOW OR HIDE A PANEL

You can show or hide accessory windows, also called panels and inspectors, by using commands in the Window menu.

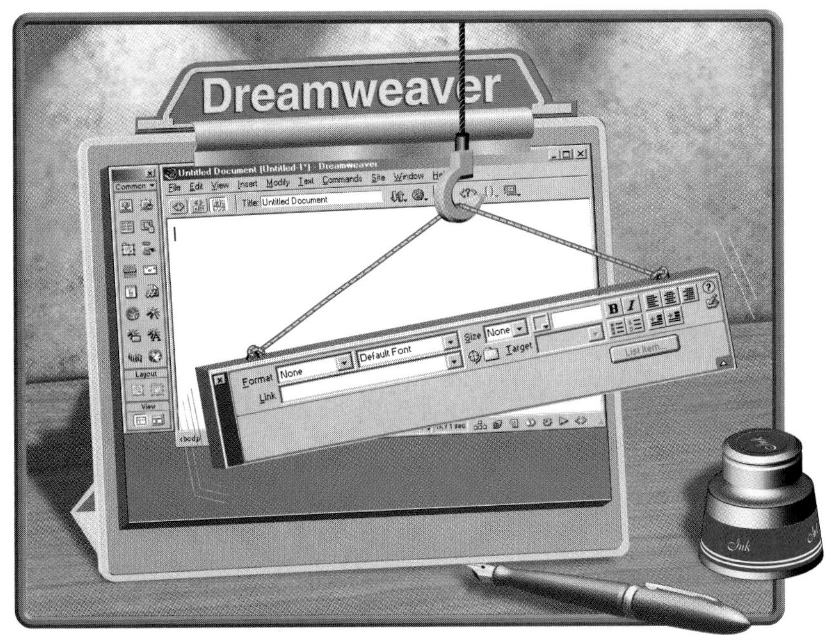

SHOW OR HIDE A PANEL

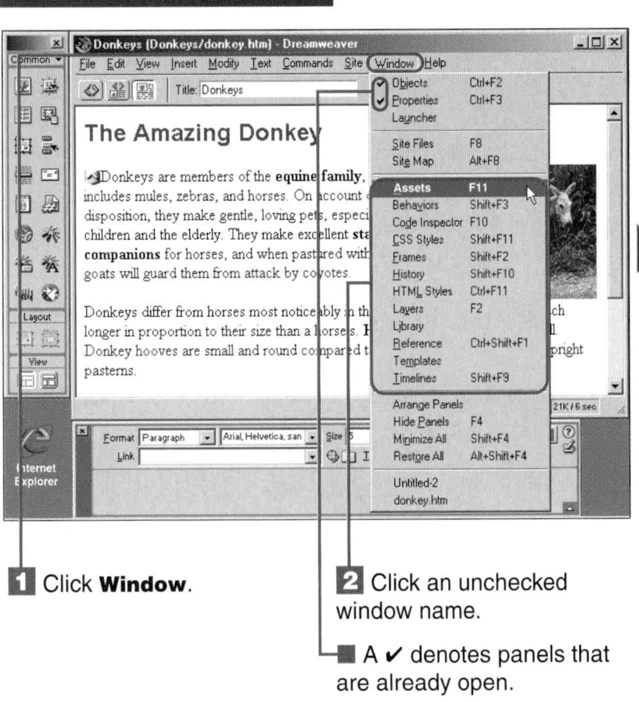

1 Click **Window**.

2 Click an unchecked window name.

■ A ✔ denotes panels that are already open.

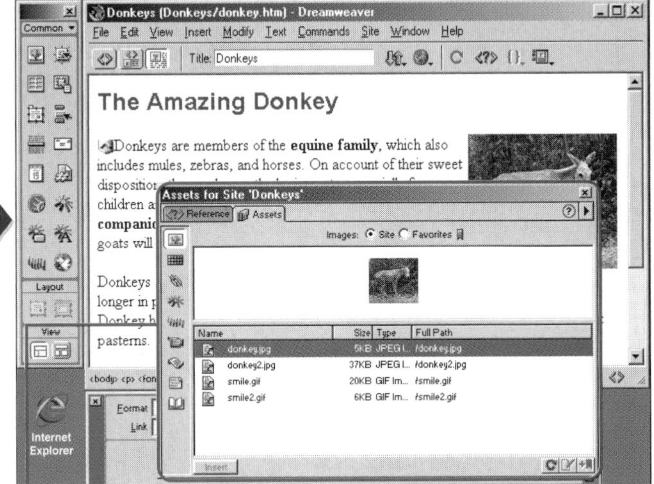

■ Dreamweaver shows the panel.

■ To hide a window, click **Window** and the checked window name.

■ You can click **Window** and **Hide Panels** to hide everything except the Document window.

ADD OBJECTS WITH THE OBJECTS PANEL

You can use the Objects panel to insert objects such as images, tables, and layers into the Document window. The panel has a drop-down menu at the top, allowing you to view different sets of object-insertion buttons.

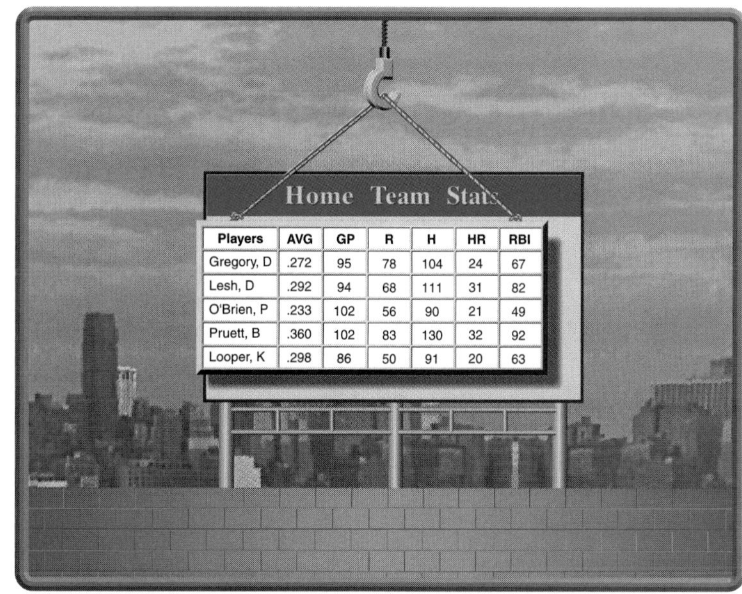

Home Team Stats
Players AVG GP R H HR RBI
Gregory, D .272 95 78 104 24 67
Lesh, D .292 94 68 111 31 82
O'Brien, P .233 102 56 90 21 49
Pruett, B .360 102 83 130 32 92
Looper, K .298 86 50 91 20 63

ADD OBJECTS WITH THE OBJECTS PANEL

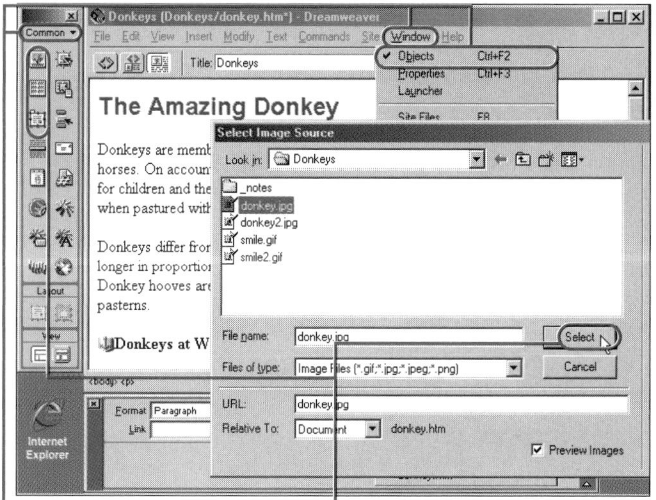

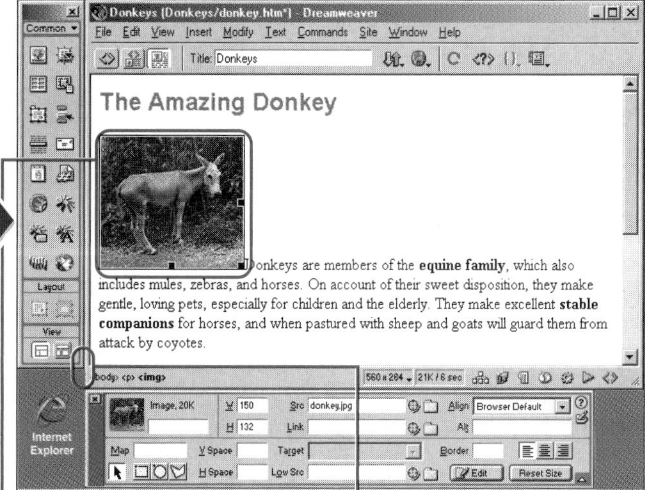

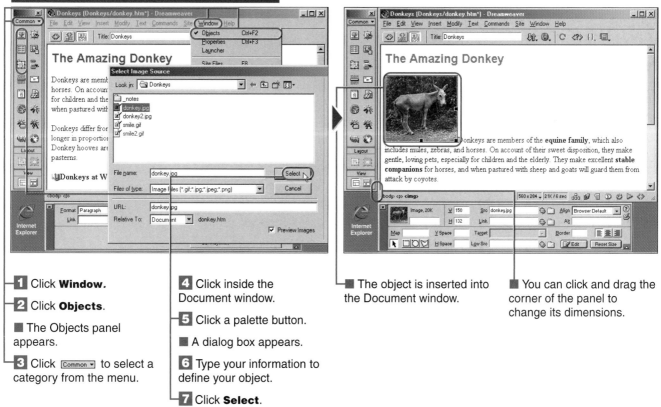

1 Click **Window.**

2 Click **Objects**.

■ The Objects panel appears.

3 Click Common to select a category from the menu.

4 Click inside the Document window.

5 Click a palette button.

■ A dialog box appears.

6 Type your information to define your object.

7 Click **Select**.

■ The object is inserted into the Document window.

■ You can click and drag the corner of the panel to change its dimensions.

CORRECT ERRORS WITH THE HISTORY PANEL

The History panel keeps track of the commands you perform in Dreamweaver and allows you to undo your changes by backtracking through those commands. This is a convenient way to correct errors.

CORRECT ERRORS WITH THE HISTORY PANEL

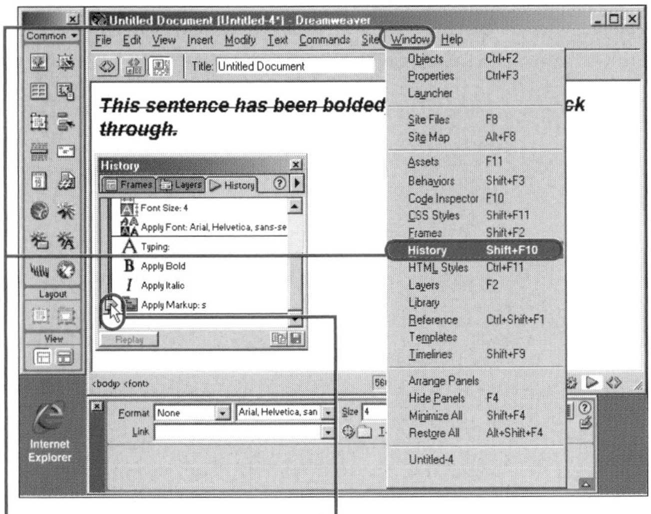

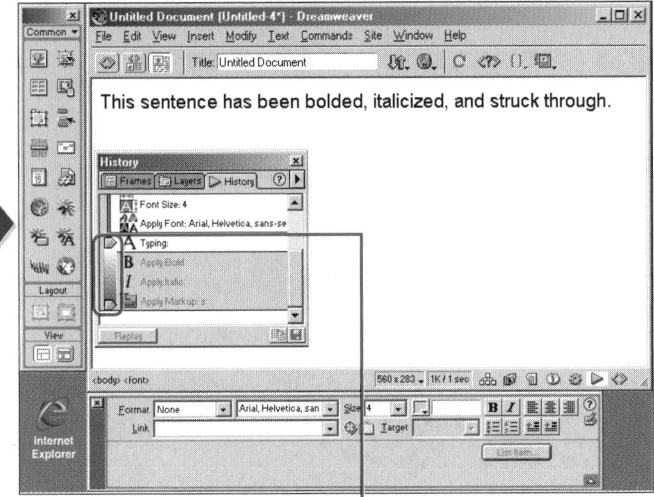

1 Click **Window.**

2 Click **History**.

■ The History panel appears.

■ The History panel records the commands you perform in Dreamweaver.

3 To undo one or more commands, click and drag the slider upward.

■ The page reverts to its previous state.

■ To redo the commands, click and drag the slider downward.

EXIT DREAMWEAVER

You can exit Dreamweaver after you finish using the program.

You should always exit Dreamweaver and all other programs like Flash and Fireworks before turning off your computer.

EXIT DREAMWEAVER

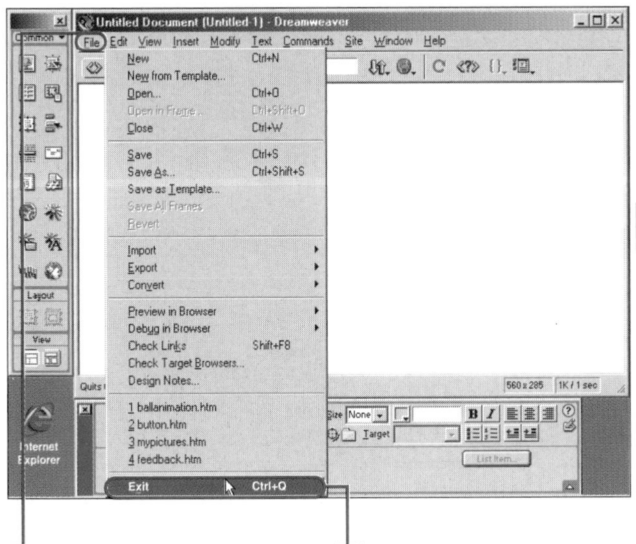

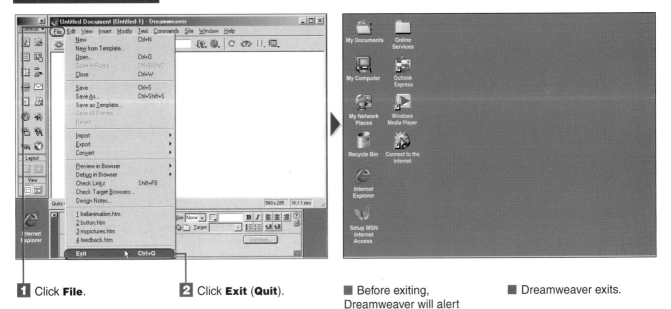

1 Click **File**.

2 Click **Exit** (**Quit**).

■ Before exiting, Dreamweaver will alert you to any documents open that have unsaved changes, allowing you to save them.

■ Dreamweaver exits.

SET UP A LOCAL SITE

Before creating your Web pages, you need to define a local site for storing the information in your site, such as your HTML documents Fireworks image files, and Flash movies. Defining a local site allows you to manage your Web site files in the Site window.

See Chapter 23 for more information on managing your Dreamweaver Web site.

SET UP A LOCAL SITE

1 Click **Site**.

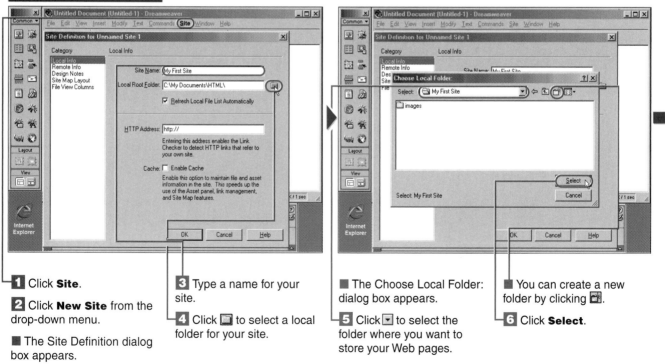

2 Click **New Site** from the drop-down menu.

■ The Site Definition dialog box appears.

3 Type a name for your site.

4 Click to select a local folder for your site.

■ The Choose Local Folder: dialog box appears.

5 Click to select the folder where you want to store your Web pages.

■ You can create a new folder by clicking .

6 Click **Select**.

Why is it important to keep all my Web site files in a single folder on my computer?

Keeping everything in the same folder enables you to easily transfer your site files to a Web server without changing the organization of the files (see Chapter 23 for more information). If you do not organize your site files on the Web server the same as they are organized on your local computer, hyperlinks will not work and images will not display properly.

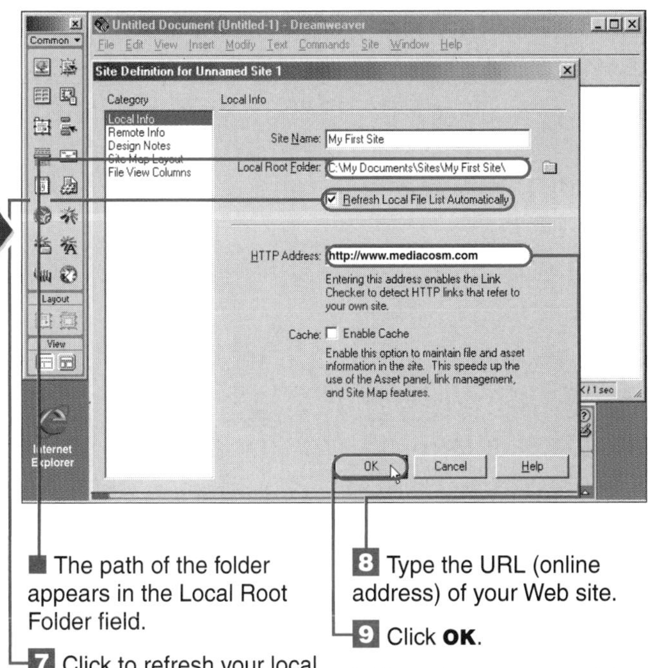

■ The path of the folder appears in the Local Root Folder field.

7 Click to refresh your local file list every time you download files (☐ changes to ☑).

8 Type the URL (online address) of your Web site.

9 Click **OK**.

■ A window appears asking if you want to create a site cache.

10 Click **Create**.

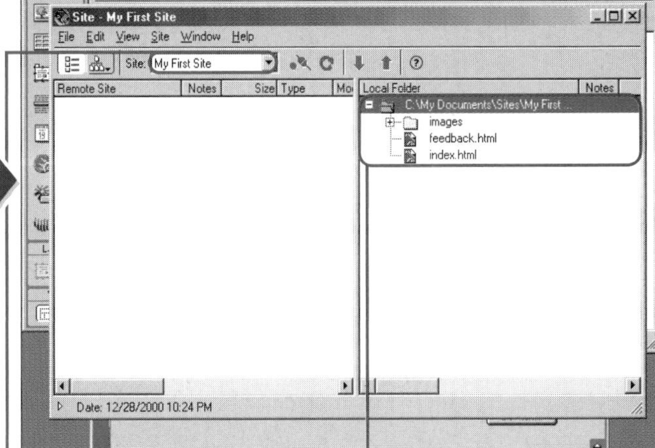

■ The Site window appears with the new site selected.

■ Any files or folders already in the local site folder appear in the right pane of the window.

OPEN A WEB PAGE

You can open an existing Web page in Dreamweaver to view and modify its structure.

OPEN A WEB PAGE

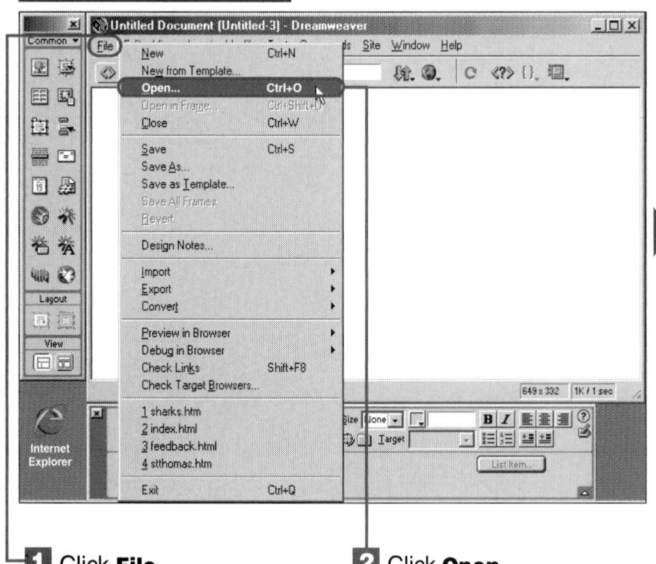

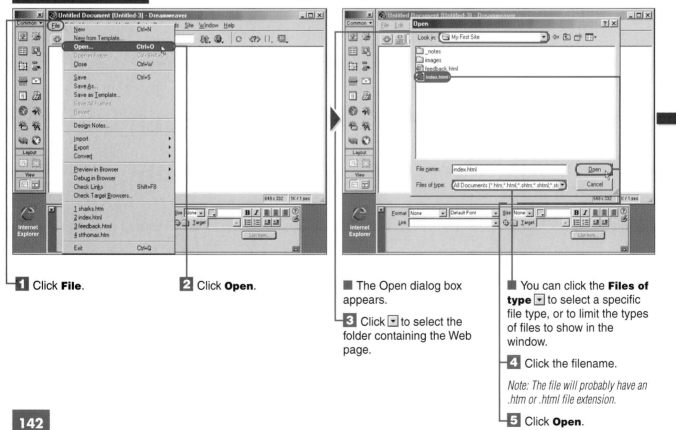

1 Click **File**.

2 Click **Open**.

■ The Open dialog box appears.

3 Click ▼ to select the folder containing the Web page.

■ You can click the **Files of type** ▼ to select a specific file type, or to limit the types of files to show in the window.

4 Click the filename.

Note: The file will probably have an .htm or .html file extension.

5 Click **Open**.

Can I open Web pages created in HTML editors other than Dreamweaver?

Yes. You can open any HTML file in Dreamweaver, no matter where it was created. You can also open non-HTML text files; however, the layout of such Web pages may look haphazard in Dreamweaver because they do not include HTML formatting.

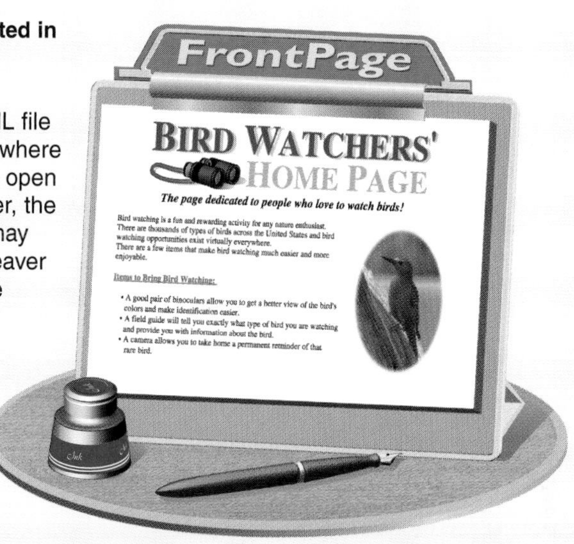

■ The file opens in a Document window.

■ You can switch between open Web pages by selecting their filenames under the Window menu.

■ Open files also appear on the Windows toolbar.

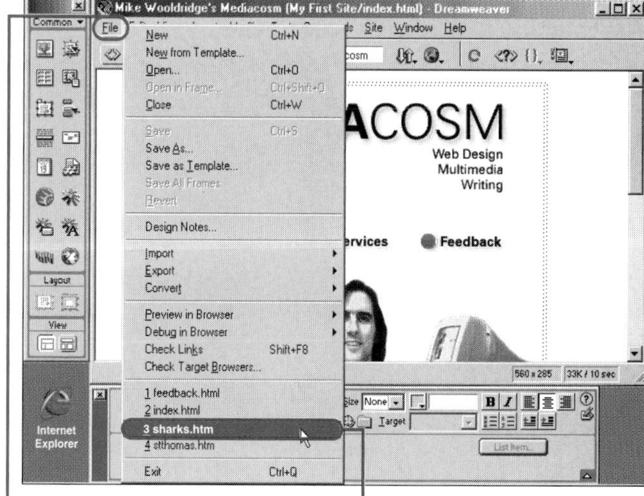

OPEN A RECENTLY OPENED PAGE

1 Click **File**.

■ A list of your last four files opened is listed.

2 Click the file you want to open.

CREATE A NEW WEB PAGE

You can open a new, blank page in Dreamweaver and then add text, images, and other elements from Fireworks or Flash to create a new Web page design.

CREATE A NEW WEB PAGE

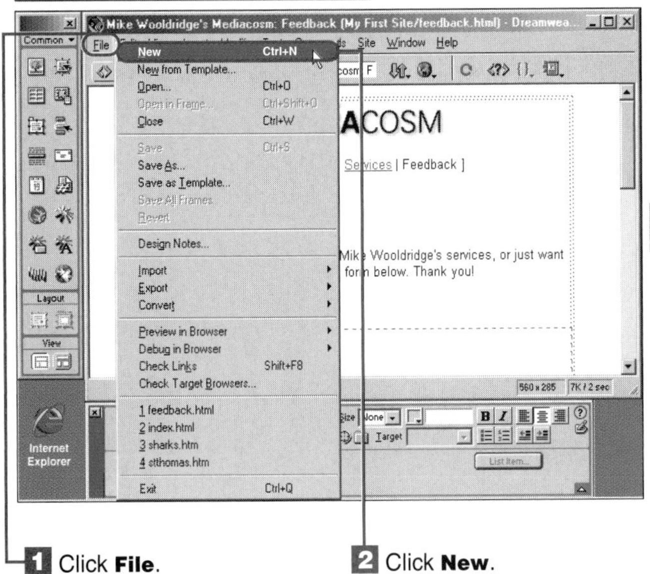

1 Click **File**.

2 Click **New**.

■ An untitled Document window appears.

Note: The page name and filename are untitled until you save the page. See page 58 for instructions.

■ The new file also appears on the Windows toolbar.

ADD A WEB PAGE TITLE

A Web page title appears in the title bar when a page opens in a Web browser. Adding a Web page title makes the page easily identifiable by viewers and search engines.

ADD A WEB PAGE TITLE

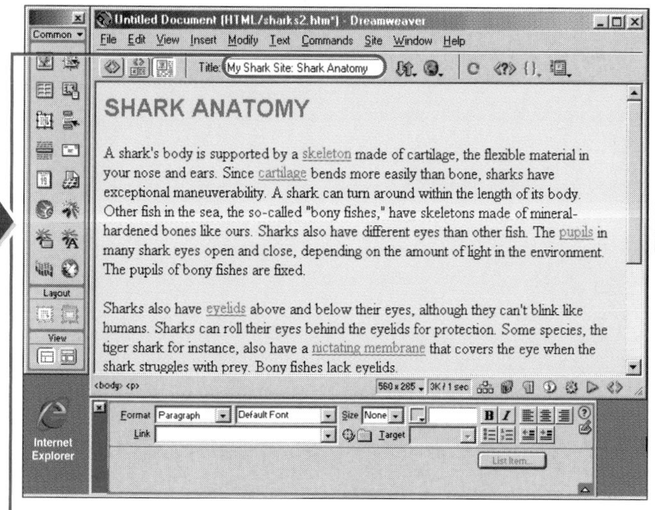

1 Type a name for your Web page.

2 Press Enter (Return).

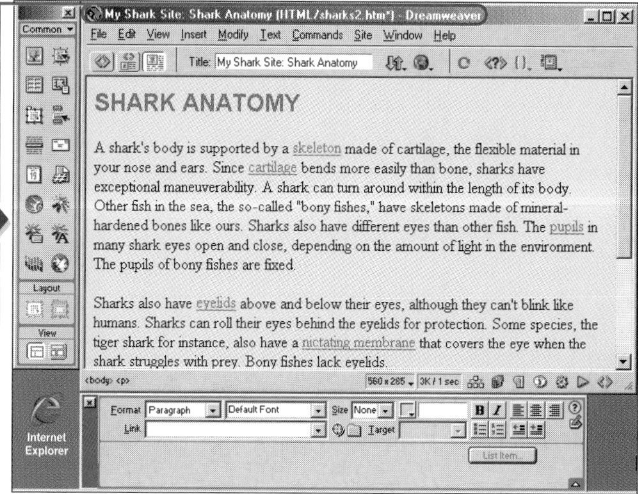

■ The title appears in the title bar of the Document window.

SAVE A WEB PAGE

You should save your Web page before closing or transferring the page to a remote site (see Chapter 23). It is also a good idea to save all your files frequently to prevent work from being lost due to power outages or system failures. If you accidentally save a wrong version, you can revert back to the previously saved file version.

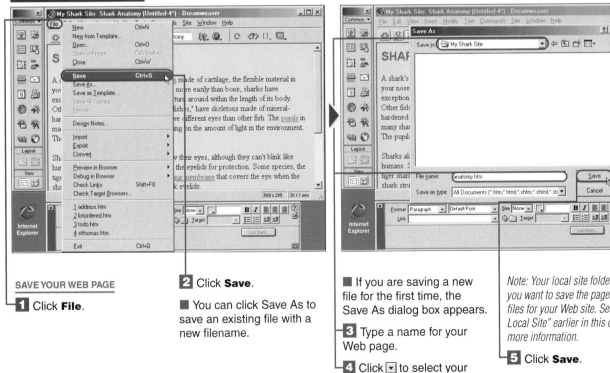

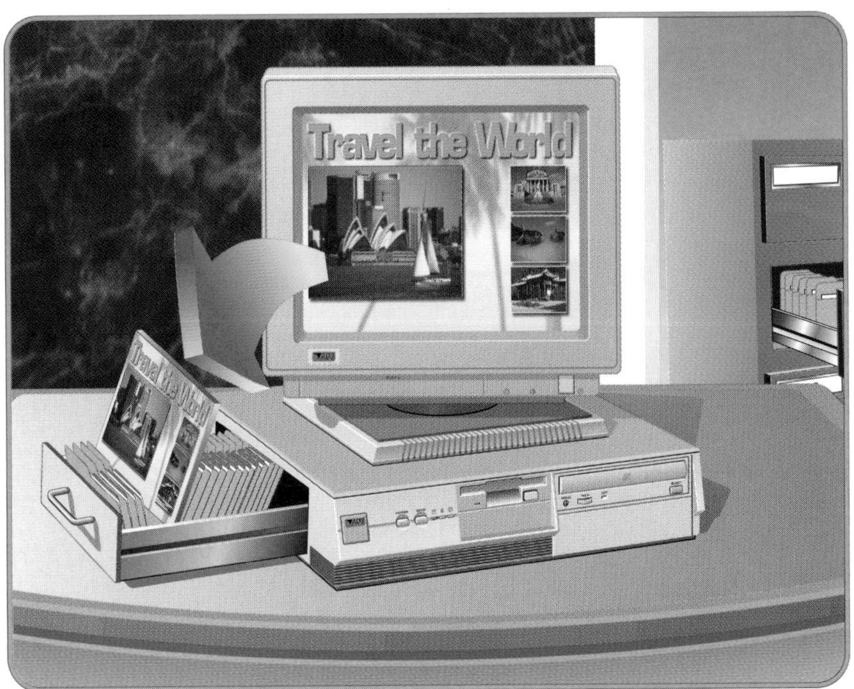

SAVE A WEB PAGE

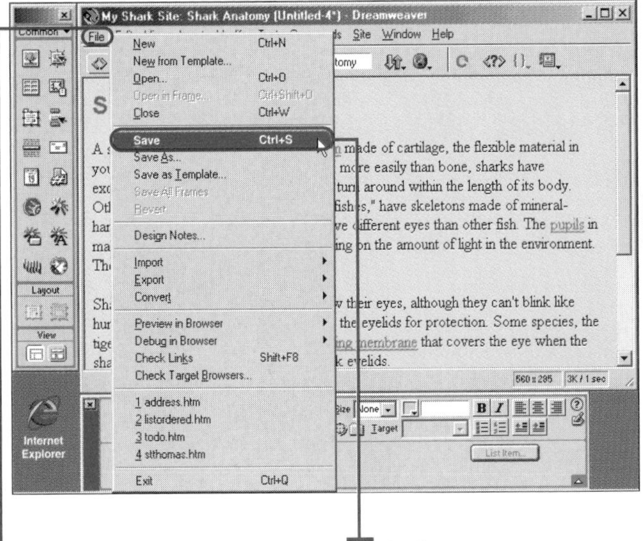

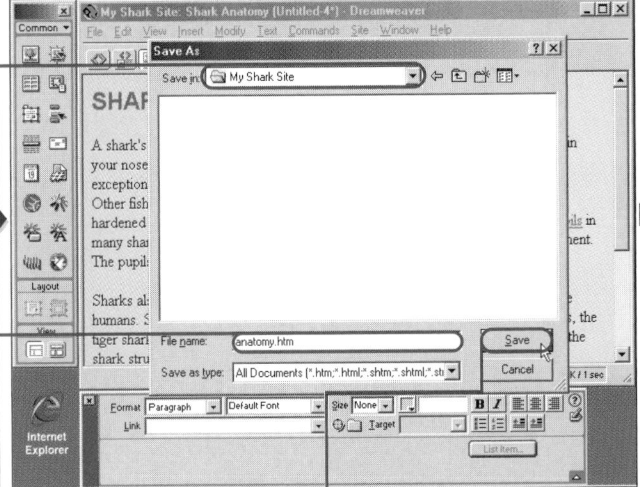

SAVE YOUR WEB PAGE

1 Click **File**.

2 Click **Save**.

■ You can click Save As to save an existing file with a new filename.

■ If you are saving a new file for the first time, the Save As dialog box appears.

3 Type a name for your Web page.

4 Click ▾ to select your local site folder.

Note: Your local site folder is where you want to save the pages and other files for your Web site. See "Set Up a Local Site" earlier in this chapter for more information.

5 Click **Save**.

How should I store the files for my Web site on my computer?

You should save all the files for your Web site in the folder that you defined as the local root folder (see "Set up a Local Site" earlier in this chapter). Keeping all the files of the site in this folder (or in subfolders inside this folder) makes it easier to hyperlink between local files, and transfer files to a remote Web server.

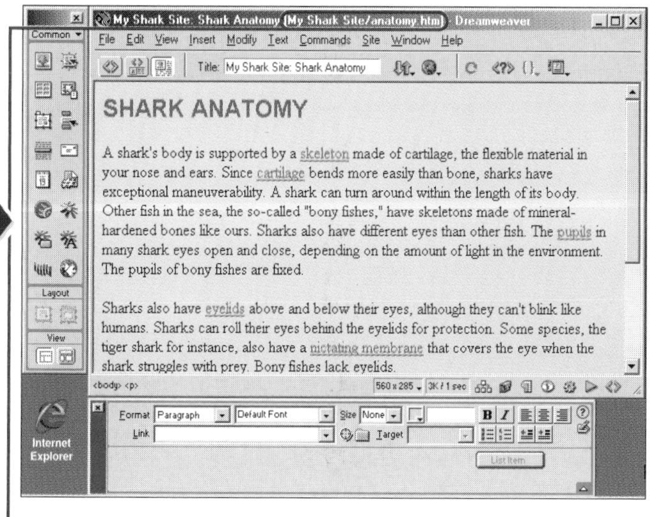

■ The Web page saves, and the filename and path appears in the title bar.

■ You can click ☒ to close the page.

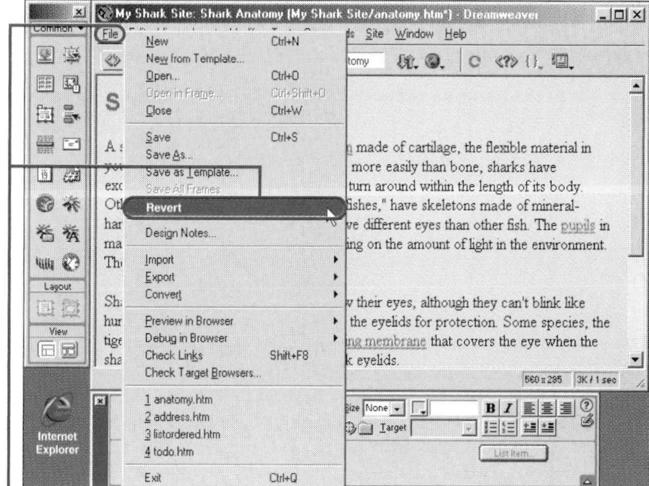

REVERT TO YOUR LAST SAVED VERSION

1 Click **File**.

2 Click **Revert**.

■ The page reverts to the previously saved version. All the changes made since last saving are lost.

EXPLORE STRUCTURAL TAGS

You define the basic structure of every HTML document with several basic tags. To view the HTML of a Web page, click the Code View icon in the Document window or Code Inspector in the Window menu.

<html> TAGS

Opening and closing `<html>` tags begin and end every HTML document.

<head> TAGS

Opening and closing `<head>` tags surround descriptive and accessory information for a page. This includes `<title>` and `<meta>` tag content.

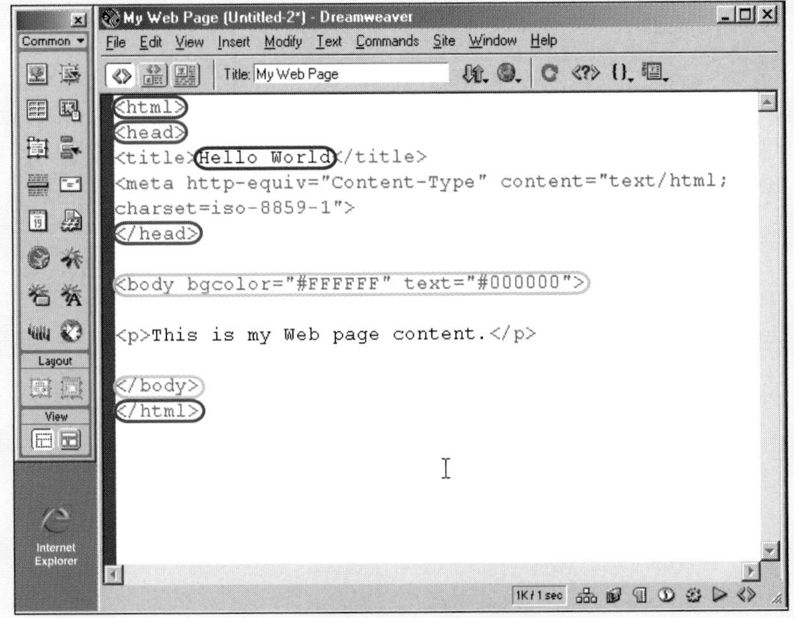

<body> TAGS

Opening and closing `<body>` tags surround content that appears inside the Web browser window. The `bgcolor` and text attributes of the `<body>` tag define the background and text color.

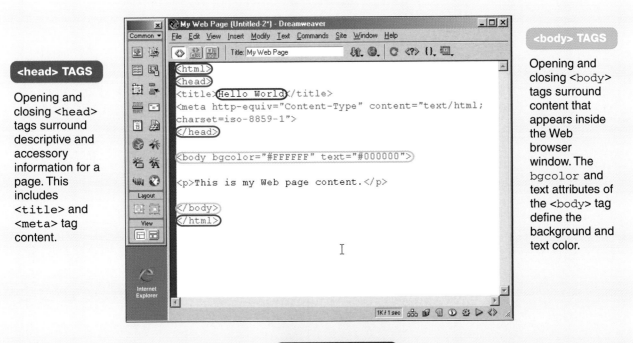

PAGE TITLE

The content inside the opening and closing `<title>` tags is displayed in the Document window title bar.

EXPLORE TEXT-FORMATTING TAGS

You can format the style of sentences, words, and characters with text-formatting tags. To view the HTML of a Web page, click a Code View icon in the Document window or Code Inspector in the Windows menu.

CODE VIEW

<font> TAG

The <font> tag controls various characteristics of text on a Web page.

<size> ATTRIBUTE

The <size> attribute goes inside the <font> tag and specifies the size of text.

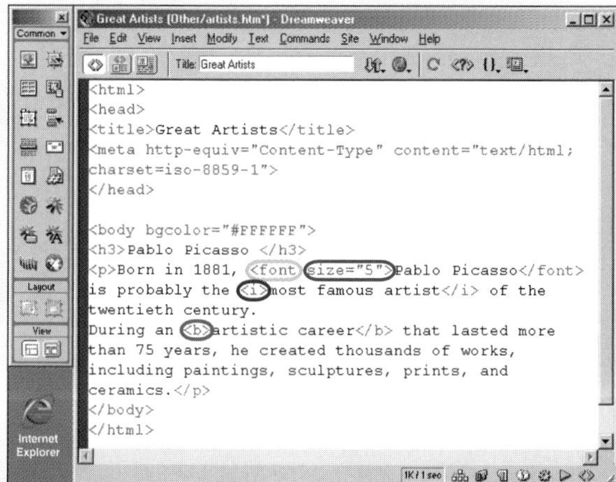

<b> TAG

The <b> tag defines text as bold.

<i> TAG

The <i> tag defines text as italic.

DESIGN VIEW

This page features text with a different font size, as well as bold and italic text.

FONT SIZE

ITALIC TEXT

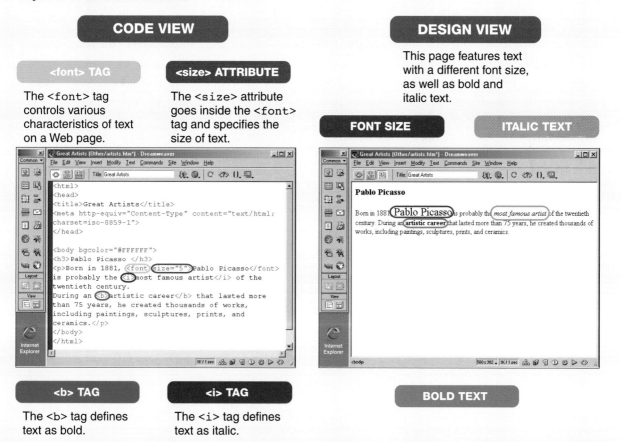

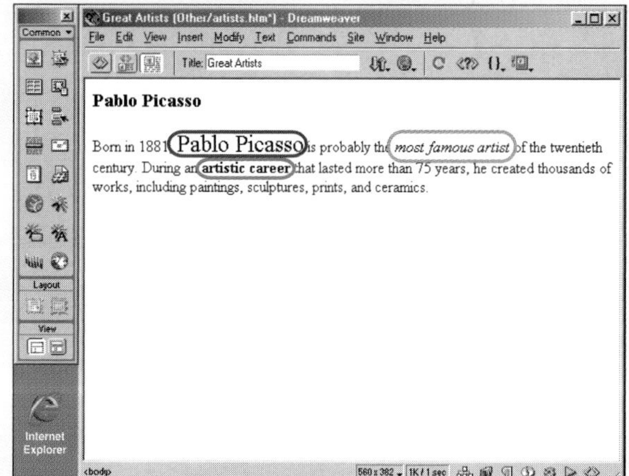

BOLD TEXT

VIEW AND EDIT THE SOURCE CODE

You can switch to Code View in the Document window to inspect and edit the HTML and other code of a Web page.

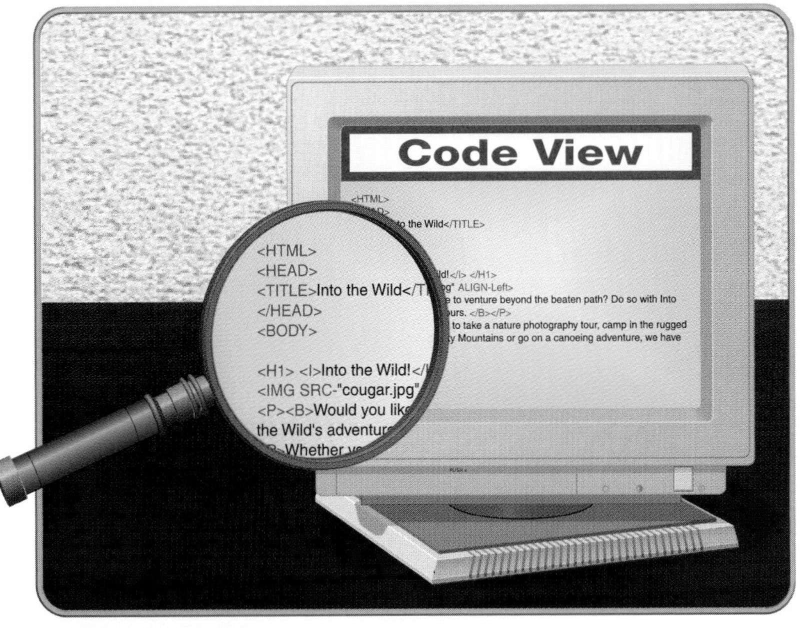

You will probably do most of your work in Design View, which displays your page approximately as it will be viewed in a Web browser.

VIEW AND EDIT THE SOURCE CODE

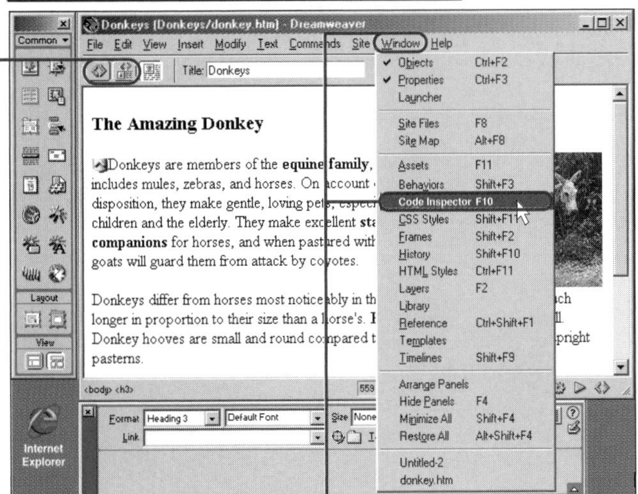

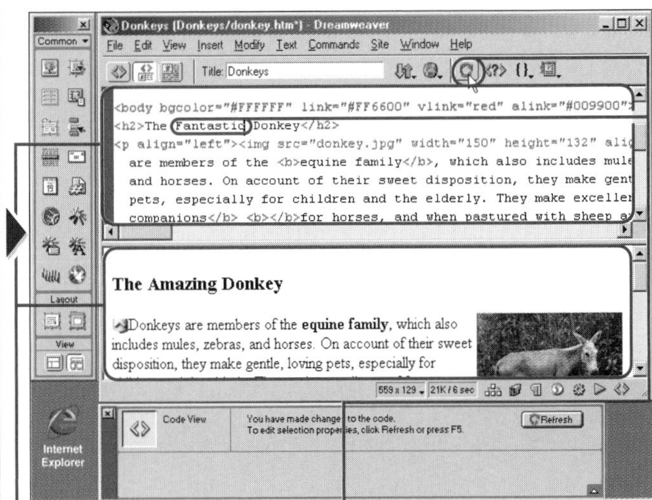

1 Click a code-viewing option (example: **Code and Design Views** button).

■ Clicking the **Code View** button ( ) displays the source code of your page in the Document window.

■ Clicking the **Code and Design Views** button ( ) splits the window and displays both your source code and the design in the Document window.

■ Selecting **Code Inspector** under the Window menu displays the code in a separate window.

■ The Code and Design Views appear in the Document window.

■ The HTML and other code appear in one pane.

■ The design view appears in the other pane.

2 Click in the code to edit the text, or add or modify the HTML.

3 Click the **Refresh** button ( ).

How do I turn on line numbers in Code View, or make code wrap at the right edge of the window?

Both of these options (and others) are available by clicking the **Options** button at the top of the Document window when you are in Code View.

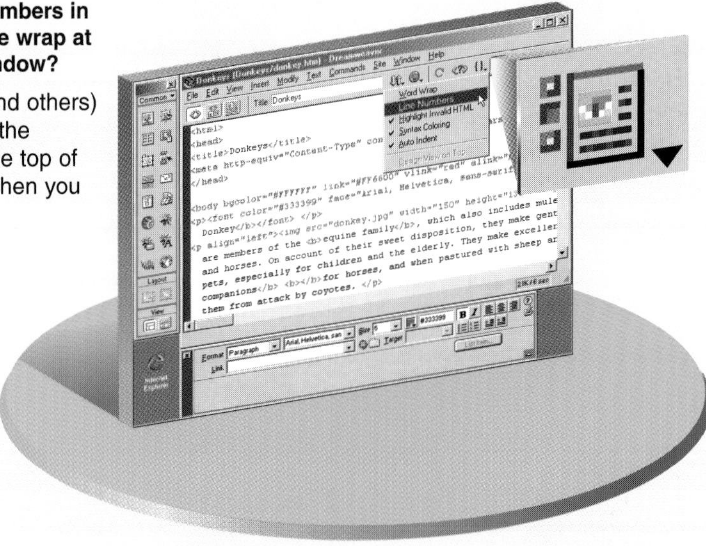

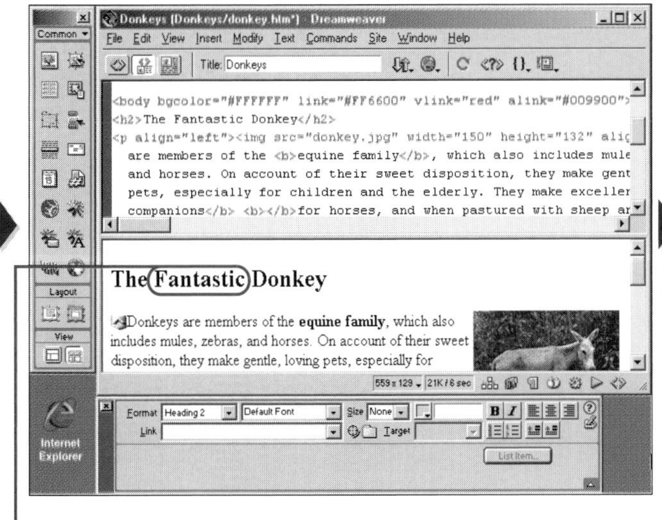

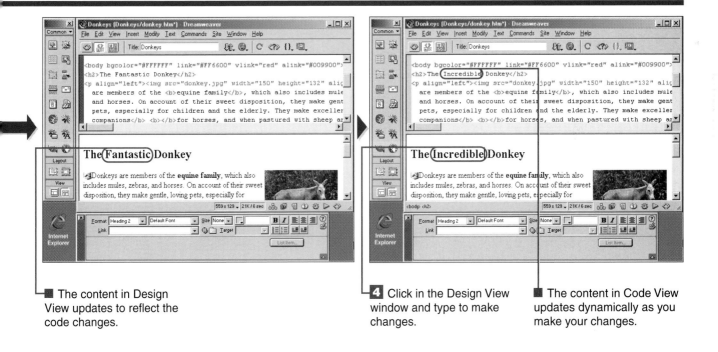

■ The content in Design View updates to reflect the code changes.

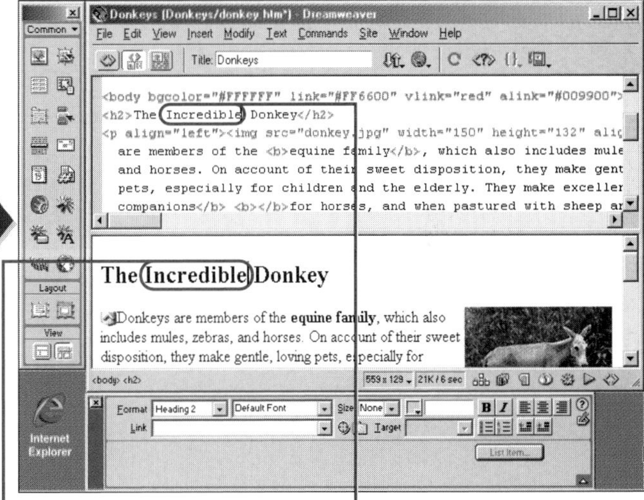

4 Click in the Design View window and type to make changes.

■ The content in Code View updates dynamically as you make your changes.

CREATE AND ALIGN PARAGRAPHS

You can organize text on your Web page by creating and aligning paragraphs. This makes it easier to display and read information.

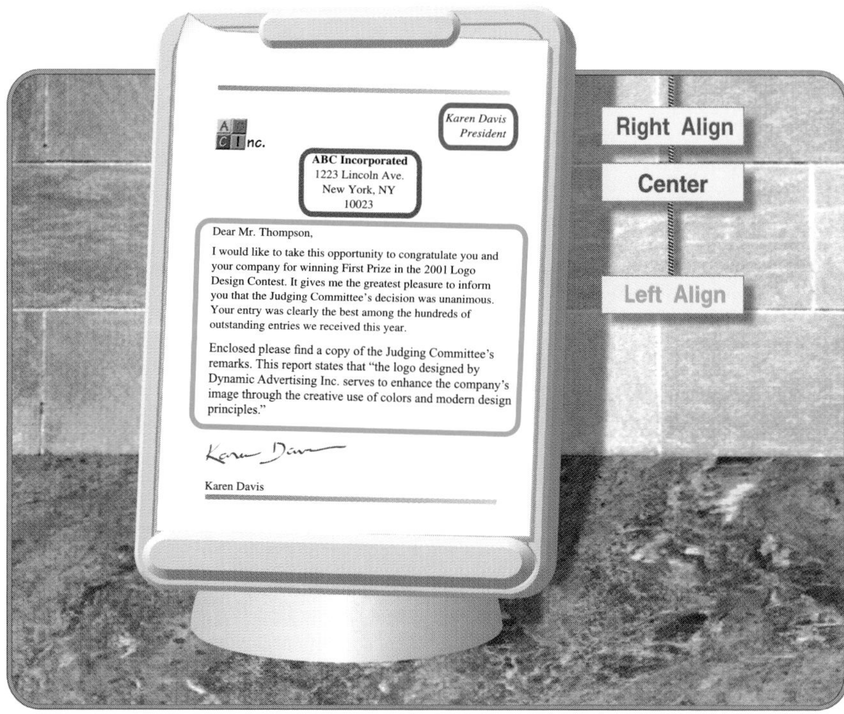

CREATE AND ALIGN PARAGRAPHS

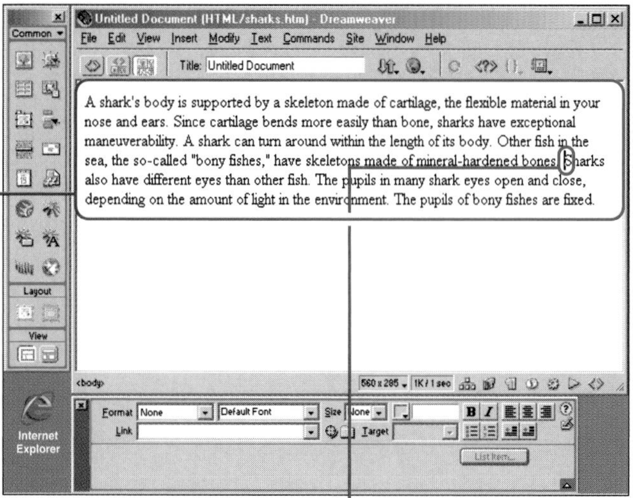

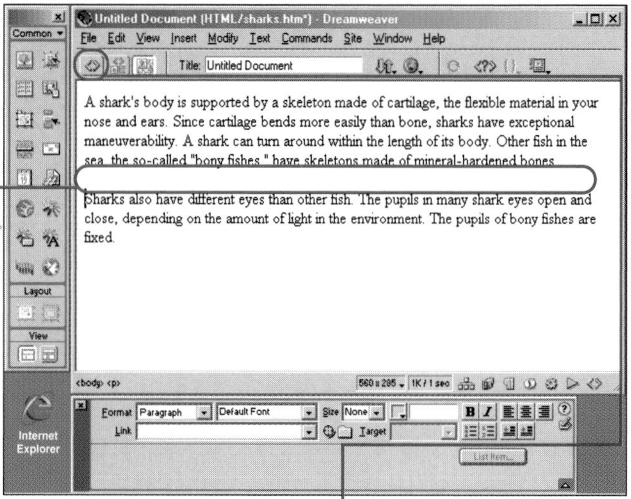

CREATE A PARAGRAPH

1 Type the text for your Web page into the Document Window.

2 Move the cursor where you want a paragraph break.

3 Press Enter (Return).

■ A blank line appears between the blocks of text, separating the text into paragraphs.

■ Click the **Code View** button ( ) to view the page's HTML.

What controls the width of the paragraphs on my Web page?

The width of your paragraphs depends on the width of the Web browser window. When a user changes the size of the browser window, the widths of the paragraphs also change. That way, the user always sees all the text of the paragraphs.

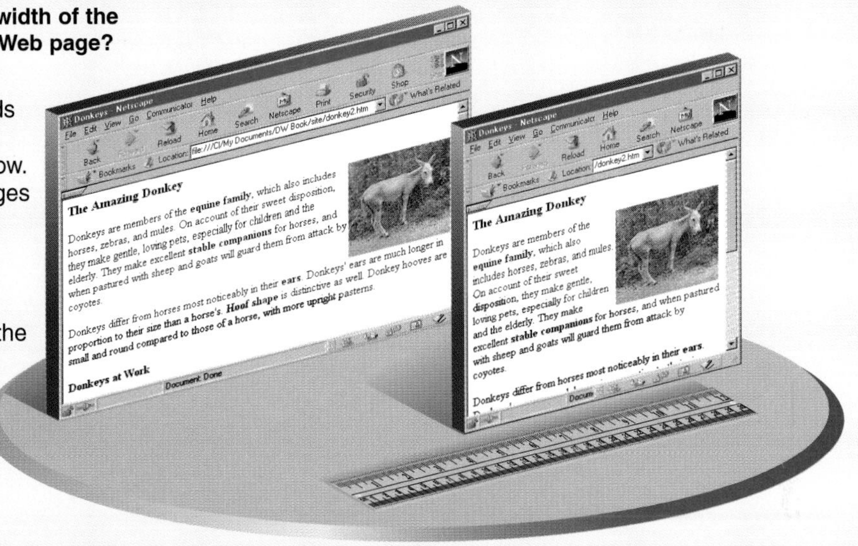

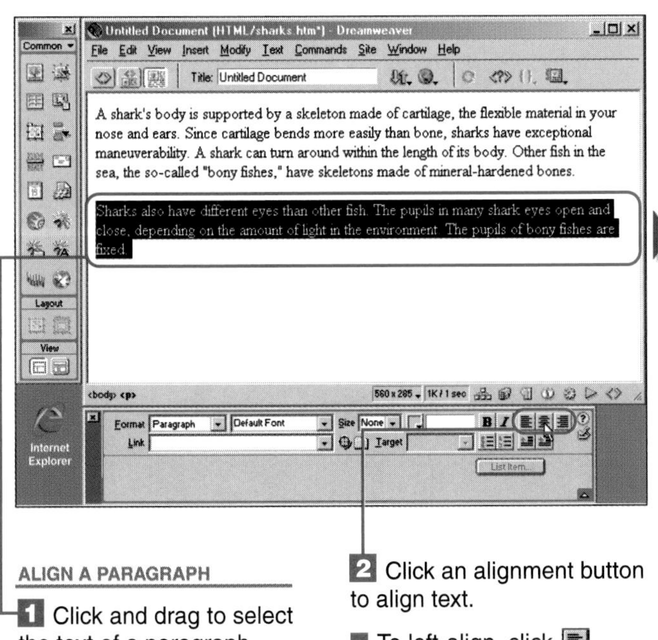

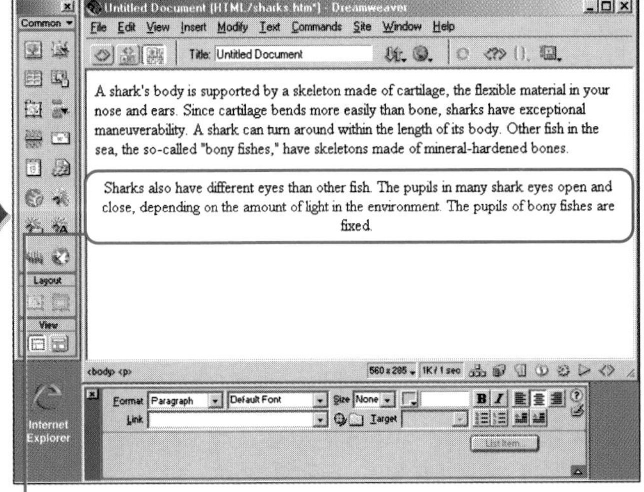

ALIGN A PARAGRAPH

1 Click and drag to select the text of a paragraph.

2 Click an alignment button to align text.

■ To left-align, click ▤. To center-align, click ▤. To right-align, click ▤.

■ The paragraph appears center-aligned.

Note: Paragraphs appear left-aligned by default.

CREATE A NEW HEADING

You can add headings to structure the text on your Web page hierarchically with titles and subtitles. You can also align headings to add emphasis to text.

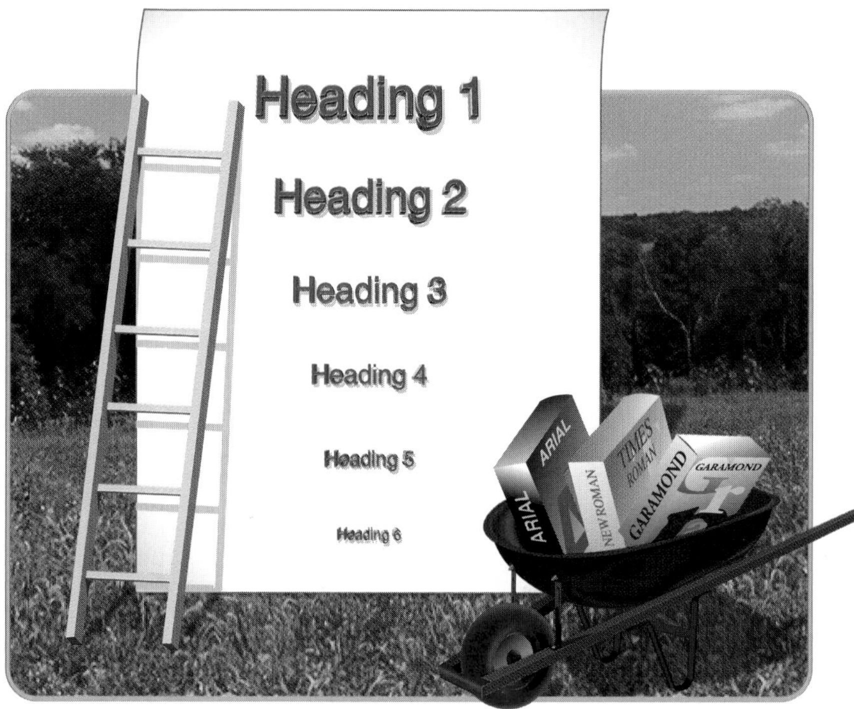

CREATE A NEW HEADING

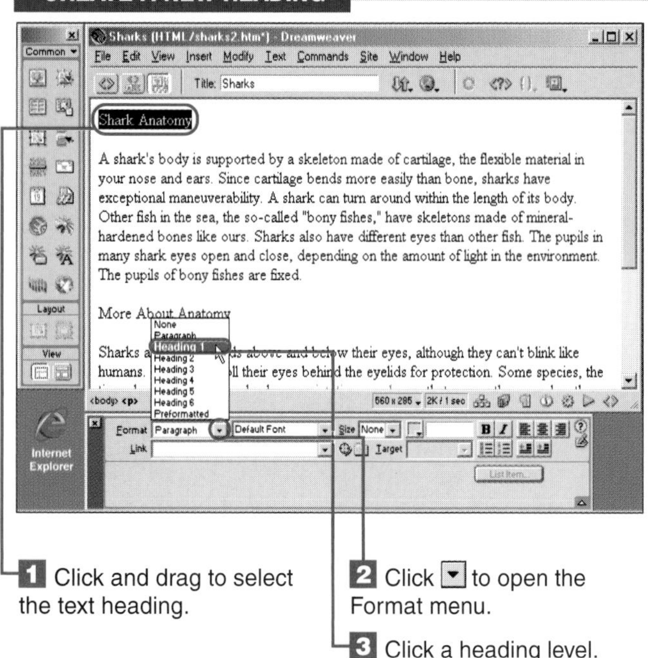

1 Click and drag to select the text heading.

2 Click ▼ to open the Format menu.

3 Click a heading level.

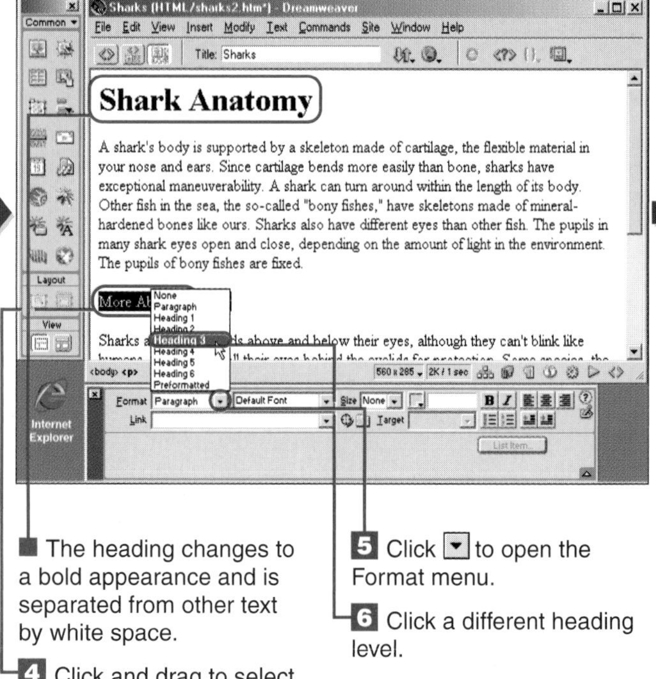

■ The heading changes to a bold appearance and is separated from other text by white space.

4 Click and drag to select more text.

5 Click ▼ to open the Format menu.

6 Click a different heading level.

What heading levels should I use to format my text?

Headings 1, 2, and 3 are often used for titles and subtitles. Heading 4 is similar to a bold version of default text. Headings 5 and 6 are often used for copyright and disclaimer information in page footers.

Decadence Chocolates Online

We've supplied the Seattle area with the finest chocolates in the world for over 20 years. Now our imported Swiss and German chocolates are available online for delivery across the United States and Canada!

Gift Boxes

An elegant card containing a message you supply is included with each gift box you order.

Gift Boxes for Every Occasion

Happy Anniversary!
Delivered with a single long-stemmed rose.
Happy Birthday!
Delivered with three helium-filled balloons.
Thank You!
Delivered with five carnations in the colors of your choice.
Valentine's Day
Receive a 10% discount if you order before January 20.

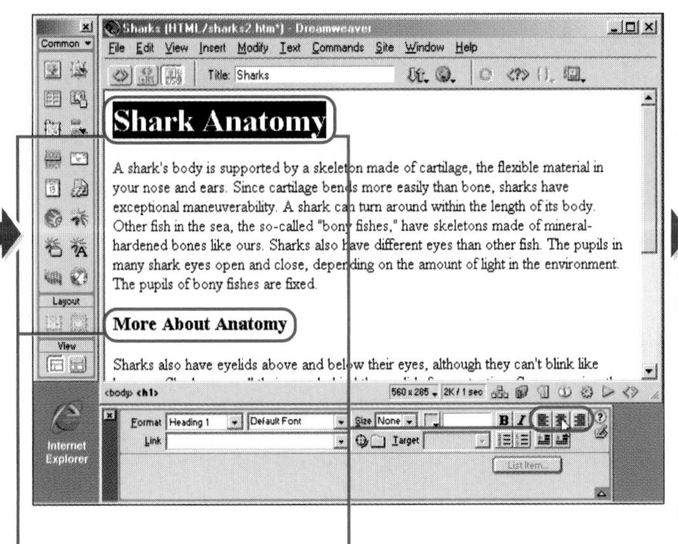

■ The second heading appears different from the first.

Note: The greater the heading level, the smaller the text formatting.

ALIGN HEADING TEXT

1 Click and drag to select some heading text.

2 Click , , or to align.

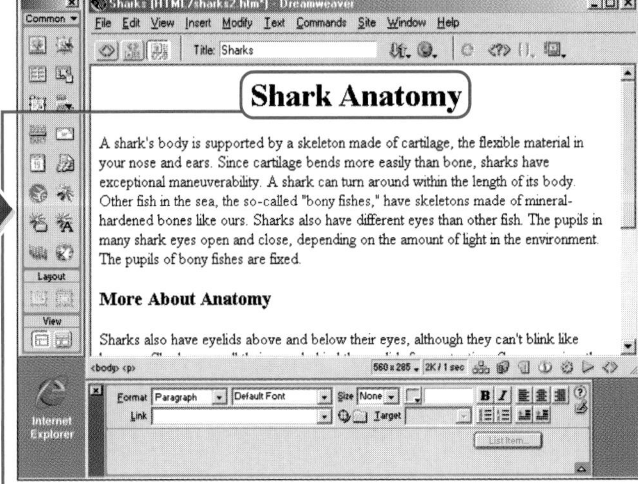

■ The heading text is aligned on the page.

CREATE LINE BREAKS

Line breaks are an alternative to paragraph breaks, which add more space between lines of text (see the section "Create and Align Paragraphs.")

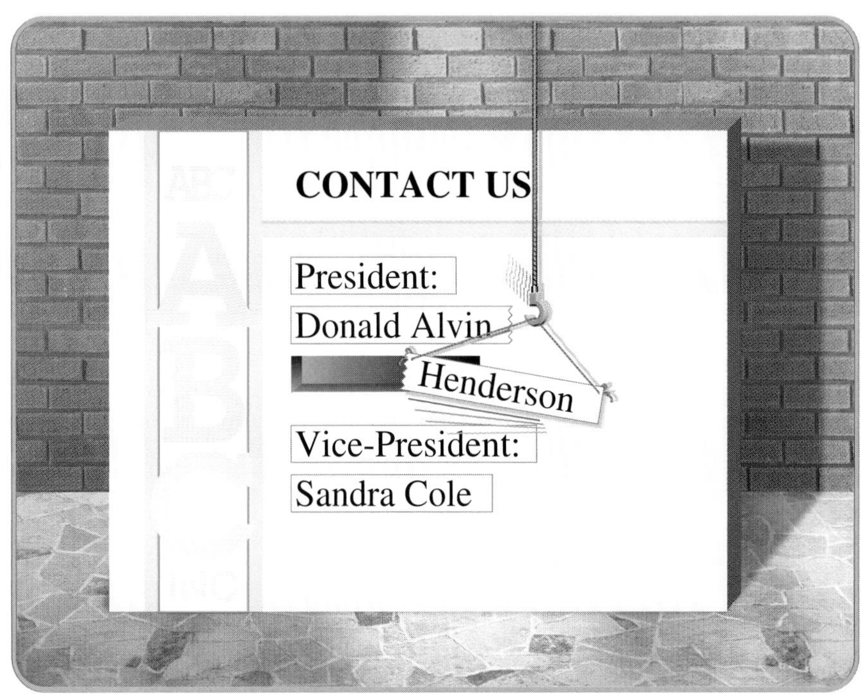

Adding line breaks to your page allows you to keep adjacent lines of related text close together.

CREATE LINE BREAKS

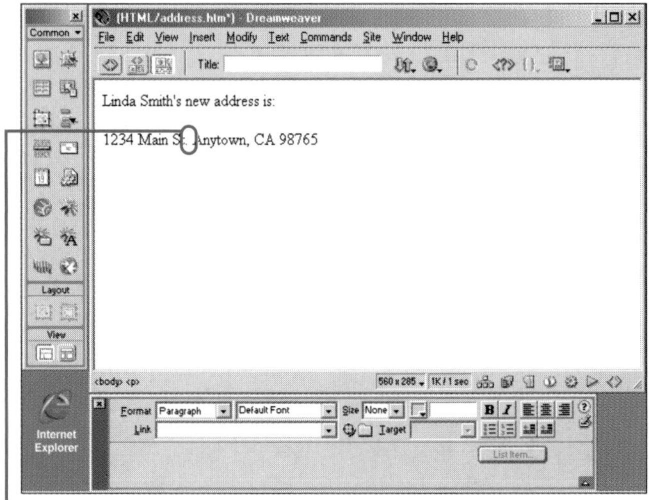

1 Click where you want the line of text to break.

2 Press Shift + Enter (Shift + Return).

■ A line break is added.

Note: You can insert multiple line breaks to add more space between lines of text.

INDENT PARAGRAPHS

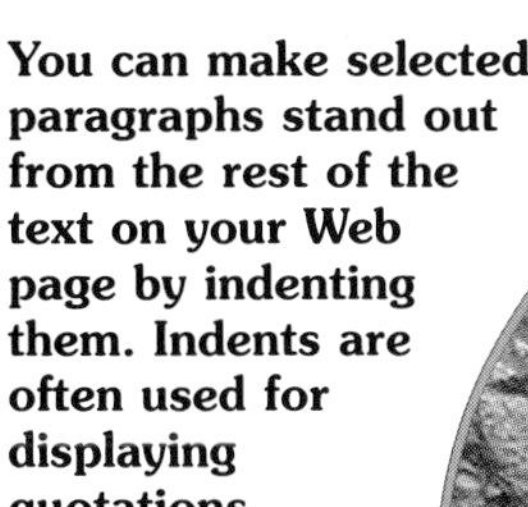

You can make selected paragraphs stand out from the rest of the text on your Web page by indenting them. Indents are often used for displaying quotations.

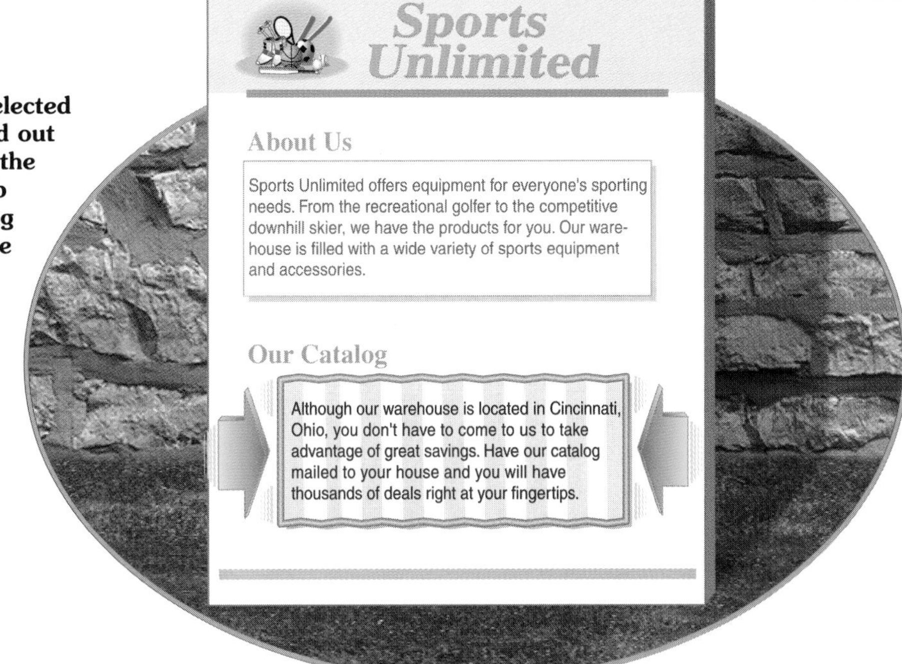

Sports Unlimited
About Us
Sports Unlimited offers equipment for everyone's sporting needs. From the recreational golfer to the competitive downhill skier, we have the products for you. Our warehouse is filled with a wide variety of sports equipment and accessories.
Our Catalog
Although our warehouse is located in Cincinnati, Ohio, you don't have to come to us to take advantage of great savings. Have our catalog mailed to your house and you will have thousands of deals right at your fingertips.

INDENT PARAGRAPHS

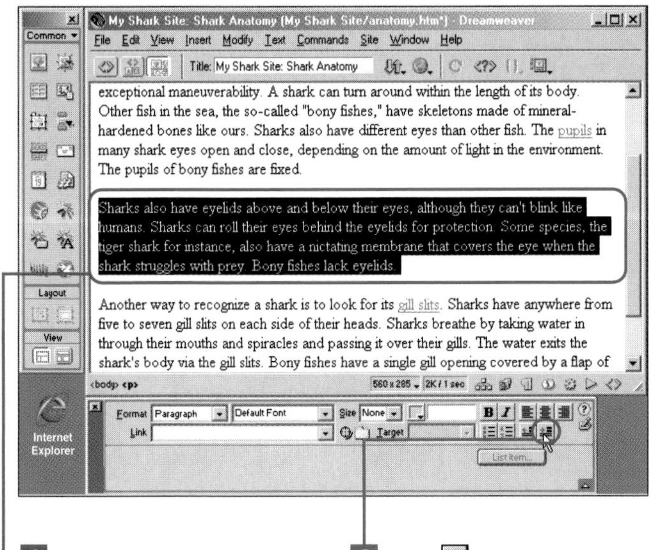

1 Click and drag to select a paragraph.

2 Click to indent the text.

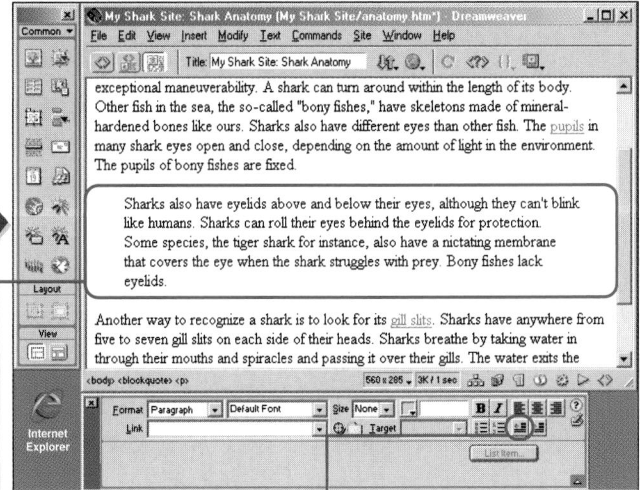

■ Additional space appears in both the left and right margins of the paragraph.

■ Repeat steps **1** and **2** to indent a paragraph further.

■ You can outdent an indented paragraph by clicking .

CHANGE FONT STYLE

To add variety or to emphasize certain elements to your Web page, you can change the font style of your text.

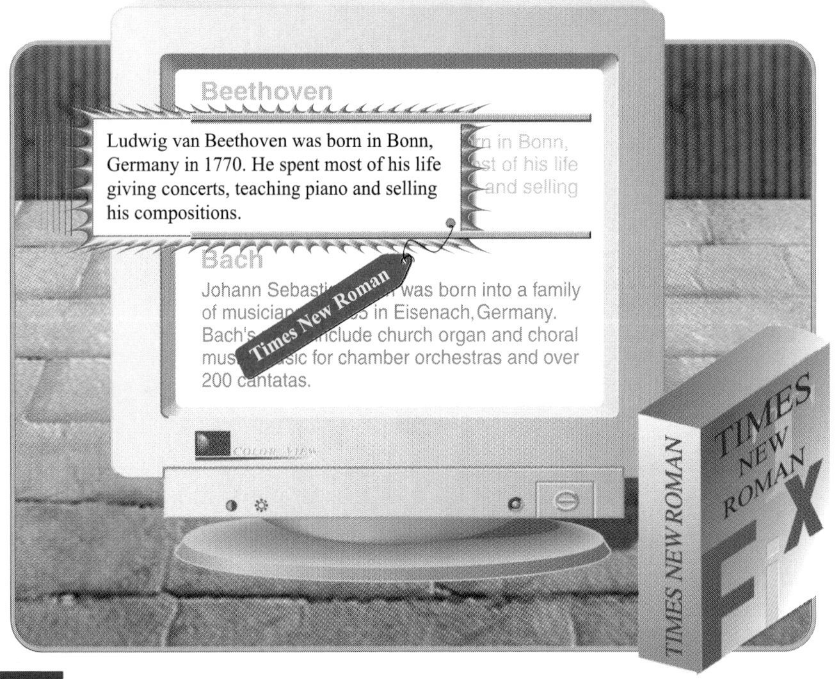

You can also customize the fonts on your Web pages by using Style Sheets (see Chapter 22.)

CHANGE FONT STYLE

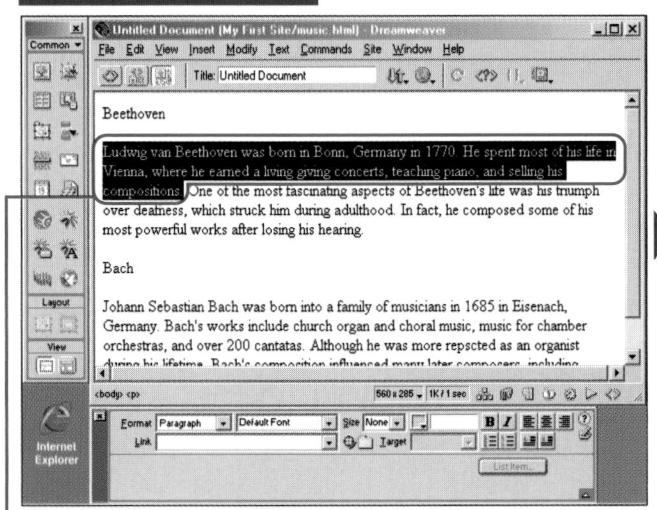

1 Click and drag to select the text.

2 Click **Text**.

3 Click **Font**.

4 Click a list of fonts.

Note: A font must be installed on the user's computer to display in the browser. A list specifies alternate styles if the user does not have certain fonts installed.

How are fonts categorized?

The two most common categories of fonts are *serif* fonts and *sans-serif* fonts. Serif fonts are distinguished by the decorations on the ends of their lines. Common serif fonts include Times New Roman, Palatino, and Garamond. Sans-serif fonts lack these decorations. Common sans-serif fonts include Arial, Verdana, and Helvetica.

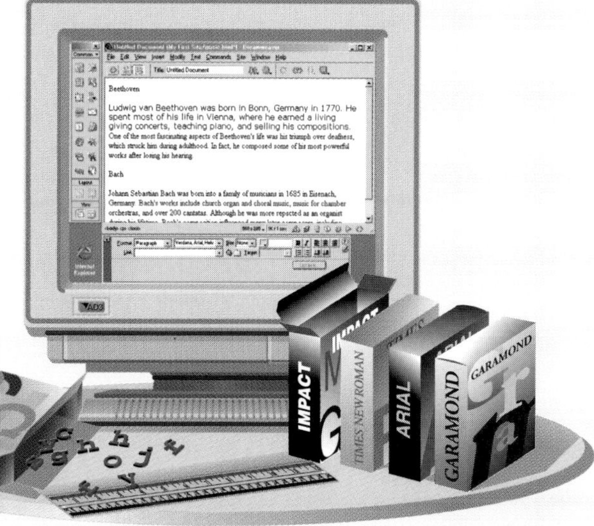

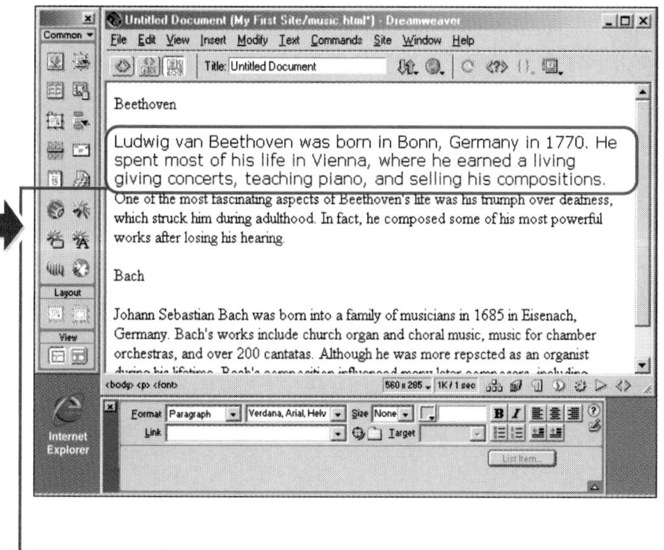

■ The text changes to the new font.

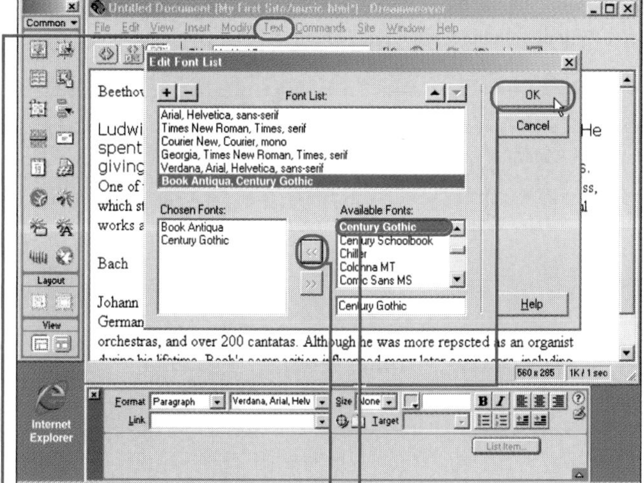

ADD AN ENTRY TO THE FONT MENU

1 Repeat steps 2 and 3 from the facing page and then click **Edit Font List** from the Text submenu.

■ The fonts installed on your computer appears in the Available Fonts list.

2 Click a font.

3 Click «.

■ Repeat steps 1 to 4 to create an entry that is a list of fonts.

4 Click **OK**.

CREATE BOLD OR ITALIC TEXT

You can emphasize text on your Web page with bold or italic styles.

You can also control the style of text on your Web page using Style Sheets (see Chapter 22.)

CREATE BOLD TEXT

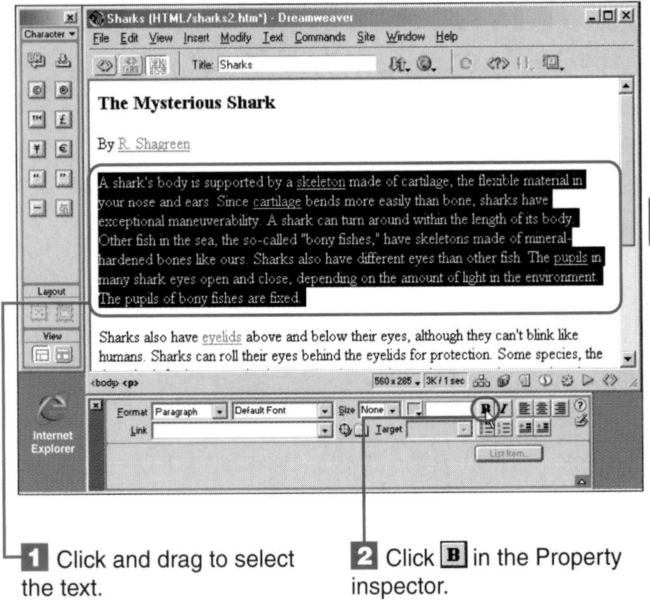

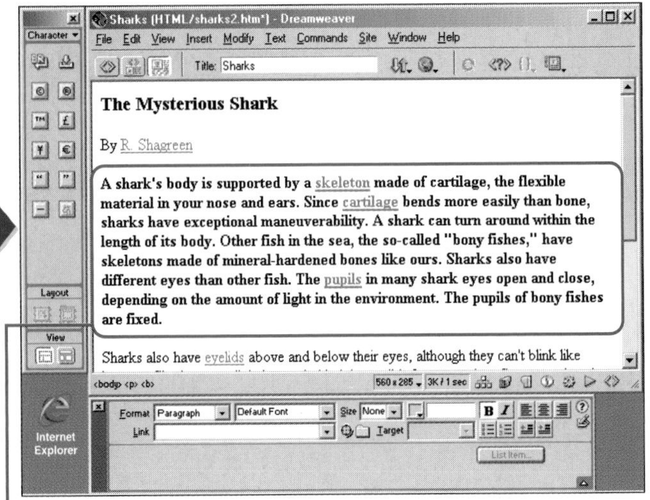

1 Click and drag to select the text.

2 Click **B** in the Property inspector.

■ The bold text has a heavier weight.

What other kinds of styles are available besides bold and italic?

You can create other styles of text besides bold and italic using commands in the **Text** and **Style** menus. The styles include Underline, Strikethrough, and Teletype (typewriter style). Many of the styles listed in the Style menu produce effects identical to bold or italic.

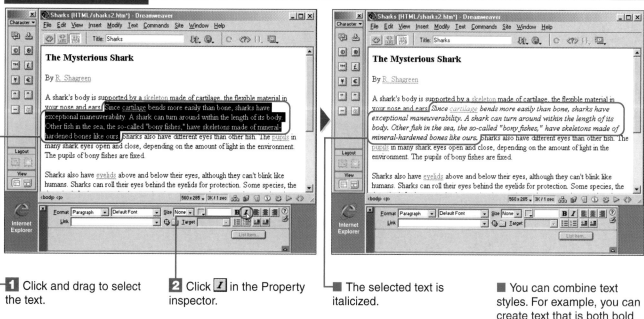

CREATE ITALIC TEXT

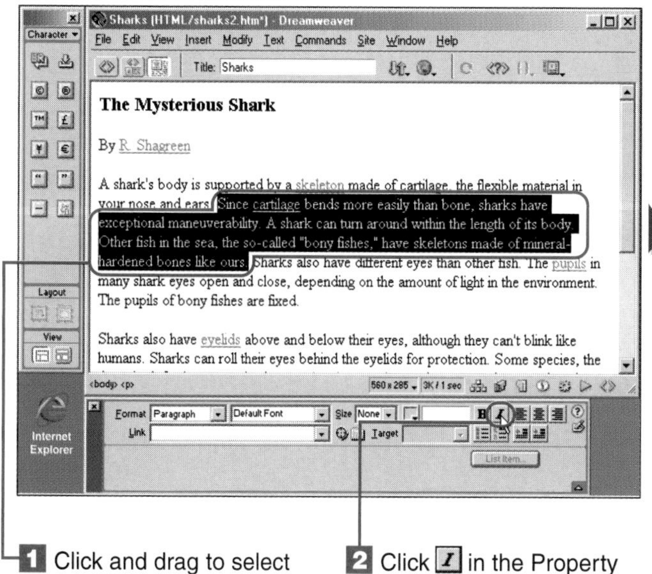

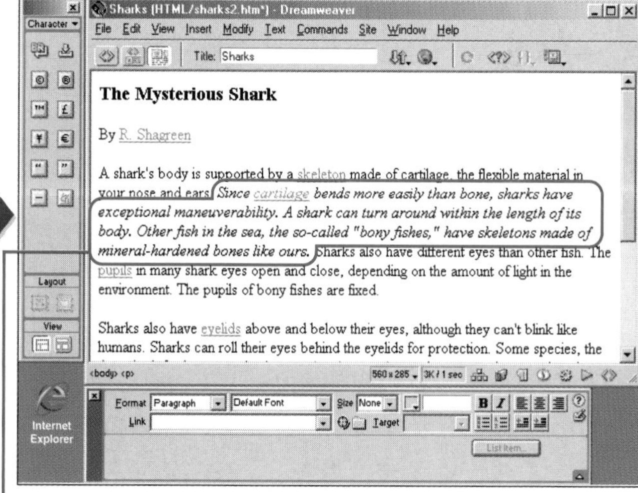

1 Click and drag to select the text.

2 Click *I* in the Property inspector.

■ The selected text is italicized.

■ You can combine text styles. For example, you can create text that is both bold and italic.

INSERT AN IMAGE INTO A WEB PAGE

Different types of images, including clip art, digital camera images, and scanned photos, can be inserted into your Web page. Many of these images can be created and edited using Fireworks.

You can also place a colored border around your image once it is on the page.

INSERT AN IMAGE INTO A WEB PAGE

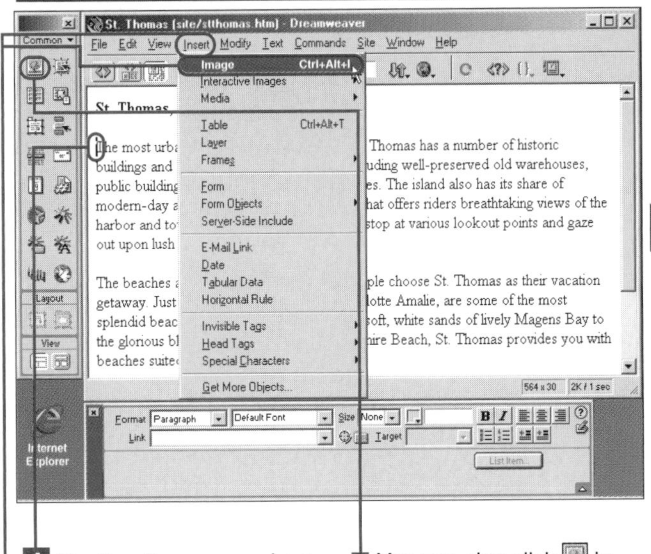

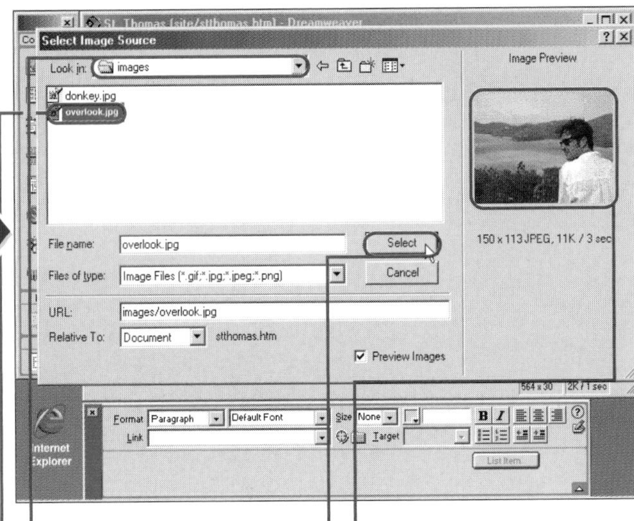

1 Position the cursor where you want to insert the image.

2 Click **Insert**.

3 Click **Image**.

■ You can also click [icon] in the Objects panel.

■ The Select Image Source dialog box appears.

4 Click [▾] to select the folder containing the image.

5 Click the image file that you want to insert into your Web page.

Note: Most Web image files will end in `.gif` *(for GIF files) or* `.jpg` *(for JPEG files).*

■ A preview of the image appears.

Note: If you want to insert an image that exists at an external Web address, you can type the address into the URL field.

6 Click **Select**.

What are the file formats for Web images?

The majority of the images you see on Web pages are GIF or JPEG files. Both GIF and JPEG are compressed file formats, which means they excel at storing image information in a small amount of file space. GIF is best for flat-color illustrations and other images that contain a limited number of colors (it only supports a maximum of 256 colors in an image). JPEG excels at storing photographic information (it supports millions of colors in an image). You insert GIF and JPEG files into your Web page by using the steps described on page 88.

JPEG

GIF

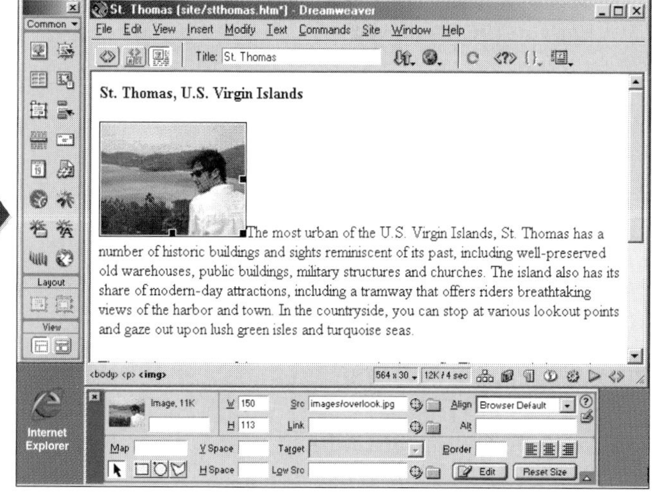

■ The image appears where you positioned your cursor in the Web page.

■ To delete an image, click the image and press Delete.

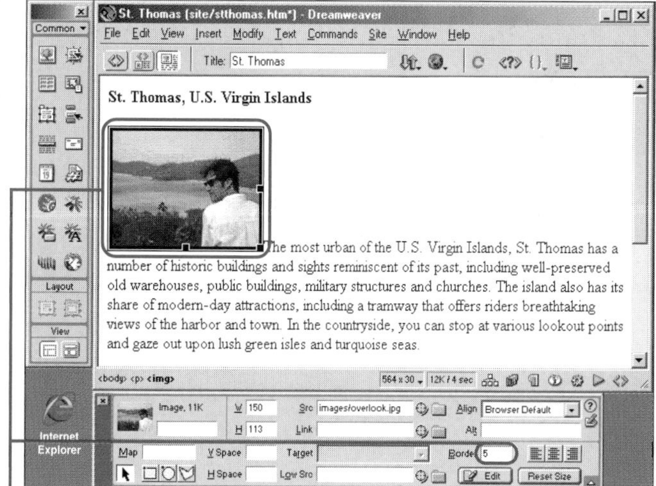

ADD A BORDER TO AN IMAGE

1 Click the image to select it.

2 Type the width (in pixels) into the Border field.

3 Press Enter (Return).

■ A border appears around the image in the same color the same as the text.

Aligning the image to one side of a Web page allows you to wrap text around it. Wrapping text around images enables you to fit more information onto the screen and gives your Web pages a more professional look.

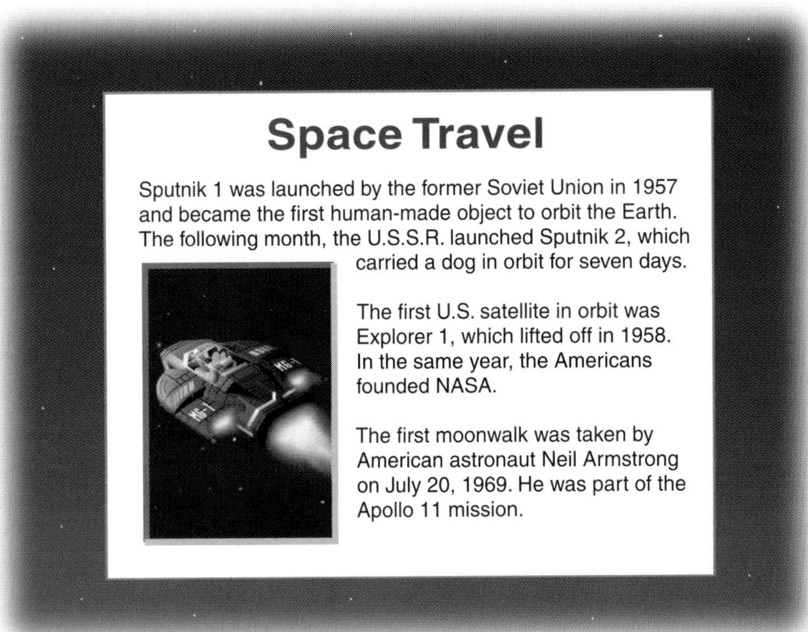

Space Travel
Sputnik 1 was launched by the former Soviet Union in 1957 and became the first human-made object to orbit the Earth. The following month, the U.S.S.R. launched Sputnik 2, which carried a dog in orbit for seven days.
The first U.S. satellite in orbit was Explorer 1, which lifted off in 1958. In the same year, the Americans founded NASA.
The first moonwalk was taken by American astronaut Neil Armstrong on July 20, 1969. He was part of the Apollo 11 mission.

WRAP TEXT AROUND AN IMAGE

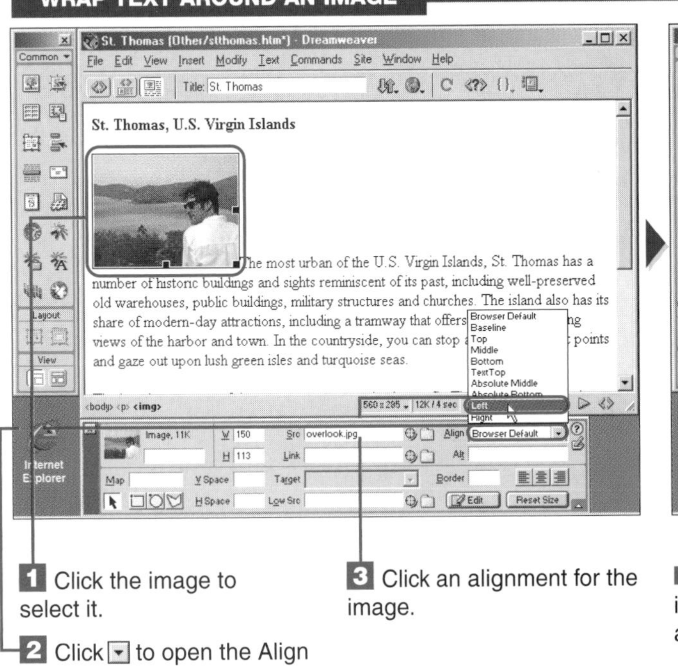

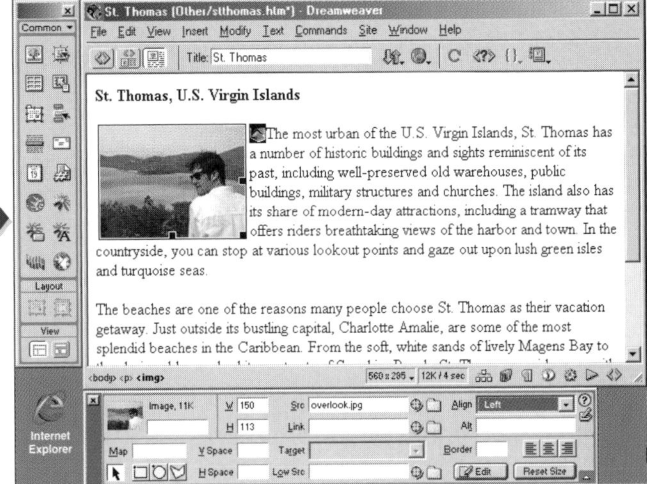

1 Click the image to select it.

2 Click ▾ to open the Align drop-down menu.

3 Click an alignment for the image.

■ The text flows around the image according to the alignment you selected.

■ In this example, text flows to the right of the left-aligned image.

How can I tell how much file space my images and text are taking up on my Web page?

The total size of your page appears in kilobytes (K) on the status bar. The total size includes the size of your HTML file, the size of your images, and the size of anything else on the page. Next to the size is the estimated download time for the page. You can specify how Dreamweaver estimates the download speed in your Preferences. (See "Set Preferences" in Chapter 2.)

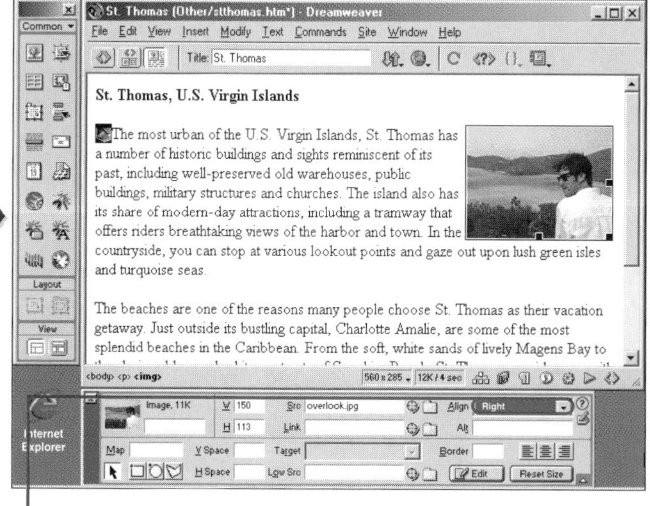

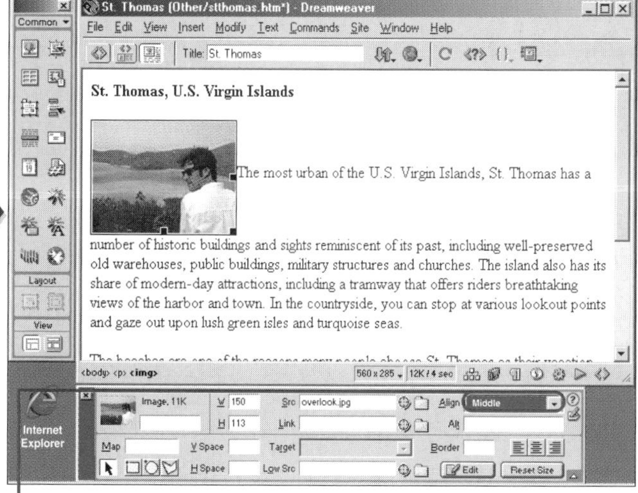

■ You can select other options from the Align drop-down menu for different wrapping effects (example: **Right Align**).

■ In this example, text flows to to the left of the right-aligned image.

■ In this example, the image has been middle-aligned on the page.

CHANGE THE SIZE OF AN IMAGE

You can resize an image for your Web page to make it fit better. Three methods for doing this are changing the image's pixel dimensions; clicking and dragging the corner of an image; and changing the image's proportional size.

CHANGE THE SIZE OF AN IMAGE

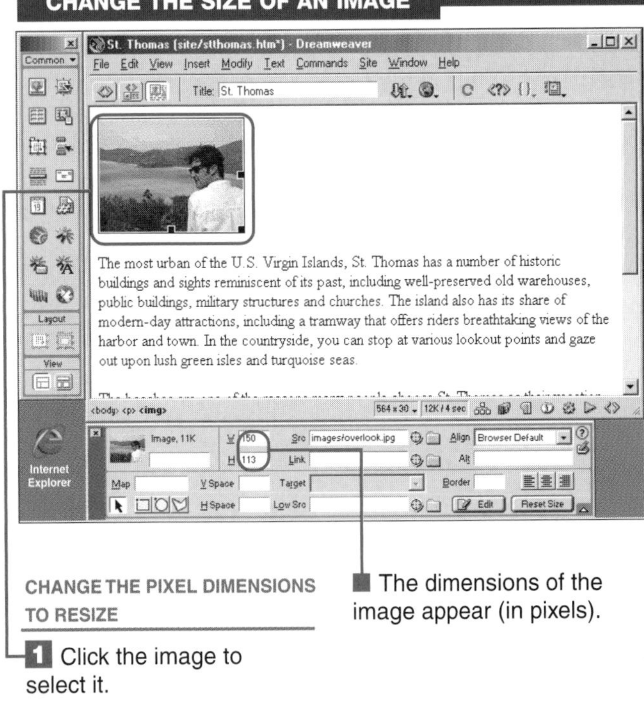

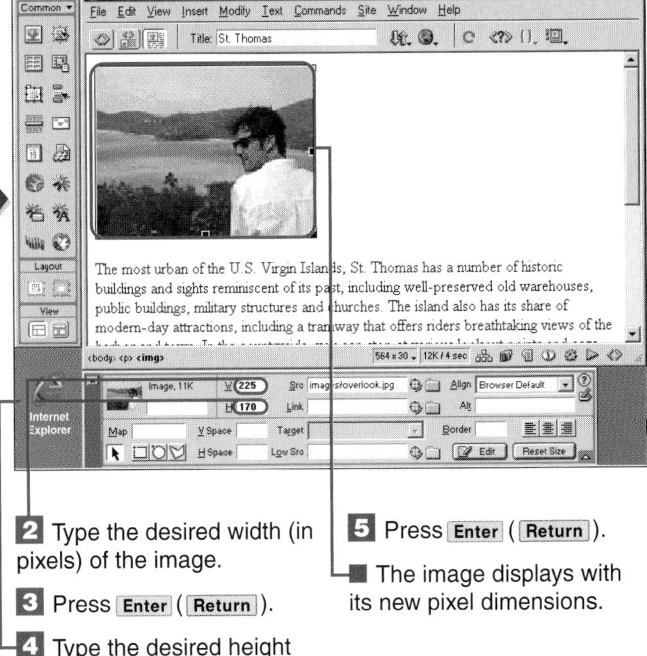

CHANGE THE PIXEL DIMENSIONS TO RESIZE

1 Click the image to select it.

■ The dimensions of the image appear (in pixels).

2 Type the desired width (in pixels) of the image.

3 Press Enter (Return).

4 Type the desired height (in pixels) of the image.

5 Press Enter (Return).

■ The image displays with its new pixel dimensions.

What is the best way to change the dimensions of a Web-page image?

The best way to change the dimensions of a Web-page image is by using Fireworks, which enables you to adjust the image's real height and width and save it as a new file. This maximizes the quality of the image and minimizes the image's file size.

Using Dreamweaver to change the image size stretches or shrinks the original image to fit the new dimensions, but does not change the real dimensions of the file. Sometimes this results in an image on a Web page that has reduced quality compared to the original.

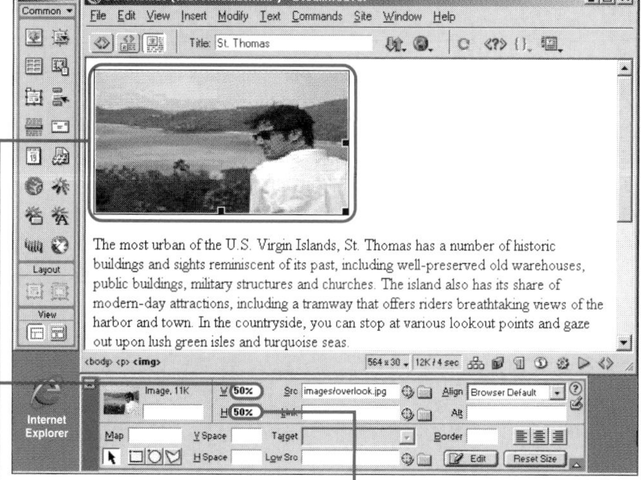

CLICK AND DRAG TO RESIZE

1 Click the image to select it.

2 Drag the handle at the edge of the image.

■ To constrain proportions, press and hold Shift as you drag a corner.

■ The image expands or contracts to its new dimensions.

CHANGE THE PROPORTIONAL SIZE TO RESIZE

1 Click the image to select it.

2 Type the desired percentage of the width.

3 Press Enter (Return).

4 Type the desired percentage of the height.

5 Press Enter (Return).

■ The image displays as a percentage of the browser window (not as a percentage of its original size).

ADD A BACKGROUND IMAGE

You can incorporate a background image to add texture to your Web page. Background images appear beneath any text or images on your page. These images can be easily created using Fireworks.

ADD A BACKGROUND IMAGE

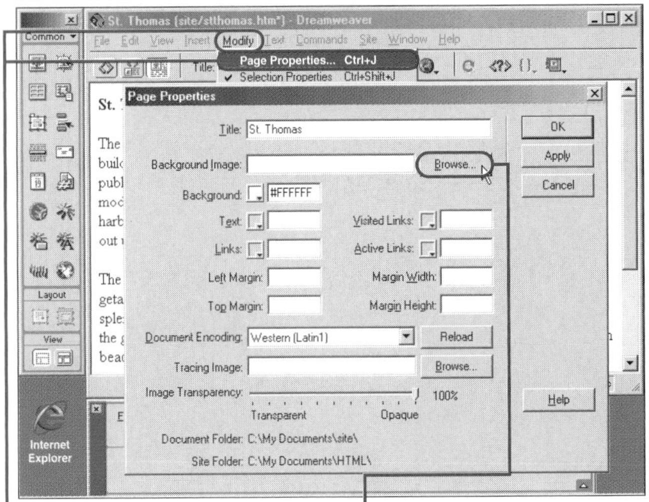

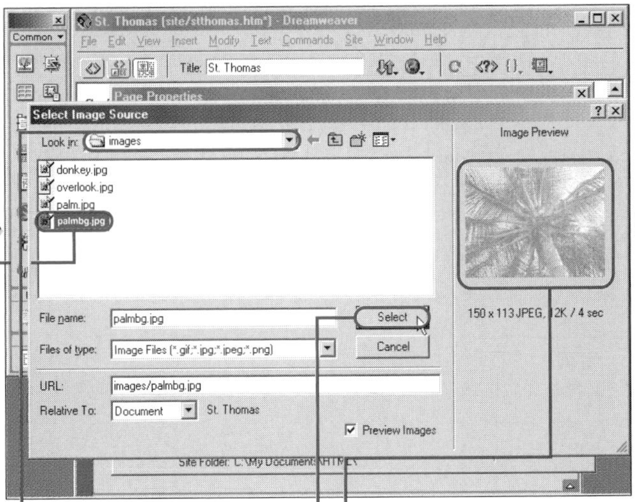

1 Click **Modify**.

2 Click **Page Properties** to open the Page Properties dialog box.

3 Click **Browse** to open the Select Image Source dialog box.

4 Click ▾ to select the folder containing the background image file.

5 Click the background image that you want to insert.

■ A preview image appears.

6 Click **Select**.

What types of images make good backgrounds?

Typically, images that do not clash with the text and other content in the foreground make good background images. You do not want your background image to overwhelm the rest of the page.

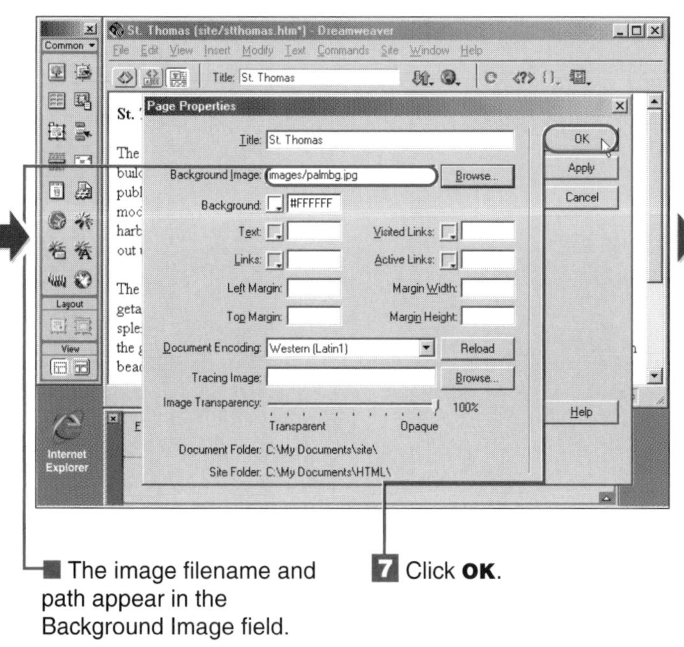

■ The image filename and path appear in the Background Image field.

7 Click **OK**.

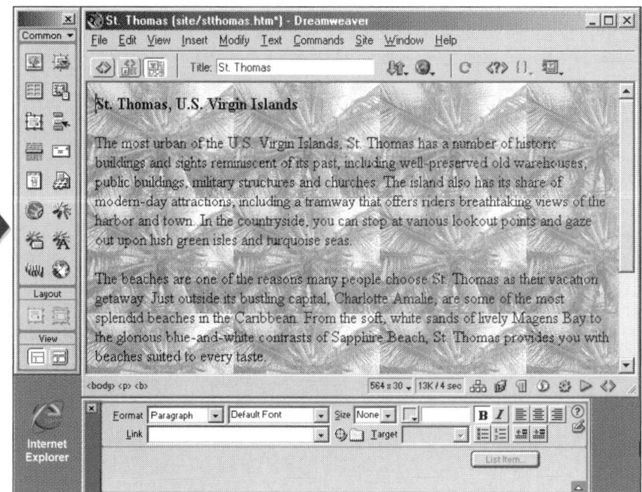

■ The image appears as a background on the Web page.

Note: If necessary, the image tiles horizontally and vertically to fill the entire window.

INSERT MULTIMEDIA

You can insert video clips and other multimedia to add life to your Web page. These include adding animations created with Flash, such as spinning logos or mini-movies.

INSERT MULTIMEDIA

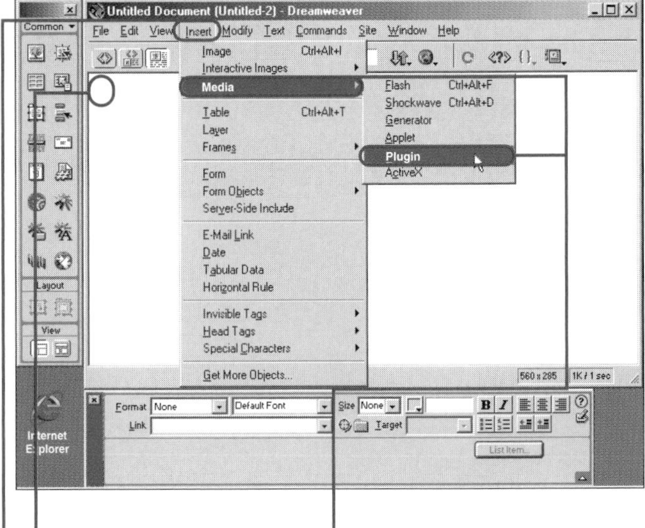

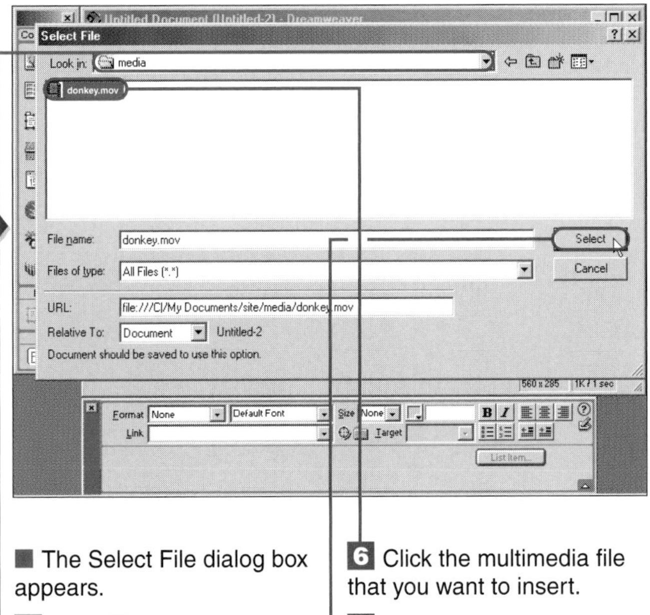

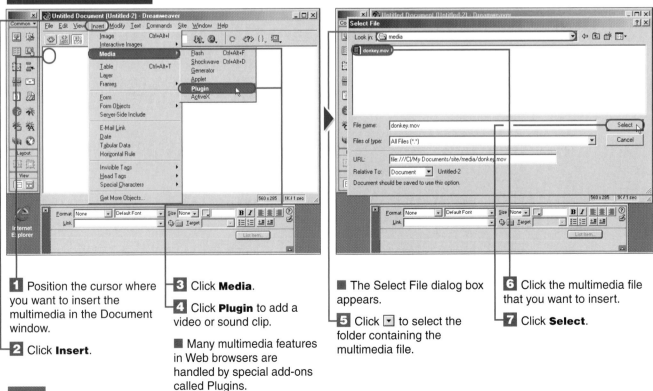

1 Position the cursor where you want to insert the multimedia in the Document window.

2 Click **Insert**.

3 Click **Media**.

4 Click **Plugin** to add a video or sound clip.

■ Many multimedia features in Web browsers are handled by special add-ons called Plugins.

■ The Select File dialog box appears.

5 Click ▾ to select the folder containing the multimedia file.

6 Click the multimedia file that you want to insert.

7 Click **Select**.

What should I consider when adding multimedia content to my site?

You can add video clips, sounds and interactive features such as Flash to jazz up a Web site. But remember that some users will not be able to view the content because their browsers do not support it and that some users are unwilling to spend the time to download and install a Plugin.

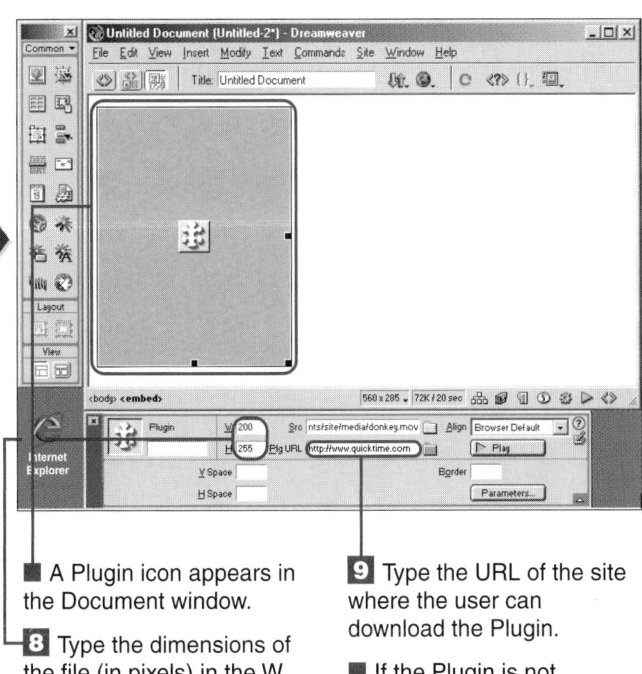

■ A Plugin icon appears in the Document window.

8 Type the dimensions of the file (in pixels) in the W (width) and H (height) fields.

9 Type the URL of the site where the user can download the Plugin.

■ If the Plugin is not installed on a user's browser, the browser will ask if the user wants to visit the site to download the Plugin.

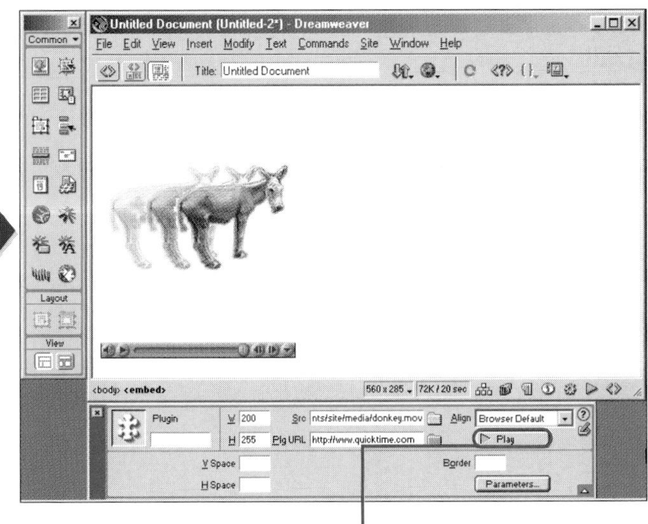

■ You can test some multimedia files, such as QuickTime movies, in the Document window.

10 Click Play to test the multimedia file.

CREATE HYPERLINKS TO OTHER PAGES ON YOUR WEB SITE

You can create a hyperlink that allows readers to move from one page of your Web site to another. Once the link is in place you can view the linked page in Dreamweaver.

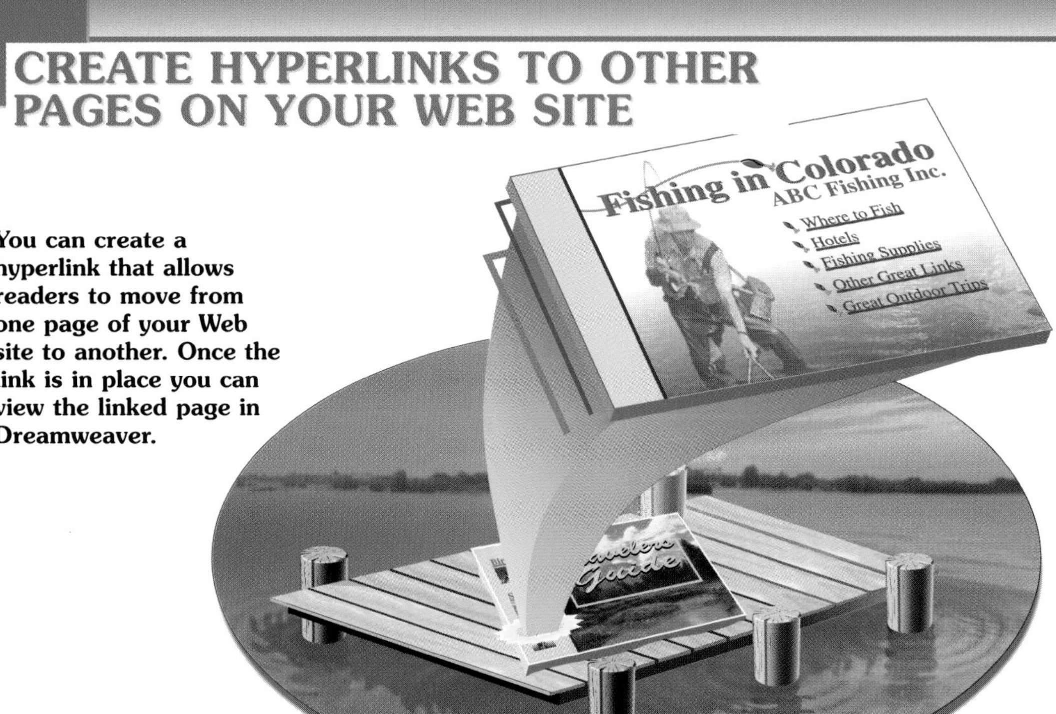

HYPERLINK TO ANOTHER PAGE ON YOUR SITE

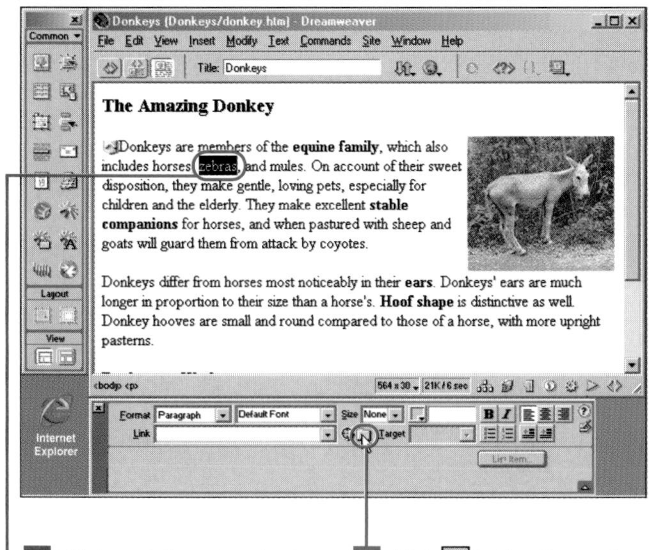

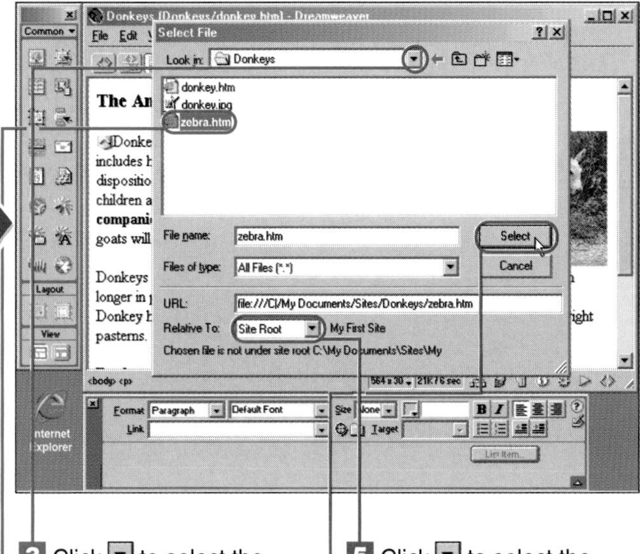

1 Click and drag to select the text that you want to turn into a hyperlink.

2 Click [folder icon] in the Properties Inspector to open the Select File dialog box.

3 Click [drop-down arrow] to select the folder containing the destination page.

4 From the list menu, click the HTML file to which you want to link.

5 Click [drop-down arrow] to select the type of link path (document-relative or root-relative).

6 Click **Select**.

How should I organize the files that make up my Web site?

You should keep the files that make up your Web site in the folder that you define as your local site folder (see Chapter 14). This makes creating links between your pages easier and ensures that all the links work correctly when you transfer the files to a live Web server (see Chapter 24).

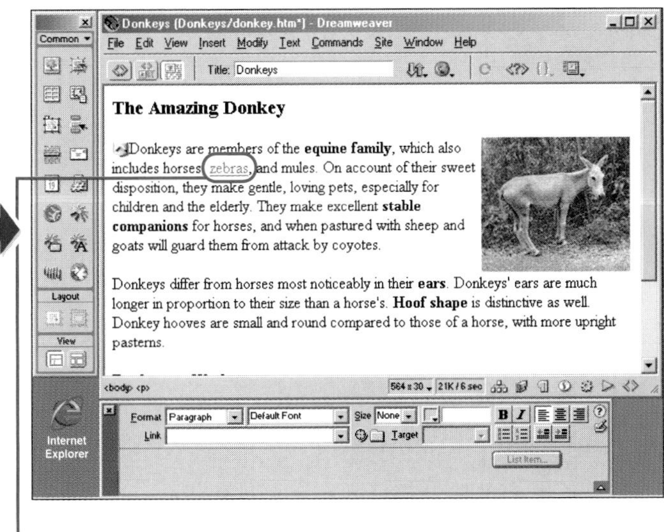

■ The new hyperlink appears in color and underlined.

■ Hyperlinks are not clickable in the Document window.

■ You can also test the link by previewing the file in a Web browser.

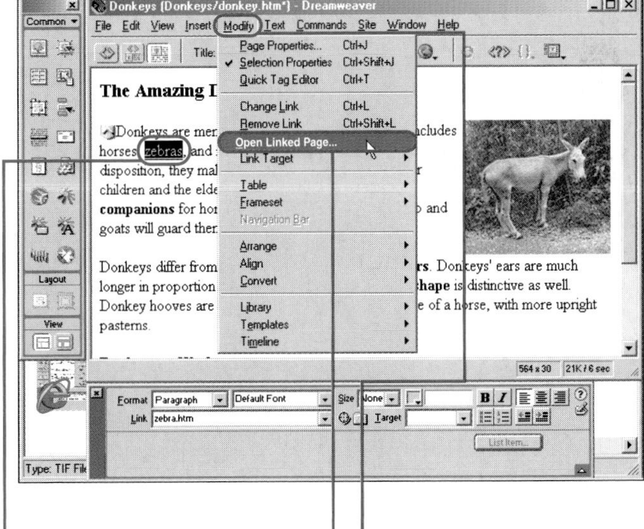

OPEN THE LINKED PAGE

1 Click and drag to select the text of the hyperlink whose destination you want to open.

2 Click **Modify**.

3 Click **Open Linked Page**.

■ The link destination opens in a Document window.

CREATE HYPERLINKS TO ANOTHER WEB SITE

You can give viewers access to additional information about topics by linking to pages in other Web sites.

HYPERLINK TO ANOTHER WEB SITE

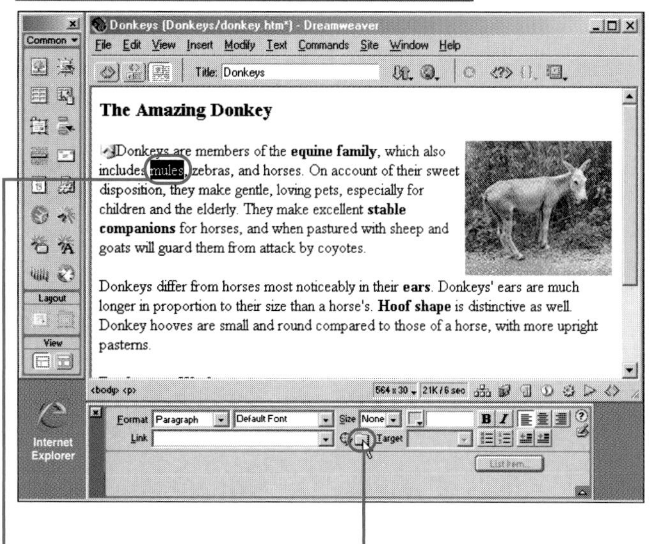

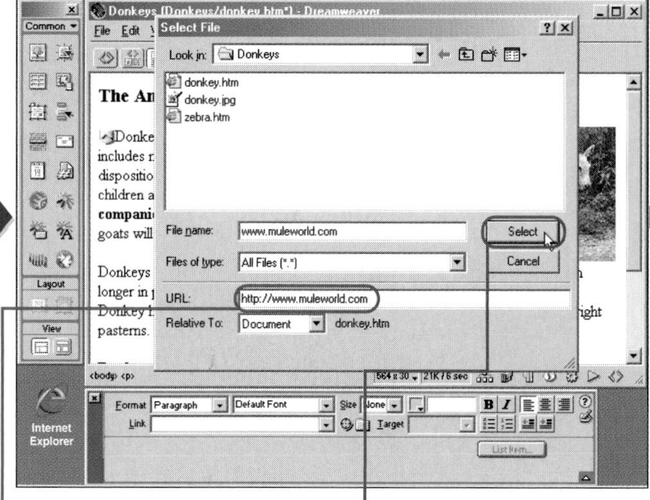

1 Click and drag to select the text that you want to turn into a hyperlink.

2 Click in the Properties Inspector to open the Select File dialog box.

3 Type the Web address of the destination page (include the **http://**) in the URL field.

4 Click **Select**.

How do I make sure my links to other Web sites always work?

You usually have no control over the Web pages on other sites to which you have linked. If you have linked to a Web page whose file is later renamed or taken offline, your viewer will receive an error message when they click the link. Maintain your site by periodically testing your links.

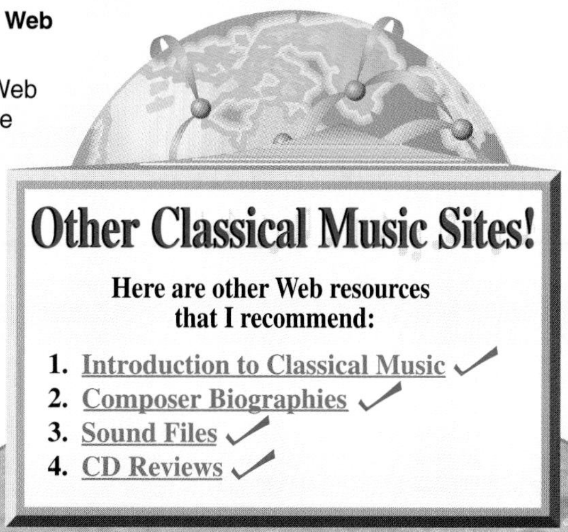

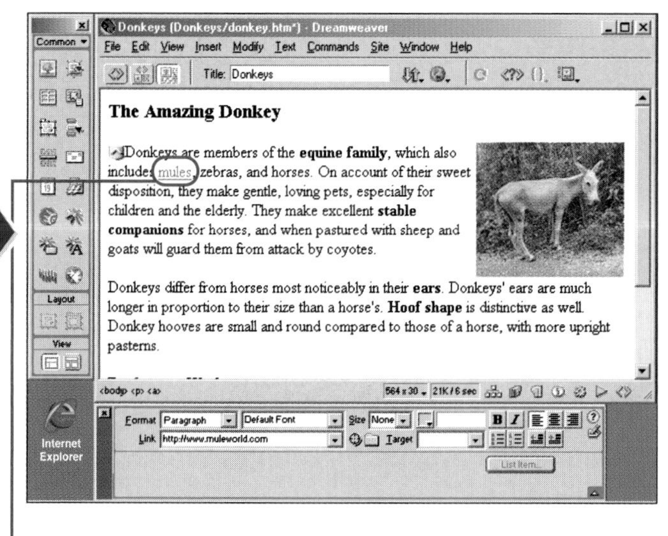

■ The new hyperlink appears colored and underlined.

■ Hyperlinks are not clickable in the Document window.

■ You can test the link by previewing the file in a Web browser.

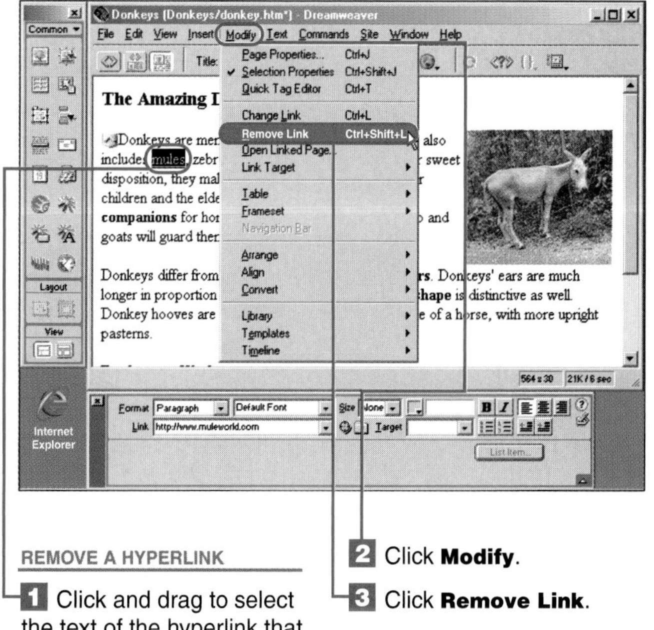

REMOVE A HYPERLINK

1 Click and drag to select the text of the hyperlink that you want to remove.

2 Click **Modify**.

3 Click **Remove Link**.

An image hyperlink allows users to click an image to go to another Web page. You can use Fireworks to create these images for your Web site.

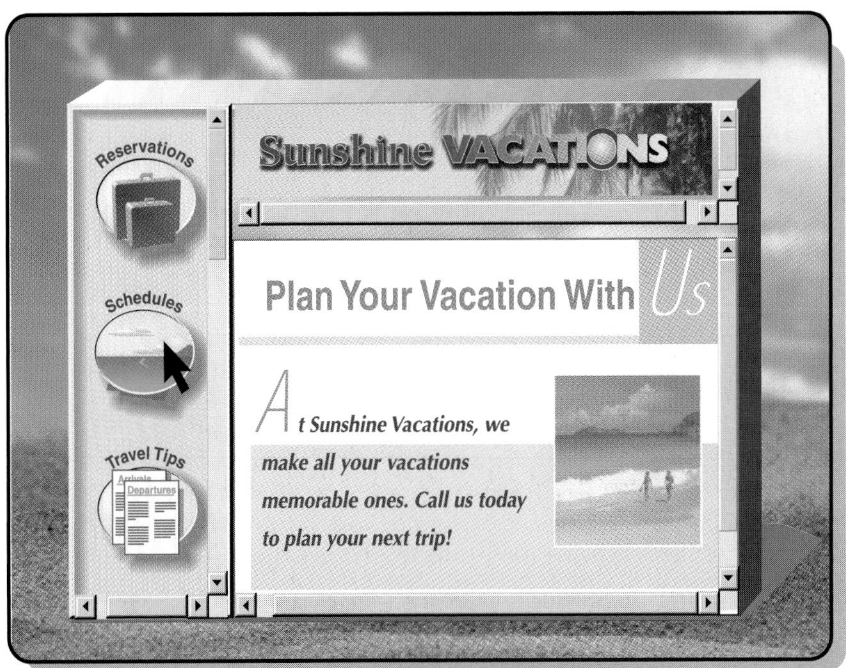

CREATE IMAGE HYPERLINKS

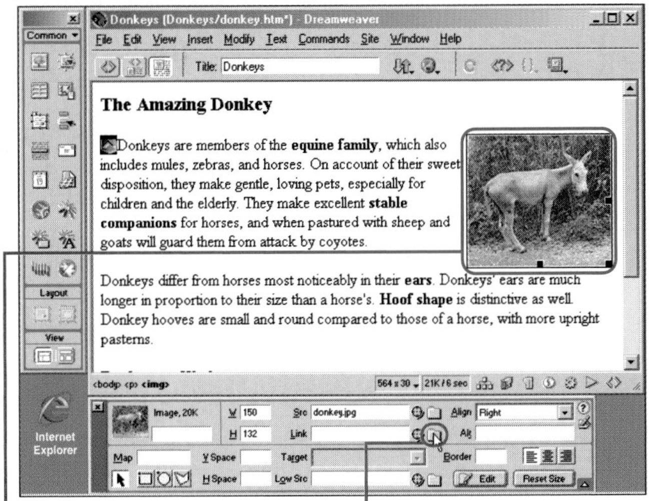

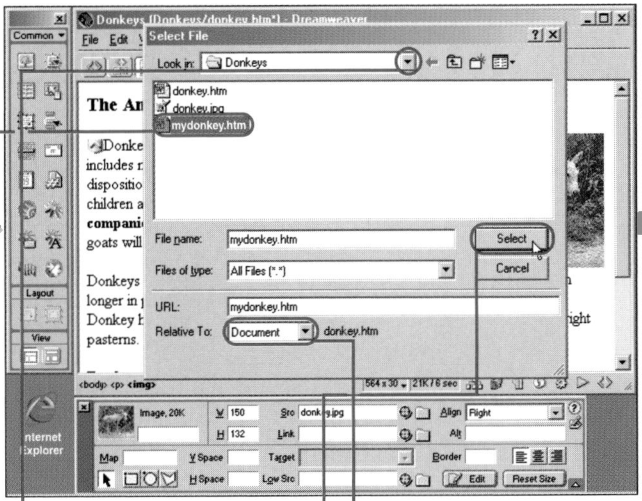

CREATE AN IMAGE HYPERLINK

1. Click the image that you want to make into a hyperlink.
2. Click [folder icon] in the Properties inspector to open the Select File dialog box.
3. Click [▼] to select the folder containing the destination page.
4. From the list menu, click the HTML file to which you want to link.
5. Click [▼] to select the type of link path (document-relative or root-relative).
6. Click **Select**.

How do I create a navigation bar for my Web page?

Many Web sites include a set of hyperlink buttons on the top, side, or bottom of each page. These buttons let viewers navigate to the main pages of the Web site. You can create these buttons using image-editing software such as Macromedia Fireworks.

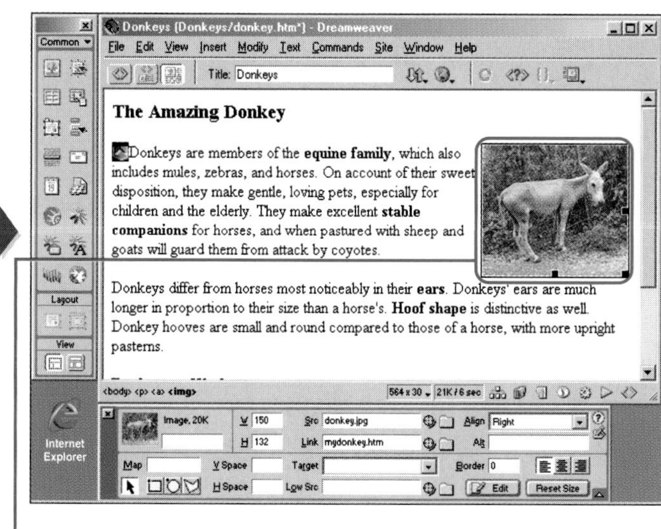

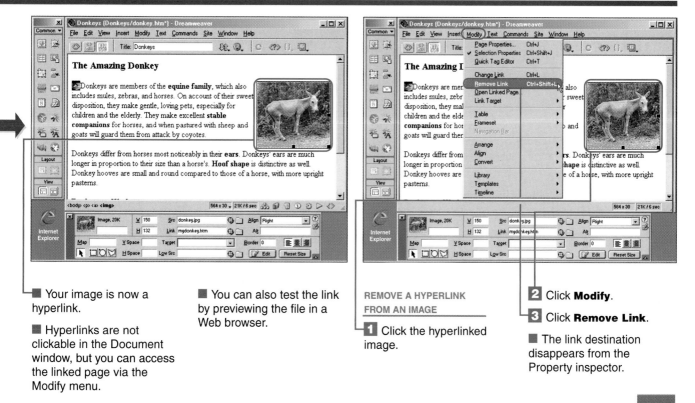

■ Your image is now a hyperlink.

■ Hyperlinks are not clickable in the Document window, but you can access the linked page via the Modify menu.

■ You can also test the link by previewing the file in a Web browser.

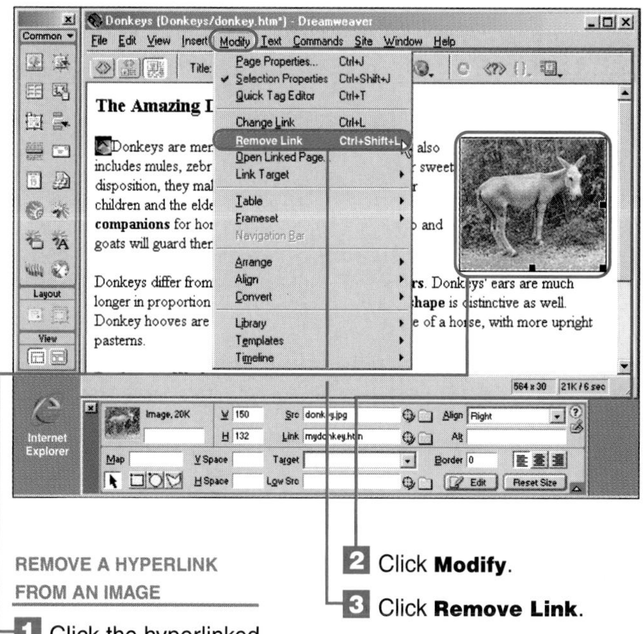

REMOVE A HYPERLINK FROM AN IMAGE

1 Click the hyperlinked image.

2 Click **Modify**.

3 Click **Remove Link**.

■ The link destination disappears from the Property inspector.

CREATE HYPERLINKS TO CONTENT ON THE SAME WEB PAGE

You can create a hyperlink to other content on the same Web page. Same-page hyperlinks are useful when a page is very long.

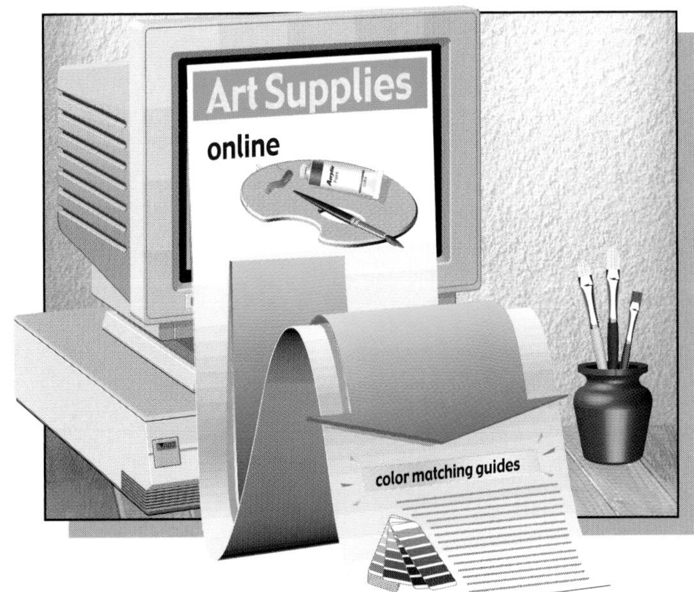

HYPERLINK TO CONTENT ON THE SAME WEB PAGE

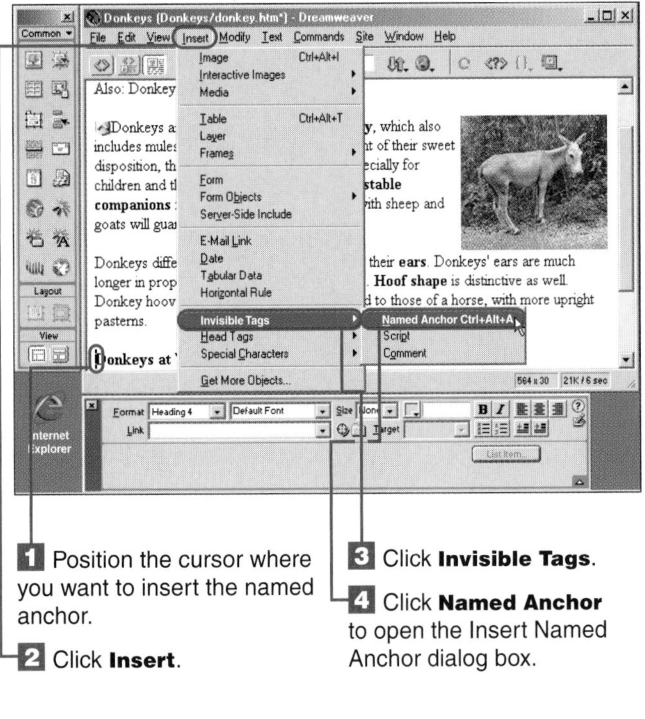

1 Position the cursor where you want to insert the named anchor.

2 Click **Insert**.

3 Click **Invisible Tags**.

4 Click **Named Anchor** to open the Insert Named Anchor dialog box.

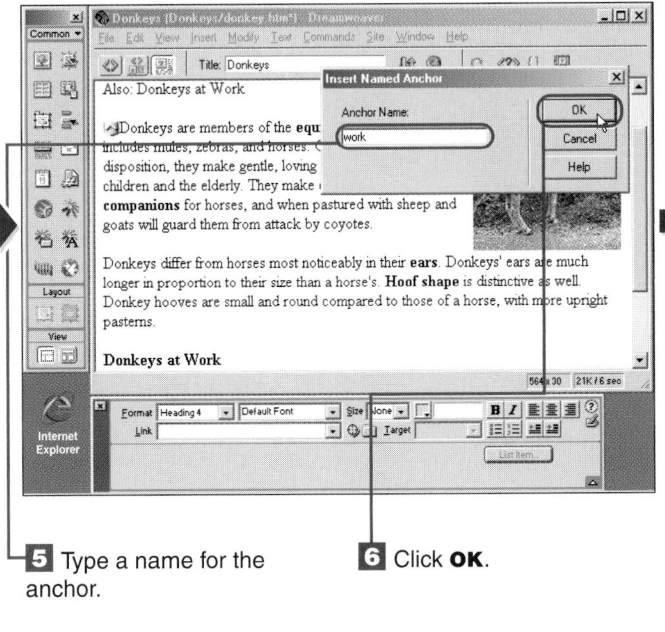

5 Type a name for the anchor.

6 Click **OK**.

How can I use same-page hyperlinks?

If you have a Web page that is a glossary, same-page links let you link to different parts of the glossary from a hyperlink menu at the top of the page.

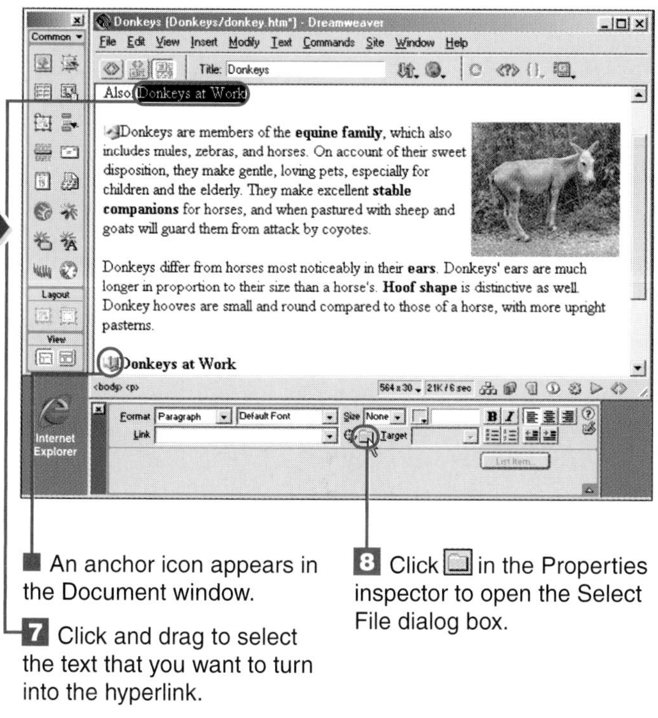

■ An anchor icon appears in the Document window.

7 Click and drag to select the text that you want to turn into the hyperlink.

8 Click ▭ in the Properties inspector to open the Select File dialog box.

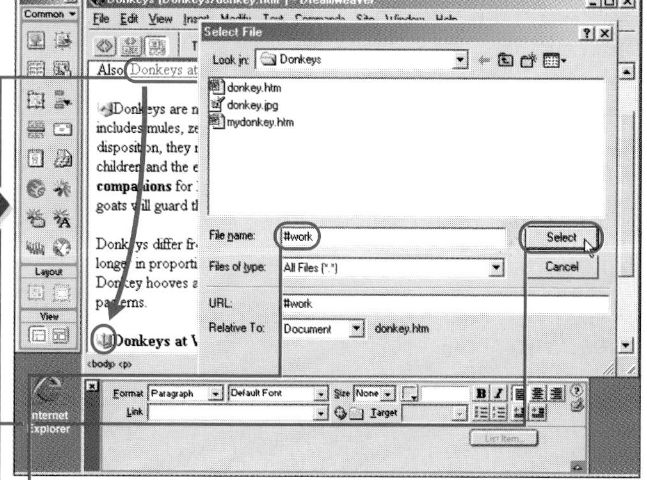

9 Type a pound sign (#) followed by the name of the anchor.

10 Click **Select**.

■ The new hyperlink links to the named anchor.

■ The new hyperlink is not clickable in the Document window.

■ You can test the link by previewing the file in a Web browser.

CREATE HYPERLINKS TO OTHER FILES

Hyperlinks do not have to lead just to other Web pages. You can link to other file types, such as Fireworks image files, word processing documents, or Flash multimedia files.

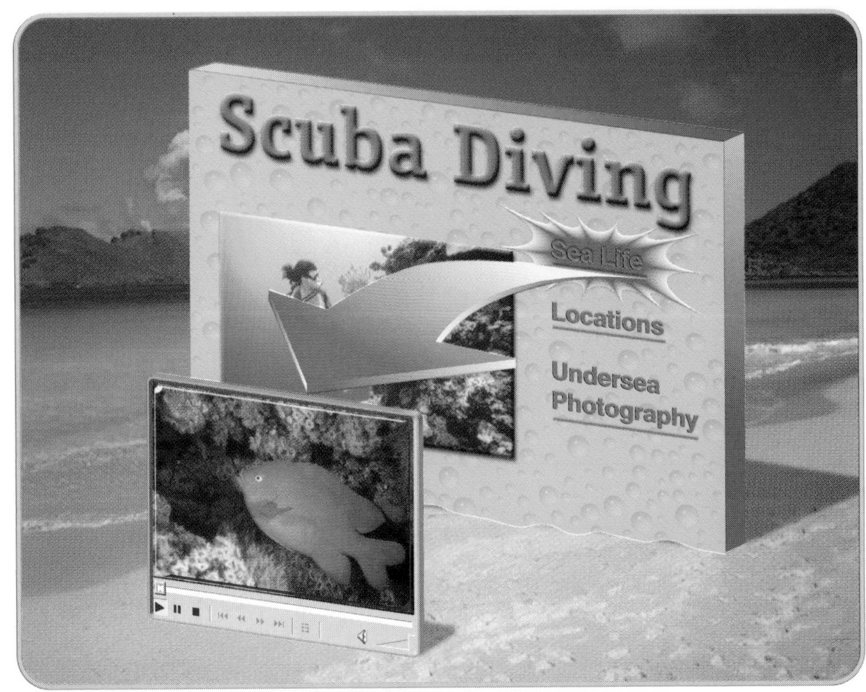

HYPERLINK TO OTHER FILES

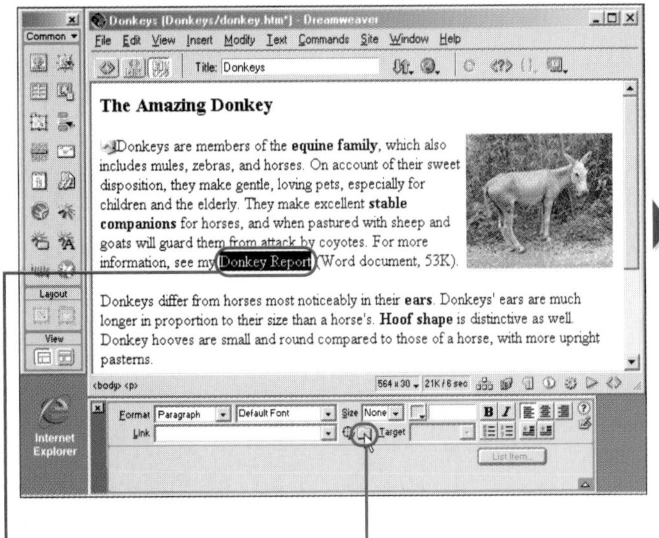

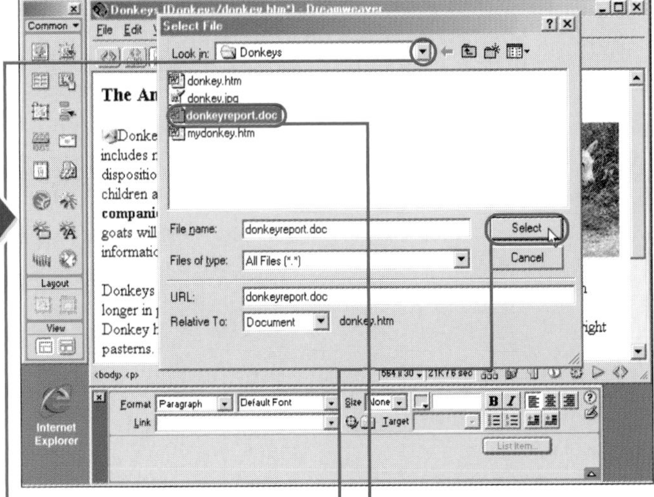

1 Click and drag to select the text that you want to turn into the hyperlink.

2 Click in the Properties inspector to open the Select File dialog box.

3 Click to select the folder containing the destination file.

4 From the list menu, click the file to which you want to link.

5 Click **Select**.

How do users see files that are not HTML documents?

What users see when they click links to other types of files depends on how their Web browser is configured and what applications they have on their computer. For instance, if you link to a Flash movie, users need to have Flash plug-in software installed on their computer to see the movie. If a user does not have the software installed, the browser typically asks if the user wants to download the file and save it so they can view it later (after they have installed the correct software).

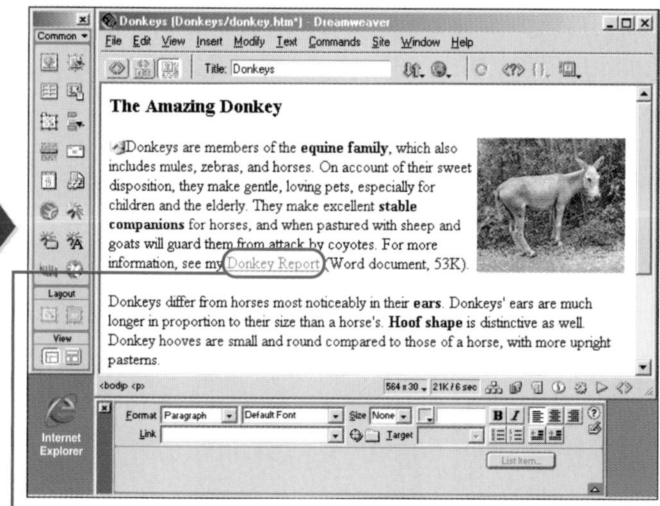

■ The new hyperlink appears in color and underlined.

■ Hyperlinks are not clickable in the Document window.

■ You can test the link by previewing the file in a Web browser.

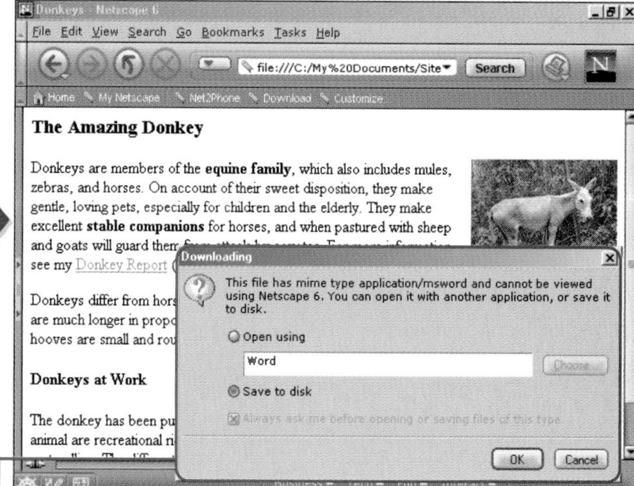

■ The particular browser is not configured to view the type of file that was linked. When you click a Web page link in a browser, an alert box appears asking whether the user wants to open the document with another application or save it.

INSERT A TABLE INTO YOUR WEB PAGE

You can organize content into columns and rows by inserting tables into your Web page. A default table has table borders but you can turn these off, making them invisible.

Team	Games	Wins	Losses	Ties	Points
The Chargers	10	9	1	0	18
Sluggers	10	8	1	1	17
The Champs	10	7	2	1	15
The Eagles	10	5	5	0	10
Barry's Battalion	10	3	7	0	6
The Professionals	10	2	8	0	4
Baseball Bombers	10	1	9	0	2

INSERT A TABLE

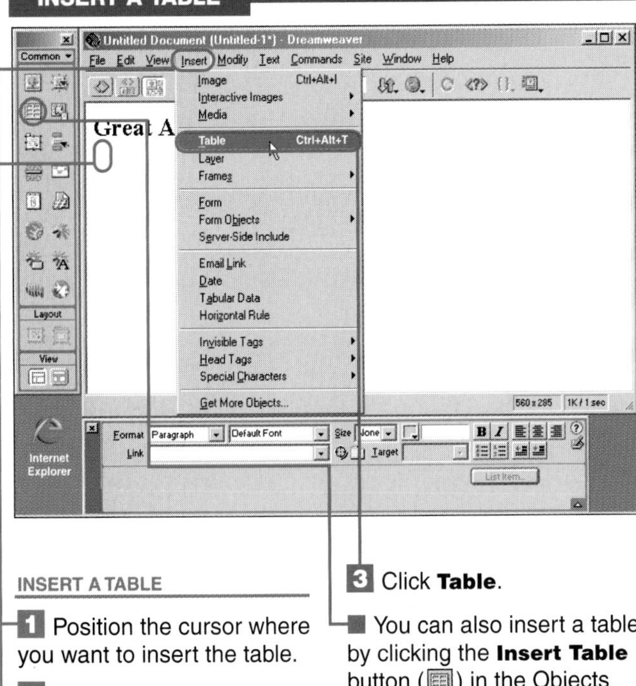

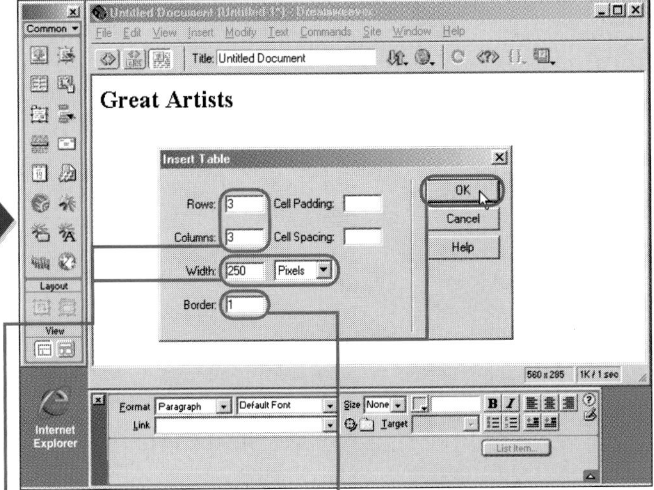

INSERT A TABLE

1 Position the cursor where you want to insert the table.

2 Click **Insert**.

3 Click **Table**.

■ You can also insert a table by clicking the **Insert Table** button (▦) in the Objects panel menu.

■ The Insert Table dialog box appears.

4 Type the number of rows and columns in your table.

5 Type the width of your table.

■ You can set the width in pixels or as a percentage by clicking ▼ and selecting your choice of measurements.

6 Type a border size in pixels.

7 Click **OK**.

How do I change the appearance of the content inside my table?

You can specify the size, style, and color of text inside a table the same way you do outside of a table (see Chapter 15). Likewise, you can control the appearance of an image inside a table the same way you can control it outside a table (see Chapter 16).

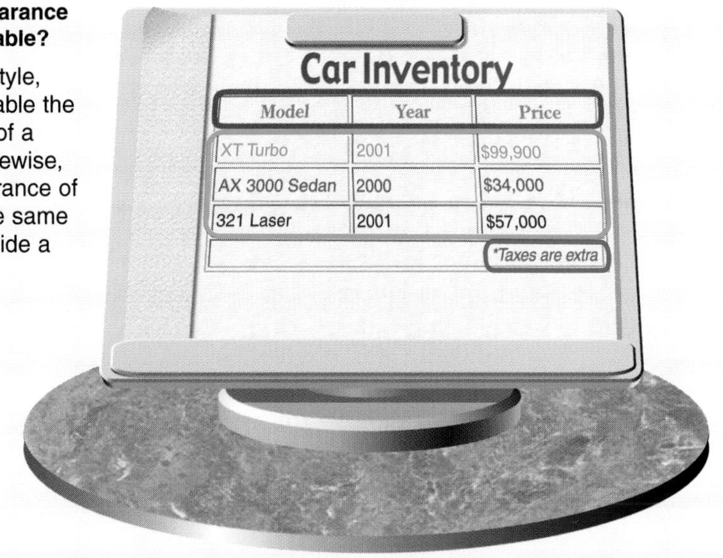

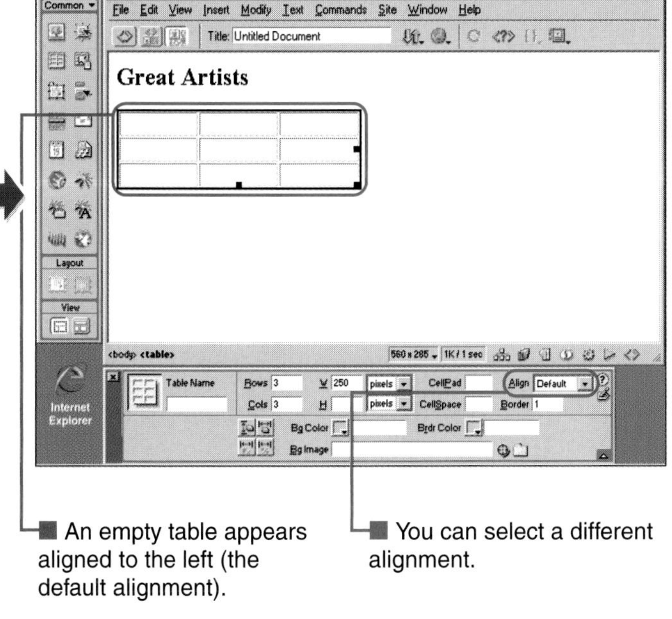

■ An empty table appears aligned to the left (the default alignment).

■ You can select a different alignment.

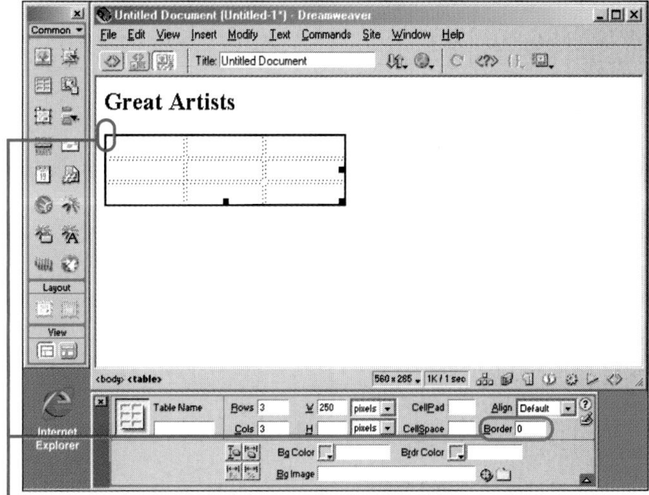

TURN OFF TABLE BORDERS

1 Click the upper-left corner of the table to select it.

2 Type **0** in the Border field.

3 Press Enter (Return).

■ Dashed lines define the turned off borders.

■ The dashed lines do not display when you open the page in a Web browser.

INSERT CONTENT INTO A TABLE

You can fill the cells of your table with text, images, form elements, and other tables.

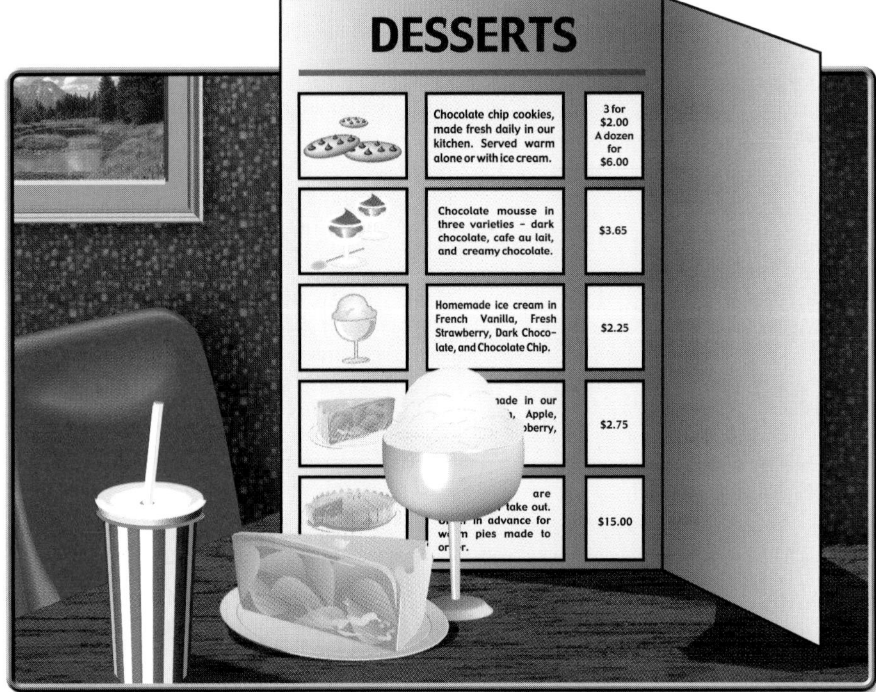

INSERT CONTENT INTO A TABLE

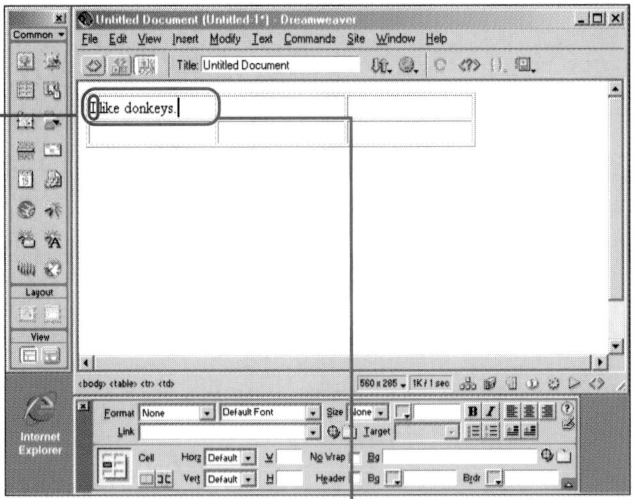

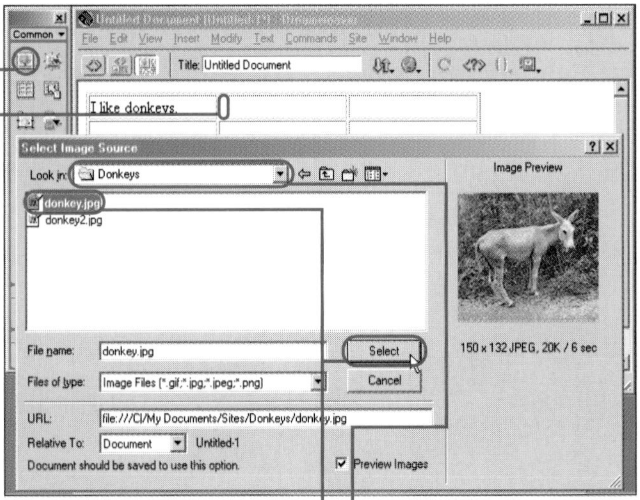

INSERT TEXT

1 Click inside a table cell.

2 Type your text in the cell.

Note: See Chapter 15 for instructions on formatting your text.

INSERT AN IMAGE

1 Click inside a table cell.

2 Click the image button.

3 Click the drop-down arrow to select the folder containing your image.

4 Click the name of your image file.

5 Click **Select**.

How can I add captions to Fireworks images on my Web page?

The best way to add a caption to the top, bottom, or side of a Fireworks image is by creating a two-celled table. Place the image in one cell and the caption in the other. You can then adjust the table's size and alignment to fit the captioned image in with the rest of your page's content.

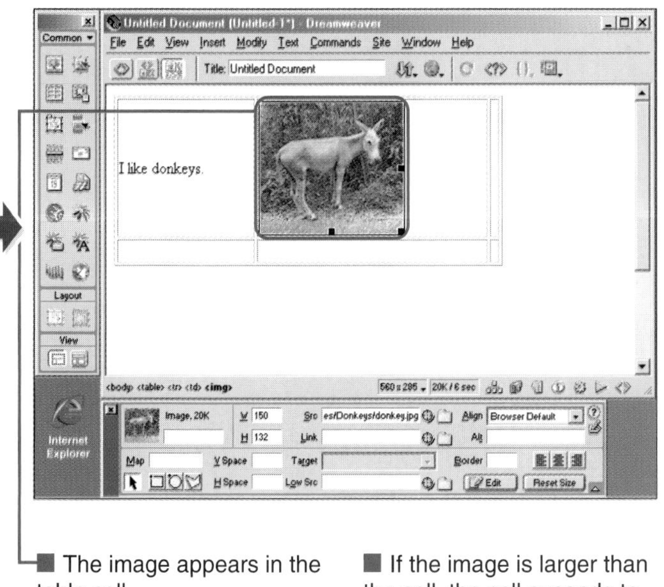

■ The image appears in the table cell.

■ If the image is larger than the cell, the cell expands to accommodate the image.

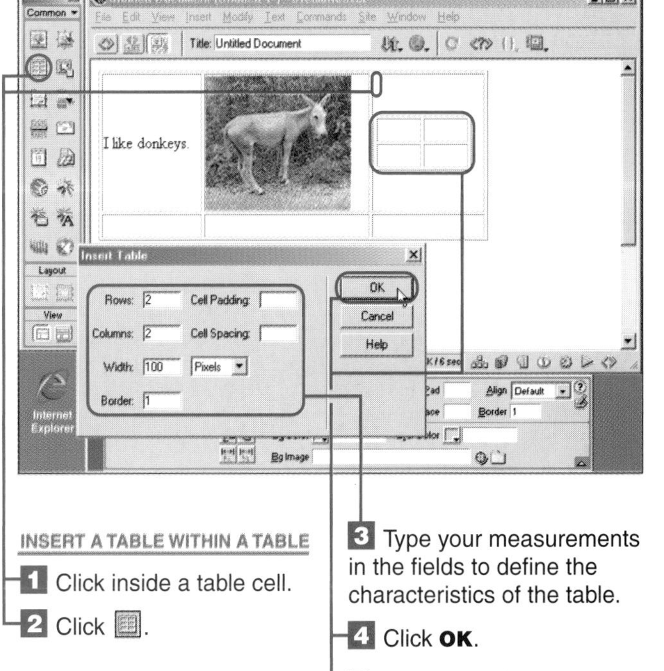

INSERT A TABLE WITHIN A TABLE

1 Click inside a table cell.

2 Click ▦.

3 Type your measurements in the fields to define the characteristics of the table.

4 Click **OK**.

■ The new table appears inside the table cell.

CHANGE THE TABLE BACKGROUND

You can change the table background to complement the style of your Web page. You can change a table's background color or fill the table's background with an image.

CHANGE THE TABLE BACKGROUND

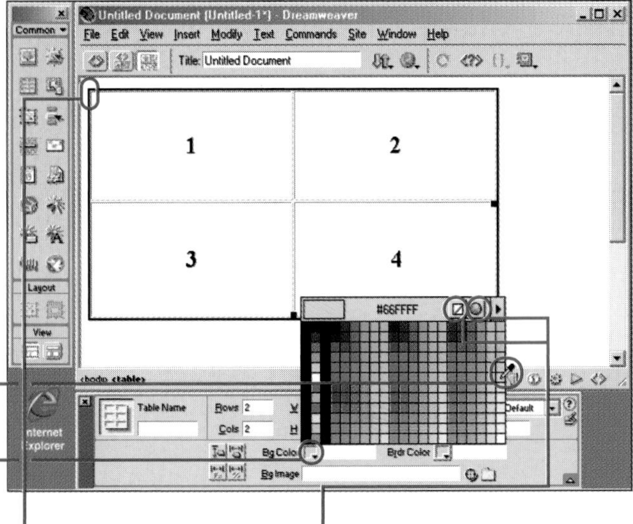

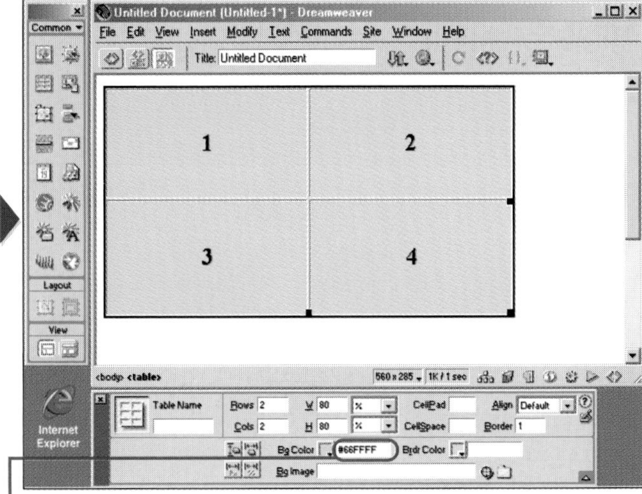

1 Click the upper-left corner of the table to select it.

2 Click **Bg Color** ( ) to open the color menu.

3 Click a color from the menu using the eyedropper tool ( ).

■ You can click the **System Color Picker** button ( ) to select a custom color.

■ You can click the **Default Color** button ( ) to specify no color.

■ The color fills the background of the table.

■ You can also type a color name or a hexadecimal color code directly.

Note: See Chapter 16 for more information on Web color.

How can I change the background of a table cell?

Click inside a cell and then specify the background color using the Bg Color or a background image by clicking .

ADD A BACKGROUND IMAGE TO A TABLE

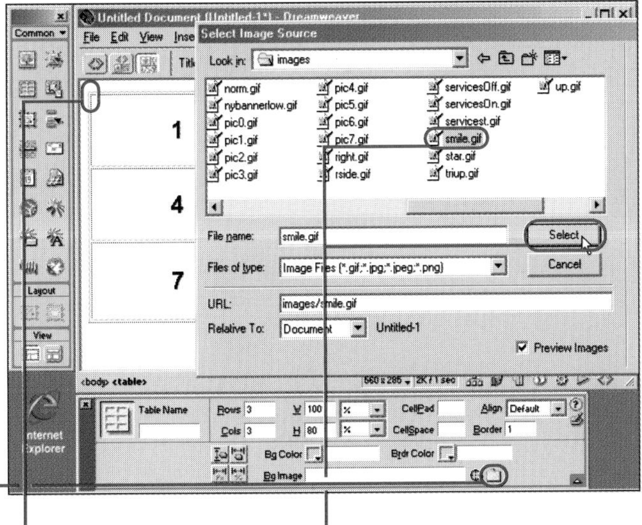

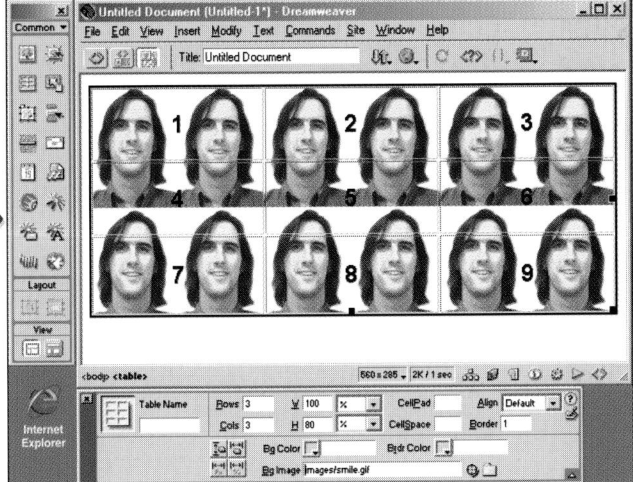

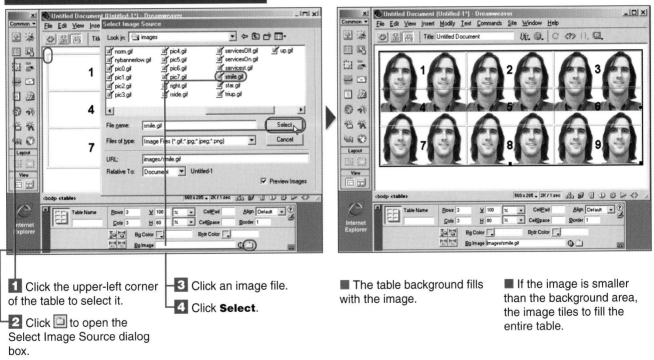

1 Click the upper-left corner of the table to select it.

2 Click to open the Select Image Source dialog box.

3 Click an image file.

4 Click **Select**.

■ The table background fills with the image.

■ If the image is smaller than the background area, the image tiles to fill the entire table.

INSERT OR DELETE A ROW OR COLUMN

You can insert new rows or columns into your table to add table content, or delete rows or cells to remove unused cells.

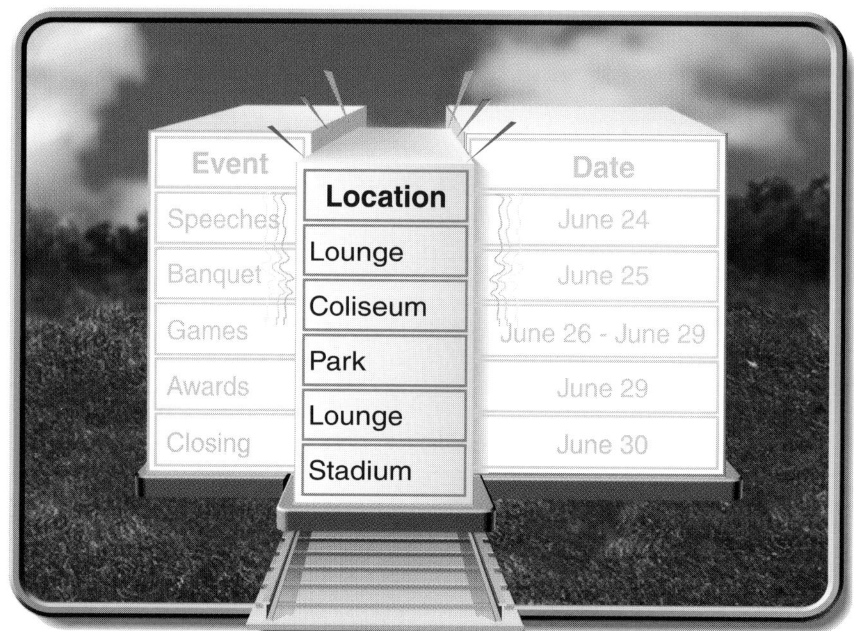

INSERT A ROW OR COLUMN

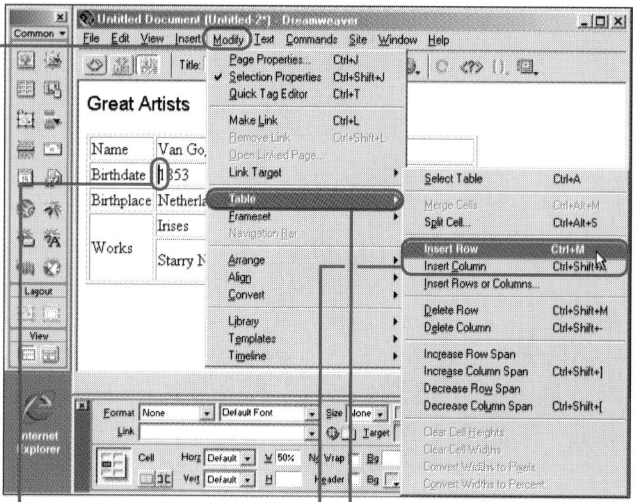

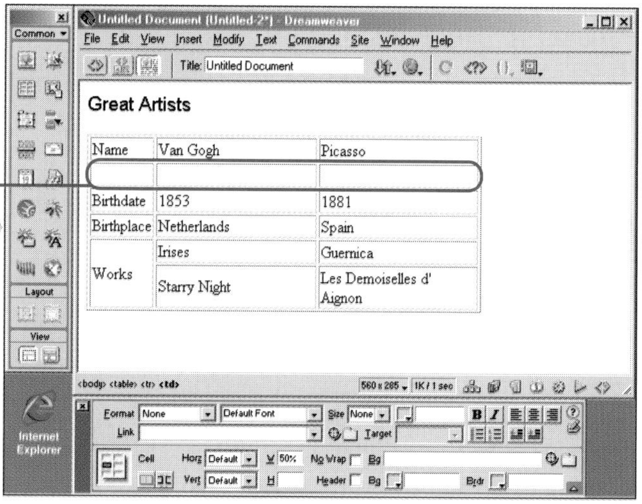

1 Click a cell directly below where you want to insert a row.

2 Click **Modify**.

3 Click **Table**.

4 Click **Insert Row** or **Insert Column**.

■ An empty row or column appears in the table.

■ To insert multiple rows or columns, repeat steps **1** to **4**.

What happens to the content of a deleted cell?

It is deleted as well. Dreamweaver does not warn you if the cells you are deleting in a table contain content. If you accidentally remove content when deleting rows or columns, you can click **Edit** and then **Undo** to undo the last command.

DELETE A ROW OR COLUMN

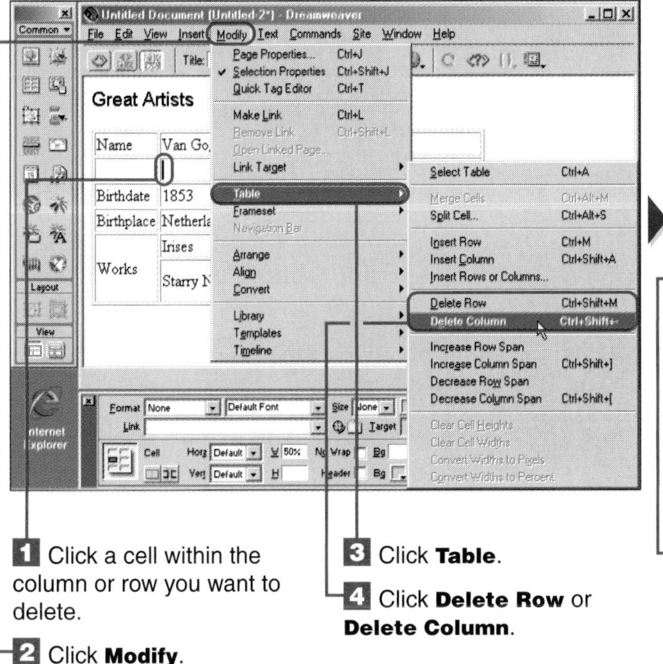

1 Click a cell within the column or row you want to delete.

2 Click **Modify**.

3 Click **Table**.

4 Click **Delete Row** or **Delete Column**.

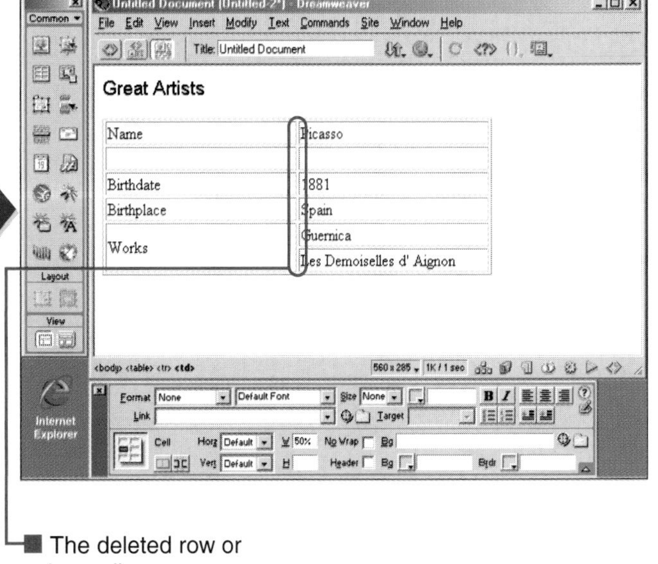

■ The deleted row or column disappears.

CREATE A LAYOUT TABLE

You can easily create tables that determine the layout of content in a Web page. Layout tables typically take up the entire dimensions of the page and have their borders turned off.

CREATE A LAYOUT TABLE

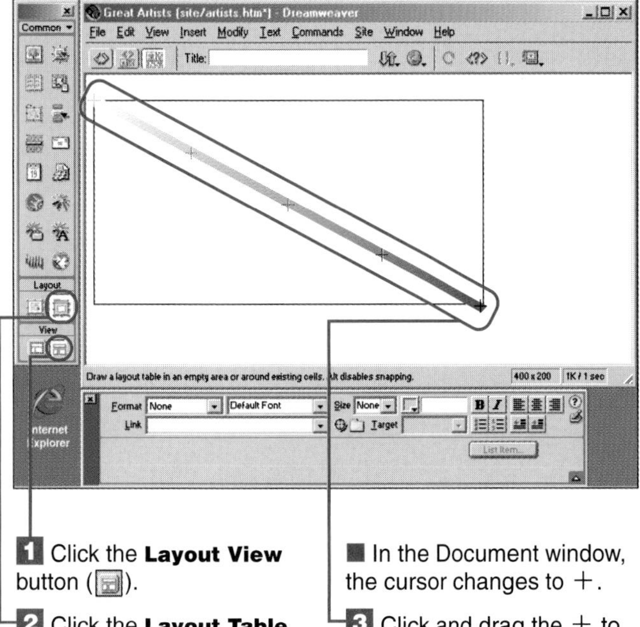

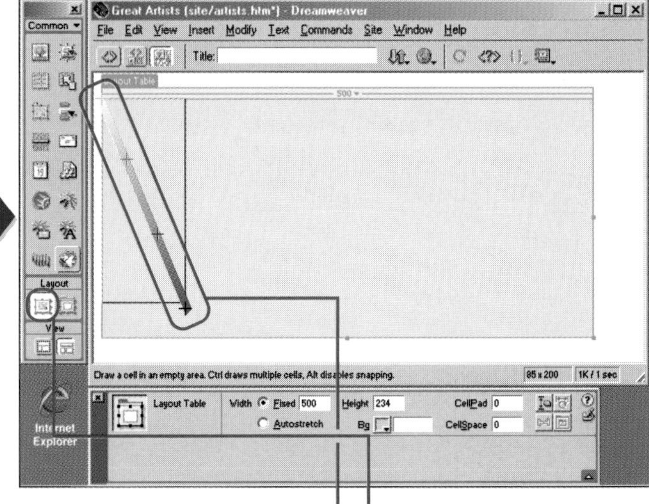

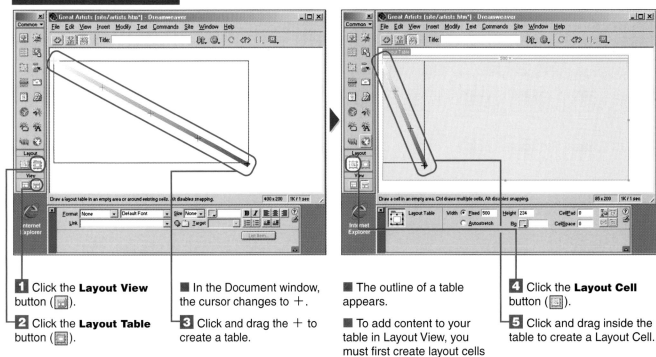

1 Click the **Layout View** button (▢).

2 Click the **Layout Table** button (▢).

■ In the Document window, the cursor changes to +.

3 Click and drag the + to create a table.

■ The outline of a table appears.

■ To add content to your table in Layout View, you must first create layout cells in your table.

4 Click the **Layout Cell** button (▢).

5 Click and drag inside the table to create a Layout Cell.

What can I do that will help me draw my layout table cells precisely?

Turn on the grid feature by clicking **View**, **Grid**, and then **Show Grid**. To customize the grid, click **Edit Grid** under the Grid submenu. Options include changing the grid square size and specifying that table and cell edges snap to the grid edges when they are near them.

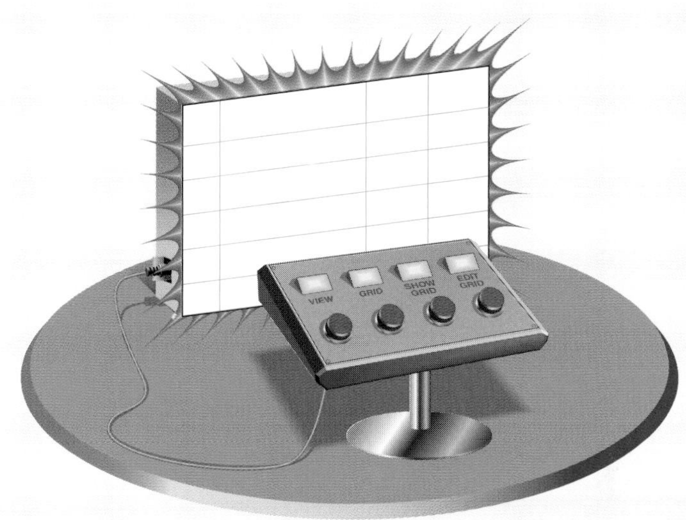

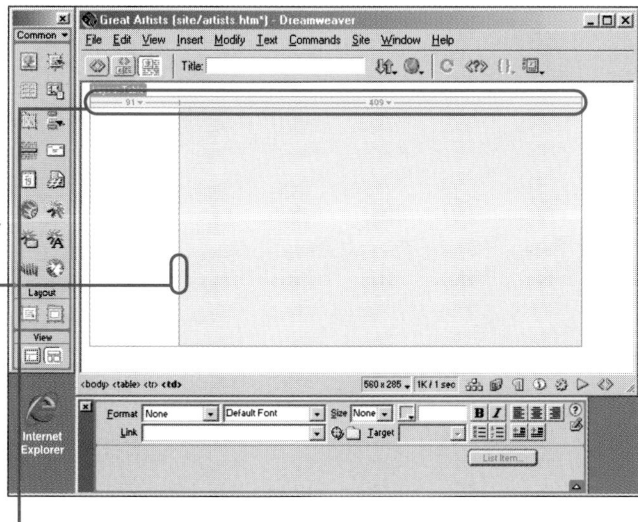

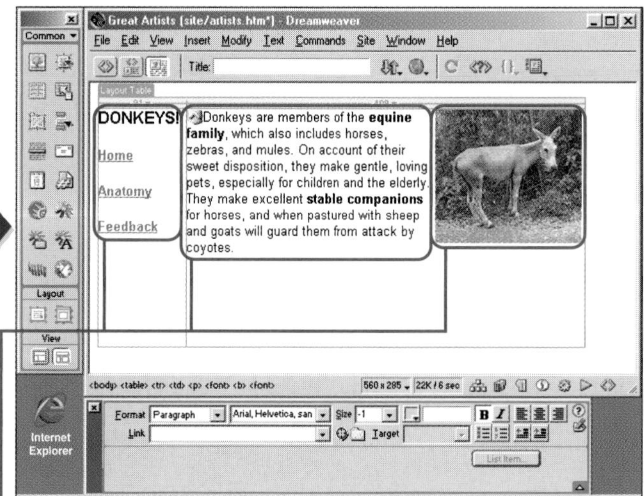

■ The sizes of the table columns appear at the top in pixels.

■ You can adjust the size and position of a cell by clicking and dragging its edge.

Note: See the section "Rearrange a Layout Table" for more information.

■ You can click again to draw more cells.

6 Insert content into your cells in Standard View.

Note: You can insert content in Layout View the same way you do in Standard View. See "Insert Content in a Table" earlier in this chapter for more information.

■ To change the properties of a table cell, click the cell's edge and make changes in the Property inspector.

REARRANGE A LAYOUT TABLE

You can easily change the size and the arrangement of a table's cells in Layout View.

REARRANGE A LAYOUT TABLE

CHANGE THE SIZE OF A CELL

1 Click the edge of a layout cell.

2 Click and drag a side or corner handle.

■ The layout cell resizes.

■ You cannot overlap other layout cells that you have defined.

How do I delete a layout cell or table?

Click the edge of the cell, and then press Delete. Dreamweaver will replace the space with gray, non-editable cells. Similarly, you can delete a layout table by clicking the table's top tab and pressing Delete.

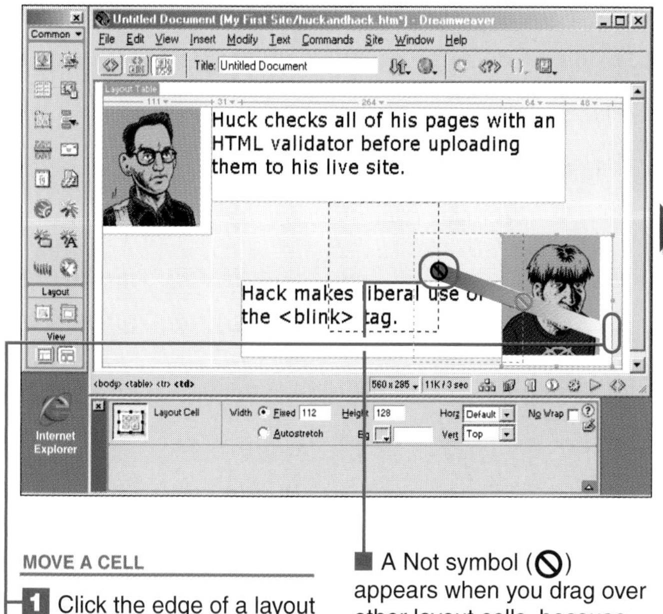

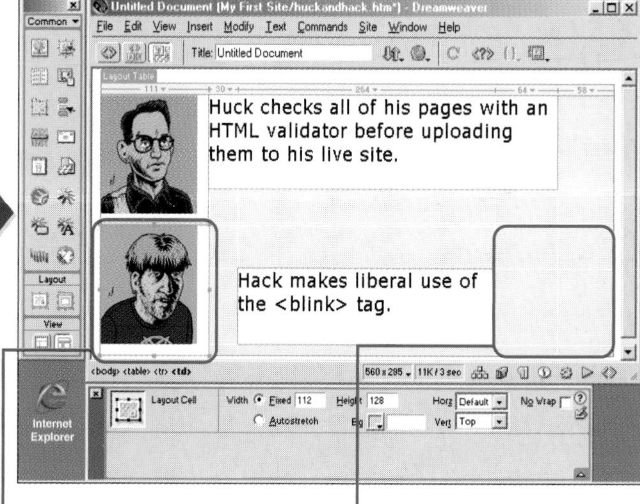

MOVE A CELL

1 Click the edge of a layout cell.

2 Click and drag the edge of the cell (do not click and drag a handle).

■ A Not symbol (⊘) appears when you drag over other layout cells, because cells cannot overlap.

3 Move the layout cell into its new position and release the mouse.

■ Undefined cells in the table adjust their sizes to make room for the cell's new position.

SET UP A FORM

You set up a form on your Web page by first creating a container that holds the text fields, menus, and other form elements. This container gets assigned the Web address of the form handler — the program that processes the submitted form.

SET UP A FORM

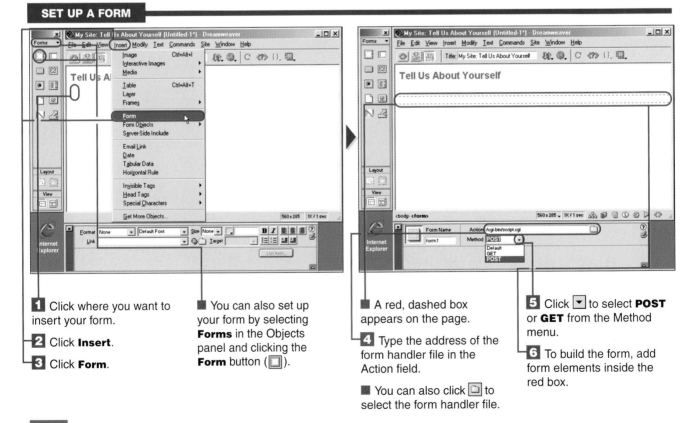

1 Click where you want to insert your form.

2 Click **Insert**.

3 Click **Form**.

■ You can also set up your form by selecting **Forms** in the Objects panel and clicking the **Form** button (▢).

■ A red, dashed box appears on the page.

4 Type the address of the form handler file in the Action field.

■ You can also click ▢ to select the form handler file.

5 Click ▾ to select **POST** or **GET** from the Method menu.

6 To build the form, add form elements inside the red box.

ADD A TEXT FIELD TO A FORM

You can add a text field to enable viewers to submit text through your form. Text fields are probably the most common form elements, enabling users to enter names, addresses, brief answers to questions, and other short pieces of text.

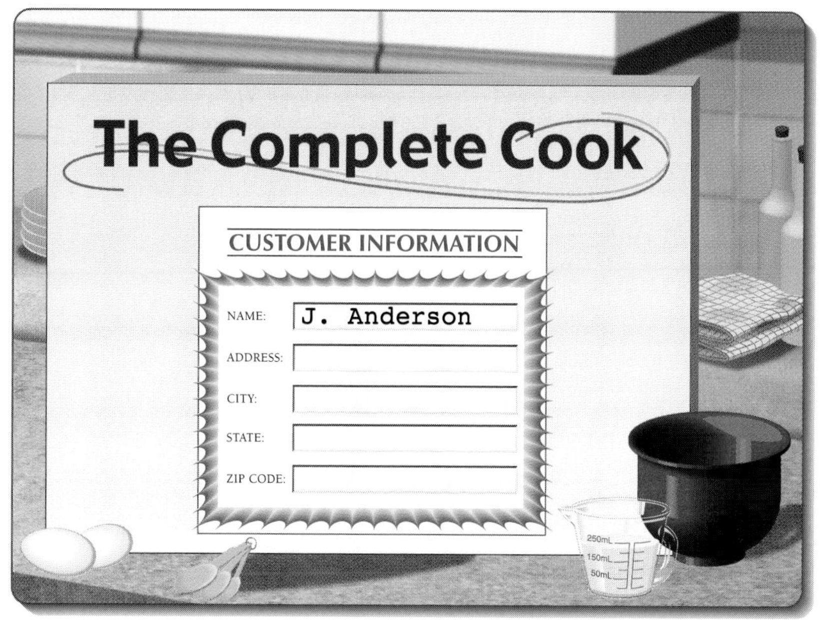

ADD A TEXT FIELD TO A FORM

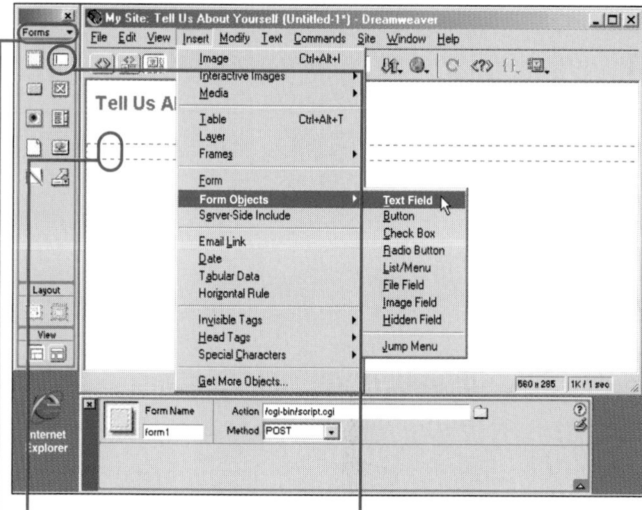

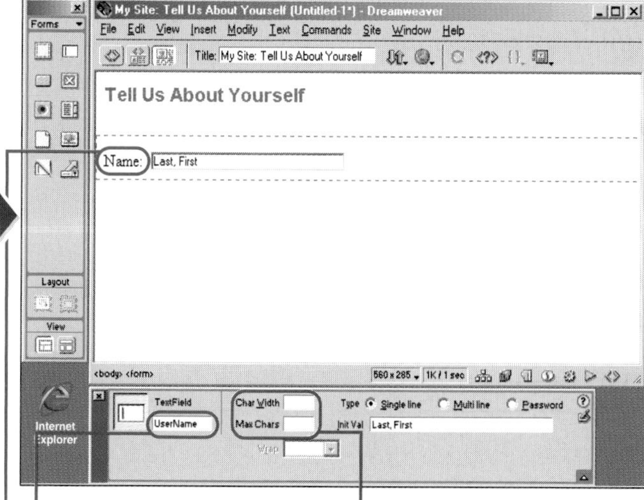

1 Click inside the form container where you want to insert the text field.

Note: See the section "Set Up a Form" earlier in this chapter to set up a form.

2 Select **Forms** in the Objects panel.

3 Click the **Text Field button** (▭).

■ A text field appears in your form. The Single line radio button is selected by default.

4 Type a field name in the text field.

■ This name lets the browser distinguish the field from other form elements.

5 Type a label for the text field so that users know what to enter.

■ You can set other options for text fields in these dialogs, such as maximum visible field width and maximum field character length.

ADD CHECK BOXES TO A FORM

Check boxes enable you to present multiple options in a form, and allow the user to select one, several, or none of the options.

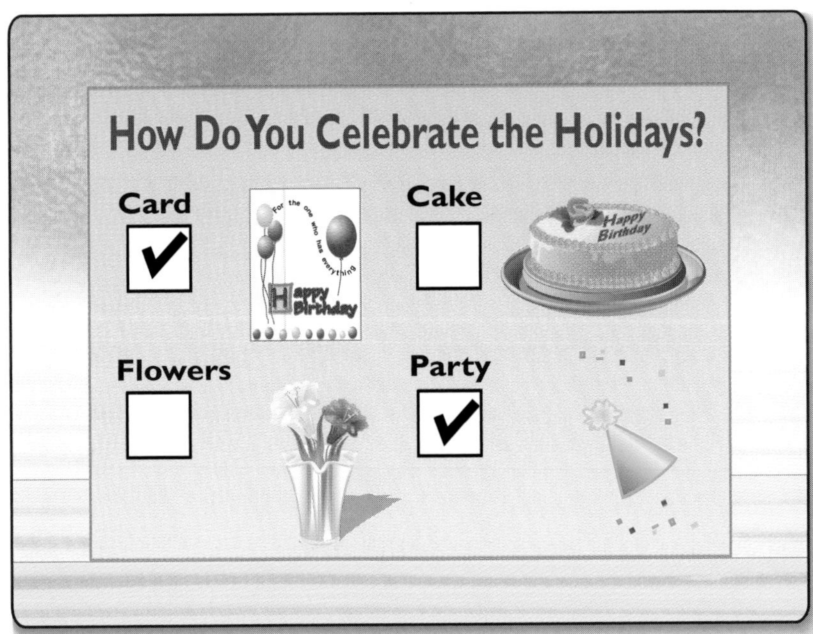

ADD CHECK BOXES TO A FORM

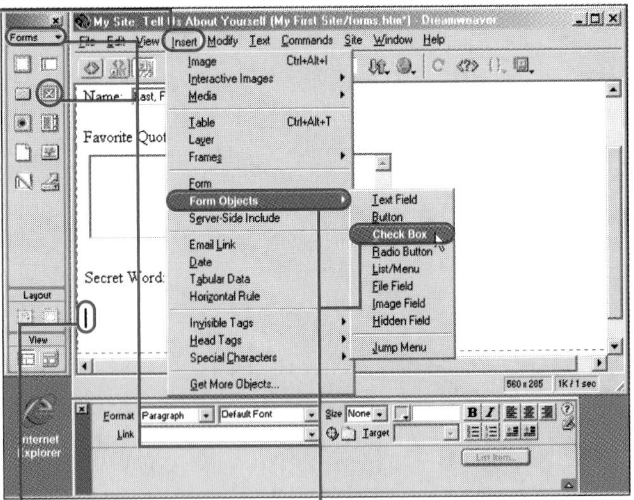

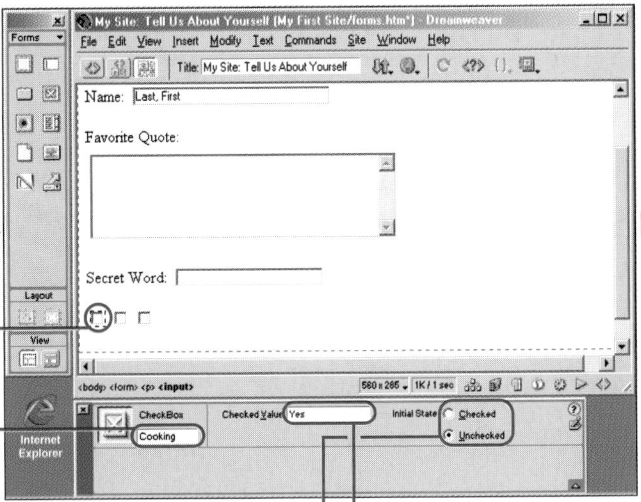

1 Click inside the form container where you want to insert your check boxes.

Note: See the section "Set Up a Form" to set up a form.

2 Click **Insert**.

3 Click **Form Objects**.

4 Click **Check Box**.

■ You can also select **Forms** in the Objects panel and click the **Insert Check Box** button (☒).

5 Repeat steps **2** to **4** until you have the desired number of check boxes in your Web page.

6 Click a check box.

7 Type a name for the check box.

8 Type a Checked Value for the check box.

■ This value is assigned to the box when the user checks it.

9 Click **Checked** or **Unchecked** (○ changes to ◉) to select the initial status.

Can I have several different groups of check boxes in the same form?

Yes. How you organize the check boxes in a form — in one group, several groups, or each check box by itself — is up to you. Because each box has a unique name, the visual organization of the boxes does not matter to the form handler.

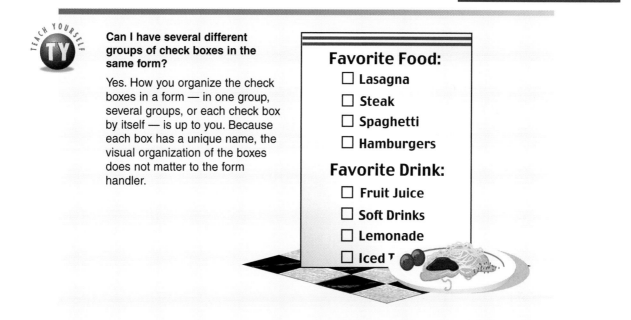

Favorite Food:
☐ Lasagna
☐ Steak
☐ Spaghetti
☐ Hamburgers

Favorite Drink:
☐ Fruit Juice
☐ Soft Drinks
☐ Lemonade
☐ Iced T

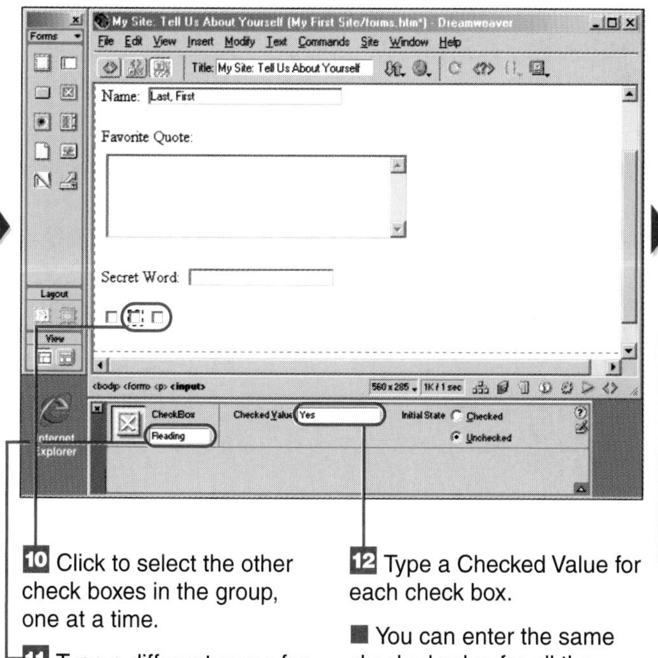

10 Click to select the other check boxes in the group, one at a time.

11 Type a different name for each check box.

12 Type a Checked Value for each check box.

■ You can enter the same checked value for all the boxes.

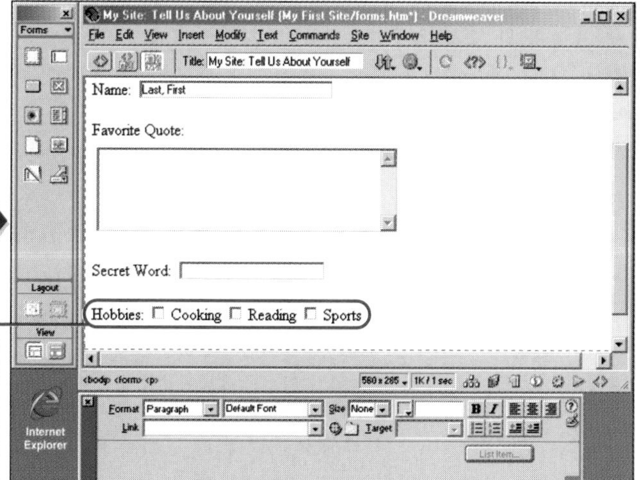

13 Label the check boxes so that users can identify what to check.

ADD RADIO BUTTONS TO A FORM

You can let users select one option from a set of several options by adding a set of radio buttons to your form. With radio buttons, a user cannot select more that one option from a set.

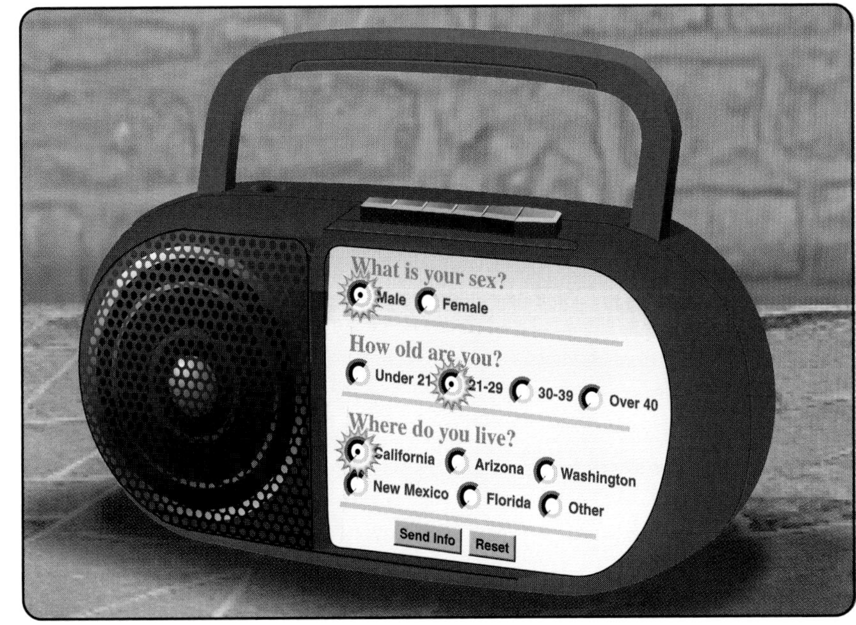

ADD RADIO BUTTONS TO A FORM

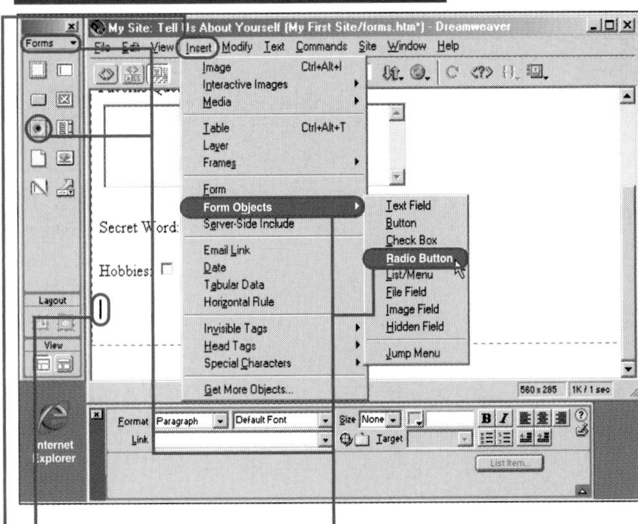

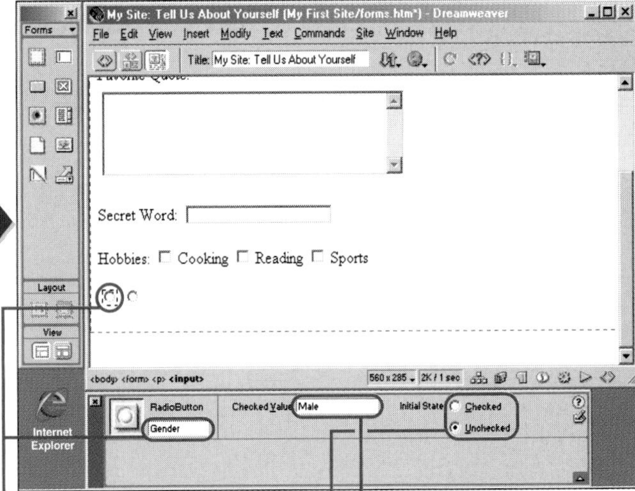

1 Click inside the form container where you want to insert your radio buttons.

Note: See the section "Set Up a Form" to set up a form.

2 Click **Insert**.

3 Click **Form Objects**.

4 Click **Radio Button**.

■ You can also select **Forms** in the Objects panel and click the **Insert Radio Button** button (◙).

5 Repeat steps **2** to **4** until you have the desired number of radio buttons in your Web page.

6 Click a radio button.

7 Type a name for the radio button.

8 Type a Checked Value for the radio button.

■ This value is assigned to the box when the user checks it.

9 Click **Checked** or **Unchecked** (○ changes to ◉) to select the initial status.

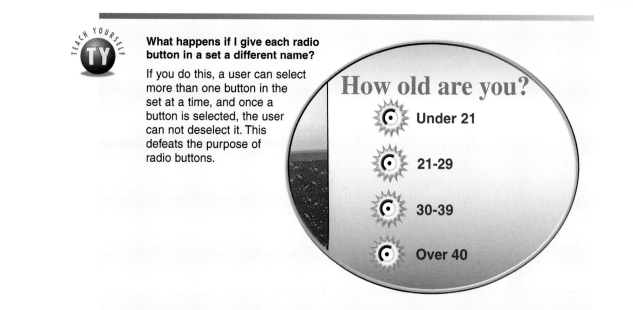

What happens if I give each radio button in a set a different name?

If you do this, a user can select more than one button in the set at a time, and once a button is selected, the user can not deselect it. This defeats the purpose of radio buttons.

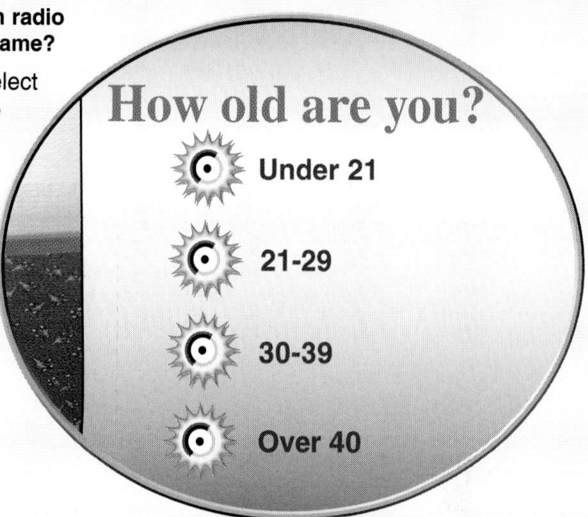

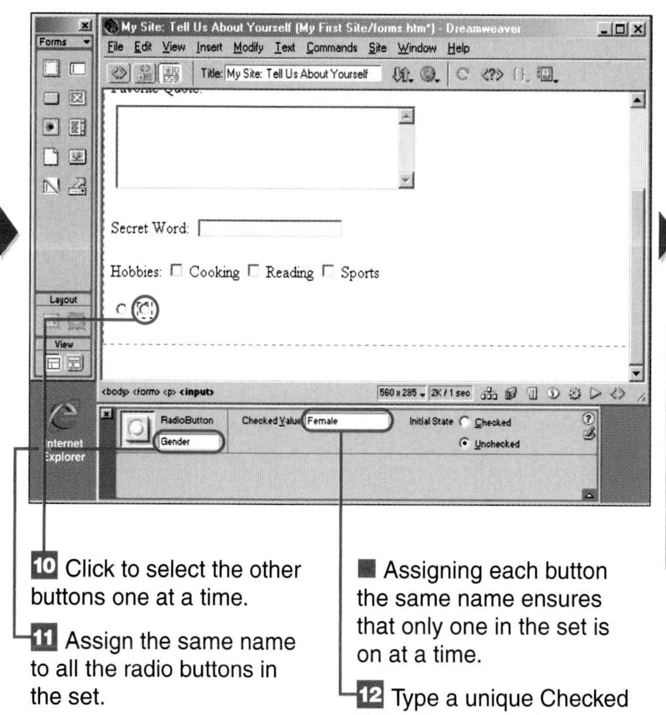

10 Click to select the other buttons one at a time.

11 Assign the same name to all the radio buttons in the set.

■ Assigning each button the same name ensures that only one in the set is on at a time.

12 Type a unique Checked Value for each radio button.

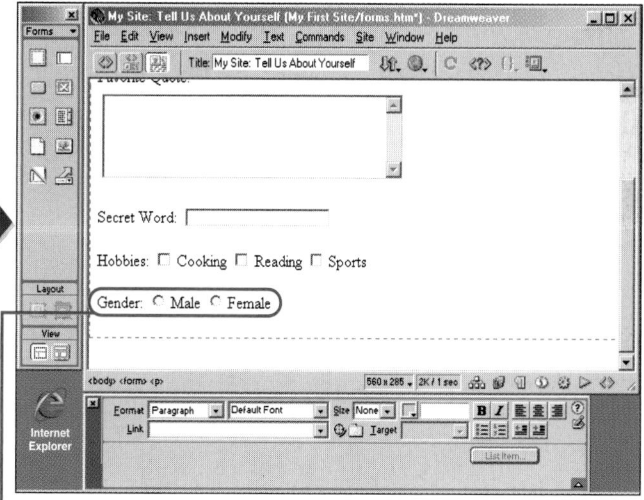

13 Label the radio buttons so that users can identify what to select.

ADD A MENU TO A FORM

A menu enables users to choose one option from a list of options. Because it hides the information until a user clicks it, a menu enables you to put a long list of options in a small amount of space.

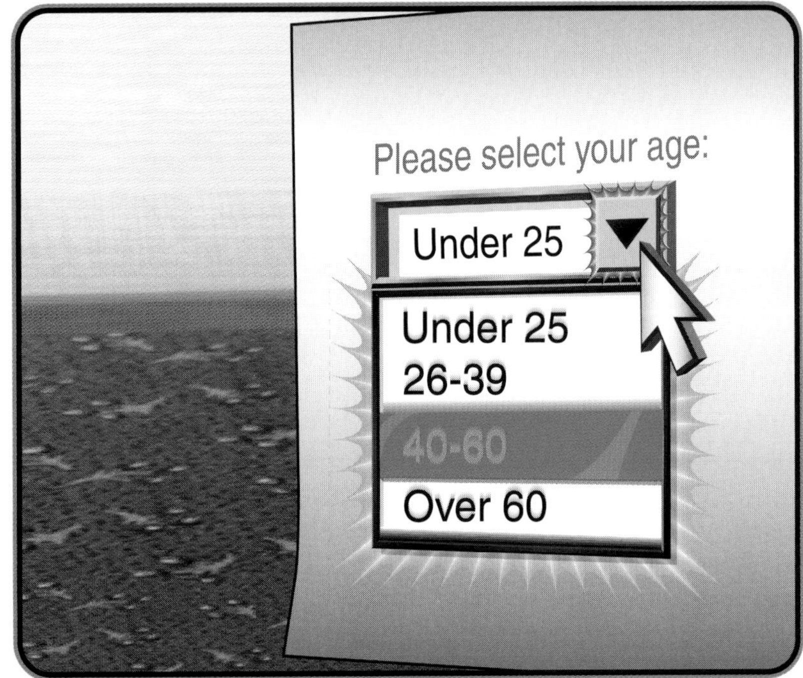

ADD A MENU TO A FORM

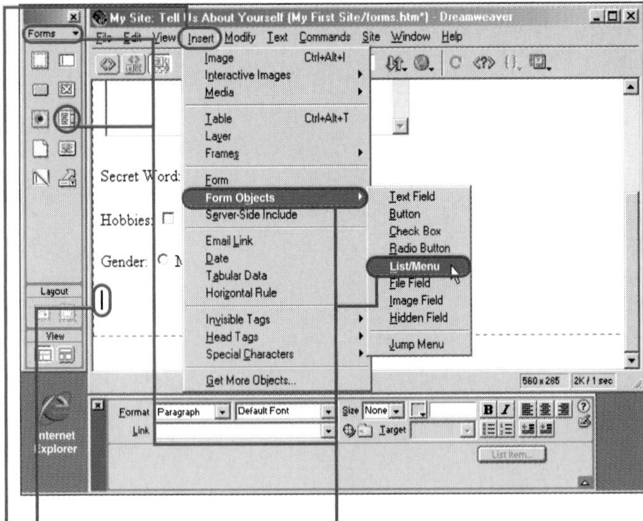

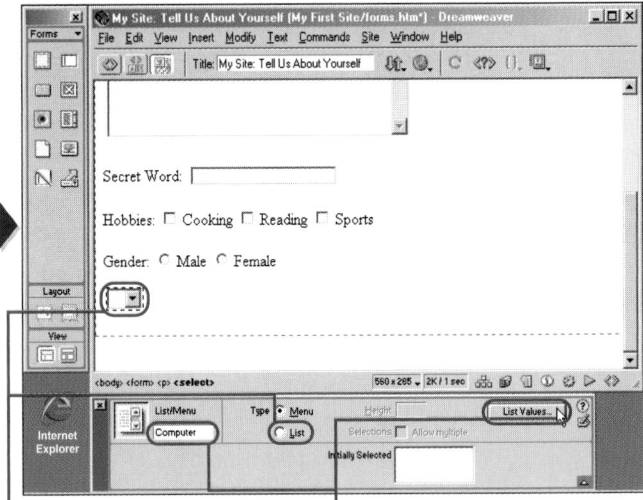

1 Click inside the form container where you want to insert the menu.

Note: See the section "Set Up a Form" earlier in this chapter to set up a form.

2 Click **Insert**.

3 Click **Form Objects**.

4 Click **List/Menu**.

- You can also select **Forms** in the Objects panel and click the **Insert List/Menu** button (▤).

- A menu appears in your Web page.

5 Click the menu to select it.

- To display a list instead of a menu, you can click **List** (○ changes to ◉).

Note: See the section "Add a List to a Form" later in this chapter for details on adding a list to a form.

6 Type a name for the menu.

7 Click **List Values** to open the dialog box.

What determines the width of a menu?

The widest item determines the width of the menu. To change the width, you can change the width of your item descriptions.

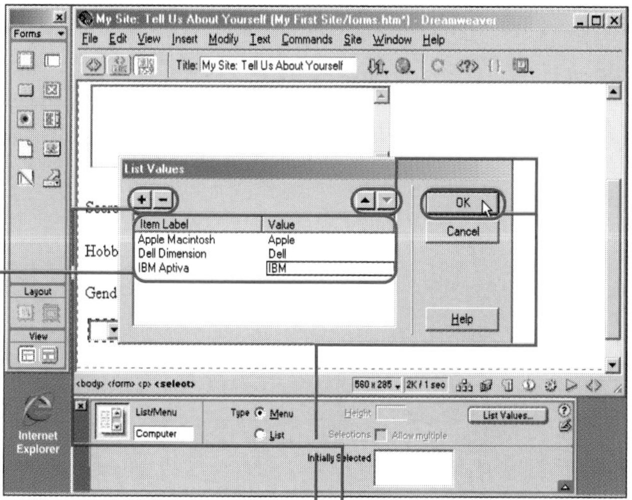

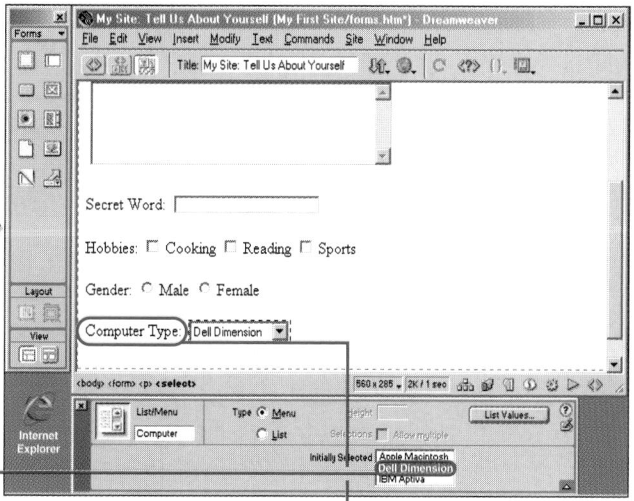

8 Type an item label and a value for each menu item.

■ The labels appear in the menu on your page. The values are sent to the form handler.

■ Click the + or − buttons to add or delete entries.

■ Select an item and click ▲ or ▼ to reposition items.

9 After entering all of your items, click **OK**.

10 Click the item that you want initially selected when the page loads.

11 Type a label that describes the menu.

ADD A LIST TO A FORM

A list allows a user to choose one option from a list of options. You can also create a list that allows a user to choose multiple options from your list.

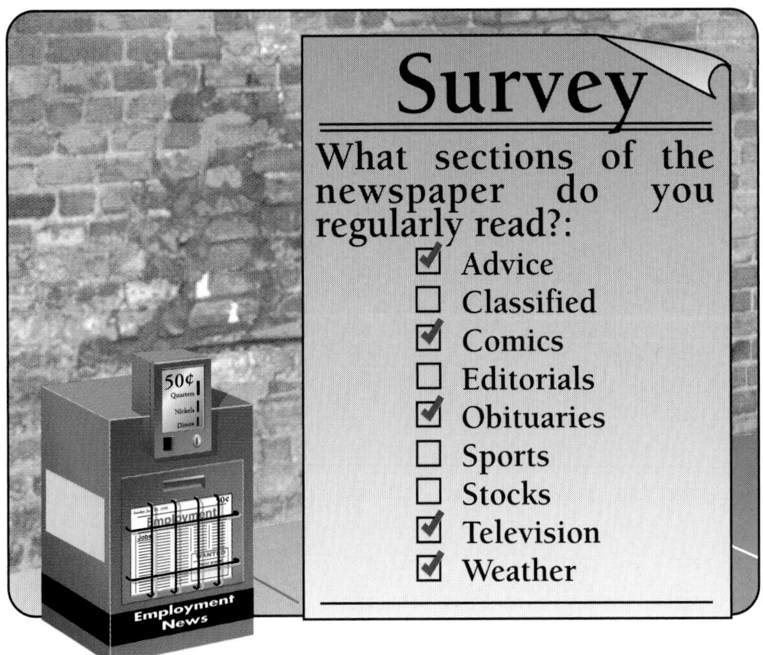

ADD A LIST TO A FORM

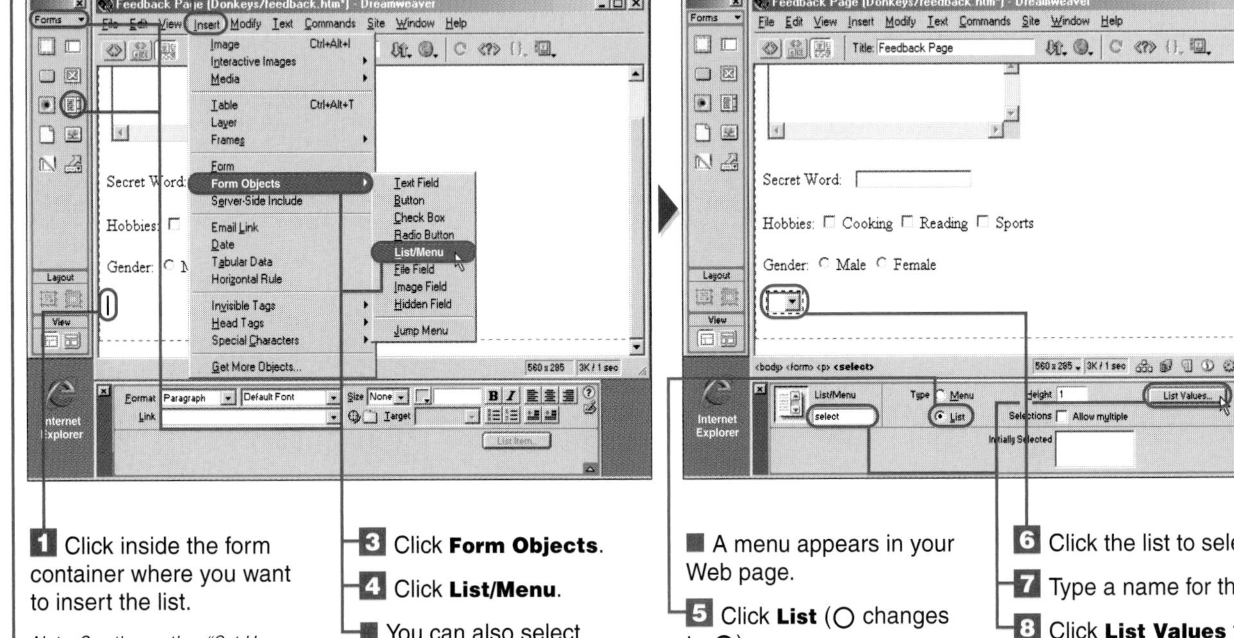

1 Click inside the form container where you want to insert the list.

Note: See the section "Set Up a Form" earlier in this chapter to set up a form.

2 Click **Insert**.

3 Click **Form Objects**.

4 Click **List/Menu**.

■ You can also select **Forms** in the Objects panel and click the **Insert List/Menu** button ( ).

■ A menu appears in your Web page.

5 Click **List** (○ changes to ◉).

■ To choose multiple options, click the **Allow multiple** check box and then enter the number of preferences in the **Height** field.

6 Click the list to select it.

7 Type a name for the list.

8 Click **List Values** to open the dialog box.

When should I use a list instead of check boxes?

Both elements can let your viewers choose several options from a set of options in your form. Lists let you combine your set of options into a relatively small space; check boxes let your viewers have a clearer view of all the options that are available. The best choice depends on the type of information you are presenting and the space available.

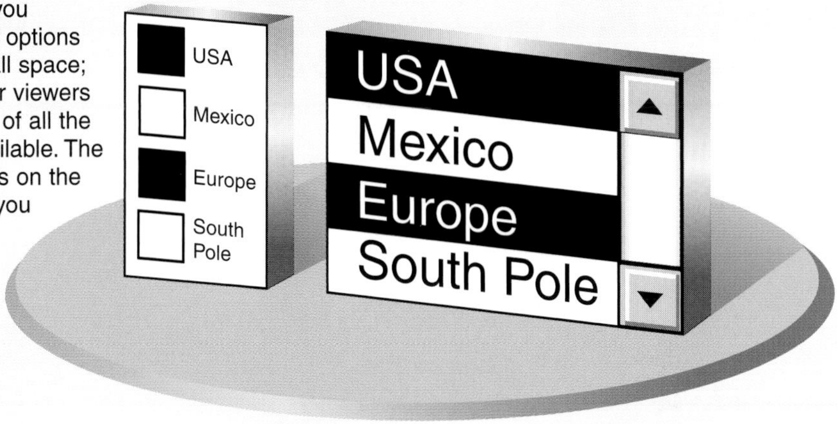

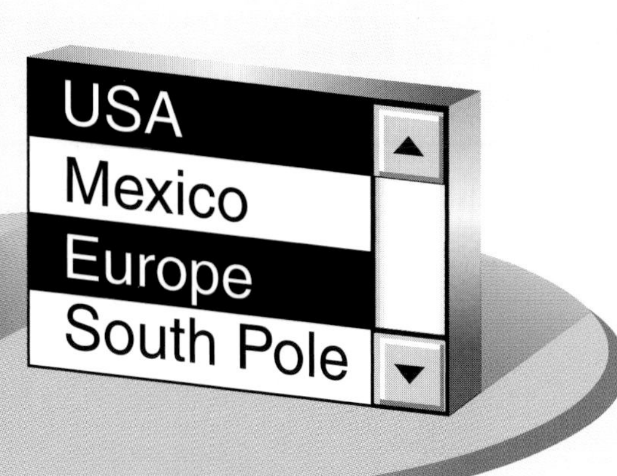

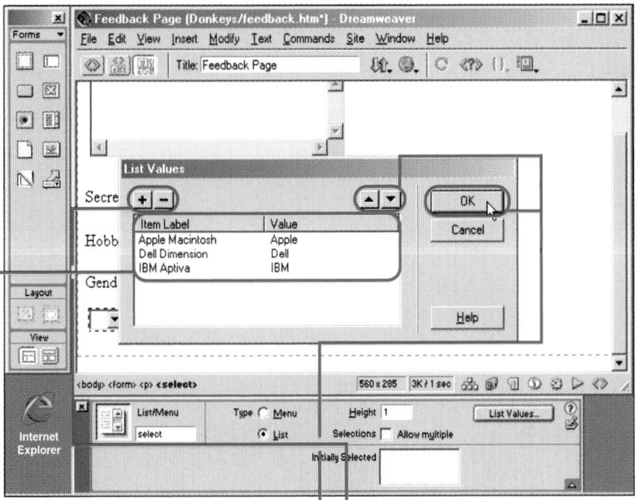

9 Type an item label and a value for each item.

■ The labels appear in the list on your page. The values are sent to the form handler.

■ You can click + or − to add or delete entries.

■ You can select an item and click ▲ or ▼ to reposition items.

10 After entering all of your items, click **OK**.

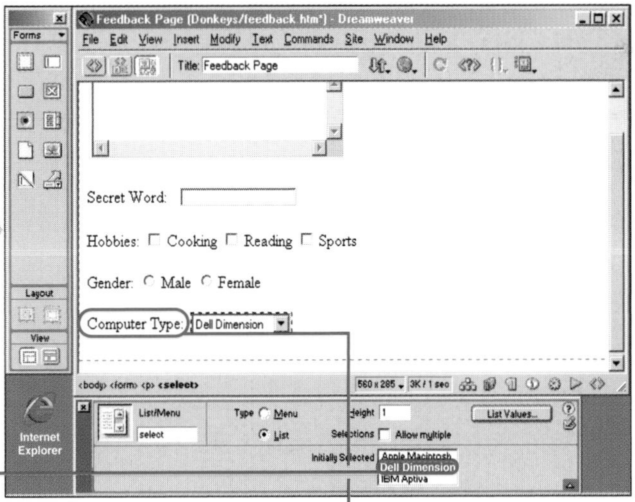

11 Click the item that you want initially selected when the page loads.

12 Type a label that describes the list.

VALIDATE A FORM

You can double-check the information a user enters in a form to make sure it is valid. The validation process can include checking that postal codes have the correct number of characters and that e-mail addresses are in the correct format.

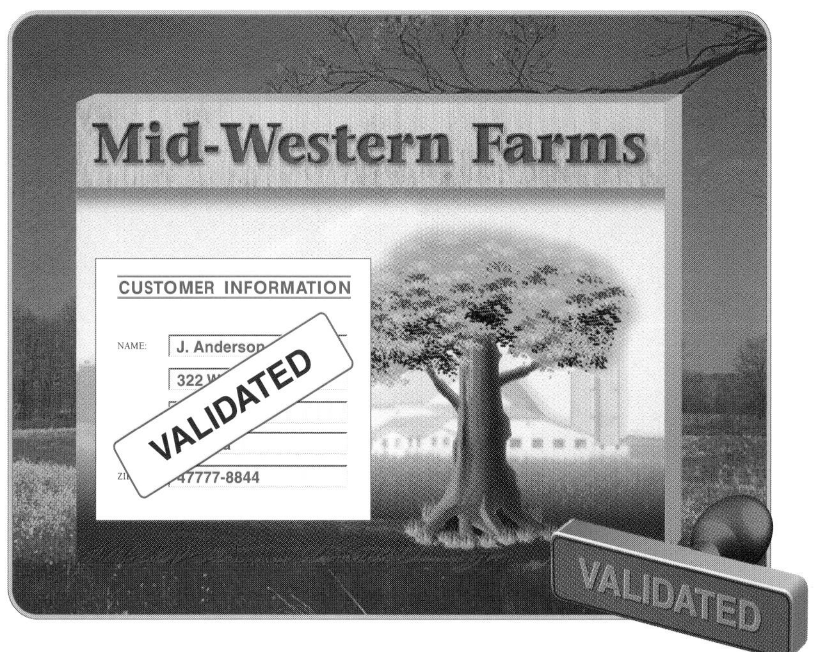

VALIDATE A FORM

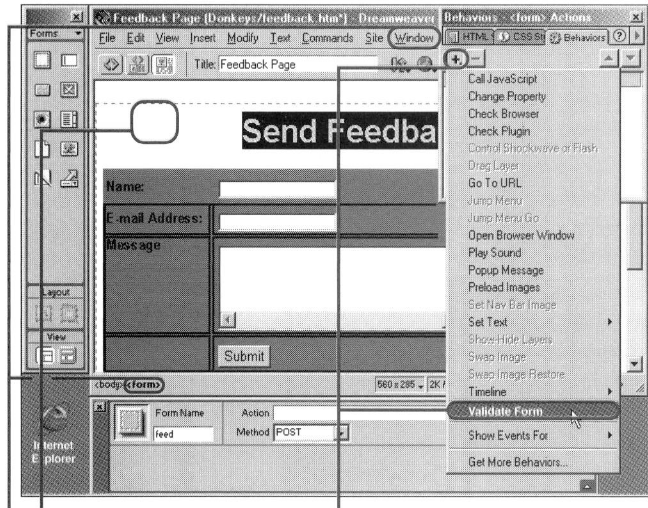

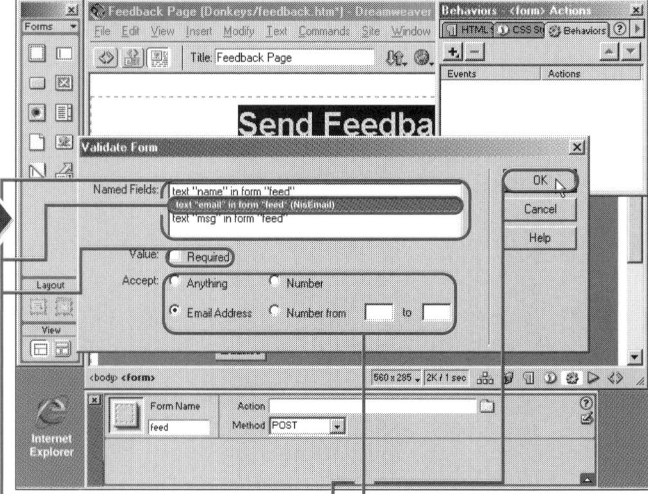

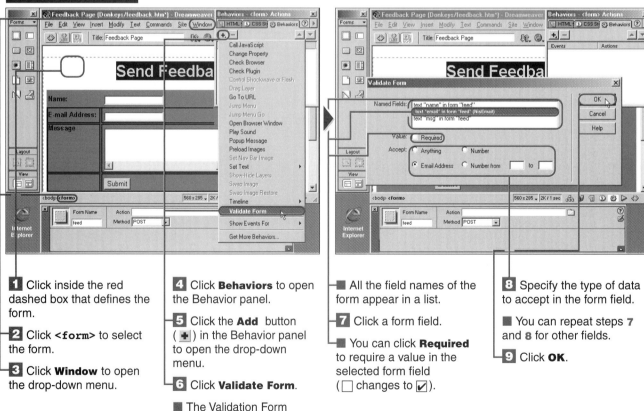

1 Click inside the red dashed box that defines the form.

2 Click **<form>** to select the form.

3 Click **Window** to open the drop-down menu.

4 Click **Behaviors** to open the Behavior panel.

5 Click the **Add** button (+) in the Behavior panel to open the drop-down menu.

6 Click **Validate Form**.

■ The Validation Form dialog box appears.

■ All the field names of the form appear in a list.

7 Click a form field.

■ You can click **Required** to require a value in the selected form field (☐ changes to ☑).

8 Specify the type of data to accept in the form field.

■ You can repeat steps **7** and **8** for other fields.

9 Click **OK**.

What browser events can trigger validation?

If you need to validate a single field in a form, you can use the `onBlur` event to trigger validation. `OnBlur` causes validation to occur when the user clicks away from the field. If you need to validate multiple fields, you can use `onSubmit` for the trigger. `OnSubmit` causes validation to occur after the user clicks the **Submit** button.

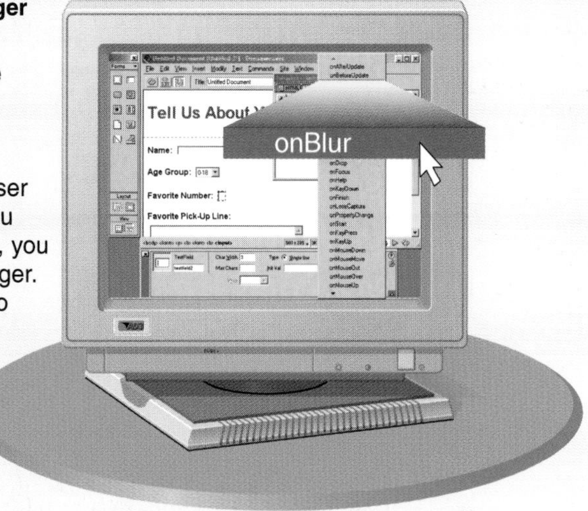

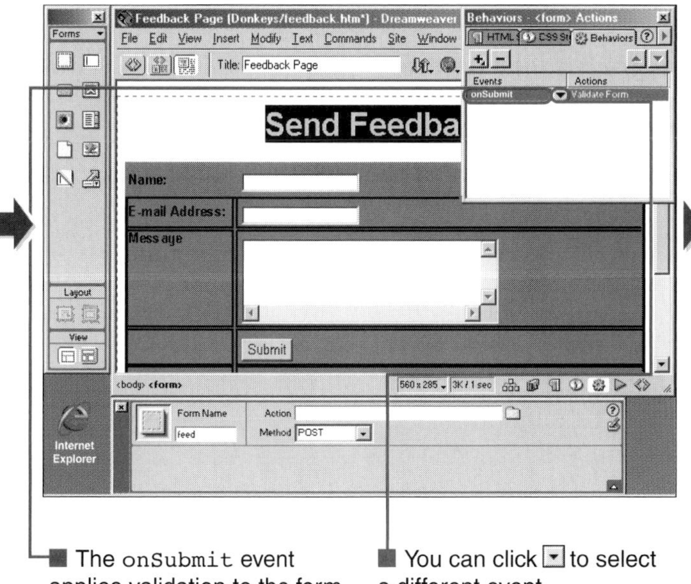

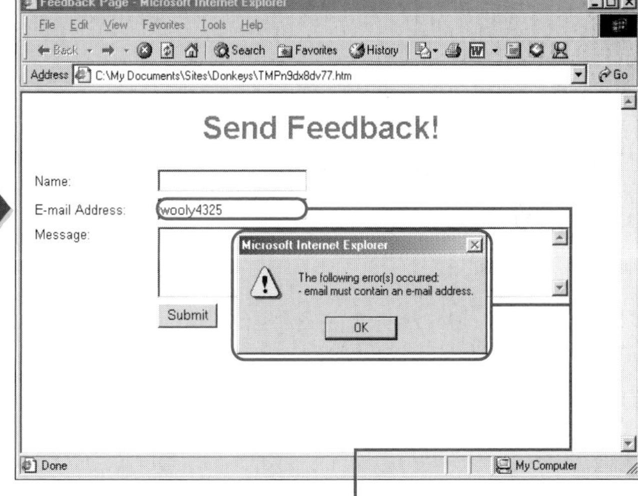

■ The `onSubmit` event applies validation to the form when the user clicks the submit button.

■ You can click ▼ to select a different event.

10 Preview the Web page in a browser.

■ If you submit the form with invalid content (example: an invalid e-mail address), the browser generates a pop-up alert.

DIVIDE A PAGE INTO FRAMES

You can split a Document window vertically to create a frameset with left and right frames, or split it horizontally to create a frameset with top and bottom frames.

You can also choose a predefined frameset for your site. See the section "Insert a Predefined Frameset" later in the chapter.

DIVIDE A PAGE INTO FRAMES

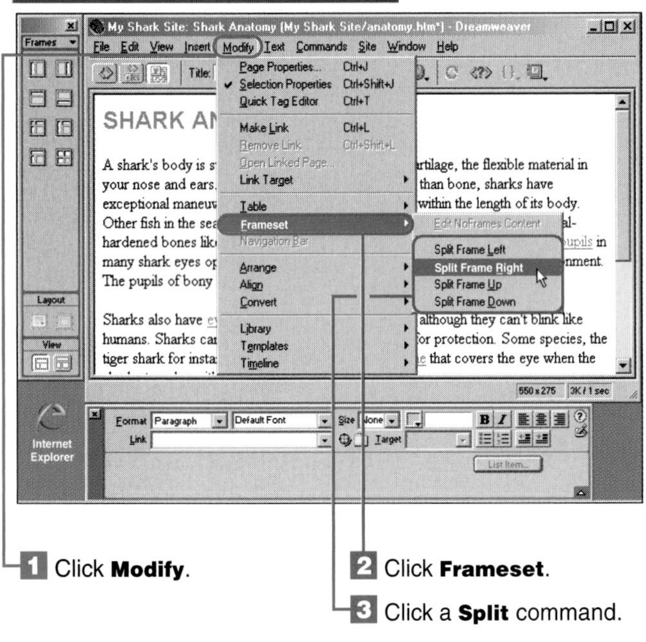

1 Click **Modify**.

2 Click **Frameset**.

3 Click a **Split** command.

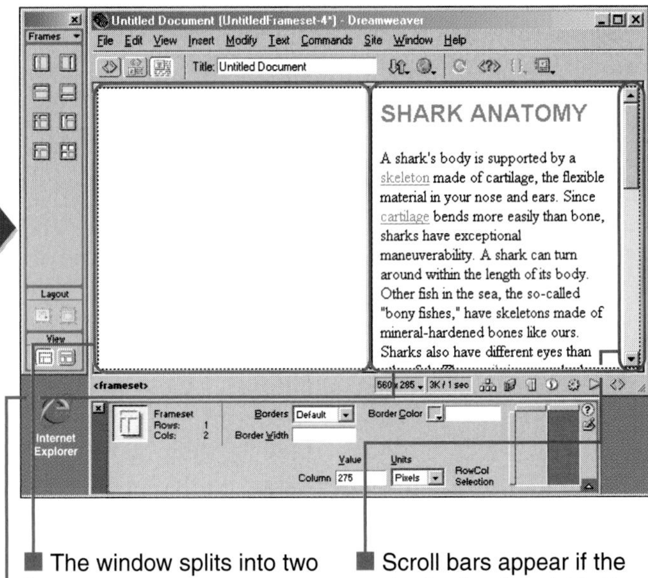

■ The window splits into two frames.

■ If content existed in the original page, it shifts to one of the new frames.

■ Scroll bars appear if the content extends outside the frame borders.

Note: See page 178 for instructions on how to add content to a new frame.

INSERT A PREDEFINED FRAMESET

You can easily create popular frame styles using the predefined framesets located in the Objects panel.

INSERT A PREDEFINED FRAMESET

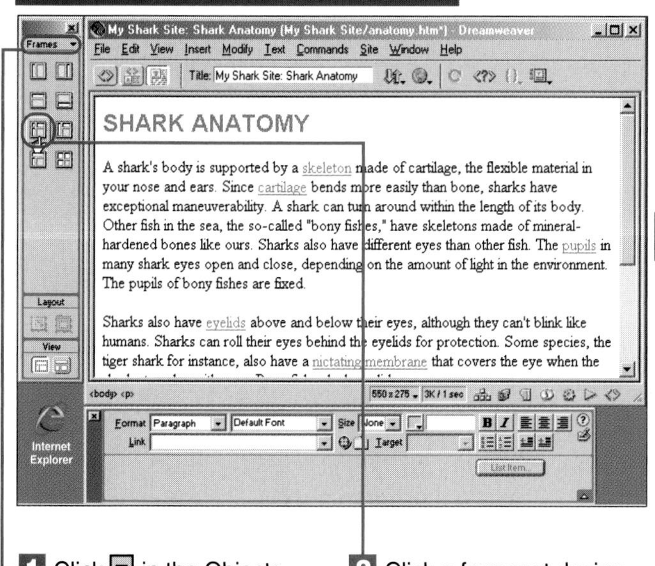

1 Click ▼ in the Objects panel menu and select **Frames**.

2 Click a frameset design (for example: ▣).

■ Dreamweaver applies the frameset to your page.

■ If content existed in the original page, it shifts to one of the new frames.

■ Scroll bars appear if the content extends outside the frame borders.

Note: See the section "Add Content to a Frame" later in this chapter for instructions on how to add content to a new frame.

NAME A FRAME

To create hyperlinks that can work between your frames, you need to give your frames names. The name tells where the hyperlink destination should open in the frameset.

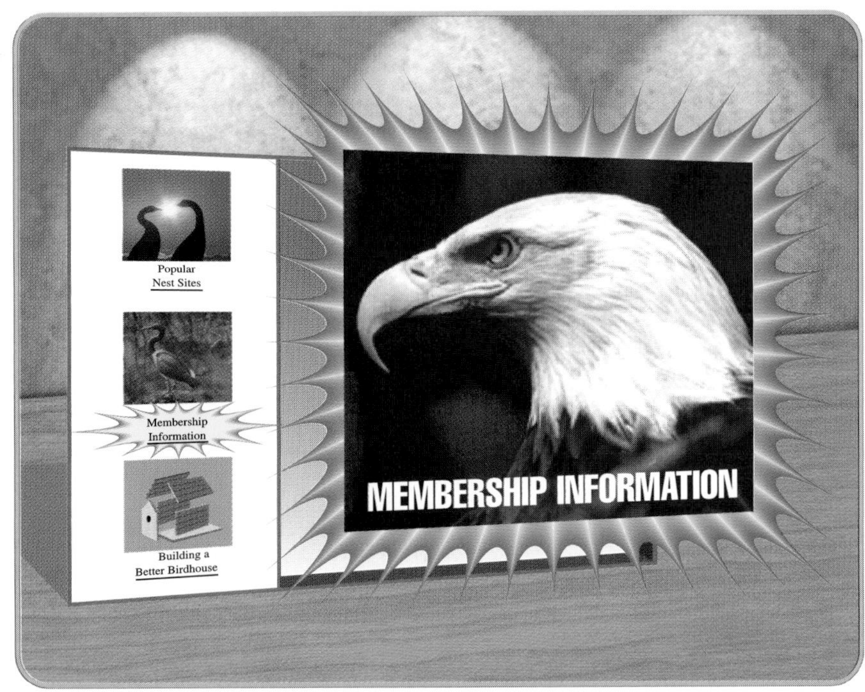

NAME A FRAME

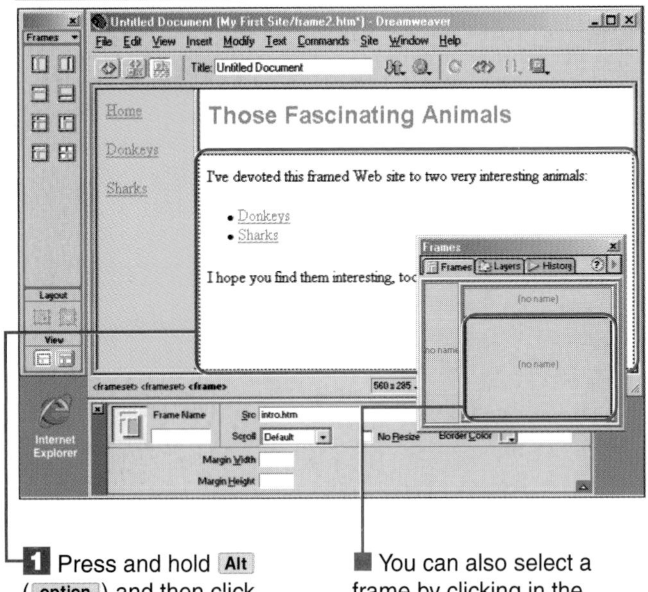

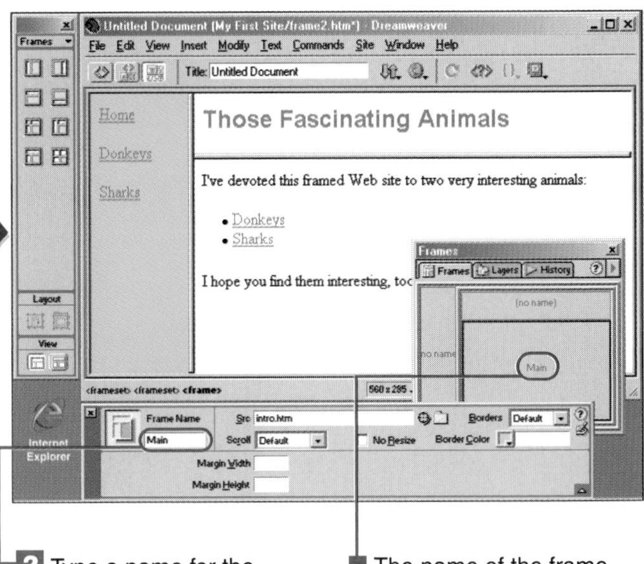

1 Press and hold **Alt** (**option**) and then click inside a frame to select it.

■ You can also select a frame by clicking in the Frames panel (click **Window** and then **Frames** to display the panel).

2 Type a name for the frame.

3 Press **Enter** (**Return**).

■ The name of the frame appears in the Frames panel.

DELETE A FRAME

You can delete a frame if you want to make your frameset less complicated.

DELETE A FRAME

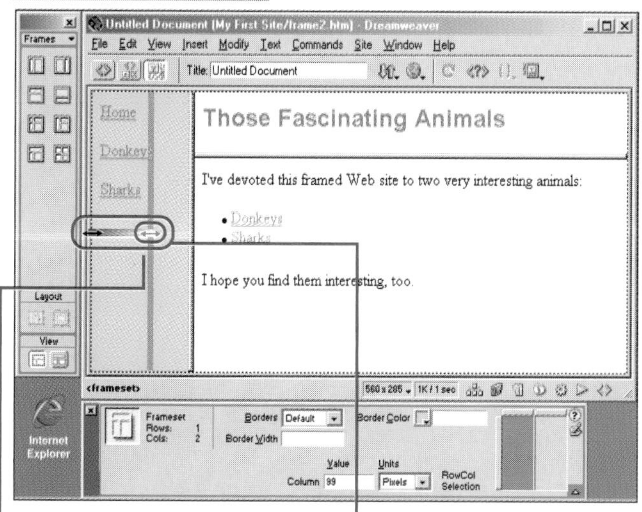

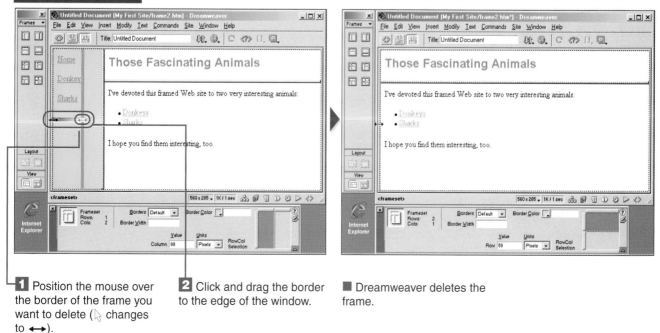

1 Position the mouse over the border of the frame you want to delete (↖ changes to ↔).

2 Click and drag the border to the edge of the window.

■ Dreamweaver deletes the frame.

ADD CONTENT TO A FRAME

You can add content to a frame by inserting an existing HTML document into the frame. You can also add content by typing text or inserting elements such as images and tables, just as you would in an unframed page.

ADD CONTENT TO A FRAME

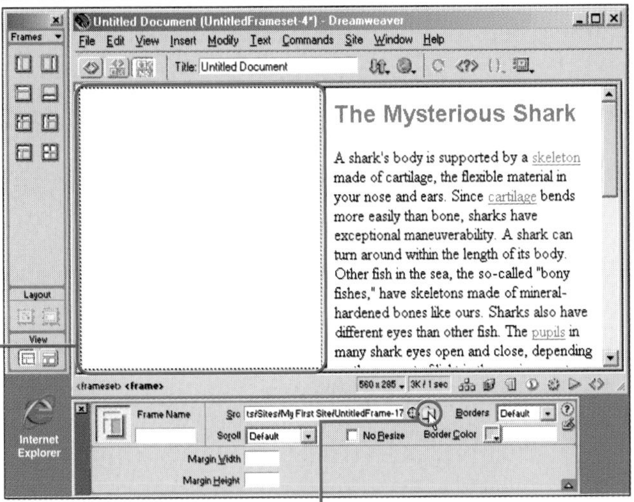

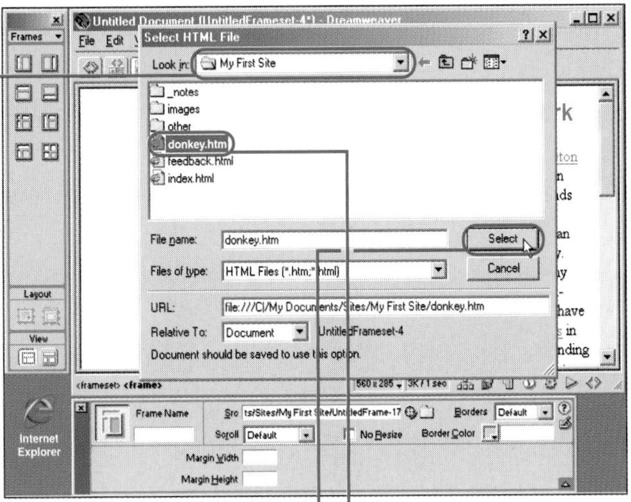

OPEN AN EXISTING HTML FILE IN A FRAME

1 Press and hold **Alt** (**option**) and then click inside a frame to select it.

■ You can also select a frame by clicking in the Frames panel (click **Window** and then **Frames** to display the Frames panel).

2 Click [icon] to open the HTML File dialog box.

3 Click ▼ to select the folder that contains the HTML file.

4 Click the file.

5 Click **Select**.

Can I load a page from the Web into a frame on my Web site?

Yes. You can insert an external Web-page address into the URL field in the Select HTML File dialog box (see steps **3** to **5** on page 178). Because Dreamweaver cannot display external files, the Web page will not appear in the Document window. However, it will appear if you preview your site in a Web browser.

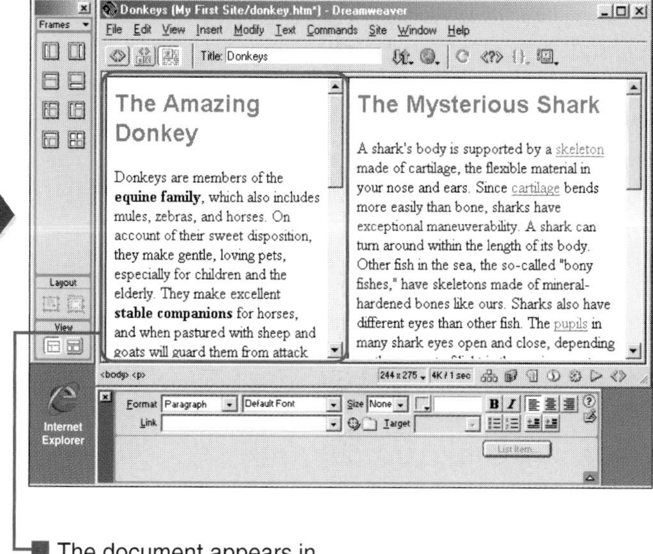

■ The document appears in the frame.

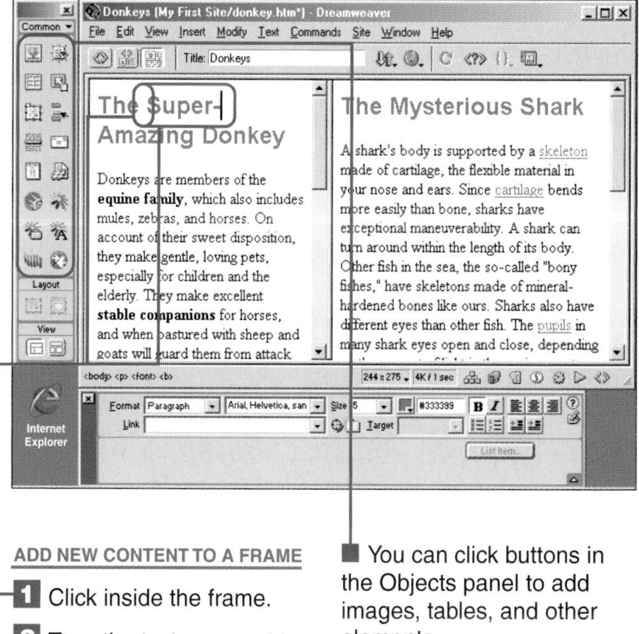

ADD NEW CONTENT TO A FRAME

1 Click inside the frame.

2 Type the text you want to display.

■ You can click buttons in the Objects panel to add images, tables, and other elements.

Note: See Chapter 13 for more information on using the Objects panel.

CHANGE FRAME DIMENSIONS

You can change the dimensions of a frame to attractively and efficiently display the information inside it.

CHANGE FRAME DIMENSIONS

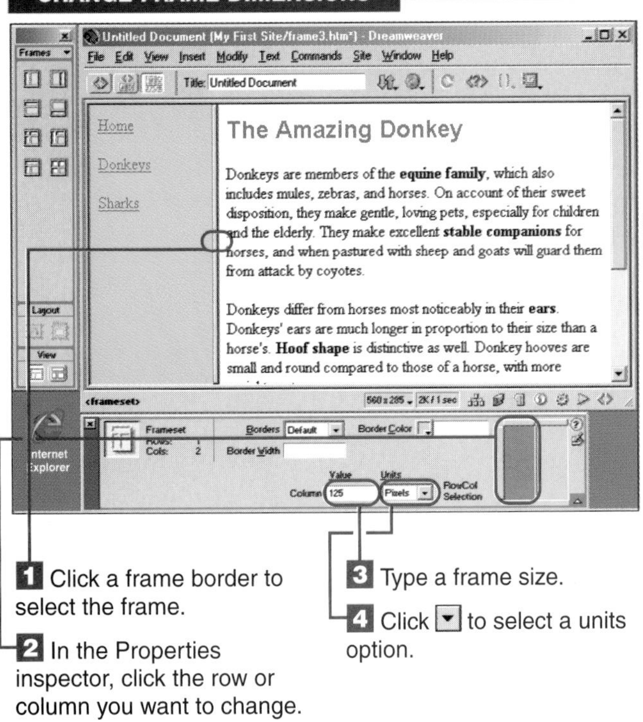

1 Click a frame border to select the frame.

2 In the Properties inspector, click the row or column you want to change.

3 Type a frame size.

4 Click ▾ to select a units option.

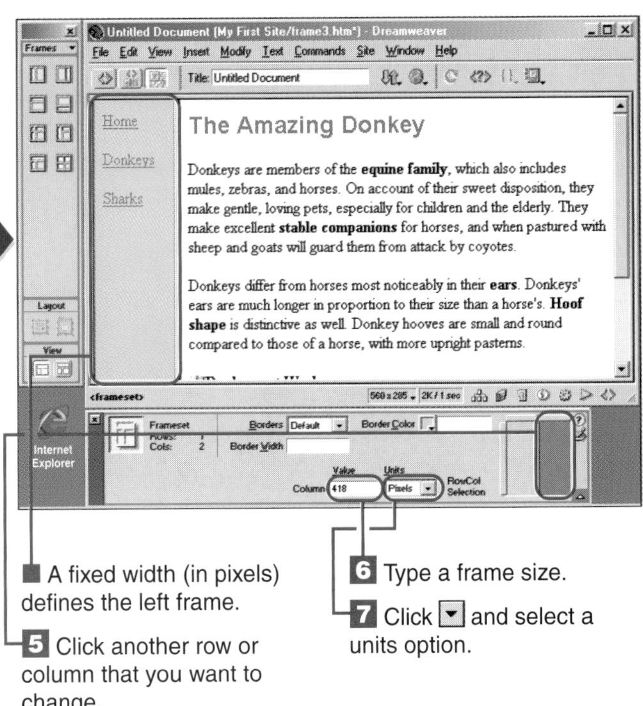

■ A fixed width (in pixels) defines the left frame.

5 Click another row or column that you want to change.

6 Type a frame size.

7 Click ▾ and select a units option.

Is there a shortcut for changing the dimensions of frames?

Yes. You can click and drag a frame border to adjust the dimensions of a frame quickly. The values in the Properties inspector will change as you drag.

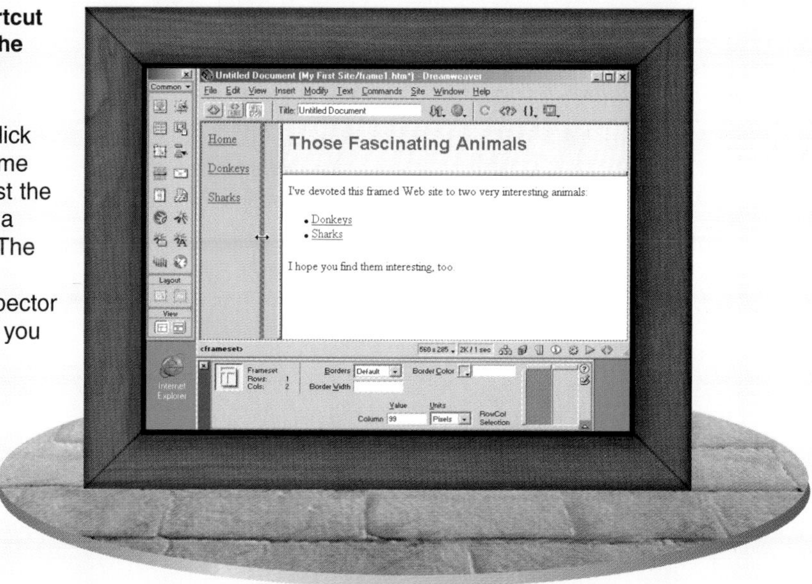

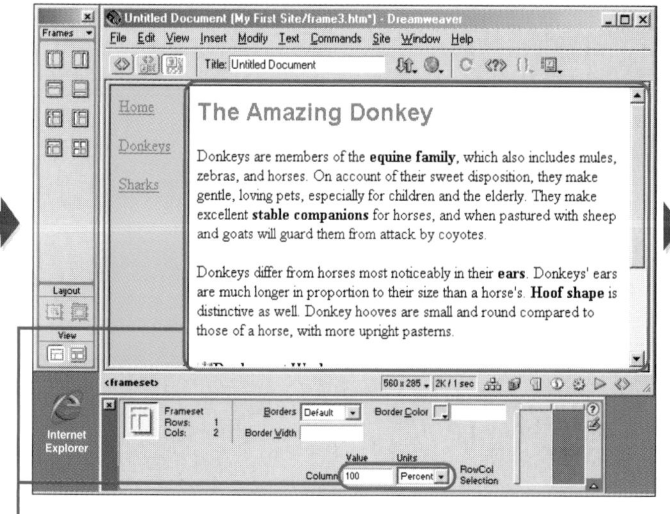

■ A percentage width defines the right frame. The right frame takes up the remaining space in the browser window.

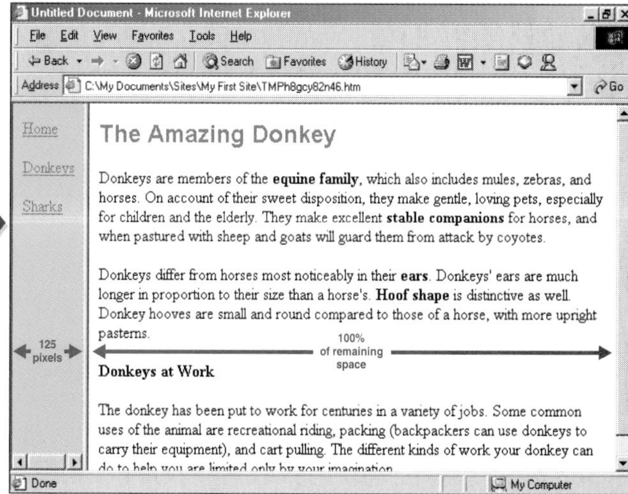

8 Preview the page in a Web browser.

■ The frameset displays as Dreamweaver defines it.

HYPERLINK TO A FRAME

You can create a hyperlink that opens a page in a different frame. You will want to do this for frames that contain navigation hyperlinks.

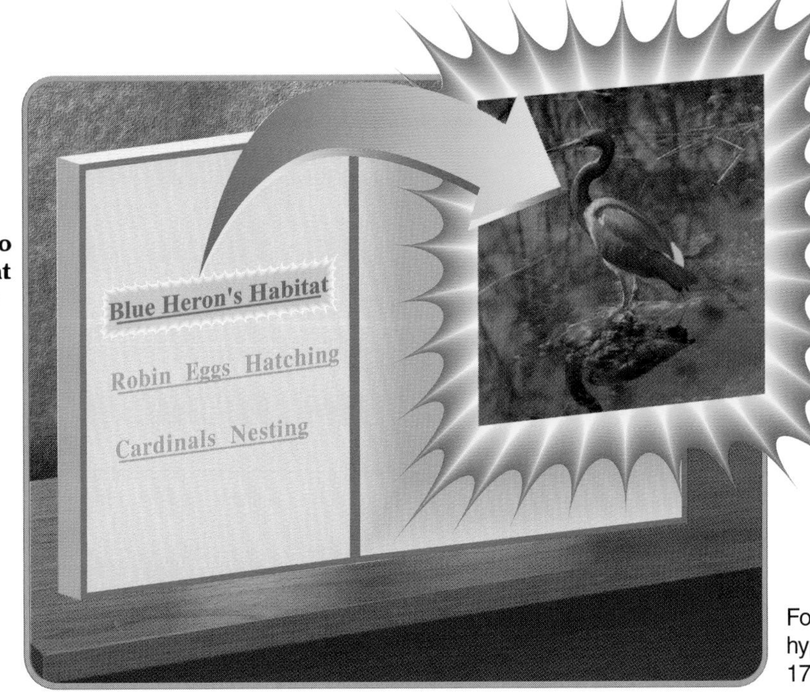

For more information about hyperlinking, see Chapter 17.

HYPERLINK TO A FRAME

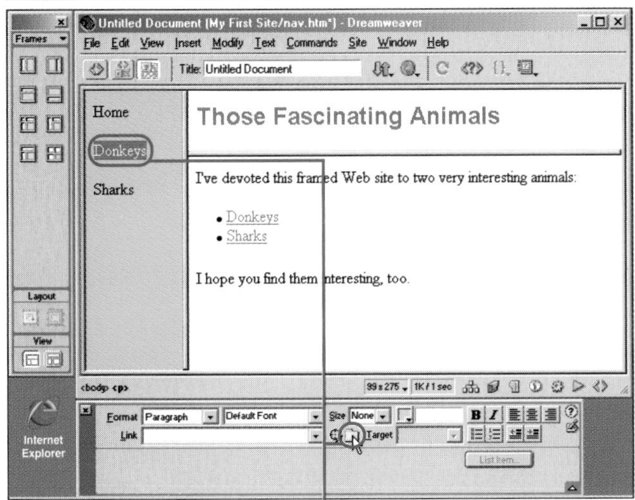

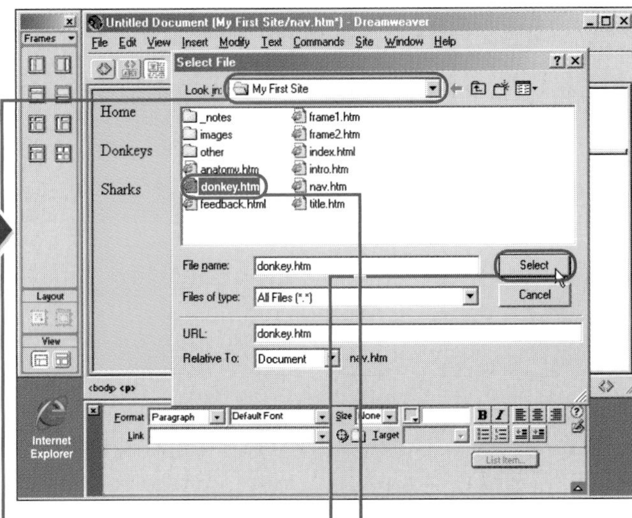

1 Assign names to your frames.

Note: See the section "Name a Frame" for instructions on how to name a frame.

2 Click and drag to select the text or image that you want to turn into a hyperlink.

3 Click ▢ to open the Select File dialog box.

4 Click ▾ to select the folder containing the destination file.

5 Click the destination file.

6 Click **Select**.

What happens if I select _top for my hyperlink target?

Selecting `_top`, instead of a frame name, opens the hyperlink destination on top of any existing framesets. This action takes the user out of an existing frameset in a site.

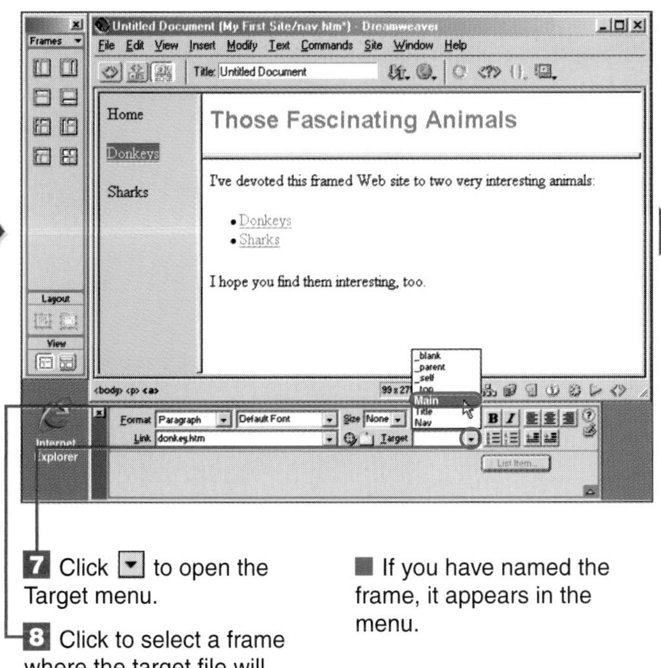

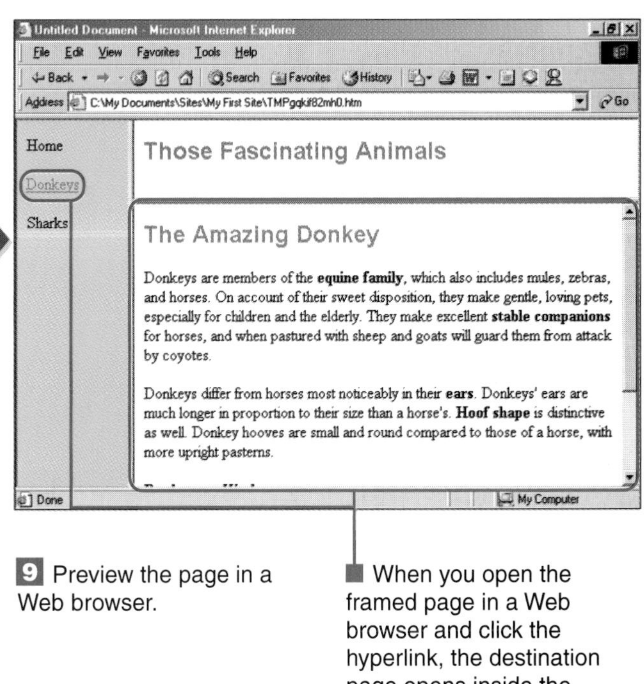

7 Click ▾ to open the Target menu.

8 Click to select a frame where the target file will open.

■ If you have named the frame, it appears in the menu.

9 Preview the page in a Web browser.

■ When you open the framed page in a Web browser and click the hyperlink, the destination page opens inside the targeted frame.

SAVE A FRAMED SITE

Saving your framed site requires you to save the HTML documents that appear in the frames as well as the frameset that defines how the frames are organized.

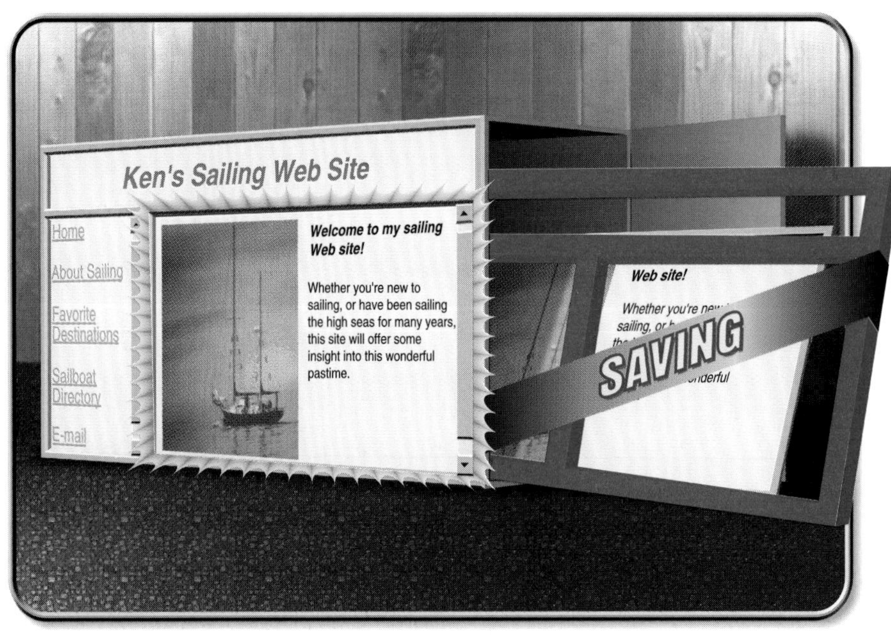

You need to save all of the documents before you can upload your site.

SAVE A FRAMED SITE

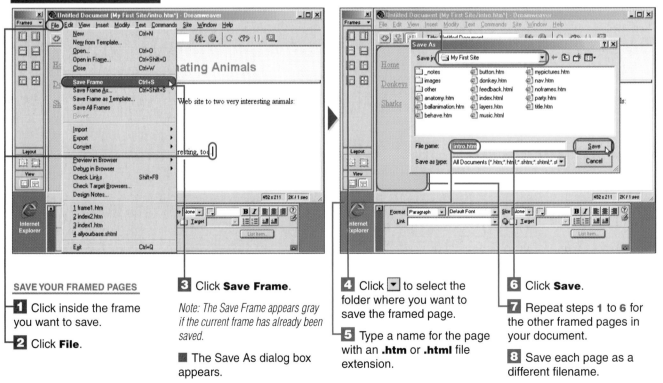

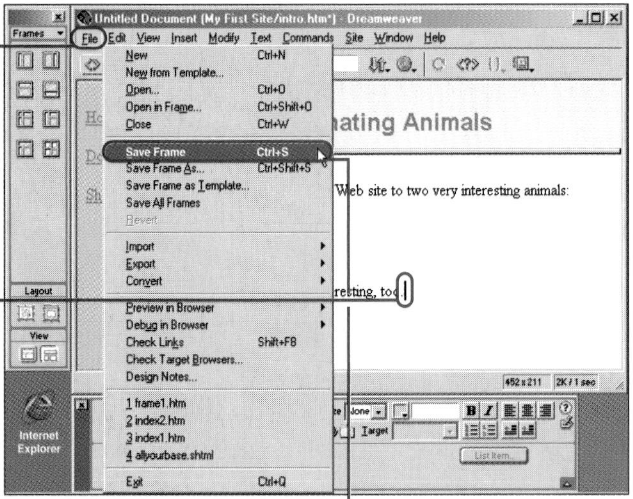

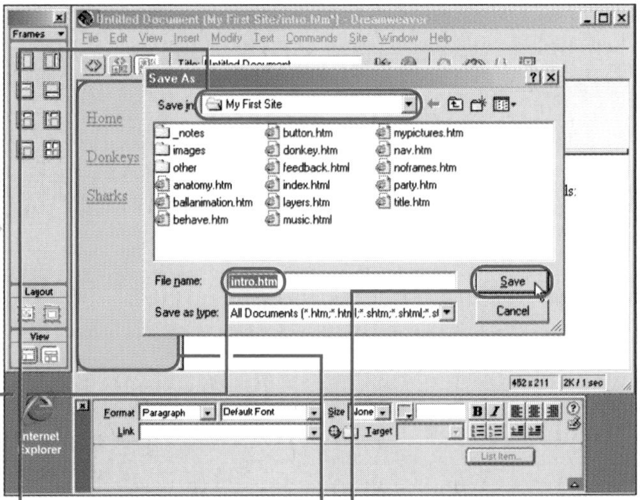

SAVE YOUR FRAMED PAGES

1 Click inside the frame you want to save.

2 Click **File**.

3 Click **Save Frame**.

Note: The Save Frame appears gray if the current frame has already been saved.

■ The Save As dialog box appears.

4 Click ▾ to select the folder where you want to save the framed page.

5 Type a name for the page with an **.htm** or **.html** file extension.

6 Click **Save**.

7 Repeat steps **1** to **6** for the other framed pages in your document.

8 Save each page as a different filename.

Is there a shortcut for saving all the pages of my framed site?

Yes. You can click **File** and then **Save All Frames**. This will save all the framed pages and framesets that make up your site. This is definitely a time saver!

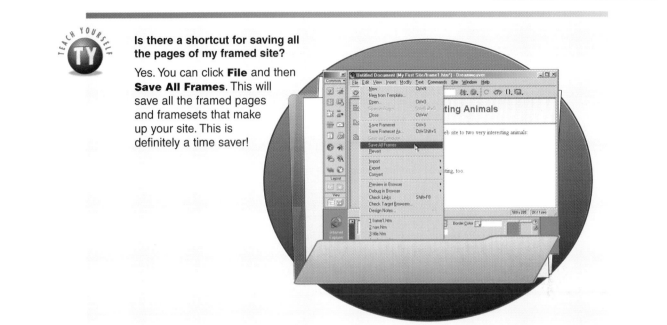

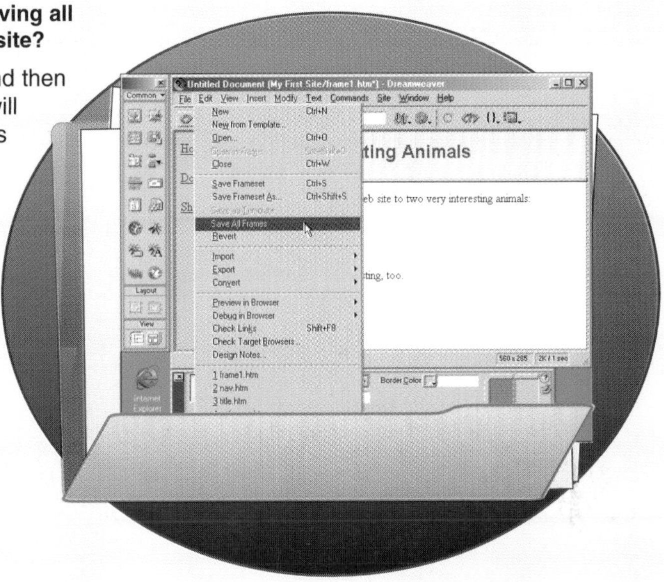

SAVE THE FRAMESET

1 Click anywhere on the frame border to select the frameset.

2 Click **File**.

3 Click **Save Frameset As**.

■ The Save As dialog box appears.

4 Click ▼ to select the folder where you want to save the frameset.

5 Type a name for the frameset with an **.htm** or **.html** file extension.

6 Click **Save**.

CREATE A LIBRARY ITEM

You can define text, images, and other Dreamweaver, Flash, or Fireworks objects as library items. Library items enable you to insert such page elements quickly without having to re-create them from scratch every time.

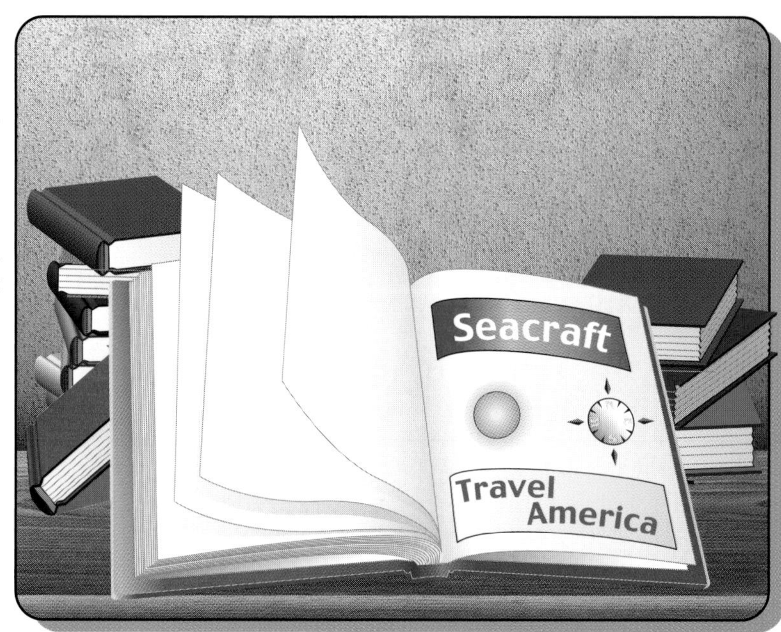

If you edit a library item, Dreamweaver can automatically update each instance of the item throughout your site.

CREATE A LIBRARY ITEM

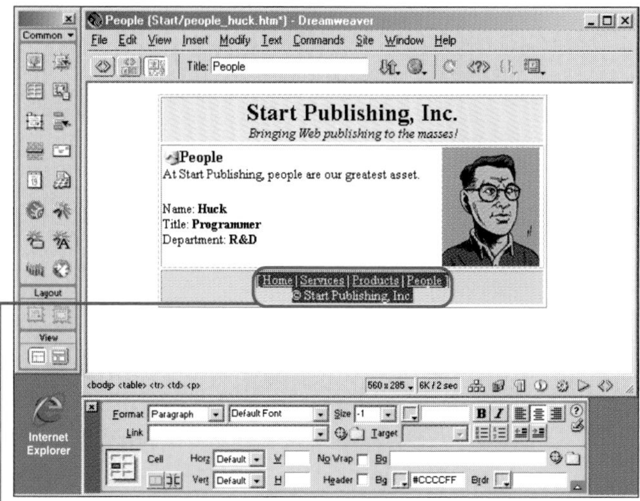

1 Click and drag to select the part of your page that you want to define as a library item.

Note: To create library items for your Web pages, you must define a local site. See Chapter 14 to set up a local site.

■ You can create Library items from any elements that appear in the body of an HTML document. These elements include text, images, tables, forms, layers, and multimedia.

2 Click **Modify**.

3 Click **Library**.

4 Click **Add Object To Library**.

What page elements should I consider defining as library items?

Anything that appears multiple times in a Web site is a good candidate to become a library item. These elements include headers, footers, navigational menus, contact information, and disclaimers. Corporate logos created in Fireworks or button animations created in Flash are also good candidates.

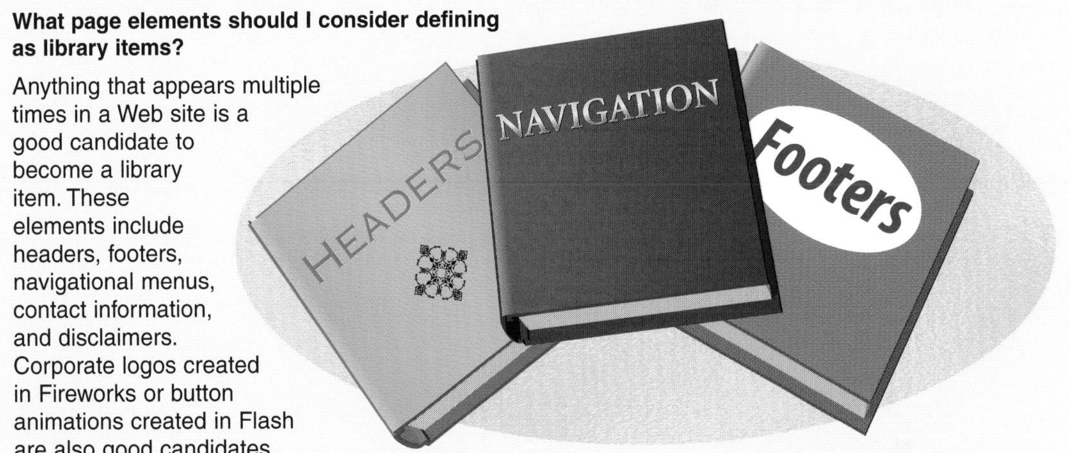

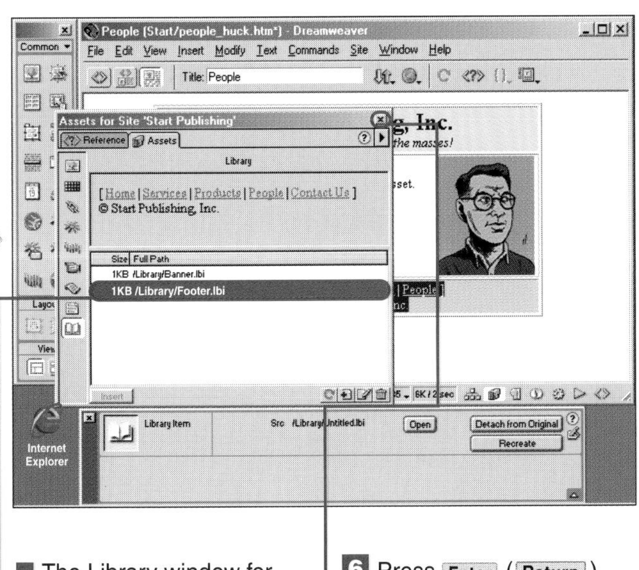

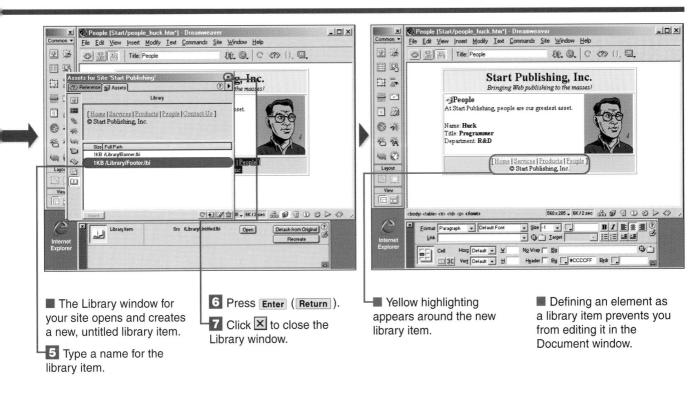

■ The Library window for your site opens and creates a new, untitled library item.

5 Type a name for the library item.

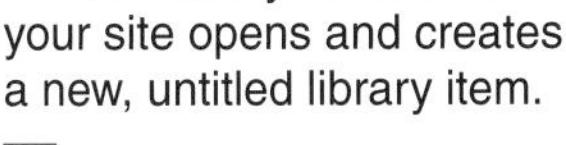

6 Press Enter (Return).

7 Click ☒ to close the Library window.

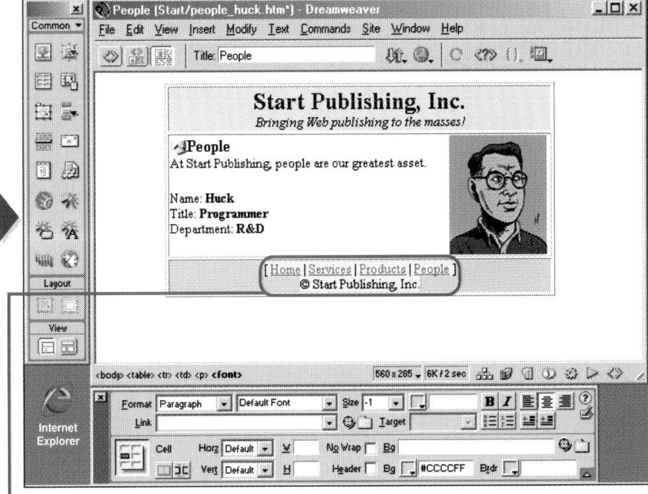

■ Yellow highlighting appears around the new library item.

■ Defining an element as a library item prevents you from editing it in the Document window.

INSERT A LIBRARY ITEM

Inserting an element onto your page from the library saves you from having to create it from scratch. It also ensures that the element is identical to other instances of that library item in your site.

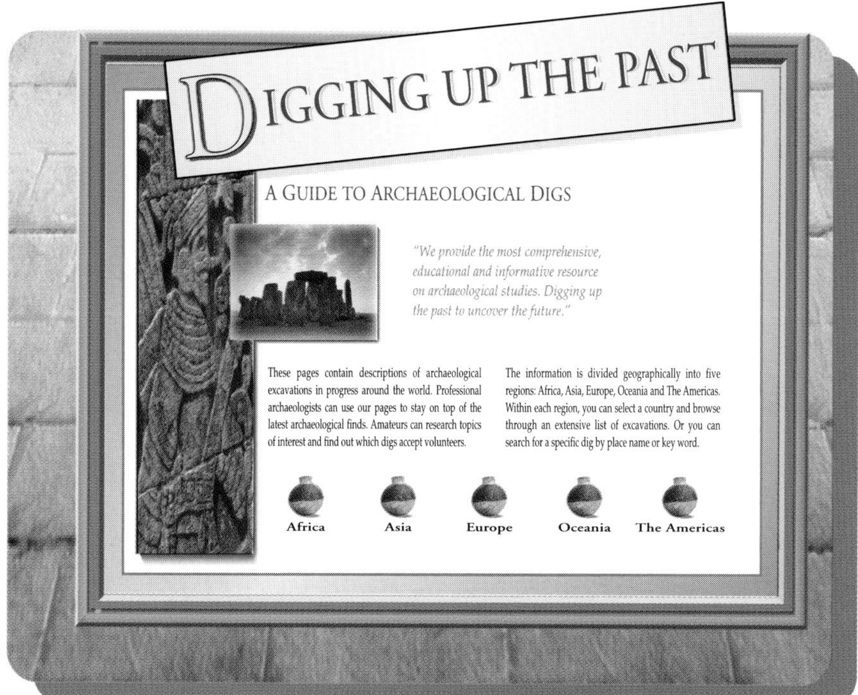

INSERT A LIBRARY ITEM

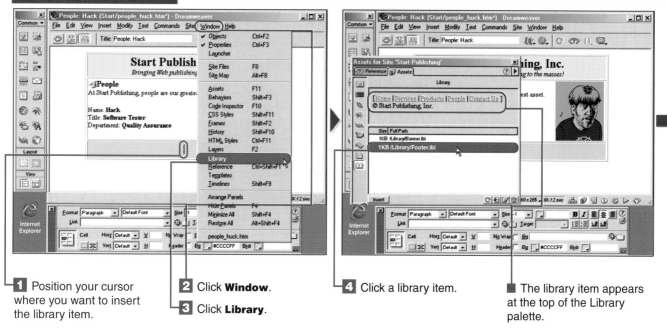

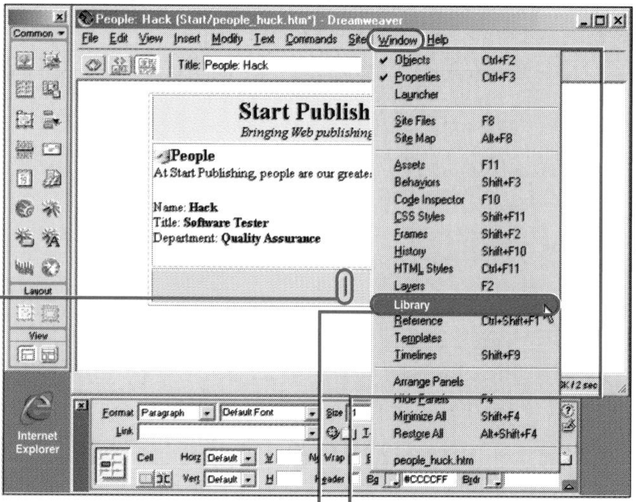

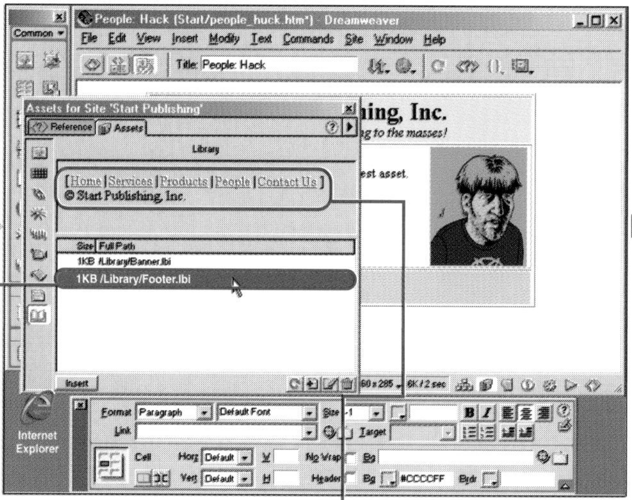

1 Position your cursor where you want to insert the library item.

2 Click **Window**.

3 Click **Library**.

4 Click a library item.

■ The library item appears at the top of the Library palette.

How do I edit a library item that has been inserted into a page?

Instances of library items in your pages are locked, and cannot be edited. To edit a library item, you need to edit the original version of that item from the library. You can also detach an instance of a library item from the library for editing, but then the instance is no longer a part of the library. See the section "Edit a Library Item and Update Your Website" later in this chapter.

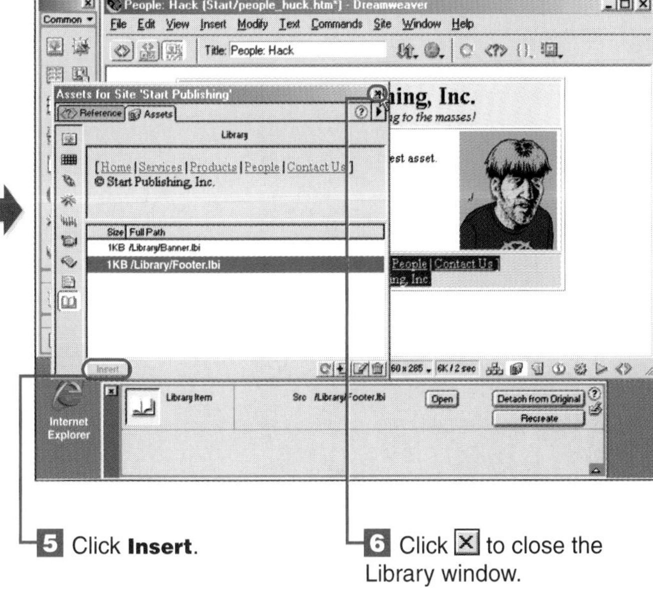

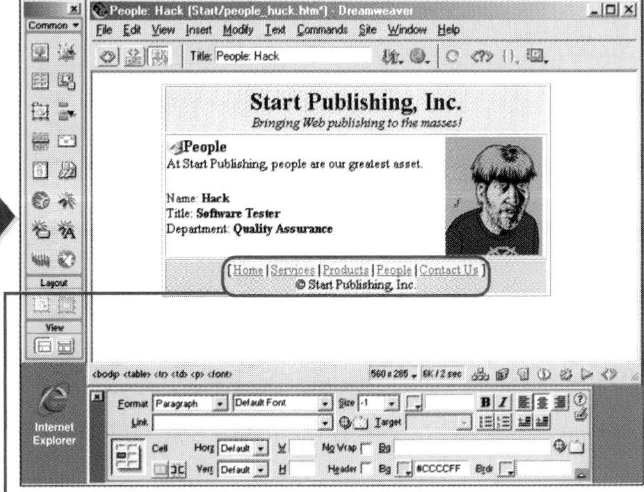

5 Click **Insert**.

6 Click ☒ to close the Library window.

■ Dreamweaver inserts the library item, which is highlighted in yellow, in the Document window.

EDIT A LIBRARY ITEM AND UPDATE YOUR WEB SITE

You can edit a library item and then automatically update all the pages in your site that feature that item. This feature can save you time when maintaining a Web site.

EDIT A LIBRARY ITEM AND UPDATE YOUR WEB SITE

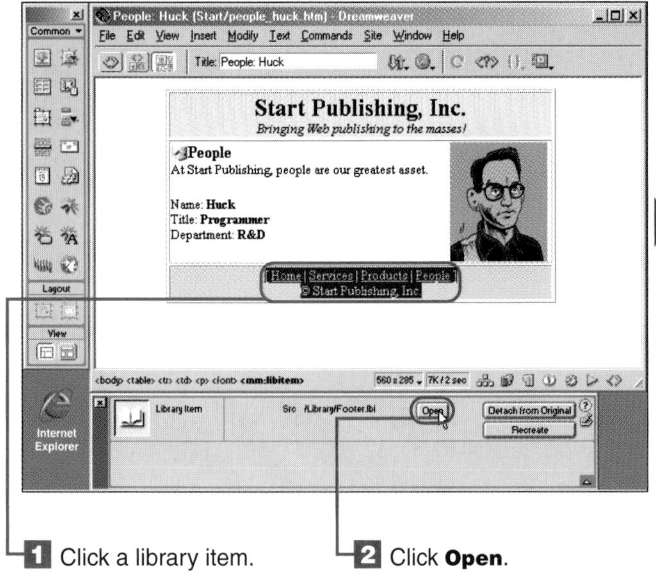

1 Click a library item.

2 Click **Open**.

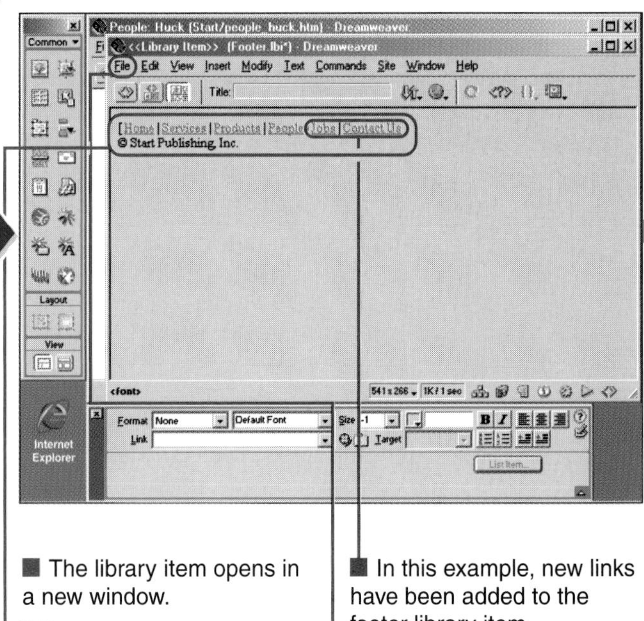

■ The library item opens in a new window.

3 Edit the library item.

■ In this example, new links have been added to the footer library item.

4 Click **File**.

5 Click **Save**.

What will my pages look like after I have edited a library item and updated my site?

All the pages in your site that contain an instance of the library item will have those instances replaced with the edited version. By using the library feature, you can make a change to a single library item and have hundreds of Web pages updated automatically.

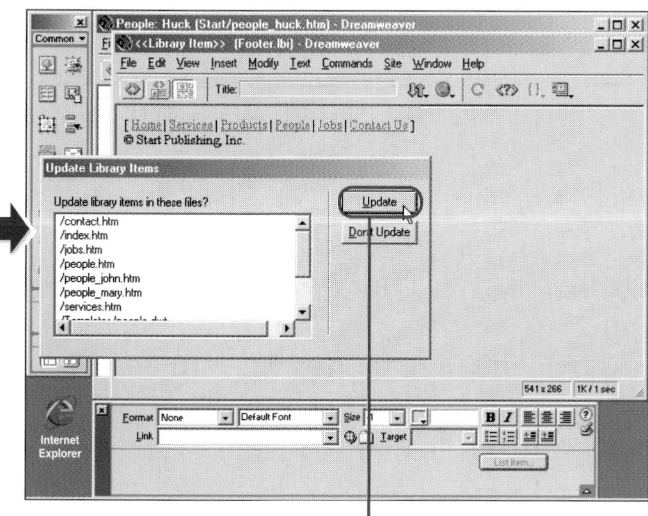

■ An alert box asks if you want to update all the instances of the library item in the site.

6 Click **Update**.

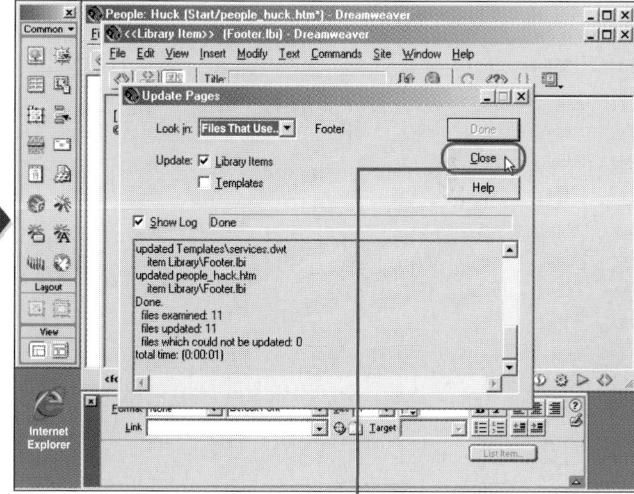

■ A dialog box shows the progress of the updates.

7 After Dreamweaver finishes updating the site, click **Close**.

CREATE A TEMPLATE

To help you save time, you can create generic template pages to use as starting points for new pages.

CREATE A TEMPLATE

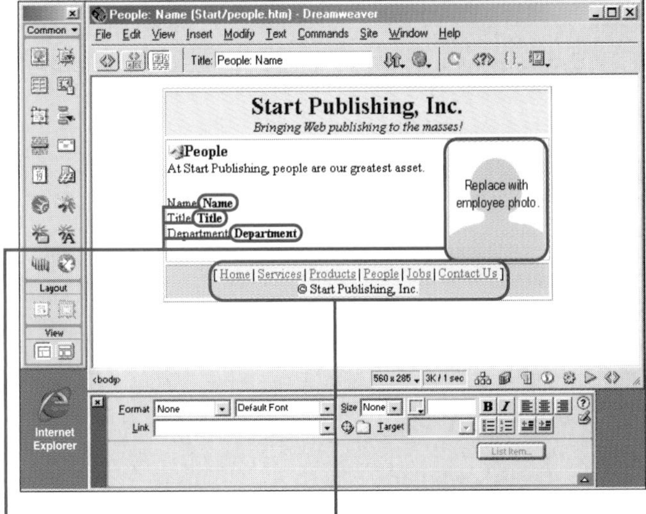

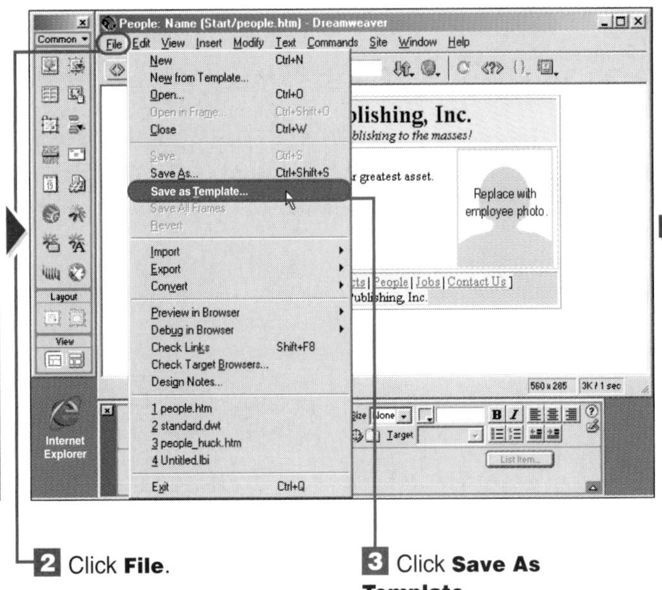

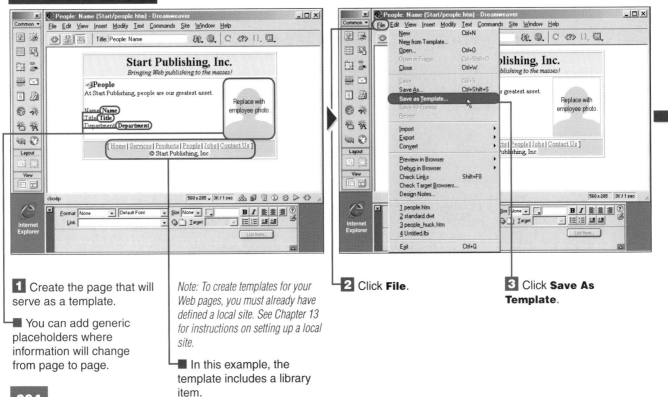

1 Create the page that will serve as a template.

■ You can add generic placeholders where information will change from page to page.

Note: To create templates for your Web pages, you must already have defined a local site. See Chapter 13 for instructions on setting up a local site.

■ In this example, the template includes a library item.

2 Click **File**.

3 Click **Save As Template**.

What are the different types of content in a template?

A template contains two types of content: editable and locked. After you create a new Web page based on a template, you can only change the parts of the new page that are defined as editable. To change locked content, you must edit the original template.

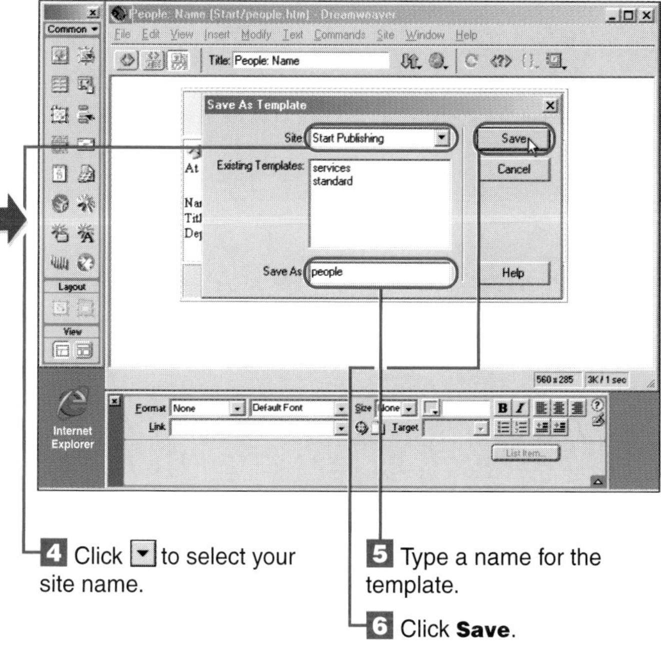

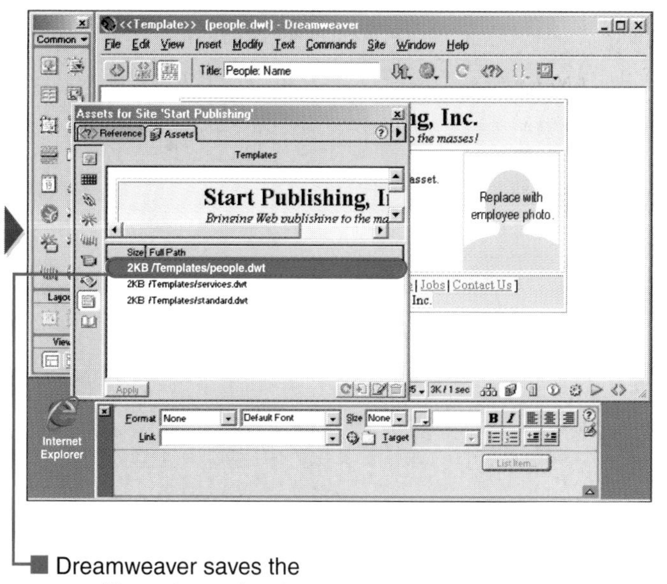

4 Click ▾ to select your site name.

5 Type a name for the template.

6 Click **Save**.

■ Dreamweaver saves the page with a `.dwt` extension in the Templates folder.

EDIT A TEMPLATE AND UPDATE YOUR WEB SITE

You can make changes to an original template file and then have Dreamweaver update other pages that were based on that template. This enables you to make wholesale changes to the page design of your site in seconds.

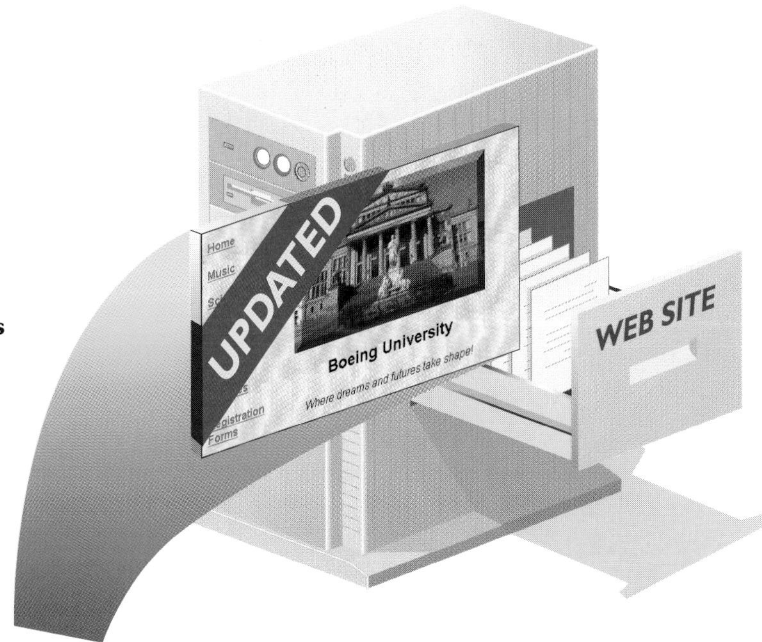

EDIT A TEMPLATE AND UPDATE YOUR WEB SITE

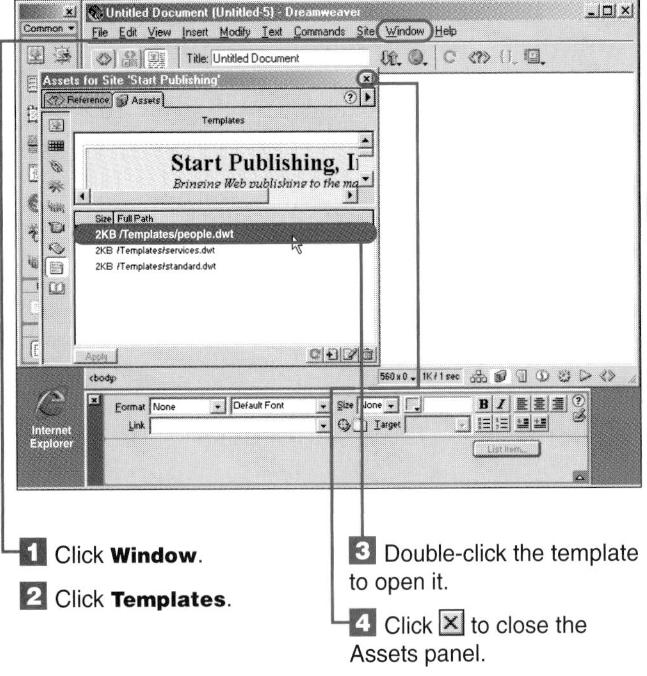

1 Click **Window**.

2 Click **Templates**.

3 Double-click the template to open it.

4 Click ☒ to close the Assets panel.

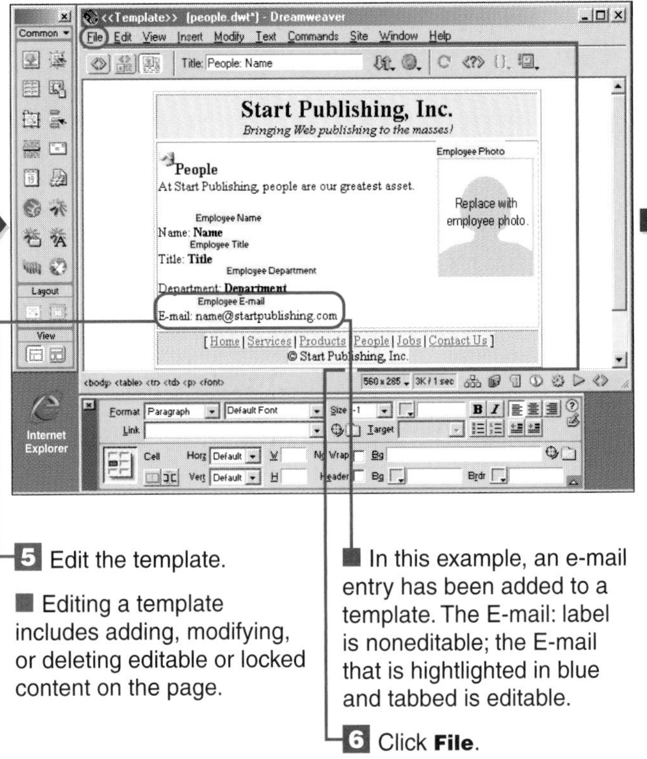

5 Edit the template.

■ Editing a template includes adding, modifying, or deleting editable or locked content on the page.

■ In this example, an e-mail entry has been added to a template. The E-mail: label is noneditable; the E-mail that is hightlighted in blue and tabbed is editable.

6 Click **File**.

7 Click **Save**.

How does Dreamweaver store page templates?

Dreamweaver stores page templates in a folder called *Templates* inside the local site folder. You can open templates by clicking **File**, **Open**, and then the ▼ to select the **Templates** folder. After opening the Templates folder, click to select a template file. (You can also open templates from inside the Assets panel.)

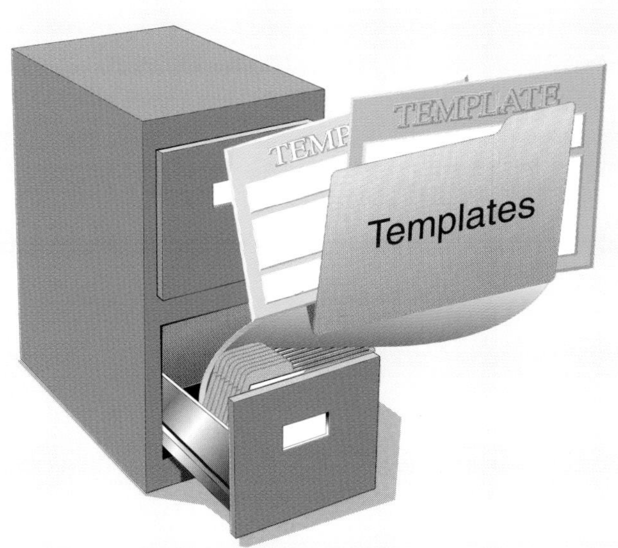

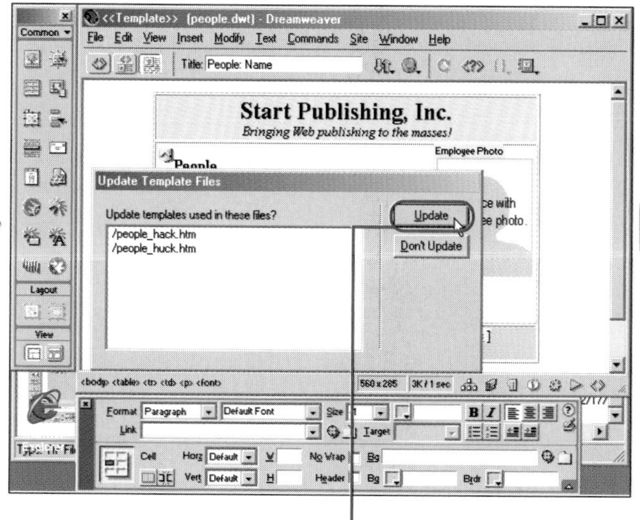

■ An alert box appears asking if you want to update all the pages that are based on the template.

8 Click **Update**.

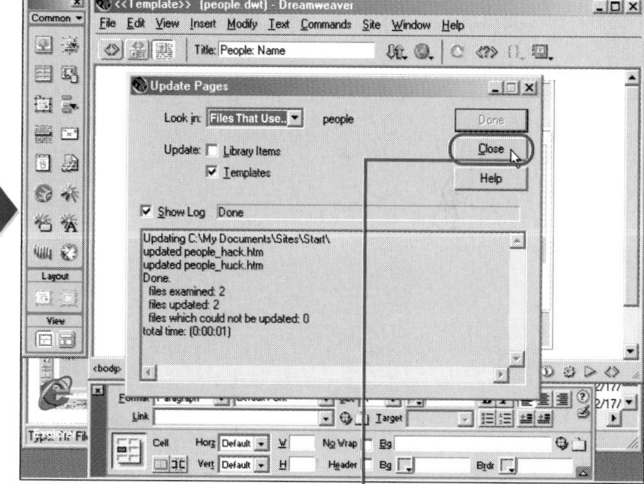

■ A dialog box shows the progress of the updates.

9 After Dreamweaver finishes updating the site, click **Close**.

CREATE A NEW HTML STYLE

Dreamweaver allows you to save time by saving complicated text styles in the HTML Styles window. You can easily use them later.

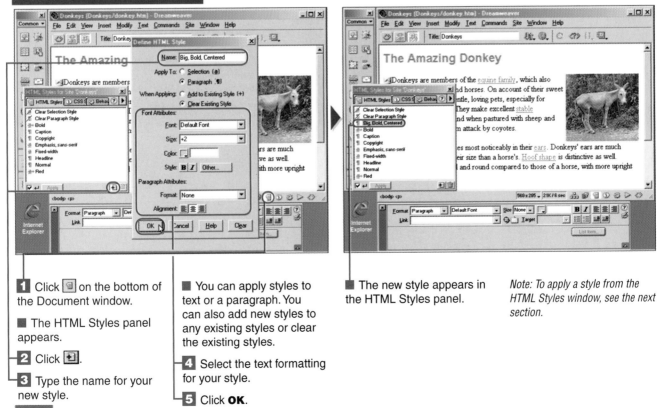

CREATE A NEW HTML STYLE

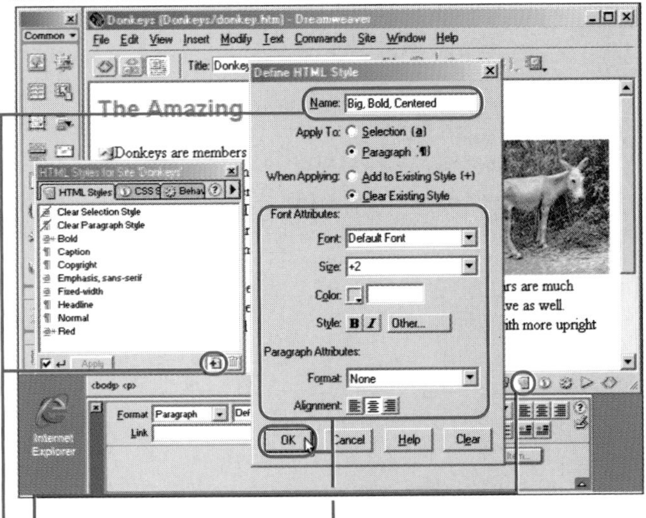

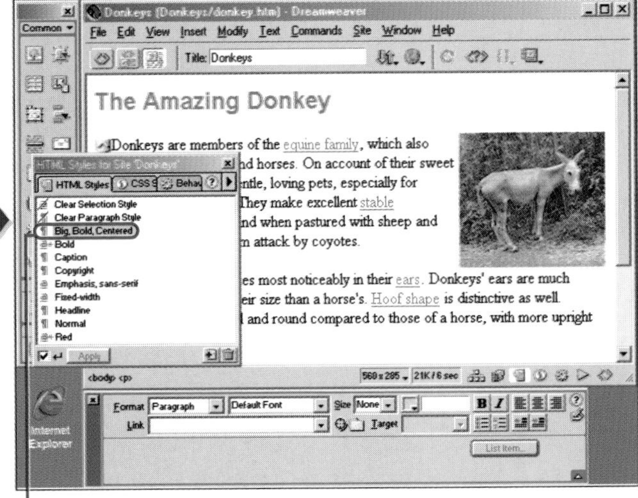

1 Click [icon] on the bottom of the Document window.

■ The HTML Styles panel appears.

2 Click [icon].

3 Type the name for your new style.

■ You can apply styles to text or a paragraph. You can also add new styles to any existing styles or clear the existing styles.

4 Select the text formatting for your style.

5 Click **OK**.

■ The new style appears in the HTML Styles panel.

Note: To apply a style from the HTML Styles window, see the next section.

APPLY HTML STYLES

You can format text using the HTML Styles panel, which allows you to apply complicated style with a single click.

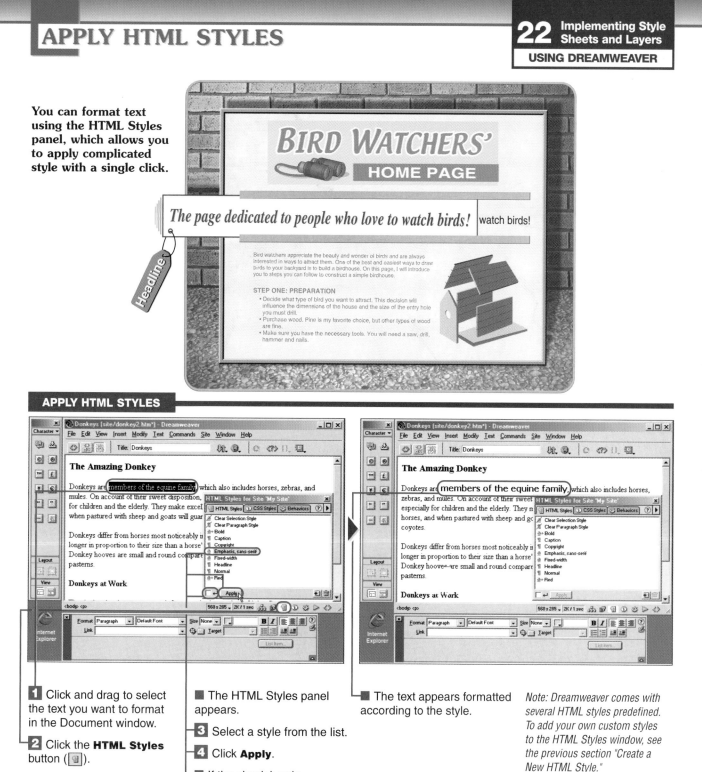

APPLY HTML STYLES

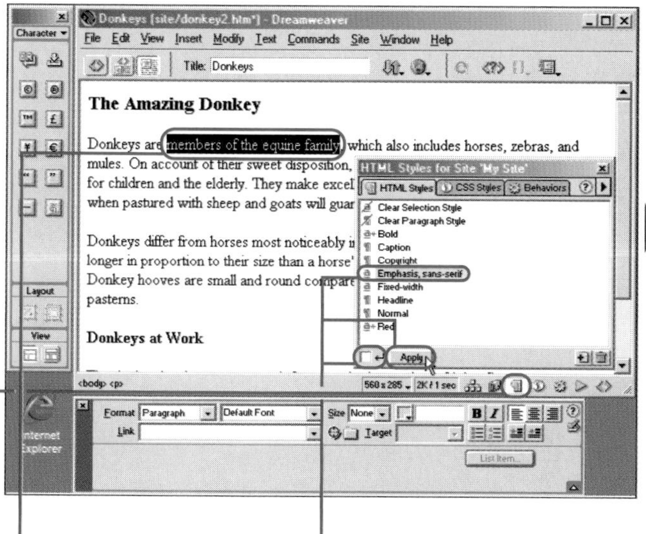

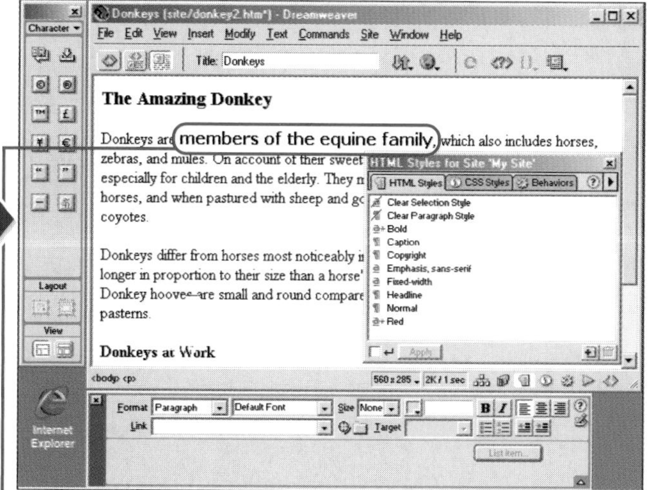

1 Click and drag to select the text you want to format in the Document window.

2 Click the **HTML Styles** button (▤).

■ You can also click **Window** and then **HTML Styles**.

■ The HTML Styles panel appears.

3 Select a style from the list.

4 Click **Apply**.

■ If the check box is selected, the style applies automatically.

■ The text appears formatted according to the style.

Note: Dreamweaver comes with several HTML styles predefined. To add your own custom styles to the HTML Styles window, see the previous section "Create a New HTML Style."

CUSTOMIZE AN HTML TAG

You can use style sheets to customize the style that is applied by an HTML tag. This capability gives you control over how HTML makes the text and other content on your page appear.

CUSTOMIZE AN HTML TAG

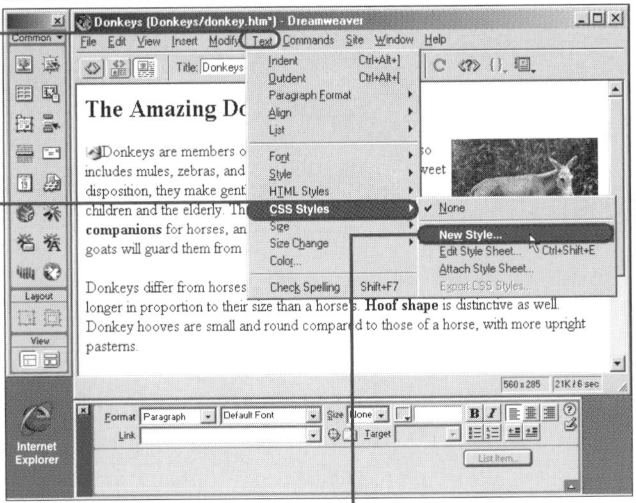

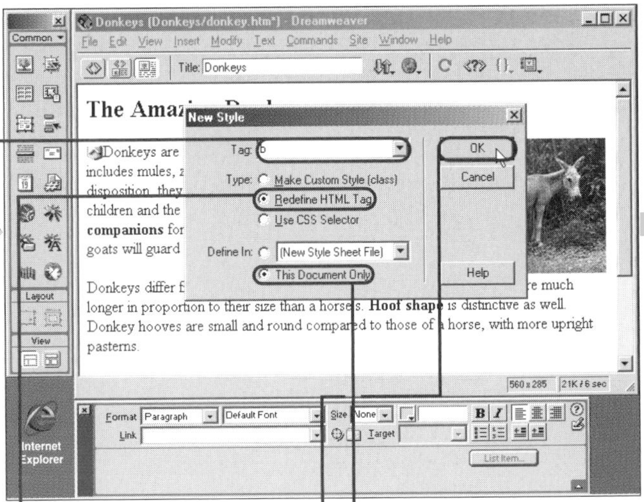

1 Click **Text**.

2 Click **CSS Styles**.

3 Click **New Style** to open the New Style dialog box.

4 Click **Redefine HTML Tag** (○ changes to ◉).

5 Click ▾ to select a tag from the list.

6 Click **This Document Only** to create an embedded style sheet (○ changes to ◉).

7 Click **OK**.

How do I edit the style that I have applied to a tag?

Click **Text**, **CSS Styles**, and then **Edit Style Sheet**. A dialog box displays the current customized tags and style-sheet classes. Click the tag and then click **Edit**.

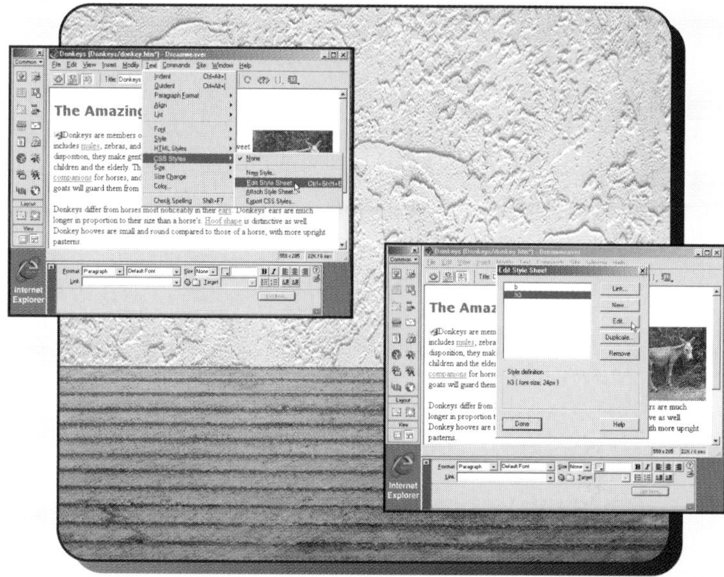

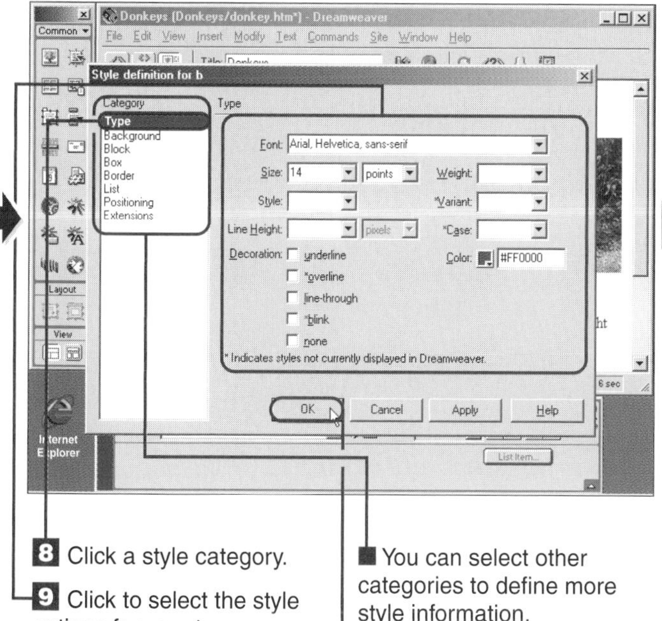

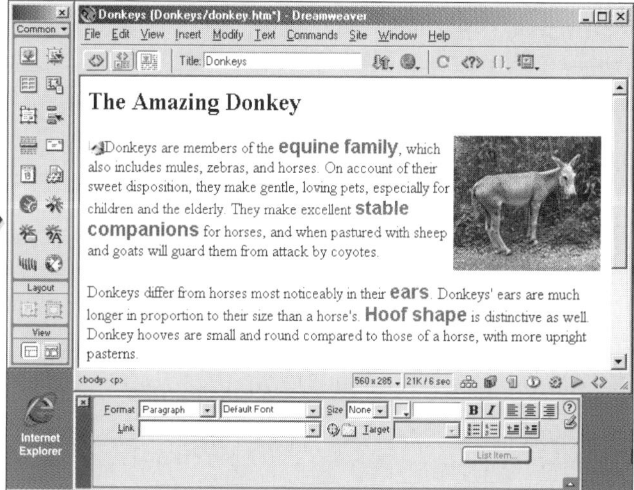

8 Click a style category.

9 Click to select the style options for your tag.

■ In the Type category, you can click ▾ and ☑ options to customize font characteristics.

■ You can select other categories to define more style information.

10 Click **OK** to accept your options.

■ Dreamweaver adds the new style to any content formatted with the redefined tag (example: **<b> tag**).

■ You can also apply the style by formatting new content with the tag.

CREATE A CLASS

You can define specific style attributes as a style sheet *class*. You can then apply that class to elements on your Web page.

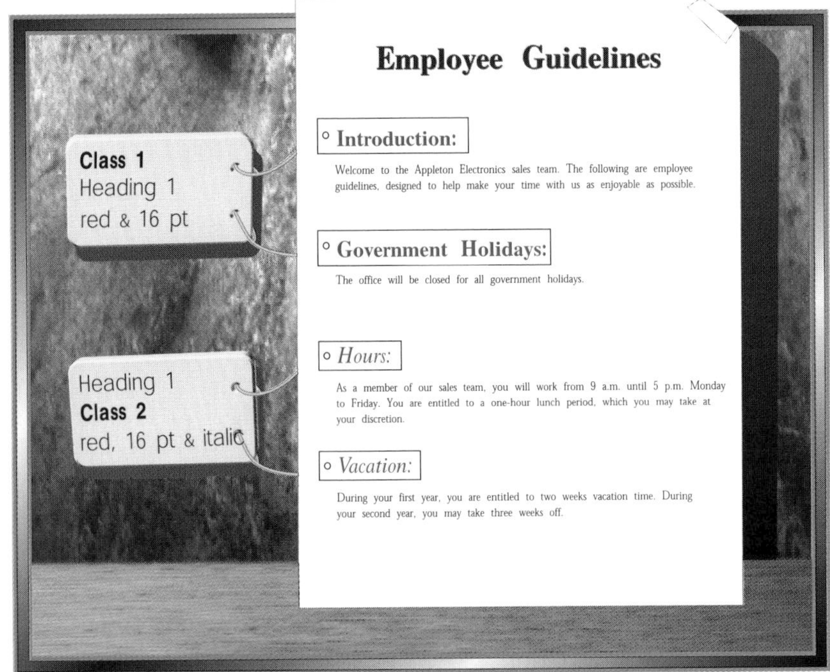

CREATE A CLASS

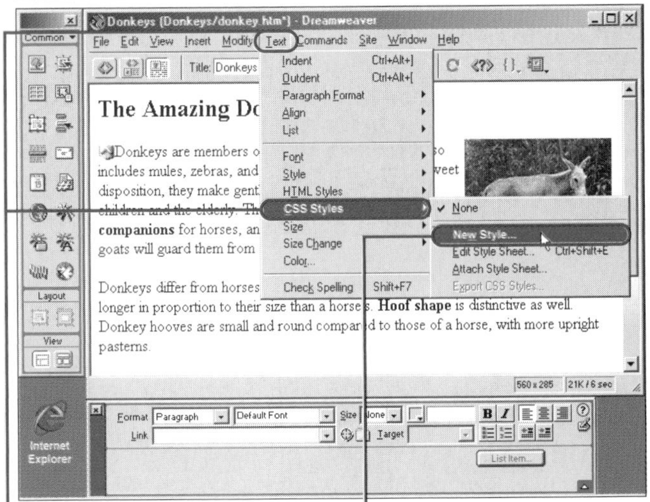

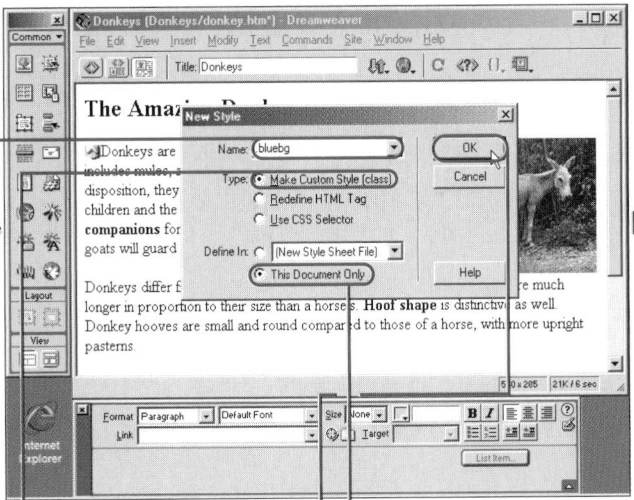

1. Click **Text**.
2. Click **CSS Styles**.
3. Click **New Style** to open the New Style dialog box.
4. Click **Make Custom Style (class)** (○ changes to ◉).
5. Type the name of the class.

   Note: Class names must begin with a period (.).
6. Click **This Document Only** to create an embedded Style sheet (○ changes to ◉).
7. Click **OK**.

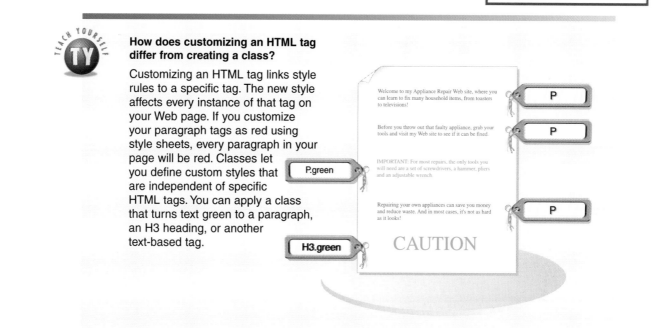

How does customizing an HTML tag differ from creating a class?

Customizing an HTML tag links style rules to a specific tag. The new style affects every instance of that tag on your Web page. If you customize your paragraph tags as red using style sheets, every paragraph in your page will be red. Classes let you define custom styles that are independent of specific HTML tags. You can apply a class that turns text green to a paragraph, an H3 heading, or another text-based tag.

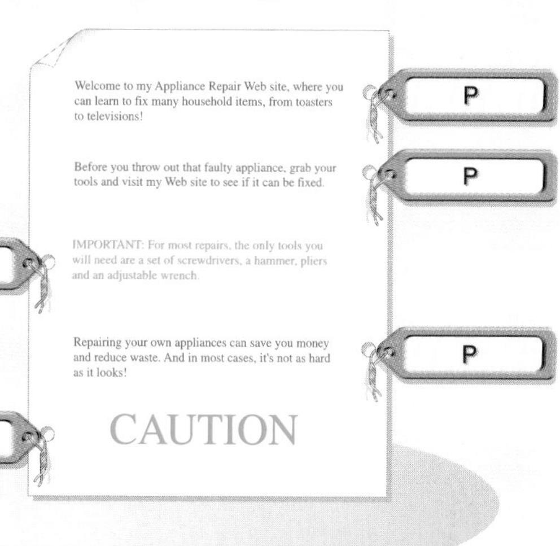

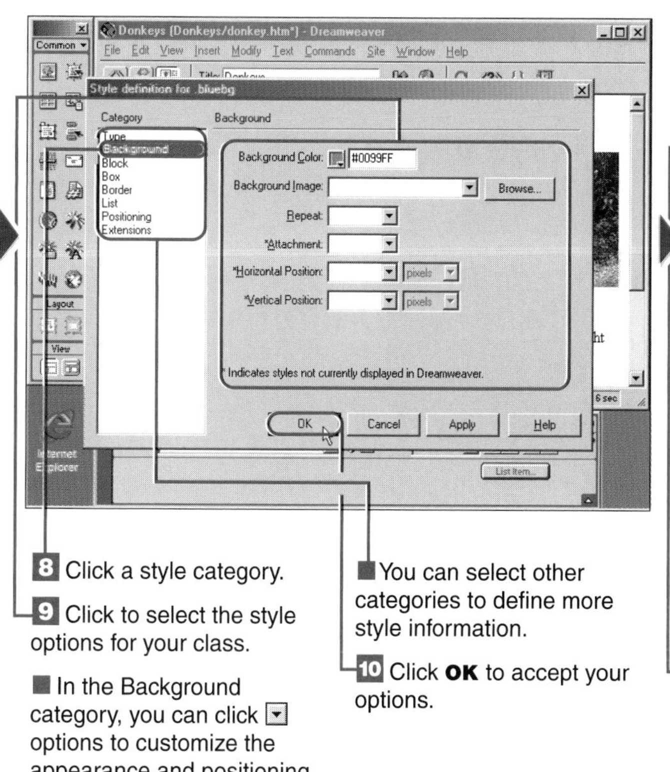

8 Click a style category.

9 Click to select the style options for your class.

■ In the Background category, you can click ▾ options to customize the appearance and positioning of the background.

■ You can select other categories to define more style information.

10 Click **OK** to accept your options.

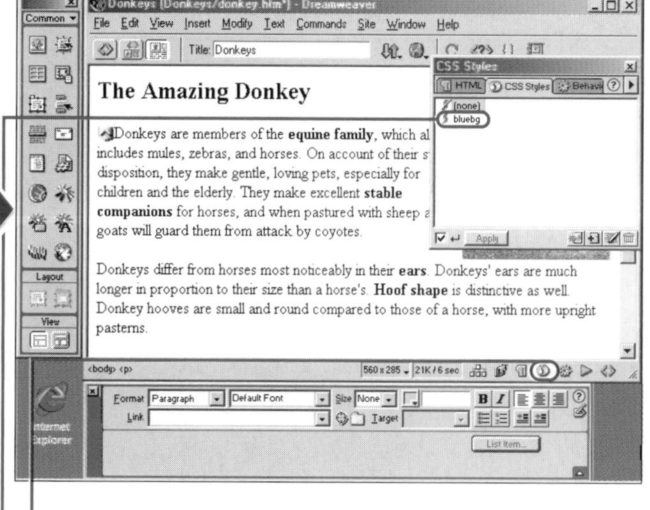

11 Click the **CSS Styles** button ( ) to open the CSS Styles panel.

■ The new class appears in the panel.

■ The new class has no effect on your content until you apply it.

Note: See the next section "Apply a Class" for instructions on applying a class.

APPLY A CLASS

You can apply a style-sheet class to elements on your Web page. This enables you to change the color, font, size, background, and other characteristics of content on your page.

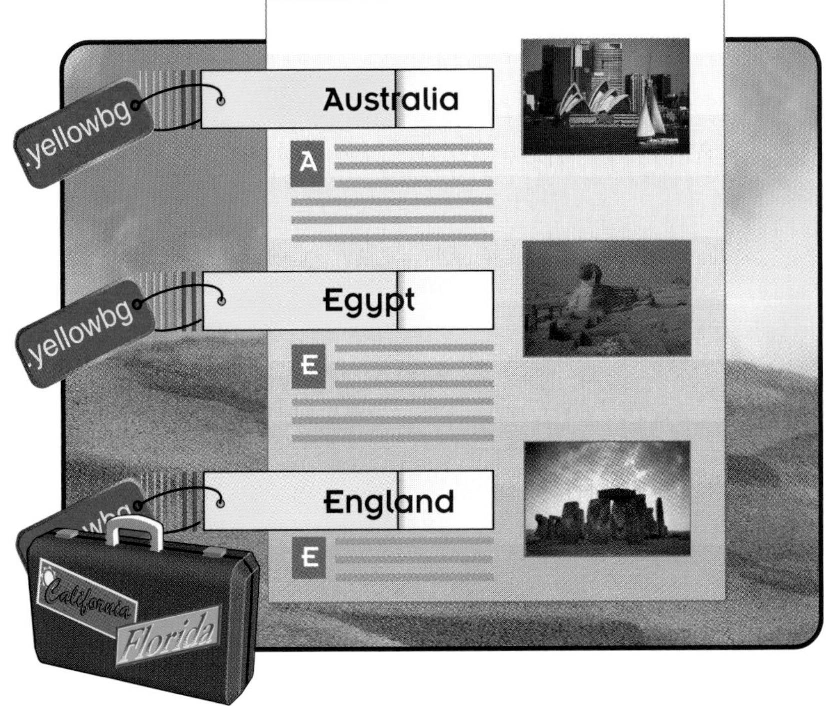

APPLY A CLASS

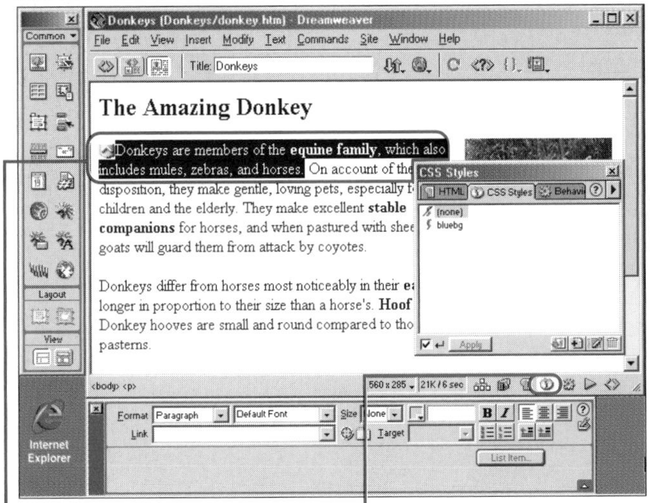

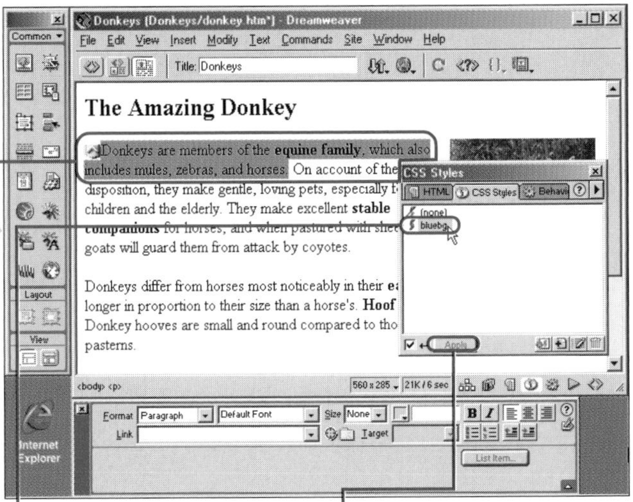

APPLY A CLASS TO AN OBJECT

1 Click and drag to select the object to which you want to apply the class.

2 Click the **CSS Style** button ( ) to open its panel.

3 Click a class.

■ Dreamweaver applies the style-sheet class to the selected content in the Document window.

■ If the Apply check box is unchecked, you can click the **Apply** button to apply the selected class.

Does Dreamweaver display all the styles that I apply to my pages?

Dreamweaver can display only a subset of the style rules that it lets you define. Style rules that are marked with an * in the Style Definitions dialog box cannot be displayed. You need to open the page in a style-sheet-capable browser to view these styles. Some of the styles that Dreamweaver cannot display include borders, word and letter spacing, and list characteristics.

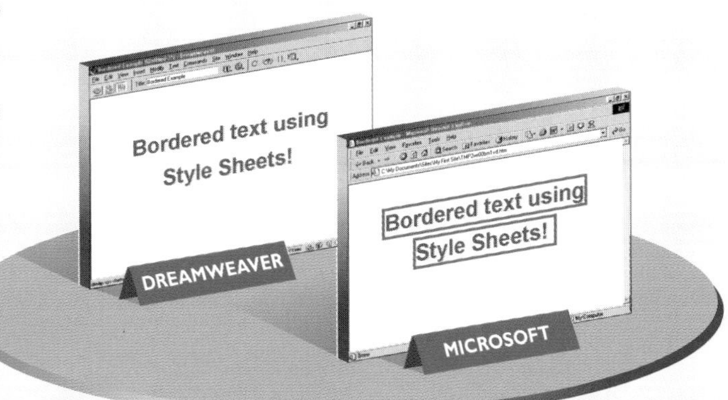

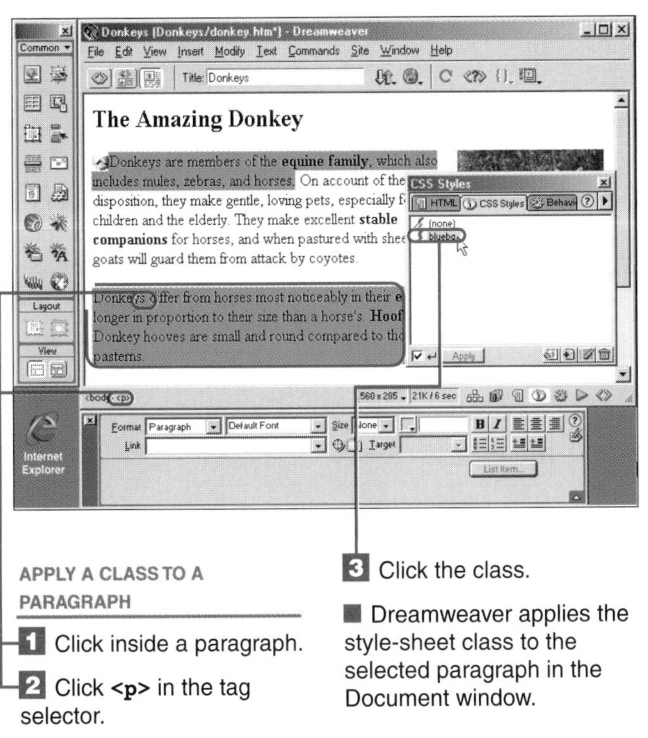

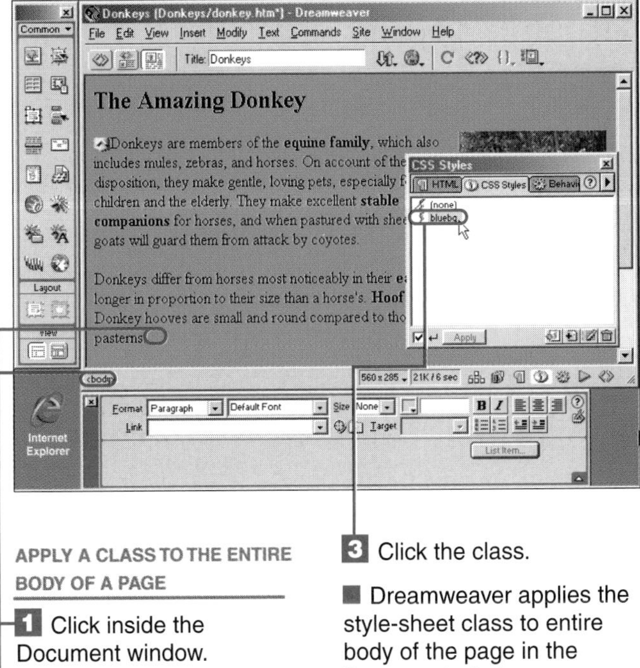

APPLY A CLASS TO A PARAGRAPH

1 Click inside a paragraph.

2 Click <p> in the tag selector.

3 Click the class.

■ Dreamweaver applies the style-sheet class to the selected paragraph in the Document window.

APPLY A CLASS TO THE ENTIRE BODY OF A PAGE

1 Click inside the Document window.

2 Click <body> in the tag selector.

3 Click the class.

■ Dreamweaver applies the style-sheet class to entire body of the page in the Document window.

EDIT A STYLE SHEET CLASS

You can edit the style rules of a class. This changes all the instances where you have applied the class on your pages.

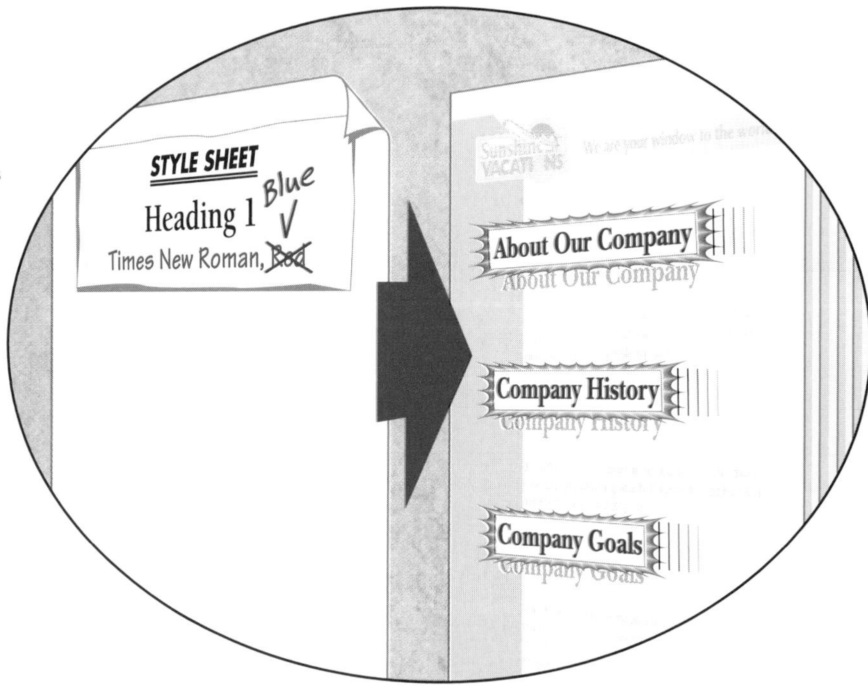

EDIT A STYLE SHEET CLASS

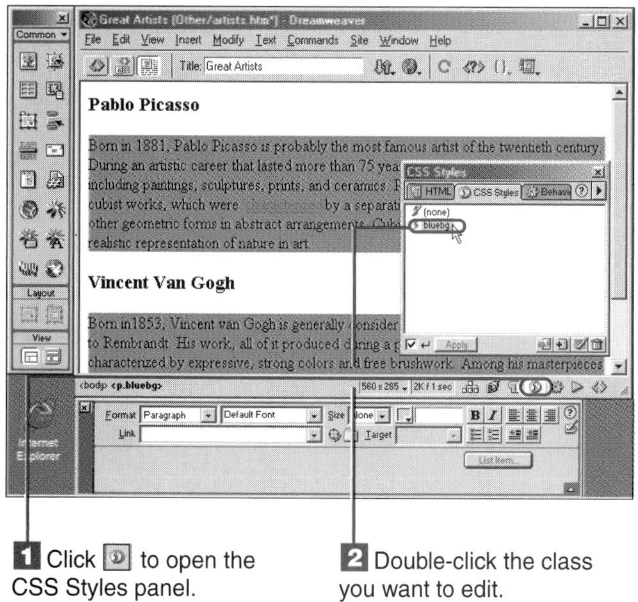

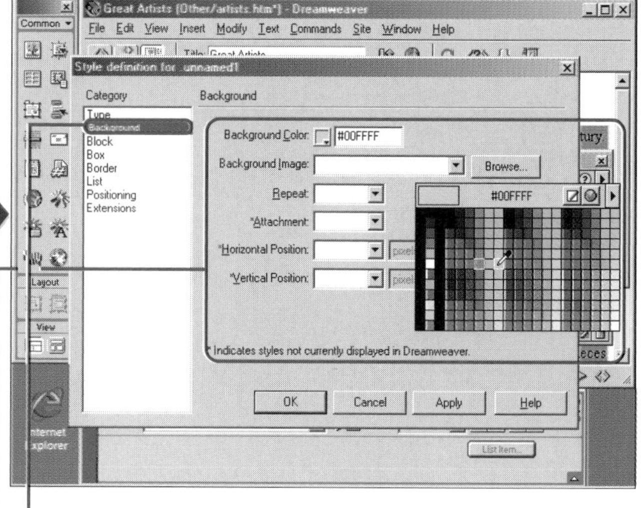

1 Click to open the CSS Styles panel.

■ The CSS Styles panel displays the classes available to that page.

2 Double-click the class you want to edit.

3 Click a style category.

4 Edit the style definitions in the dialog box.

■ In this example, the background color has been changed to a different shade of blue.

What are some type-based features that I can apply with style sheets that I cannot with HTML?

Style sheets let you specify a numeric value for font weight, enabling you to apply varying degrees of boldness (instead of just a single boldness setting as with HTML). This works only with certain fonts. You can also define type size in absolute units (pixels, points, picas, in, cm, or mm) or relative units (ems, exs, or percentage). HTML offers no such choices of units.

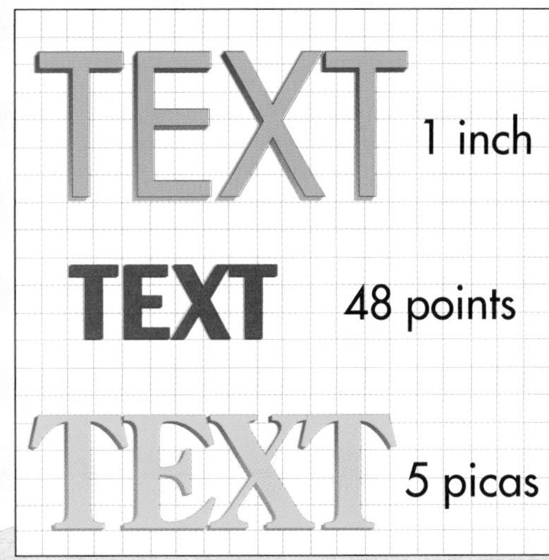

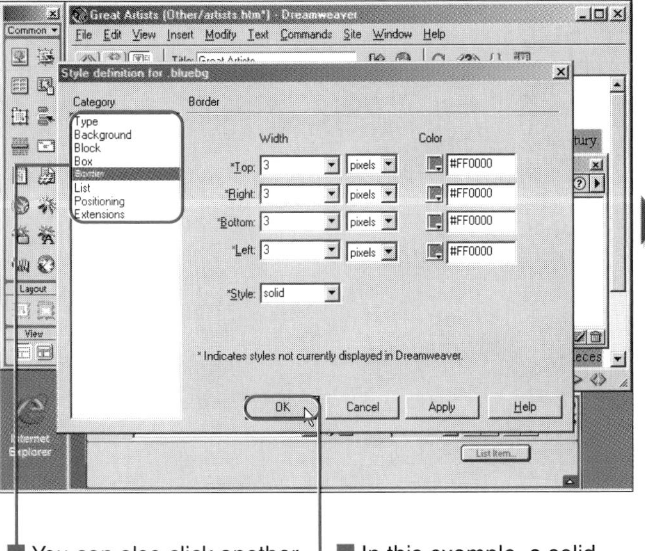

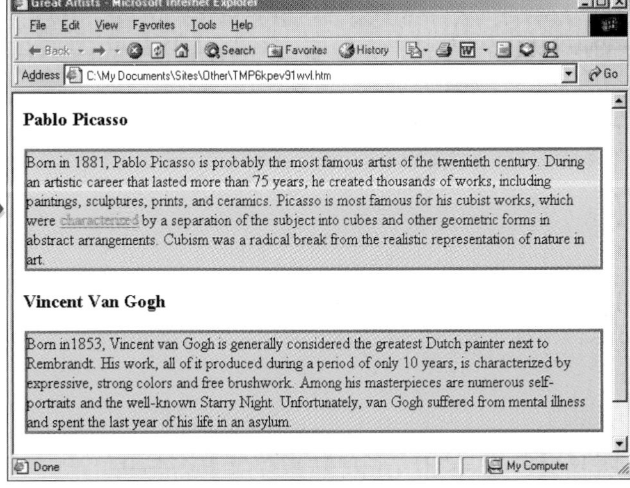

■ You can also click another category to modify more style definitions.

■ In this example, a solid red border has also been added to the class.

5 Click **OK**.

6 Preview the page in a Web browser.

■ The page appears with the edited class applied.

Note: Dreamweaver cannot display some style definitions, for example, border styles. Therefore you must open the page in a Web browser to see the full effect of your edits.

CREATE A LAYER

Layers let you create rectangular areas that float above the other content on your page. You can fill these areas with different types of content and position them precisely in the browser window.

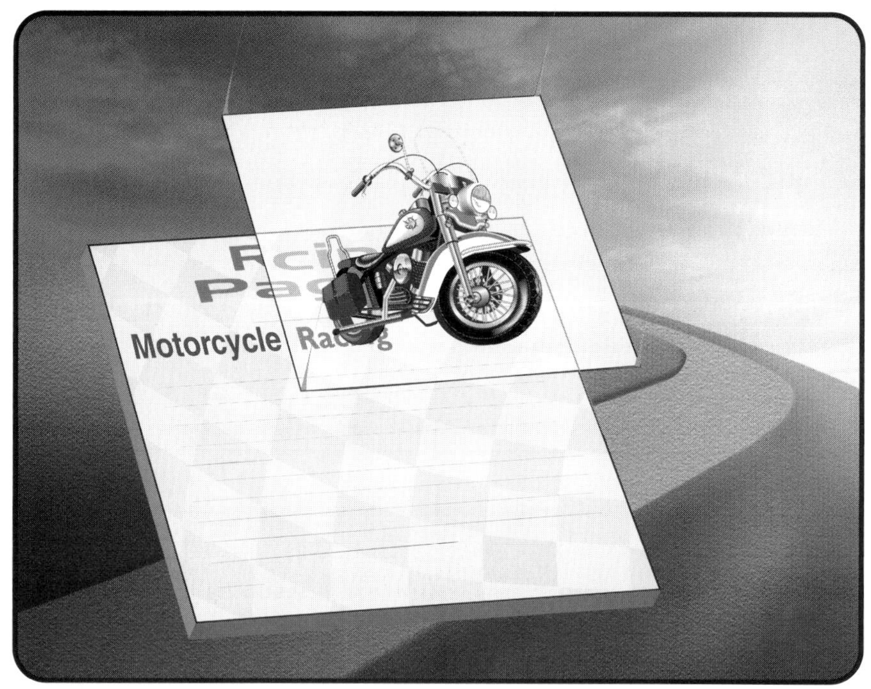

CREATE A LAYER

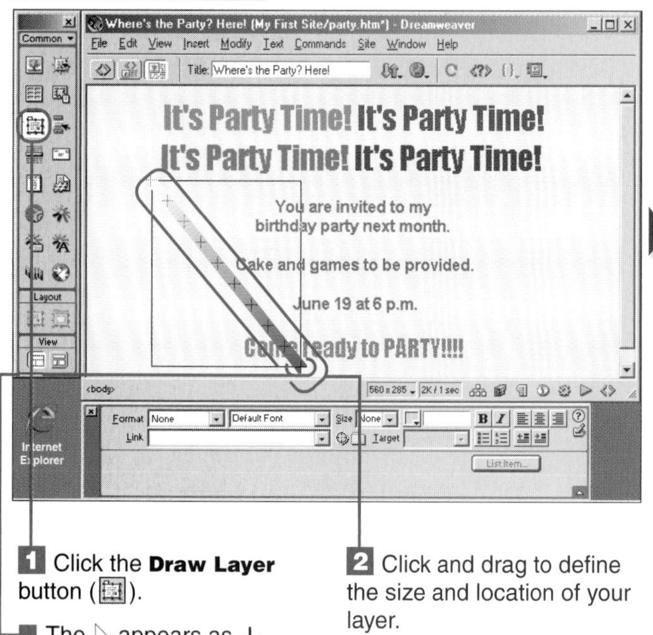

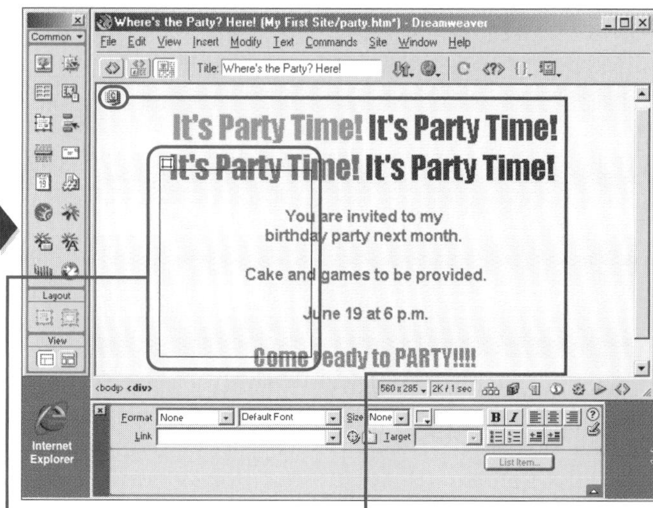

1 Click the **Draw Layer** button ( ).

■ The appears as +.

2 Click and drag to define the size and location of your layer.

■ Dreamweaver inserts a layer into the page. Layers are removed from the normal flow of the page and can sit on top of other content.

■ An icon represents where the layer code was inserted. You can click the icon to select the layer.

How do I place one layer inside another?

Open the Preferences dialog box (click **Edit** and then **Preferences**). Click the **Layers** category and make sure the **Nesting** check box is checked. Close the window and click the **Insert Layer** button on the Objects panel. Click and drag inside an existing layer to nest a new layer inside it. When a layer is nested inside another, the layer's icon appears inside the enclosing layer.

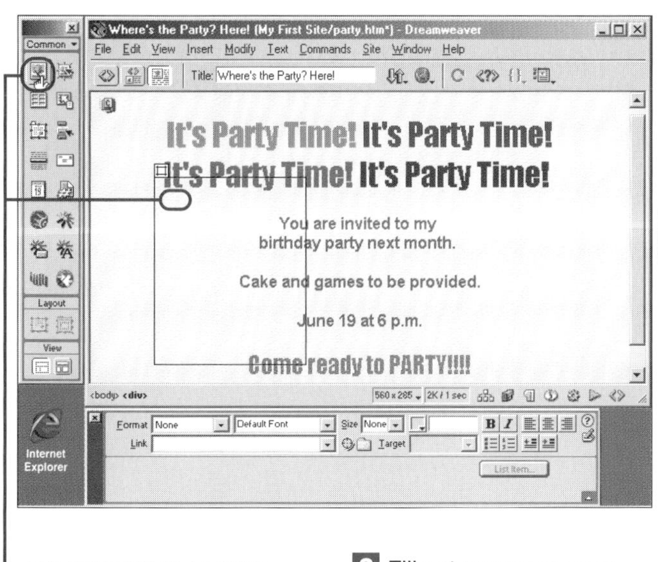

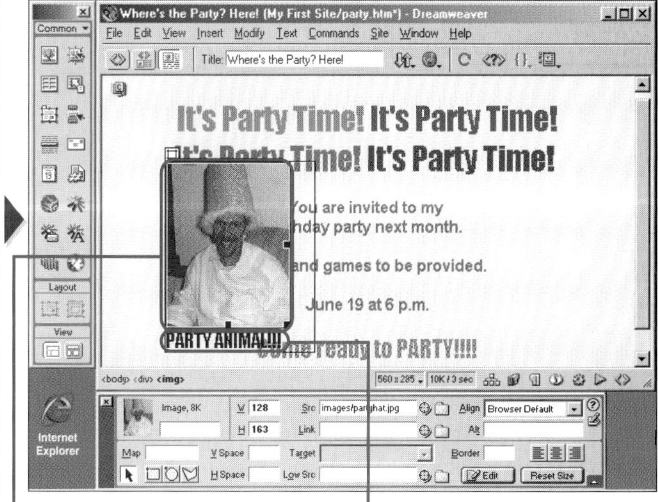

ADD CONTENT TO A LAYER

1 Click inside the layer.

2 Click a button in the Objects panel to insert an object.

3 Fill out any necessary dialog boxes to define and insert the object.

■ In this example, an image object appears inside the layer.

■ To add text, you can click inside the layer and type. You can also style the text in a layer.

RESIZE AND REPOSITION LAYERS

Every layer has specific position and dimension settings that define its place on the page. You can adjust the position and dimensions of a layer to make it fit attractively with the rest of the content on your page.

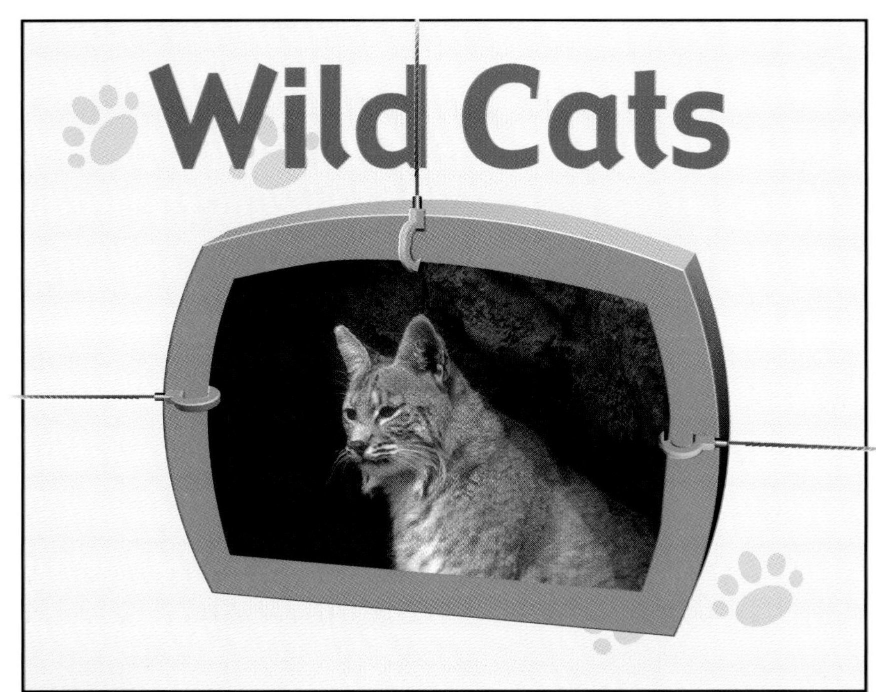

RESIZE AND REPOSITION LAYERS

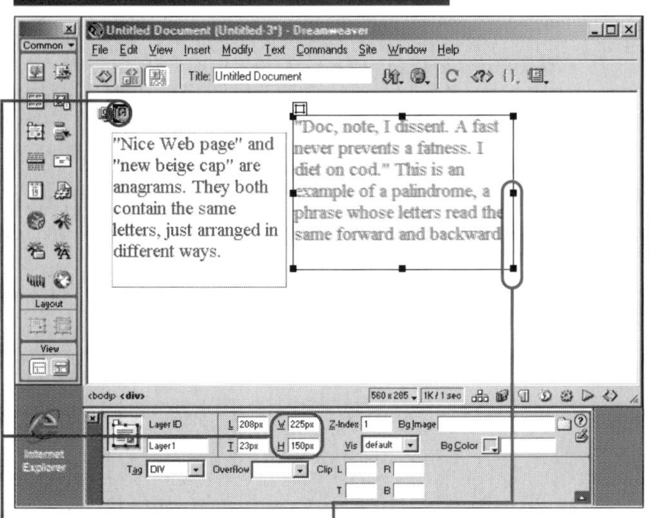

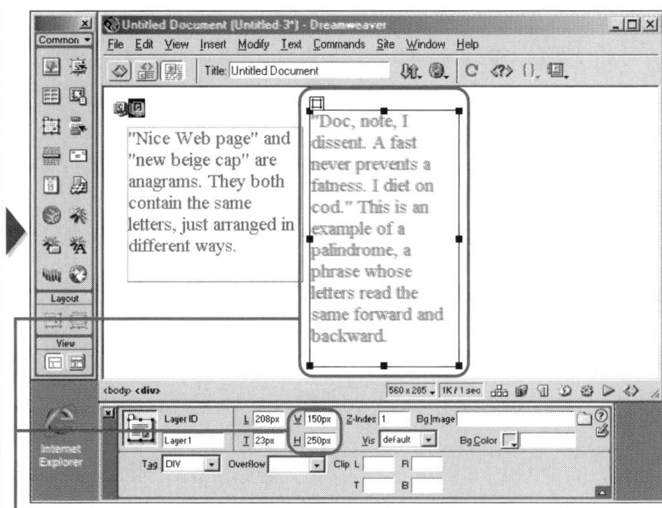

RESIZE A LAYER

1 Click the **Layer** button ( ) to select the layer.

2 Type the new width of the layer in the W field and the new height of the layer in the H field.

■ Label the values **px** for pixels, **in** for inches, or **cm** for centimeters.

■ You can also click and drag on the layer's border handles to change its dimensions.

■ Dreamweaver applies the new dimensions to the layer.

How do I change a layer's visibility?

Select a layer, and then adjust the Vis (Visibility) menu in the Property inspector. The menu lets you make a layer visible or invisible, or have it inherit its characteristic from its parent (the enclosing layer).

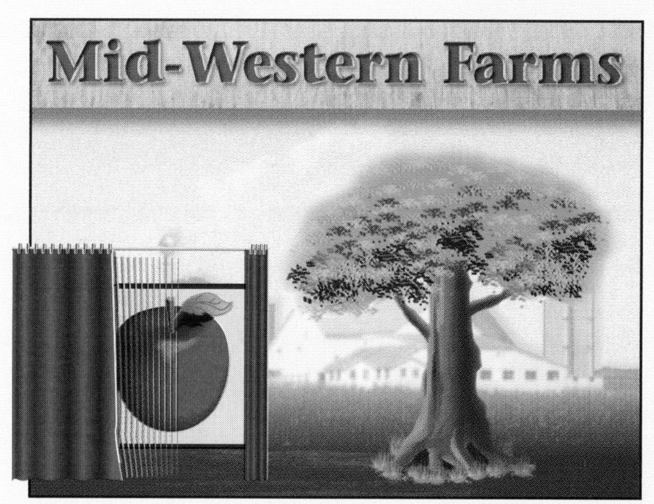

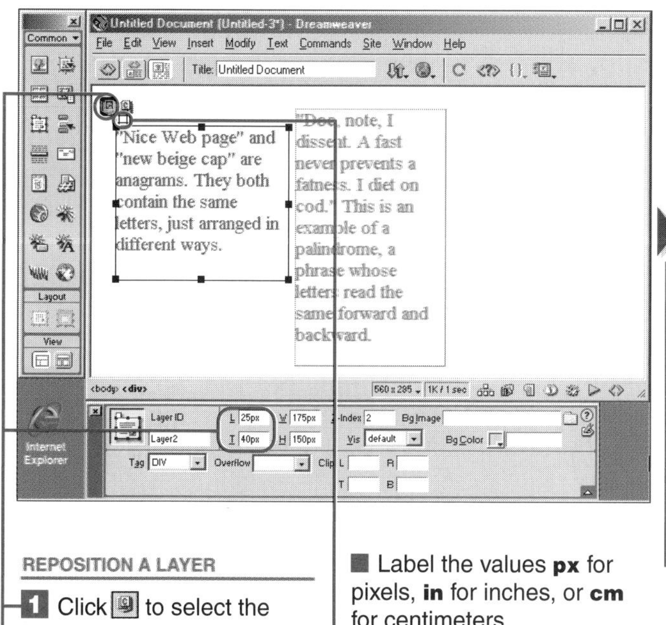

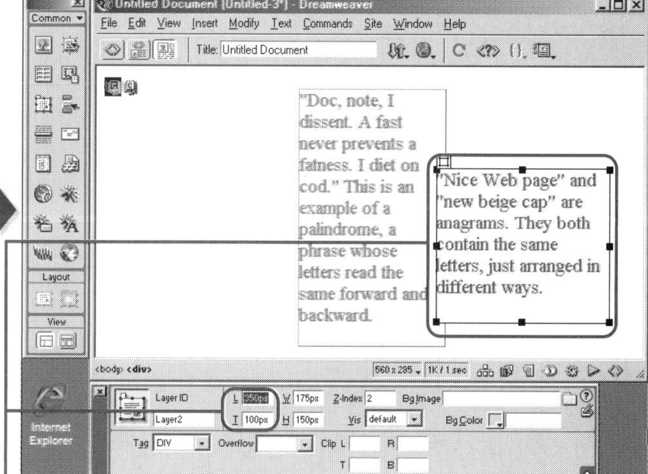

REPOSITION A LAYER

1 Click (select icon) to select the layer.

2 Type the new distance from the left side of the window in the L field and the new distance from the top of the window in the T field.

- Label the values **px** for pixels, **in** for inches, or **cm** for centimeters.

- You can also click and drag the **Layer** tab (▣) to change a layer's position.

- Dreamweaver applies the new positioning to the layer.

CREATE A STRAIGHT-LINE ANIMATION

You can create a timeline animation that moves a layer in a straight line on your page. A straight-line animation is a quick and easy way to enliven a page that otherwise consists of static text and images.

CREATE A STRAIGHT-LINE ANIMATION

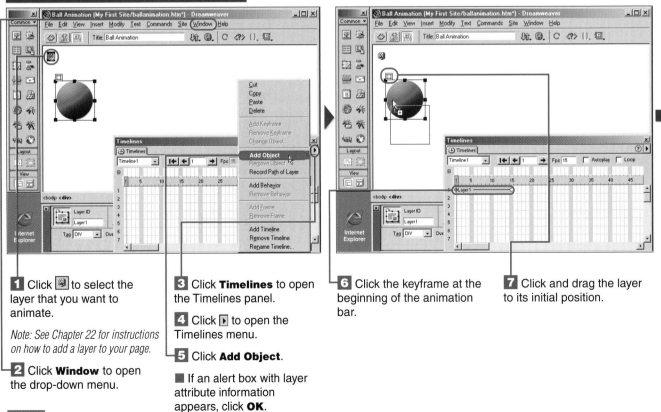

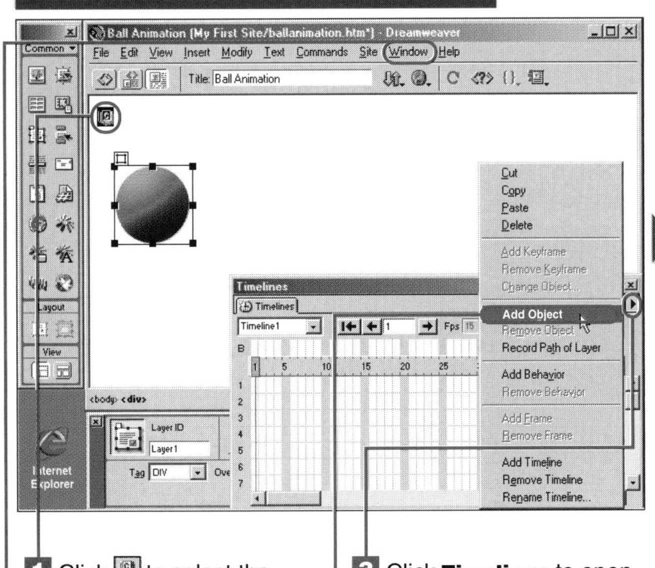

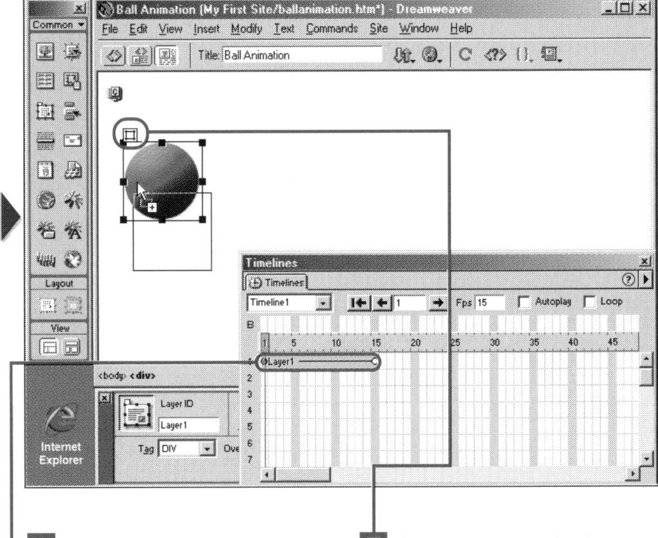

1 Click [icon] to select the layer that you want to animate.

Note: See Chapter 22 for instructions on how to add a layer to your page.

2 Click **Window** to open the drop-down menu.

3 Click **Timelines** to open the Timelines panel.

4 Click [icon] to open the Timelines menu.

5 Click **Add Object**.

■ If an alert box with layer attribute information appears, click **OK**.

6 Click the keyframe at the beginning of the animation bar.

7 Click and drag the layer to its initial position.

Can I create several straight-line animations on a single Web page?

Yes. Put each piece of content that you want to animate in its own layer, then define an animation bar in the Timelines inspector for each layer. (To add each additional animation bar to the Timelines inspector, click a layer and use the Add Object command in the Timelines menu.)

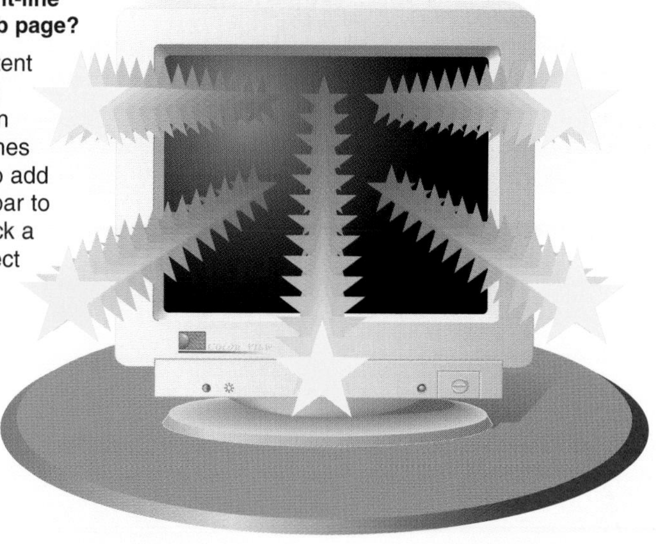

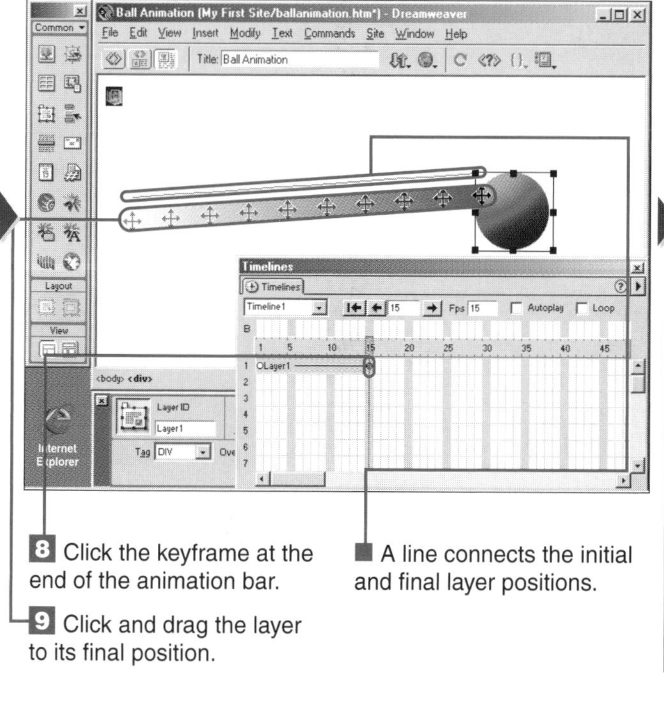

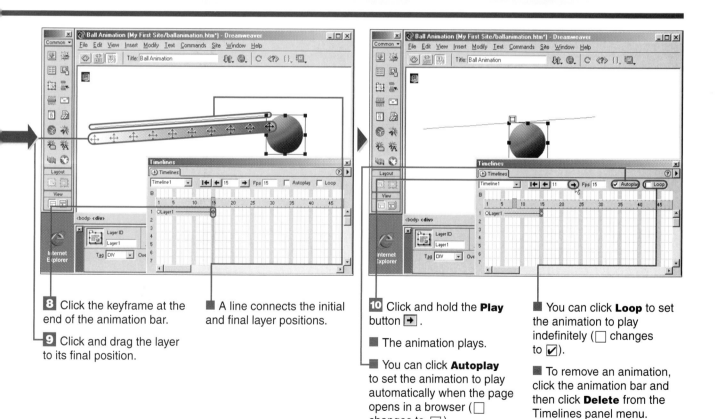

8 Click the keyframe at the end of the animation bar.

9 Click and drag the layer to its final position.

■ A line connects the initial and final layer positions.

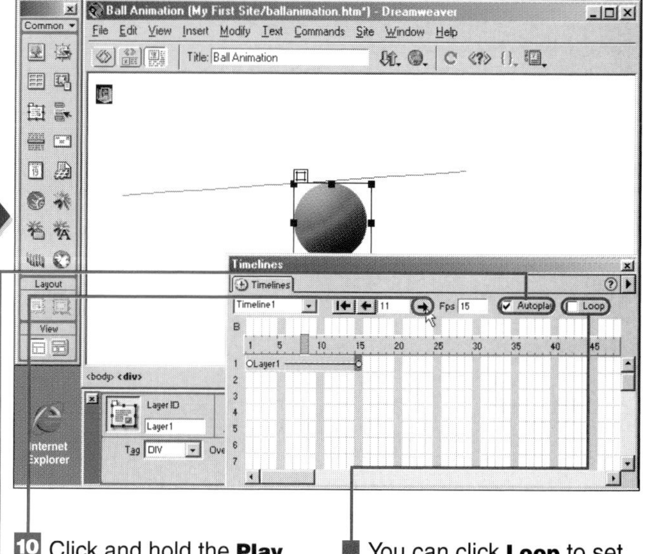

10 Click and hold the **Play** button (➔).

■ The animation plays.

■ You can click **Autoplay** to set the animation to play automatically when the page opens in a browser (☐ changes to ☑).

■ You can click **Loop** to set the animation to play indefinitely (☐ changes to ☑).

■ To remove an animation, click the animation bar and then click **Delete** from the Timelines panel menu.

CREATE AN ANIMATION BY DRAGGING A PATH

You can create animations that loop or curve by dragging a layer along the intended path and have Dreamweaver record the path as the layer moves. Recording a path can save you time because it lets you avoid having to assign keyframes.

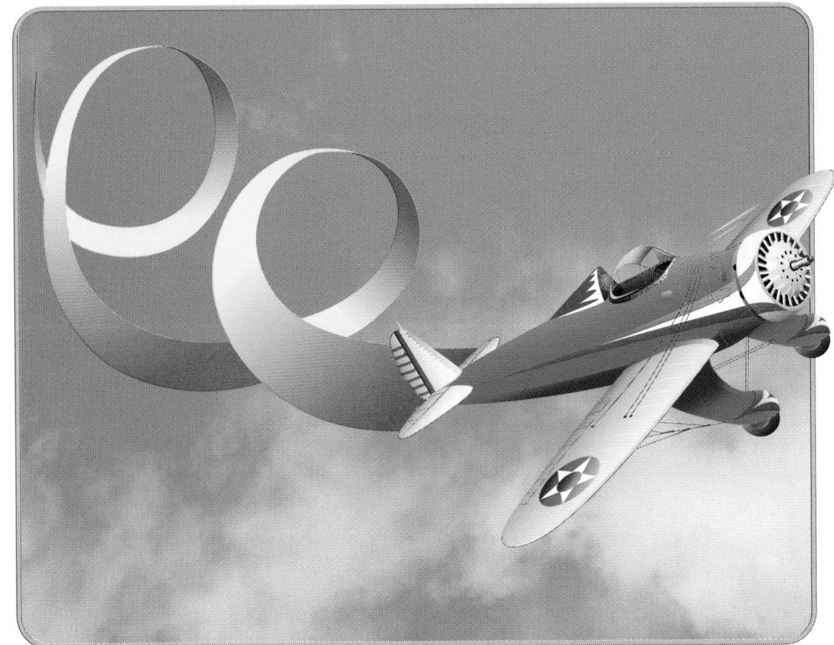

CREATE AN ANIMATION BY DRAGGING A PATH

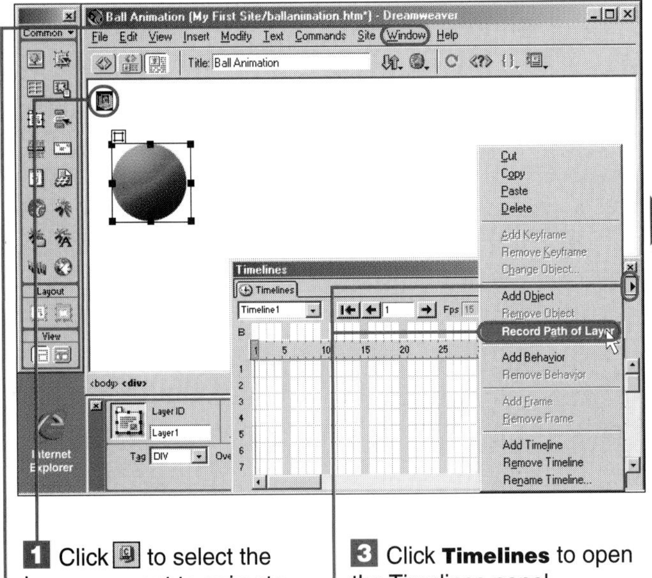

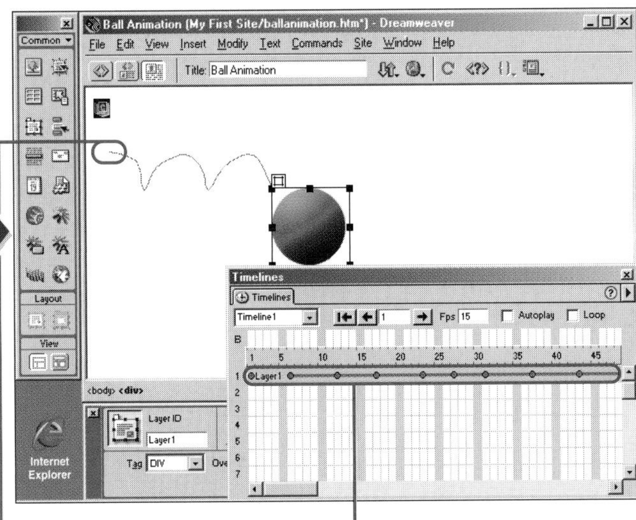

1 Click ▣ to select the layer you want to animate.

Note: See Chapter 22 for instructions on how to add a layer to your page.

2 Click **Window** to open the drop-down menu.

3 Click **Timelines** to open the Timelines panel.

4 Click ▸ to open the Timelines menu.

5 Click **Record Path of Layer**.

6 Click and drag the layer along the intended animation path.

*Note: If after dragging, an alert box with layer attribute information appears, click **OK**.*

■ Dreamweaver creates an animation bar describing the recorded path.

Can I cause a layer to rotate using timelines?

You cannot use timelines to rotate the content that is inside a layer. The animated content in the layer must stay perpendicular to the browser window as it moves. (One way to put rotating content on your page is to create it as an animated GIF file. You can create animated GIFs in Macromedia Fireworks.)

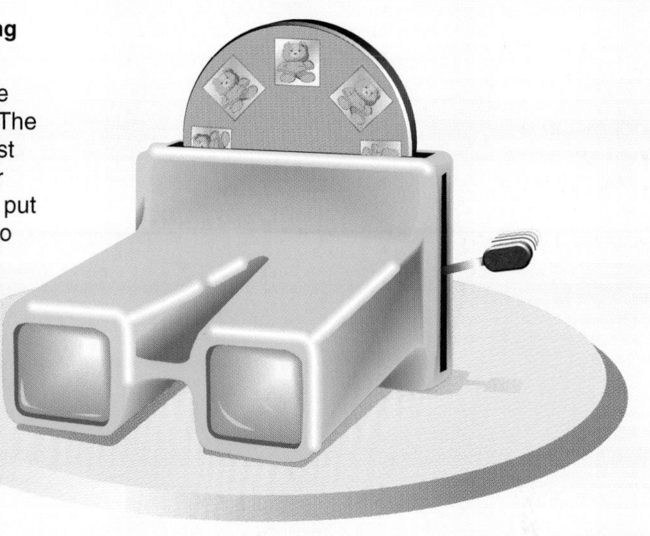

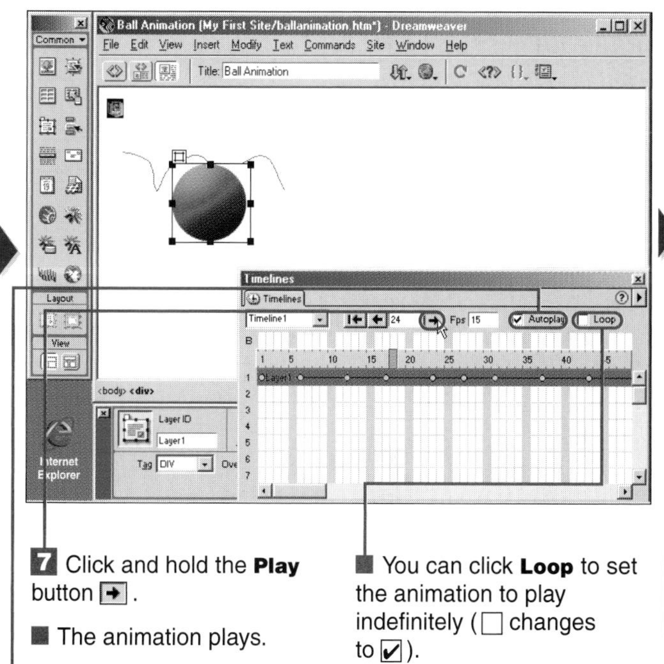

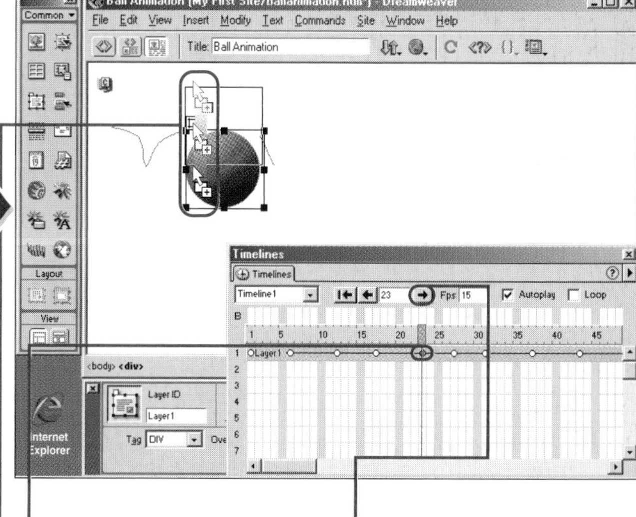

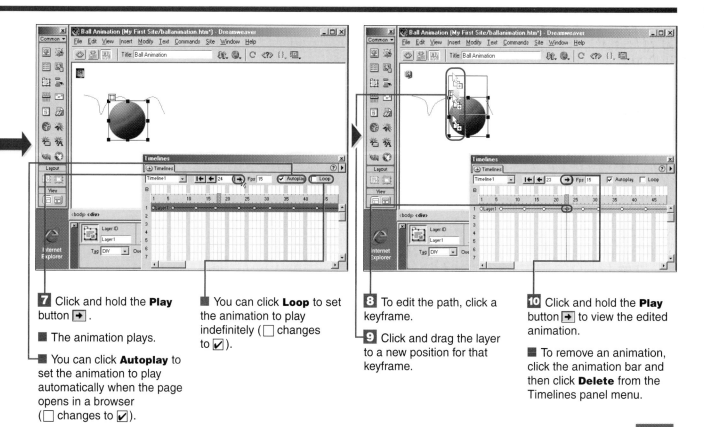

7 Click and hold the **Play** button.

■ The animation plays.

■ You can click **Autoplay** to set the animation to play automatically when the page opens in a browser (☐ changes to ☑).

■ You can click **Loop** to set the animation to play indefinitely (☐ changes to ☑).

8 To edit the path, click a keyframe.

9 Click and drag the layer to a new position for that keyframe.

10 Click and hold the **Play** button to view the edited animation.

■ To remove an animation, click the animation bar and then click **Delete** from the Timelines panel menu.

CREATE A FLASHING ANIMATION

You can change the visibility, dimensions, and Z-index of a layer along a timeline to make a layer blink, change size, or change order in a stack of layers.

CREATE A FLASHING ANIMATION

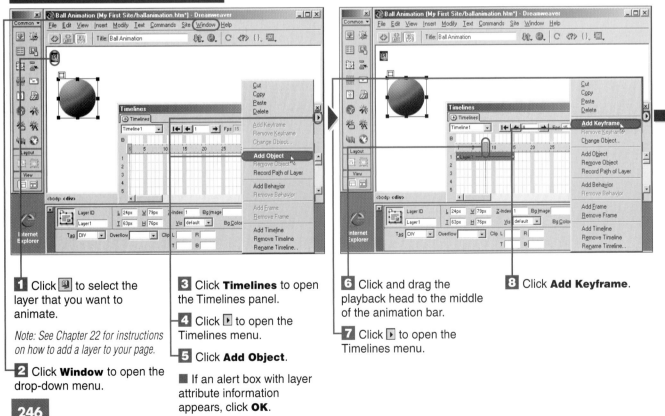

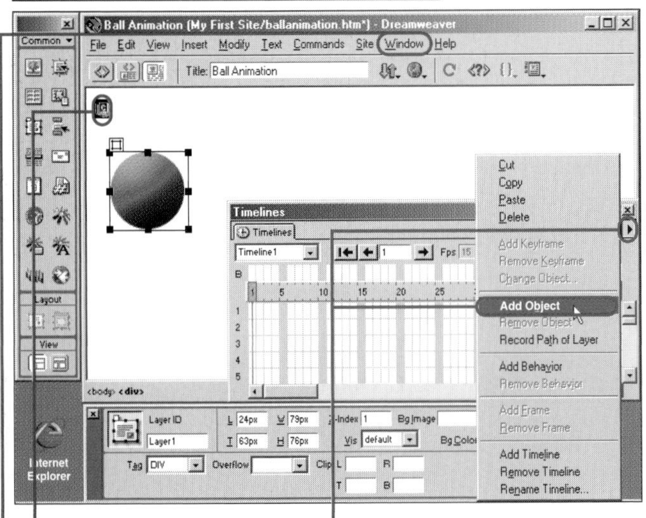

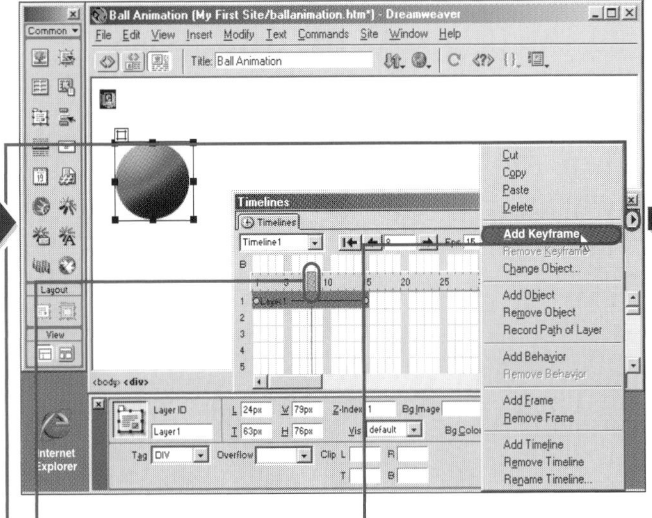

1 Click [icon] to select the layer that you want to animate.

Note: See Chapter 22 for instructions on how to add a layer to your page.

2 Click **Window** to open the drop-down menu.

3 Click **Timelines** to open the Timelines panel.

4 Click [icon] to open the Timelines menu.

5 Click **Add Object**.

■ If an alert box with layer attribute information appears, click **OK**.

6 Click and drag the playback head to the middle of the animation bar.

7 Click [icon] to open the Timelines menu.

8 Click **Add Keyframe**.

How do I shuffle positions of overlapping layers in a timeline?

Change the Z-indexes of the layers at a keyframe in the timeline. Layers are stacked according to what their Z-indexes are relative to other layers (the greater the Z-index, the lower the position in the stack). You can specify a layer's Z-index in the Property inspector.

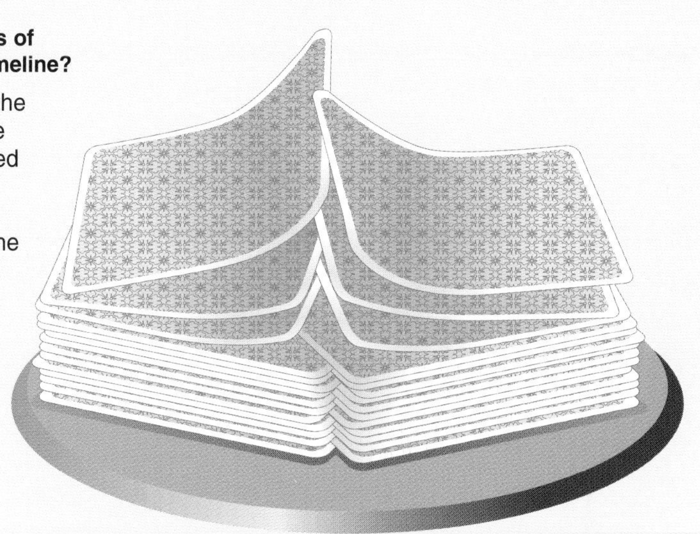

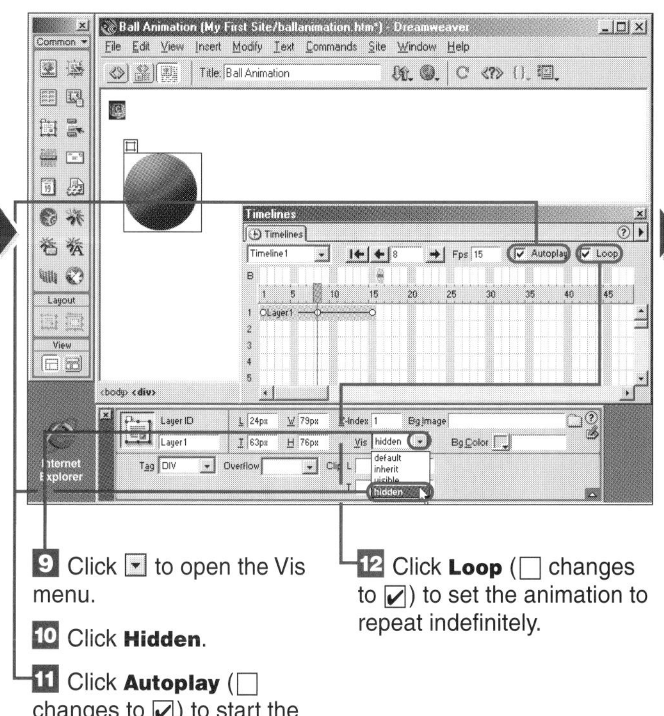

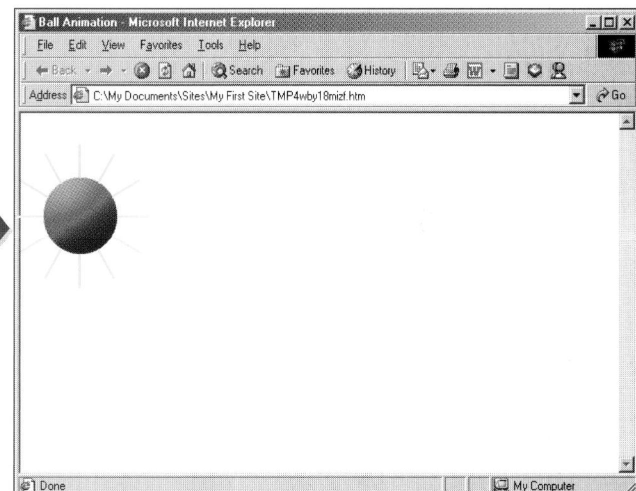

9 Click ▾ to open the Vis menu.

10 Click **Hidden**.

11 Click **Autoplay** (☐ changes to ☑) to start the animation when the page opens.

12 Click **Loop** (☐ changes to ☑) to set the animation to repeat indefinitely.

13 Preview the Web page in a browser.

■ The object flashes on and off indefinitely.

CHANGE ANIMATION SPEED

You can speed up or slow down a timeline animation by changing its frame rate or by adjusting the number of frames that make up the animation.

CHANGE ANIMATION SPEED

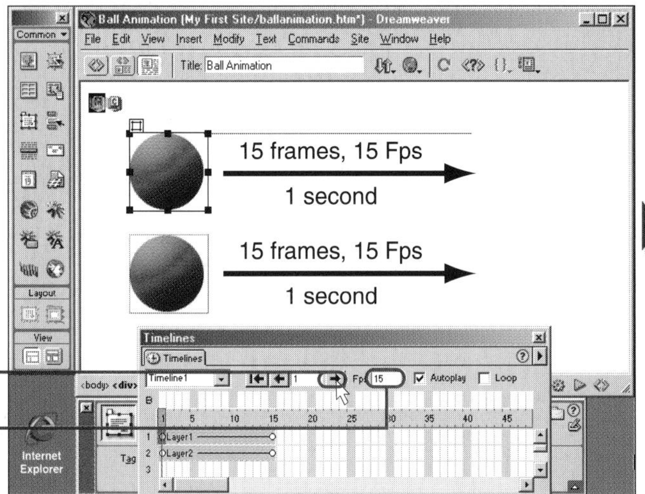

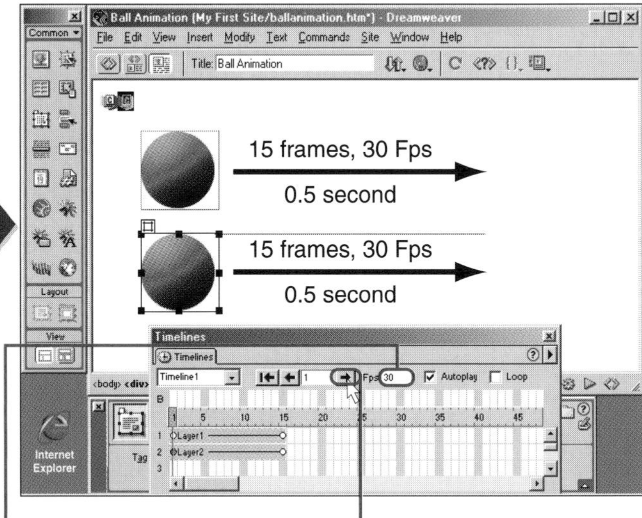

CHANGE THE FRAME RATE

1 Click and hold the **Play** button to preview the timeline animations on a page.

2 Type a new fps (frames-per-second) value for the animations (example: **30 frames-per-second**).

■ A higher value increases the animation speed, and a lower value decreases the animation speed.

■ The change in the fps rate affects all the animations in the timeline equally.

3 To preview the modified animations, click and hold the **Play** button.

How high should I set my frame rate for animations?

Most browsers running on average computer systems will not be able to display animations at rates faster than 15 frames per second. You will most likely want to use this rate as your ceiling. If you are running many animations on a page, and want to make sure all users will be able to play them smoothly, you may want to decrease the frame rate to less than 15 fps.

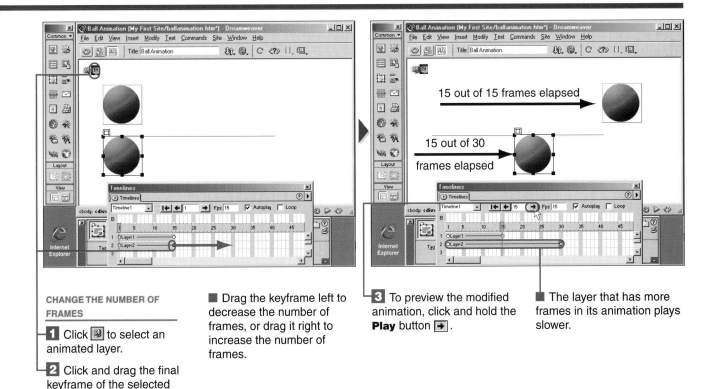

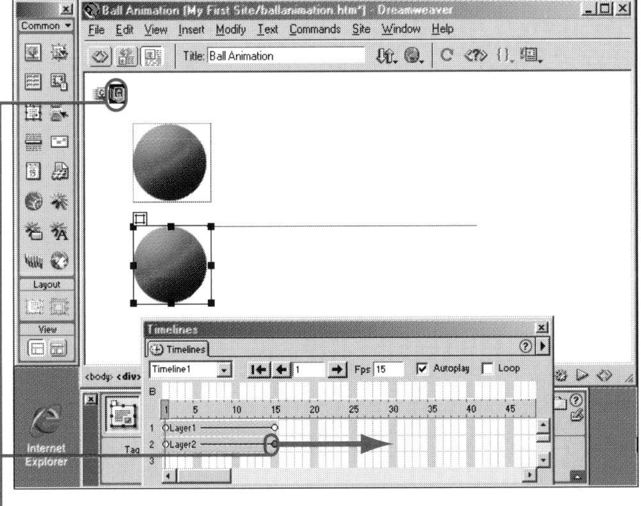

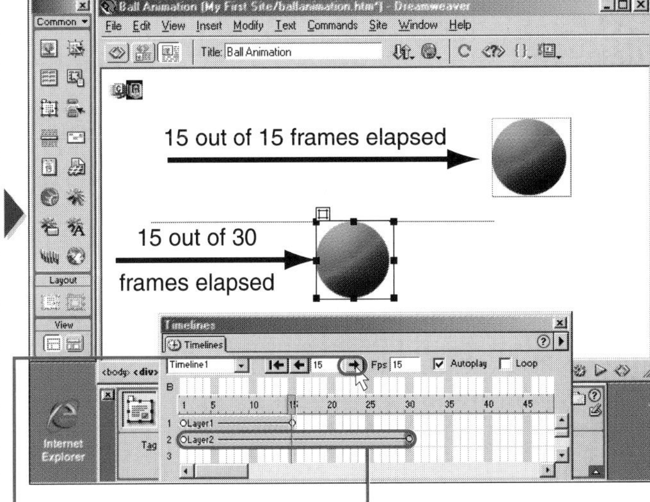

CHANGE THE NUMBER OF FRAMES

1 Click [icon] to select an animated layer.

2 Click and drag the final keyframe of the selected layer.

■ Drag the keyframe left to decrease the number of frames, or drag it right to increase the number of frames.

3 To preview the modified animation, click and hold the **Play** button [icon].

■ The layer that has more frames in its animation plays slower.

SET UP A REMOTE SITE

The remote site is the place where your site's files are made available to the rest of the world. You set up a remote site by specifying a directory on a Web server where your site will be hosted.

SET UP A REMOTE SITE

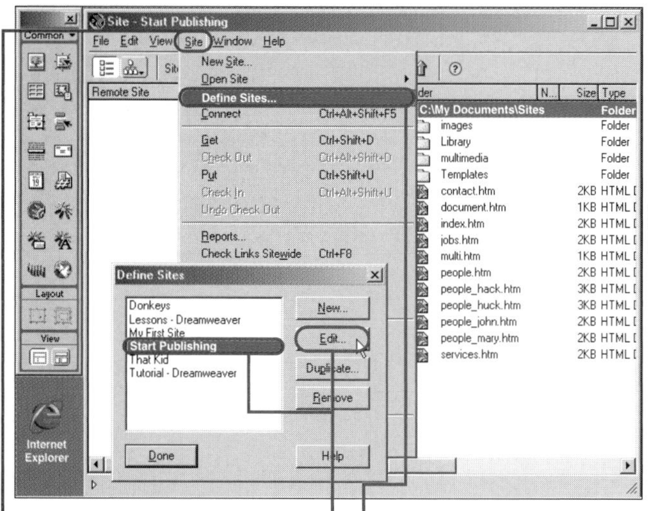

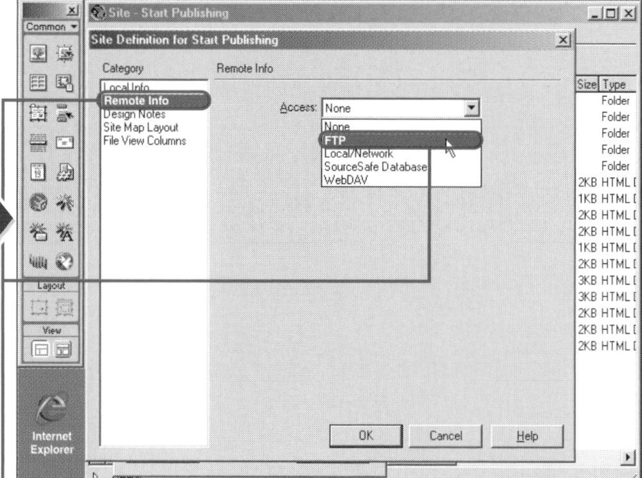

1 Set up a local site.

Note: See Chapter 14 for instructions on setting up a local site and opening the Site window.

2 Open the Site window.

3 Click **Site**.

4 Click **Define Sites**.

■ The Define Sites dialog box appears.

5 Click a site name from the list.

6 Click **Edit**.

■ The Site Definition dialog box appears.

7 Click **Remote Info**.

8 Click ▾ to select an access method.

9 Click **FTP**.

■ If your Web server is mounted as a network drive (Windows) or as an AppleTalk or NFS server (Mac), or if you are running a Web server on your local machine, click **Local/Network**.

What happens if I change my Internet service provider (ISP) and need to move my site to a different server?

You will need to change your remote site settings to enable Dreamweaver to connect to the new ISP's server. Your local site settings can stay the same.

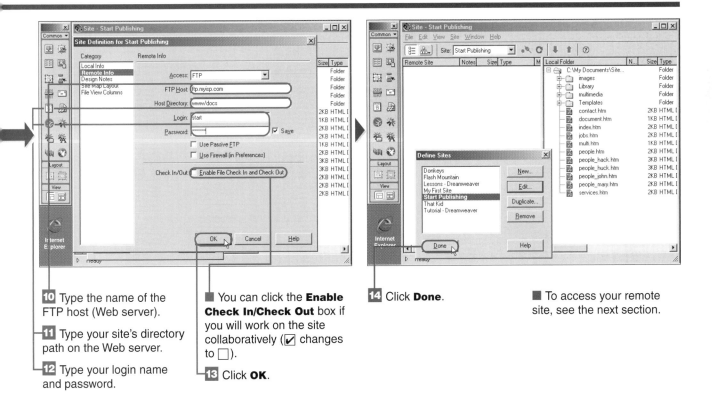

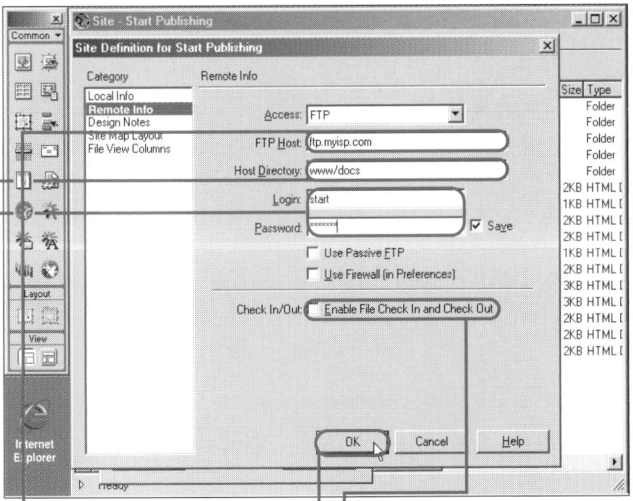

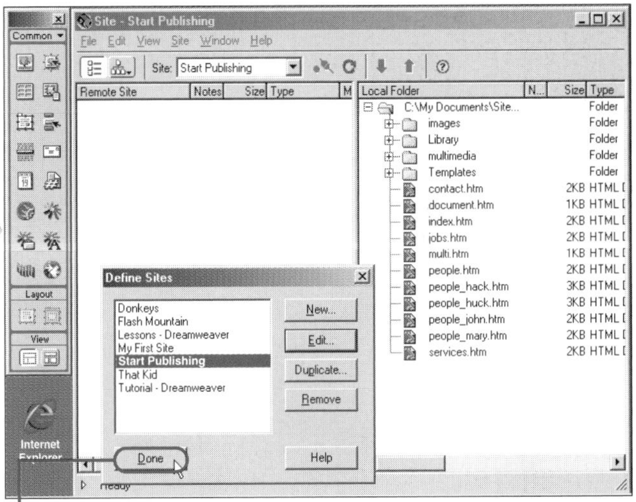

10 Type the name of the FTP host (Web server).

11 Type your site's directory path on the Web server.

12 Type your login name and password.

■ You can click the **Enable Check In/Check Out** box if you will work on the site collaboratively (☑ changes to ☐).

13 Click **OK**.

14 Click **Done**.

■ To access your remote site, see the next section.

CONNECT TO A REMOTE SITE

You can connect to the Web server that hosts your remote site and transfer files between it and your computer. Dreamweaver connects to the Web server by a process known as *File Transfer Protocol*, or FTP.

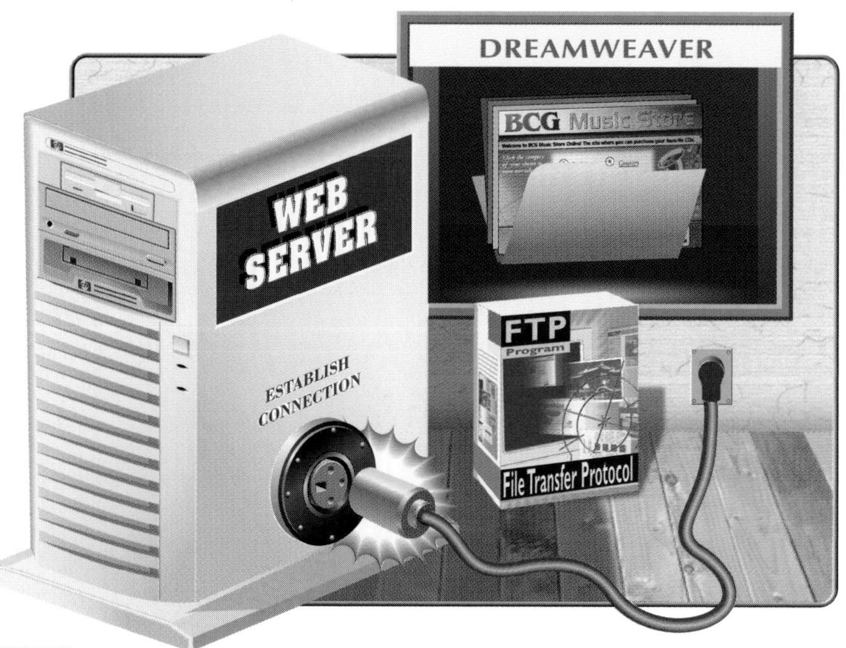

CONNECT TO A REMOTE SITE

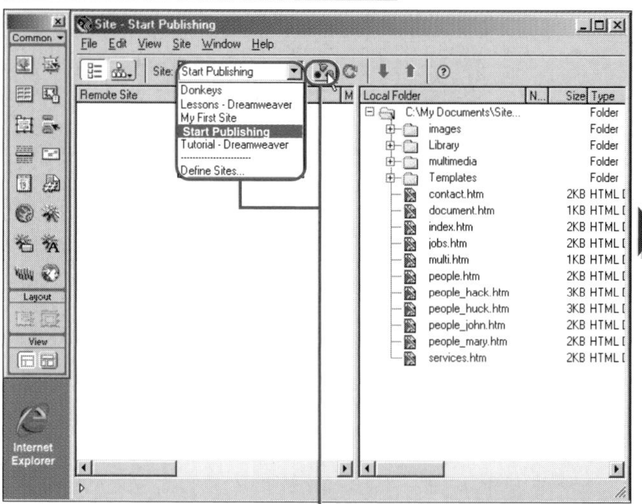

1 Set up a local site.

Note: See Chapter 14 for instructions on setting up a local site.

2 Set up a Remote Site.

Note: See "Set Up a Remote Site" earlier in this chapter for instructions.

3 Open the Site window.

Note: See Chapter 14 for instructions on opening the Site window.

4 Click ▾ to select your Web site.

5 Click the **Connect** button (🔌).

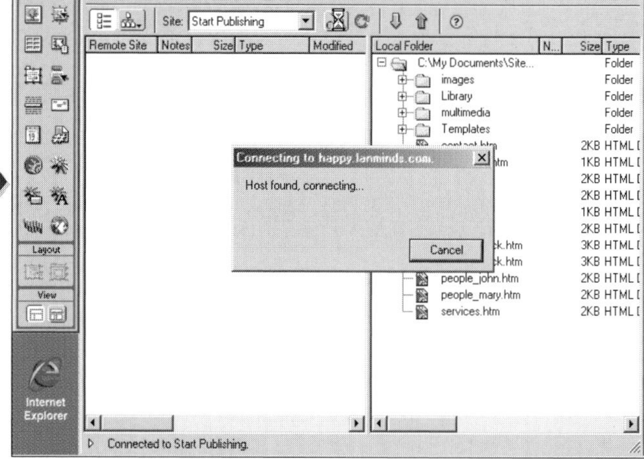

■ Dreamweaver attempts to connect to the remote site.

Note: If it cannot connect to the site, Dreamweaver displays an alert box. If you have trouble connecting, double-check the host information you entered for the remote site.

How do I keep Dreamweaver from prematurely disconnecting from the Web server?

You can click **Edit**, **Preferences**, and then **Site**. Then you can adjust the time that Dreamweaver lets pass between commands before it logs you off the server (the default is 30 minutes). Note that Web servers also have a similar setting on their end. So the server, not Dreamweaver, may sometimes log you off.

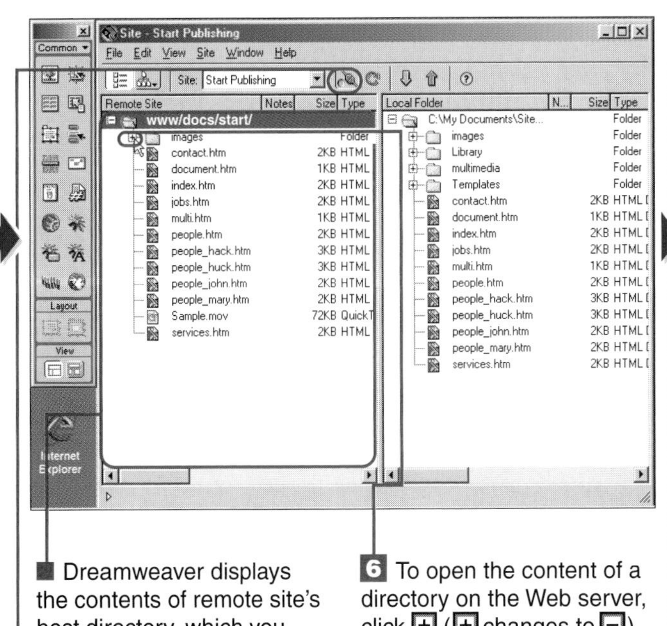

■ Dreamweaver displays the contents of remote site's host directory, which you specified when you set up the remote site.

■ changes to .

6 To open the content of a directory on the Web server, click ⊞ (⊞ changes to ⊟).

■ Dreamweaver displays the contents of the directory.

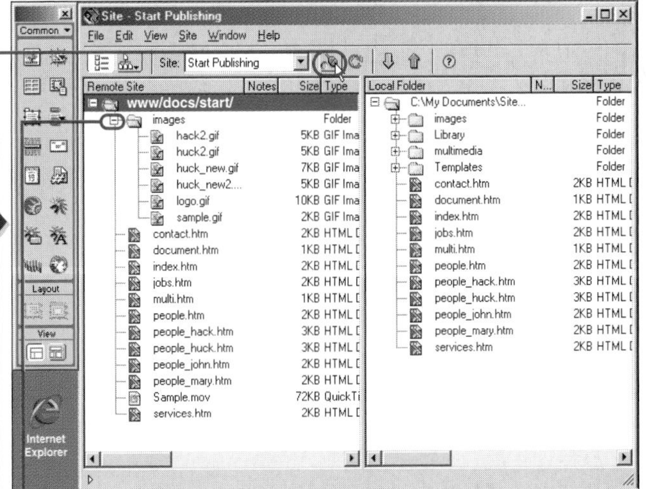

■ You can click ⊟ to close a directory.

7 Click to disconnect from the Web server.

■ Dreamweaver automatically disconnects from a Web server if you do not transfer any files for 30 minutes. You can change the disconnect period in Preferences.

UPLOAD FILES

You can upload site files from Dreamweaver to your remote site to make the files available to others on the Web.

UPLOAD FILES

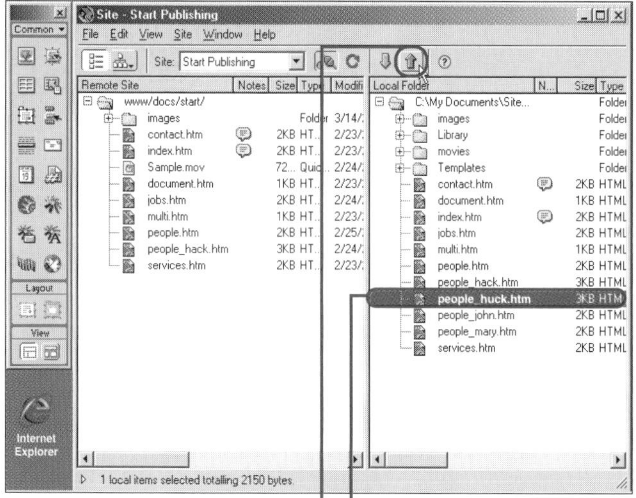

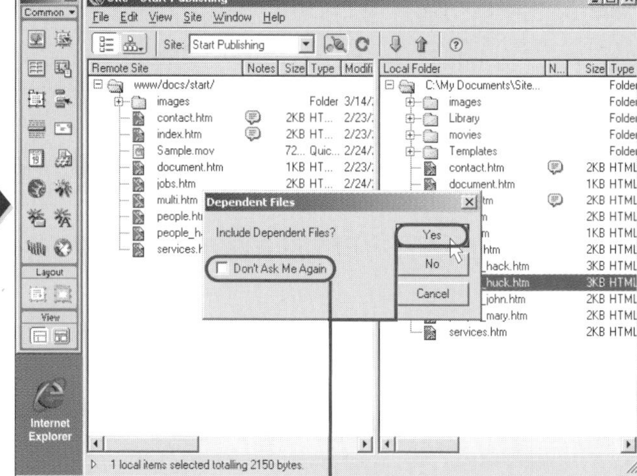

1 Connect to the Web server by using the Site window.

Note: See the previous section for instructions.

2 Click the file you want to upload.

3 Click the **Put** button (⇧).

■ An alert box appears asking if you want to include dependent files.

Note: Dependent files are images and other files associated with a particular Web page.

■ If you are uploading a frameset, dependent files include the files for each frame in the frameset.

4 Click **Yes**.

■ You can click here to avoid the alert box in the future (☐ changes to ☑).

How do I stop a file transfer in progress?

You can click the **Stop Sign** button, which appears at the bottom of the Document window while a transfer is in progress. You can also press Esc (⌘ +).

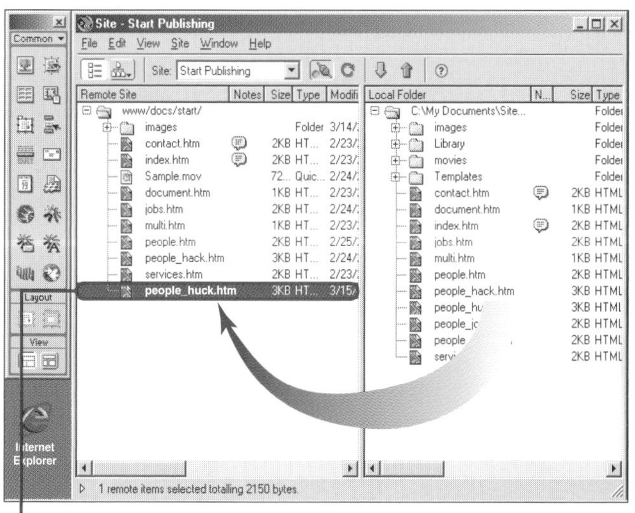

■ The files transfer from your computer to the Web server.

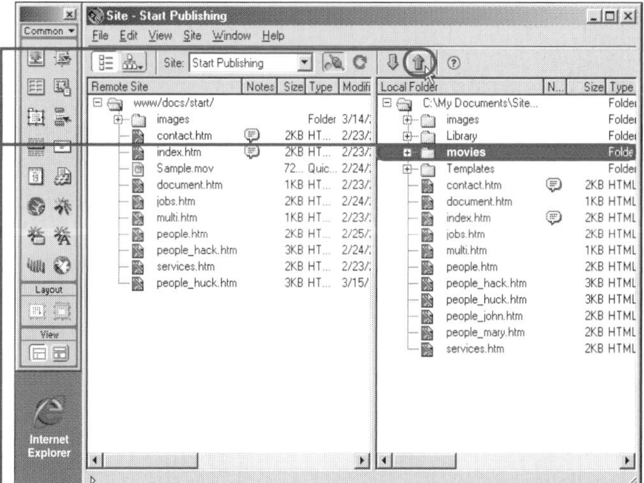

UPLOAD A FOLDER

1 Click a folder in the right pane.

2 Click ⇧.

■ Dreamweaver transfers the folder and its contents from your computer to the Web server.

DOWNLOAD FILES

You can download files from your remote site to Dreamweaver if you need to retrieve duplicate copies from the Web server.

DOWNLOAD FILES

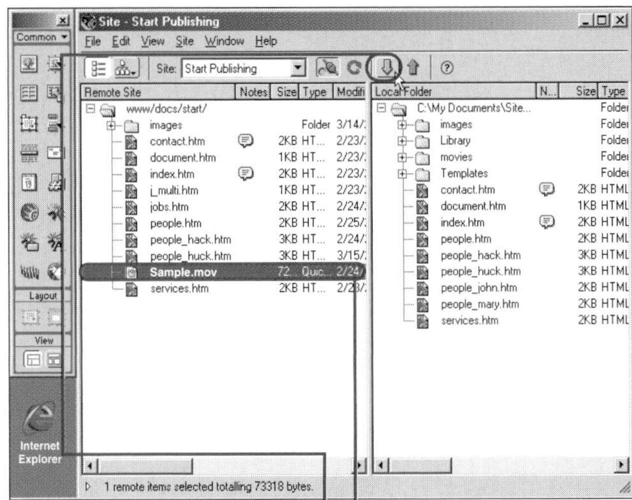

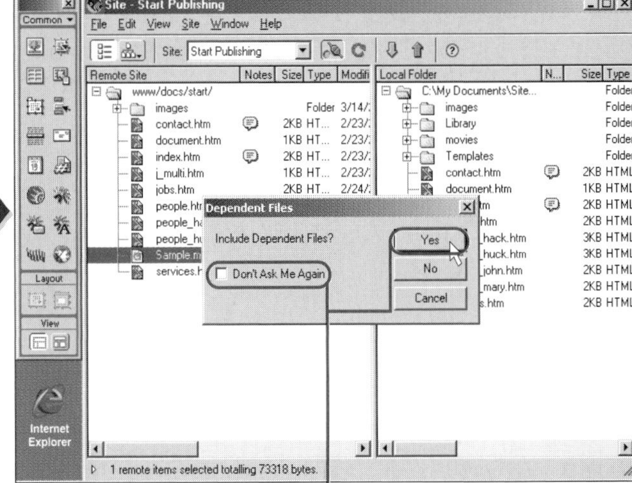

1 Connect to the Web server by using the Site window.

Note: See the section "Connect to a Remote Site" earlier in this chapter for instructions.

2 Click the file you want to download.

3 Click the **Get** button (⇩).

■ An alert box appears asking if you want to include dependent files.

Note: Dependent files are images and other files that are associated with a particular Web page.

■ If you are downloading a frameset, dependent files include the files for each frame in the frameset.

4 Click **Yes** to download dependent files.

■ You can click here to avoid the alert box in the future (☐ changes to ☑).

Where does Dreamweaver log errors that occur during transfer?

Dreamweaver logs all transfer activity (including errors) in a file-transfer log. You can view it by clicking **Window** (Windows) or **Site** (Mac), and then **Site FTP log.**

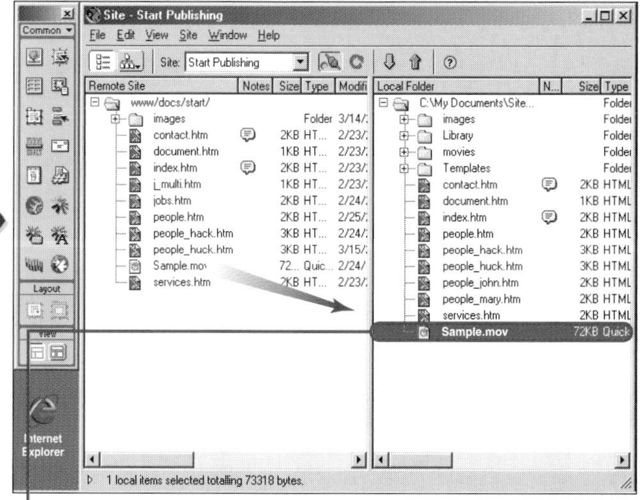

■ The file transfers from the Web server to your computer.

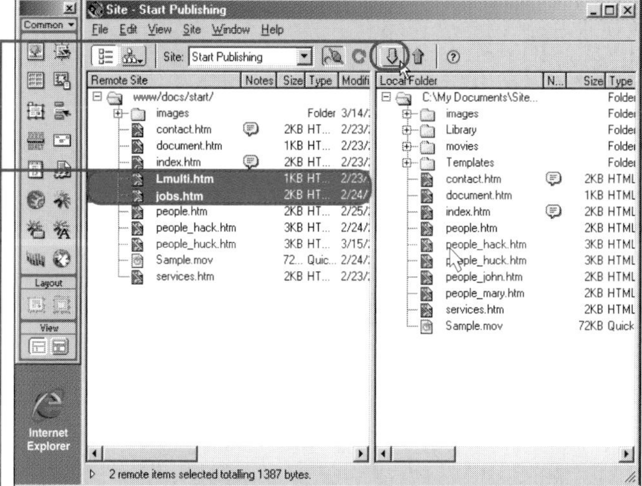

DOWNLOAD MULTIPLE FILES

1 Press and hold Ctrl (Shift) and then click to select the files you want to download.

2 Click ⇩.

■ The files transfer from your the Web server to your computer.

Home
Australia
Europe
Tips
Contact
MORE
BACK
HOME PAGE
FORWARD

Part 3

Using Fireworks

25 Fireworks Basics
Pages 260-273

26 Working with Text
Pages 274-287

27 Working with Objects
Pages 288-307

28 Working with Images
Pages 308-325

29 Applying Effects
Pages 326-341

30 Creating Buttons and Navigation Bars
Pages 342-357

31 Creating Hotspots and Image Maps
Pages 358-365

32 Slicing Images
Pages 366-377

33 Creating Rollovers
Pages 378-385

34 Optimizing Graphics
Pages 386-393

35 Exporting Objects and Slices
Pages 394-401

36 Integrating Graphics with HTML Editors
Pages 402-409

START FIREWORKS

You can start Fireworks to create graphics to use on your Dreamweaver Web pages.

START FIREWORKS

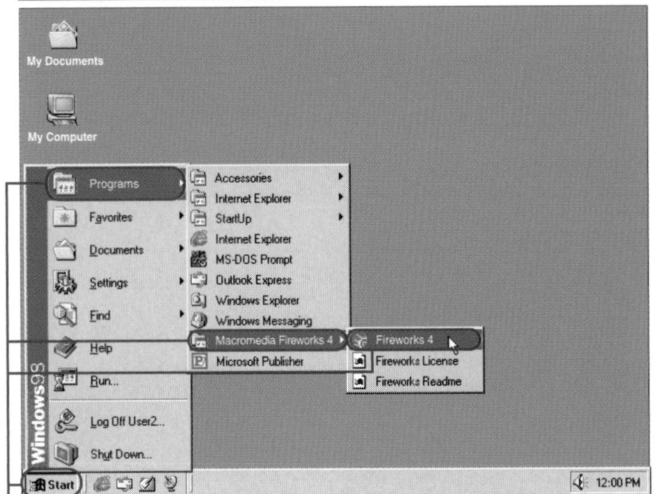

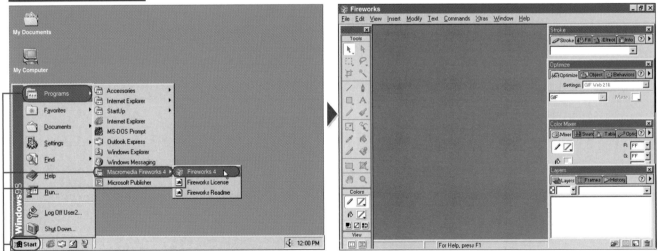

1. Click **Start**.
2. Click **Programs**.
3. Click **Macromedia Fireworks 4**.
4. Click **Fireworks 4**.

Note: To start Fireworks on a Macintosh, open the Macromedia Fireworks folder and double-click the Fireworks icon ( ).

■ The Macromedia Fireworks window appears with the tools you need to begin work.

Note: For information about the Fireworks tools, see "Using Panels."

VIEW PREVIEWS

THE ORIGINAL VIEW TAB

A new document opens in the Original view. You can use the Original view to create graphics, text, and hotspots and to edit images.

THE PREVIEW VIEW TAB

The Preview view tab lets you view images, text, or graphics as they will appear in a Web browser. Preview view also shows you details about the file, including file size and download time. You can even play animations in Preview view.

THE 2-UP VIEW

The 2-Up view gives details about the document in different formats, allowing you to compare document formats side-by-side. The first view lists the size of the original file, and the second view lists the size of the same file in a common Web page format, such as GIF or JPEG. The second view also lists other information, such as the number of colors used.

THE 4-UP VIEW

With the 4-Up view, you can compare up to four different versions of your document. The 4-Up view enables you to change colors, formats, and other options to find the smallest file size with the most acceptable quality for your image or graphic.

CREATE A NEW DOCUMENT

You can create a new document that holds text, images, animations, and other graphics that you can use on your Dreamweaver Web pages.

CREATE A NEW DOCUMENT

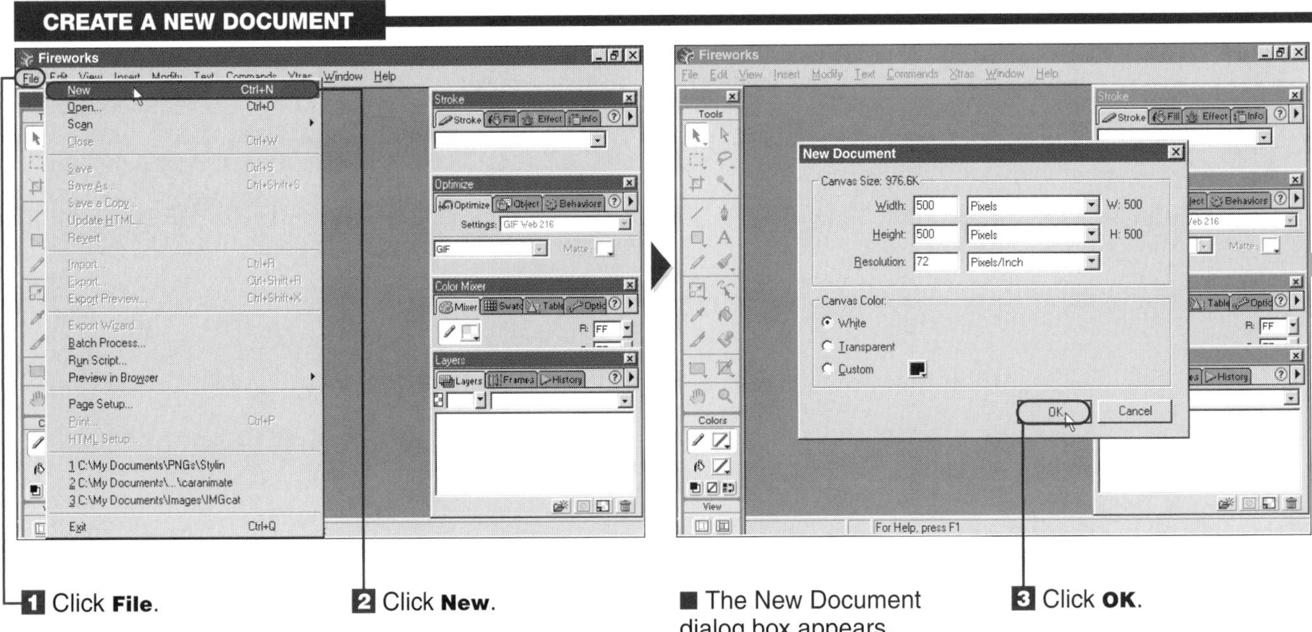

1 Click **File**.

2 Click **New**.

■ The New Document dialog box appears.

3 Click **OK**.

What file format is the new Fireworks document?

The standard format of a Fireworks document is the Fireworks file format, also called Portable Network Graphic (PNG). The PNG format lets you use a large variety of colors in your Web page designs.

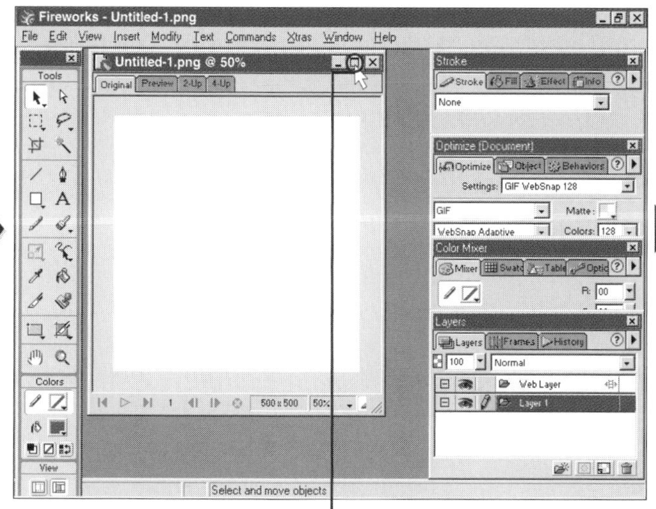

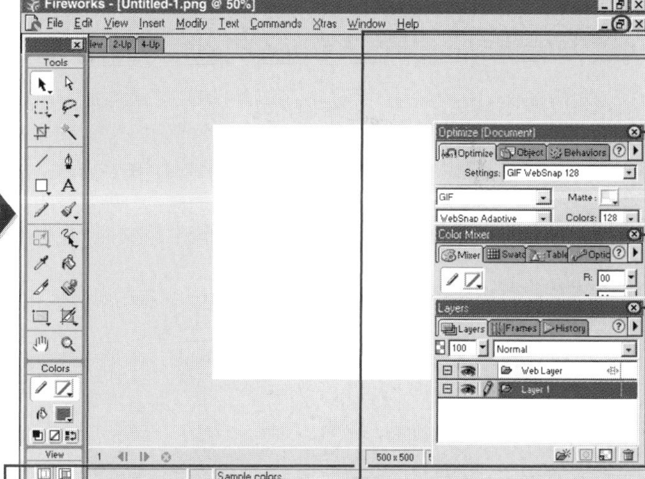

■ The new document appears on the screen.

MAXIMIZE THE DOCUMENT (PC ONLY)

1 Click ☐ in the document window to view the entire document.

■ The document window is maximized.

■ Click ☒ to close one or more of the panels to better view the document.

■ Click 🗗 to change the document window back to the reduced size.

MODIFY CANVAS SIZE

You can change the size of a document if you want to work with a large image or add more text to the page.

MODIFY CANVAS SIZE

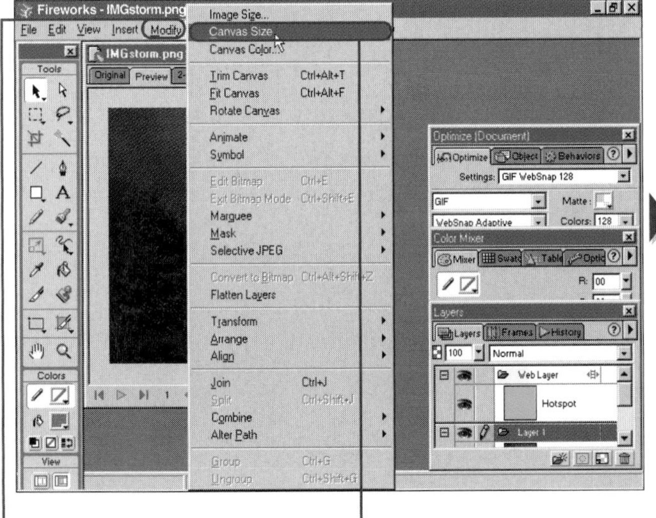

1 Click **Modify**.

2 Click **Canvas Size**.

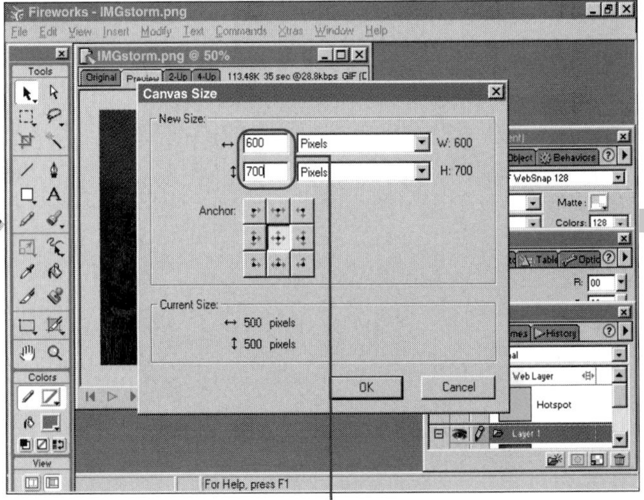

■ The Canvas Size dialog box appears.

3 Type a new size in the width and height boxes.

What is a pixel?

A *pixel* is a tiny square of color that is a part of a larger image. A photograph of fruit, for example, contains thousands of pixels.

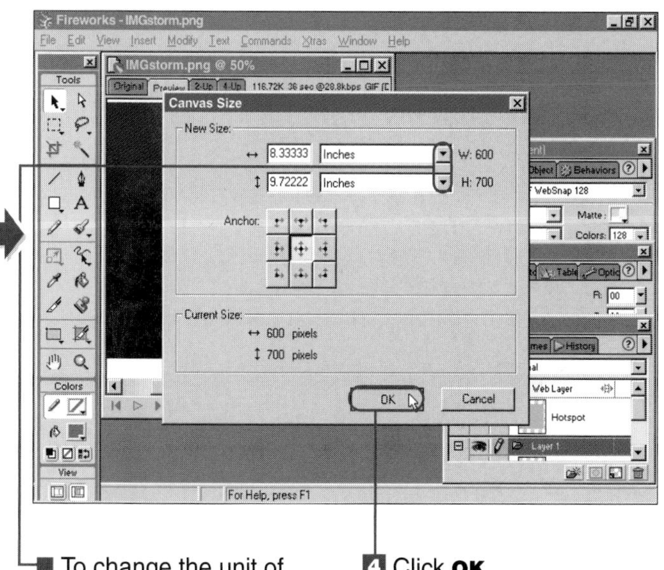

■ To change the unit of measure, you can click the W or H box ▾ and click **Pixels**, **Inches**, or **Centimeters**.

4 Click **OK**.

■ The document changes to the new size.

■ You can use the horizontal and vertical scroll bars to view more of the page.

CHANGE CANVAS COLOR

You can change the background color of your document from white to any color in the available palette.

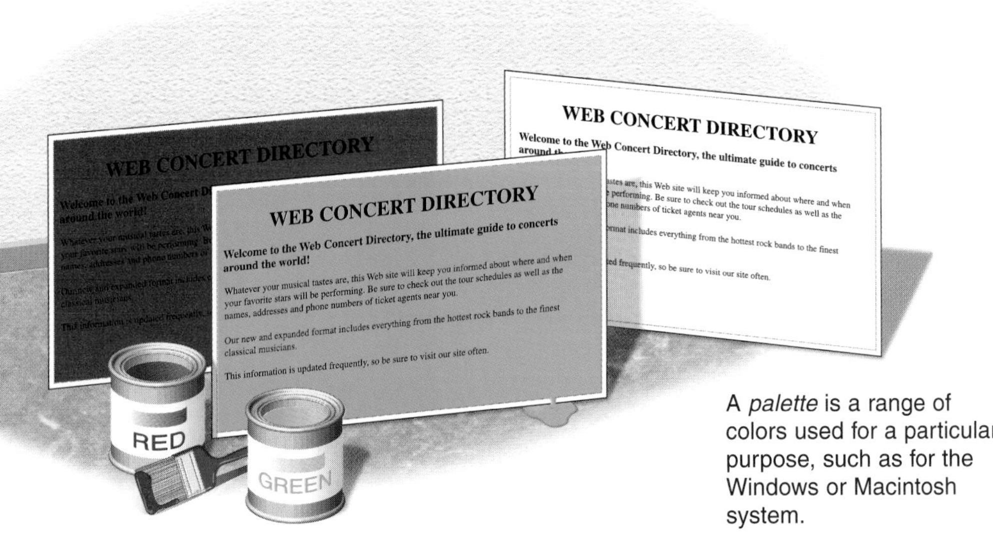

A *palette* is a range of colors used for a particular purpose, such as for the Windows or Macintosh system.

CHANGE CANVAS COLOR

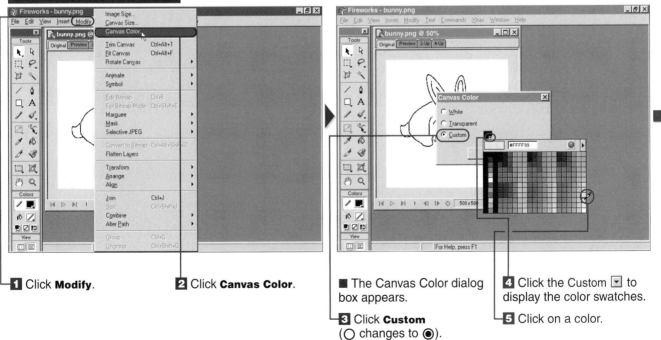

1 Click **Modify**.

2 Click **Canvas Color**.

■ The Canvas Color dialog box appears.

3 Click **Custom** (○ changes to ◉).

4 Click the Custom ▾ to display the color swatches.

5 Click on a color.

Why do I need a background color when I am making buttons to use on my Dreamweaver Web page?

A background color in Fireworks is not necessary. You can use the background color in Fireworks to match the background color of your Web page, if you want.

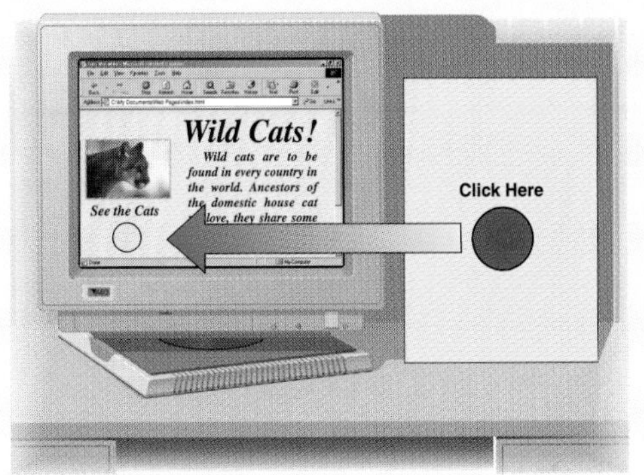

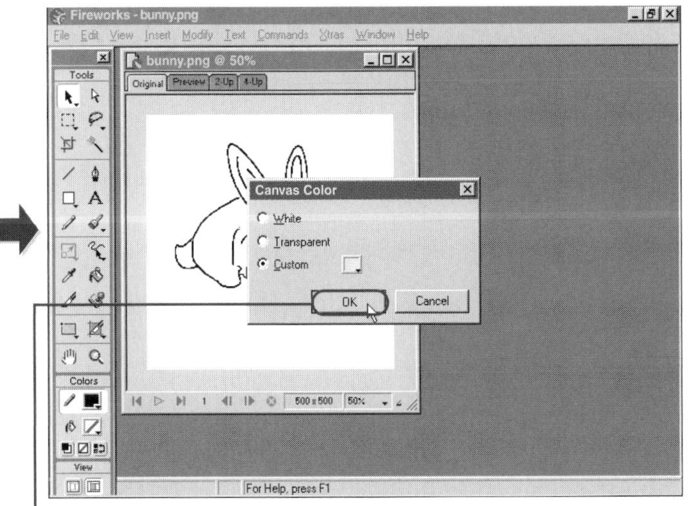

6 Click **OK**.

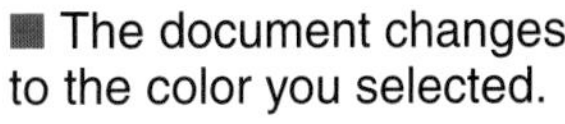

■ The document changes to the color you selected.

SAVE A DOCUMENT

You should save your document to store the page for future use. This lets you later edit and print the document.

You should regularly save your work to protect yourself from losing recent changes.

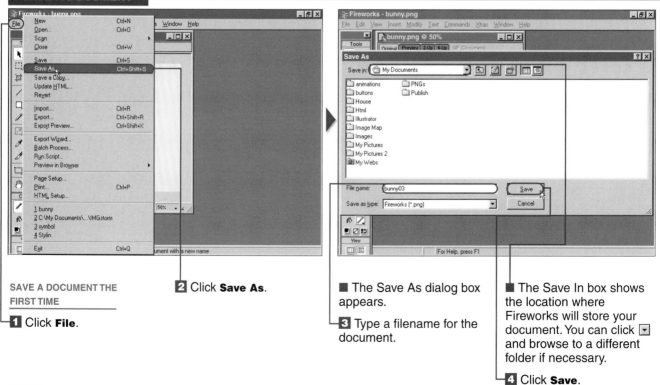

SAVE A DOCUMENT

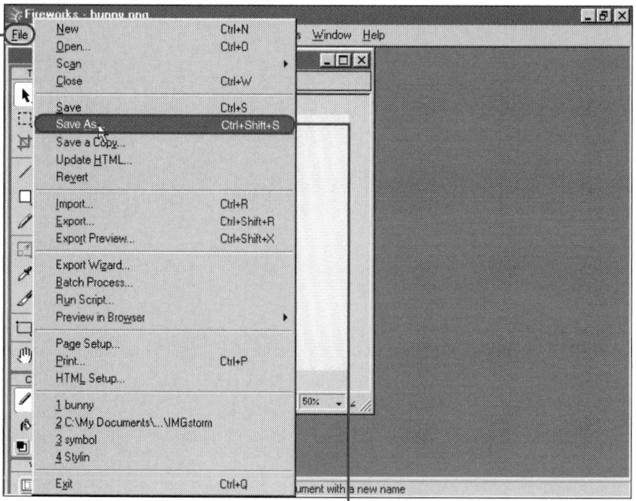

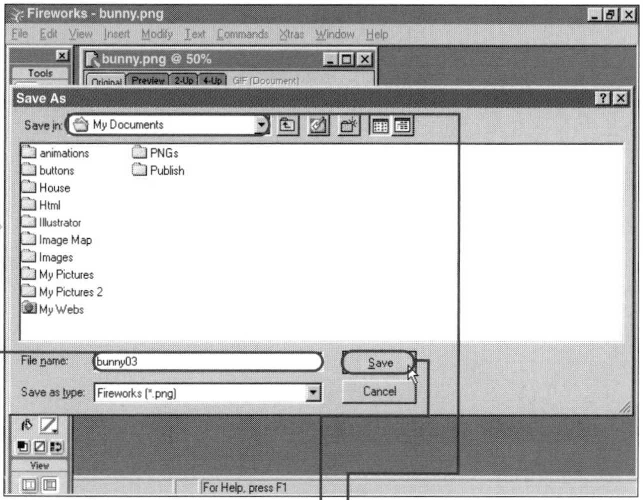

SAVE A DOCUMENT THE FIRST TIME

1 Click **File**.

2 Click **Save As**.

■ The Save As dialog box appears.

3 Type a filename for the document.

■ The Save In box shows the location where Fireworks will store your document. You can click ▼ and browse to a different folder if necessary.

4 Click **Save**.

How can I save a copy of my document?

Start by saving the document and giving it a name. Then choose **Save As** again from the File menu but give the document a different filename. You can even place the copy of the file in a different location on the computer.

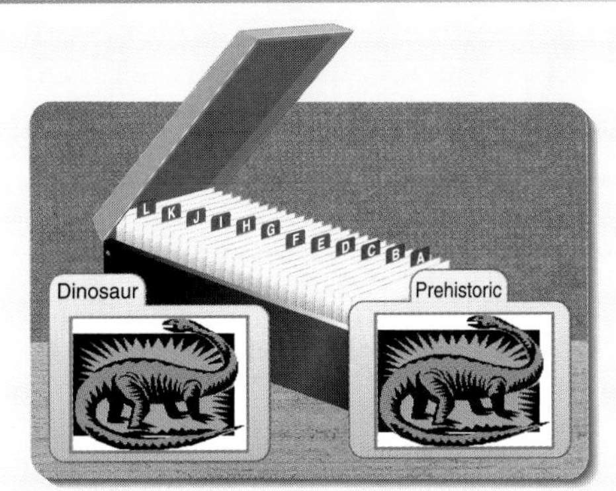

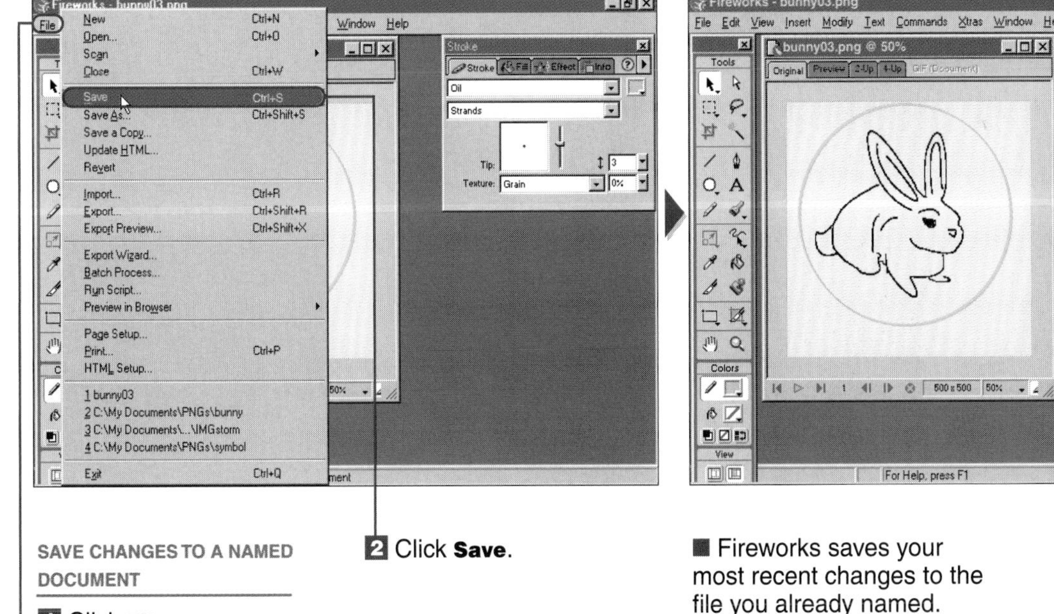

SAVE CHANGES TO A NAMED DOCUMENT

1 Click **File**.

2 Click **Save**.

■ Fireworks saves your most recent changes to the file you already named.

OPEN AN EXISTING DOCUMENT

You can open a document you previously saved so that you can edit or print the document.

OPEN AN EXISTING DOCUMENT

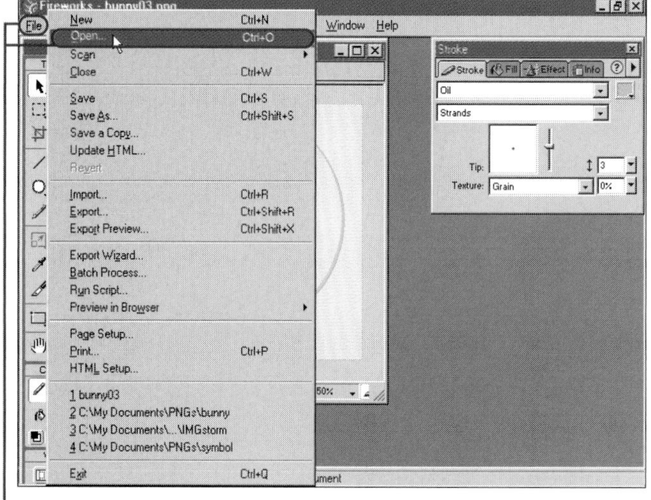

1 Click **File**.

2 Click **Open**.

Note: You do not have to close other documents that you already have open. Fireworks can have multiple documents open at the same time.

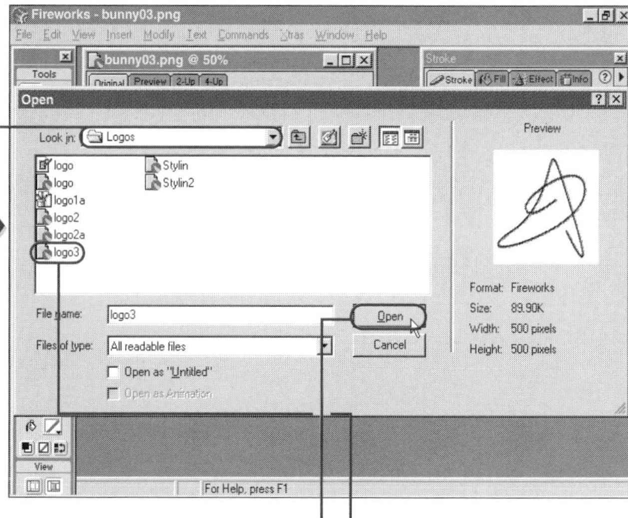

■ The Open dialog box appears.

3 Click ▾ and browse to the folder that contains the document that you want to open.

4 Click the name of the document.

5 Click **Open**.

How many documents can I have open at one time?

You can have five, ten, or more documents open at the same time, but you should close the documents that you are not currently using. When you have multiple documents open, your computer uses more memory and slows down.

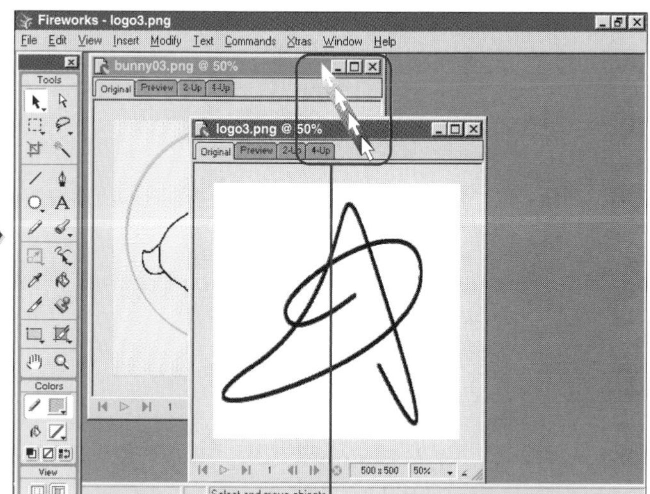

■ The opened document appears on-screen.

MOVE THE DOCUMENT WINDOW

1 Click and drag the title bar of the document window to move it.

WORK IN ANOTHER DOCUMENT WINDOW

1 Click anywhere in the other document window to bring it forward.

CLOSE A DOCUMENT

You can close a document when you are finished working with it. Closing the document does not close Fireworks.

CLOSE A DOCUMENT

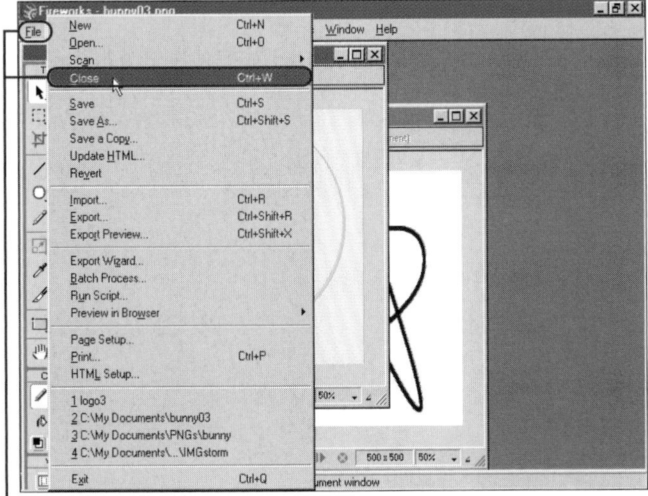

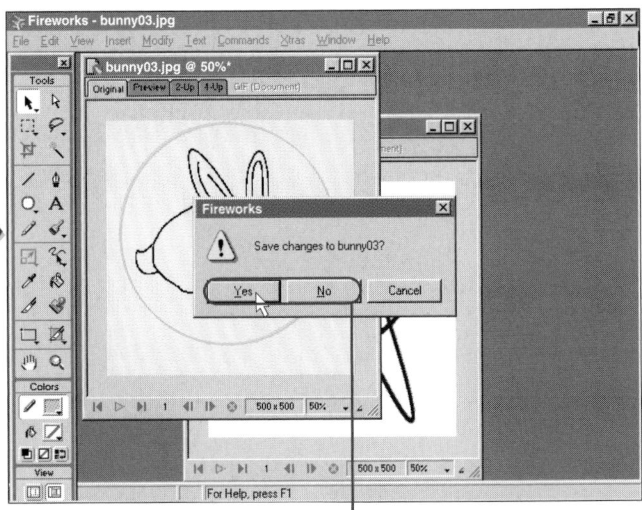

1 Click **File**.

2 Click **Close**.

Note: You should always save your document before you close it (see the section "Save a Document").

■ If you have not saved your document, Fireworks displays a dialog box that asks you if you want to save your changes.

3 Click **Yes** to save the document or **No** if you do not want to save your changes.

■ The document disappears from the screen.

UNDO AND REDO A CHANGE

You can undo most changes you make in Fireworks, such as changing canvas color. You may need to undo a change when the action you took was an accident or a mistake. You can also redo a change after you undo it.

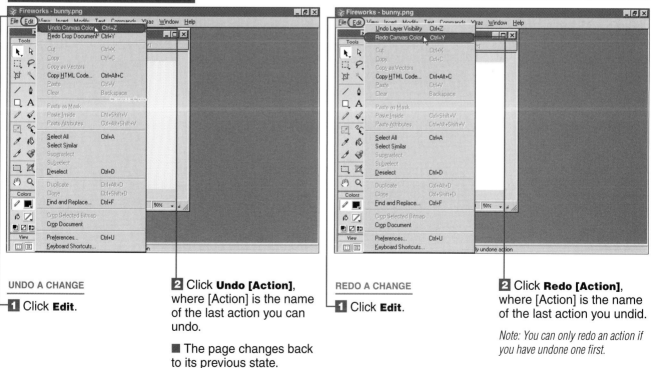

UNDO AND REDO A CHANGE

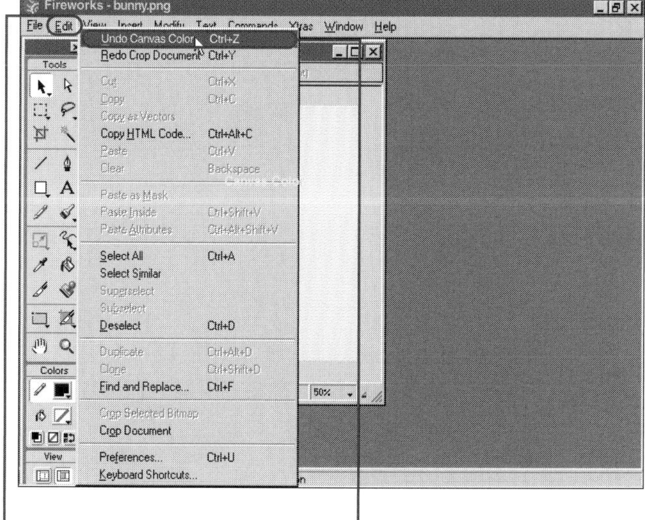

UNDO A CHANGE

1. Click **Edit**.
2. Click **Undo [Action]**, where [Action] is the name of the last action you can undo.

■ The page changes back to its previous state.

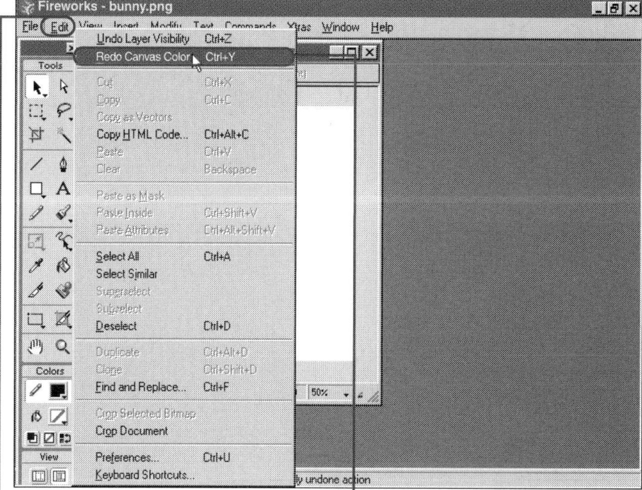

REDO A CHANGE

1. Click **Edit**.
2. Click **Redo [Action]**, where [Action] is the name of the last action you undid.

Note: You can only redo an action if you have undone one first.

ENTER AND EDIT TEXT

You can enter text in Fireworks to use for headings or logos. You can also edit the text you enter.

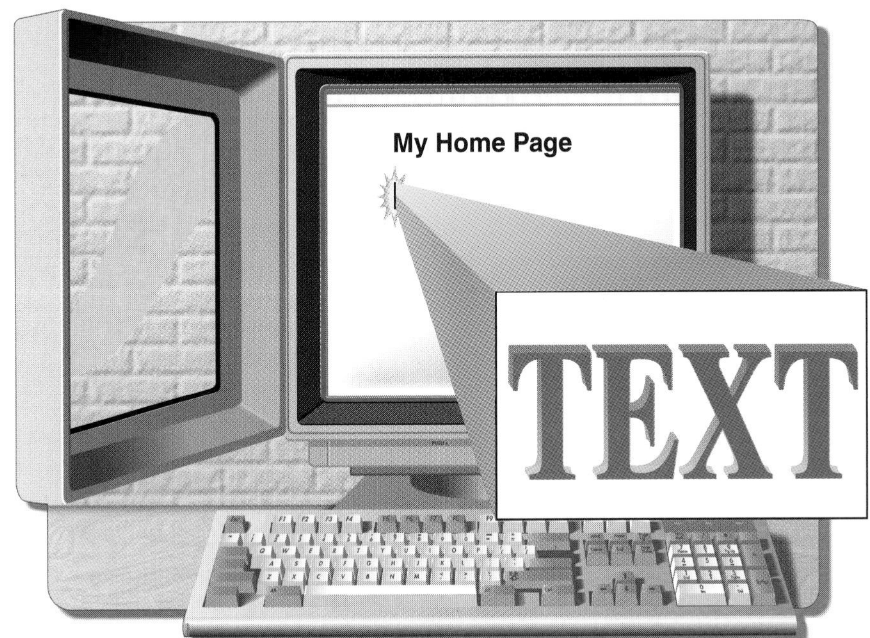

ENTER AND EDIT TEXT

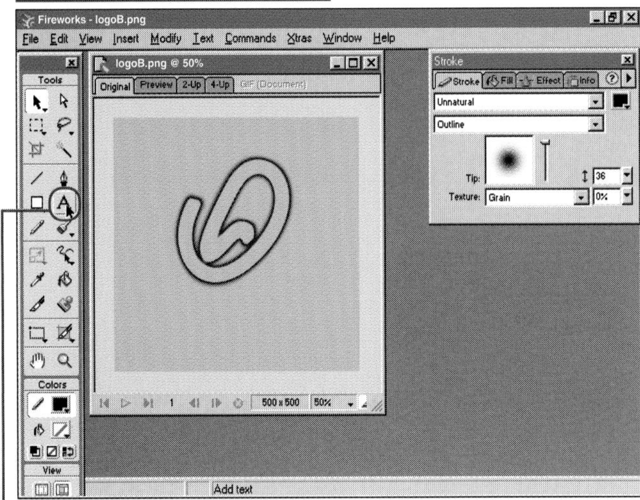

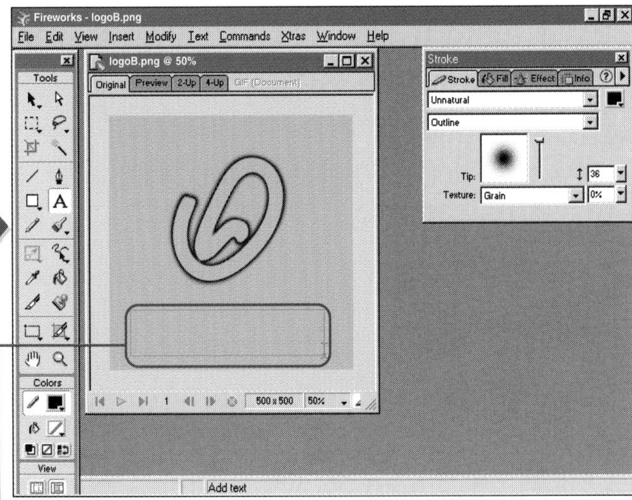

1 Click the Add Text tool button (A).

2 Click and drag I on the document page to draw a bounding box.

Note: If you create a bounding box, text automatically wraps to the next line.

Is there a way I can type directly onto the page?

No. You must use the Text Editor to enter and edit all text in Fireworks. You can also use the Text Editor to resize text and otherwise format the text (see the section "Select and Format Text with the Text Editor").

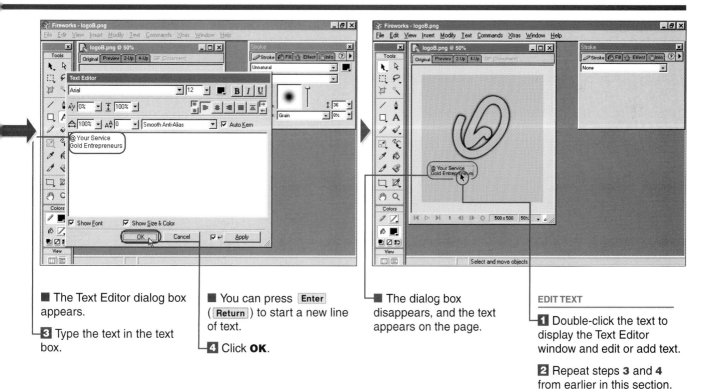

■ The Text Editor dialog box appears.

3 Type the text in the text box.

■ You can press **Enter** (**Return**) to start a new line of text.

4 Click **OK**.

■ The dialog box disappears, and the text appears on the page.

EDIT TEXT

1 Double-click the text to display the Text Editor window and edit or add text.

2 Repeat steps **3** and **4** from earlier in this section.

SELECT TEXT AND CHANGE THE FONT SIZE

You can use the Text Editor to format your text, such as change the text color or font.

SELECT TEXT

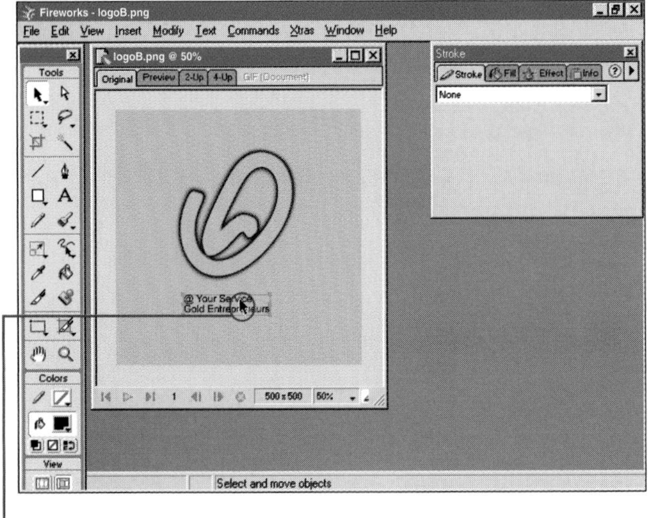

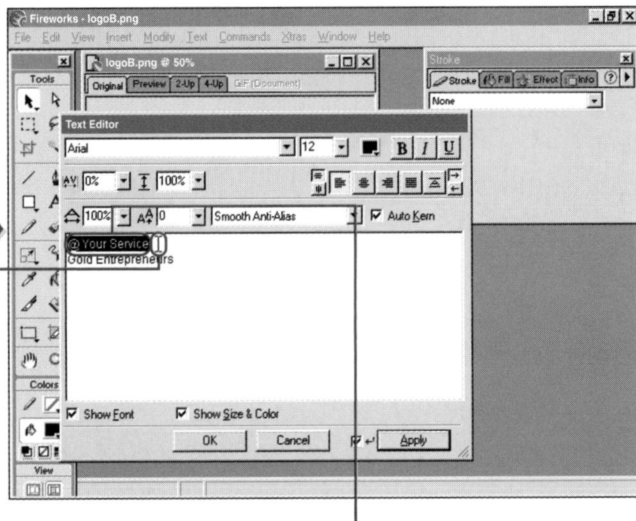

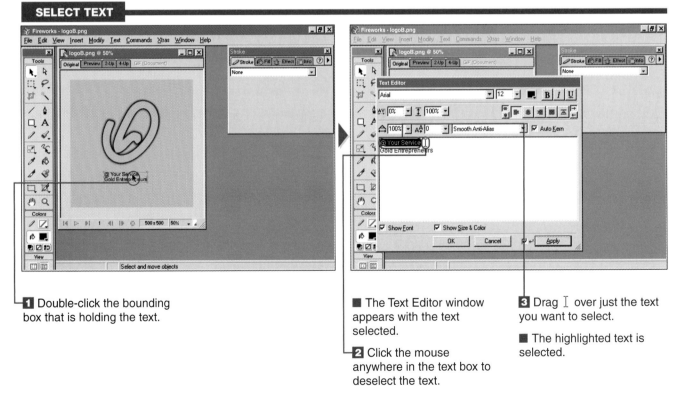

1 Double-click the bounding box that is holding the text.

■ The Text Editor window appears with the text selected.

2 Click the mouse anywhere in the text box to deselect the text.

3 Drag I over just the text you want to select.

■ The highlighted text is selected.

How does Fireworks measure the size of the text?

Fireworks measures the height of the text in points. A point is a traditional typesetting measurement. There are 72 points to an inch.

CHANGE THE FONT SIZE

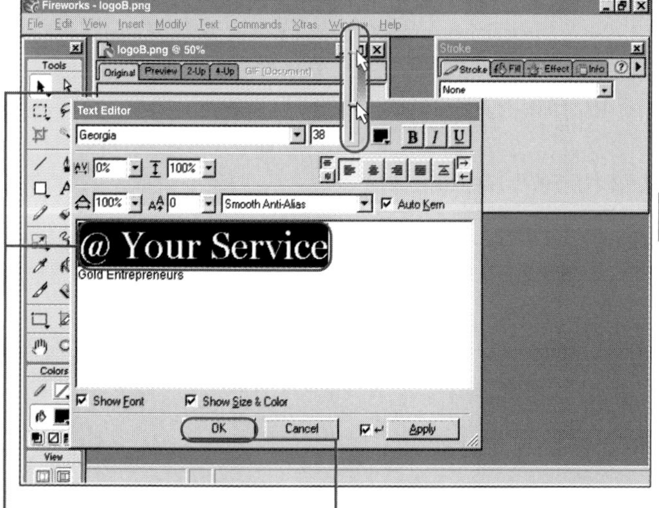

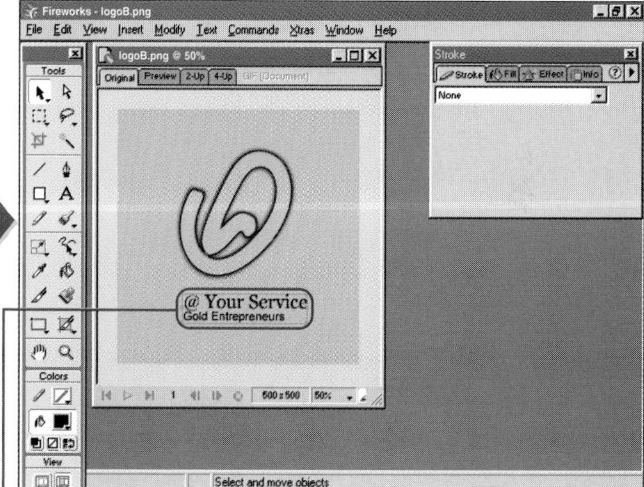

1 In the Text Editor, select the text.

2 Click ▾ and drag the slider to the size that you want.

Note: You can also select the number in the Size box and type a new size value.

3 Click **OK**.

■ The text appears in the document at the new size you selected.

CHANGE THE FONT STYLE

You can use different fonts to make headings eye-catching.

You should be careful to use fonts and text sizes that are easy to read.

CHANGE THE FONT STYLE

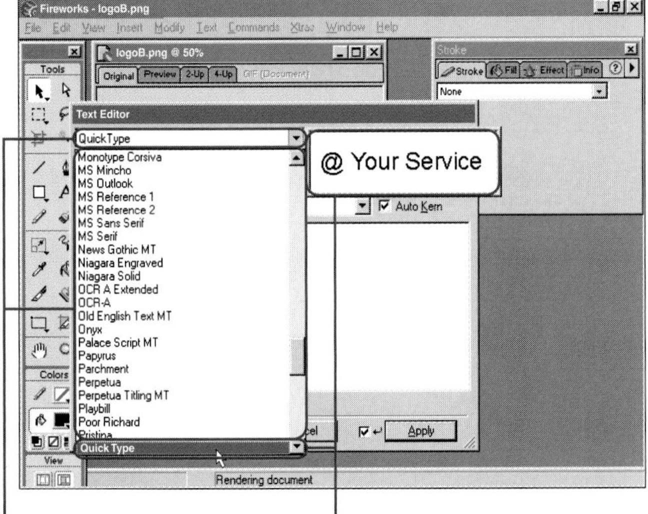

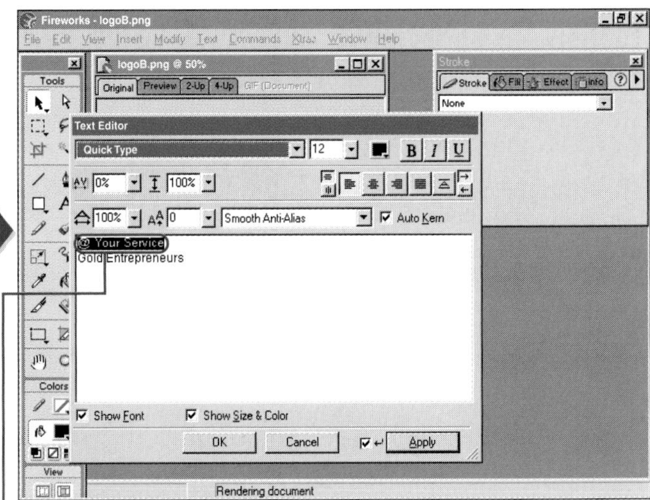

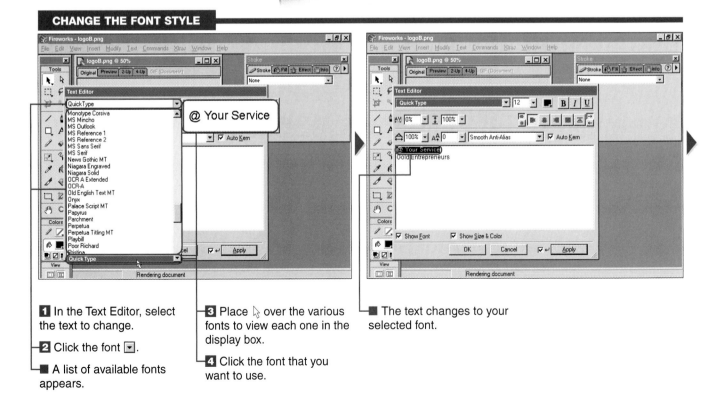

1 In the Text Editor, select the text to change.

2 Click the font ▾.

■ A list of available fonts appears.

3 Place ↖ over the various fonts to view each one in the display box.

4 Click the font that you want to use.

■ The text changes to your selected font.

Can I format only one or two lines of the text in a text box?

Yes. Select only the text that you want to format in the Text Editor. You can select other text and format it differently.

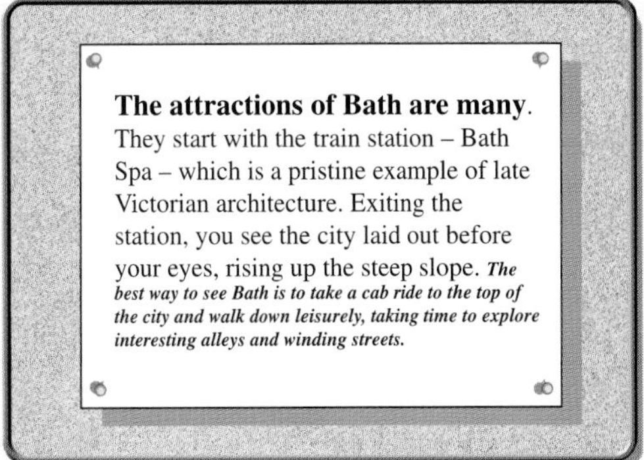

The attractions of Bath are many.
They start with the train station – Bath Spa – which is a pristine example of late Victorian architecture. Exiting the station, you see the city laid out before your eyes, rising up the steep slope. The best way to see Bath is to take a cab ride to the top of the city and walk down leisurely, taking time to explore interesting alleys and winding streets.

CHANGE THE FONT STYLE (CONTINUED)

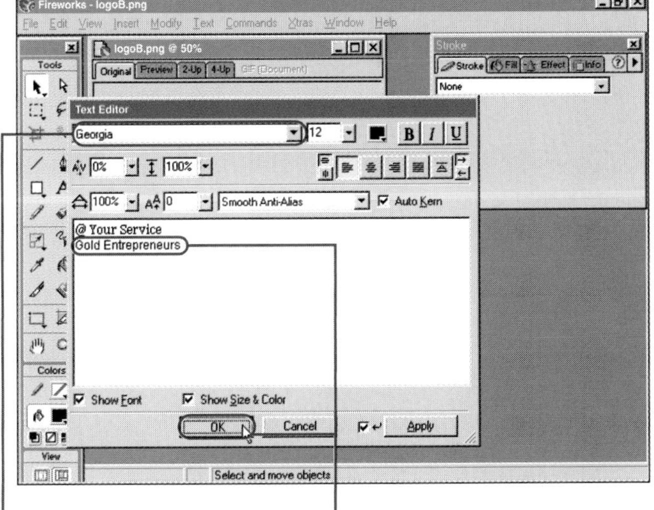

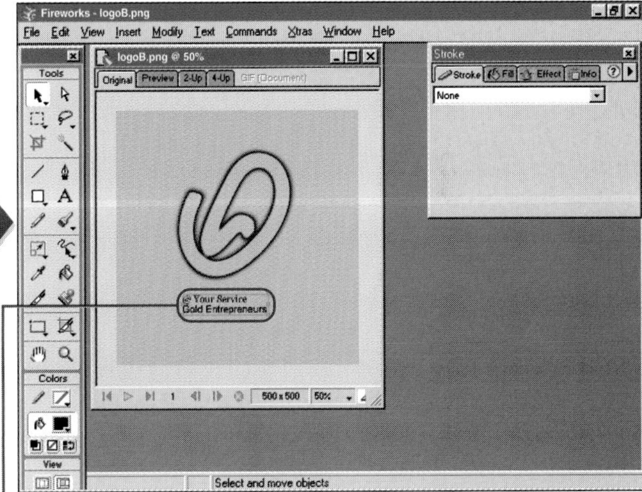

■ If you do not like the font, you can change it by repeating steps **2** through **4**.

■ You can also change the font of other text showing in the Text Editor.

5 Click **OK**.

■ The changed text appears in the Fireworks document.

You can use the Text Editor to change the color of text and text attributes. Attributes are bold, italic, and underline.

CHANGE TEXT COLOR

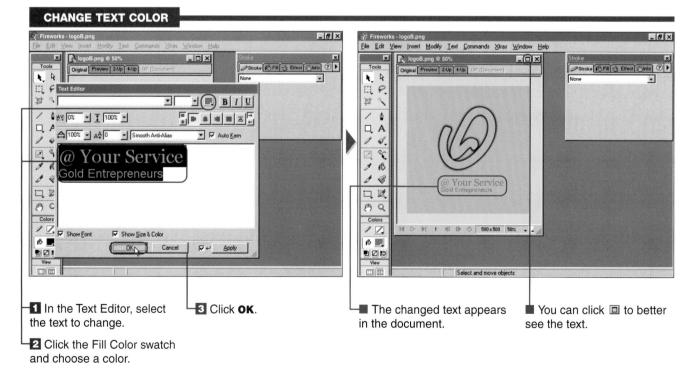

1 In the Text Editor, select the text to change.

2 Click the Fill Color swatch and choose a color.

3 Click **OK**.

■ The changed text appears in the document.

■ You can click ▣ to better see the text.

Are there any colors that are best to use for text on a Web page?

Yes. If you have a dark background on your Dreamweaver Web page, use light-colored text. For light backgrounds, use dark text. The most important rule to remember is that the text should be easy to read.

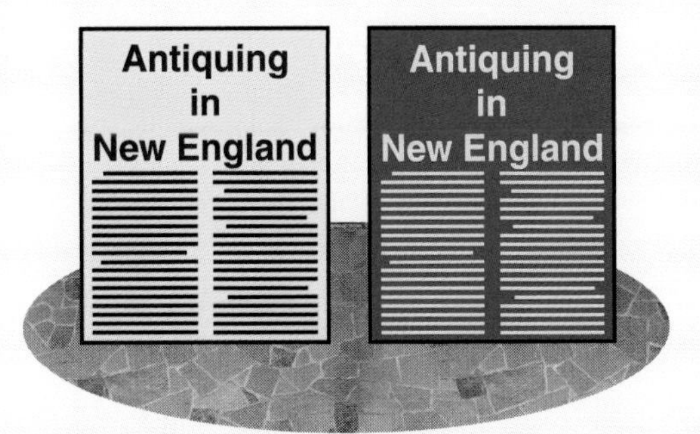

MAKE TEXT BOLD OR ITALIC

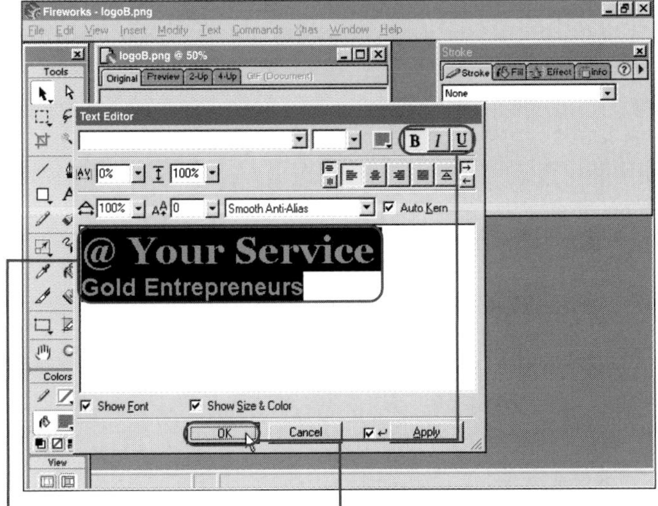

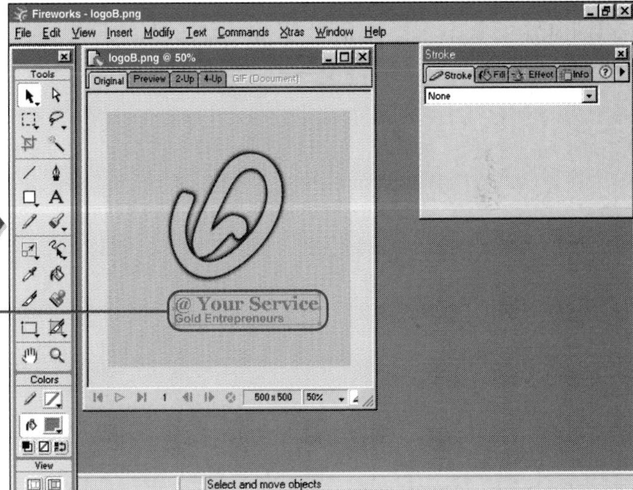

1 In the Text Editor, select the text to change.

2 Click **B** to apply bold, *I* for italic, or U for underline.

Note: You can apply one, two, or all three attributes to the text.

3 Click **OK**.

■ The changed text appears in the document.

CHANGE TEXT ORIENTATION AND ALIGNMENT

You can set text orientation to vertical or horizontal. You can also set text alignment within a text frame.

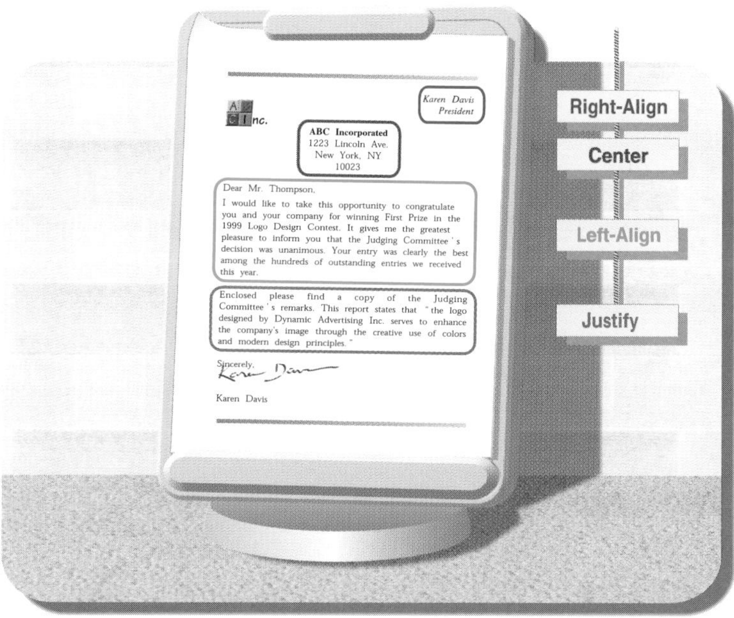

CHANGE TEXT ORIENTATION

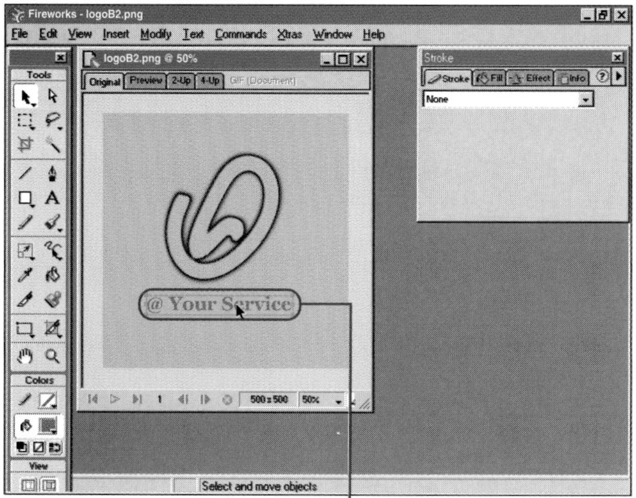

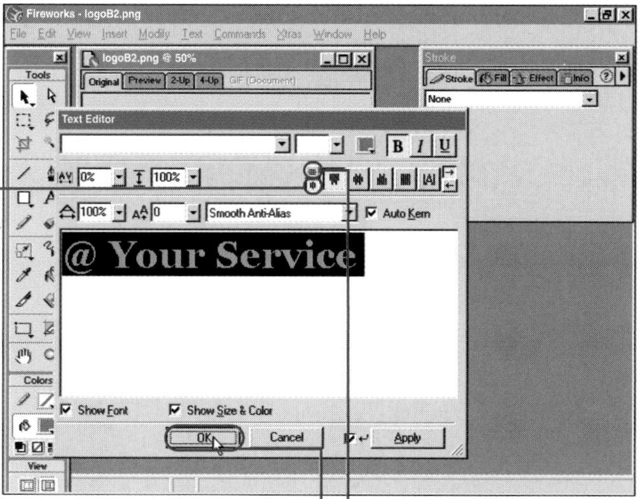

Note: The default setting is for horizontal orientation.

1 Double-click the bounding box to open the Text Editor.

2 Click the Vertical Text button ( ).

■ The text in the document changes to a vertical alignment.

■ You can click the Horizontal Text button ( ) to change orientation back.

3 Click **OK**.

What if I want two lines of text side-by-side with a vertical orientation?

You should put each line of text in a separate bounding box. Because vertical text is difficult to read, make sure that you use only one or two words of text in vertical alignment, such as in logos.

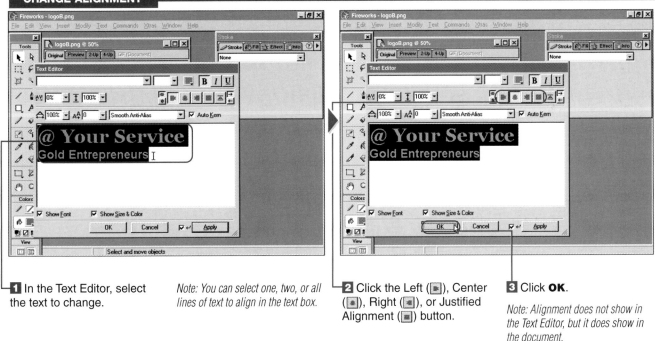

CHANGE ALIGNMENT

1 In the Text Editor, select the text to change.

Note: You can select one, two, or all lines of text to align in the text box.

2 Click the Left (▤), Center (▤), Right (▤), or Justified Alignment (▤) button.

3 Click **OK**.

Note: Alignment does not show in the Text Editor, but it does show in the document.

MOVE OR COPY TEXT

You can move a text bounding box in the document page so that you can better see it or place it near another graphic. You can also copy text within a document or to another document.

marks the Boston Cycling
takes place April 10.
e event is aimed at raising money for
unity profile of the Boston Cycling
Participants are asked to solicit pledges from
hen everyone involved will enter a five-mile
ark Williams
ident Boston Cycling Cl

MOVE TEXT

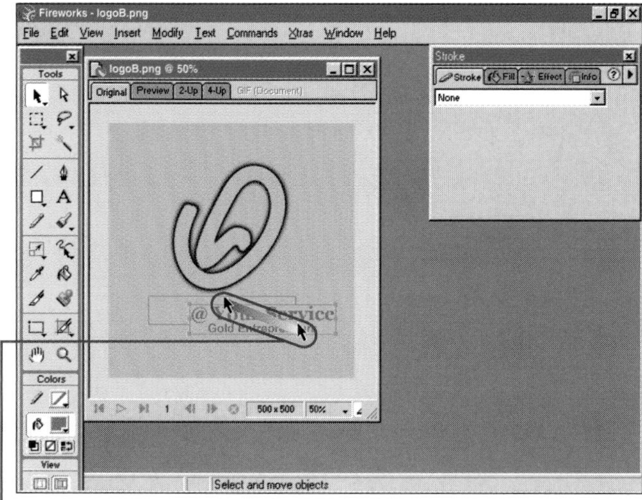

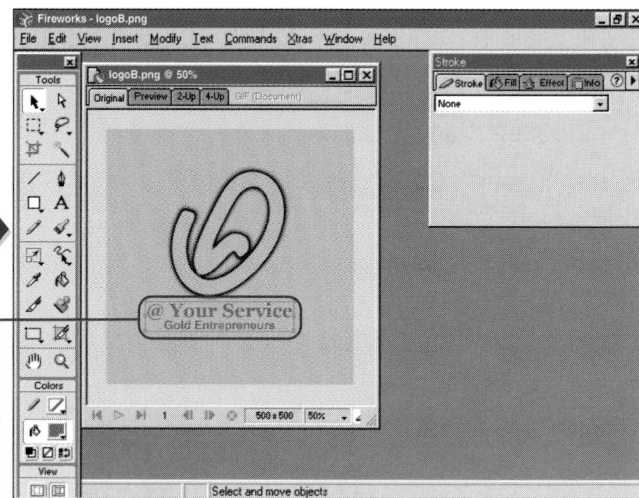

1 Click the bounding box and drag it to the new position.

Note: When you move ↖ over an object, the object becomes outlined in red. Click the object to select it, and the outline turns blue.

■ The text appears in its new location.

What happens if I click and drag one of the small squares on the bounding box?

The six small squares located on the corners and ends of the bounding box are called *handles.* If you click and drag a handle, you can enlarge the text block frame horizontally but not vertically. The text adjusts its alignment within the text block frame, but otherwise, the text does not change.

COPY AND PASTE TEXT

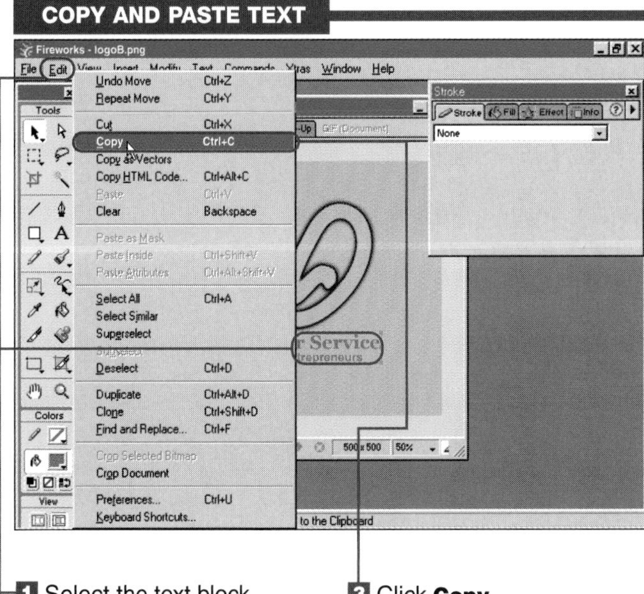

1 Select the text block.

2 Click **Edit**.

3 Click **Copy**.

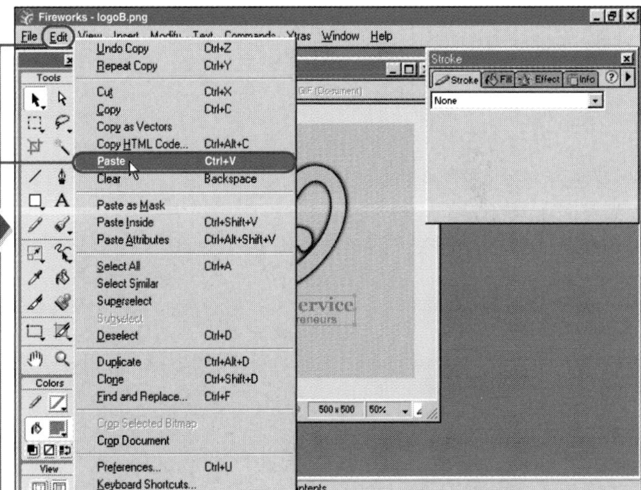

*Note: You can paste the text to another document window by opening or displaying the window before steps **4** and **5**.*

4 Click **Edit**.

5 Click **Paste**.

■ The pasted object appears on top of the original.

■ You can move the pasted object down the page to view it.

IMPORT TEXT

You can import text from other programs, such as a word-processing program.

IMPORT TEXT

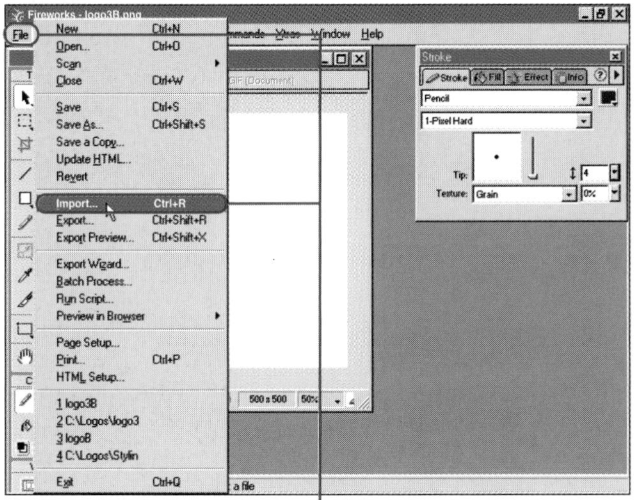

Note: You must save the text in RTF or ASCII format in the word processor before you can import it to Fireworks.

1 Click **File**.

2 Click **Import**.

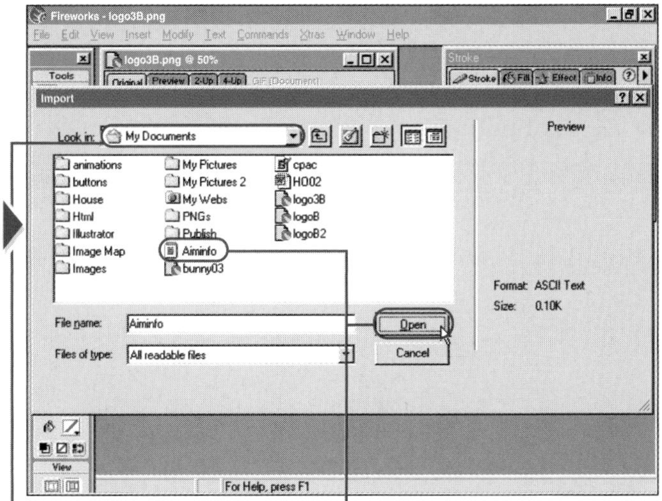

■ The Import dialog box appears.

3 Click ▾ and browse to a different folder if necessary.

4 Click the file that you want to import.

5 Click **Open**.

My text imported in the wrong font and type size. Why?

Fireworks imports the text to fit a default bounding box in a default text size. You can change the font, text size, and other text characteristics in the Text Editor. Changes you make to the text appear only in Fireworks, not in the original word processing program.

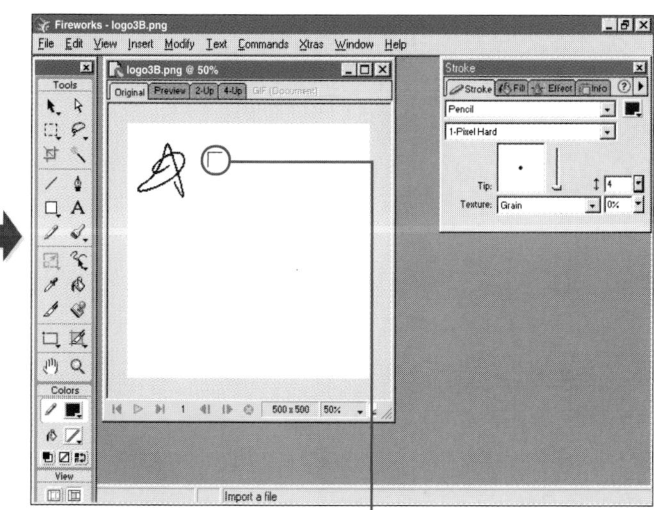

■ The mouse pointer changes to ⌜.

6 Click ⌜ on the document page.

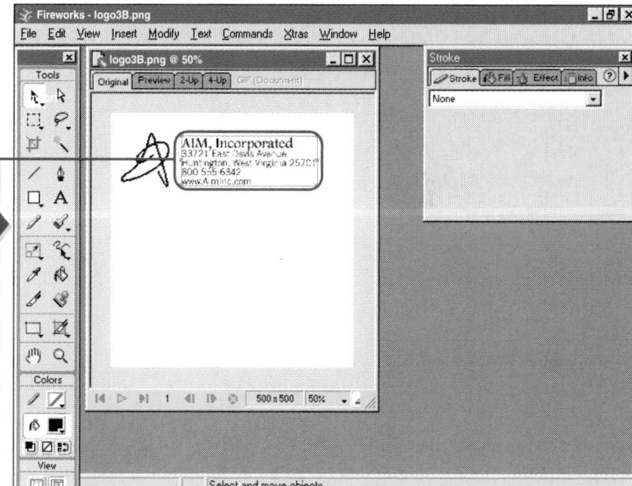

■ The imported text flows into the frame.

Note: You can double-click the text block to change the text size. See "Select Text" and "Change Font Size" earlier in this chapter.

Note: For information about attaching text to a path, see Chapter 4.

DRAW LINES AND CURVES

You can draw straight or curved lines. Lines are useful for separating text or objects or for creating drawings.

In Fireworks, lines are also called *paths.*

DRAW A STRAIGHT LINE

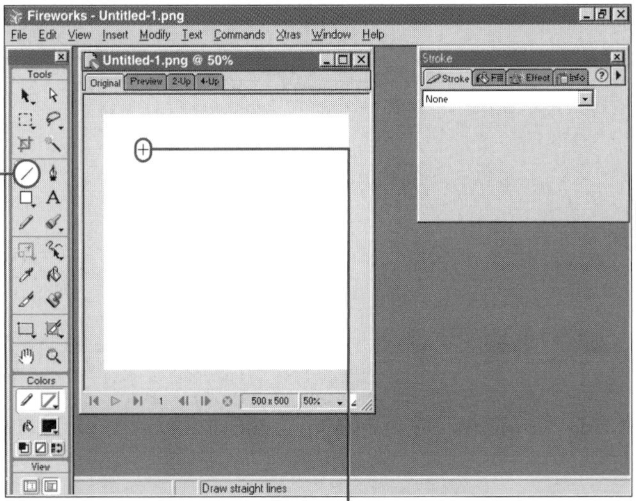

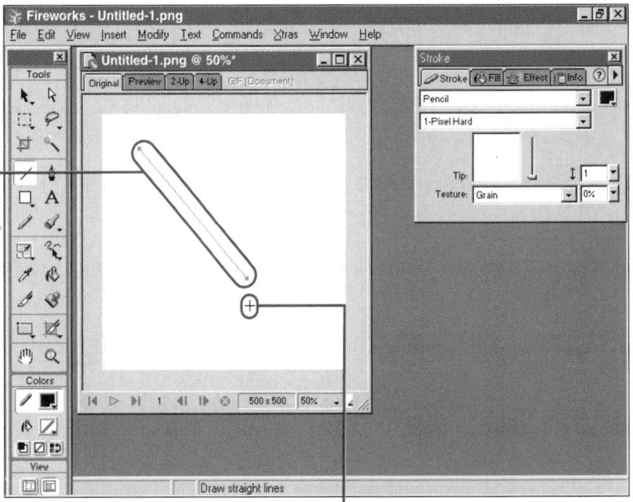

1 Click the Line tool button ( ).

2 Position the mouse cursor on the page (changes to +).

3 Click and drag to create the line.

■ The cursor continues to display as + until you click another tool, such as the Selection Pointer tool ( ).

How can I create a perfectly horizontal or vertical line?

To create a horizontal, vertical, or 45-degree angled line, hold the Shift key as you draw the line, and Fireworks snaps the line into place when you release the mouse button. When you complete drawing the line, release the mouse button and then release the Shift key.

DRAW FREEFORM LINES

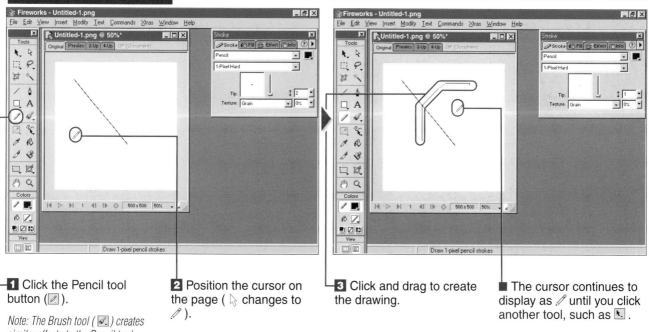

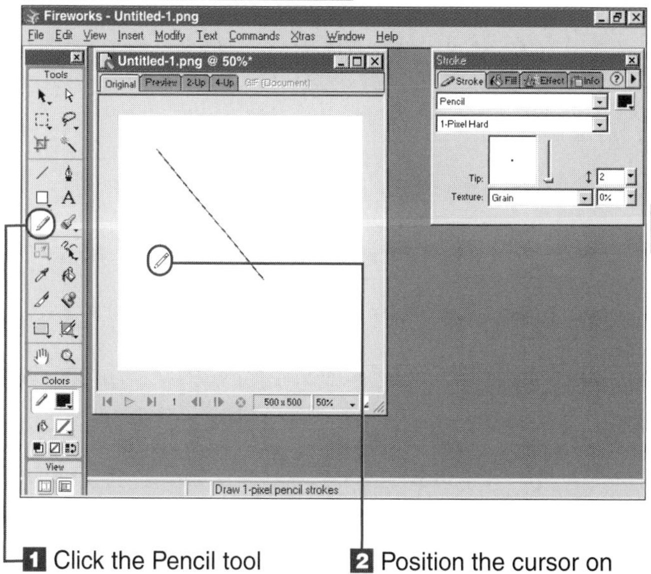

1 Click the Pencil tool button (Pencil).

Note: The Brush tool (Brush) creates similar effects to the Pencil tool.

2 Position the cursor on the page (↖ changes to ✎).

3 Click and drag to create the drawing.

■ The cursor continues to display as ✎ until you click another tool, such as ↖.

CONTINUED

DRAW LINES AND CURVES

Although you can draw freeform lines with the Brush and Pencil tools, you can draw smoother curves with the Pen tool. The Pen tool uses Bezier curves to create smooth-flowing lines.

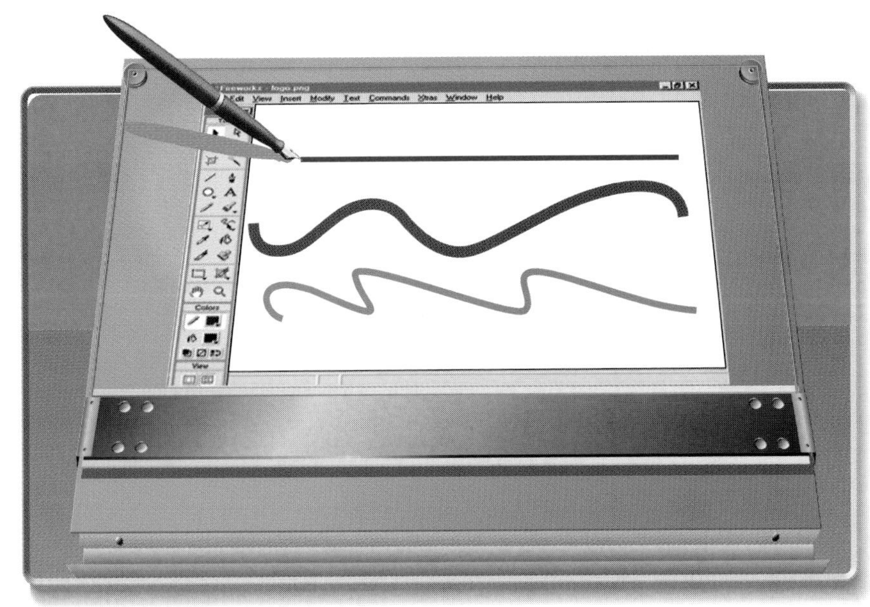

A *Bezier curve* is a smooth curve segment automatic-ally formed between two points.

DRAW BEZIER CURVES

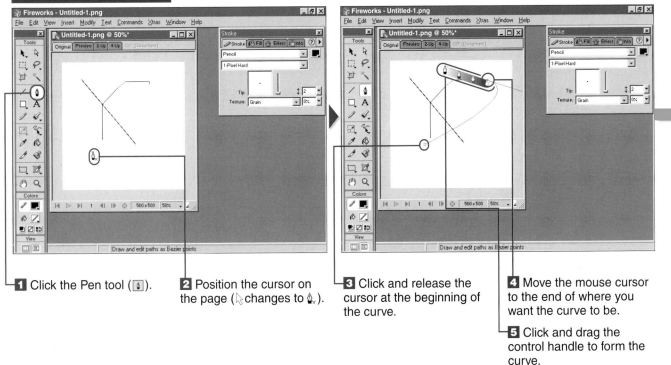

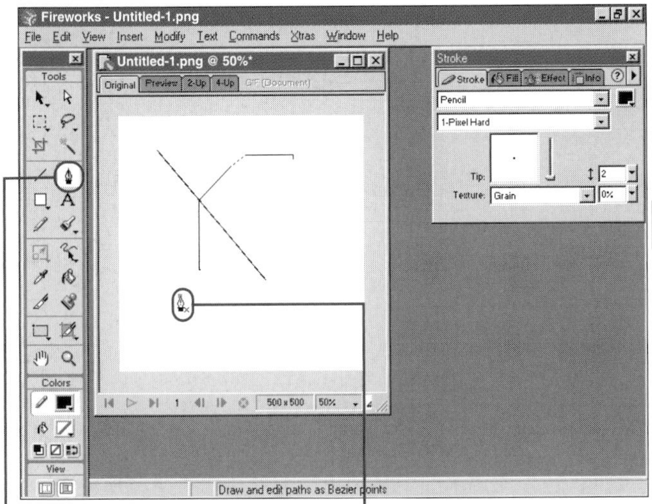

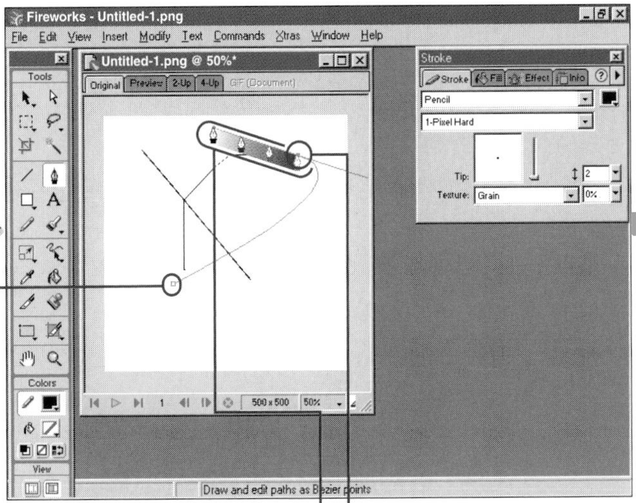

1 Click the Pen tool ( ).

2 Position the cursor on the page (changes to).

3 Click and release the cursor at the beginning of the curve.

4 Move the mouse cursor to the end of where you want the curve to be.

5 Click and drag the control handle to form the curve.

Can I use the lines I draw to create a shape?

Yes, you can create a shape by moving the Pen, Pencil, or Brush tool over the beginning point of the line. You can then fill the shape like you would any other shape you create. See "Apply a Fill" later in this chapter.

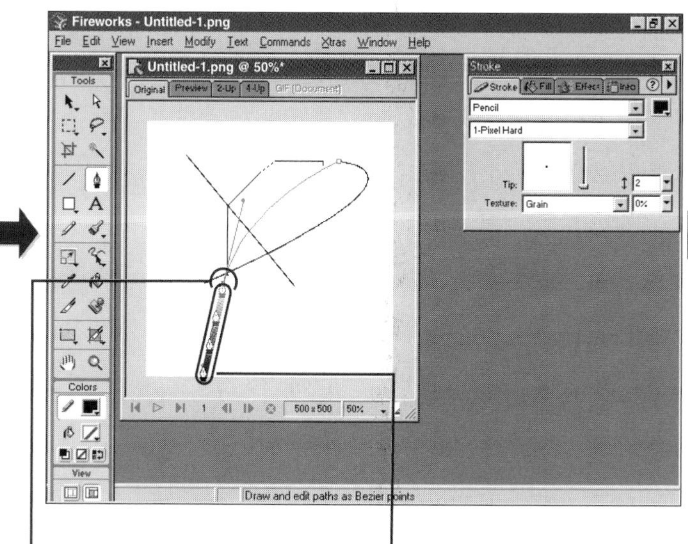

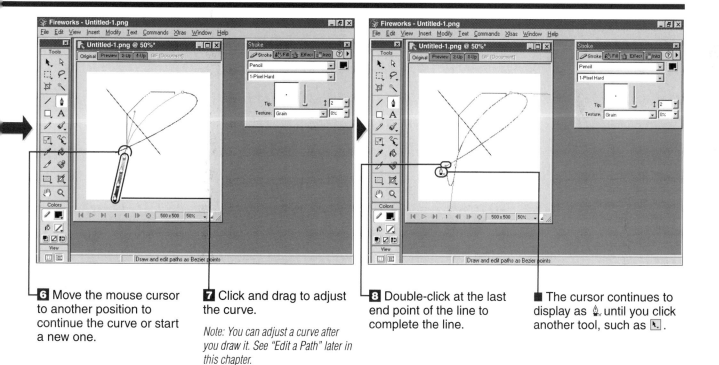

6 Move the mouse cursor to another position to continue the curve or start a new one.

7 Click and drag to adjust the curve.

Note: You can adjust a curve after you draw it. See "Edit a Path" later in this chapter.

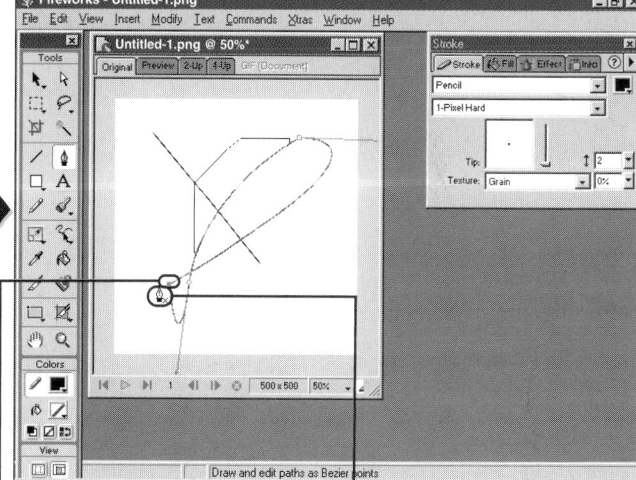

8 Double-click at the last end point of the line to complete the line.

■ The cursor continues to display as the Pen cursor until you click another tool, such as the Pointer tool.

You can change the path any line takes after you draw it.

EDIT A PATH

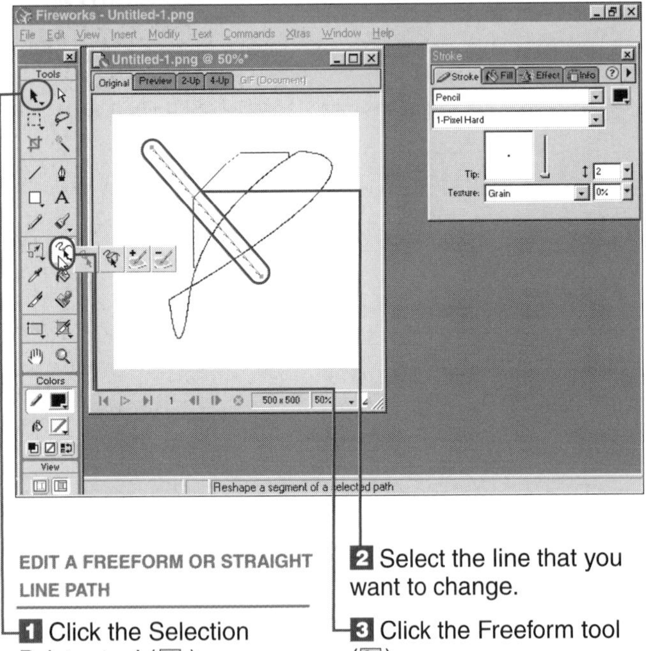

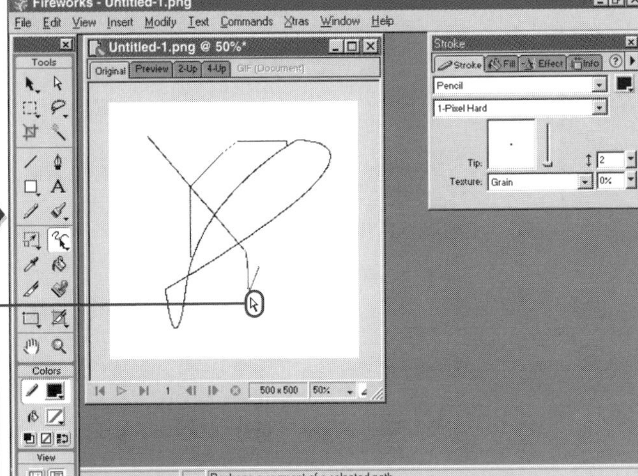

EDIT A FREEFORM OR STRAIGHT LINE PATH

1 Click the Selection Pointer tool ( ).

2 Select the line that you want to change.

3 Click the Freeform tool ( ).

4 Click within the line and drag the line to alter a line segment.

Note: You must select a new path again before you can edit with the Freeform tool.

Can I use the Freeform tool on a Bezier curve?

Yes, you can, but you will lose the smooth rounded curves if you use the Freeform tool on a Bezier curve.

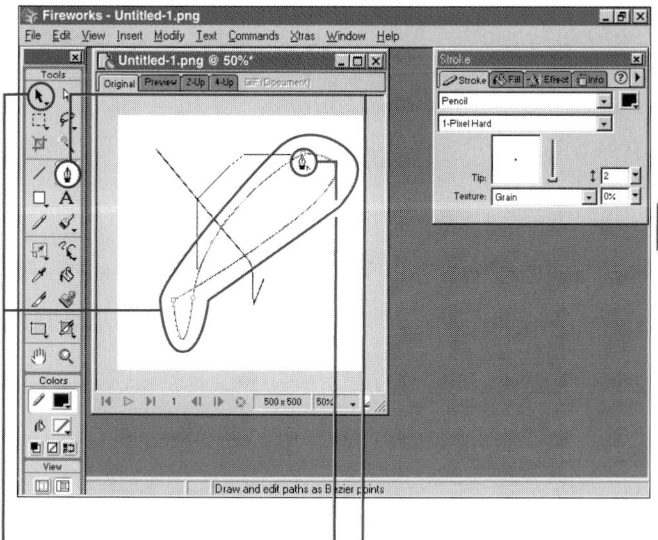

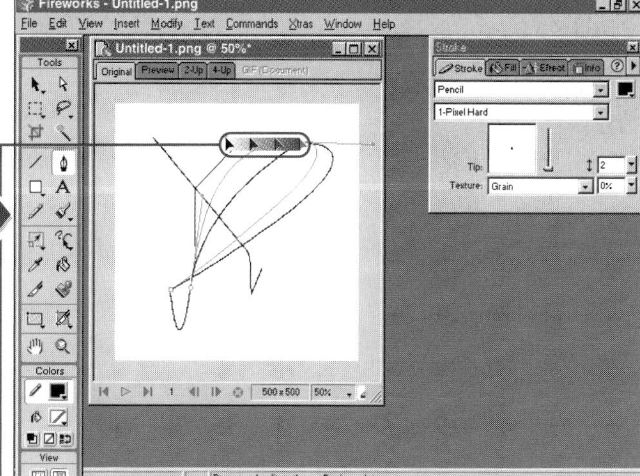

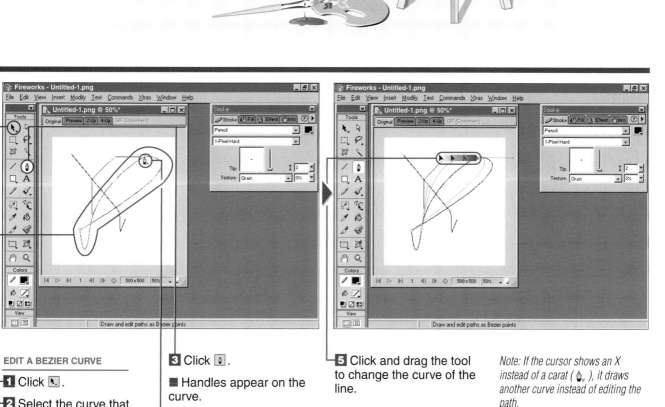

EDIT A BEZIER CURVE

1 Click [pointer tool].

2 Select the curve that you want to change.

3 Click [pen tool].

■ Handles appear on the curve.

4 Position the tool over a handle until you see a carat beside the Pen cursor (✒).

5 Click and drag the tool to change the curve of the line.

Note: If the cursor shows an X instead of a carat (✒), it draws another curve instead of editing the path.

DRAW A SHAPE

You can draw shapes, such as a button or a bar, to use in your Dreamweaver Web Pages.

DRAW A SHAPE

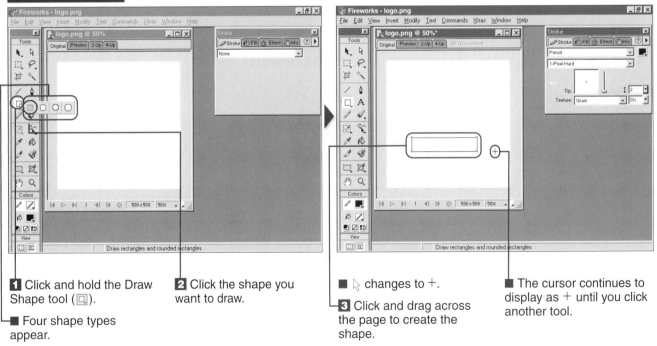

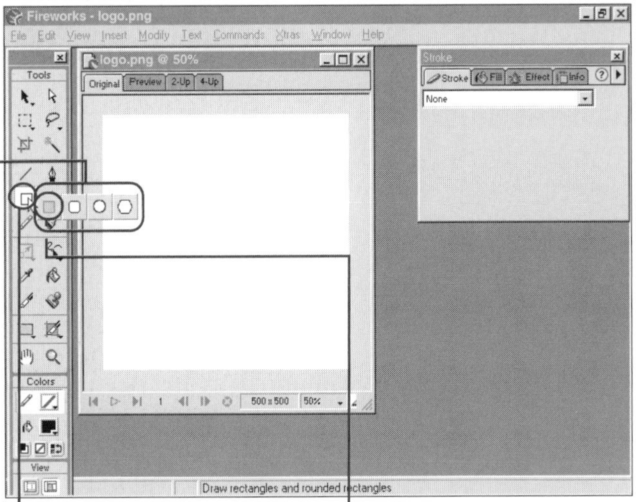

■1 Click and hold the Draw Shape tool (▢).

■ Four shape types appear.

■2 Click the shape you want to draw.

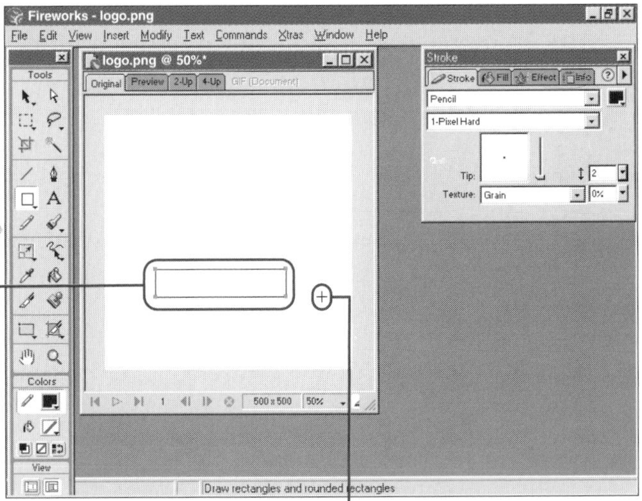

■ ↖ changes to +.

■3 Click and drag across the page to create the shape.

■ The cursor continues to display as + until you click another tool.

How does Fireworks choose the stroke for the shapes I draw?

The stroke you use to draw a shape is the default stroke — pencil. If you change the stroke, Fireworks uses that stroke for all objects you draw until you change the stroke again. Fills work the same way. Fireworks uses no fill until you change the fill for an object.

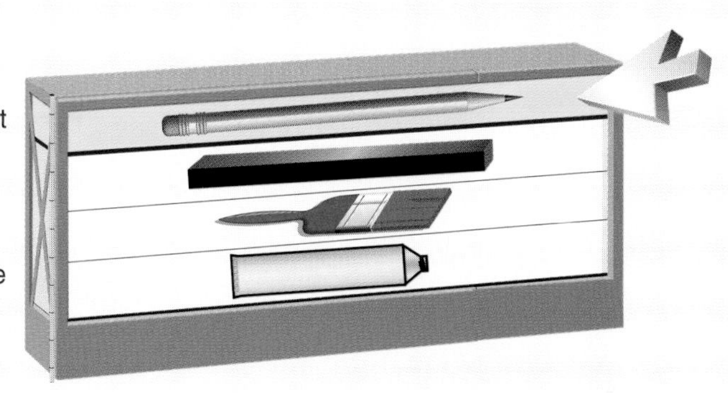

DRAW A PERFECT SQUARE OR CIRCLE

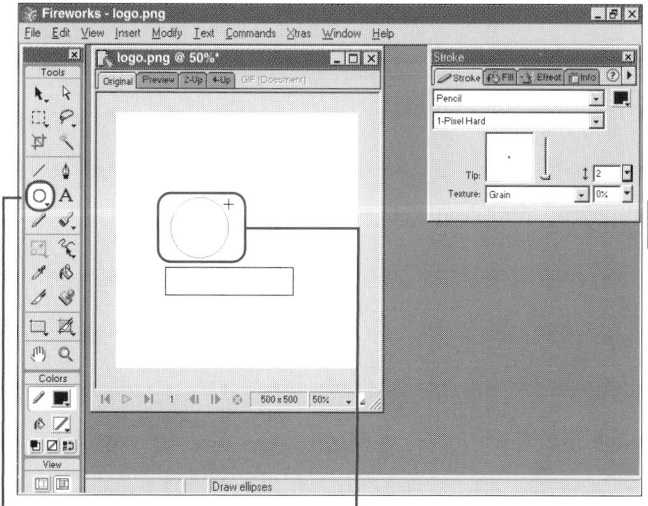

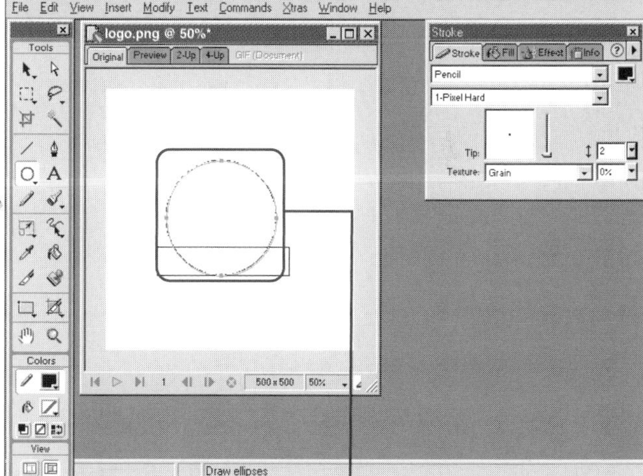

1 Click and hold ▭ and, from the box that appears, select the Draw Rectangle tool (▭) for a square or the Draw Ellipse tool (○) for a circle.

2 Press and hold down the Shift key as you draw the square or circle.

3 Release the mouse button and the Shift key.

■ The result is a perfect square or circle.

APPLY A FILL

You can fill a shape with color or pattern such as tweed.

APPLY A FILL

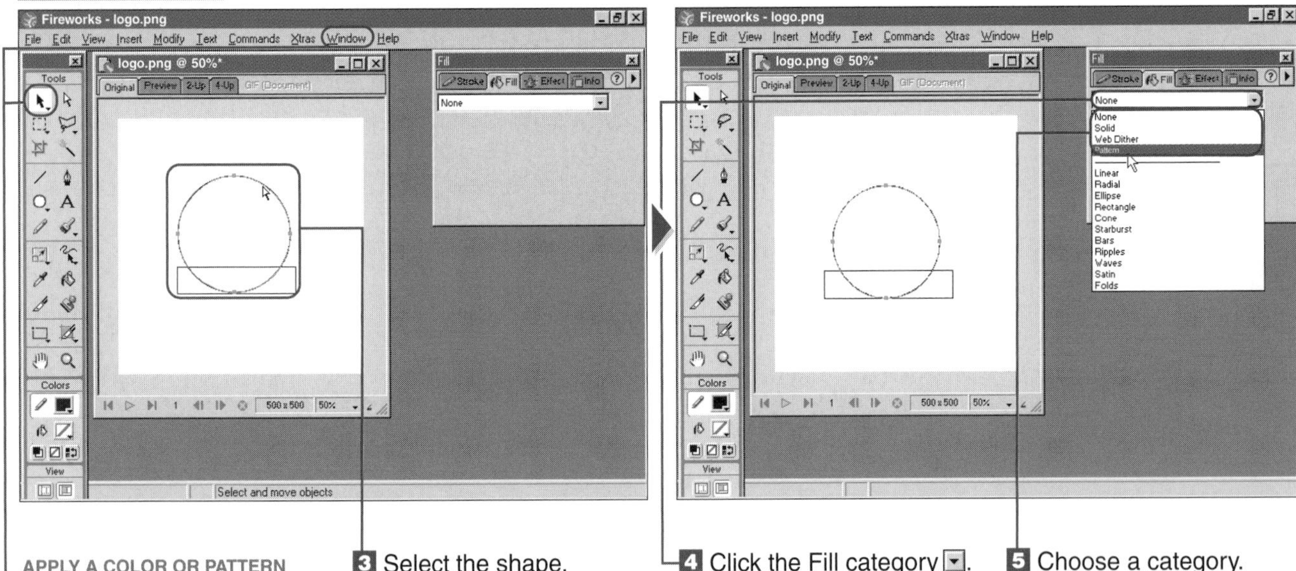

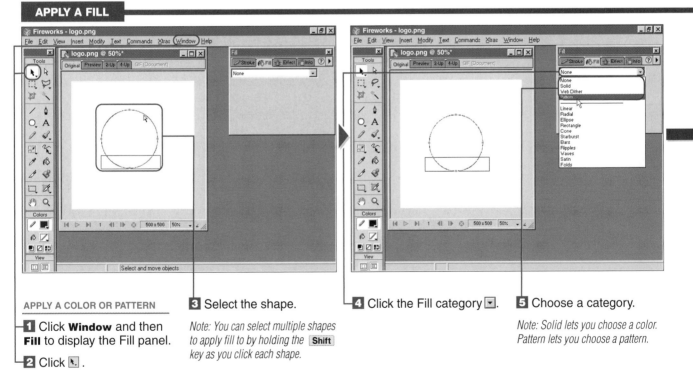

APPLY A COLOR OR PATTERN

1 Click **Window** and then **Fill** to display the Fill panel.

2 Click ⬉.

3 Select the shape.

Note: You can select multiple shapes to apply fill to by holding the **Shift** *key as you click each shape.*

4 Click the Fill category ▾.

5 Choose a category.

Note: Solid lets you choose a color. Pattern lets you choose a pattern.

How does Fireworks choose which solid color or pattern to display initially?

The first pattern Fireworks displays is Berber, and the first solid color is black. After that, Fireworks displays the last color or pattern you chose in the Fill box.

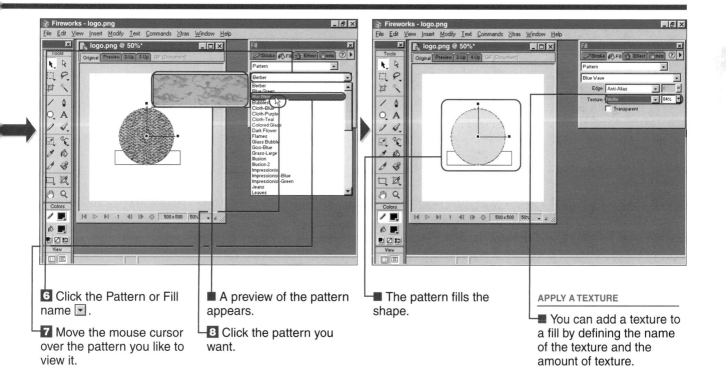

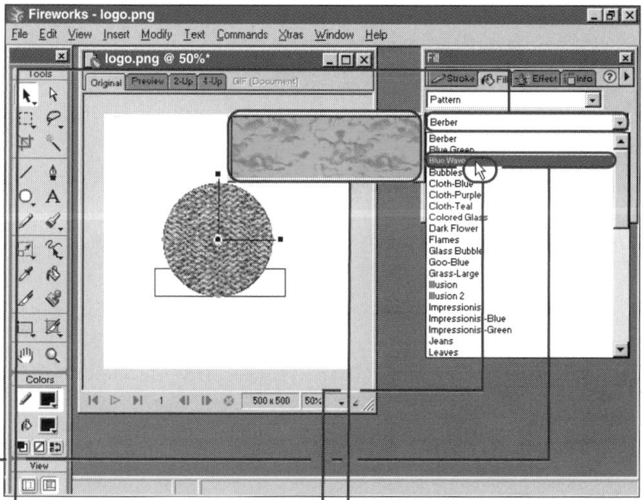

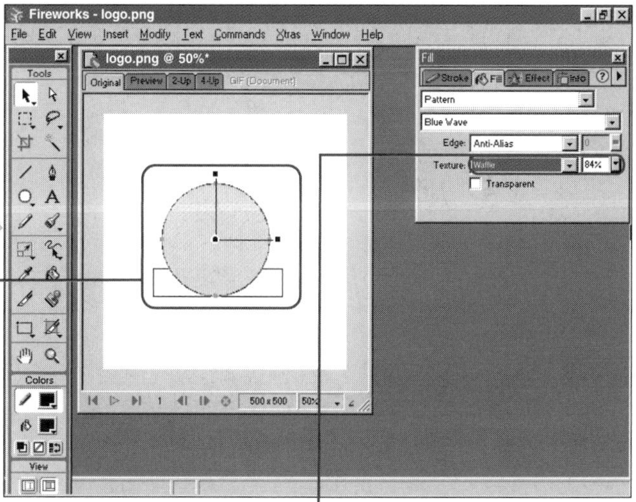

6 Click the Pattern or Fill name ▾.

7 Move the mouse cursor over the pattern you like to view it.

■ A preview of the pattern appears.

8 Click the pattern you want.

■ The pattern fills the shape.

APPLY A TEXTURE

■ You can add a texture to a fill by defining the name of the texture and the amount of texture.

You can add colors to your graphics that will look good in any browser that views your Dreamweaver Web Page.

Use Web-safe colors for the best results.

OPEN A PALETTE IN THE SWATCHES PANEL

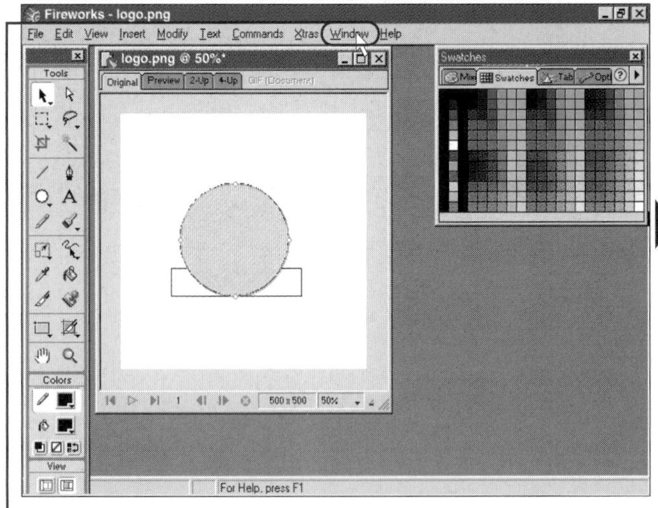

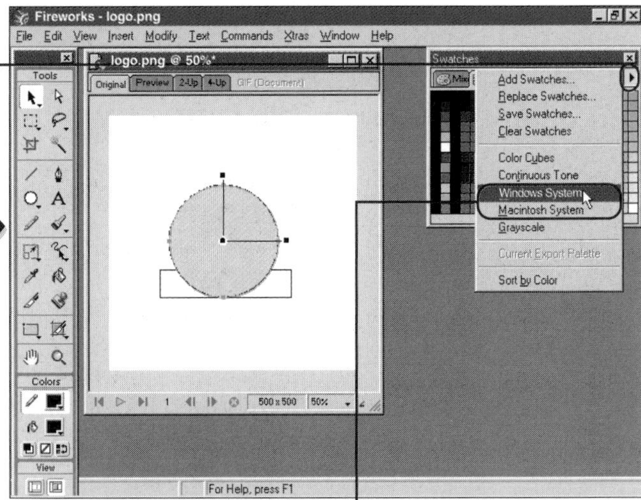

1 Click **Window** and then **Swatches** to display the Swatches panel.

Note: You can hide or display the other panels.

2 Click the Swatches panel Options pop-up (▶).

3 Click **Windows System** or **Macintosh System**.

■ Colors common to Windows or the Macintosh appear.

What are Web-safe colors?

Web-safe colors are colors that are common to both the PC and Macintosh and to each of the major browsers on those systems. It is a good idea to design your Dreamweaver Web graphics with Web-safe colors.

SORT THE COLORS IN THE SWATCHES PANEL

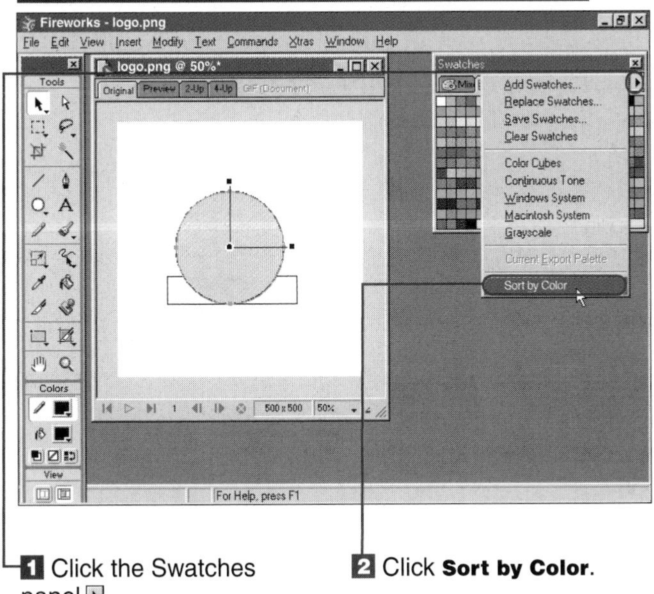

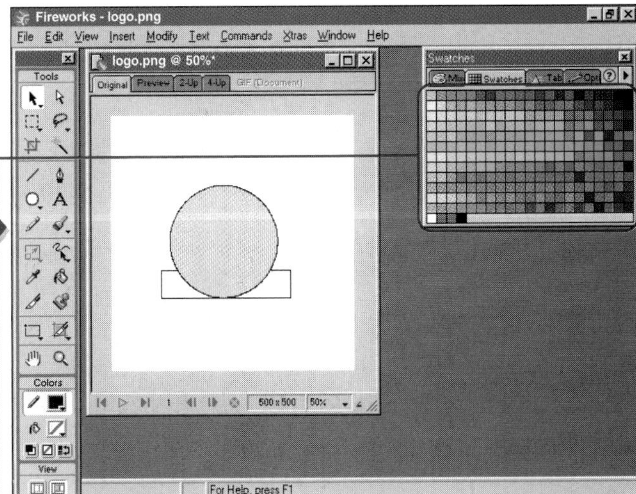

1 Click the Swatches panel ▶.

2 Click **Sort by Color**.

■ The colors in the Swatches panel sort.

■ You can choose matching colors easily.

CONTINUED

You can use colors that are not in the swatches, such as a special logo color.

Some colors you pick may not look the same in all browsers.

MIX A COLOR

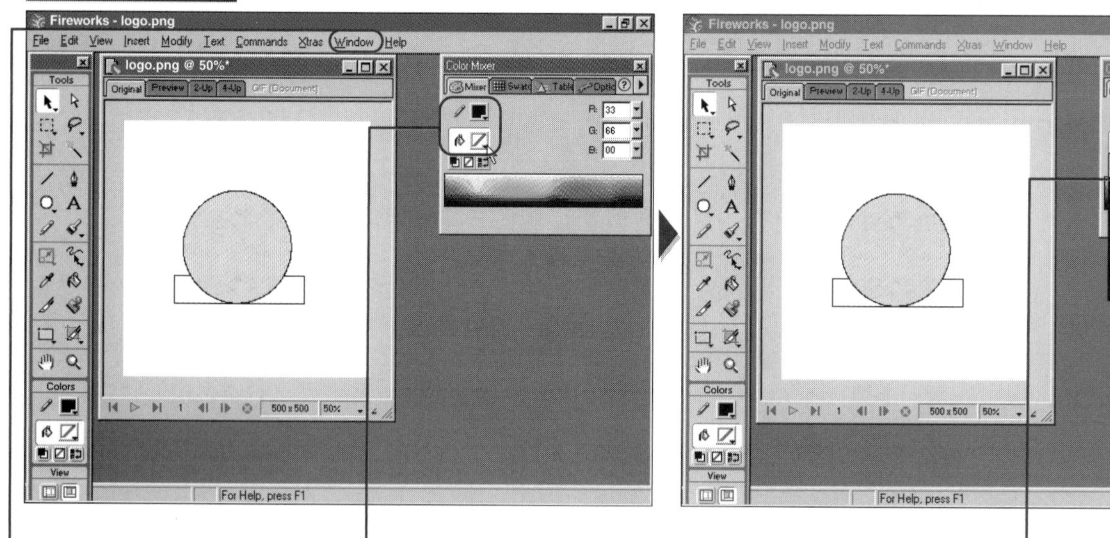

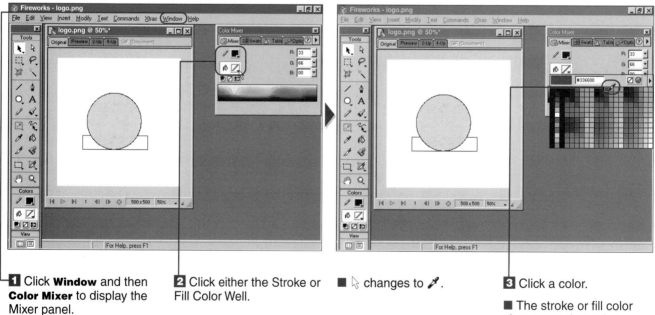

1 Click **Window** and then **Color Mixer** to display the Mixer panel.

2 Click either the Stroke or Fill Color Well.

■ ↖ changes to the eyedropper.

3 Click a color.

■ The stroke or fill color changes to that color.

What if I made changes to the stroke and fill but want to change them back to their original colors?

Click the Default Colors button (■) in the Mixer panel. The colors change back. You cannot undo this step.

ADD A COLOR TO THE SWATCHES PANEL

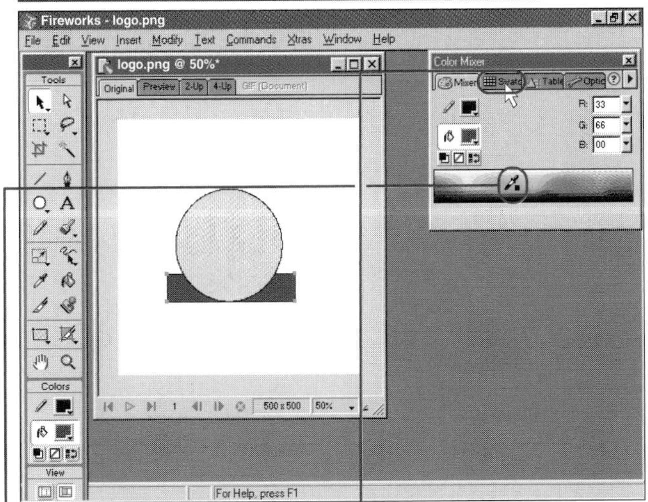

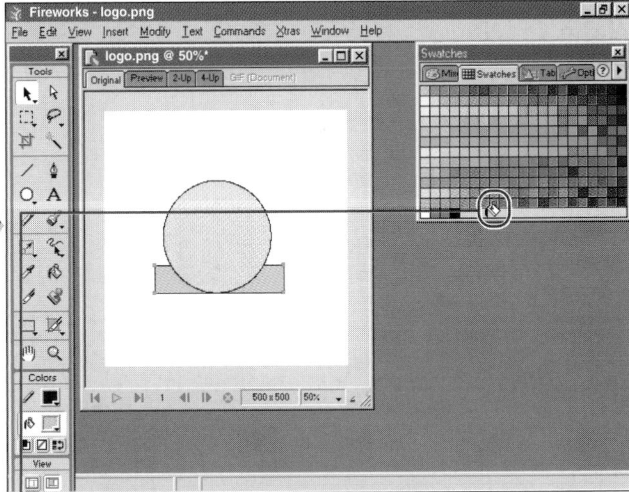

1 In the Mixer panel, click ✎ on the color you want to add.

2 Click the **Swatches** tab.

Note: The color will also replace either the stroke or fill color.

3 Move the mouse cursor to the bottom of the Swatches panel (✎ changes to ◈) and click.

■ The new color appears in the Swatches panel.

ARRANGE OBJECTS

You can arrange objects in layers on the page so that some objects are on top of others.

Arranging objects gives the design depth.

ARRANGE OBJECTS

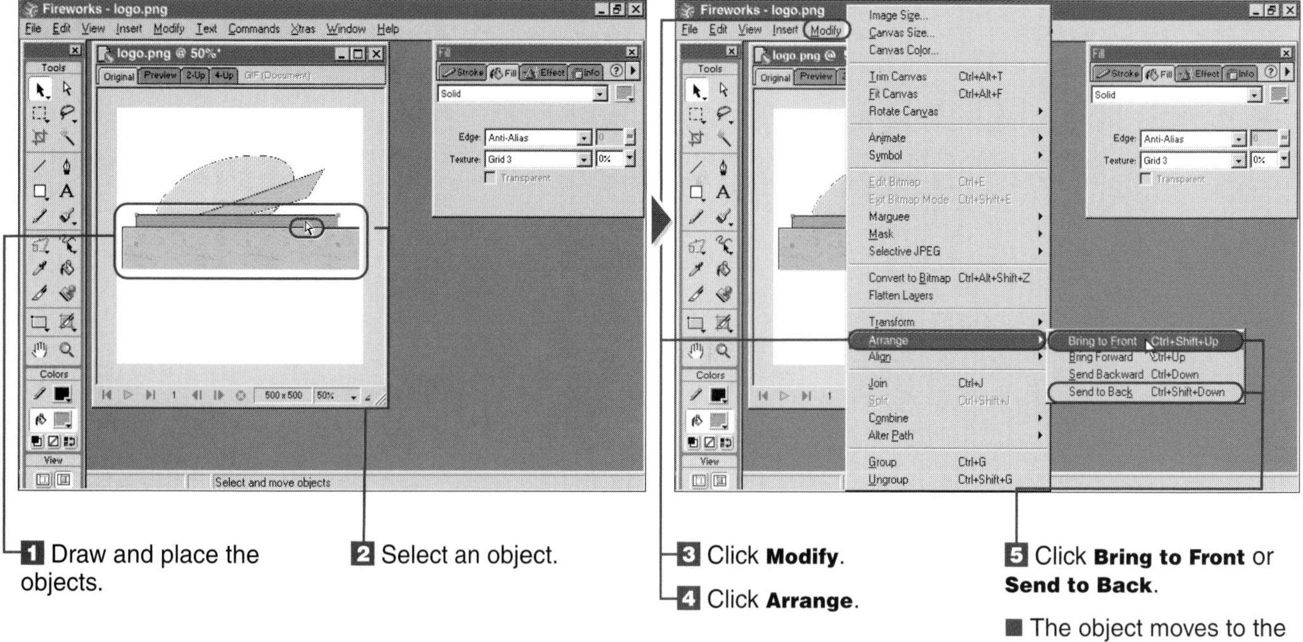

1 Draw and place the objects.

2 Select an object.

3 Click **Modify**.

4 Click **Arrange**.

5 Click **Bring to Front** or **Send to Back**.

■ The object moves to the top or bottom of the stack.

Can I arrange multiple objects at one time?

Yes, you can select multiple objects and bring them all forward or send them all back. The selected objects remain in their original stacking order.

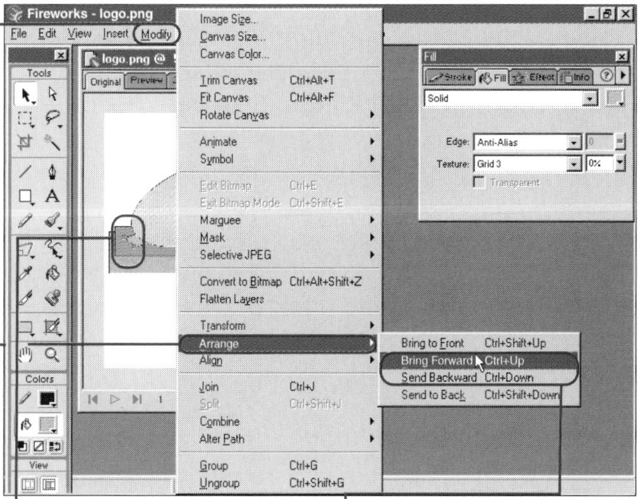

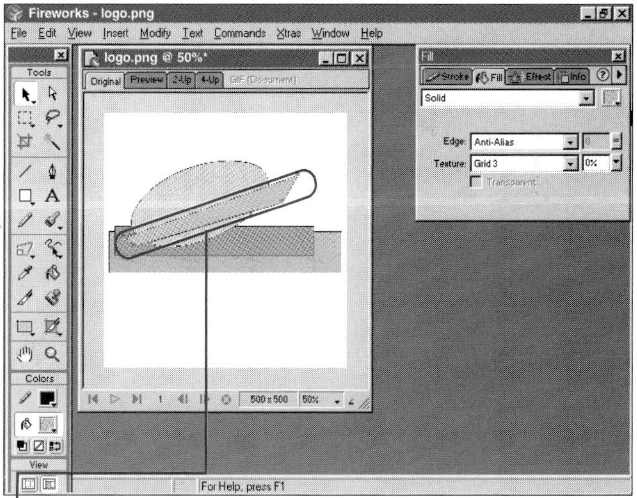

6 Select an object.

7 Click **Modify**.

8 Click **Arrange**.

9 Click **Bring Forward** or **Send Backward**.

■ The object moves up or down one layer in the stack.

GROUP OBJECTS

You can group objects to apply one stroke or fill to multiple objects at once.

A group of objects act as one object.

GROUP OBJECTS

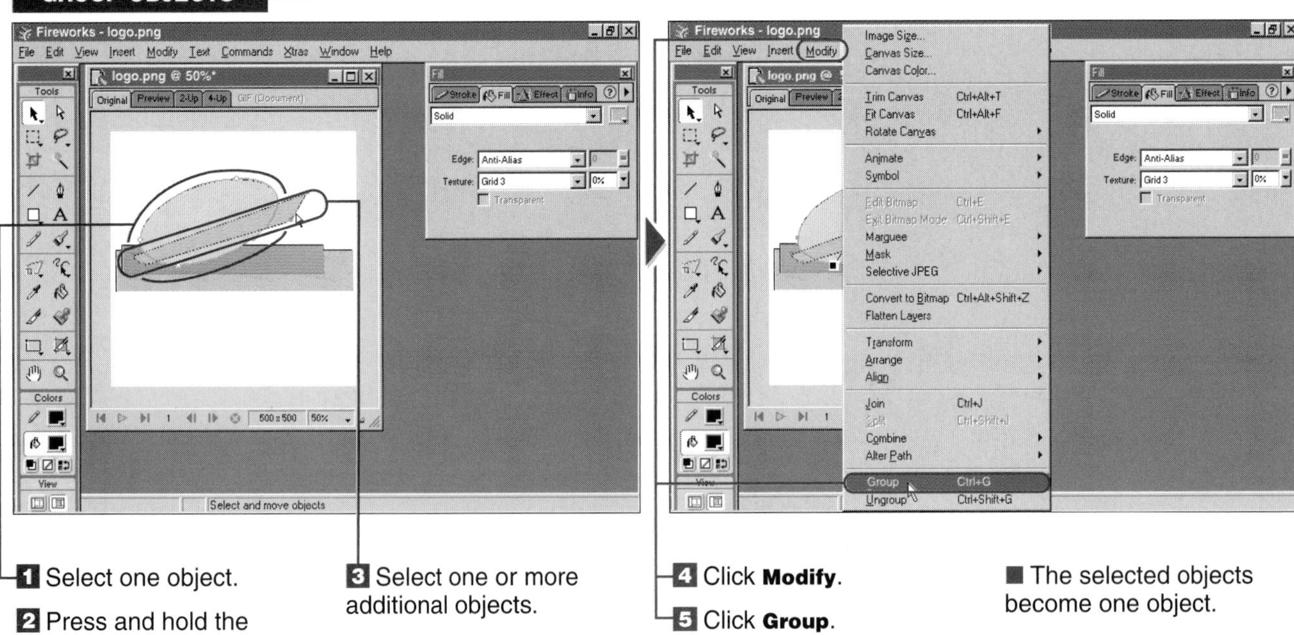

1 Select one object.

2 Press and hold the Shift key.

3 Select one or more additional objects.

4 Click **Modify**.

5 Click **Group**.

■ The selected objects become one object.

Why would I want to ungroup an object?

You ungroup an object when you want to edit or format one of the objects within the group. You can always group the selected objects again later.

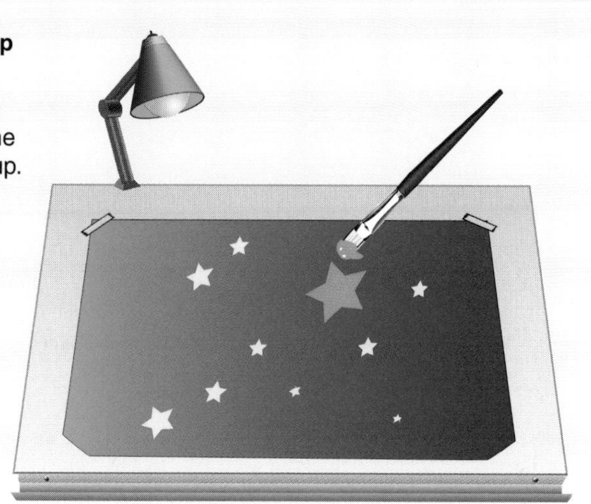

UNGROUP OBJECTS

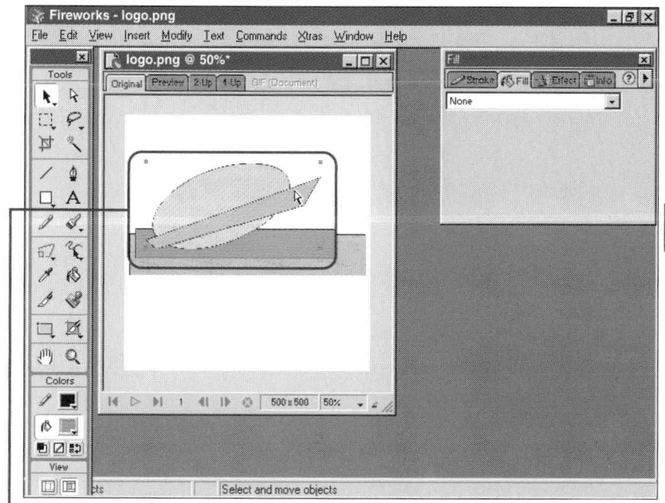

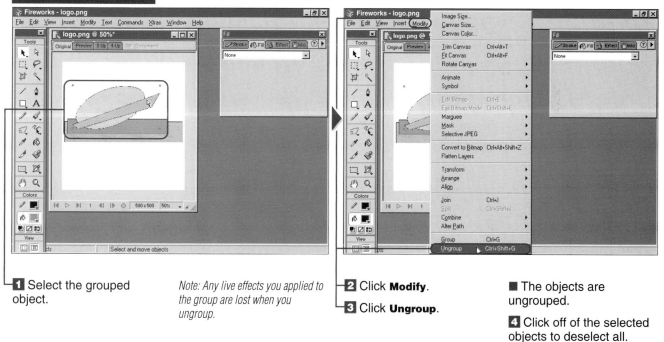

1 Select the grouped object.

Note: Any live effects you applied to the group are lost when you ungroup.

2 Click **Modify**.

3 Click **Ungroup**.

■ The objects are ungrouped.

4 Click off of the selected objects to deselect all.

IMPORT AN OBJECT

You can import objects you created in other applications, such as Adobe Illustrator.

When importing BMP, JPEG, GIF, and TIFF images, you can follow these same steps.

IMPORT AN OBJECT

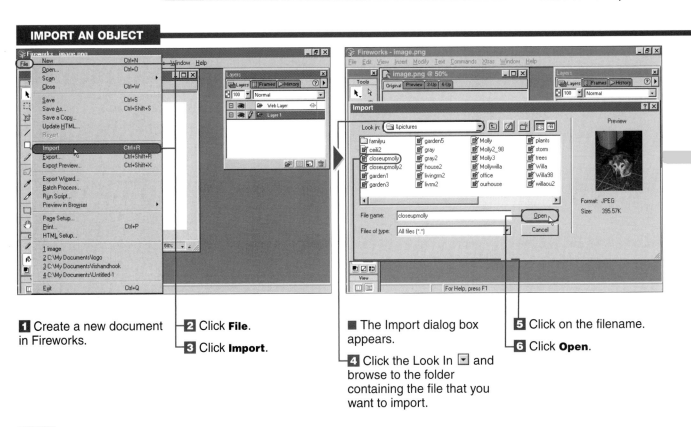

1 Create a new document in Fireworks.

2 Click **File**.

3 Click **Import**.

■ The Import dialog box appears.

4 Click the Look In ▾ and browse to the folder containing the file that you want to import.

5 Click on the filename.

6 Click **Open**.

How do I import an object with layers?

You can import objects from applications that apply layers, such as Photoshop. Fireworks displays an additional dialog box after you import. The dialog box contains options for using layers, such as Maintain Layers and Share Layers.

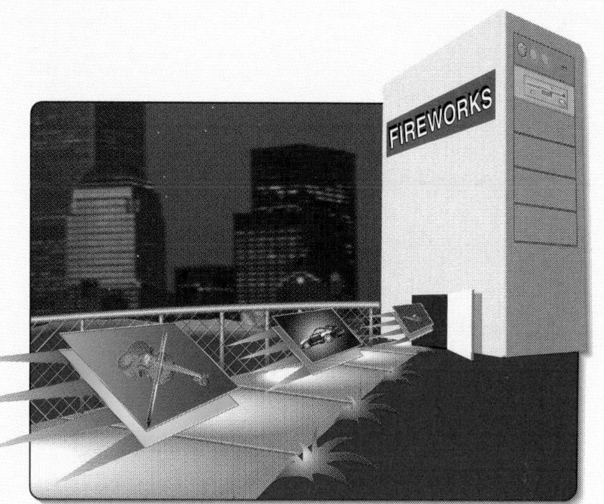

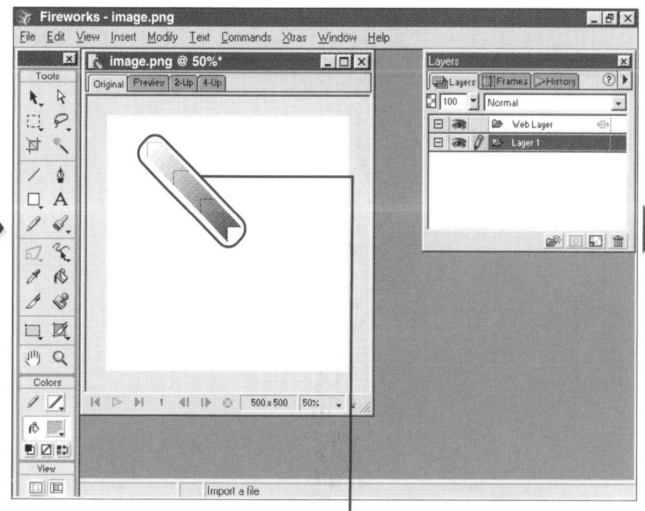

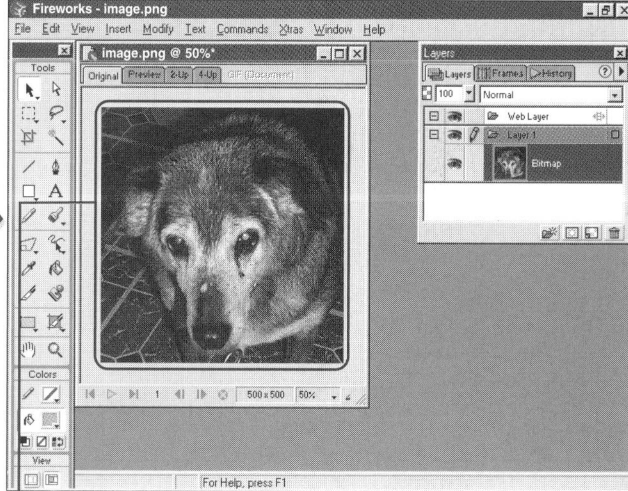

■ ↖ changes to the import cursor (⌜).

■ You can click and drag the cursor to specify the final size of the object.

7 Click the page to insert the object at its original size.

MODIFY AN IMAGE

You can modify an image's size to make it fit the space on your Dreamweaver Web page. You can also change the print size for printing hard copies of an image.

CHANGE THE IMAGE SIZE

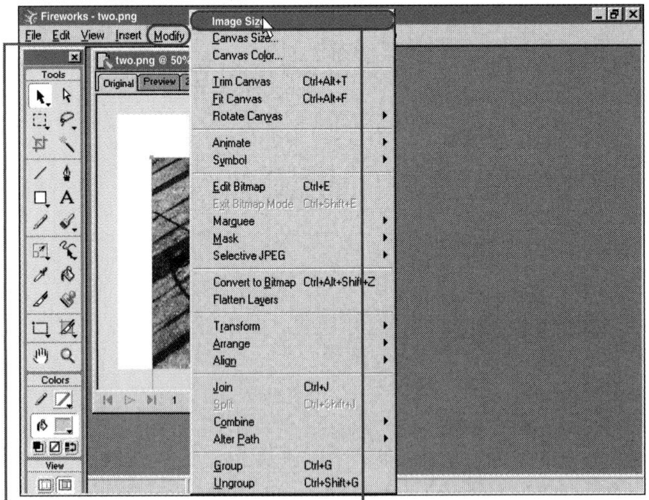

Note: You must select an image before you can modify it.

1 Click **Modify**.

2 Click **Image Size**.

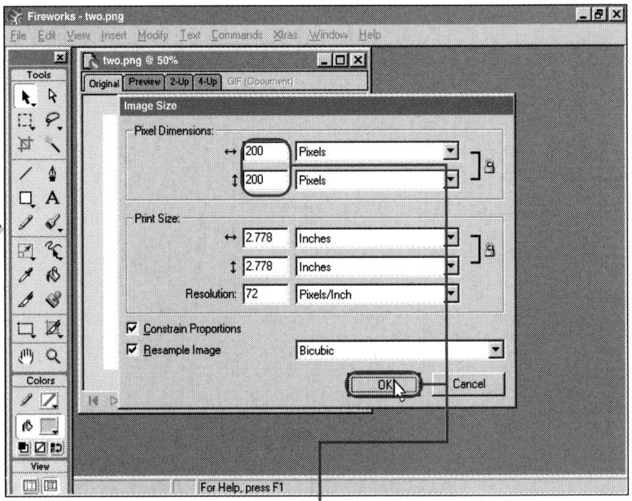

■ The Image Size dialog box appears.

Note: If the image is for use on a Web page, use the pixel dimensions to set the size.

3 Type the new size in pixels.

4 Click **OK**.

What is the difference between the pixel dimensions and the print size?

The pixel dimension defines the number of pixels in the image, which describes the size of the image on-screen. The print size defines the size of the image if you printed it.

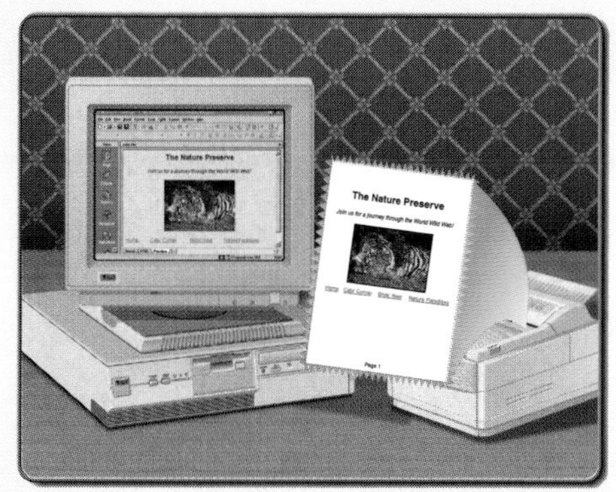

CHANGE THE PRINT SIZE

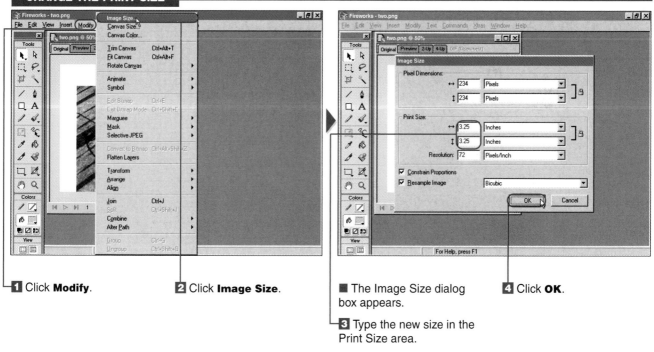

1 Click **Modify**.

2 Click **Image Size**.

■ The Image Size dialog box appears.

3 Type the new size in the Print Size area.

4 Click **OK**.

CONTINUED

MODIFY AN IMAGE

You can set the on-screen or printed resolution of the image to change its size or quality. You can constrain an image to its proportional dimensions so the image does not distort when its size changes.

CHANGE THE IMAGE RESOLUTION

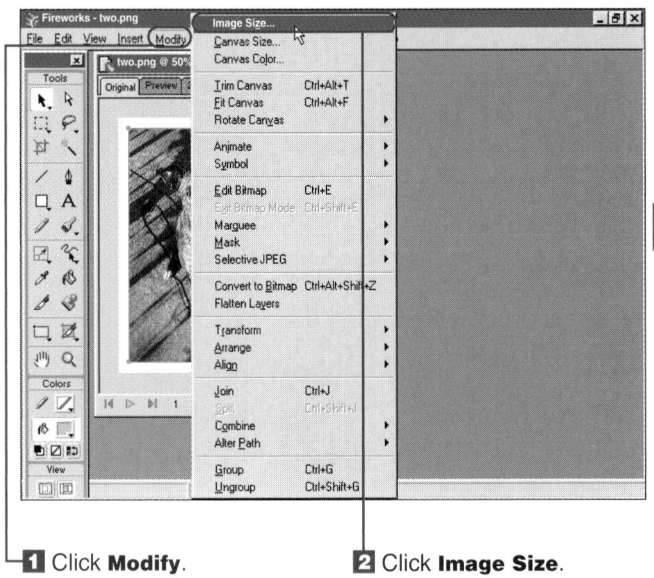

1 Click **Modify**.

2 Click **Image Size**.

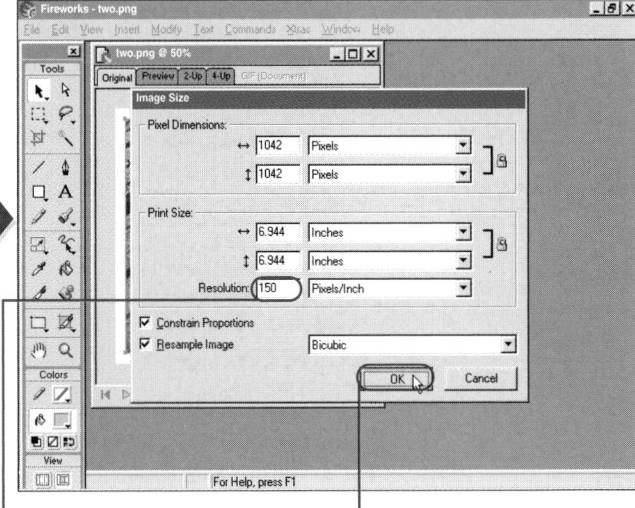

■ The Image Size dialog box appears.

3 Type in the new resolution.

Note: When you change the resolution, the pixel dimensions change as well.

4 Click **OK**.

What does resolution control?

Resolution for an online image sets the size of the image. The higher the resolution, the larger the image. Resolution for a printed image, however, determines the quality of the image.

CONSTRAIN IMAGE PROPORTIONS

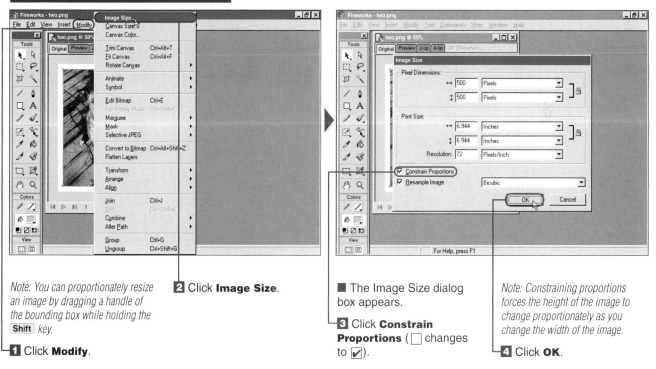

Note: You can proportionately resize an image by dragging a handle of the bounding box while holding the **Shift** *key.*

1 Click **Modify**.

2 Click **Image Size**.

■ The Image Size dialog box appears.

3 Click **Constrain Proportions** (☐ changes to ☑).

Note: Constraining proportions forces the height of the image to change proportionately as you change the width of the image.

4 Click **OK**.

CROP AN IMAGE

You can crop an image to remove unwanted parts of the image.

CROP AN IMAGE

1 Click **Edit**.

2 Click **Crop Selected Bitmap**.

3 Click and drag the mouse on any handle.

When would I crop an image?

Crop an image when you want to remove an item or part of the image from a picture. For example, you may want to crop a picture if you took it from too far away.

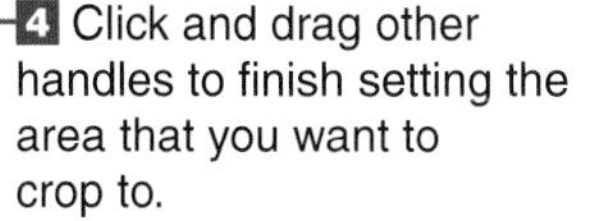
4 Click and drag other handles to finish setting the area that you want to crop to.

5 Double-click the image.

■ The image is cropped.

SELECT AND MOVE PIXELS

Although you can select an image with the mouse pointer, you can also select an entire image or a part of it with the Marquee or Lasso tools.

SELECT AND MOVE PIXELS WITH THE MARQUEE TOOL

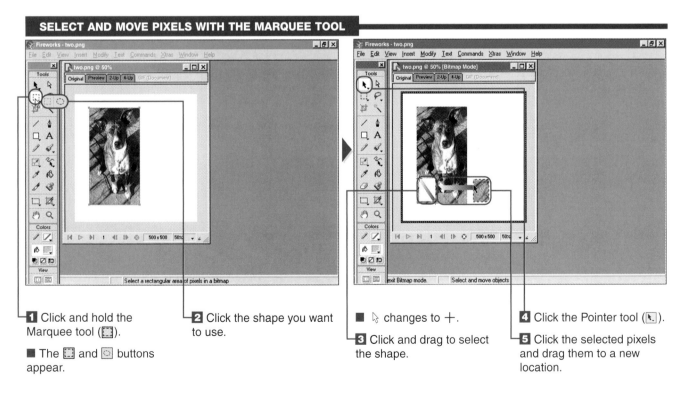

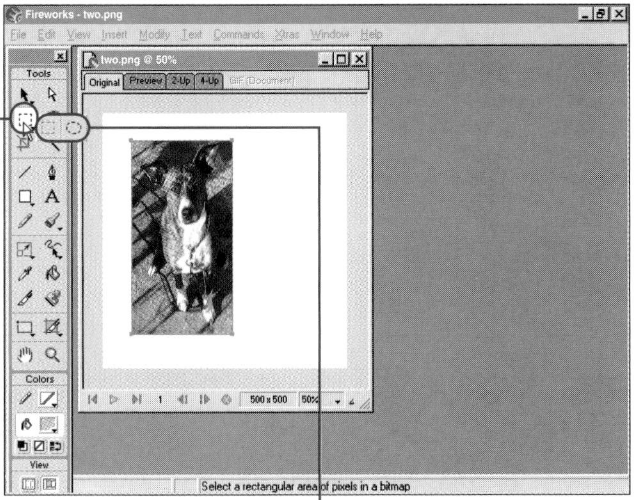

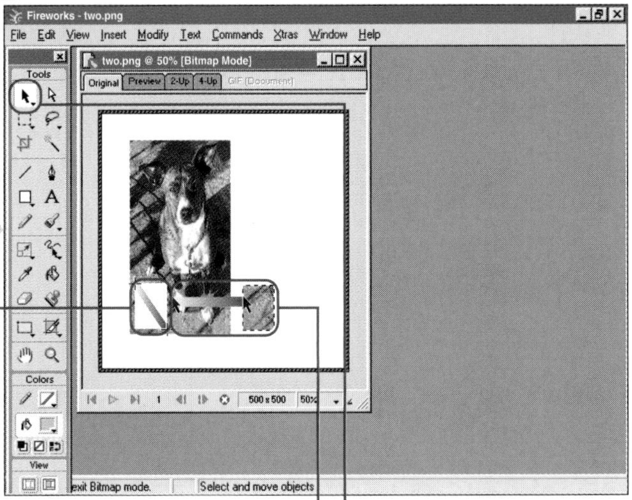

1. Click and hold the Marquee tool ( ).

■ The and buttons appear.

2. Click the shape you want to use.

■ changes to +.

3. Click and drag to select the shape.

4. Click the Pointer tool ( ).

5. Click the selected pixels and drag them to a new location.

What is the difference between the Marquee and Lasso tools?

The Marquee tool creates a rectangular, square, oval, or circular shape. The Lasso tool creates natural irregular shapes, and the polygonal lasso creates angular irregular shapes.

SELECT AND MOVE PIXELS WITH THE LASSO TOOL

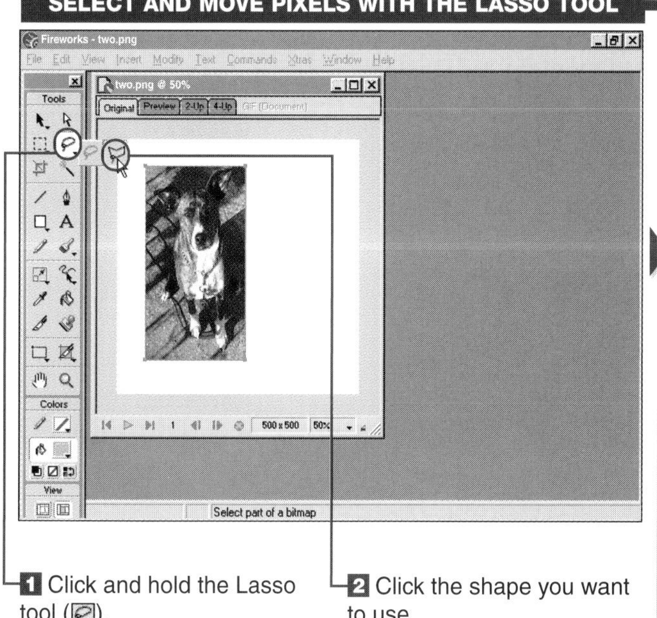

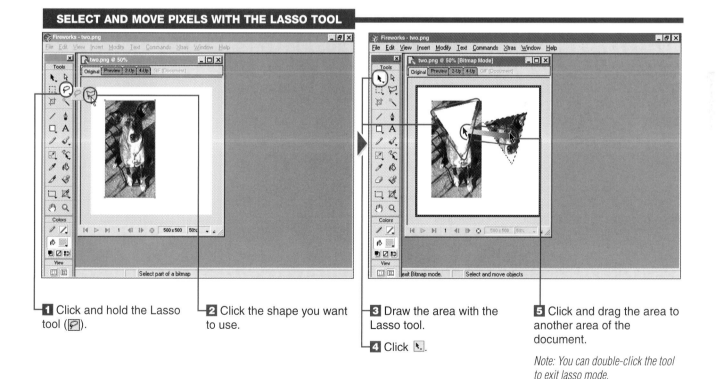

1 Click and hold the Lasso tool (lasso icon).

2 Click the shape you want to use.

3 Draw the area with the Lasso tool.

4 Click (pointer icon).

5 Click and drag the area to another area of the document.

Note: You can double-click the tool to exit lasso mode.

CONTINUED

SELECT AND MOVE PIXELS

You can select certain colors of pixels to remove them from the picture. For example, you can use the magic wand to remove a background.

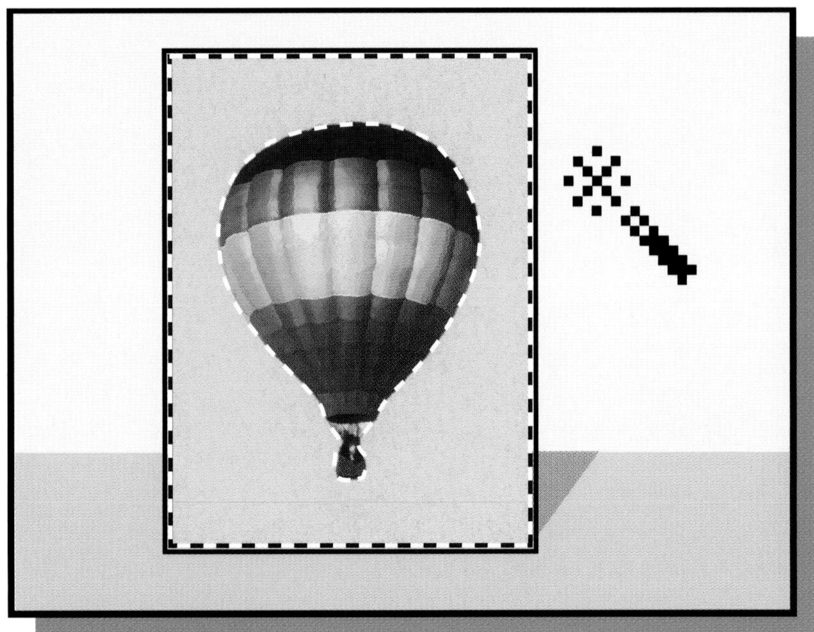

SELECT PIXELS WITH THE MAGIC WAND TOOL

1 Click the Magic Wand tool ( ).

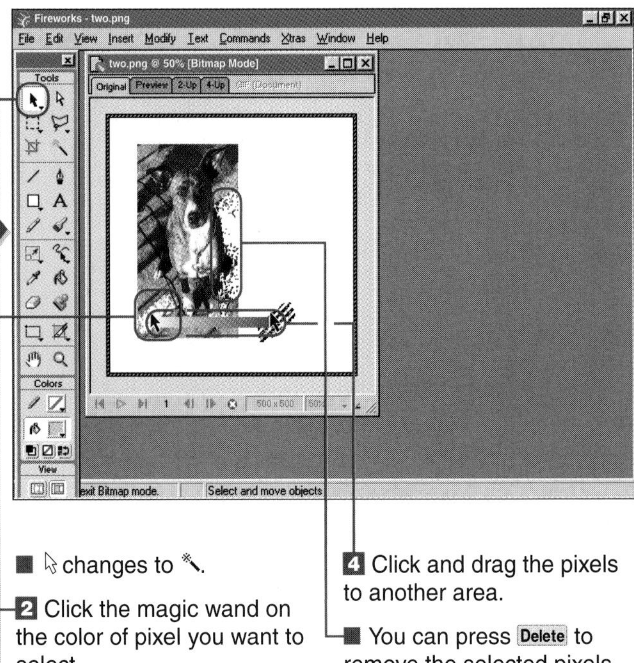

■ changes to .

2 Click the magic wand on the color of pixel you want to select.

3 Click .

4 Click and drag the pixels to another area.

■ You can press Delete to remove the selected pixels.

What do I do with the pixels I cut?

You can move the cut pixels to another part of the document or to another document by using the cut and paste commands. You can also cut the selected pixels to remove them from the image completely.

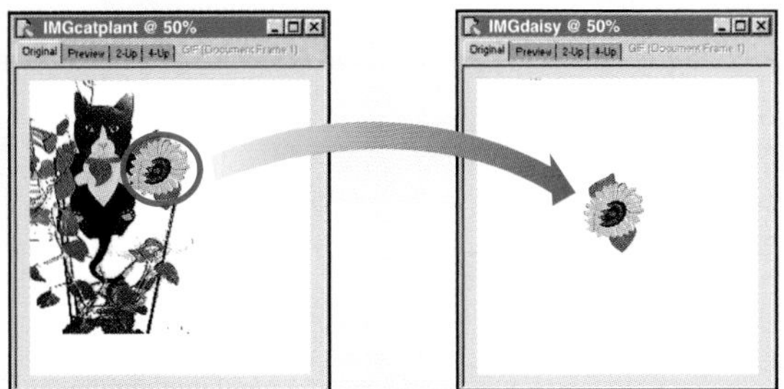

SELECT MULTIPLE AREAS

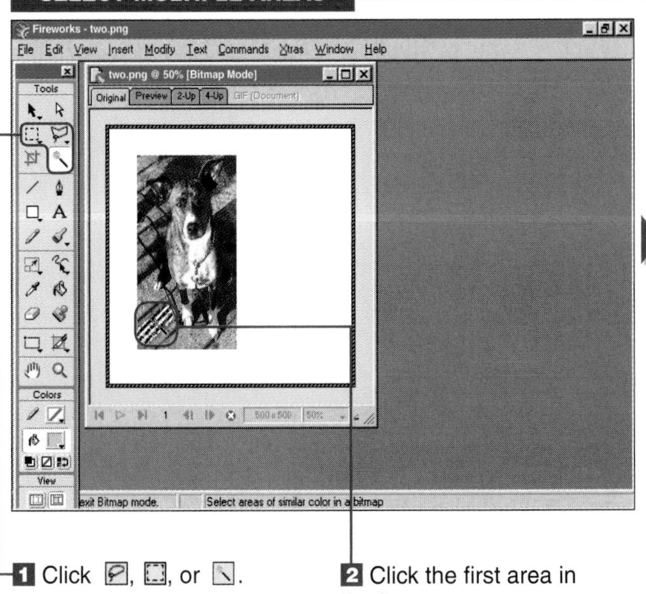

1 Click , , or .

2 Click the first area in the image.

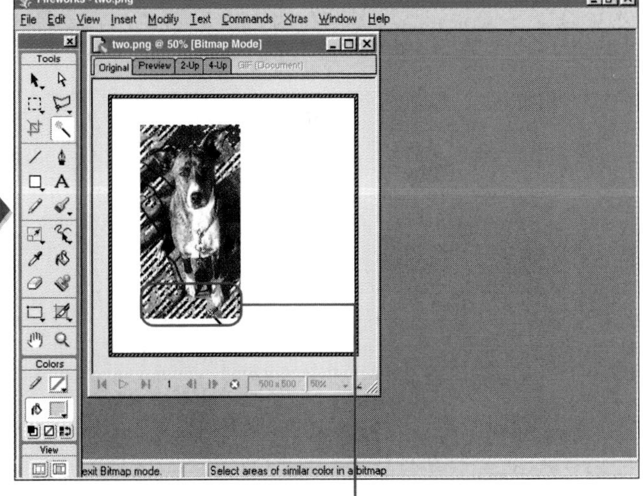

3 Press and hold the **Shift** key.

Note: You can press and hold the **Alt** *(* **option** *) key instead if you want to deselect areas.*

4 Select the other areas to be copied, moved, or removed.

ERASE PIXELS

You can erase pixels from an image with the Eraser tool.

The Eraser tool works just like a pencil eraser, but on images only.

ERASE PIXELS

1 Click the Eraser tool button (![eraser]).

■ ![arrow] changes to ![eraser].

■ You can double-click ![eraser] to display the Tool Options (Eraser Tool) panel.

2 Click the Eraser Size ![arrow] and drag the slider to change the size of the eraser point.

3 Click ■ or ● to change the shape of the eraser.

4 Click and drag the Edge Softness slider to change the edge.

Why does the area I erased look like a checkerboard?

The checkerboard indicates that the area is transparent. You can change the erased area to the canvas color or fill the area with a color of your choice.

5 Click the Eraser Color ▾.

6 Choose the option to erase to.

*Note: If you choose **Transparent**, for example, the pixels you erase become transparent.*

7 Click and drag back and forth to erase pixels.

ADJUST BRIGHTNESS AND CONTRAST

You can adjust the brightness and contrast of an image when the image is too dark or lacks clarity.

ADJUST BRIGHTNESS AND CONTRAST

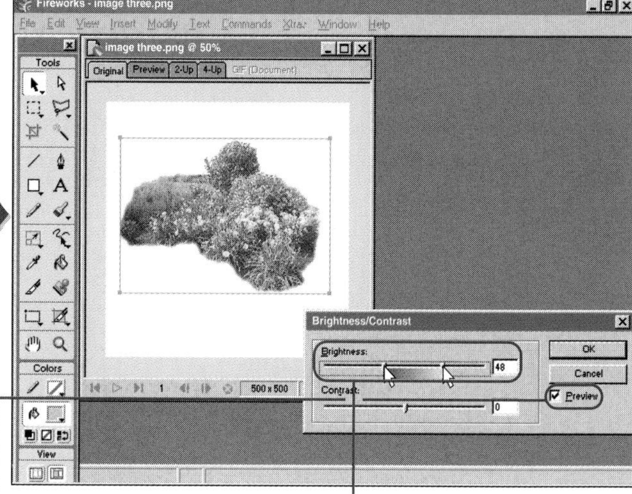

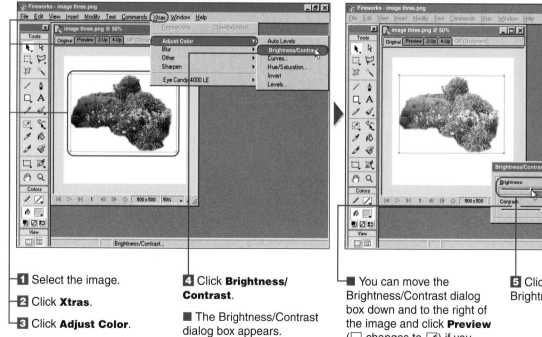

1 Select the image.

2 Click **Xtras**.

3 Click **Adjust Color**.

4 Click **Brightness/ Contrast**.

■ The Brightness/Contrast dialog box appears.

■ You can move the Brightness/Contrast dialog box down and to the right of the image and click **Preview** (☐ changes to ☑) if you want to preview your brightness and contrast changes as you make them.

5 Click and drag the Brightness slider.

How much can I adjust brightness or contrast?

Values for the brightness and contrast sliders range from -100 to 100. If an image requires more adjustment than -100 or 100, consider using another photograph.

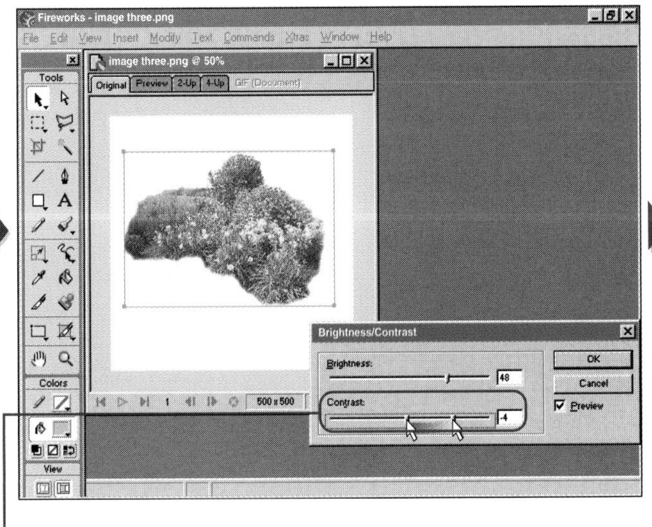

6 Click and drag the Contrast slider.

Note: You can experiment with the contrast and brightness while you view the changes in the document.

7 Click **OK**.

■ Your brightness and contrast changes appear in the image.

BLUR AN IMAGE

You can blur an image to give it an unfocused effect.

BLUR AN IMAGE

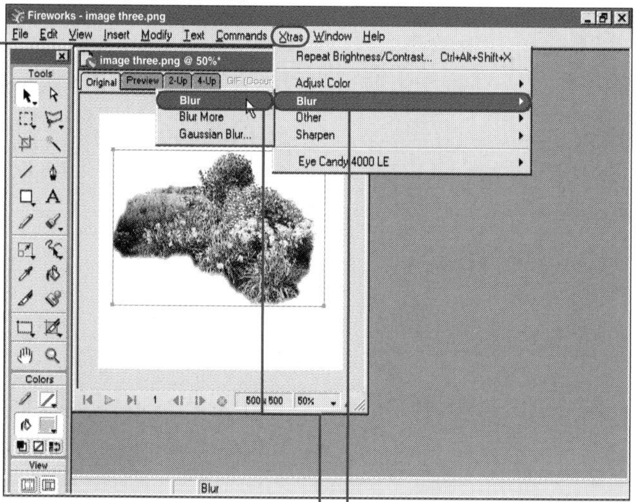

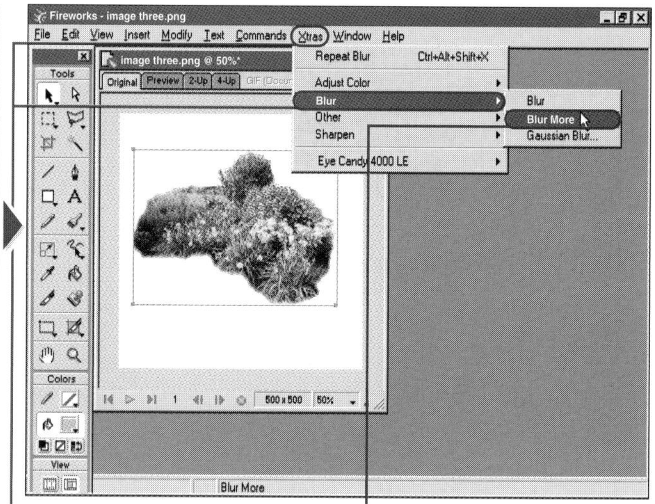

1 Click **Xtras**.

2 Click **Blur**.

3 Click **Blur**.

■ The image blurs on a very small scale.

4 Click **Xtras**.

5 Click **Blur**.

6 Click **Blur More**.

Note: Blur More blurs about three times as much as Blur.

What is a Gaussian blur?

The Gaussian Blur command applies a specific amount of blur to each pixel of the image, giving the image a hazy effect. You can adjust the Gaussian blur to make the image into colors instead of shapes.

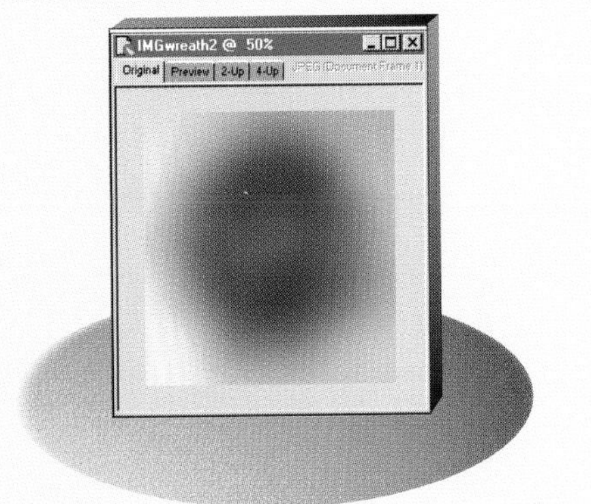

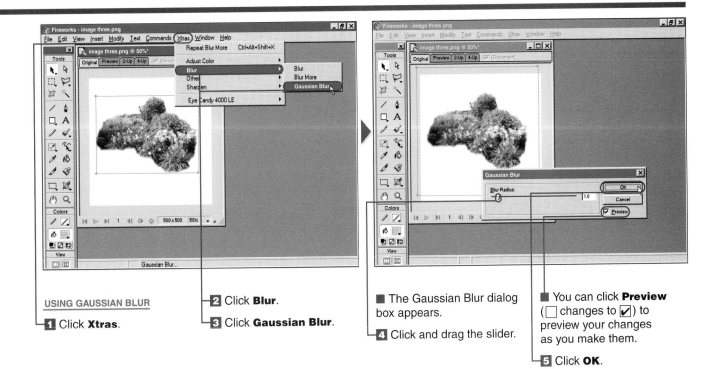

USING GAUSSIAN BLUR

1 Click **Xtras**.

2 Click **Blur**.

3 Click **Gaussian Blur**.

■ The Gaussian Blur dialog box appears.

4 Click and drag the slider.

■ You can click **Preview** (☐ changes to ☑) to preview your changes as you make them.

5 Click **OK**.

SHARPEN AN IMAGE

You can sharpen an image to bring out details and edges in your image.

SHARPEN AN IMAGE

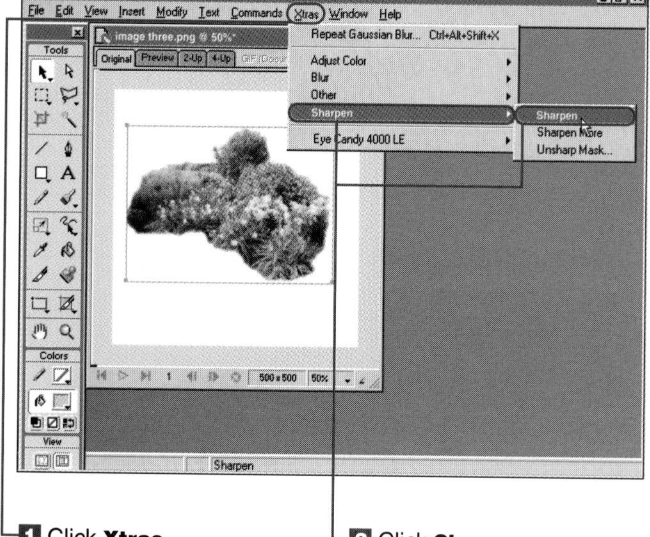

1 Click **Xtras**.

2 Click **Sharpen**.

3 Click **Sharpen**.

■ The image sharpens on a small scale.

4 Click **Xtras**.

5 Click **Sharpen**.

6 Click **Sharpen More**.

Note: Sharpen More sharpens about three times as much as Sharpen.

What is Unsharp Mask?

The Unsharp Mask command sharpens the edges of the image by adding more contrast. Unsharp Mask offers the most control in the pixel radius — which sharpens each pixel's edge.

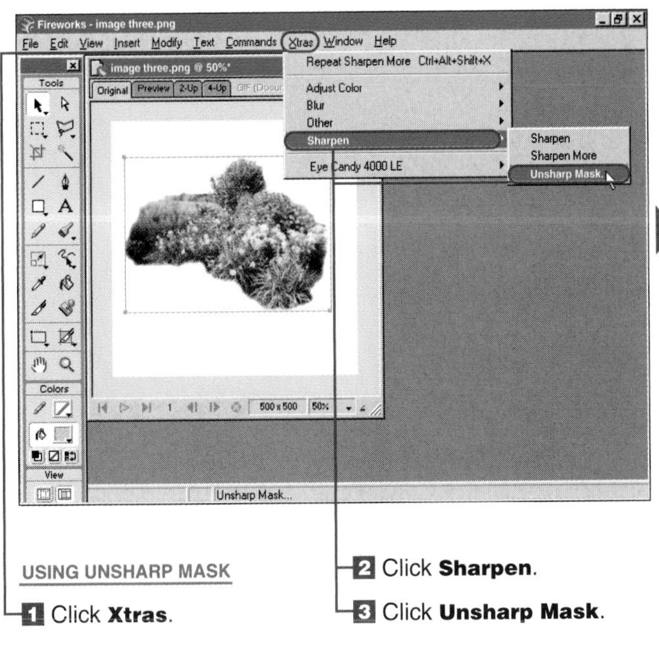

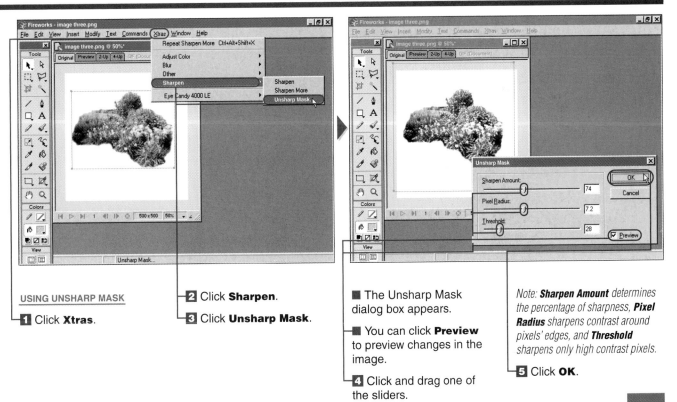

USING UNSHARP MASK

1 Click **Xtras**.

2 Click **Sharpen**.

3 Click **Unsharp Mask**.

■ The Unsharp Mask dialog box appears.

■ You can click **Preview** to preview changes in the image.

4 Click and drag one of the sliders.

*Note: **Sharpen Amount** determines the percentage of sharpness, **Pixel Radius** sharpens contrast around pixels' edges, and **Threshold** sharpens only high contrast pixels.*

5 Click **OK**.

BEVEL AND EMBOSS EDGES

You can apply two popular effects — bevel and emboss — to buttons and other graphics so that the graphics look three-dimensional. This is useful when making buttons for Dreamweaver Web pages.

BEVEL EDGES

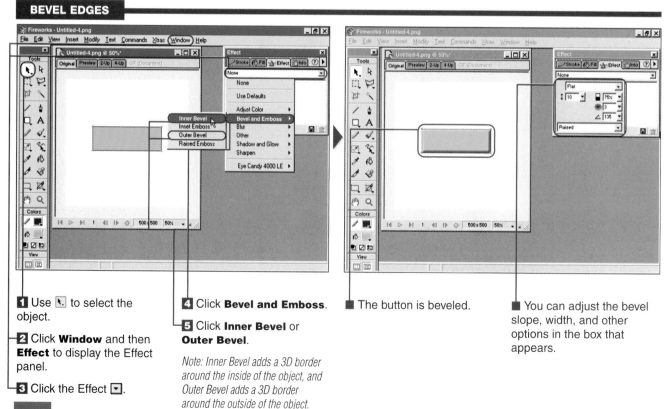

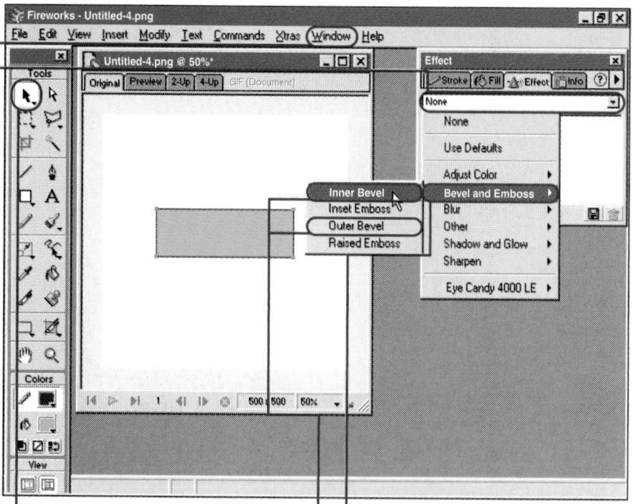

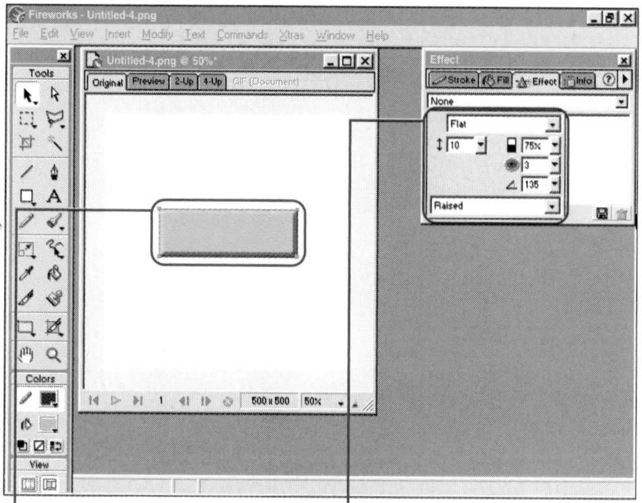

1 Use ↖ to select the object.

2 Click **Window** and then **Effect** to display the Effect panel.

3 Click the Effect ▾.

4 Click **Bevel and Emboss**.

5 Click **Inner Bevel** or **Outer Bevel**.

Note: Inner Bevel adds a 3D border around the inside of the object, and Outer Bevel adds a 3D border around the outside of the object.

■ The button is beveled.

■ You can adjust the bevel slope, width, and other options in the box that appears.

What is the difference between bevel and emboss?

The bevel applies an angled edge to either the inside or the outside of the object. Embossing adds highlights or shadows to the object to make it appear pushed in or out of the background.

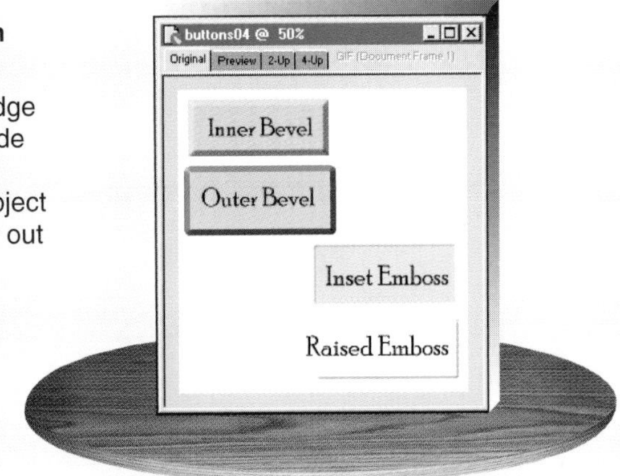

EMBOSS EDGES

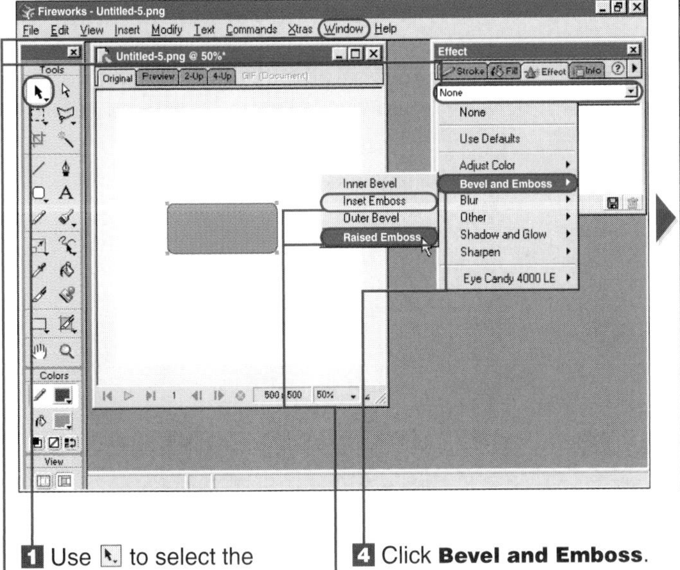

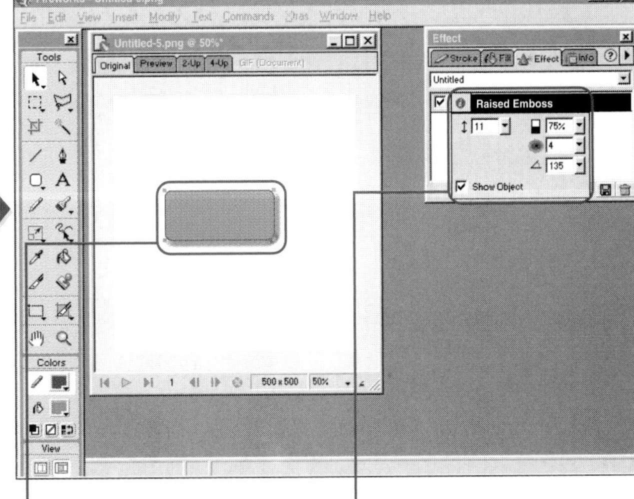

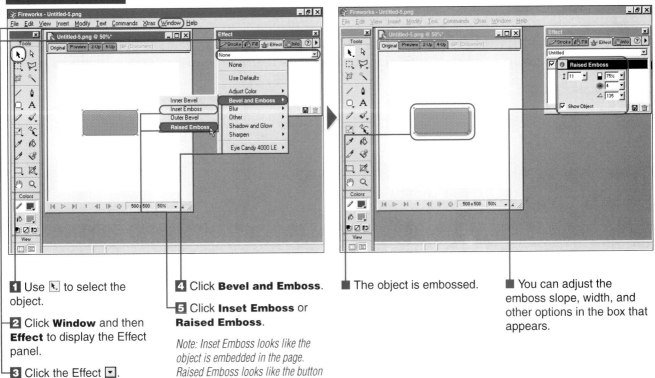

1 Use ⬉ to select the object.

2 Click **Window** and then **Effect** to display the Effect panel.

3 Click the Effect ▾.

4 Click **Bevel and Emboss**.

5 Click **Inset Emboss** or **Raised Emboss**.

Note: Inset Emboss looks like the object is embedded in the page. Raised Emboss looks like the button is hovering over the page.

■ The object is embossed.

■ You can adjust the emboss slope, width, and other options in the box that appears.

You can blur or sharpen the edges to make certain objects stand out in a graphic.

To find out how to blur or sharpen an entire image instead of just the edges, see Chapter 28.

BLUR EDGES

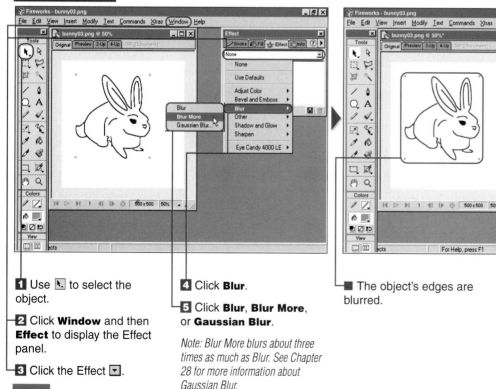

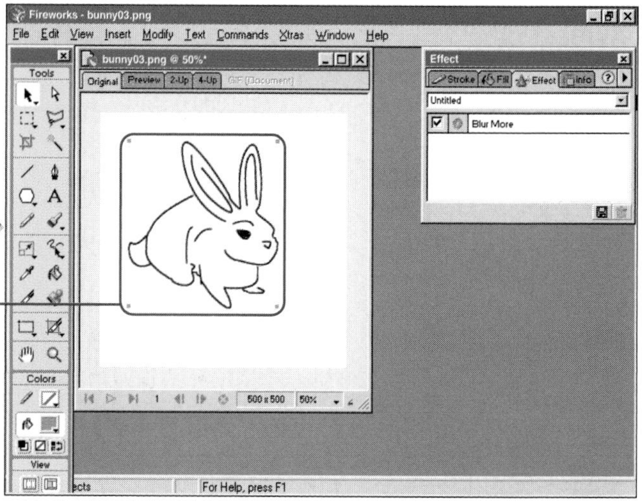

1 Use ↖ to select the object.

2 Click **Window** and then **Effect** to display the Effect panel.

3 Click the Effect ▼.

4 Click **Blur**.

5 Click **Blur**, **Blur More**, or **Gaussian Blur**.

Note: Blur More blurs about three times as much as Blur. See Chapter 28 for more information about Gaussian Blur.

■ The object's edges are blurred.

Why would I want to blur or sharpen an object?

You can blur an object in the background to add depth to your graphics. You can sharpen an object to show more detail.

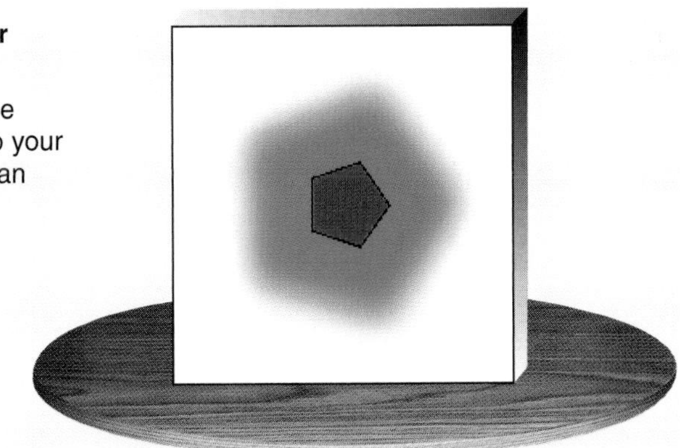

SHARPEN EDGES

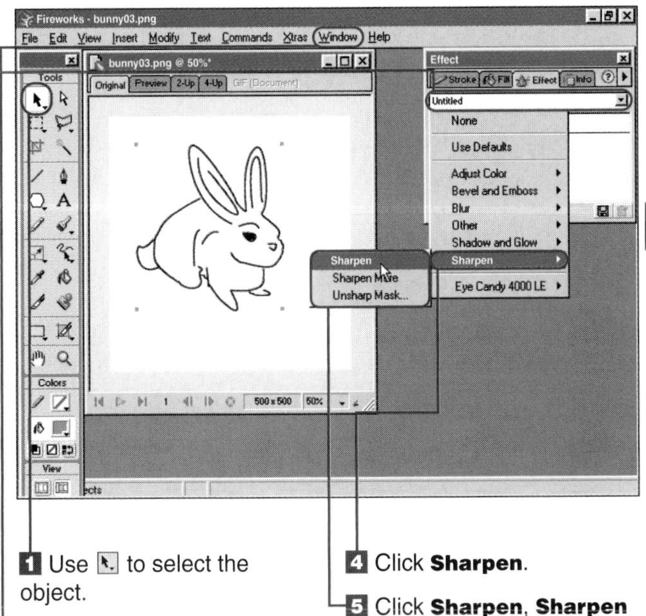

1 Use ↖ to select the object.

2 Click **Window** and then **Effect** to display the Effect panel.

3 Click the Effect ▾.

4 Click **Sharpen**.

5 Click **Sharpen**, **Sharpen More**, or **Unsharp Mask**.

Note: Sharpen More sharpens about three times as much as Sharpen. See Chapter 28 for more information about Unsharp Mask.

■ The object's edges are sharper.

Note: Sharpen works particularly well with bitmap fills.

APPLY A SHADOW

You can add a shadow to a button or other object. Shadows add depth to the graphic.

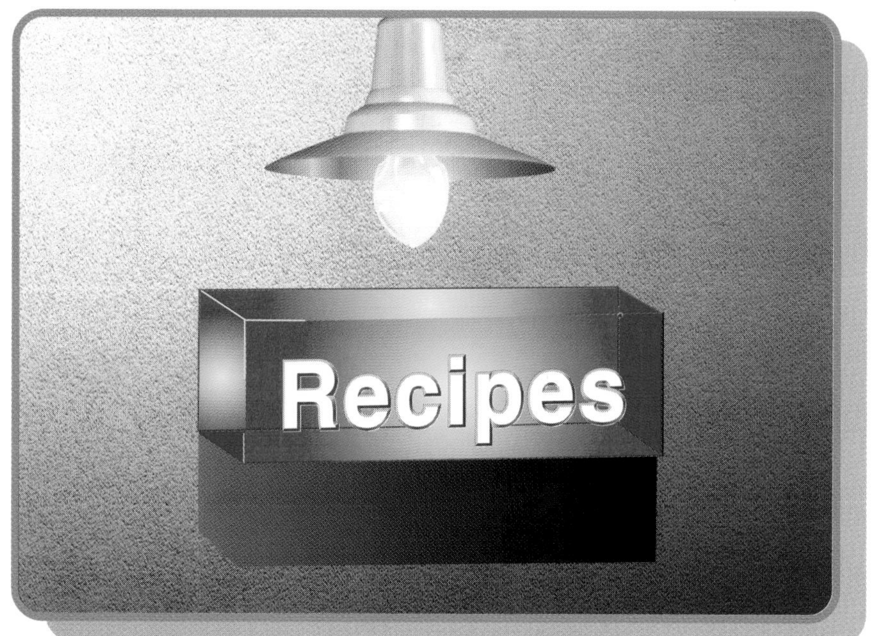

APPLY A DROP SHADOW

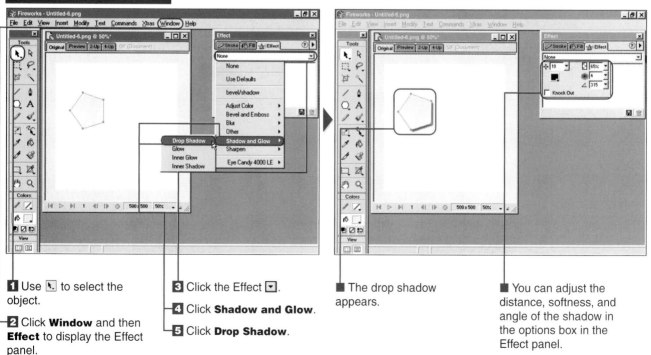

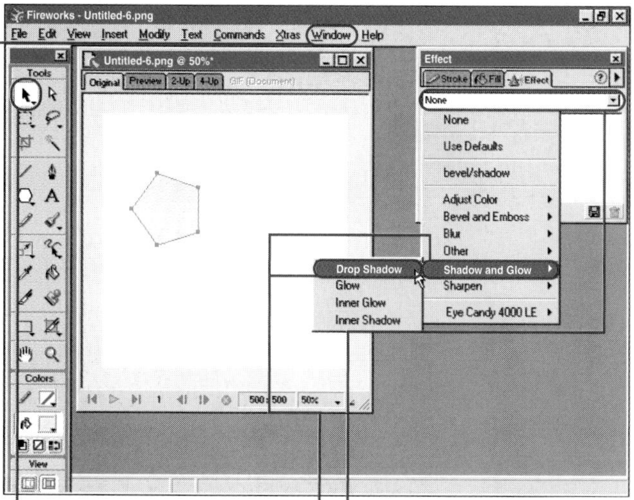

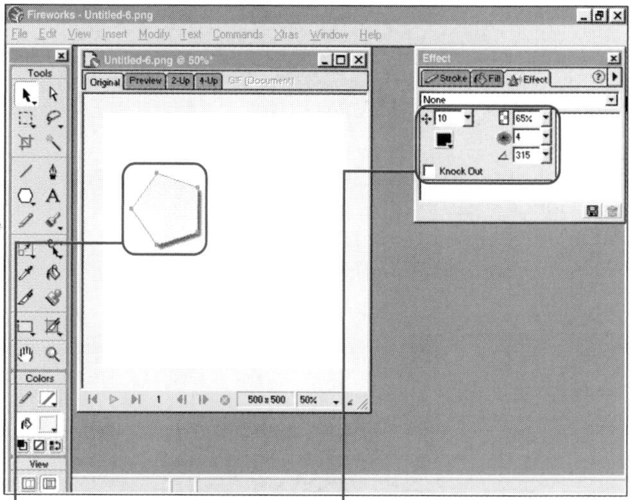

1 Use the Pointer tool to select the object.

2 Click **Window** and then **Effect** to display the Effect panel.

3 Click the Effect ▼.

4 Click **Shadow and Glow**.

5 Click **Drop Shadow**.

■ The drop shadow appears.

■ You can adjust the distance, softness, and angle of the shadow in the options box in the Effect panel.

What is the difference between a drop shadow and an inner shadow?

A drop shadow is a copy of the object offset to the outside of the object to give the illusion of depth. An inner shadow is similar but the shadow is on the inside of the object. Shadows only appear on one or two sides.

APPLY AN INNER SHADOW

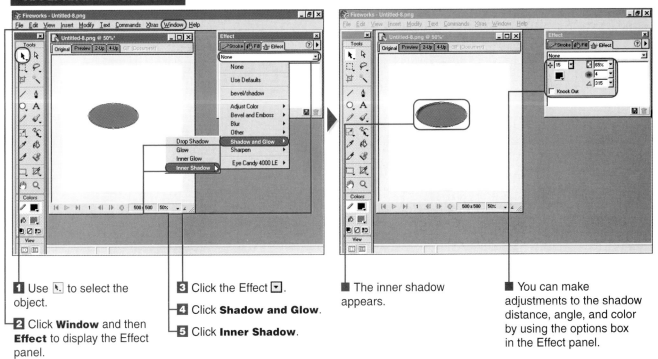

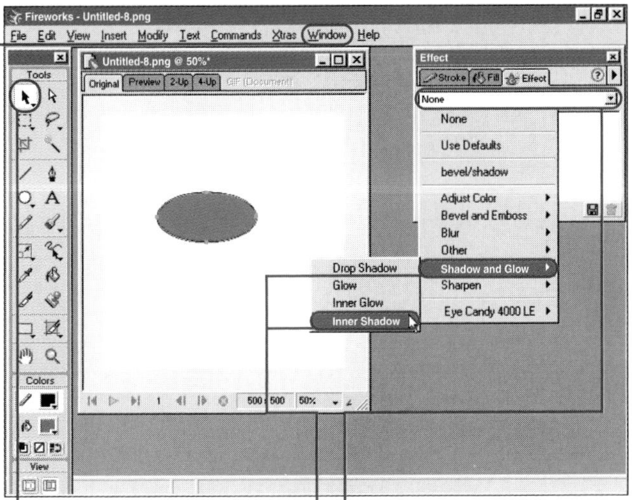

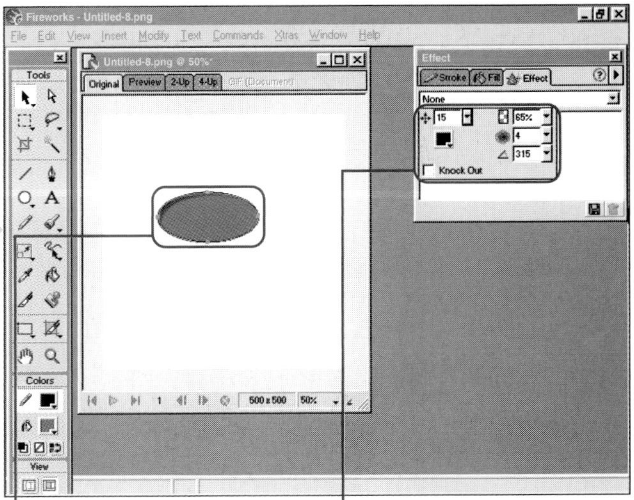

1 Use to select the object.

2 Click **Window** and then **Effect** to display the Effect panel.

3 Click the Effect .

4 Click **Shadow and Glow**.

5 Click **Inner Shadow**.

■ The inner shadow appears.

■ You can make adjustments to the shadow distance, angle, and color by using the options box in the Effect panel.

APPLY A GLOW

You can apply a glow that gives the object a border around all edges.

APPLY A GLOW

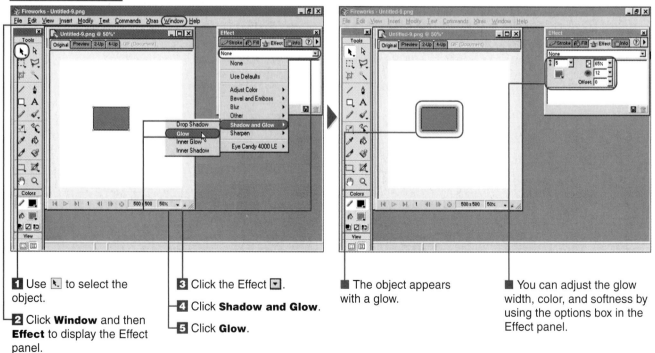

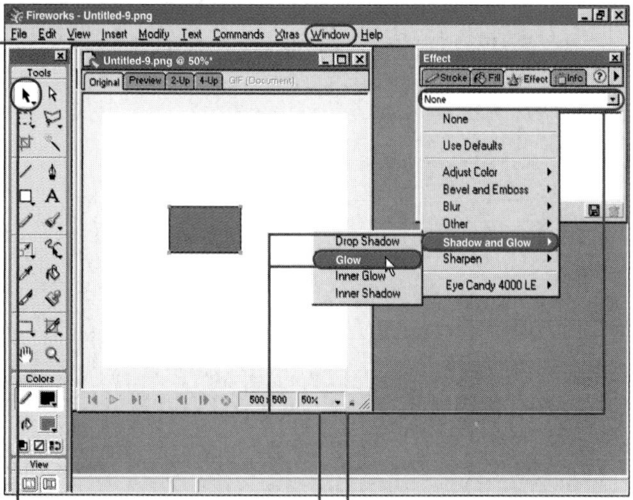

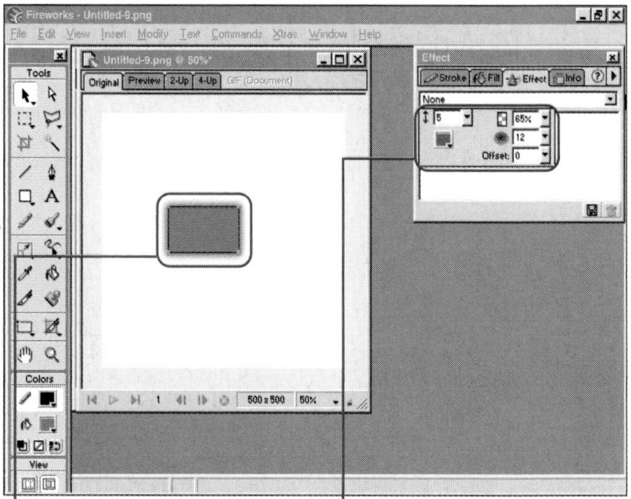

1. Use to select the object.
2. Click **Window** and then **Effect** to display the Effect panel.
3. Click the Effect .
4. Click **Shadow and Glow**.
5. Click **Glow**.

- The object appears with a glow.
- You can adjust the glow width, color, and softness by using the options box in the Effect panel.

What is the difference between a glow and an inner glow?

A glow is a border on the outside of the object making the object look raised from the page. An inner glow appears on the inside of the object's edges, making the object look recessed on the page.

APPLY AN INNER GLOW

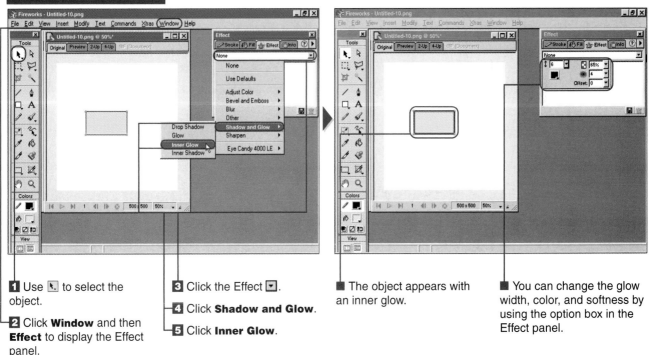

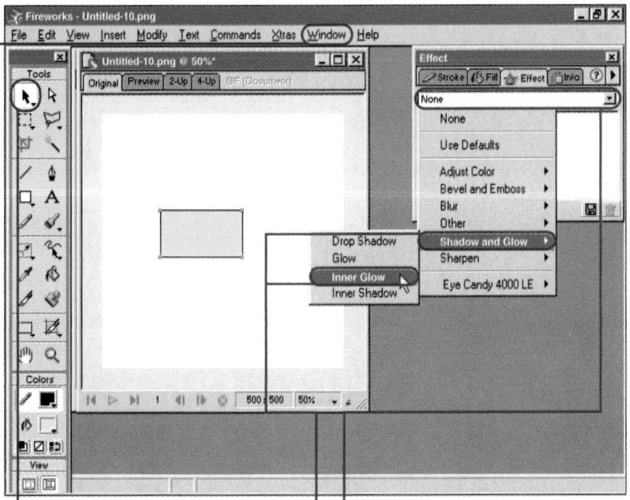

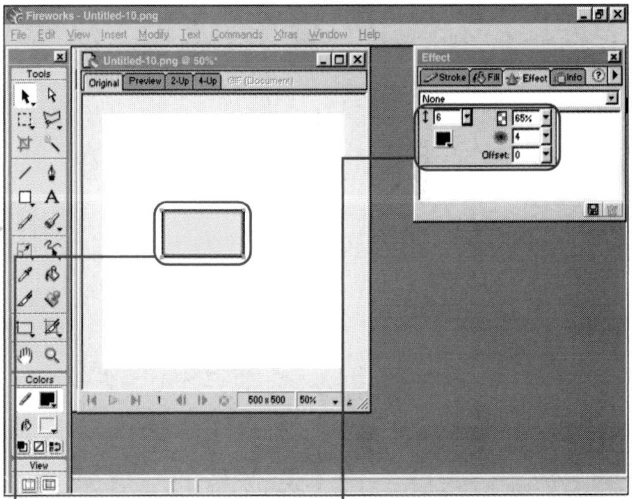

1 Use [pointer tool] to select the object.

2 Click **Window** and then **Effect** to display the Effect panel.

3 Click the Effect [dropdown arrow].

4 Click **Shadow and Glow**.

5 Click **Inner Glow**.

■ The object appears with an inner glow.

■ You can change the glow width, color, and softness by using the option box in the Effect panel.

SET DEFAULT EFFECTS

You can set default effects that you can apply to new objects, which enables you to format objects quickly and easily.

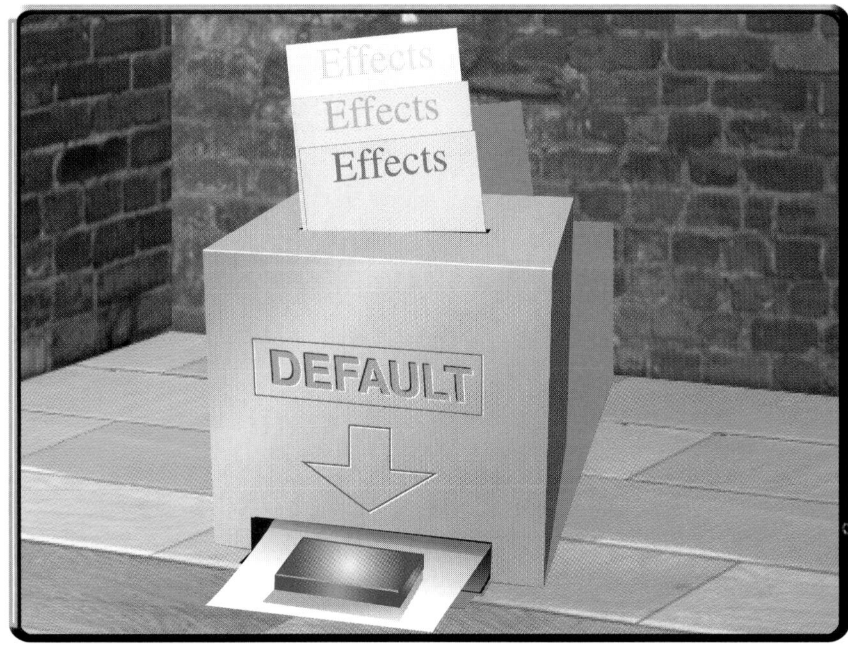

A *default* is a characteristic that you can assign to a graphic.

SET DEFAULT EFFECTS

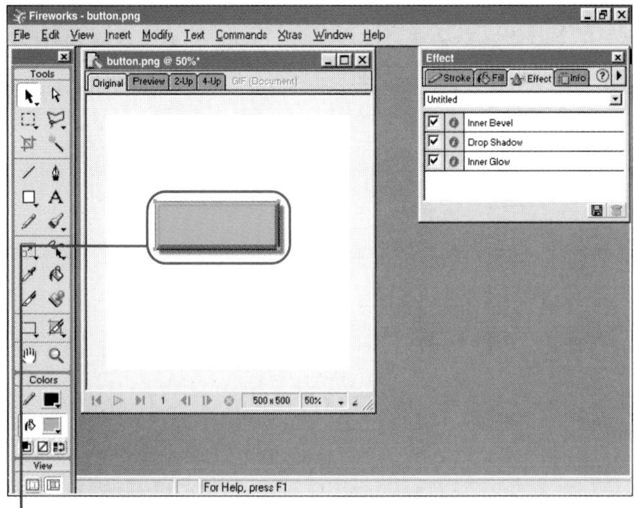

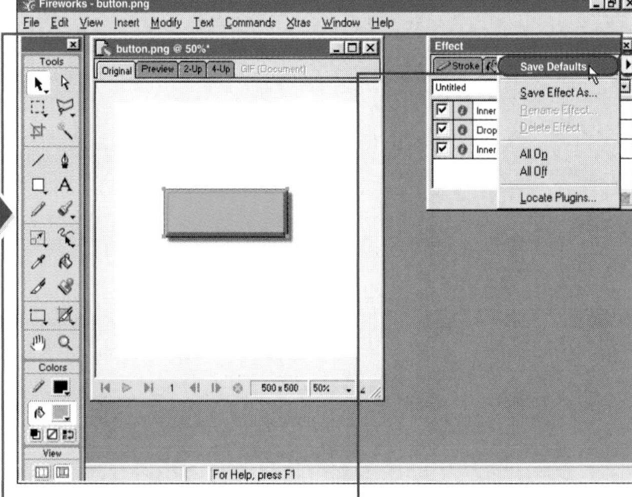

1 Apply the effects that you want to use as defaults to the object.

Note: You can change options for each effect, such as color and angle.

2 Click the Options ▶.

3 Click **Save Defaults**.

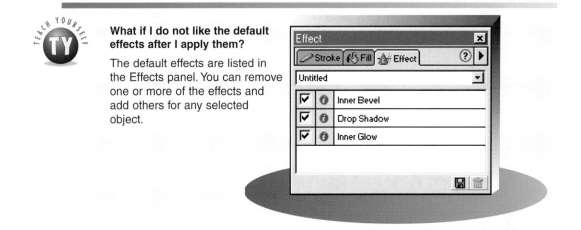

What if I do not like the default effects after I apply them?

The default effects are listed in the Effects panel. You can remove one or more of the effects and add others for any selected object.

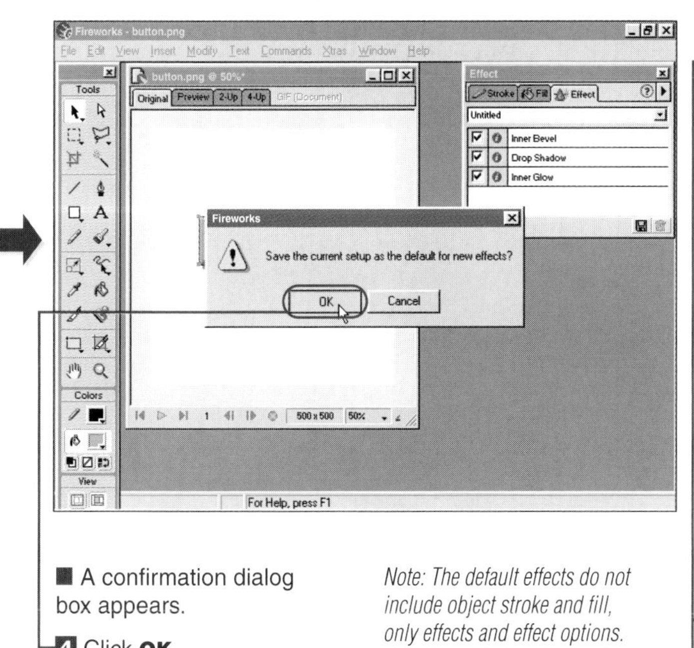

■ A confirmation dialog box appears.

4 Click **OK**.

Note: The default effects do not include object stroke and fill, only effects and effect options.

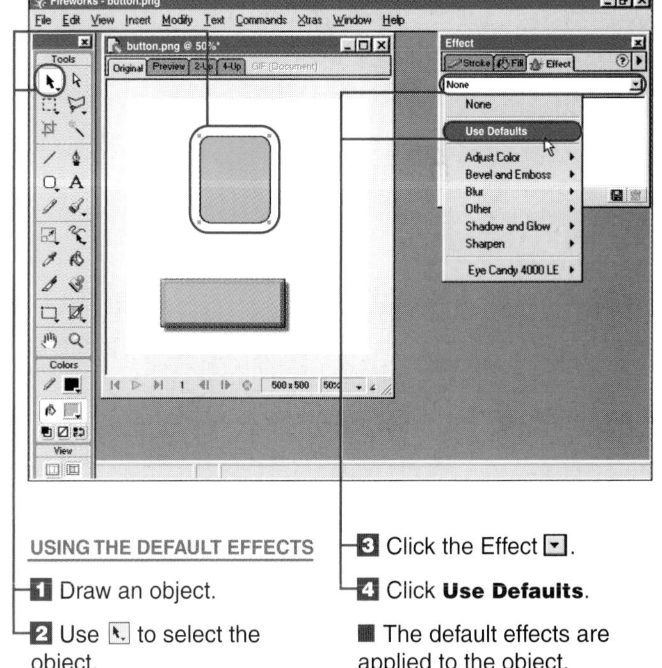

USING THE DEFAULT EFFECTS

1 Draw an object.

2 Use [pointer tool] to select the object.

3 Click the Effect [▾].

4 Click **Use Defaults**.

■ The default effects are applied to the object.

SAVE AND USE STYLES

You can use styles to save custom effects, fills, strokes, and text characteristics.

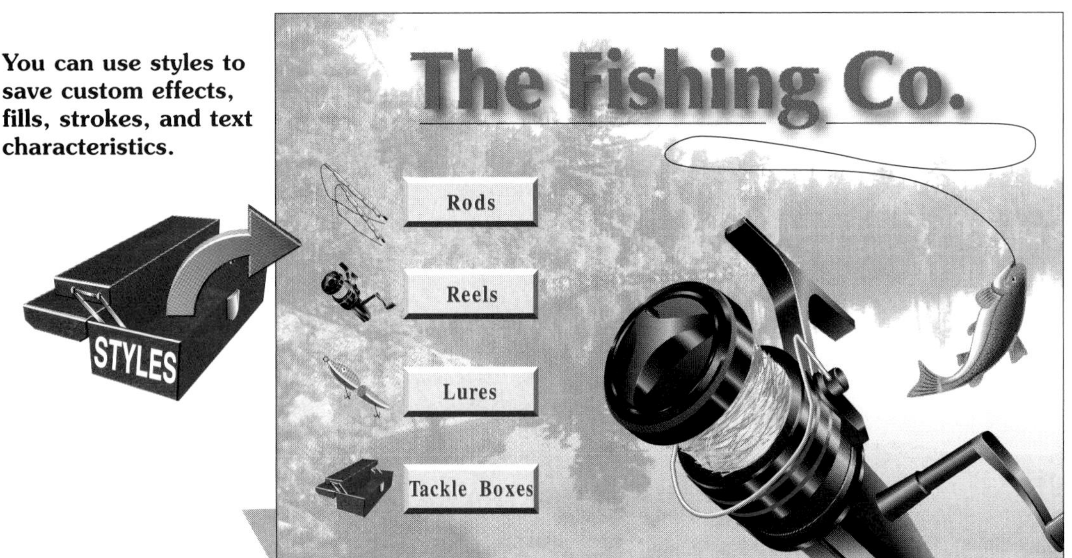

After you save a style, you can apply that style to another object with one click of the mouse.

SAVE STYLES

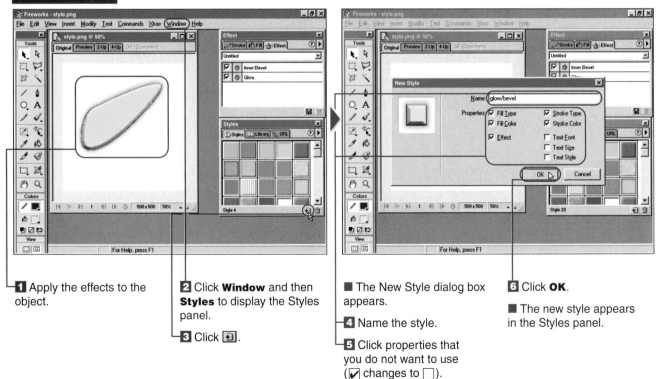

1 Apply the effects to the object.

2 Click **Window** and then **Styles** to display the Styles panel.

3 Click [icon].

■ The New Style dialog box appears.

4 Name the style.

5 Click properties that you do not want to use (☑ changes to ☐).

6 Click **OK**.

■ The new style appears in the Styles panel.

What are the other styles in the Styles panel?

Fireworks provides a variety of preset styles that you can use on your text and objects. You can apply any style in the Styles panel by following the steps shown below in "Using Styles."

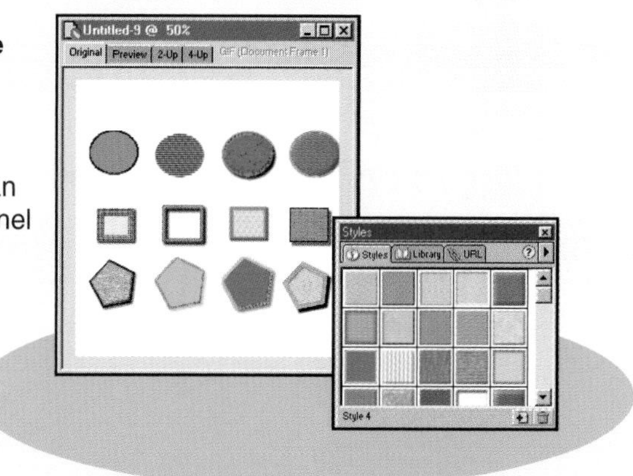

USING STYLES

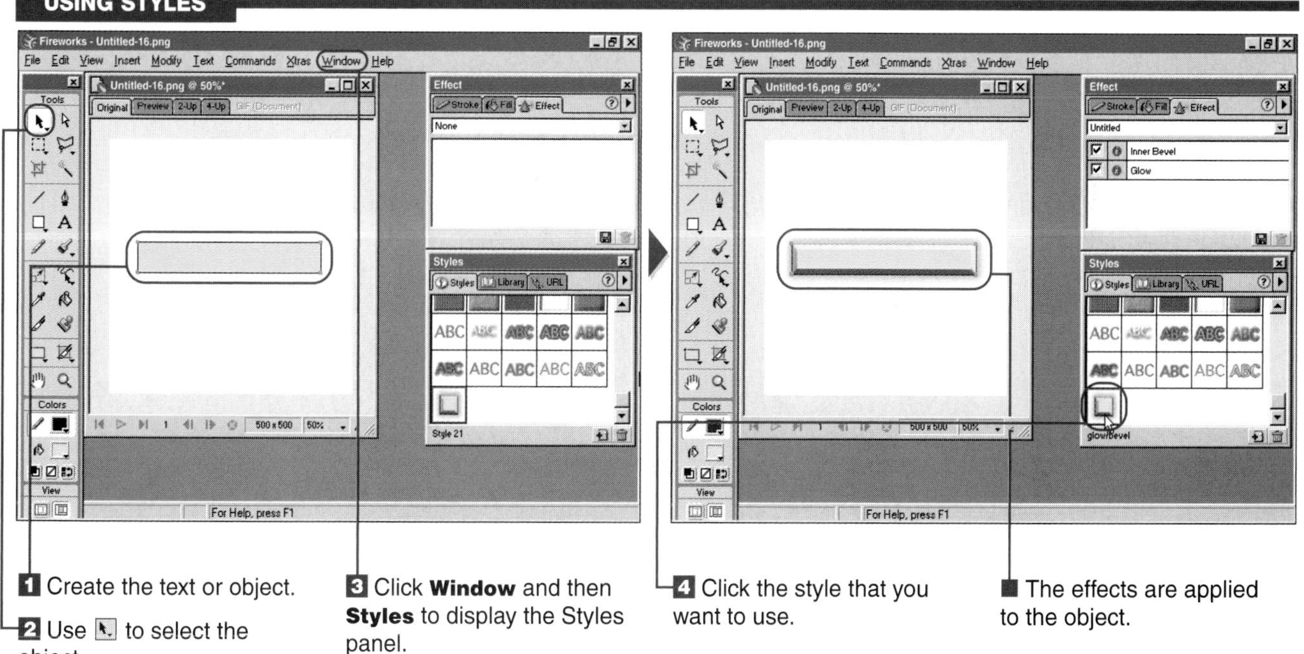

1 Create the text or object.

2 Use [select tool] to select the object.

3 Click **Window** and then **Styles** to display the Styles panel.

4 Click the style that you want to use.

■ The effects are applied to the object.

You can create a cut-out effect on an underlying image by creating a mask.

The mask blocks out part of the underlying image.

CREATE MASKS

1 Create the object or import the image to be masked.

Note: For information about importing objects, refer to Chapter 27.

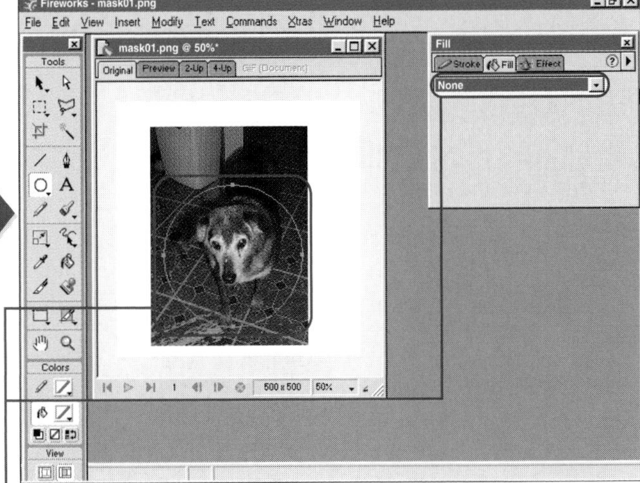

2 Create the object to be used as a mask.

3 Choose a pattern or texture for the mask or choose no fill.

Note: See Chapter 27 for information about applying a pattern or texture.

What are some common uses for masks?

You can create text with a gradient fill, blend an image into a background of patterns, or add a blurred frame to an image. Experiment with masking to create unusual effects.

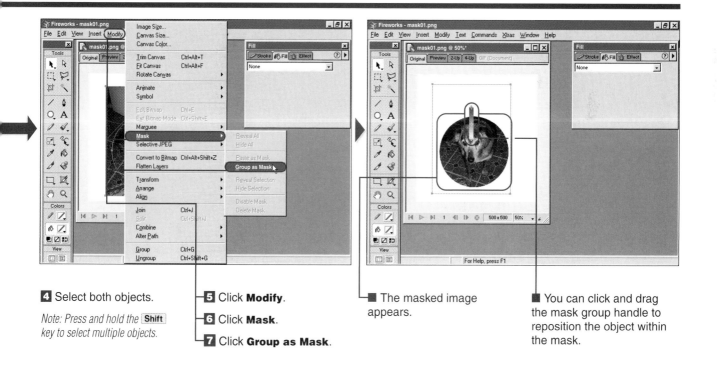

4 Select both objects.

Note: Press and hold the **Shift** *key to select multiple objects.*

5 Click **Modify**.

6 Click **Mask**.

7 Click **Group as Mask**.

■ The masked image appears.

■ You can click and drag the mask group handle to reposition the object within the mask.

EDIT MASKS

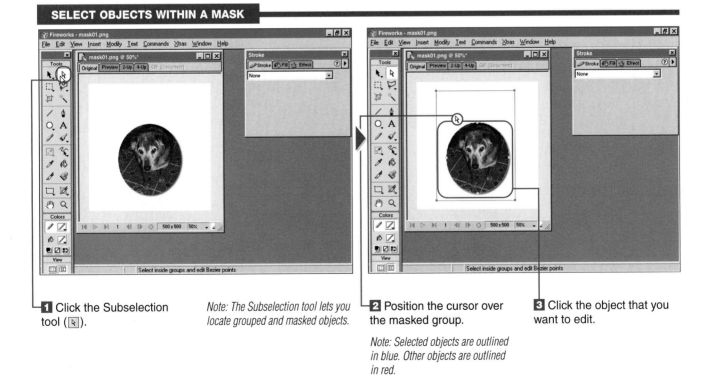

You can modify the masked group at any time in Fireworks. You first must select an object to edit it.

A *masked group* refers to the topmost object that is used as a mask plus the object that is masked.

SELECT OBJECTS WITHIN A MASK

1 Click the Subselection tool (▷).

Note: The Subselection tool lets you locate grouped and masked objects.

2 Position the cursor over the masked group.

Note: Selected objects are outlined in blue. Other objects are outlined in red.

3 Click the object that you want to edit.

When I select a masked group, which object's formatting shows up in the Effect panel?

When you select a masked group, the top object's attributes show up in the Fill panel, the Stroke panel, and the Effect panel.

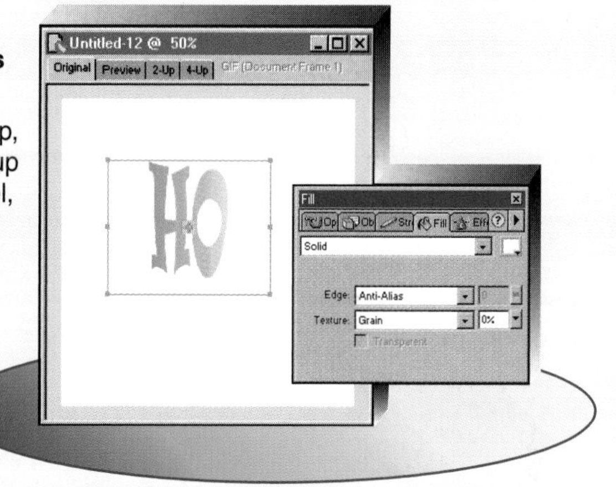

EDIT THE MASK

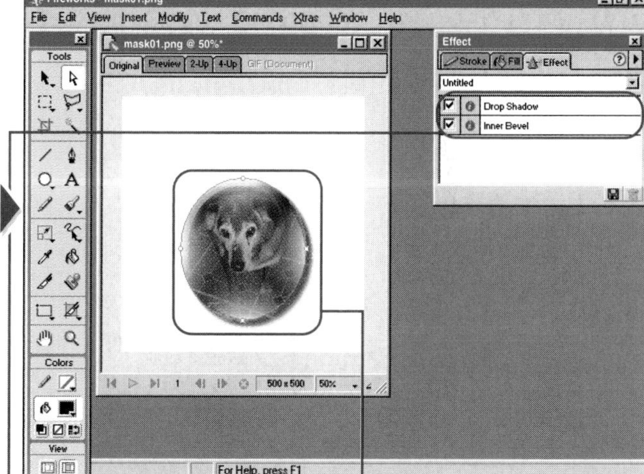

1 Select the masked object or the mask.

2 Click **Window** and then **Fill**, **Stroke**, or **Effect** to display the Fill, Stroke, or Effect panel.

Note: You can add stroke, fill, or an effect to the mask to make it more interesting.

3 Make the changes that you want to the selected object.

■ Changes appear without unmasking the group.

CREATE A BUTTON

You can create buttons that the user clicks to perform actions on a Dreamweaver Web site, such as jumping to another Web page.

Format the button using effect tools or use a button symbol from the library that comes with Fireworks.

CREATE A BUTTON

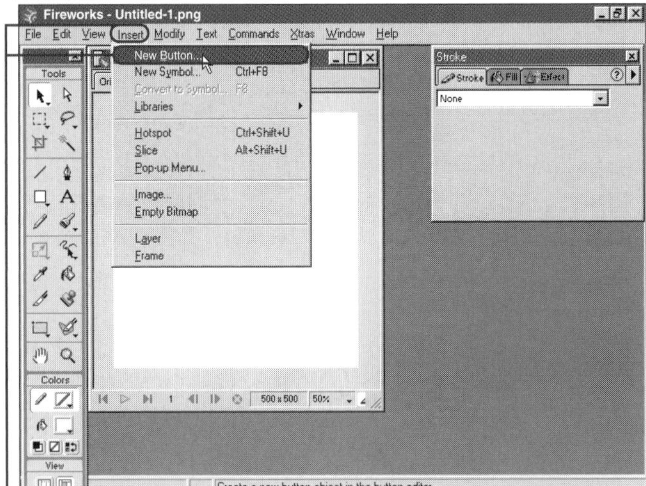

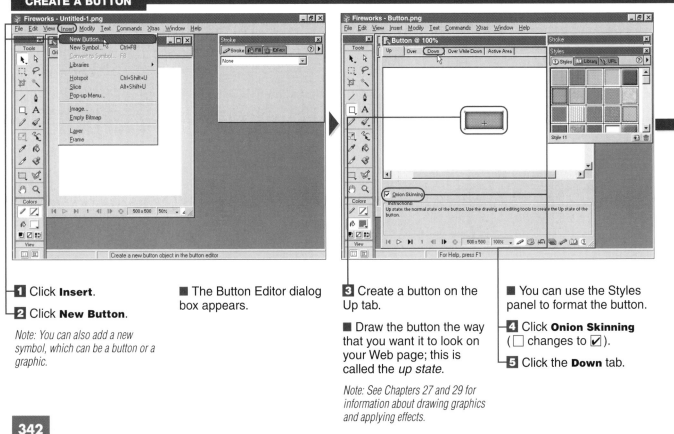

1 Click **Insert**.

2 Click **New Button**.

Note: You can also add a new symbol, which can be a button or a graphic.

■ The Button Editor dialog box appears.

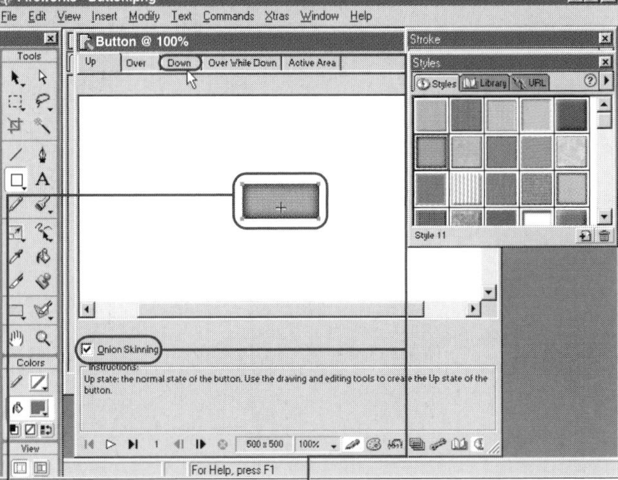

3 Create a button on the Up tab.

■ Draw the button the way that you want it to look on your Web page; this is called the *up state*.

Note: See Chapters 27 and 29 for information about drawing graphics and applying effects.

■ You can use the Styles panel to format the button.

4 Click **Onion Skinning** (☐ changes to ☑).

5 Click the **Down** tab.

What is Onion Skinning?

The Onion Skinning check box lets you see the up state button so that you can build the down state on top of it.

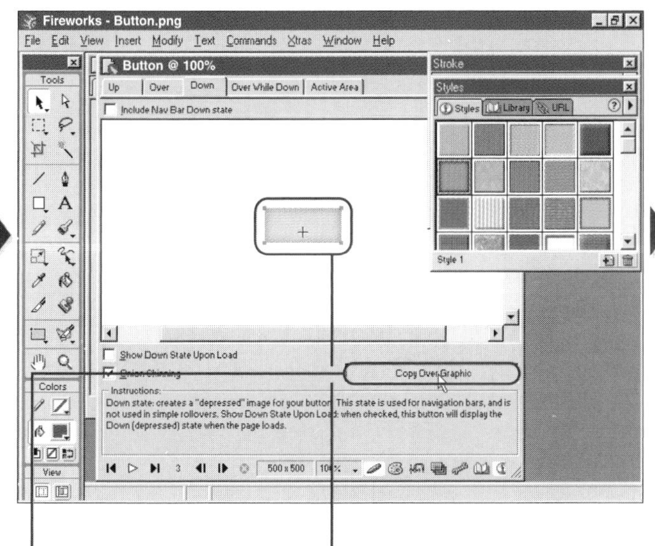

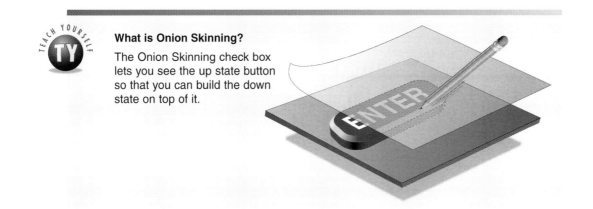

6 Click **Copy Over Graphic**.

■ An outline of the previous button appears. You can draw over the copy so that the button looks similar to the up state.

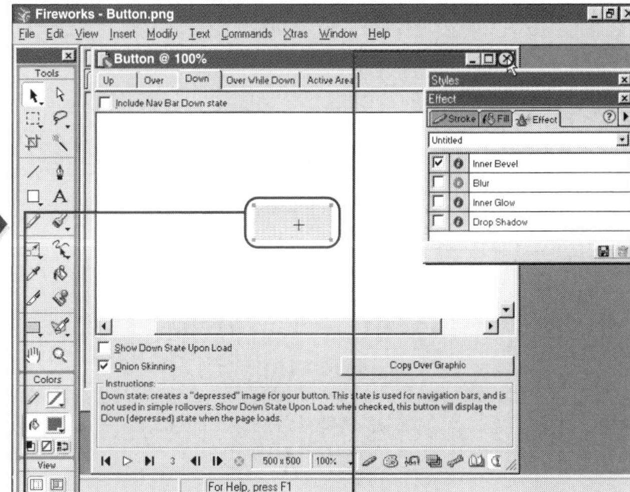

7 Create the button the way that you want it to look when it has been clicked.

Note: This is called the down state. *You can add an inner shadow or an emboss, for example (see Chapter 29).*

8 Click ☒ to close the Button Editor.

■ The button symbol appears in the Library panel and an instance appears in your document.

CONVERT AN OBJECT TO A BUTTON

You can convert any object you create into a button and then copy the button to the Button Editor.

CONVERT AN OBJECT TO A BUTTON

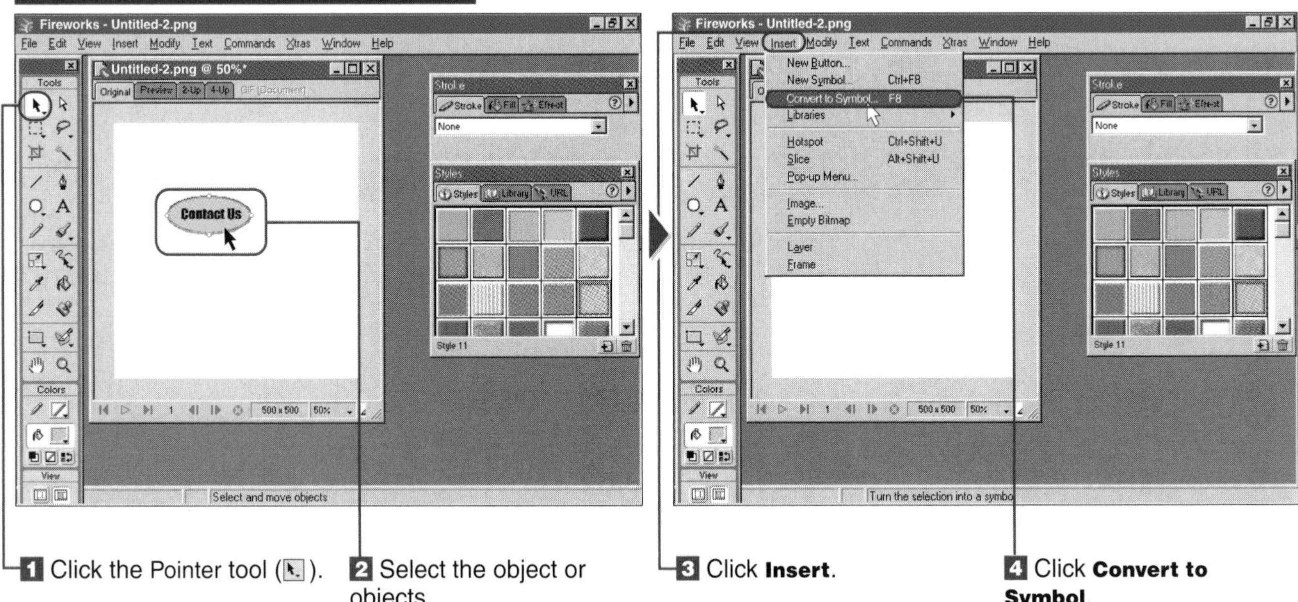

1 Click the Pointer tool (![pointer]).

2 Select the object or objects.

Note: See Chapter 27 for information about grouping multiple objects.

3 Click **Insert**.

4 Click **Convert to Symbol**.

What is a slice?

A *slice* is a part of a larger image. Slices are used to improve download time but also to create buttons for Dreamweaver Web pages. See Chapter 32 for more information.

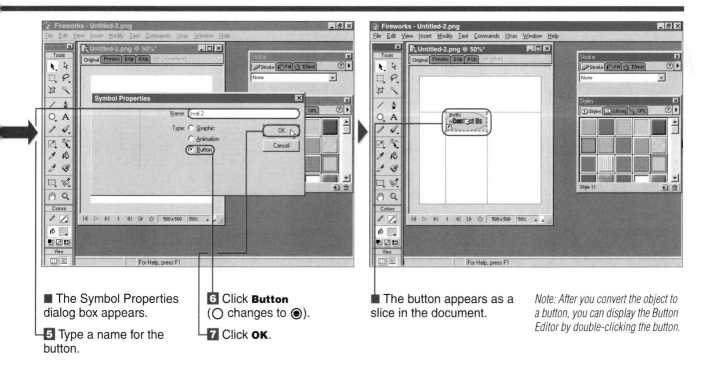

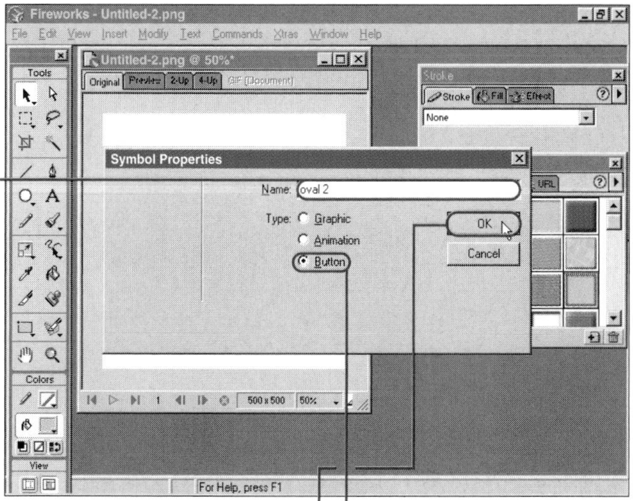

■ The Symbol Properties dialog box appears.

5 Type a name for the button.

6 Click **Button** (○ changes to ◉).

7 Click **OK**.

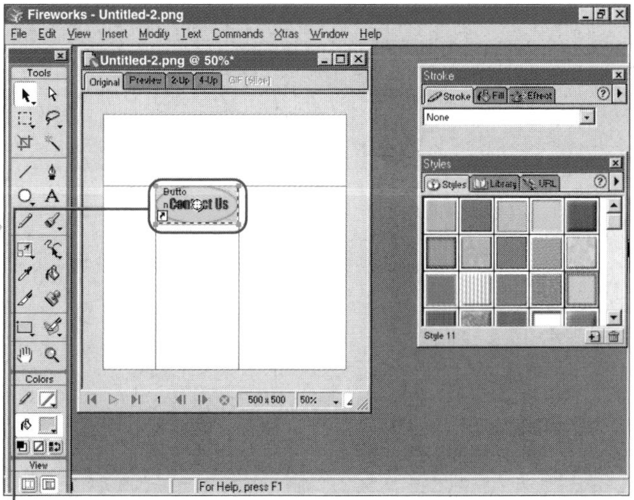

■ The button appears as a slice in the document.

Note: After you convert the object to a button, you can display the Button Editor by double-clicking the button.

COPY AND EDIT A BUTTON

You can copy a button and then edit it to change text or another part of the object.

Copying a button means that all the buttons you create for one Web page will be similar in design and pattern.

COPY A BUTTON

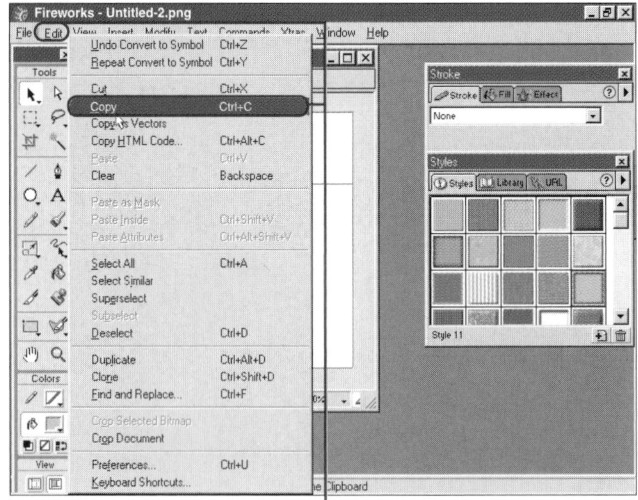

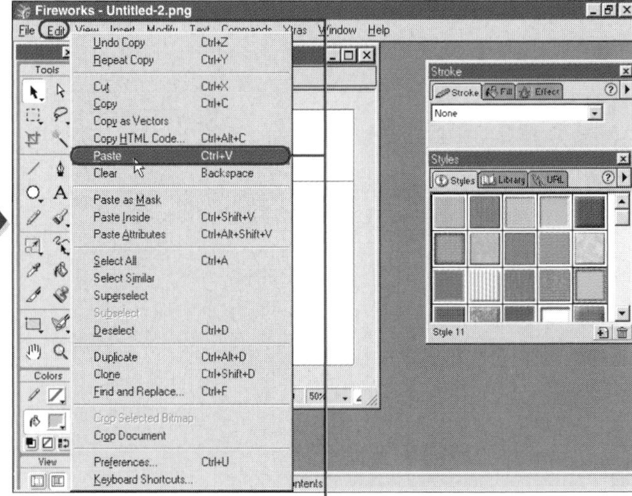

1 Select the button.

2 Click **Edit**.

3 Click **Copy**.

4 Open a new or existing document.

5 Click **Edit**.

6 Click **Paste**.

■ The copied button appears in the new document.

When I edit a copy of a button, does the original button change too?

No. You can edit an instance of a button. The original button does not change.

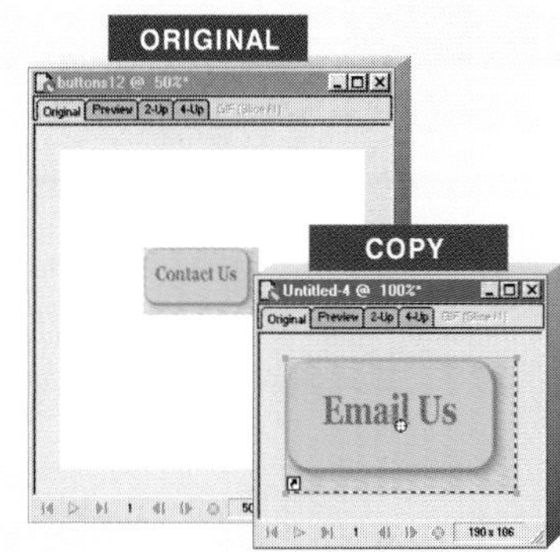

EDIT A BUTTON

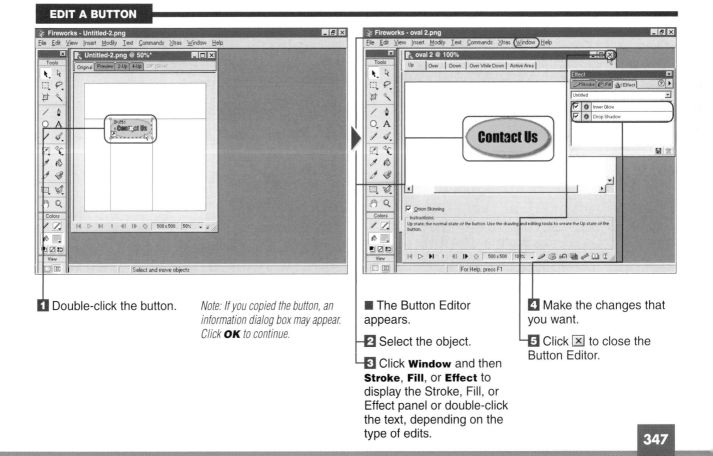

1 Double-click the button.

*Note: If you copied the button, an information dialog box may appear. Click **OK** to continue.*

■ The Button Editor appears.

2 Select the object.

3 Click **Window** and then **Stroke**, **Fill**, or **Effect** to display the Stroke, Fill, or Effect panel or double-click the text, depending on the type of edits.

4 Make the changes that you want.

5 Click ☒ to close the Button Editor.

ASSIGN A URL TO A BUTTON

You use the Link Wizard to assign a URL to buttons and other objects. The URL creates a link to another Web page.

URL stands for *Uniform Resource Locator* and is simply a Web address.

ASSIGN A URL TO A BUTTON

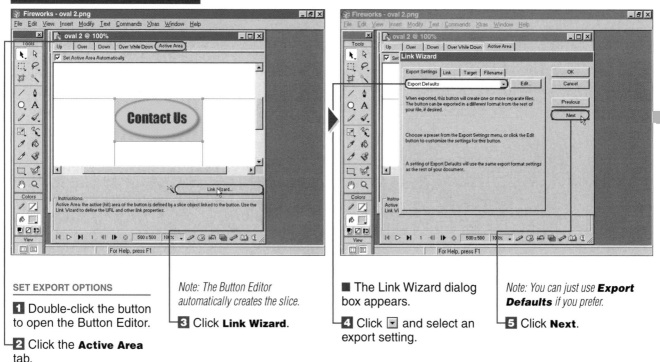

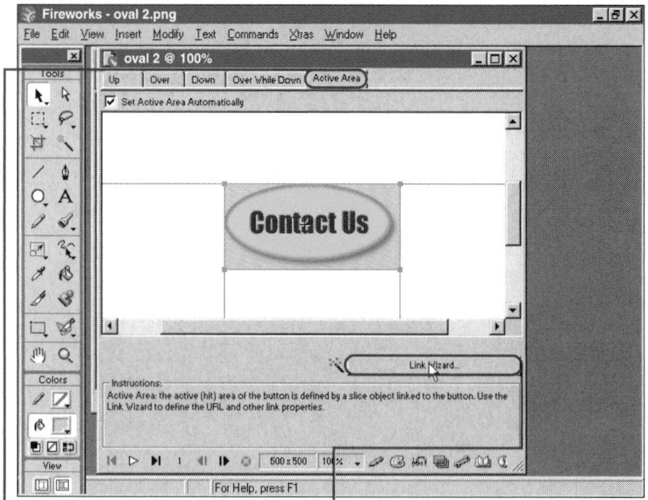

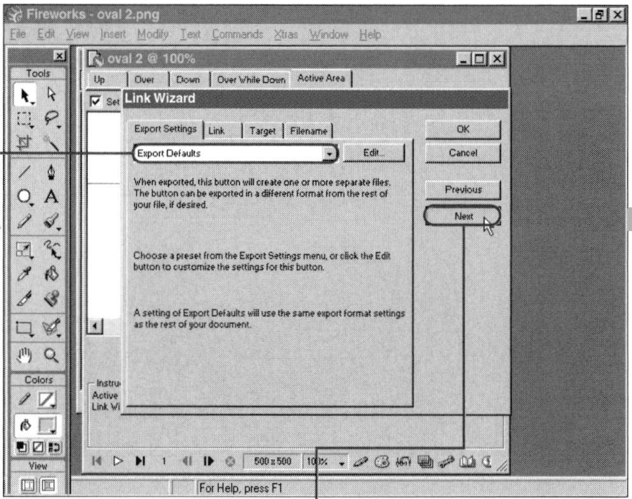

SET EXPORT OPTIONS

1 Double-click the button to open the Button Editor.

2 Click the **Active Area** tab.

Note: The Button Editor automatically creates the slice.

3 Click **Link Wizard**.

■ The Link Wizard dialog box appears.

4 Click ▾ and select an export setting.

*Note: You can just use **Export Defaults** if you prefer.*

5 Click **Next**.

What is the active area?

The *active area* is the part of the button that performs an action when clicked and is defined by creating a slice over the button. You can adjust the size of the slice if necessary.

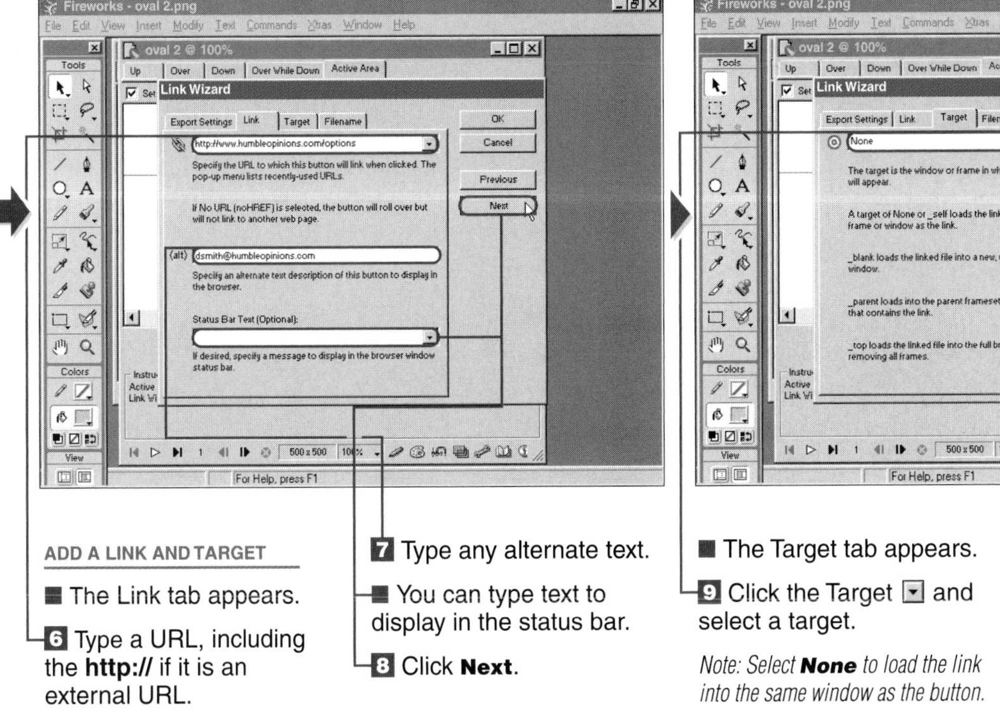

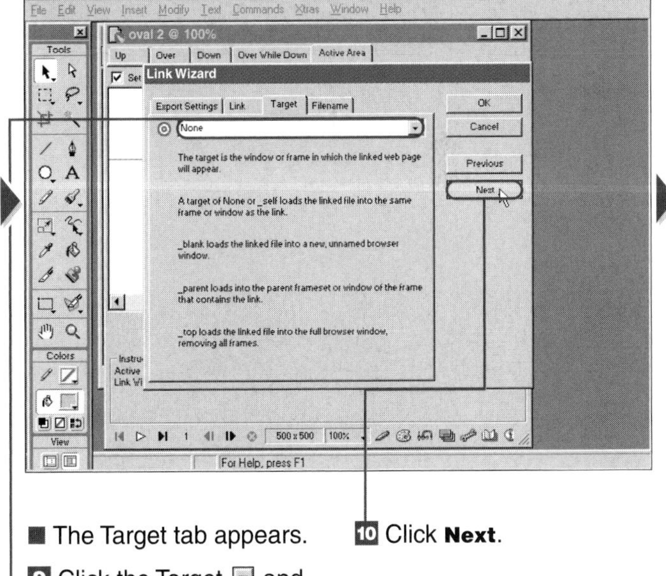

ADD A LINK AND TARGET

■ The Link tab appears.

6 Type a URL, including the **http://** if it is an external URL.

7 Type any alternate text.

■ You can type text to display in the status bar.

8 Click **Next**.

■ The Target tab appears.

9 Click the Target ▾ and select a target.

*Note: Select **None** to load the link into the same window as the button.*

10 Click **Next**.

CONTINUED

ASSIGN A URL TO A BUTTON

You can use the Link Wizard to create a file consisting of the sliced button and its assigned URL.

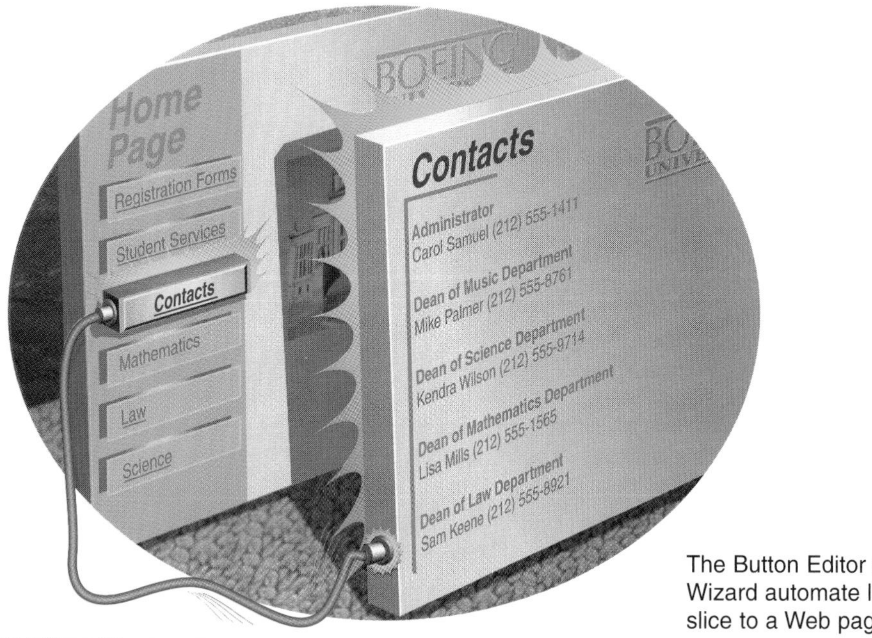

The Button Editor and Link Wizard automate linking a slice to a Web page.

ASSIGN A URL TO A BUTTON (CONTINUED)

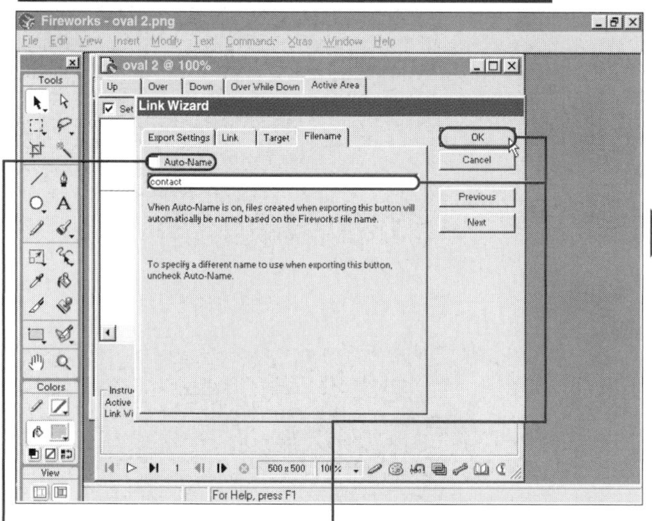

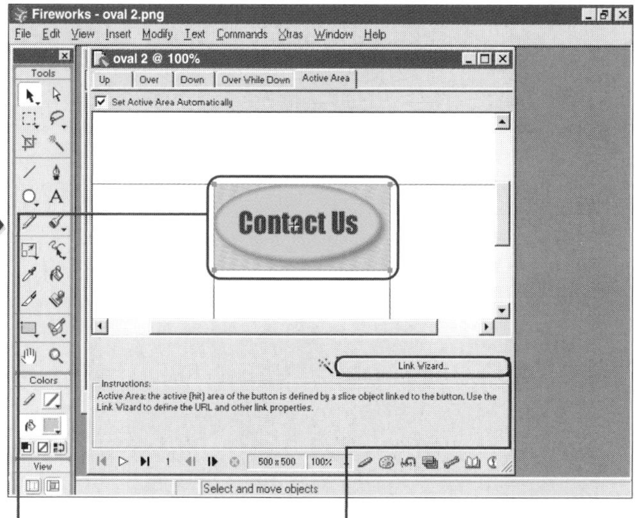

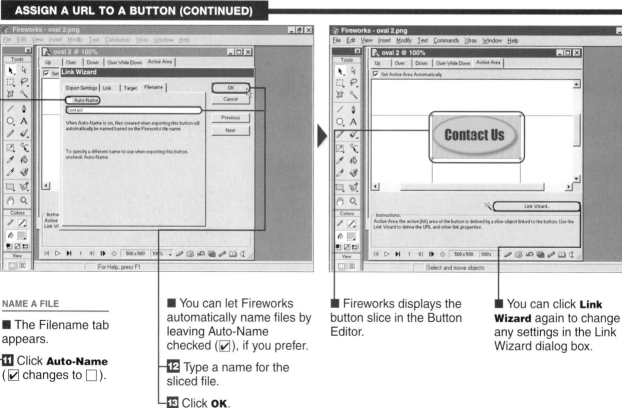

NAME A FILE

■ The Filename tab appears.

11 Click **Auto-Name** (☑ changes to ☐).

■ You can let Fireworks automatically name files by leaving Auto-Name checked (☑), if you prefer.

12 Type a name for the sliced file.

13 Click **OK**.

■ Fireworks displays the button slice in the Button Editor.

■ You can click **Link Wizard** again to change any settings in the Link Wizard dialog box.

What is the URL Library?

The URL Library stores the URLs you add to it in the URL panel. You can use URLs listed in it for multiple buttons, slices, or hotspots.

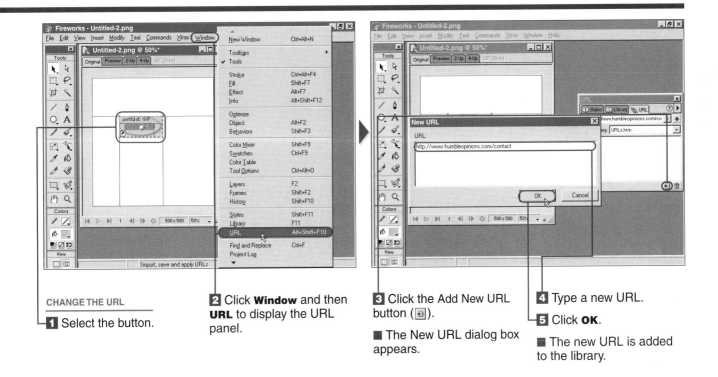

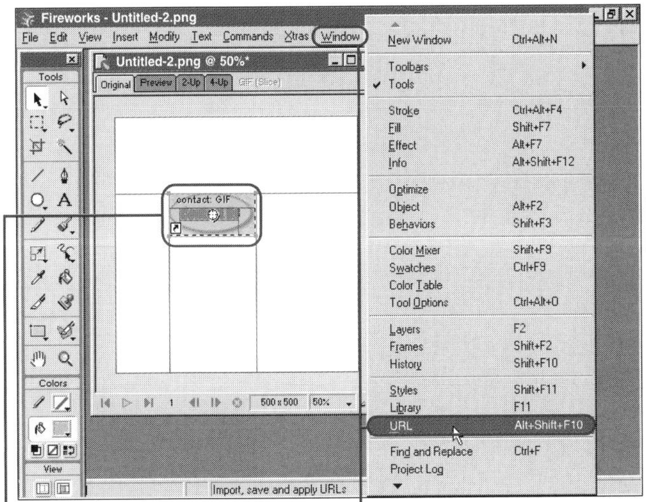

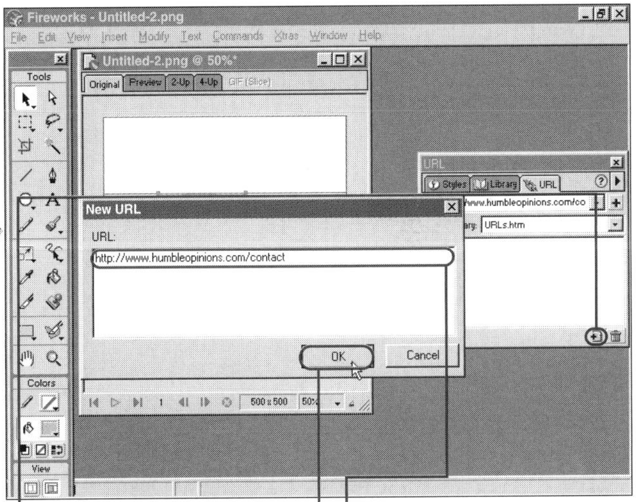

CHANGE THE URL

1 Select the button.

2 Click **Window** and then **URL** to display the URL panel.

3 Click the Add New URL button (⊞).

■ The New URL dialog box appears.

4 Type a new URL.

5 Click **OK**.

■ The new URL is added to the library.

IMPORT AND UPDATE A BUTTON

You can import buttons from other documents to use in your current document. You update buttons when you make changes to the original.

You can update and import graphic symbols and buttons.

IMPORT AND UPDATE A BUTTON

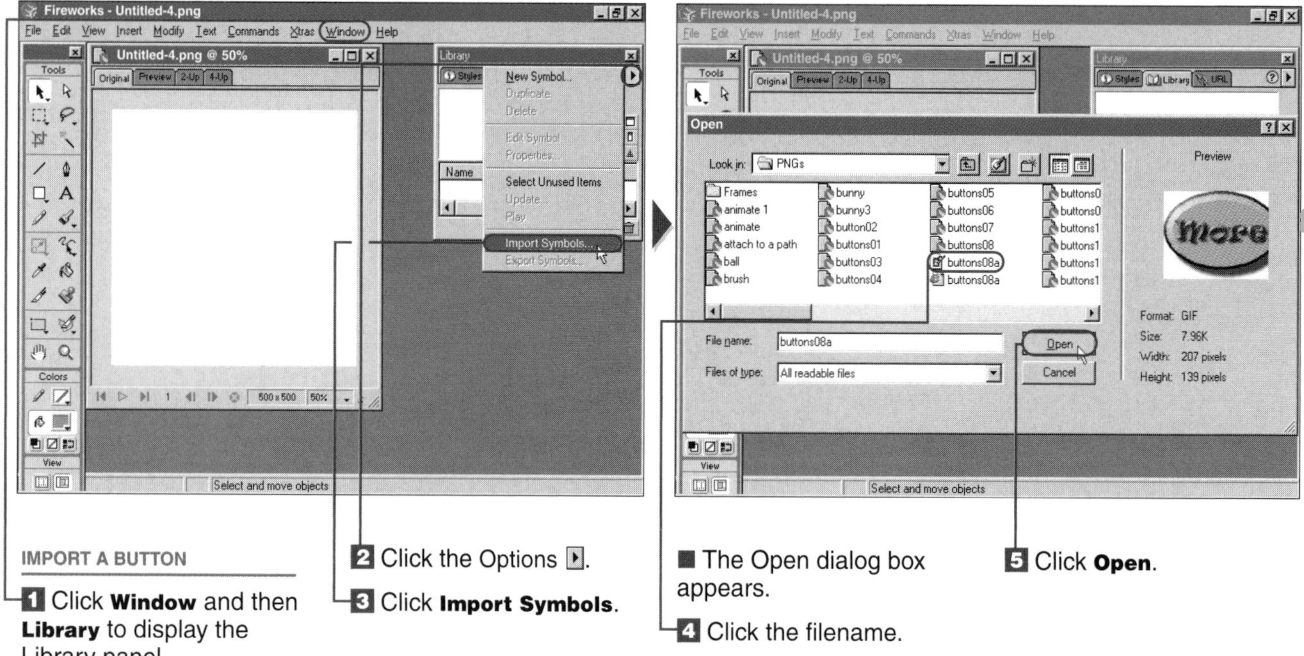

IMPORT A BUTTON

1 Click **Window** and then **Library** to display the Library panel.

2 Click the Options ▶.

3 Click **Import Symbols**.

■ The Open dialog box appears.

4 Click the filename.

5 Click **Open**.

Can I import symbols and graphics from other programs to Fireworks?

Yes. The Open dialog box displays all readable file types, including GIF, JPEG, BMP, and others.

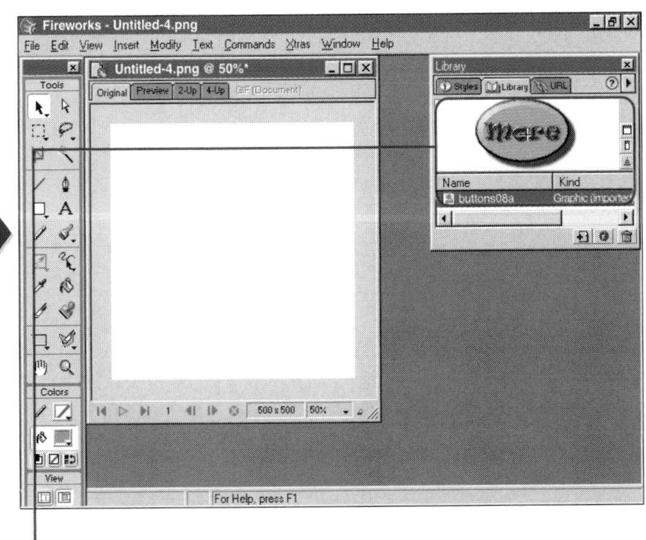

■ The button is added to the Library panel.

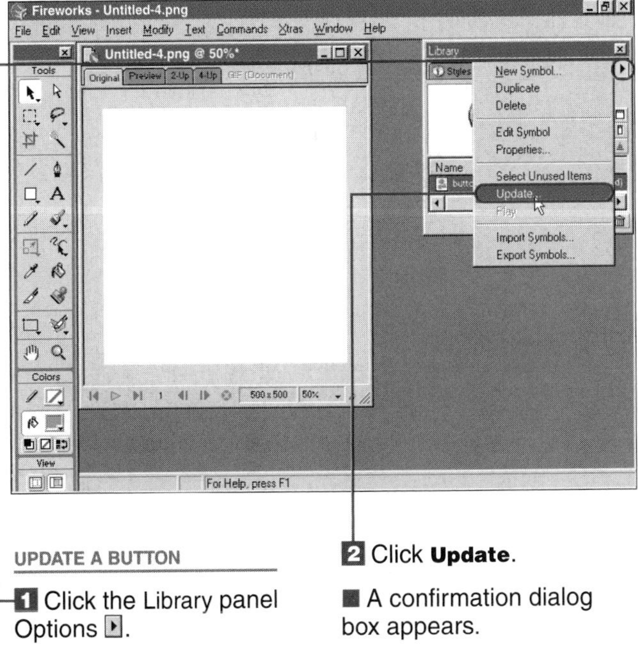

UPDATE A BUTTON

1 Click the Library panel Options ▸.

2 Click **Update**.

■ A confirmation dialog box appears.

3 Click **OK**.

CREATE A NAVIGATION BAR

You can create a navigation bar containing multiple buttons. Each button directs users to a different page on the Dreamweaver Web site.

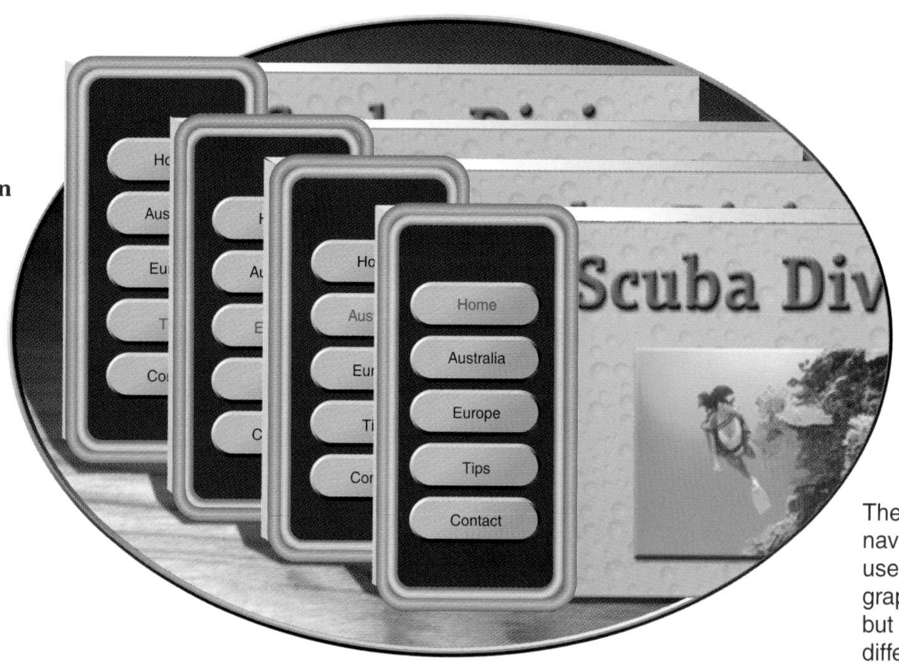

The buttons on a navigation bar use the same graphic design, but each displays different text.

CREATE A NAVIGATION BAR

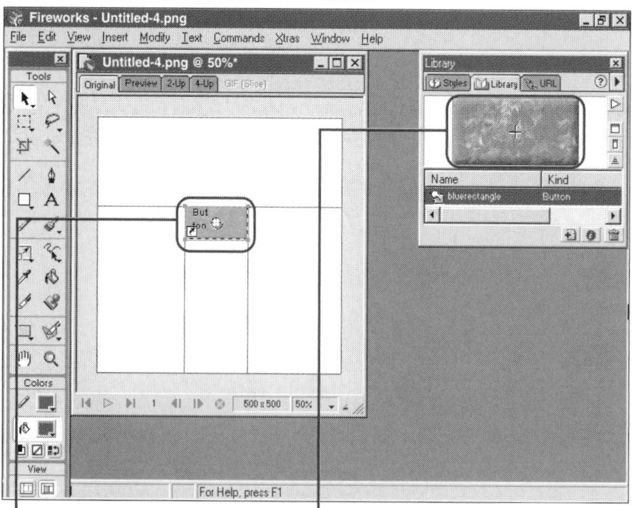

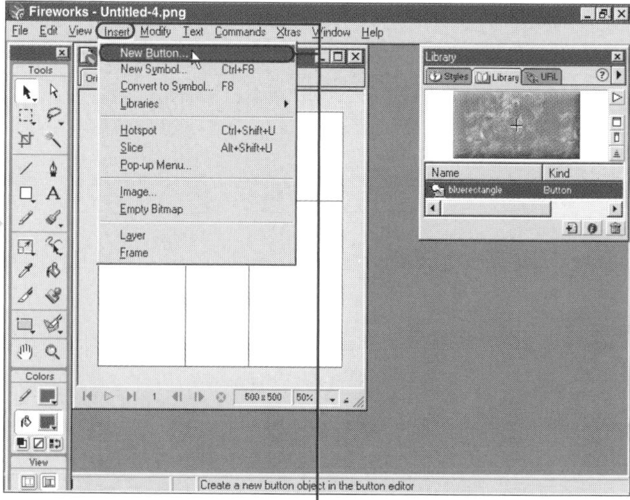

1 Create or import a button.

Note: For more information, see the sections "Create a Button" and "Import and Update a Button" earlier in this chapter.

Note: Do not add text to the new button yet.

■ The button appears in the Symbol library.

2 Move the original button to the side of the document.

■ The button symbol remains in the library.

3 Click **Insert**.

4 Click **New Button**.

Why do I keep the original button that has no text?

If you decide to change the graphic design of the button — fill, stroke, or effect — you can make changes to the original and choose that the changes be made to all instances.

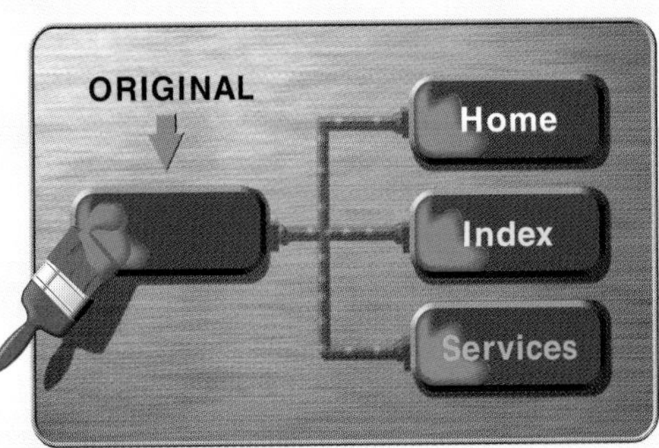

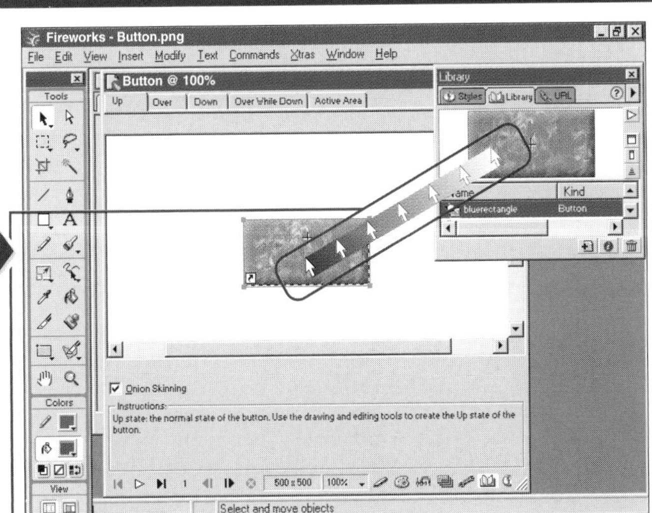

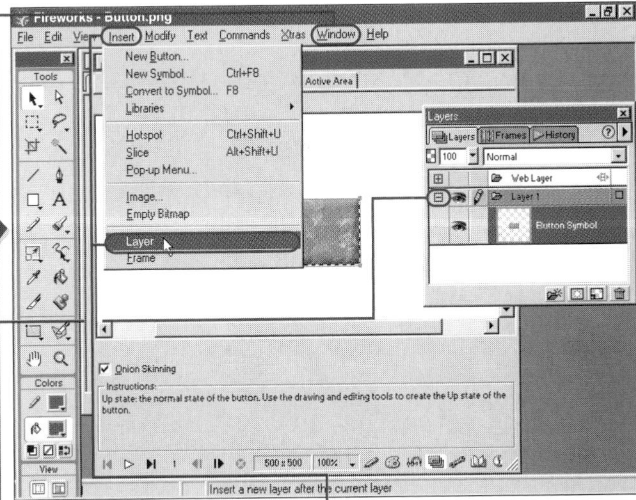

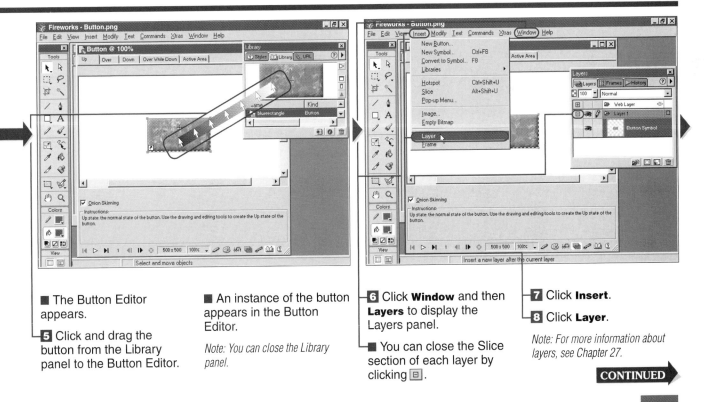

■ The Button Editor appears.

5 Click and drag the button from the Library panel to the Button Editor.

■ An instance of the button appears in the Button Editor.

Note: You can close the Library panel.

6 Click **Window** and then **Layers** to display the Layers panel.

■ You can close the Slice section of each layer by clicking ⊟.

7 Click **Insert**.

8 Click **Layer**.

Note: For more information about layers, see Chapter 27.

CONTINUED

All buttons on a navigation bar should use the same graphic design for consistency.

The same navigation bar appears on each of the Web pages in the site.

CREATE A NAVIGATION BAR (CONTINUED)

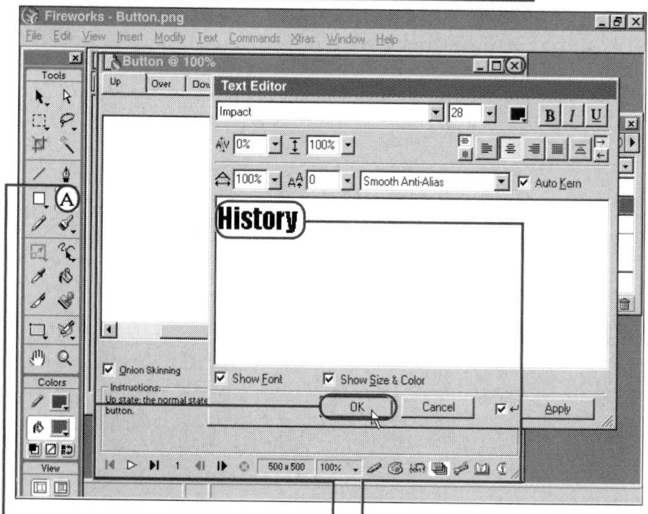

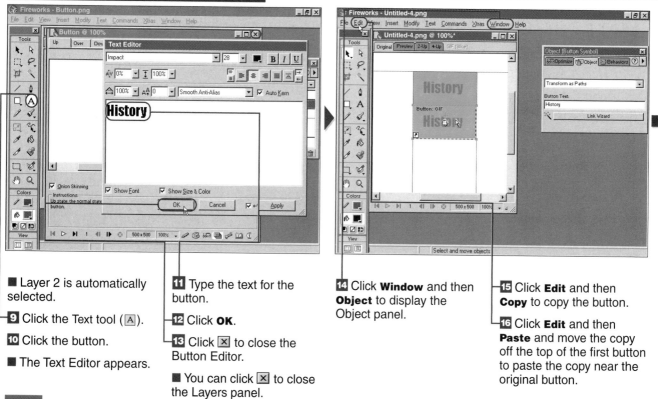

■ Layer 2 is automatically selected.

9 Click the Text tool (A).

10 Click the button.

■ The Text Editor appears.

11 Type the text for the button.

12 Click **OK**.

13 Click ☒ to close the Button Editor.

■ You can click ☒ to close the Layers panel.

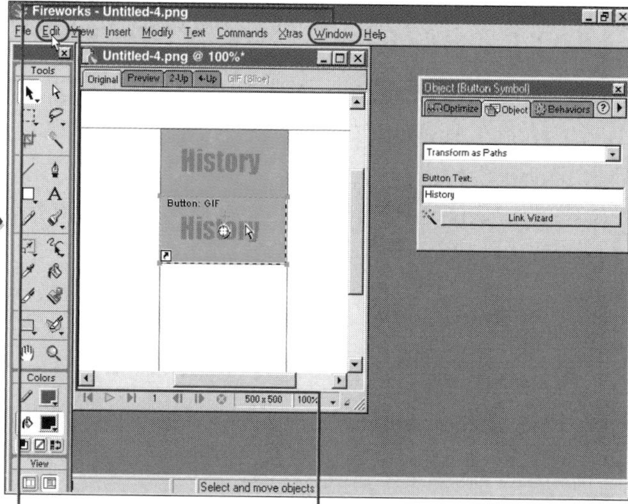

14 Click **Window** and then **Object** to display the Object panel.

15 Click **Edit** and then **Copy** to copy the button.

16 Click **Edit** and then **Paste** and move the copy off the top of the first button to paste the copy near the original button.

Can I edit a button after I create the navigation bar?

Yes. Double-click any button to edit it in the Button Editor. You have the choice of editing only the current button or all instances of the button.

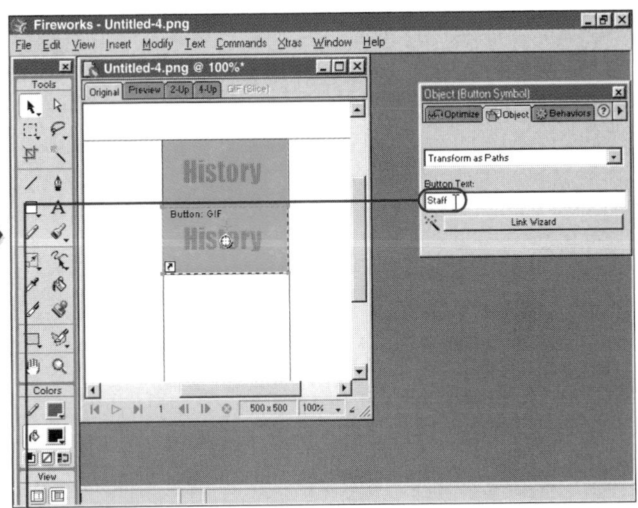

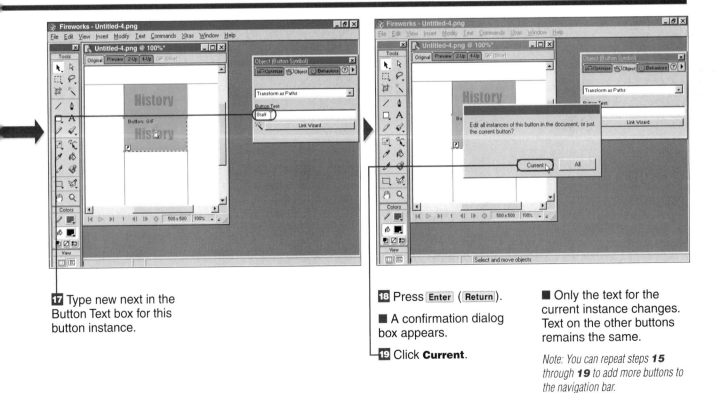

17 Type new next in the Button Text box for this button instance.

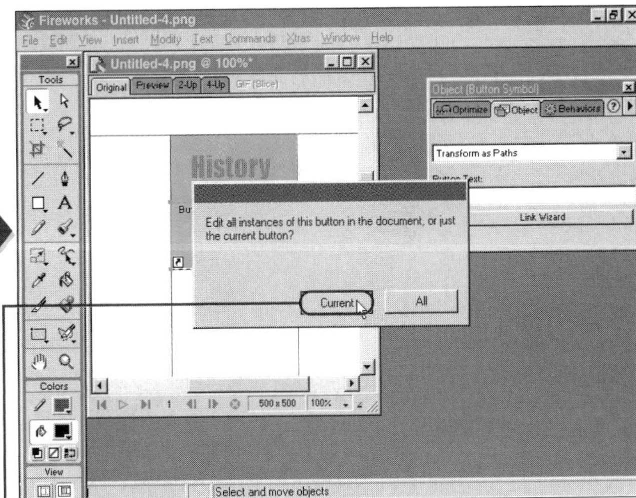

18 Press Enter (Return).

■ A confirmation dialog box appears.

19 Click **Current**.

■ Only the text for the current instance changes. Text on the other buttons remains the same.

*Note: You can repeat steps **15** through **19** to add more buttons to the navigation bar.*

CREATE OR INSERT A HOTSPOT

You can create a hotspot on any graphic or text. Hotspots can link to another area of your Dreamweaver Web page, or to a totally different Web page.

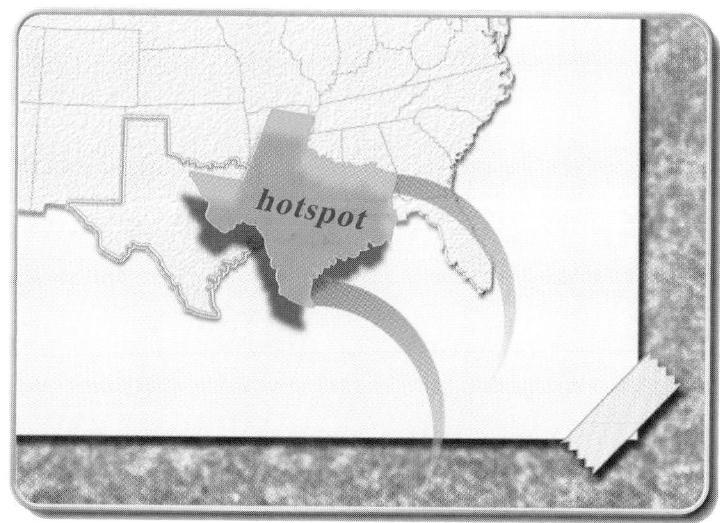

CREATE A HOTSPOT

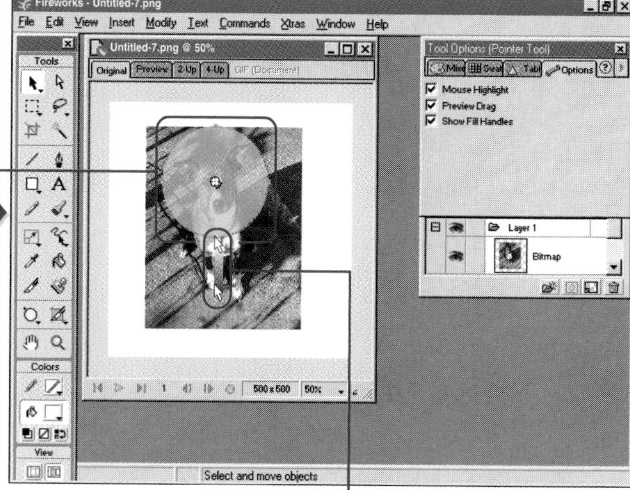

1 Click and hold the Hotspot tool ( ) and select the shape that you want to use.

Note: You can click ○ to draw circle or oval shapes, □ to draw rectangles or squares, or ▽ to draw irregular shapes.

2 Draw the circle, rectangle, or polygon.

■ The hotspot shape appears over the graphic or image.

■ You can click a handle and drag to resize the hotspot shape.

What is the difference between creating and inserting a hotspot?

Generally, you create a circle or rectangle when you want only a portion of the image to act as a hotspot. You insert a hotspot when you want to use the entire image, graphic, or text instead of just a part of it.

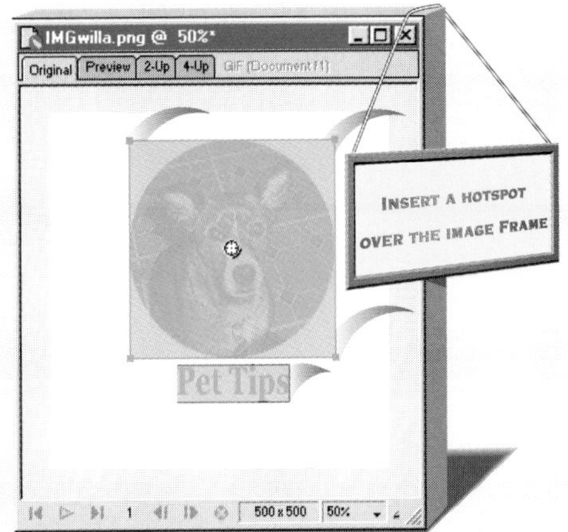

INSERT AND PREVIEW A HOTSPOT

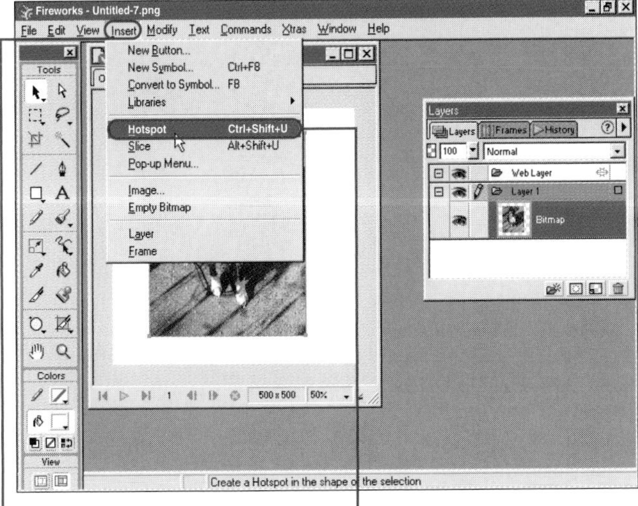

1. Select the graphic, text, or image that you want to insert as a hotspot.
2. Click **Insert**.
3. Click **Hotspot**.
   - The hotspot covers the entire graphic.
4. Click the **Preview** tab.
5. Drag ↖ over the graphic.
   - 👆 indicates a hotspot.

EDIT HOTSPOTS

You can change or convert the shape of your hotspots to better fit an image or graphic. You can change a shape by altering the size of a rectangle or circle. You convert the shape when changing a rectangle to a circle, for example.

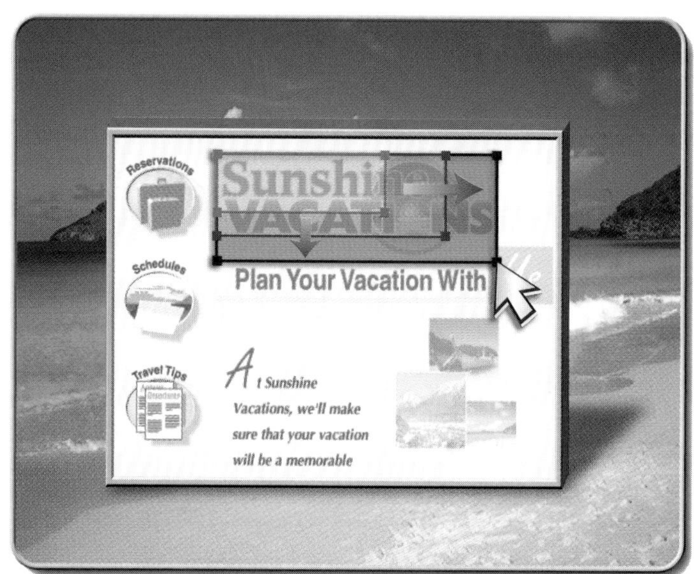

CHANGE THE HOTSPOT SHAPE SIZE

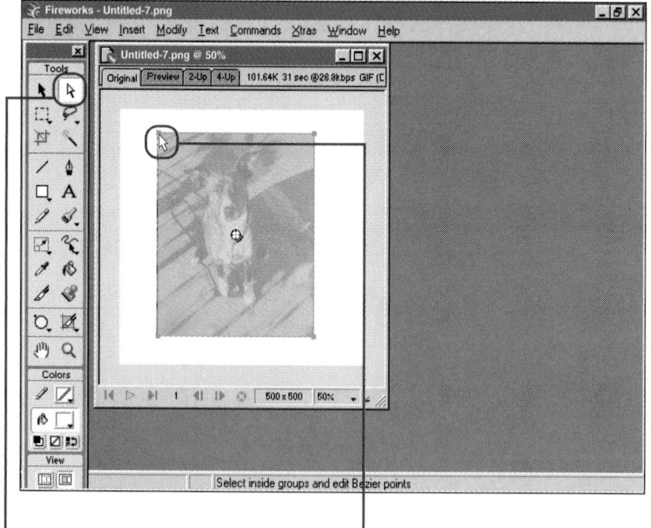

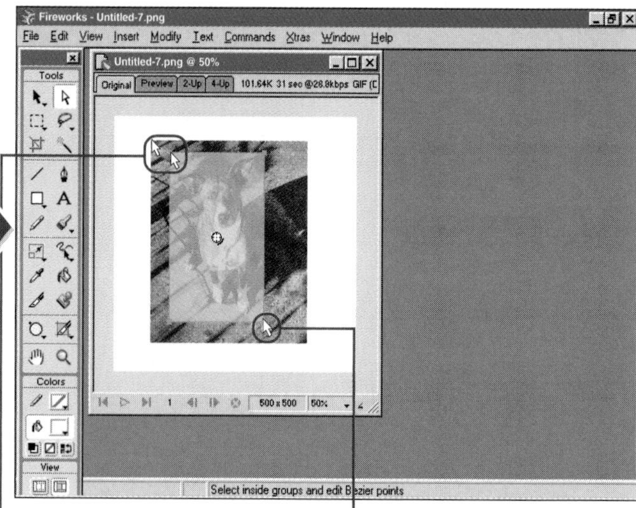

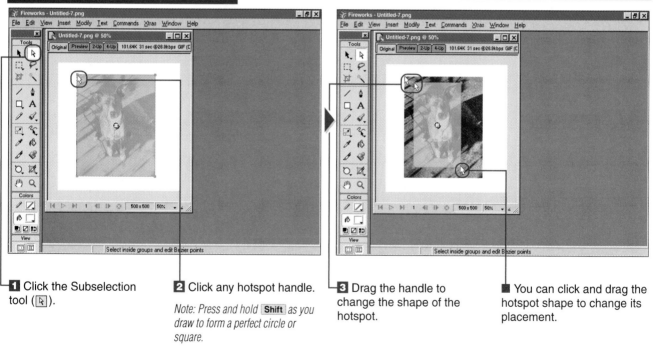

1 Click the Subselection tool (![]).

2 Click any hotspot handle.

Note: Press and hold **Shift** *as you draw to form a perfect circle or square.*

3 Drag the handle to change the shape of the hotspot.

■ You can click and drag the hotspot shape to change its placement.

Why would I want to change the color of the hotspot?

Changing the hotspot's color changes only what you see on-screen. It does not affect how the hotspot works or appears on the Web page. You can change the color to better distinguish between a hotspot and a slice, for example. For more information about slices, see Chapter 32.

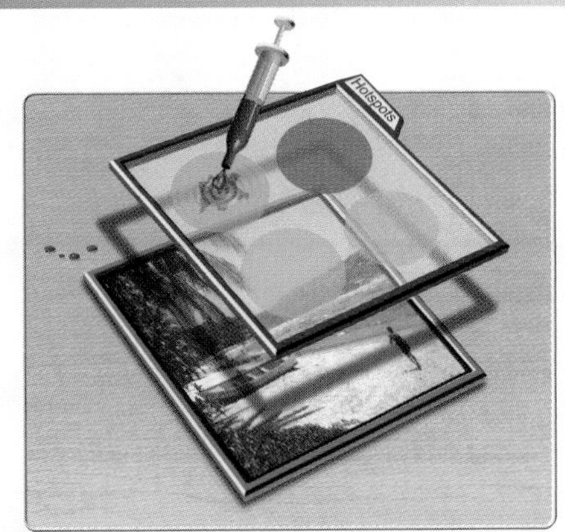

CONVERT THE HOTSPOT SHAPE

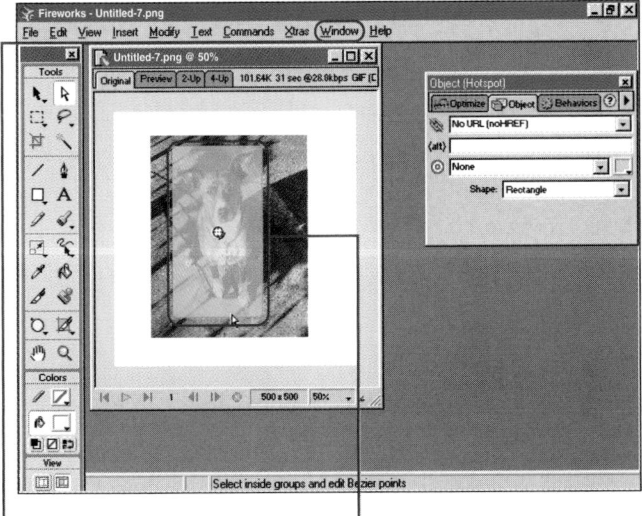

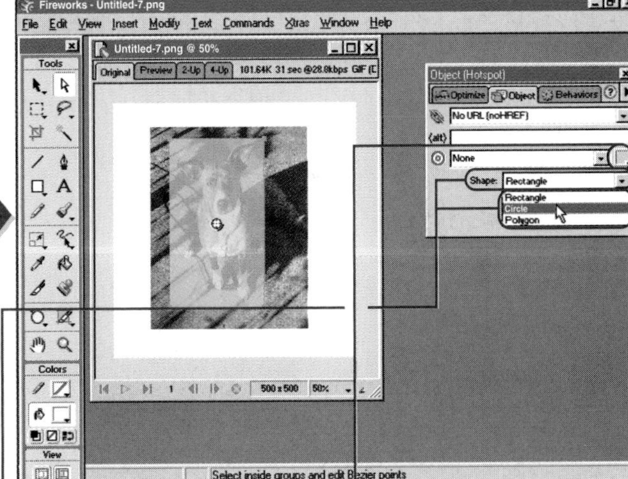

■1 Click **Window** and then **Object** to display the Object panel.

■2 Select the hotspot.

■3 Click the Shape ▼.

■4 Click the shape you want to convert to.

■ You can change the color of the hotspot by clicking the color swatch and choosing a new color.

■ Fireworks converts the shape of your hotspot.

CONTINUED

EDIT HOTSPOTS

You can scale, rotate, skew, or distort your hotspot to better define the shape of your graphic.

SCALE OR ROTATE A HOTSPOT

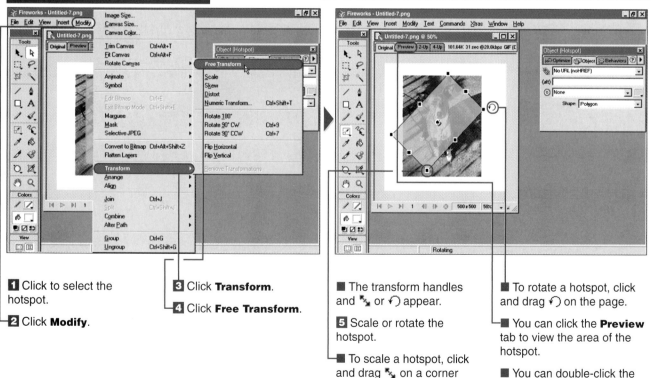

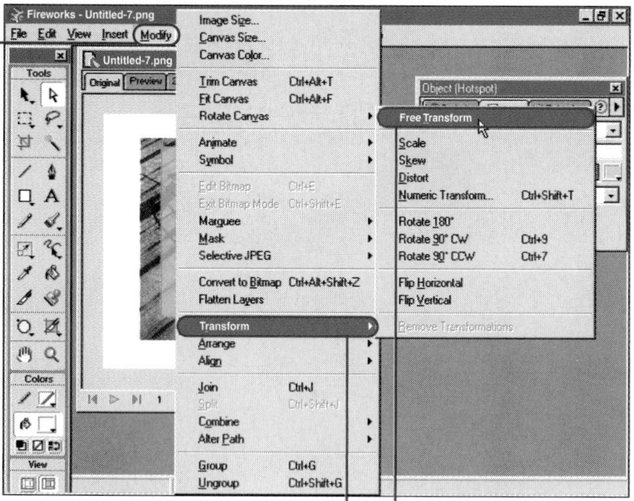

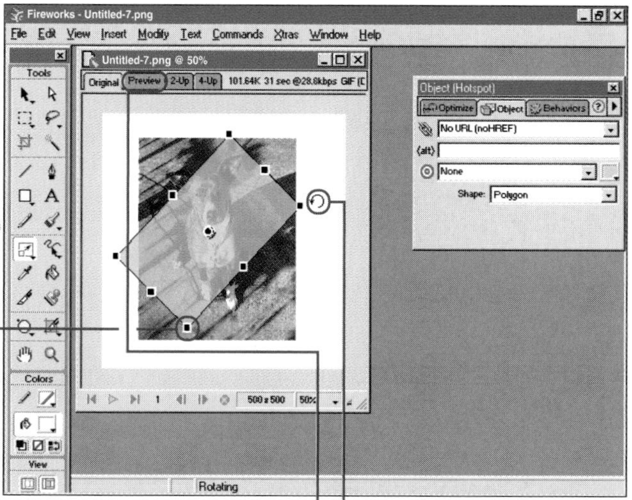

1 Click to select the hotspot.

2 Click **Modify**.

3 Click **Transform**.

4 Click **Free Transform**.

■ The transform handles and ⤡ or ↶ appear.

5 Scale or rotate the hotspot.

■ To scale a hotspot, click and drag ⤡ on a corner handle.

■ To rotate a hotspot, click and drag ↶ on the page.

■ You can click the **Preview** tab to view the area of the hotspot.

■ You can double-click the hotspot to close the transform mode.

Why would I need to transform a hotspot?

You might need to fit a hotspot to an unusual shape, such as a diamond or parallelogram. Tranforming a hotspot can help you do so: Scaling a hotspot changes its size, rotating a hotspot turns it around on the page, and skewing and distorting a hotspot enable you to change the size and shape of one or two sides.

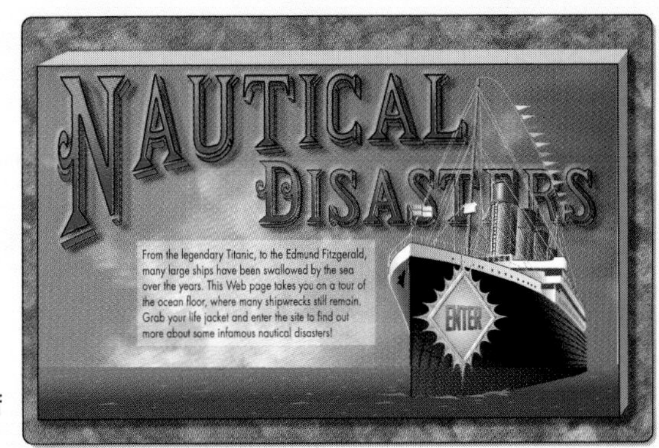

SKEW OR DISTORT A HOTSPOT

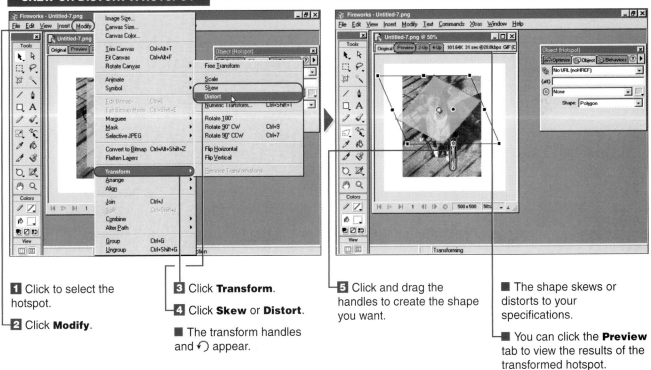

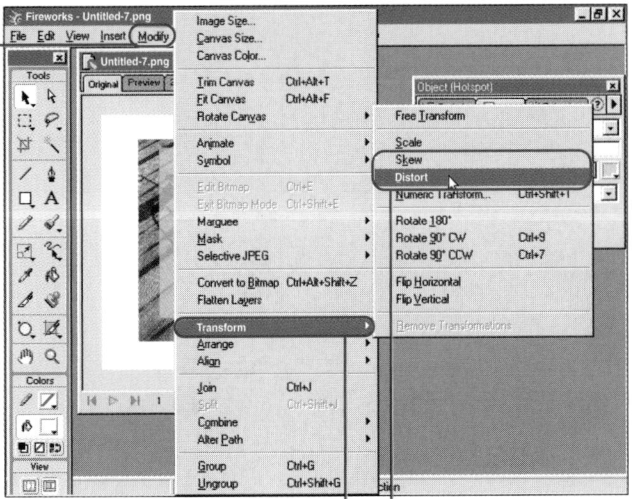

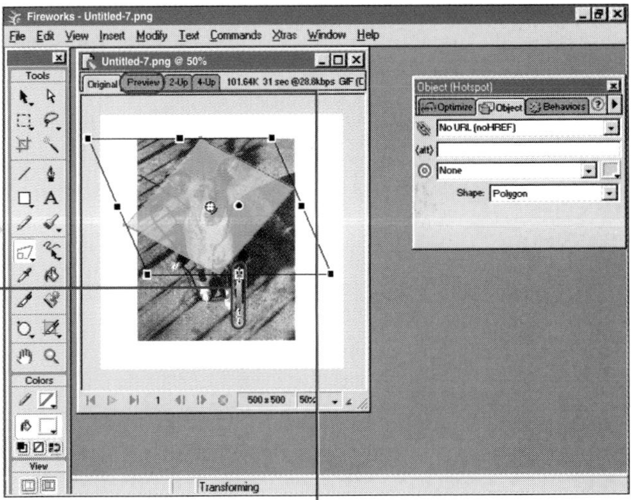

1 Click to select the hotspot.

2 Click **Modify**.

3 Click **Transform**.

4 Click **Skew** or **Distort**.

■ The transform handles and ↶ appear.

5 Click and drag the handles to create the shape you want.

■ The shape skews or distorts to your specifications.

■ You can click the **Preview** tab to view the results of the transformed hotspot.

CREATE AN IMAGE MAP

You can create an image map of your Dreamweaver Web site that helps people navigate your site.

The image map contains links to other Web pages in the site.

CREATE AN IMAGE MAP

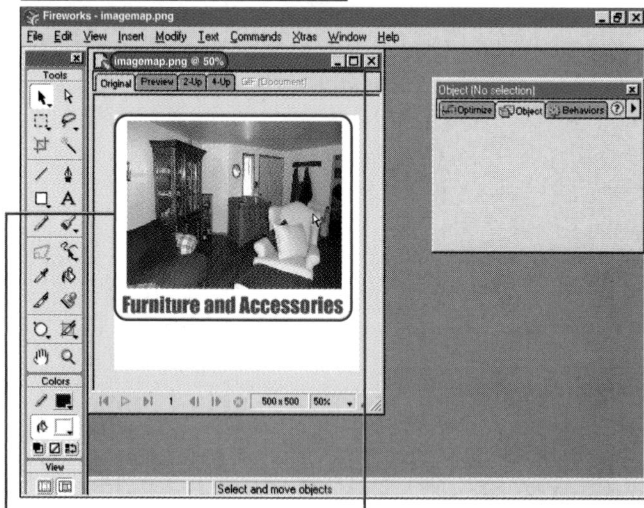

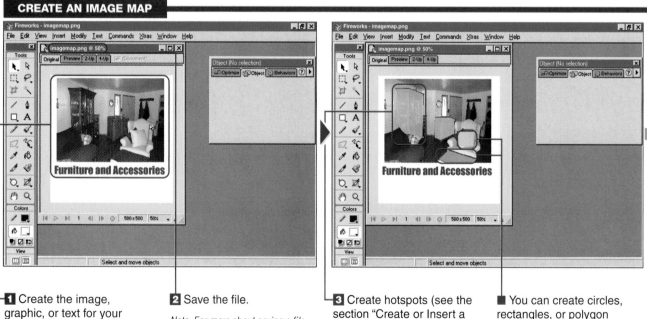

1 Create the image, graphic, or text for your image map.

Note: For more on creating text, graphics, or images, see Chapters 26, 27, and 28.

2 Save the file.

Note: For more about saving a file, see Chapter 25.

3 Create hotspots (see the section "Create or Insert a Hotspot").

■ You can create circles, rectangles, or polygon hotspots.

Is there a limit to the number of hotspots I can use in an image map?

No, you can use as many hotspots as you like. You must remember, however, that the more hotspots you use, the larger the image map file becomes. Larger files take longer to download and open on the Web.

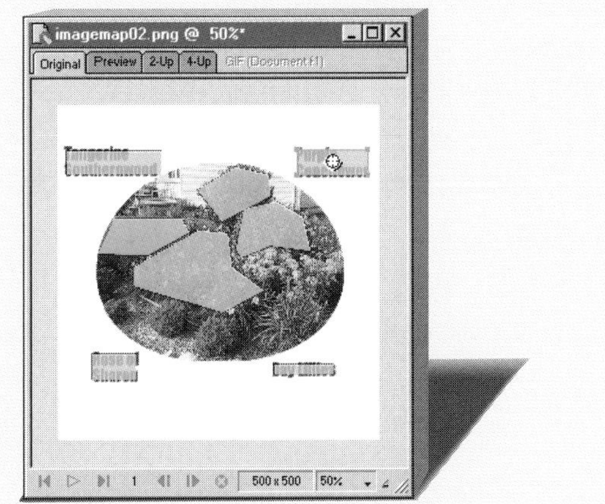

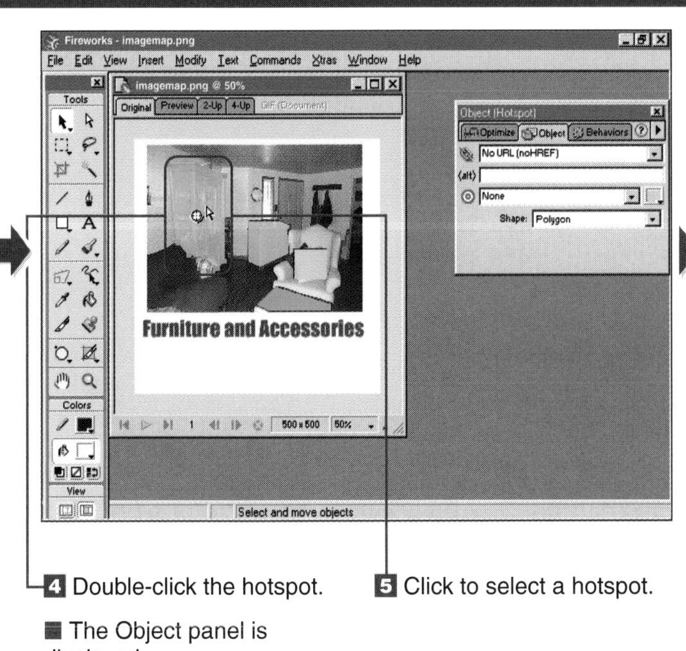

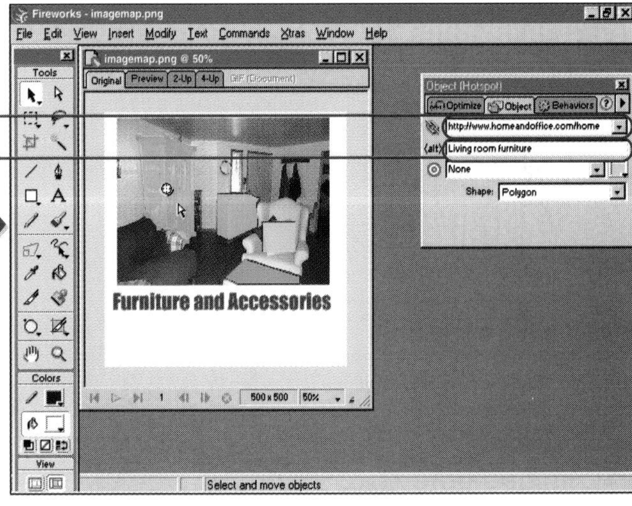

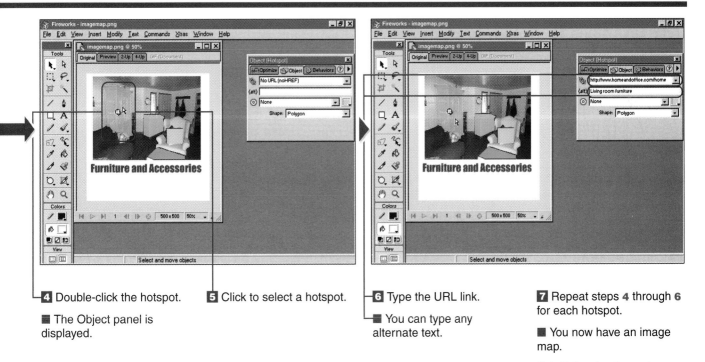

4 Double-click the hotspot.

■ The Object panel is displayed.

5 Click to select a hotspot.

6 Type the URL link.

■ You can type any alternate text.

7 Repeat steps **4** through **6** for each hotspot.

■ You now have an image map.

Note: To learn how to export an image map, see Chapter 35.

USING THE SLICE TOOLS

You can use the slice tools to create slices that are either rectangular or a polygon.

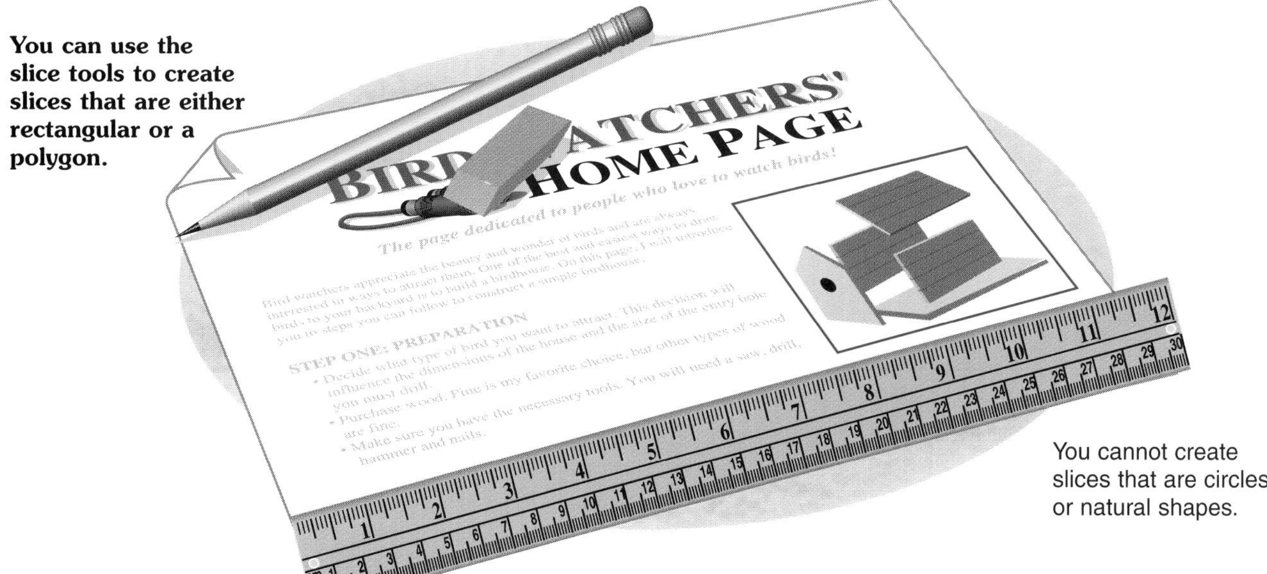

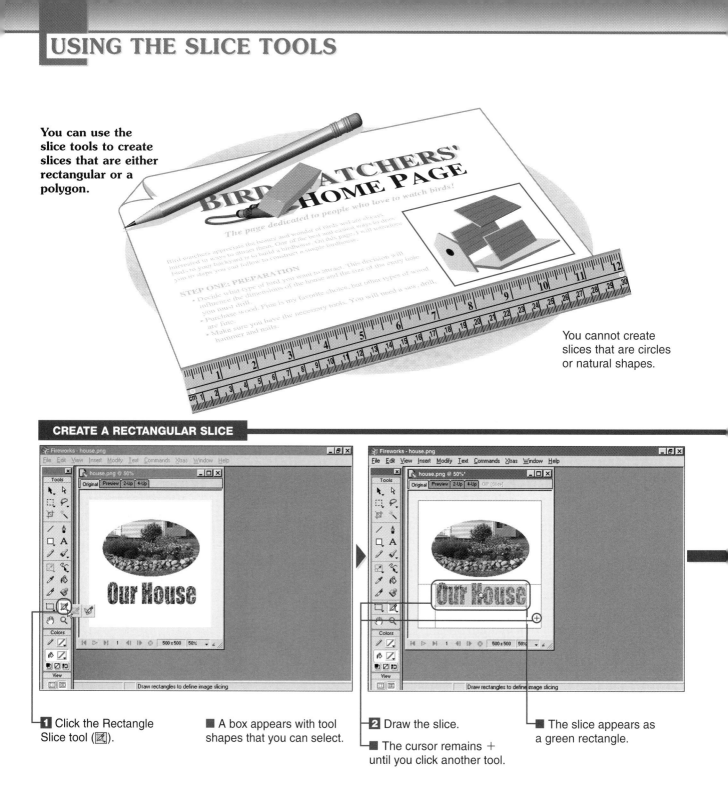

You cannot create slices that are circles or natural shapes.

CREATE A RECTANGULAR SLICE

1 Click the Rectangle Slice tool (▨).

■ A box appears with tool shapes that you can select.

2 Draw the slice.

■ The cursor remains + until you click another tool.

■ The slice appears as a green rectangle.

What are the red lines around the slice?

As you draw a slice, Fireworks adds slice guides. You use the slice guides to help you align other slices and therefore keep the number of slice files to a minimum. Having fewer slices means that the image downloads quicker.

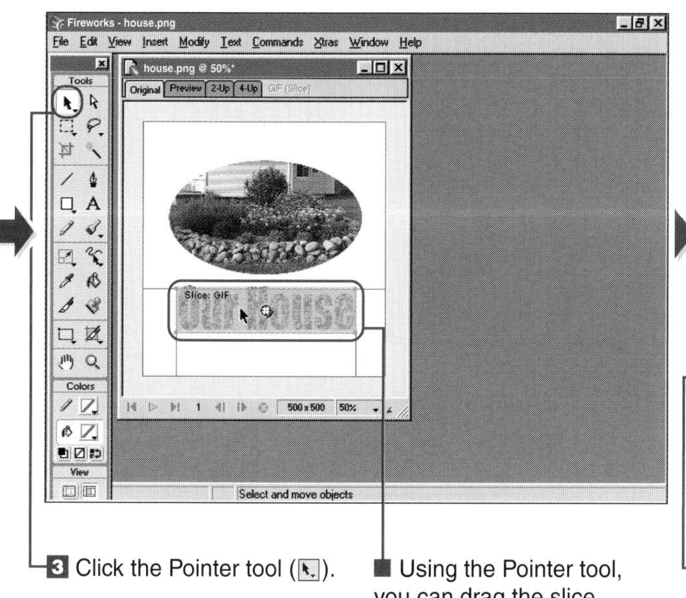

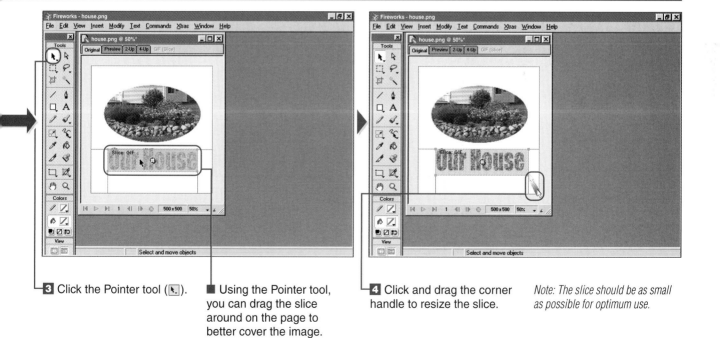

3 Click the Pointer tool ( ).

■ Using the Pointer tool, you can drag the slice around on the page to better cover the image.

4 Click and drag the corner handle to resize the slice.

Note: The slice should be as small as possible for optimum use.

CONTINUED

You can cut a polygon slice to make the slice smaller by outlining a shape that is not rectangular, such as an oval. Slicing only the image and not the background makes a more efficient and smaller slice.

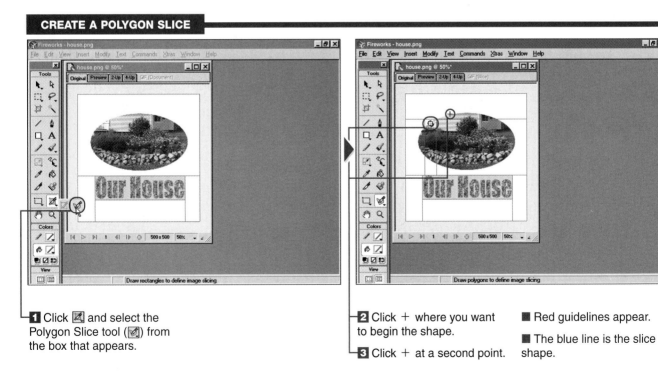

CREATE A POLYGON SLICE

1 Click and select the Polygon Slice tool from the box that appears.

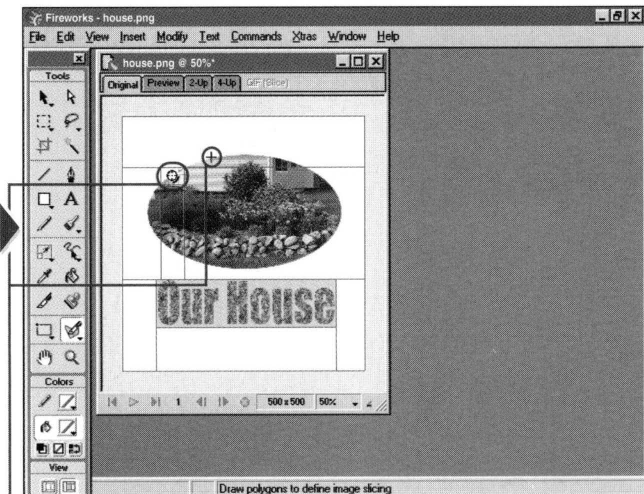

2 Click + where you want to begin the shape.

3 Click + at a second point.

■ Red guidelines appear.

■ The blue line is the slice shape.

How does Fireworks export a polygon slice?

Fireworks exports a polygon slice as a series of rectangles. A polygon slice often results in more individual files and takes longer to load on the browser. You should use a rectangle slice whenever possible to save space and time.

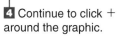

4 Continue to click + around the graphic.

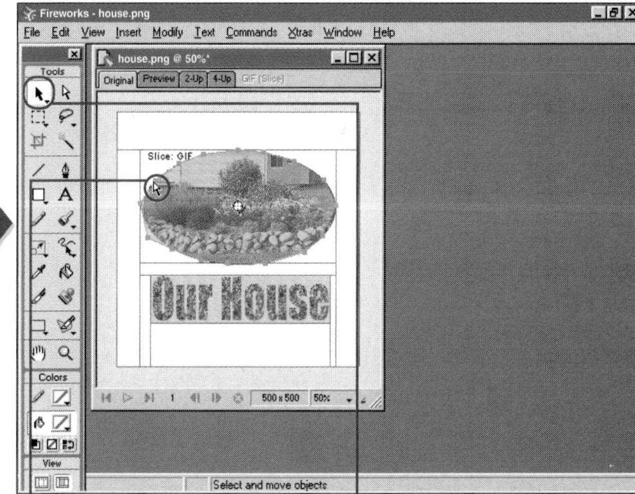

5 Click the tool on top of the first point to close the shape.

■ You are finished creating your polygon slice.

■ You can click the pointer tool to adjust the slice on the object.

HIDE OR SHOW A SLICE

You can hide a slice so that you can view or edit an image or graphic more easily.

HIDE OR SHOW A SLICE

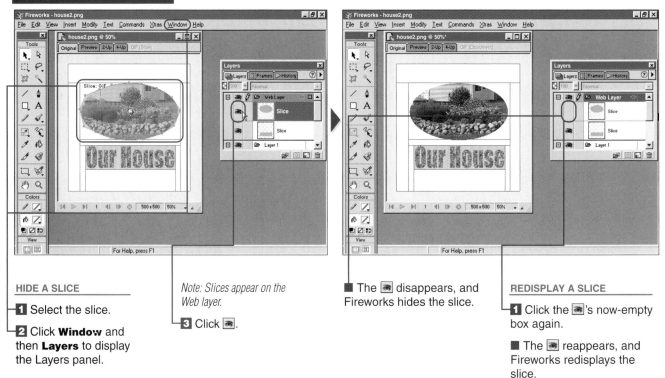

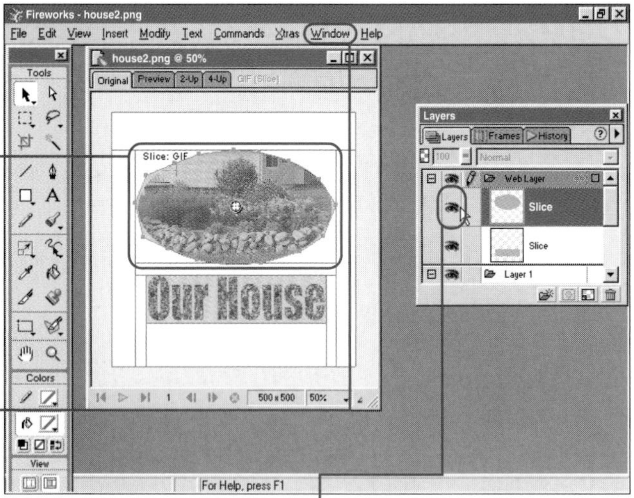

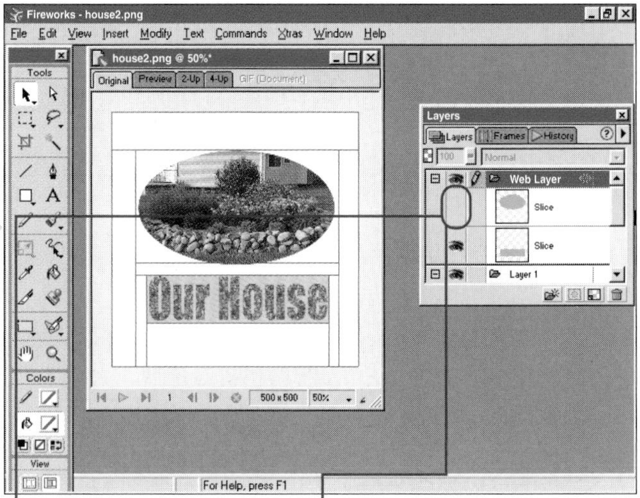

HIDE A SLICE

1 Select the slice.

2 Click **Window** and then **Layers** to display the Layers panel.

Note: Slices appear on the Web layer.

3 Click .

■ The disappears, and Fireworks hides the slice.

REDISPLAY A SLICE

1 Click the 's now-empty box again.

■ The reappears, and Fireworks redisplays the slice.

NAME A SLICE

You can manually name slices, to easily locate an image reference in the Dreamweaver HTML code.

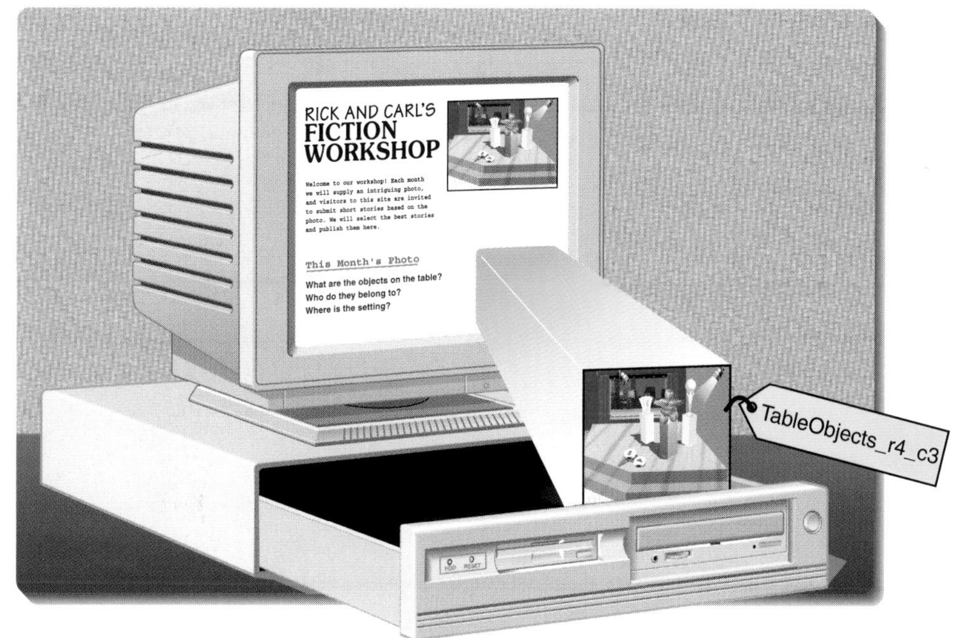

NAME A SLICE

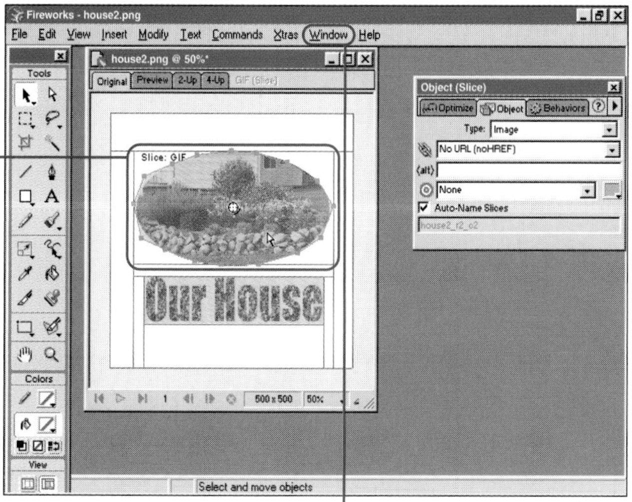

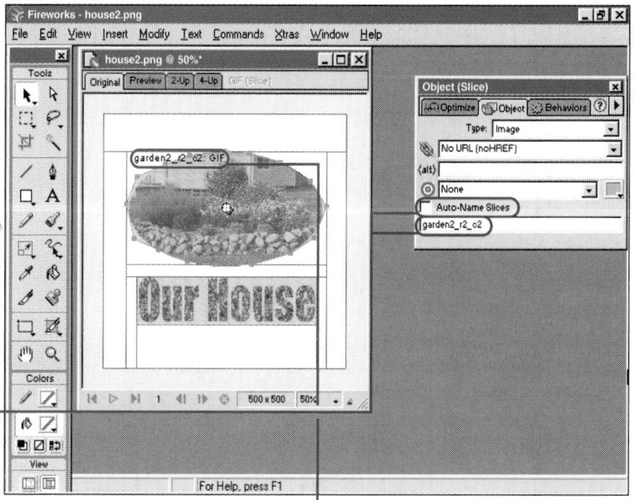

1. Select the slice.
2. Click **Window** and then **Object** to display the Object panel.
3. Click **Auto-Name Slices** (☑ changes to ☐).
4. Type the slice name.
5. Press Enter (Return).

■ The slice name changes to the one you typed.

CREATE A TEXT SLICE

You can use a text slice to display HTML text in the browser instead of an image.

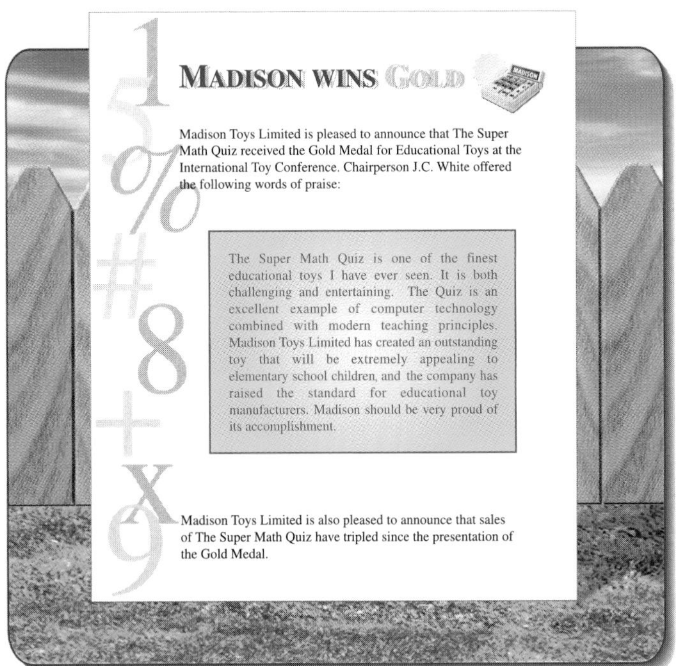

MADISON WINS GOLD
Madison Toys Limited is pleased to announce that The Super Math Quiz received the Gold Medal for Educational Toys at the International Toy Conference. Chairperson J.C. White offered the following words of praise:
The Super Math Quiz is one of the finest educational toys I have ever seen. It is both challenging and entertaining. The Quiz is an excellent example of computer technology combined with modern teaching principles. Madison Toys Limited has created an outstanding toy that will be extremely appealing to elementary school children, and the company has raised the standard for educational toy manufacturers. Madison should be very proud of its accomplishment.
Madison Toys Limited is also pleased to announce that sales of The Super Math Quiz have tripled since the presentation of the Gold Medal.

CREATE A TEXT SLICE

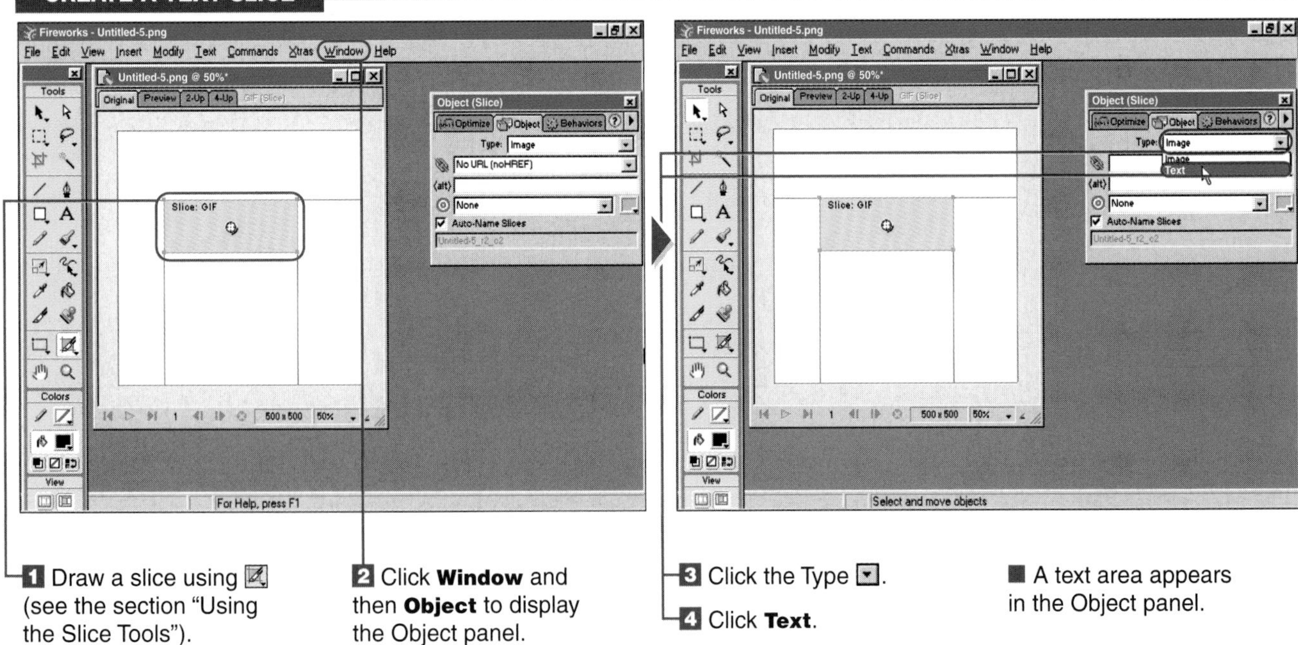

1 Draw a slice using ▨ (see the section "Using the Slice Tools").

2 Click **Window** and then **Object** to display the Object panel.

3 Click the Type ▾.

4 Click **Text**.

■ A text area appears in the Object panel.

When would I use text slices instead image slices?

You can use a text slice when you want to quickly update text on your Web site without having to create new graphics.

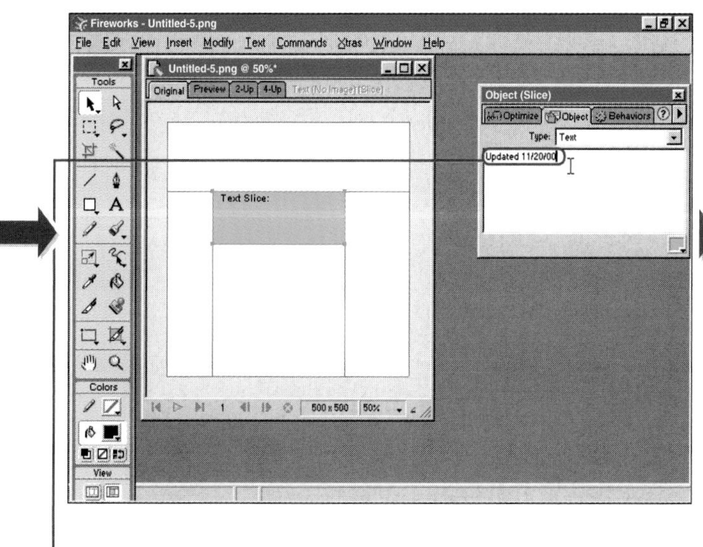

5 Type the text.

Note: The text in the slice does not appear in the Fireworks document. It does appear in a Web browser.

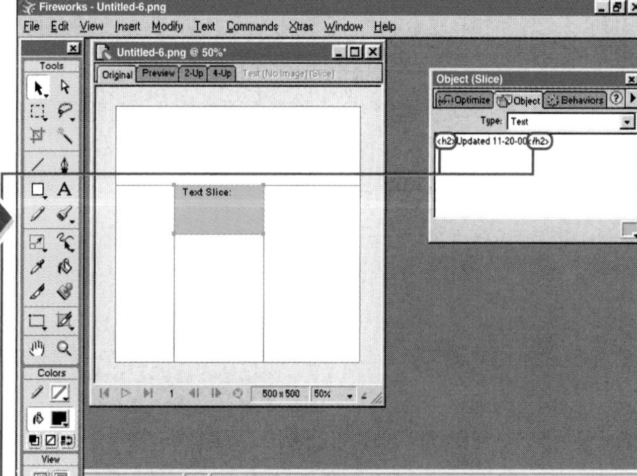

■ You can add HTML formatting tags to format the text.

Note: HTML text may look different when viewed in different browsers.

ASSIGN A URL LINK TO AN IMAGE SLICE

You can assign a URL to any slice in order to link it to another Web page.

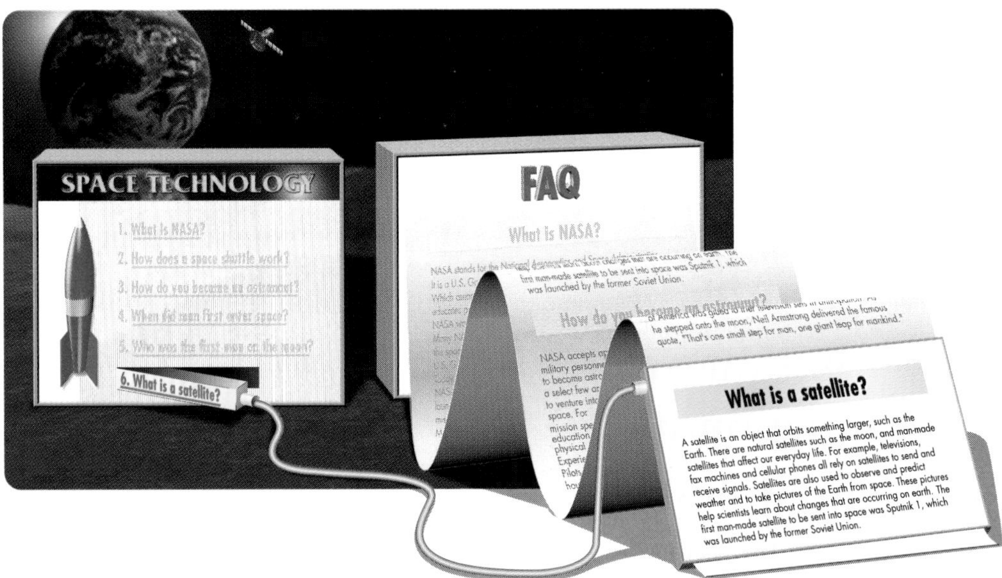

ASSIGN A URL LINK TO AN IMAGE SLICE

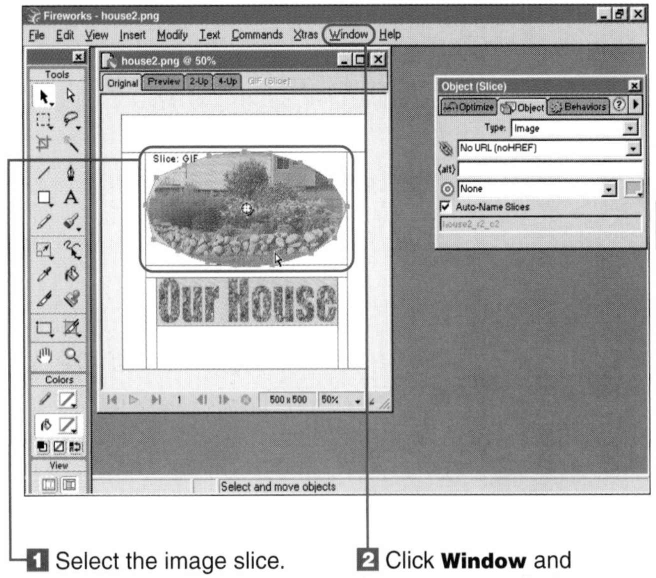

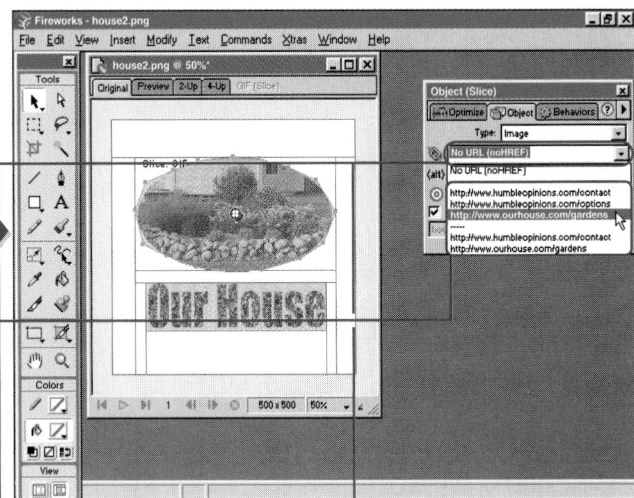

1 Select the image slice.

2 Click **Window** and then **Object** to display the Object panel.

3 Click the Current URL ▾.

4 Click the URL that you want to assign to the slice.

■ You can type the URL if it is not already in the list.

How do the URL lists in the URL Library panel and the Object panel differ?

The URL Library panel contains a list of URLs you can use in linking buttons, slices, and other graphics when you are working. In the Object panel, the URL text box describes the URL for only one object. The drop-down URL list in the Object panel comes from the URL Library. You can add URLs for use with all documents in the URL Library panel, but you can add URLs to the Object panel for use with only the current document.

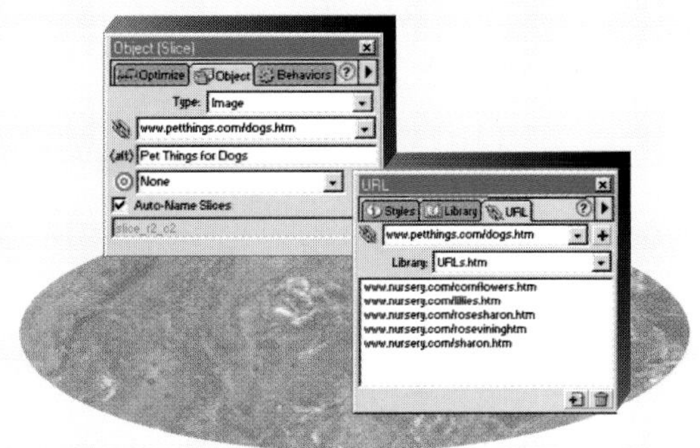

■ Optionally, type the alternate text.

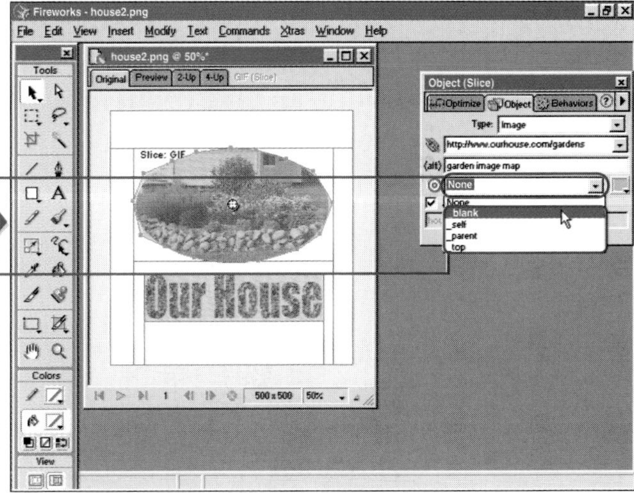

5 Click the Link Target ▼.

6 Click a link target.

■ The link target is assigned to your slice.

UPDATE AND EXPORT A SLICE

You can update and export a slice of an image or graphic instead of the entire image — for example, if you made changes to only one slice within the document.

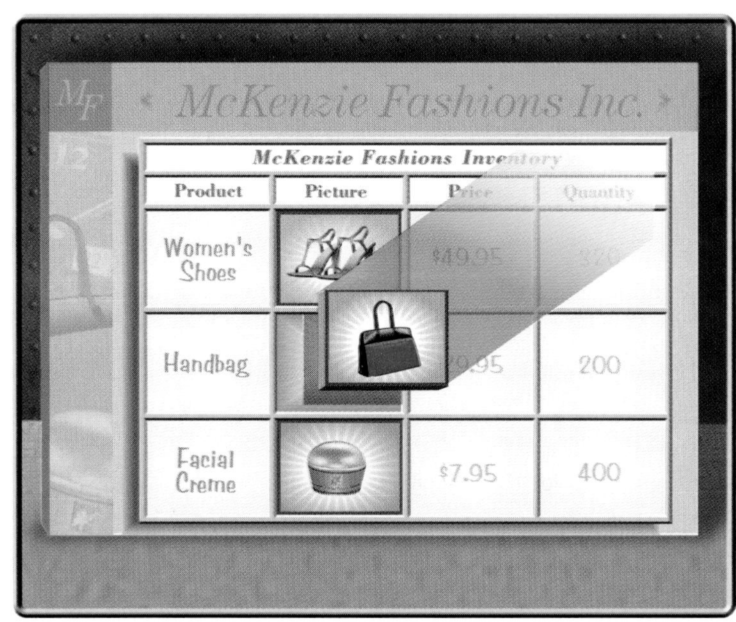

To learn about exporting slices, see Chapter 35.

UPDATE AND EXPORT A SLICE

UPDATE THE SLICE

1 Select the slice.

2 Click **Window** and then **Layers** to display the Layers panel.

3 Click (eye icon) to hide the selected slice ((eye icon) disappears).

4 Select the image or graphic.

5 Make changes to the graphic.

Note: For information about modifying images, see Chapter 28.

Why would I export a slice?

You export the slice to use in other applications, such as Dreamweaver or FrontPage. Before you export a slice, you need to optimize it first. Optimizing the slice compresses it and makes it load faster to the Web page. See Chapter 34 for information about optimizing graphics. See Chapter 35 for information about exporting graphics.

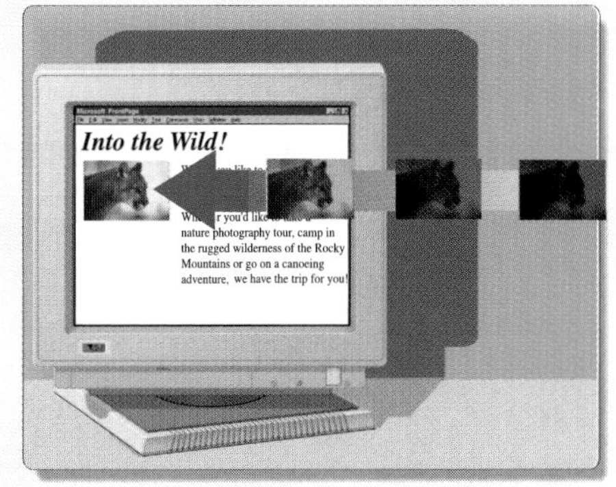

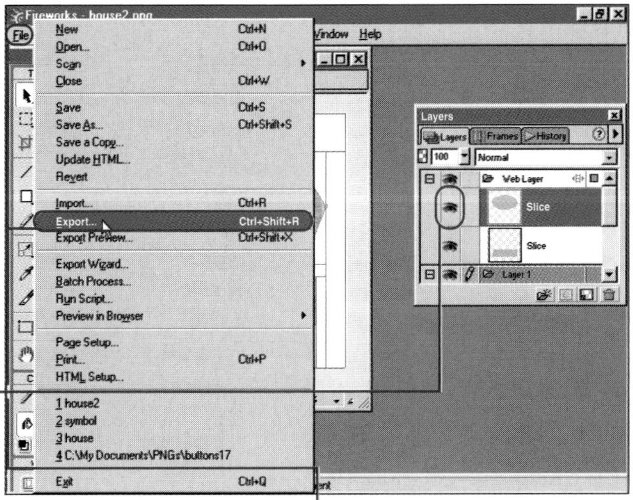

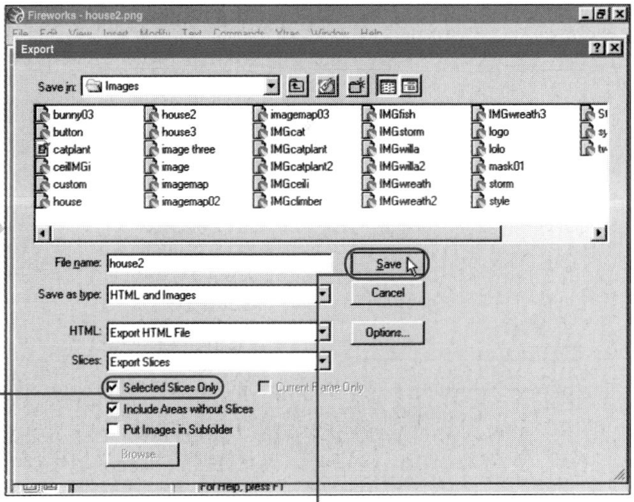

6 Click the 's now-empty box to display the slice (reappears).

EXPORT THE SLICE

7 Click **File**.

8 Click **Export**.

■ The Export dialog box appears.

9 Click **Selected Slices Only** (□ changes to ✓).

10 Click **Save**.

■ The slice is updated and exported.

CREATE A SIMPLE ROLLOVER

You can create a button or navigation bar that uses a rollover effect by using the Button Editor.

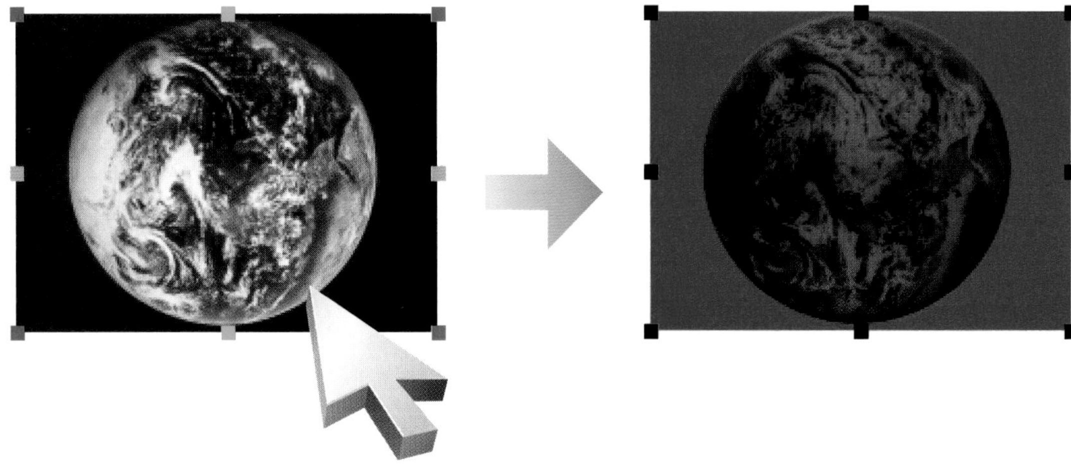

CREATE THE OVER STATE

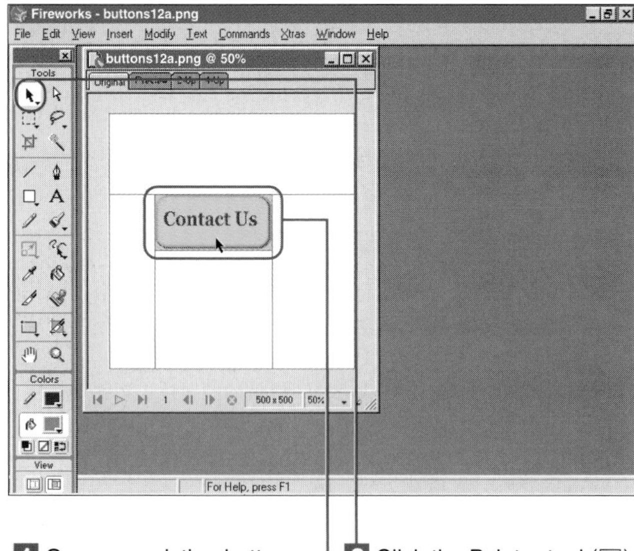

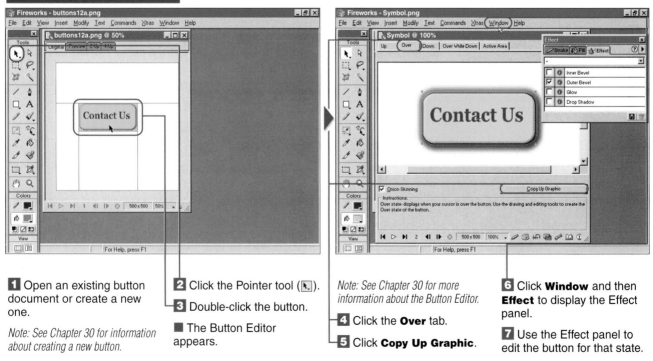

1 Open an existing button document or create a new one.

Note: See Chapter 30 for information about creating a new button.

2 Click the Pointer tool (↖).

3 Double-click the button.

■ The Button Editor appears.

Note: See Chapter 30 for more information about the Button Editor.

4 Click the **Over** tab.

5 Click **Copy Up Graphic**.

6 Click **Window** and then **Effect** to display the Effect panel.

7 Use the Effect panel to edit the button for that state.

Note: For information about the Up and Down states, see Chapter 30.

Can I use only effects to change the button in each state?

If you change the fill or stroke in one instance, that fill or stroke copies to all instances. However, you can add a new shape, button, text, or image.

CREATE THE OVER WHILE DOWN STATE

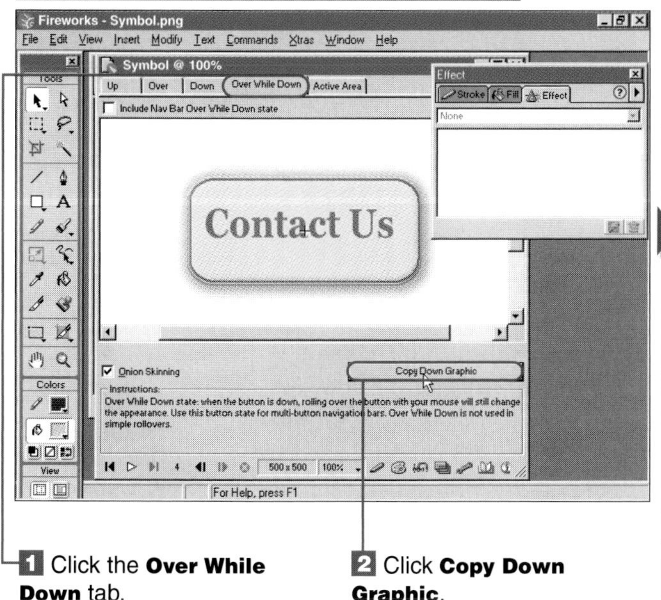

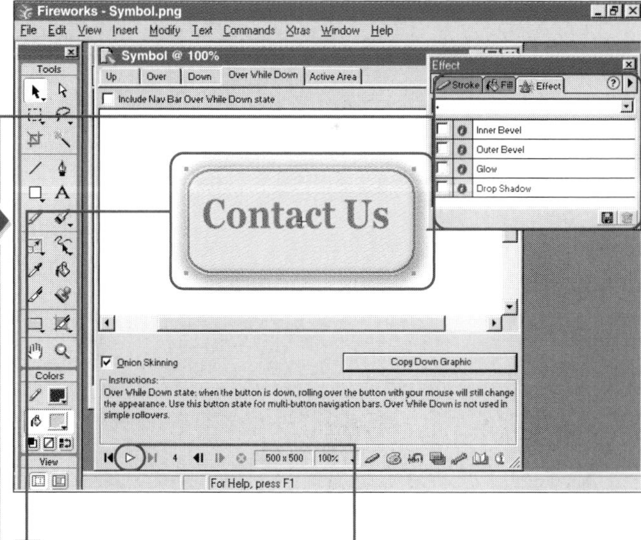

1 Click the **Over While Down** tab.

2 Click **Copy Down Graphic**.

3 Select the graphic.

4 Use the Effect panel to modify the graphic.

Note: See Chapter 29 for information about using the Effect panel.

■ You can click the Play button (▷) to see an animation of the four states.

■ You can close the Button Editor by clicking ☒.

You can apply a behavior to a hotspot or a slice to create rollovers and other actions.

ASSIGN A BEHAVIOR

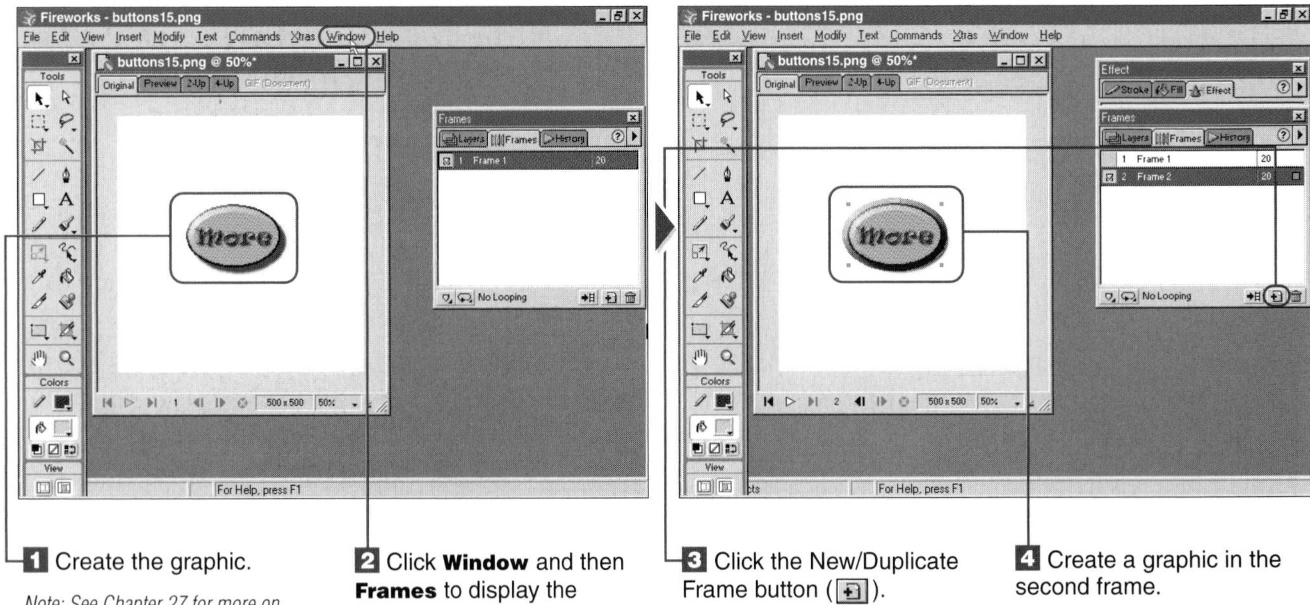

1 Create the graphic.

Note: See Chapter 27 for more on creating graphics.

2 Click **Window** and then **Frames** to display the Frames panel.

3 Click the New/Duplicate Frame button ( ).

4 Create a graphic in the second frame.

How can I create a second graphic that is similar to the first?

You can copy the original graphic. Then create a new frame and paste the graphic in that frame. You can then change the effect on either button. For more information about applying effects, see Chapter 29.

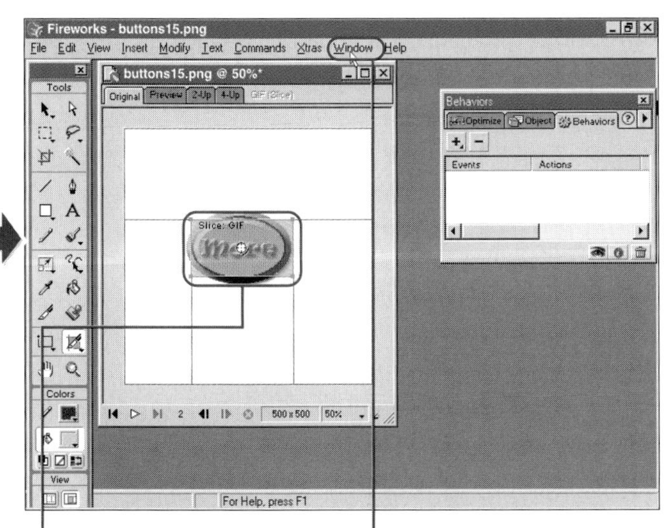

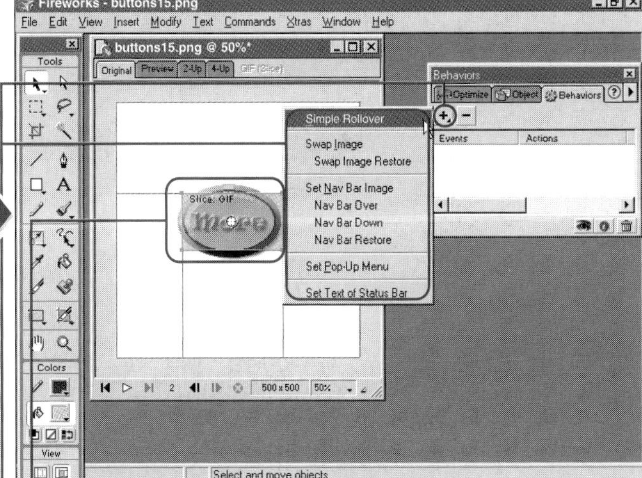

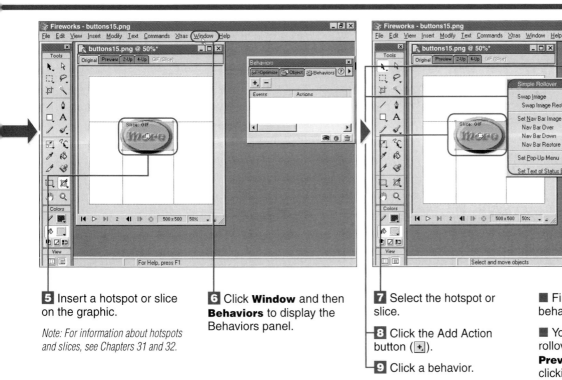

5 Insert a hotspot or slice on the graphic.

Note: For information about hotspots and slices, see Chapters 31 and 32.

6 Click **Window** and then **Behaviors** to display the Behaviors panel.

7 Select the hotspot or slice.

8 Click the Add Action button (+).

9 Click a behavior.

Note: Depending on the behavior you select, you may need to define the behavior further in a related dialog box.

- Fireworks assigns the behavior to your graphic.
- You can preview the rollover by clicking the **Preview** tab and then clicking ▷.

SWAP AN IMAGE

Using slices and behaviors, you can swap two images on your Dreamweaver Web pages in response to the cursor's movement. When you pass the cursor over one image, another image appears. When you remove the cursor, the original image returns.

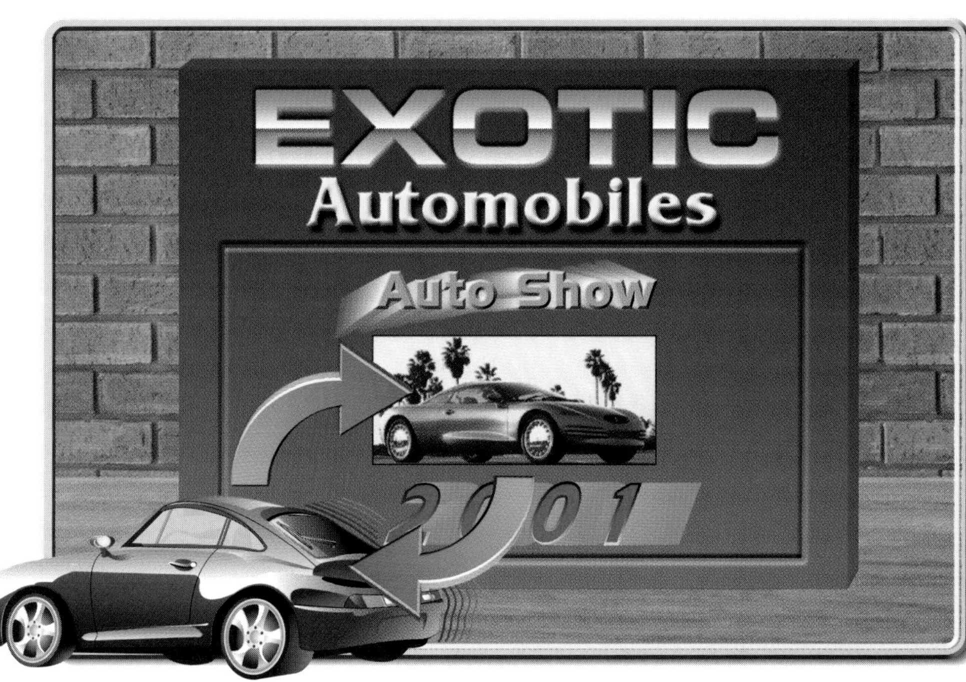

SWAP AN IMAGE

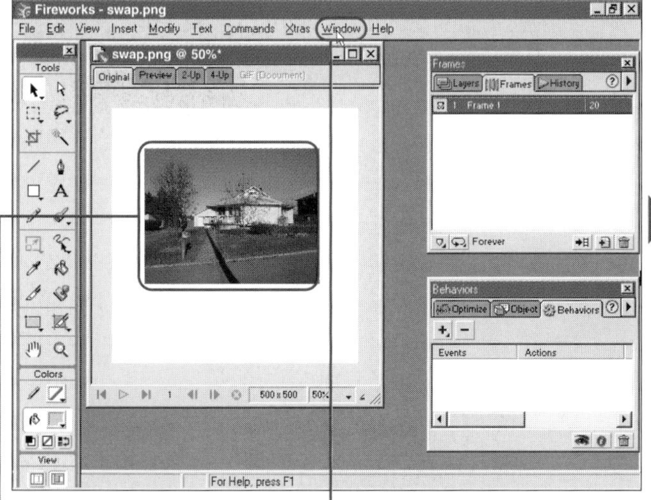

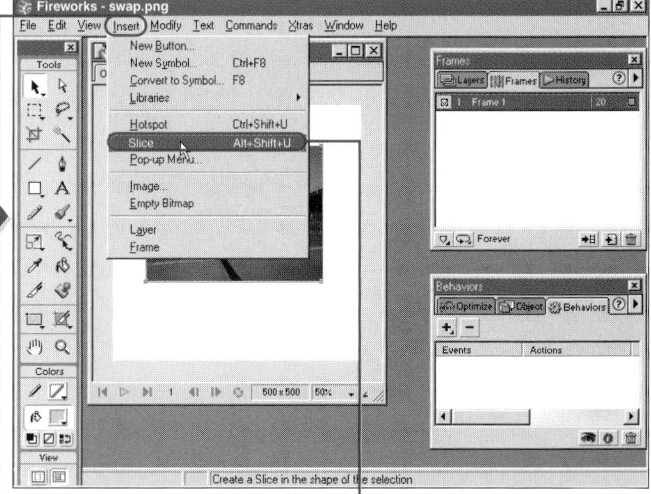

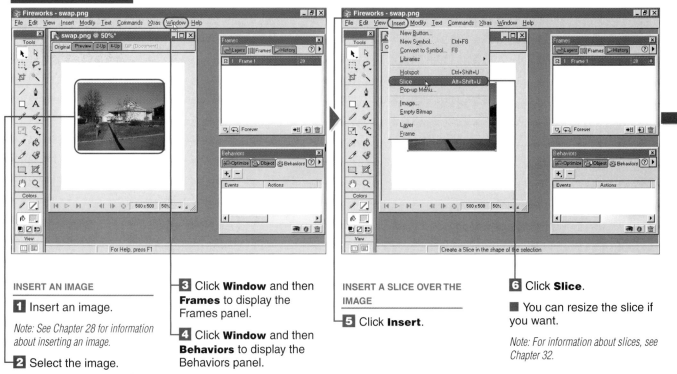

INSERT AN IMAGE

1. Insert an image.

Note: See Chapter 28 for information about inserting an image.

2. Select the image.

3. Click **Window** and then **Frames** to display the Frames panel.

4. Click **Window** and then **Behaviors** to display the Behaviors panel.

INSERT A SLICE OVER THE IMAGE

5. Click **Insert**.

6. Click **Slice**.

■ You can resize the slice if you want.

Note: For information about slices, see Chapter 32.

Should I create a larger slice or a smaller one for a rollover?

A large slice gives the Web visitor more area on which to click, and is therefore easier to see and use. However, large slices create larger files and take longer to load onto the page. Use a medium slice when in doubt.

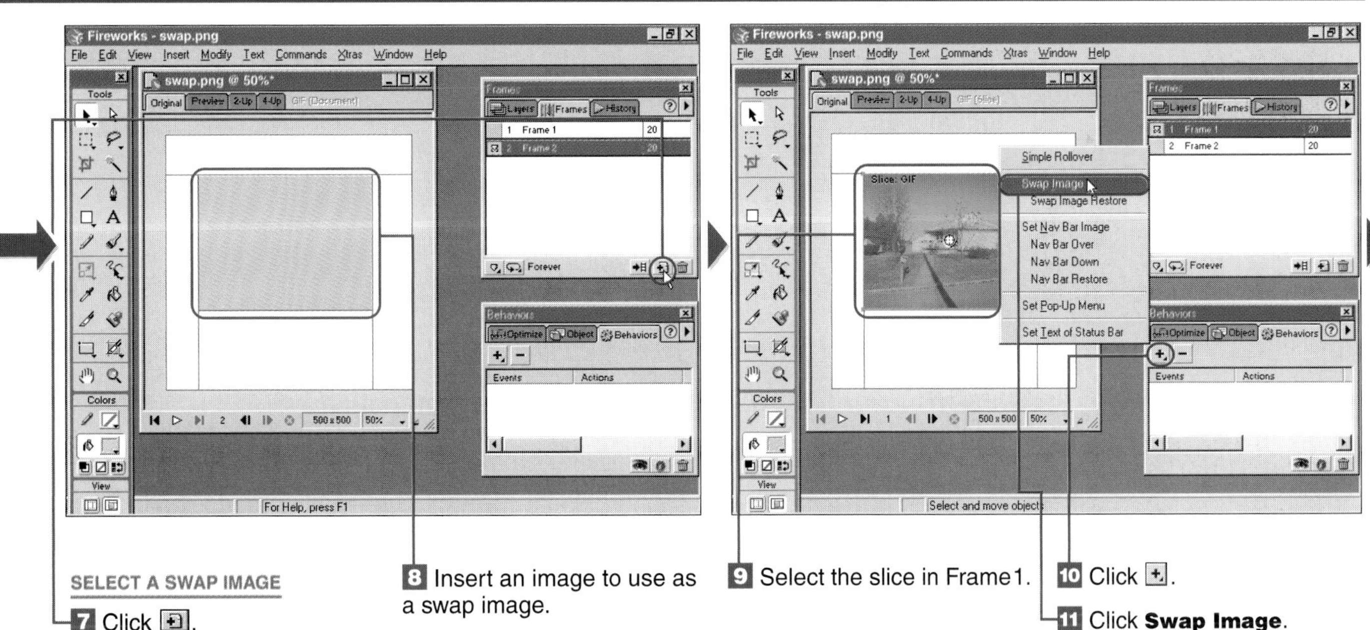

SELECT A SWAP IMAGE

7 Click ⊞.

8 Insert an image to use as a swap image.

9 Select the slice in Frame1.

10 Click ⊞.

11 Click **Swap Image**.

CONTINUED

SWAP AN IMAGE

You can choose which image Fireworks swaps with the original image, so you can try several swaps on your Dreamweaver Web page.

SWAP AN IMAGE (CONTINUED)

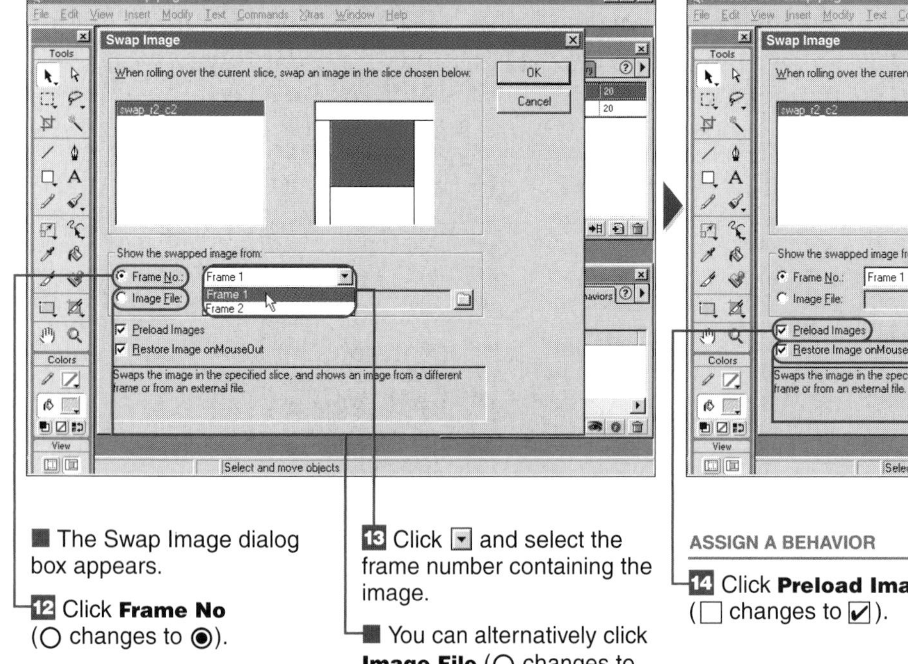

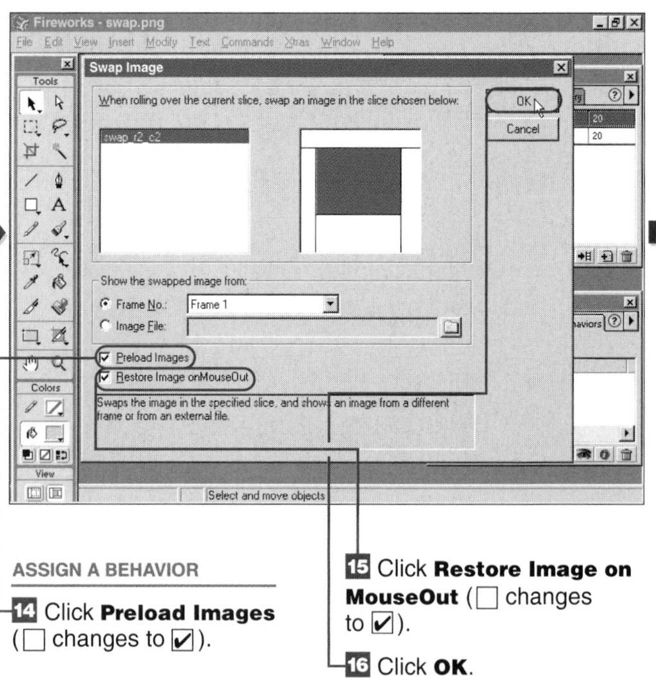

■ The Swap Image dialog box appears.

12 Click **Frame No** (○ changes to ◉).

13 Click ▾ and select the frame number containing the image.

■ You can alternatively click **Image File** (○ changes to ◉) and type the location of an image file to swap.

ASSIGN A BEHAVIOR

14 Click **Preload Images** (☐ changes to ☑).

15 Click **Restore Image on MouseOut** (☐ changes to ☑).

16 Click **OK**.

What do the Preload Images and Restore Image onMouseOut check boxes do?

Preload Images loads both images when the Web visitor opens the Dreamweaver Web page. Restore Image onMouseOut restores the first image when you move the cursor away from the image. Preload Images guarantees that there is no delay in loading the image during the mouseover.

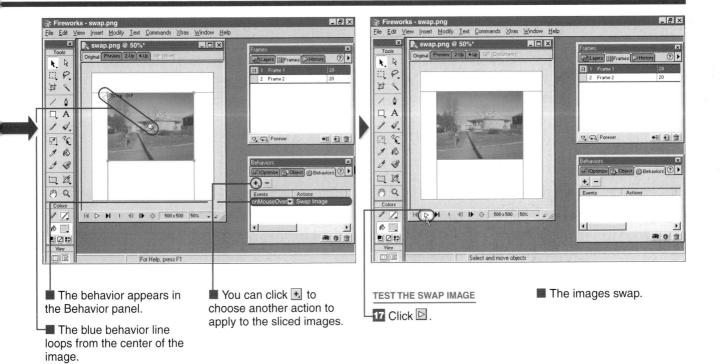

■ The behavior appears in the Behavior panel.

■ The blue behavior line loops from the center of the image.

■ You can click [+] to choose another action to apply to the sliced images.

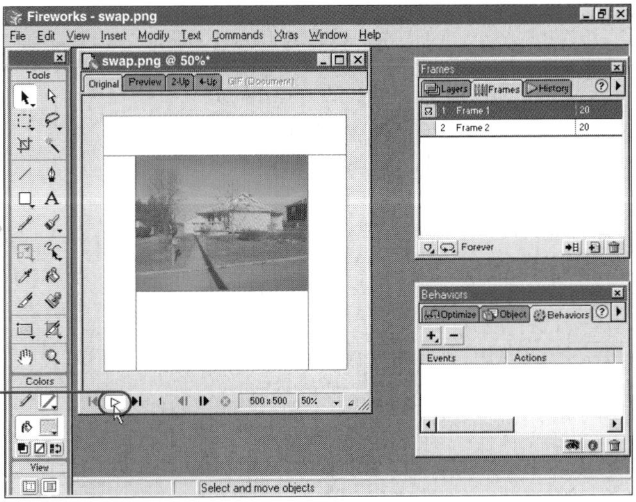

TEST THE SWAP IMAGE

17 Click [▷].

■ The images swap.

SELECT A GRAPHIC FILE FORMAT

You can use the file format that best suits the graphic so that the file loads quickly and looks its best.

FILE COMPRESSION

You want to use a file format that allows for compression so that file transfer over the Internet is fast.

GRAPHIC QUALITY

You lose some of your graphics' quality when you compress them. The different file formats have varying levels of quality because they use different types of compression. You can use the Fireworks Preview to check various formats.

PNG

Portable Network Graphic (PNG) is a flexible Web graphic format; some Web browsers, however, cannot view PNG. PNG is the original Fireworks file format. You can use PNG for line art and for images.

JPEG

The Joint Photographic Experts Group (JPEG) format is perfect for photographs, scanned images, images with textures, and gradient color objects.

GIF

The Graphics Interchange File (GIF) format is used for static or animated graphics. Use the GIF format for logos, cartoons, animations, and vector objects.

OPTIMIZE PNGS AND GIFS

You can optimize PNG and GIF graphics before you export them to make sure that they load on to the Dreamweaver Web page quickly.

You use similar optimization settings for PNGs and GIFs.

OPTIMIZE PNGS AND GIFS

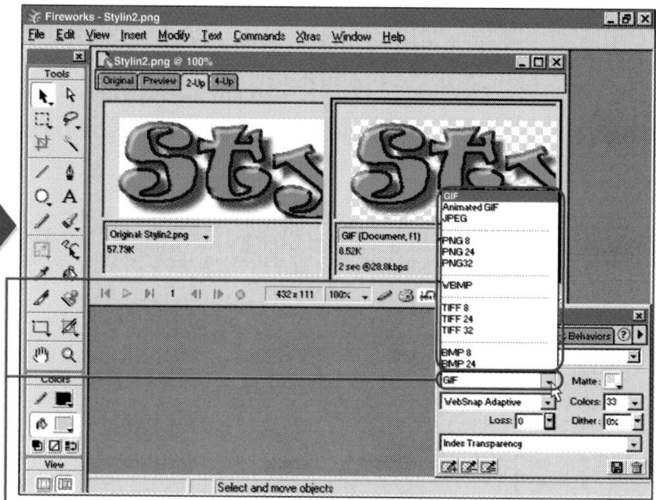

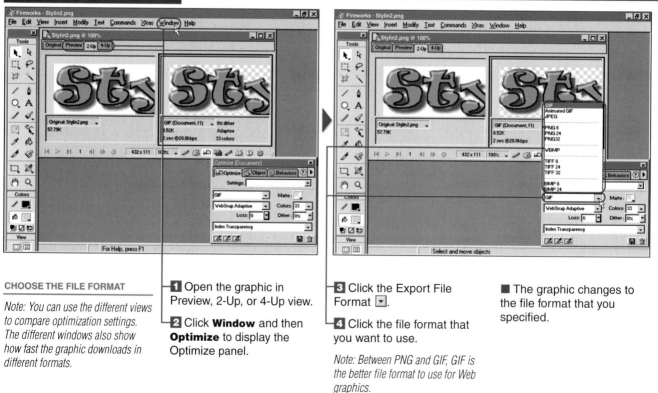

CHOOSE THE FILE FORMAT

Note: You can use the different views to compare optimization settings. The different windows also show how fast the graphic downloads in different formats.

1 Open the graphic in Preview, 2-Up, or 4-Up view.

2 Click **Window** and then **Optimize** to display the Optimize panel.

3 Click the Export File Format ▾.

4 Click the file format that you want to use.

Note: Between PNG and GIF, GIF is the better file format to use for Web graphics.

■ The graphic changes to the file format that you specified.

How does changing the indexed palette affect the changes I make in the Color Table?

The colors remain similar. The difference is whether the colors are suitable for the Web. WebSnap Adaptive or Web 216 are best for Internet graphics.

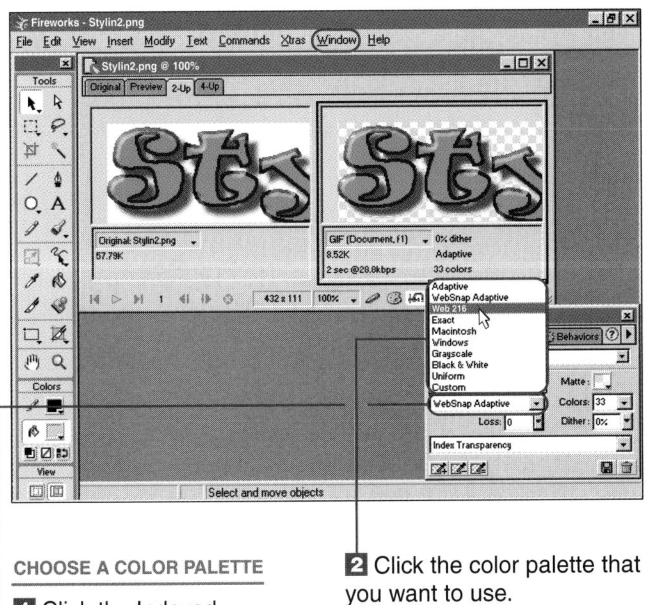

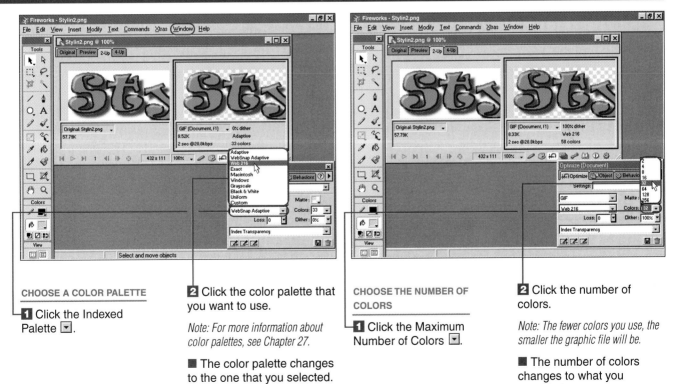

CHOOSE A COLOR PALETTE

1 Click the Indexed Palette ▼.

2 Click the color palette that you want to use.

Note: For more information about color palettes, see Chapter 27.

■ The color palette changes to the one that you selected.

CHOOSE THE NUMBER OF COLORS

1 Click the Maximum Number of Colors ▼.

2 Click the number of colors.

Note: The fewer colors you use, the smaller the graphic file will be.

■ The number of colors changes to what you specified.

CONTINUED

You can make the canvas color and other colors appear transparent so that the Dreamweaver Web page's background color shows through a portion of the graphic.

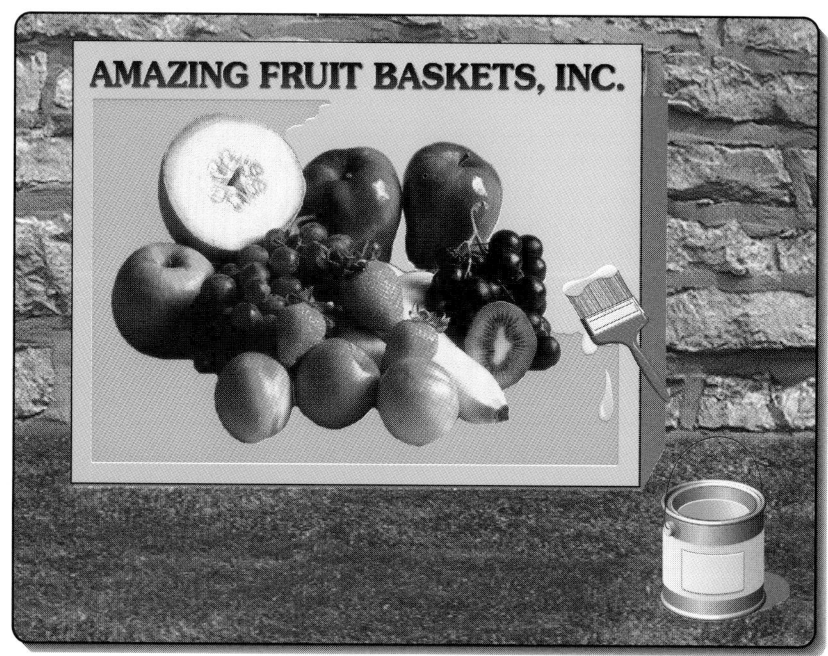

OPTIMIZE PNGS AND GIFS (CONTINUED)

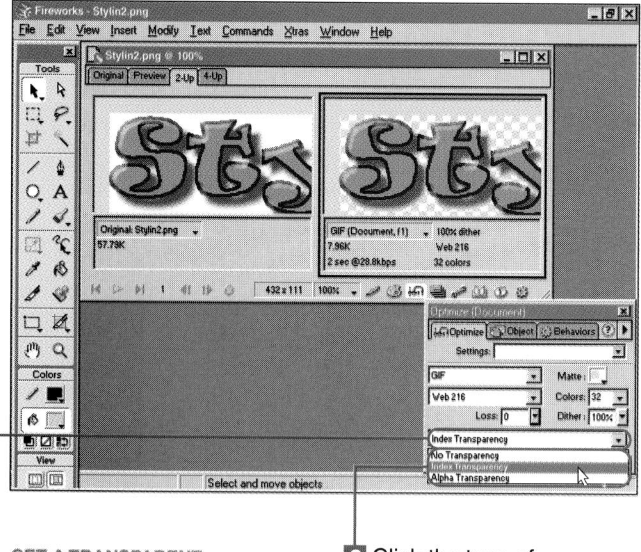

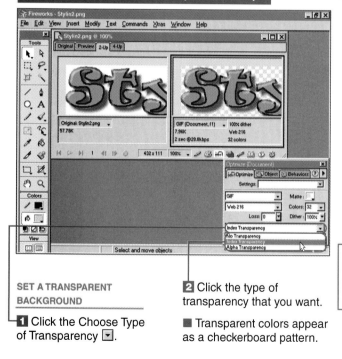

SET A TRANSPARENT BACKGROUND

1 Click the Choose Type of Transparency ▼.

2 Click the type of transparency that you want.

■ Transparent colors appear as a checkerboard pattern.

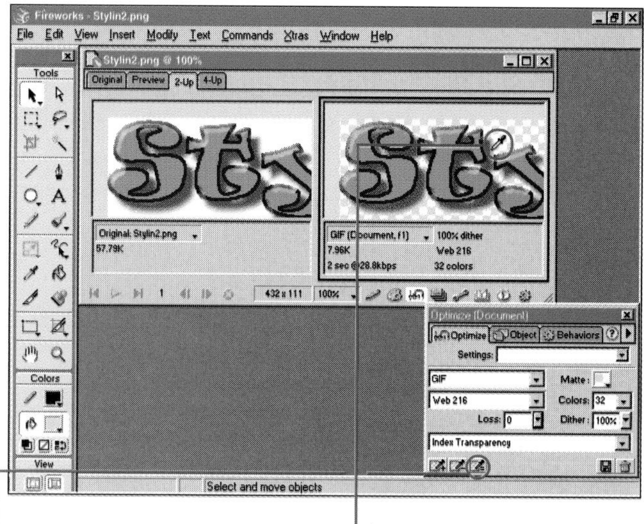

SET A TRANSPARENT COLOR

1 Click the Set Transparent Index Color button ( ) (changes to).

2 Click the color in the graphic that you want to be transparent.

■ Every instance of that color in the graphic becomes transparent.

What is the difference between index and alpha transparency?

Index transparency makes the selected color or canvas transparent. If you choose to make white transparent, for example, index transparency makes everything white in the graphic, plus the canvas, transparent. Alpha transparency makes a color appear transparent when viewed in a Web browser. You can use alpha transparency to touch up the color around a graphic so that it does not bleed into the background of the Dreamweaver Web page.

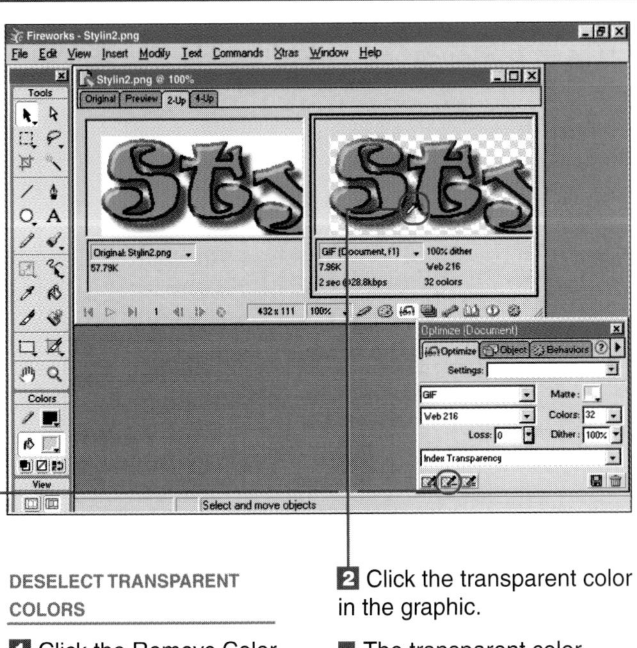

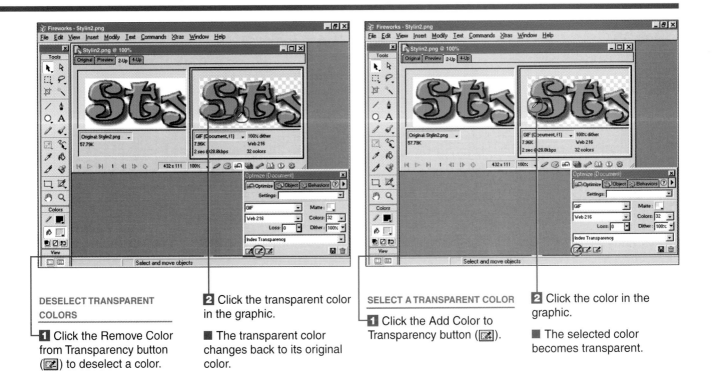

DESELECT TRANSPARENT COLORS

1 Click the Remove Color from Transparency button (▨) to deselect a color.

2 Click the transparent color in the graphic.

■ The transparent color changes back to its original color.

SELECT A TRANSPARENT COLOR

1 Click the Add Color to Transparency button (▨).

2 Click the color in the graphic.

■ The selected color becomes transparent.

OPTIMIZE JPEGS

You can optimize a JPEG to create a smaller file and speed loading time.

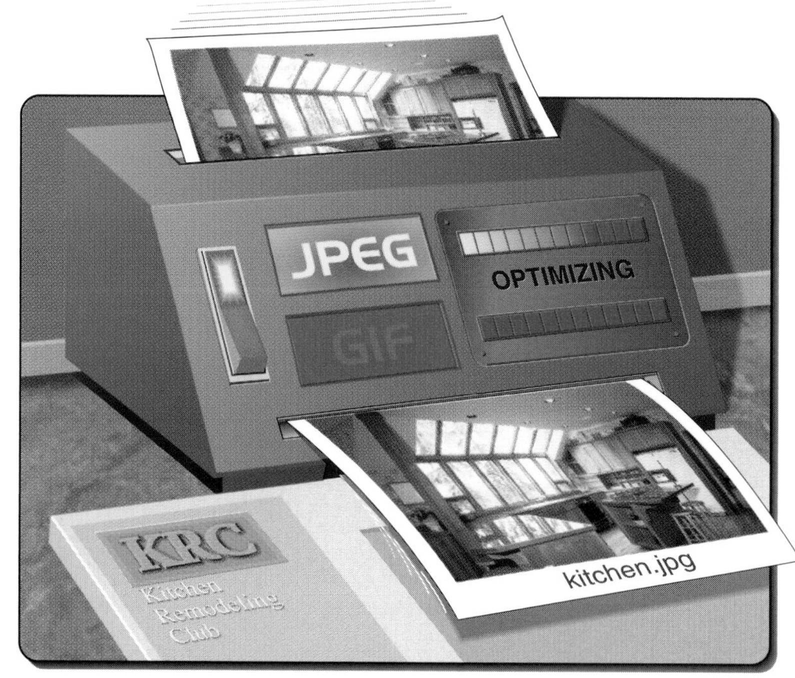

Optimizing a JPEG reduces the quality of the image.

OPTIMIZE JPEGS

1 Open the Preview, 2-Up, or 4-Up view of the image.

2 Click **Window** and then **Optimize** to display the Optimize panel.

■ If the file format is not already JPEG, you can click ▾ to change it to JPEG.

3 Click the Quality ▾.

4 Click and drag the slider to indicate the quality.

How do I decide which quality setting to use?

Quality is measured in percentage — from 0 to 100 percent. The higher the percentage, the more quality yet less compression in the graphic. You can lower the quality percentage quite a bit before you notice changes in the image.

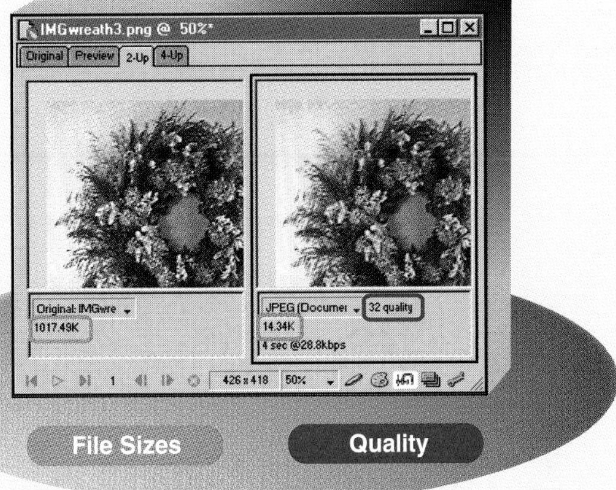

5 Click the Smoothing Level ▾.

6 Click the number that you want to use.

Note: Smoothing blurs the entire image so that the results of the compression are less noticeable. You can start with a 4 or 5 and see how the picture looks before you change it to a higher or lower number.

7 Click the Options ▸.

8 Confirm that **Remove Unused Colors** is checked.

Note: Clicking the command when it is checked removes the check mark.

■ The JPEG is optimized for export.

EXPORT AN AREA OR AN ENTIRE GRAPHIC IMAGE

You can choose to export a graphic or image from the Export Preview dialog box or from the File menu.

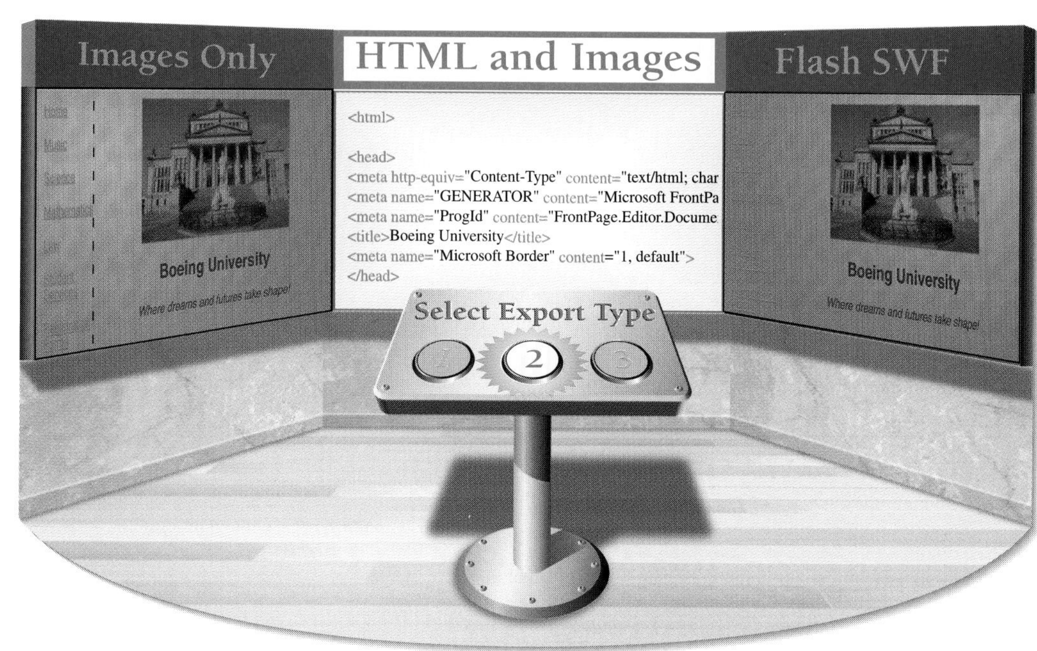

EXPORT AN ENTIRE GRAPHIC OR IMAGE

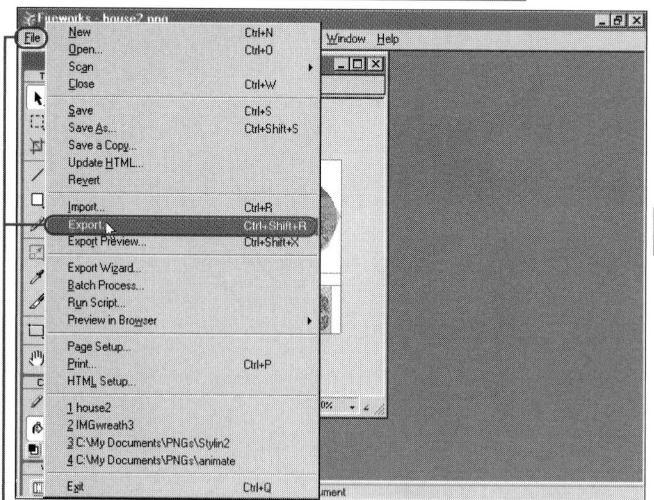

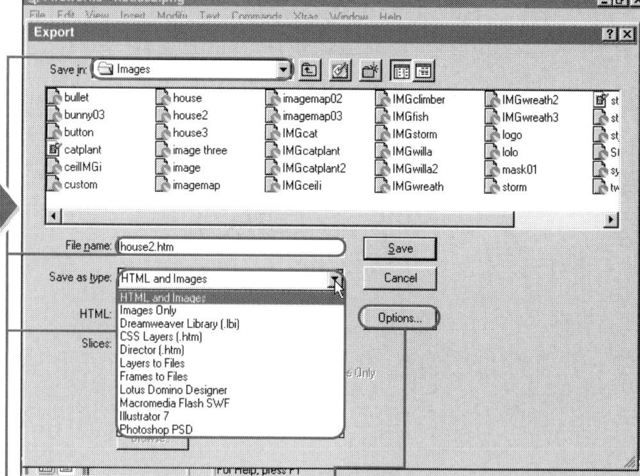

1 Click **File**.

2 Click **Export**.

*Note: From the Export Preview window, you can click **Export** to open the Export dialog box.*

■ The Export dialog box appears.

3 Click ▾ and choose a folder.

4 Type a name or accept the name that Fireworks provides.

5 Click the Save as Type ▾ and select a file type.

*Note: To export only an image, click **Images Only**.*

■ If you choose **HTML and Images**, click **Options**.

*Note: If you do not choose **HTML and Images**, skip to step **6**.*

Which file type should I save the file as?

If you export the file to another program — such as Illustrator, Flash, or Photoshop — to continue work on the file, choose that file type. If you export the file for use in another program — such as Dreamweaver or FrontPage, you can save the file as HTML and Images.

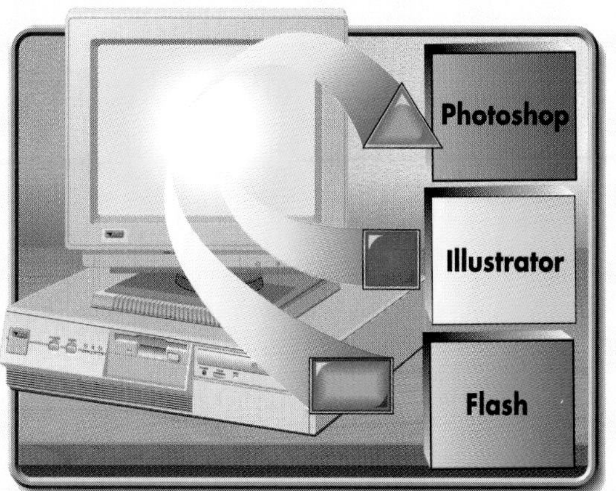

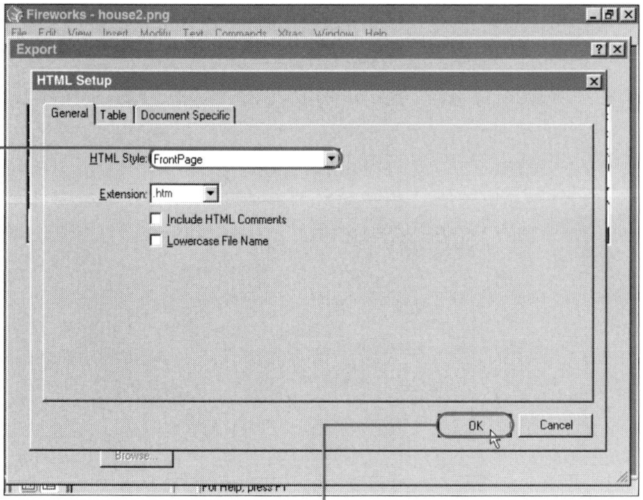

SET HTML OPTIONS (IF USING THE HTML AND IMAGES FILE TYPE)

■ Click the HTML Style ▾ and select the HTML editor that you plan to use.

Note: For more information about HTML editors, see Chapter 36.

■ Click **OK**.

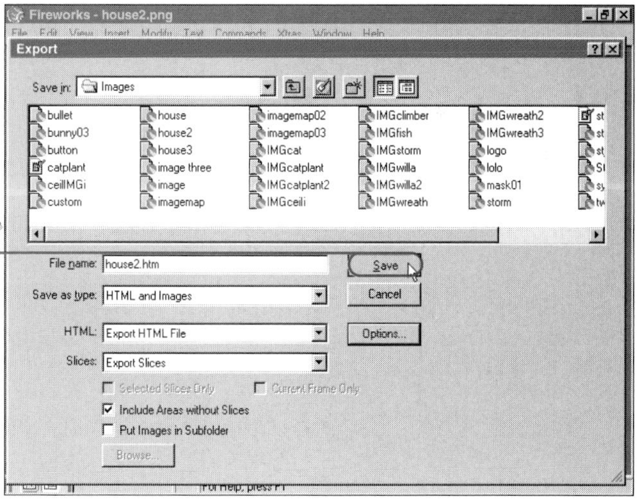

EXPORT THE IMAGE

6 Click **Save**.

■ Fireworks exports the document.

EXPORT A SLICE

You can export one slice from any graphic to save load time and limit file size on a Dreamweaver Web page.

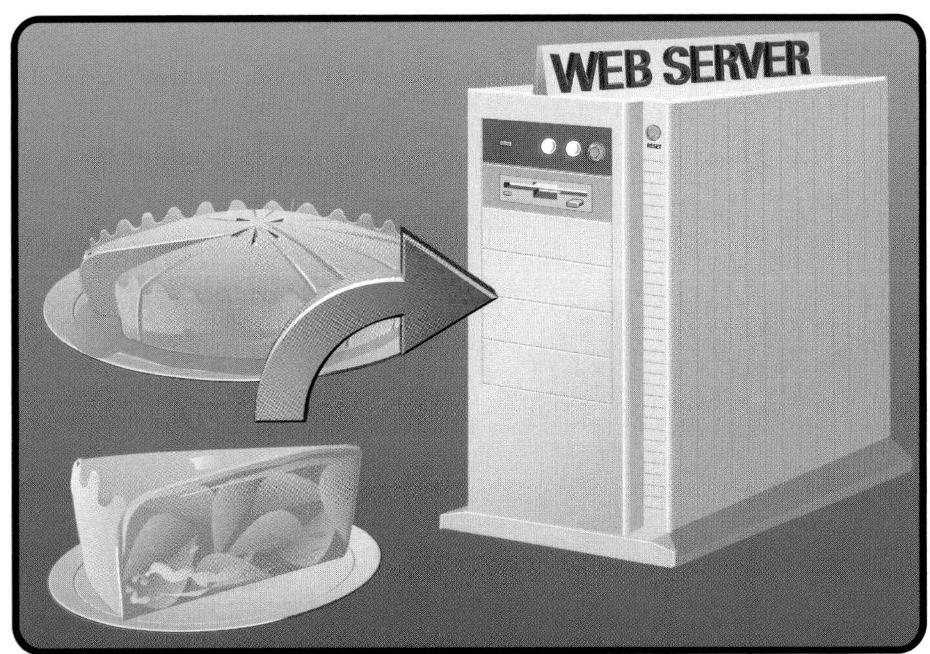

EXPORT A SLICE

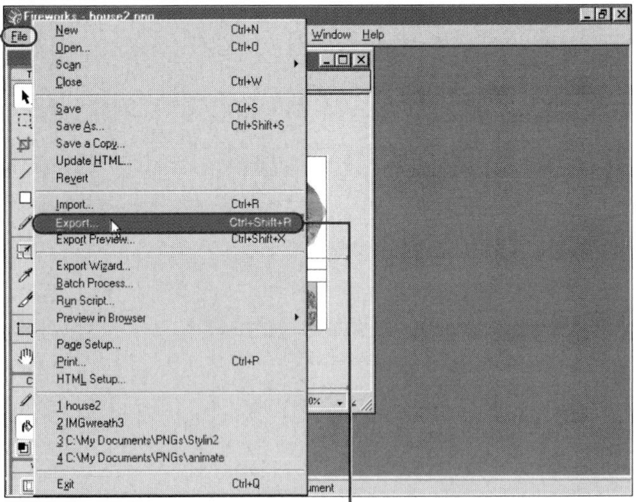

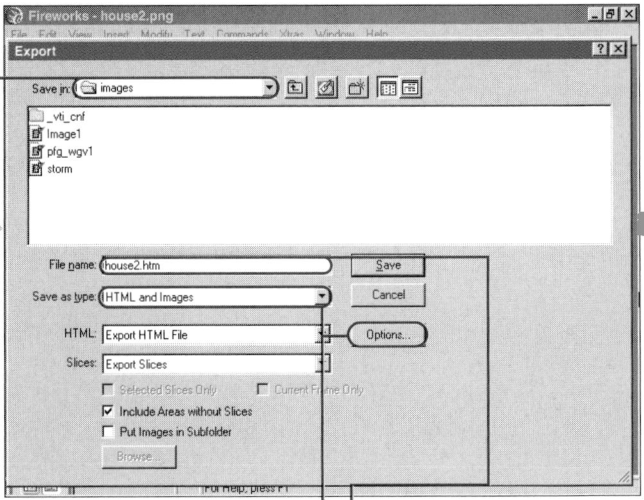

1 Select the slice.

2 Click **File**.

3 Click **Export**.

■ The Export dialog box appears.

4 Click ▾ and choose a location.

5 Type a filename.

6 Choose a file type and set HTML options if you choose the HTML format.

Should I choose Export Slices or Slice Along Guides in the Export dialog box?

Generally, choose **Export Slices.** Choose **Slice Along Guides** to divide a large image into multiple slices using the guides and only when there are no behaviors attached to the image.

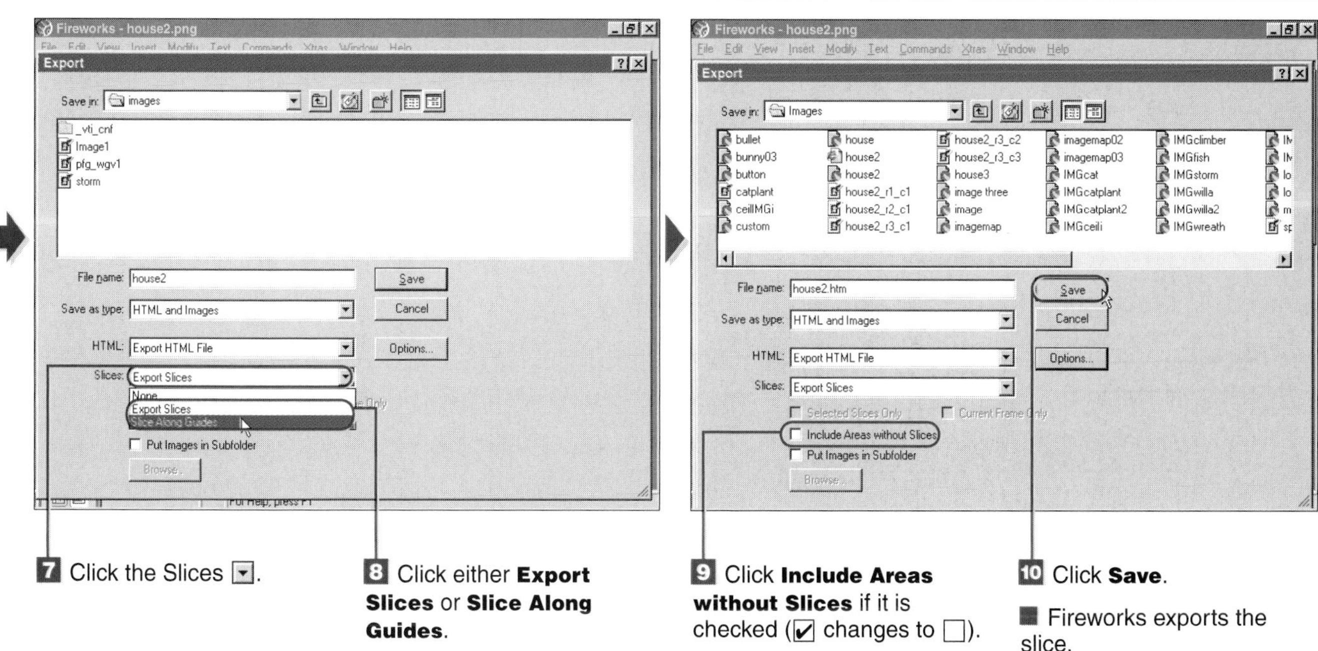

7 Click the Slices ▾.

8 Click either **Export Slices** or **Slice Along Guides**.

9 Click **Include Areas without Slices** if it is checked (☑ changes to ☐).

10 Click **Save**.

■ Fireworks exports the slice.

EXPORT LAYERS OR FRAMES

You can export layers or frames as separate image files so that each layer or frame file is smaller than the original file.

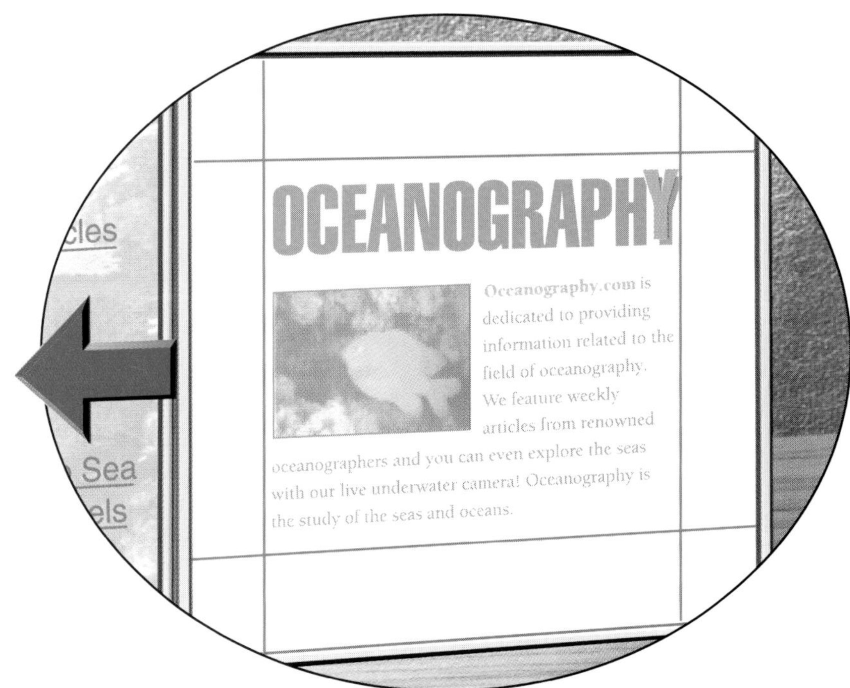

EXPORT LAYERS OR FRAMES

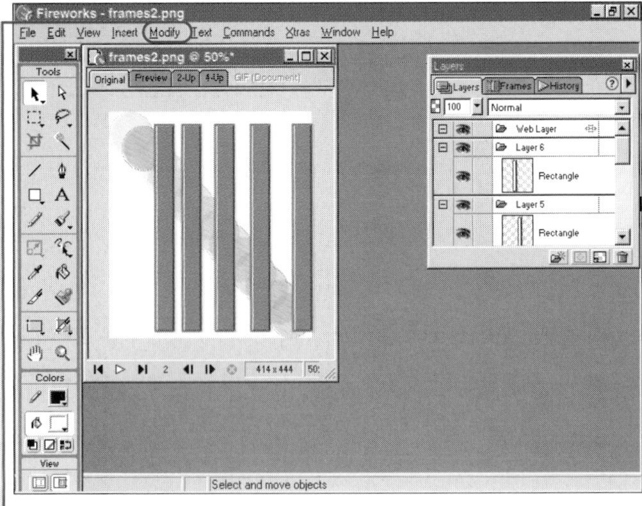

Note: Before exporting, you should optimize your graphic (see Chapter 34) and trim its canvas.

■ To trim the canvas, you can click **Modify** and then **Trim Canvas**.

■ The canvas trims to include all graphics in all frames or layers.

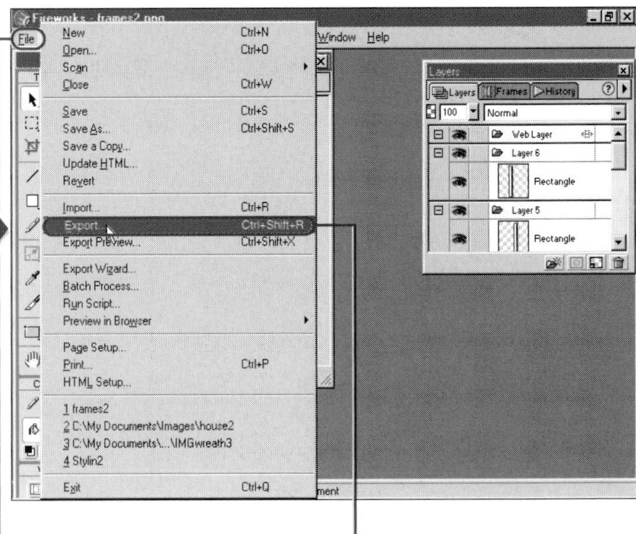

1 Click **File**.

2 Click **Export**.

How does Fireworks name files when you export a graphic or image?

When you export layers or frames, Fireworks names each file with the document name and the name of the layer or frame. For example, a frame filename may be `house_f13`; `house` is the name of the document, and `_f13` is the frame. You can change the name of the document when you type the filename in the Export dialog box.

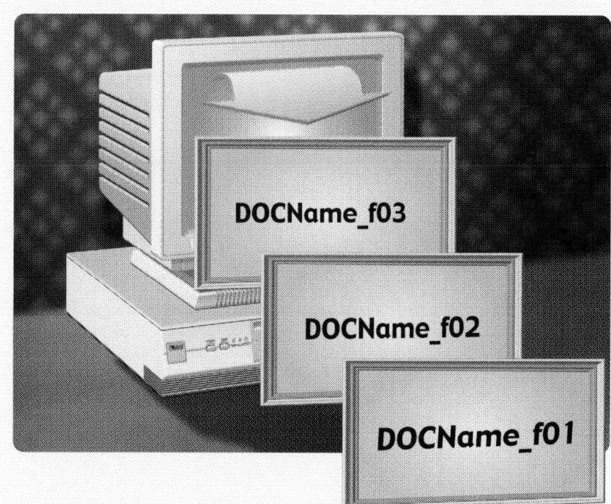

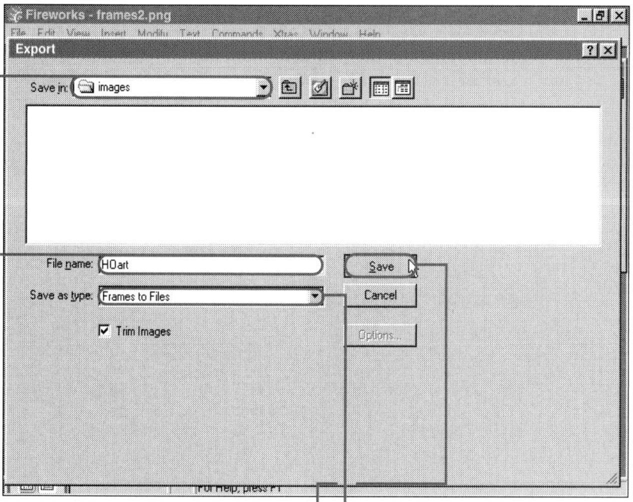

■ The Export dialog box appears.

3 Click ▾ and designate the folder to save in.

4 Type a filename.

5 Click the Save As Type ▾ and click either **Layers to Files** or **Frames to Files**, depending on which you are exporting.

6 Click **Save**.

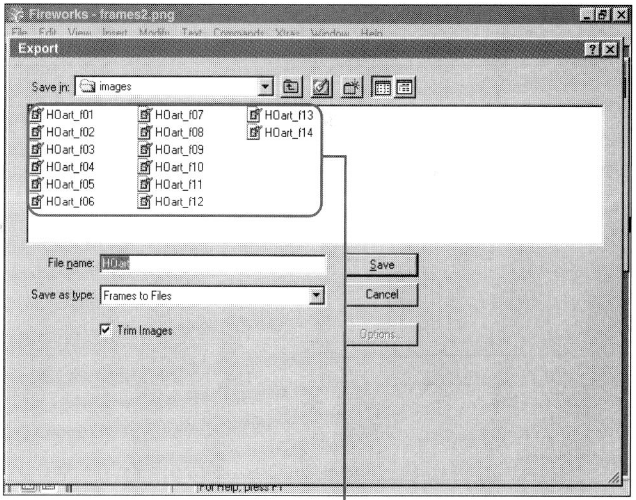

■ Fireworks saves each layer or frame to a file.

7 To view the saved filenames, click **File** and then **Export** to again open the Export dialog box.

EXPORT AN IMAGE MAP

You can export an image map to a Dreamweaver HTML file format. Until you export the image map, it does not function as an image map in the Web browser.

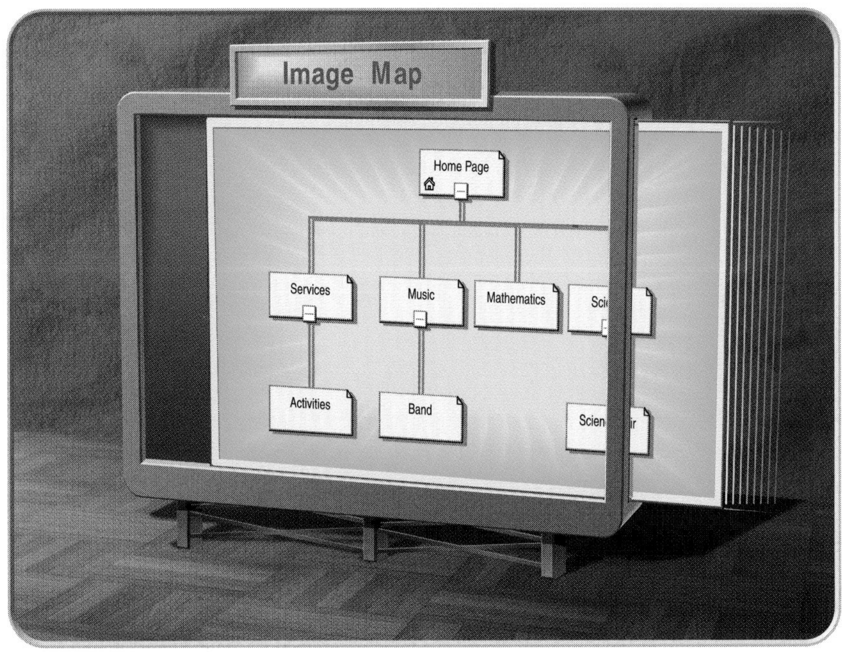

EXPORT AN IMAGE MAP

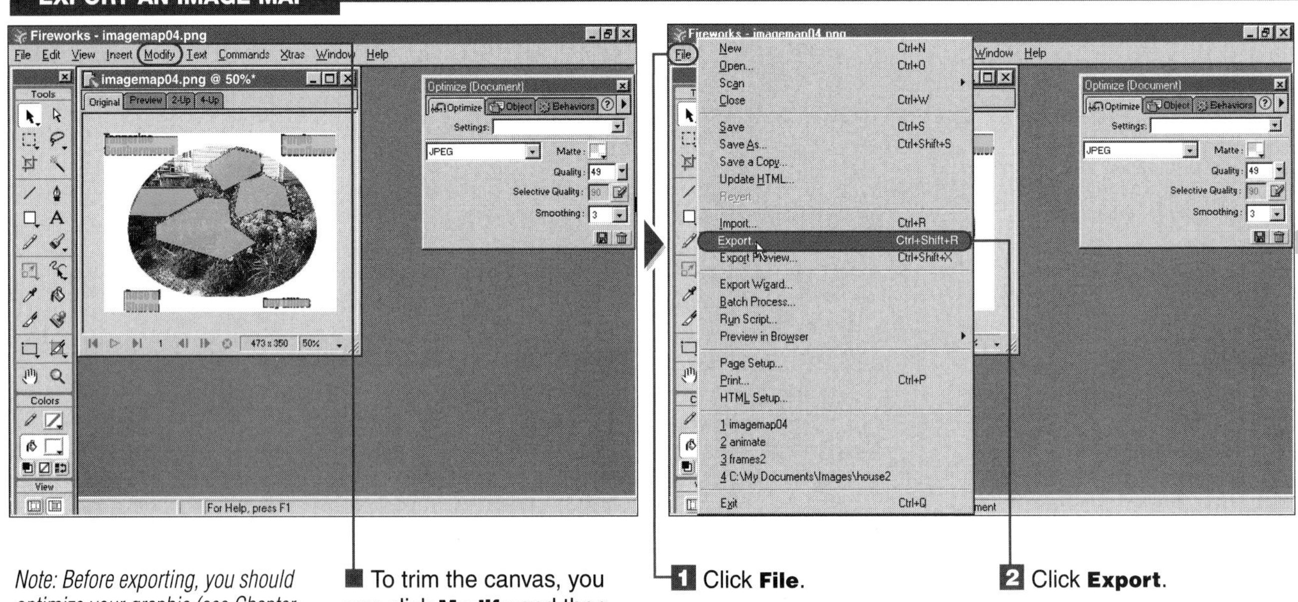

Note: Before exporting, you should optimize your graphic (see Chapter 34) and trim its canvas.

■ To trim the canvas, you can click **Modify** and then **Trim Canvas**.

1 Click **File**.

2 Click **Export**.

What does the exported image map file contain?

The exported image map file contains the graphic file, the HTML file, and all the information for hotspots and URL links.

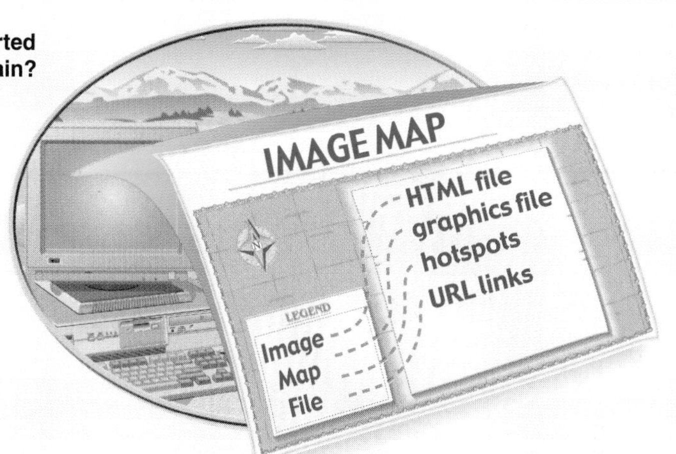

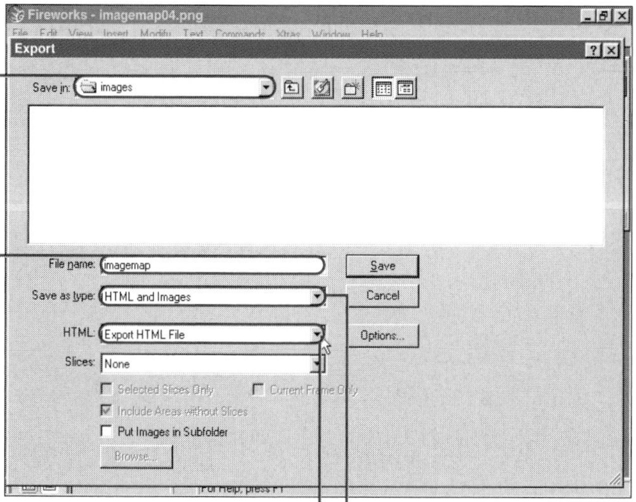

■ The Export dialog box appears.

3 Click ▼ and designate the folder to save to.

4 Type the name of the file.

5 Make sure that **HTML and Images** is selected.

6 Make sure that **Export HTML File** is selected.

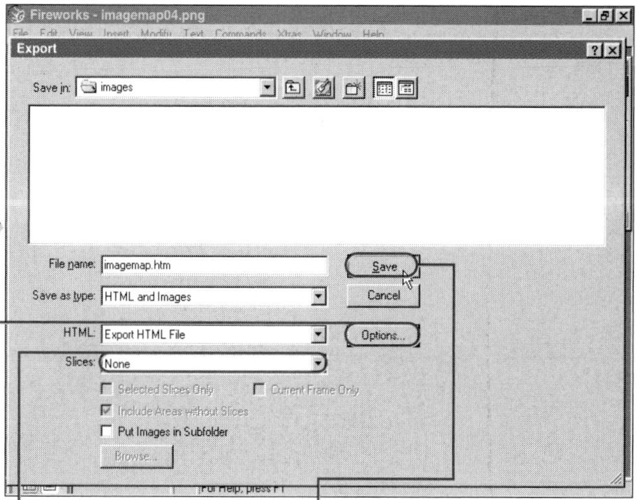

7 Click the Slices ▼ and click **None**.

8 Click **Options**.

9 In the HTML Setup dialog box, click ▼ and click the HTML editor that you want to export to.

10 Click **OK** in the HTML Setup dialog box.

11 Click **Save**.

COPY AND PASTE HTML

You can copy HTML code to the Clipboard and then paste the code into an HTML editor like Dreamweaver.

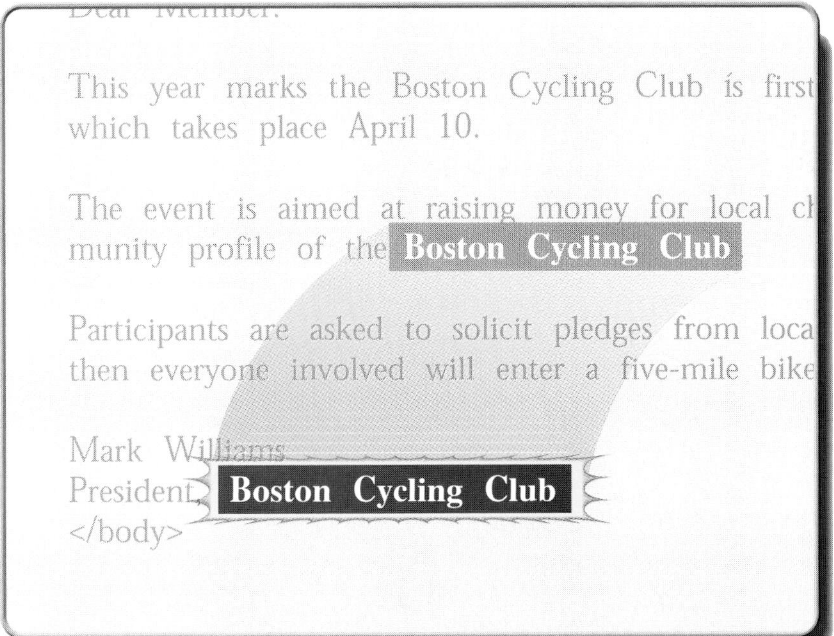

COPY AND PASTE HTML

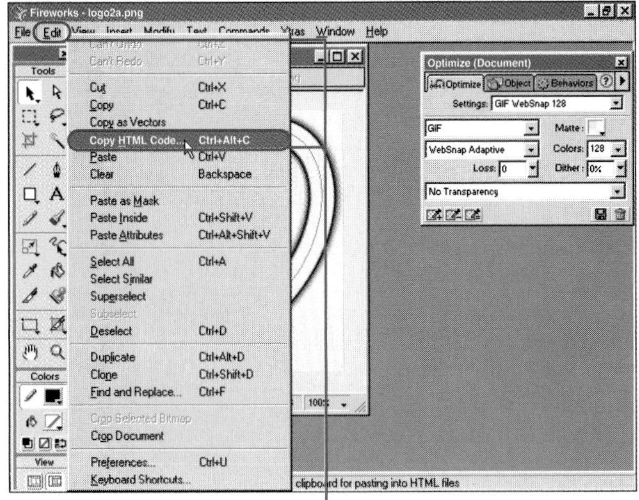

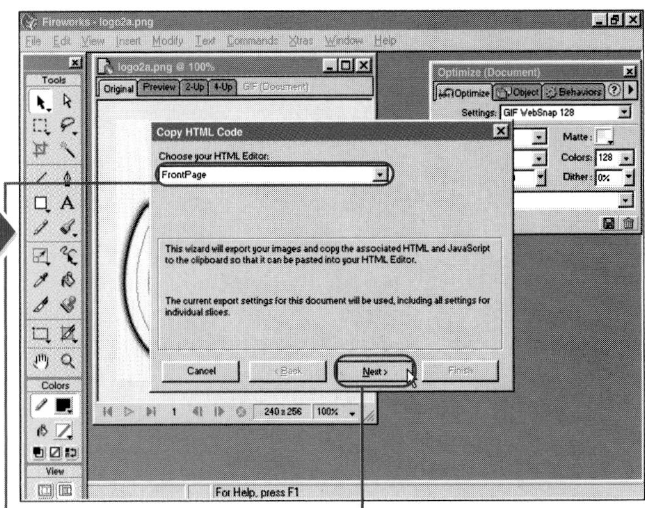

COPY HTML

Note: It is a good idea to optimize and prepare the graphic for exporting before copying and pasting the HTML (see Chapters 34 and 35).

1 Select the graphic to be copied.

2 Click **Edit**.

3 Click **Copy HTML Code**.

■ The Copy HTML Code dialog box appears.

4 Click the HTML Editor ▼ and select the editor that you plan to use.

5 Click **Next**.

Does it matter to which folder I save the HTML file?

If you are using Dreamweaver, the HTML file saves automatically to the right folder. If you use a different HTML editor, you must save the Fireworks HTML file to the same folder as the HTML document in the HTML editor.

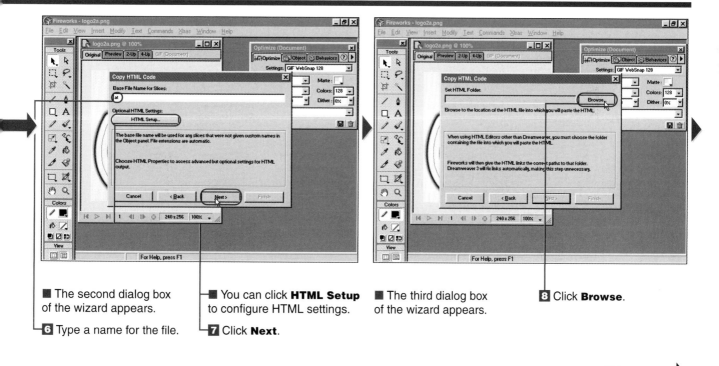

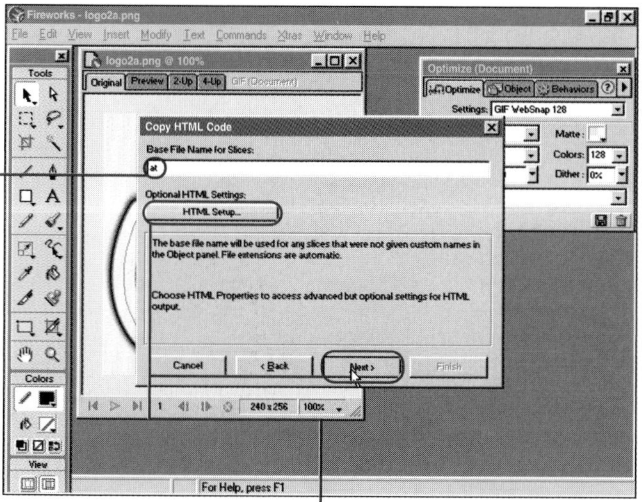

■ The second dialog box of the wizard appears.

6 Type a name for the file.

■ You can click **HTML Setup** to configure HTML settings.

7 Click **Next**.

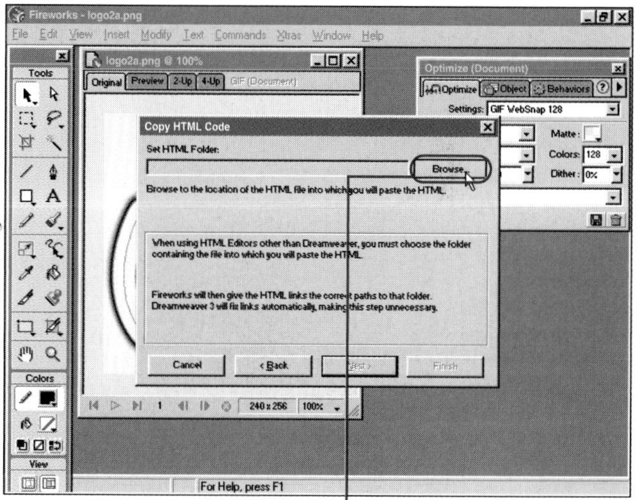

■ The third dialog box of the wizard appears.

8 Click **Browse**.

CONTINUED

COPY AND PASTE HTML

You can paste the HTML into a folder where all images are exported.

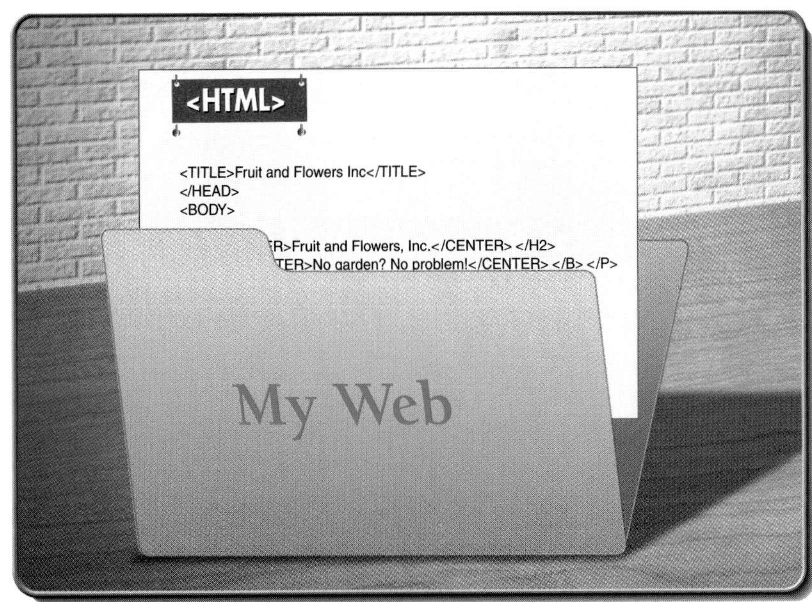

COPY AND PASTE HTML (CONTINUED)

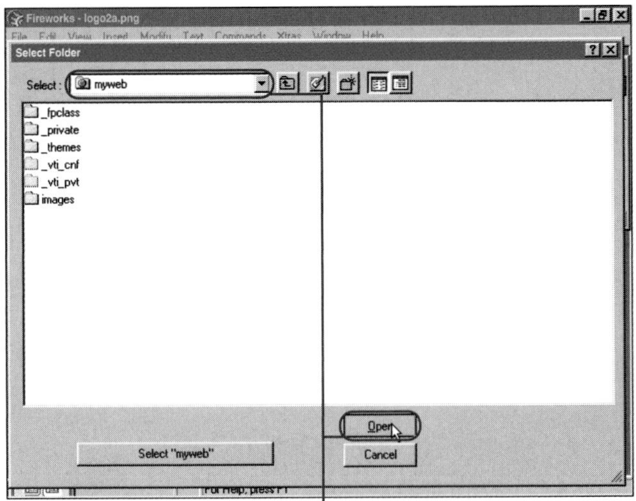

■ The Select Folder dialog box appears.

9 Click ▾ and choose the destination folder.

10 Click **Open**.

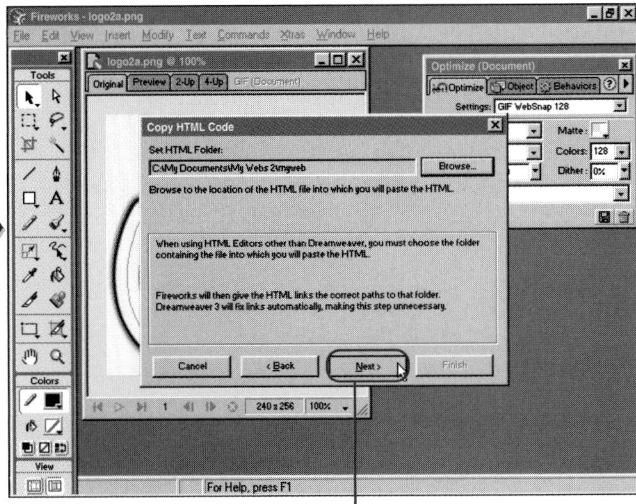

■ The Select Folder dialog box closes, returning you to the Copy HTML Code dialog box.

11 Click **Next**.

■ The next dialog box of the wizard appears, in which you choose a folder for saving your exported images.

Why do I have to set up two HTML folders?

When you choose an HTML editor other than Dreamweaver, you must set up an extra HTML folder to hold the file that you are pasting. When you choose Dreamweaver as your HTML editor, Dreamweaver automatically corrects paths and links to the file.

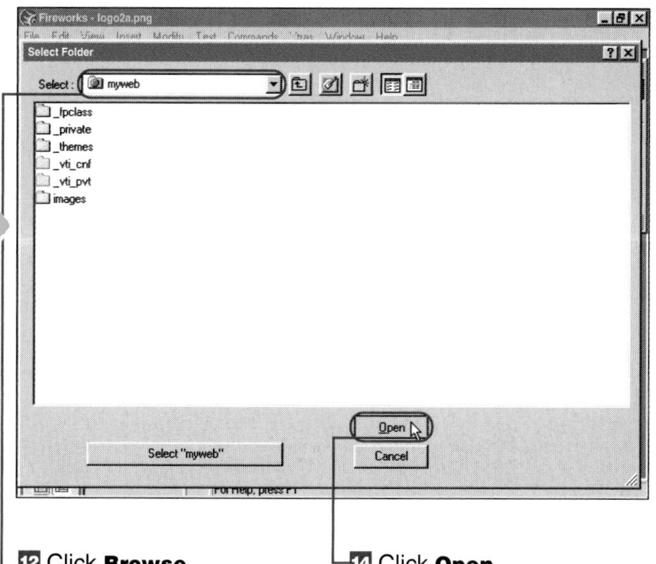

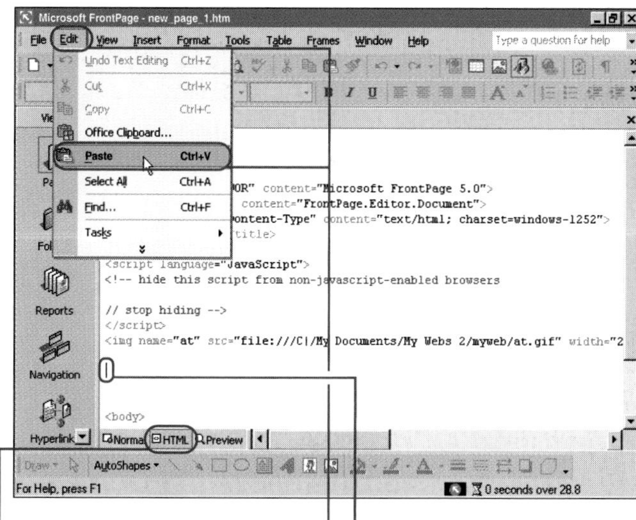

12 Click **Browse**.

■ The Select Folder dialog box appears.

13 Click ▾ and choose the destination folder.

*Note: You should use the same folder used in step **9**.*

14 Click **Open**.

15 Click **Finish** in the Copy HTML Code dialog box.

■ The HTML is copied to the clipboard, ready to be pasted.

Note: If you need to update the HTML, you can export the HTML again and overwrite the older file.

PASTE HTML

1 Open the HTML view in your HTML editor.

*Note: The procedure for performing step **1** depends on the HTML editor. In FrontPage, you click the **HTML** view tab to display the HTML view.*

2 Click to position the cursor where you want to paste the HTML.

3 Click **Edit**.

4 Click **Paste**.

■ The HTML is pasted into the document.

COPY HTML FOR SLICED OBJECTS

You can copy HTML code for a sliced object or multiple objects in the Fireworks document.

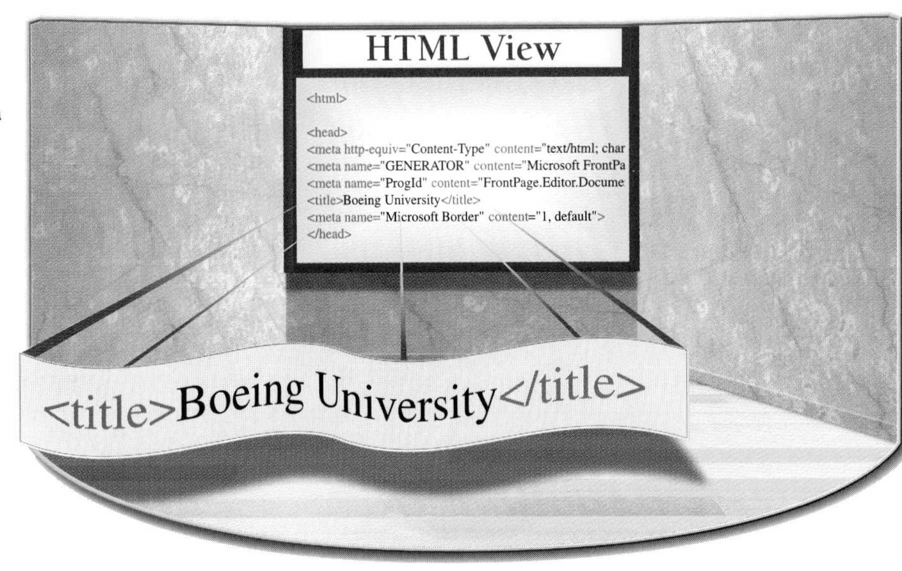

View the HTML code in a text editor and copy just the code you need.

COPY HTML FOR SLICED OBJECTS

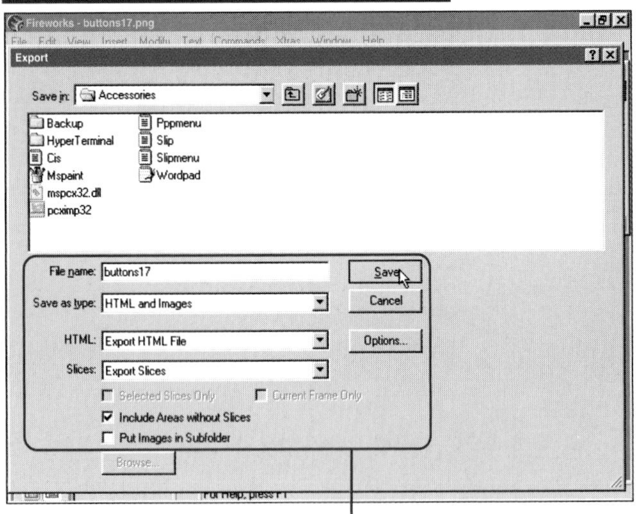

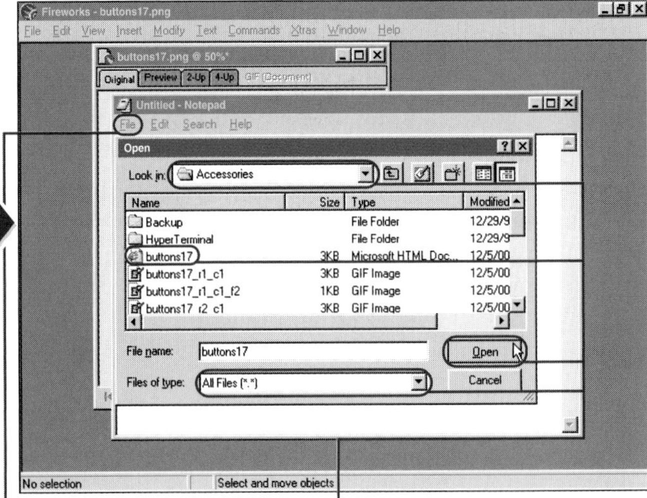

1 Select one or more slices in the Fireworks document.

2 Click **File** and then **Export**.

■ The Export dialog box appears.

3 Export the slices (see Chapter 35).

*Note: Select **HTML and Images** as the type. In the HTML Setup dialog box, select **Generic** as the HTML style.*

Note: Export the HTML file to the same folder as your HTML editor.

4 Open a text editor, such as Notepad.

5 Open the HTML document.

■ To do so in Notepad, first click **File** and then **Open**.

■ Click the Look In ▾ and browse to the folder where you exported the slice file.

■ Click the Files of Type ▾ and select **All Files**.

■ Click the name of the HTML document and then click **Open**.

How do I know what to copy from the HTML file?

Fireworks uses the `<table>` tag to identify the beginning of the slice information and the `</table>` tag to indicate the end of the slice information.

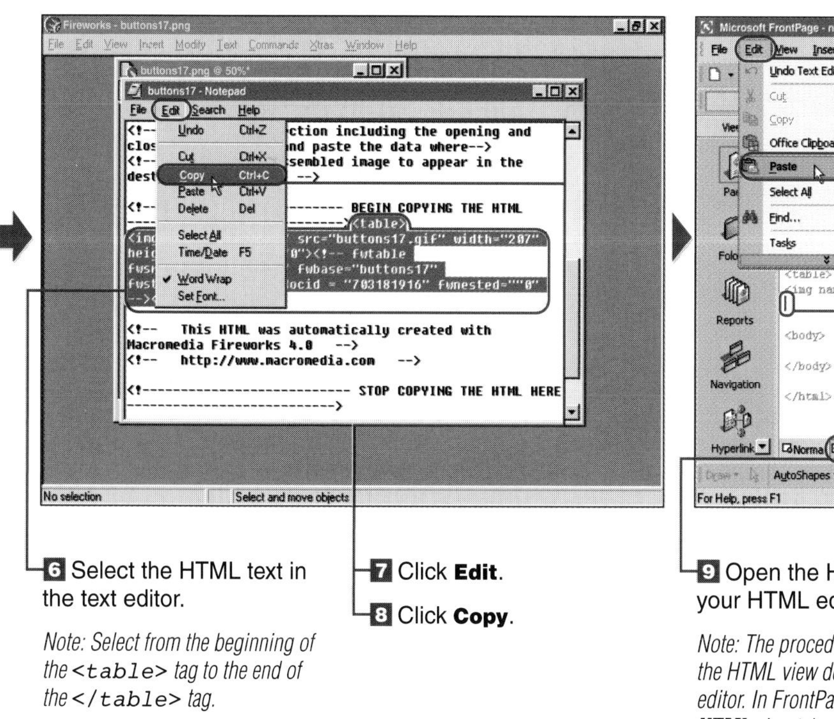

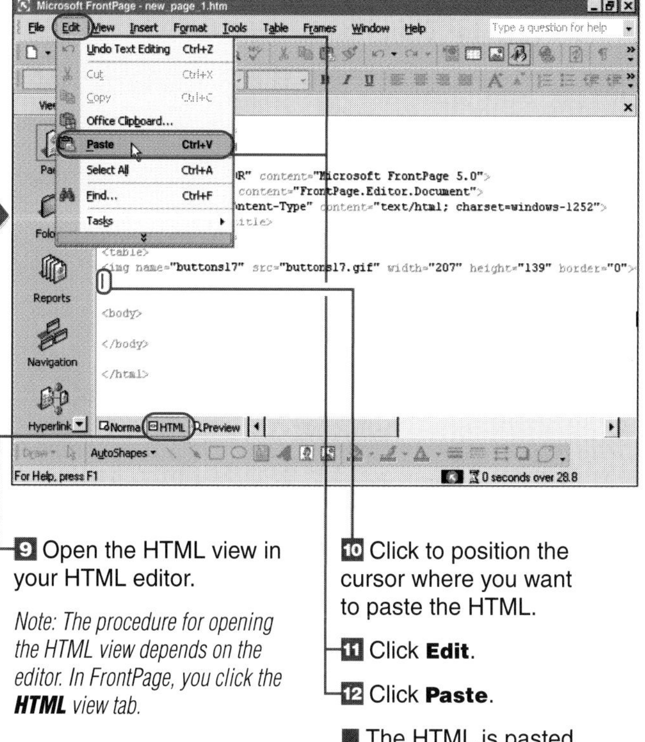

6 Select the HTML text in the text editor.

Note: Select from the beginning of the `<table>` tag to the end of the `</table>` tag.

7 Click **Edit**.

8 Click **Copy**.

9 Open the HTML view in your HTML editor.

*Note: The procedure for opening the HTML view depends on the editor. In FrontPage, you click the **HTML** view tab.*

10 Click to position the cursor where you want to paste the HTML.

11 Click **Edit**.

12 Click **Paste**.

■ The HTML is pasted into the document.

COPY JAVASCRIPT

You can copy buttons and other JavaScript from Fireworks documents to your HTML editor, such as Dreamweaver.

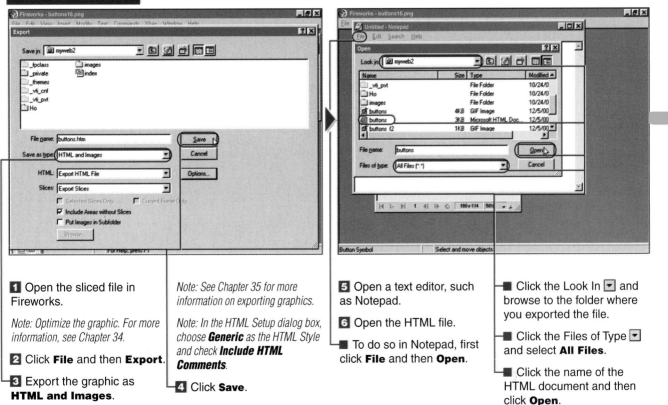

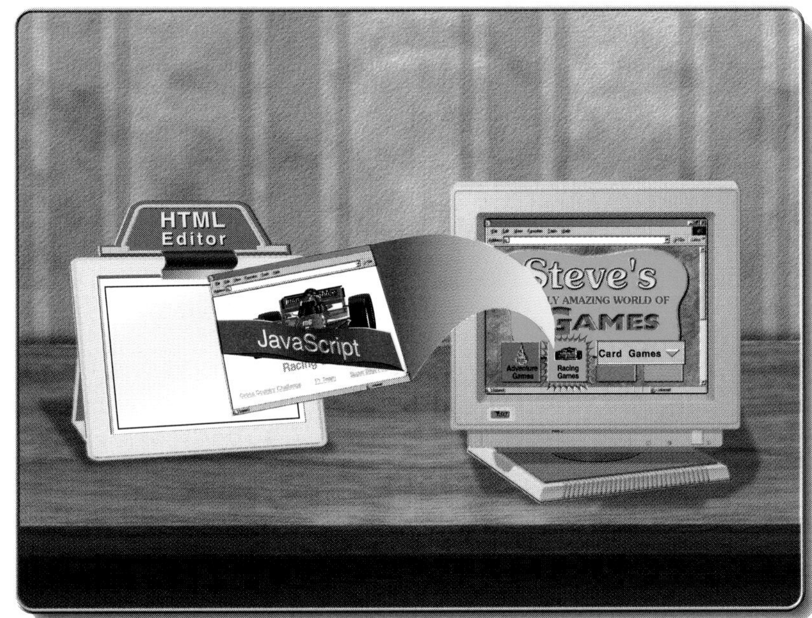

COPY JAVASCRIPT

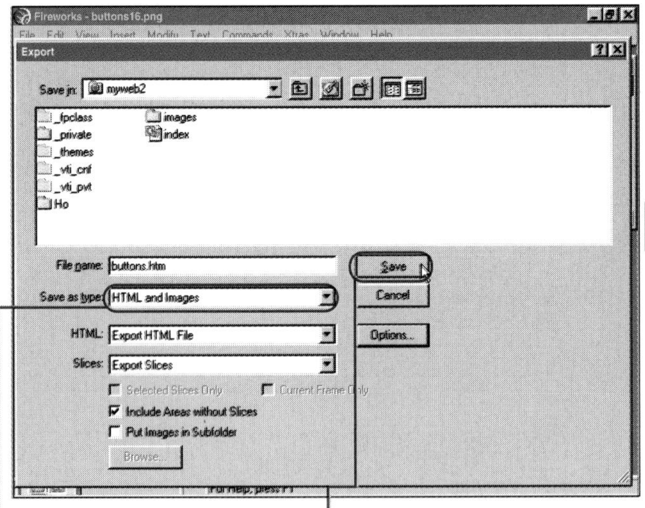

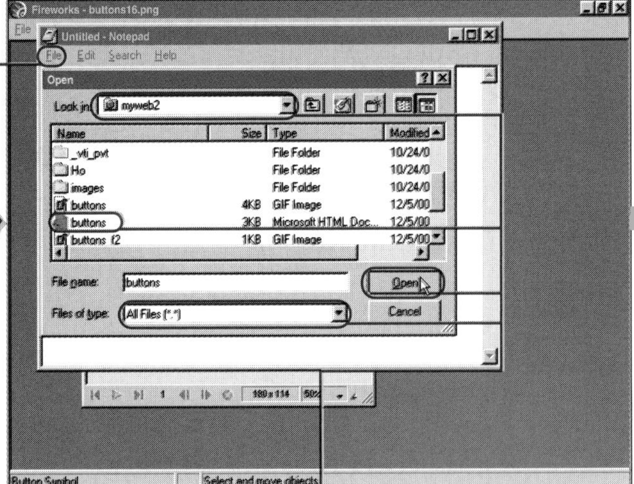

1 Open the sliced file in Fireworks.

Note: Optimize the graphic. For more information, see Chapter 34.

2 Click **File** and then **Export**.

3 Export the graphic as **HTML and Images**.

Note: See Chapter 35 for more information on exporting graphics.

*Note: In the HTML Setup dialog box, choose **Generic** as the HTML Style and check **Include HTML Comments**.*

4 Click **Save**.

5 Open a text editor, such as Notepad.

6 Open the HTML file.

■ To do so in Notepad, first click **File** and then **Open**.

■ Click the Look In ▾ and browse to the folder where you exported the file.

■ Click the Files of Type ▾ and select **All Files**.

■ Click the name of the HTML document and then click **Open**.

What are comments in the HTML file?

Multiline comments begin with <!-- and end with --> in an HTML file. *Comments* consist of notes and advice that you can read, but comments do not show up on the Web page like HTML tags and text do. Comments help you to locate the text to copy, whether for `<table>` tags, `<script>` tags, or other tags. Fireworks and HTML editors add comments to help you locate certain HTML formatting. You can also add comments yourself to your HTML files.

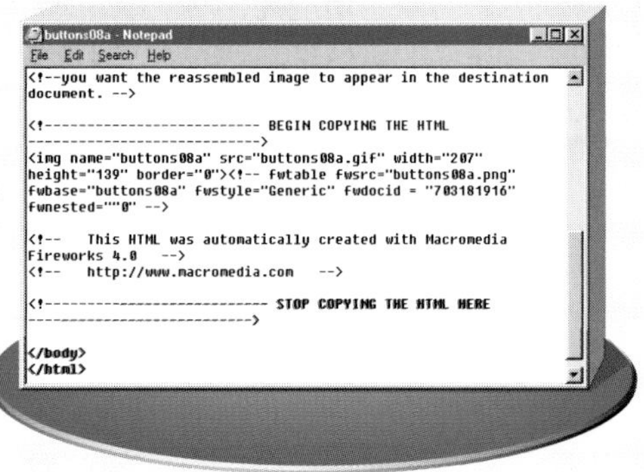

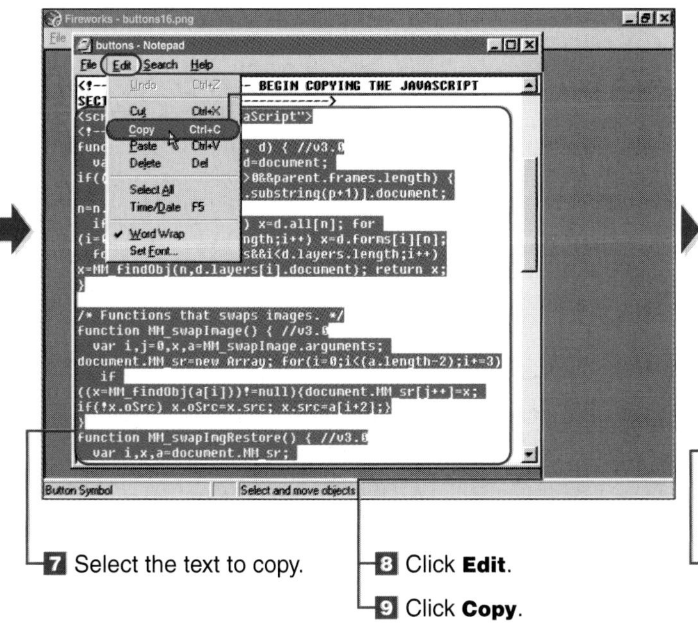

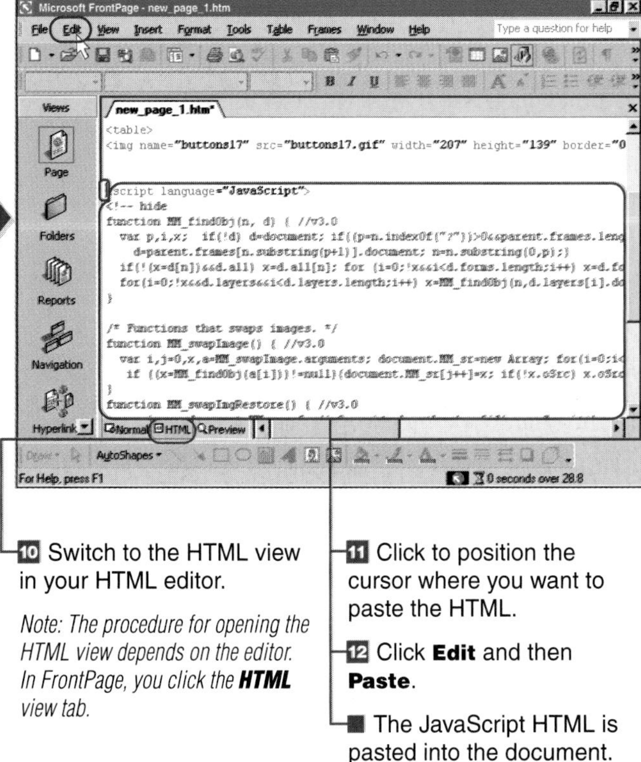

7 Select the text to copy.

8 Click **Edit**.

9 Click **Copy**.

10 Switch to the HTML view in your HTML editor.

*Note: The procedure for opening the HTML view depends on the editor. In FrontPage, you click the **HTML** view tab.*

11 Click to position the cursor where you want to paste the HTML.

12 Click **Edit** and then **Paste**.

■ The JavaScript HTML is pasted into the document.

INDEX

Numbers

2-Up view, Fireworks, 261
4-Up view, Fireworks, 261

A

accessory information, open/close <head> tags, 148
action list, font sizing, 115
actions
- adding to frames, 110–111
- button assignments, 96–99
- deleting, 99
- font sizing, 115
- frame versus object, 113
- Get URL, 117
- Load Movie, 116
- organization guidelines, 111
- Play, 114–115
- scripts, 111
- Stop, 112–113
- testing, 113
- undoing last, 69

Actions list, button action assignments, 98–99
active area, 349
Add Text tool, Fireworks, 274–275
AIF sound file format, 100
Align panel
- object alignments, 38–39
- object positioning, 31

alignments
- Fireworks text, 282–283
- movie editing, 130
- object, 38–39
- paragraphs, 152–153
- tables, 183
- text formatting, 44–45

alpha transparency, defined, 391
Alt key, keyboard shortcuts, 5
angled lines, drawing in Fireworks, 289
animated GIF, rotation method, 245
animations
- button effects, 92–95
- creating by dragging a path, 244
- deleting, 243
- flashing action, 246–247
- frame rate guidelines, 249
- frame-by-frame, 72–75
- motion tweens, 78–81
- playing straight-line, 243
- previewing, 77
- shape tweens, 84–87
- speed settings, 248–249
- straight-line, 242–243

AppleTalk, remote site setup, 250–251
Arial, sans-serif font type, 159
attributes
- bgcolor, 148
- Fireworks text 280–281
- text, 148

audio. *See* sounds
Autoplay, straight-line animation playback, 243

B

backgrounds
- canvas colors, 266–267
- images, 168–169
- setting transparent, 390
- tables, 186–187

Bandwidth Profiler
- closing, 125
- Frame by Frame Graph mode, 124–125
- frame selections, 125
- graph sizing, 124
- modem download speed testing, 123
- movie bandwidth testing, 122–125
- movie information display, 123–124
- opening, 123
- Streaming Graph mode, 124

behaviors
- assigning, 380–381
- Preload Images, 384–385
- Restore Image on MouseOut, 384–385
- swap images, 384–385
- symbol assignment, 53
- Validate Form, 204

Berber pattern, Fireworks default, 297
bevel edges, Fireworks images, 326–327
Bezier curves, drawing in Fireworks, 290–291, 293
bitmap graphics, importing, 60–61
blank keyframe, inserting, 65
block text box, 41
blocks, versus labels, 40
blur edges, Fireworks images, 328–329
blurs, image, 322–323
body <body> tag, 148
body text, class application, 235
bold <b> tag
- create bold text, 42, 160–161
- defined, 149
- heading level guidelines, 155

borders
add to an image, 163
frame size, 213
selection methods, 29
tables, 183
bounding box
drawing, 274
import text, 287
side-by-side/vertical text orientation, 283
sizing handles, 285
text selection methods, 276–277
Brightness/Contrast dialog box, Fireworks, 320–321
brightness, image settings, 320–321
browsers
full-screen movie playback, 131
opening a movie, 117
paragraph width settings, 153
play a movie, 120–121
preview a movie before publishing, 127
validation triggers, 205
button actions, versus frame actions, 113
Button Editor dialog box
button creation, 342–343
editing buttons, 347
navigation bar creation, 355–357
object to button conversion, 344–345
rollover creation, 378–379
button frames, assign sounds, 107
buttons
action assignments, 96–99
action edits, 99
active area, 349
animation effects, 92–95
assign sounds, 106–107
copy/paste, 346
create in Flash, 88
create in Fireworks, 342–343
delete actions, 99
Down state, 90
editing, 347
enable/disable, 97
frame selection, 92
Hit state, 91
import, 90, 352–353
naming conventions, 88
navigation bar creation, 354–357
object conversion, 344–345
onion skinning, 343
Over state, 89
positioning, 91
premade, 89
preview, 91
slice, 345
sound addition, 93
testing animations, 94–95
Timeline frames, 88
Up state, 89, 342
update, 352–353
URL assignments, 348–351
Buttons Library window, premade buttons, 89

C

canvas
color changes, 266–267
sizing, 264–265
trim on graphics, 398, 400
undo/redo changes, 273
Canvas Color dialog box, 266
Canvas Size dialog box, 264
captions, Fireworks images, 185
cells
colors, 187
deleting, 193
sizing with gridlines, 191
table content entry, 184
center points, object settings, 33
centimeters, Fireworks supported measurement type, 265
changes, undo/redo, 273
character format, kerning, 45
Character panel, text format, 42–43
check boxes
form addition, 196–197
organizing, 197
versus lists, 203
checkerboards, Fireworks display, 319
circles, drawing in Fireworks, 295
classes
applying, 234–235
body text application, 235
create, 232–233
paragraph application, 235
style sheet, 232
versus custom HTML tag, 233
click-and-drag
line edits, 14–15
object moves, 30
Clipboard, copy and paste HTML code, 402–405
Close button, close Flash files, 9
Code Inspector, view/edit source code, 150–151
Code view
code wrapping, 151
line numbers, 151

(continued)

Code view *(continued)*
text-formatting tags, 149
view/edit source code, 150–151
code wrap, enable, 151
color palettes, choose, 389
Color Table, changes, 389
colors
add to Swatches panel, 301
choosing number, 389
deselect transparency, 391
fills, 17
Fireworks selections, 298–301
Fireworks text, 280–281
gradient effects, 25
hotspots, 361
hyperlinks, 173
linear gradients, 25
lines, 13
make transparent, 390–391
mixing, 300–301
pixel selections, 316–317
radial gradients, 25
setting transparent, 391
symbol instance editing, 56–57
table backgrounds, 186–187
table cells, 187
transparent instance, 57
Web-safe, 299
columns, insert/delete, 188–189
commands
Basic Actions, Load Movie, 116
Basic Actions, Play, 114
Basic Actions, Stop, 112
Control, Enable Simple Buttons, 99, 107
Control, Test Movie, 59, 77, 94–95, 112, 115, 122
Debug, Customize, 123
Duplicate, 53
Edit, Copy, 285, 346, 409
Edit, Copy Frames, 69
Edit, Copy to HTML Code, 402
Edit, Crop Selected Bitmap, 312
Edit, Paste, 285, 346, 405, 407, 409
Edit, Paste Frames, 69
Edit, Redo, 273
Edit, Undo, 189, 273
Effects, Advanced, 56
Effects, Alpha, 57
File, Close, 9, 272
File, Exit, 139
File, Export, 396, 406, 408
File, Export, Selected Slices Only, 377
File, Import, 60, 100, 286, 306
File, New, 7, 144, 262
File, Open, 6, 142, 270, 406
File, Open, Templates, 227
File, Publish Preview, Default, 127
File, Publish Settings, 126, 128
File, Revert, 147
File, Save, 8, 146, 269
File, Save All Frames, 217
File, Save As, 268
File, Save As Template, 224
File, Save Frame, 216
File, Save Frameset As, 217
Font Size, Large, 115
Font Size, Medium, 115
Font Size, Small, 115
Frame by Frame Graph, 124
Gaussian Blur, 323
Insert Keyframe, 108
Insert, Blank Keyframe, 65, 93
Insert, Convert to Symbol, 52, 344
Insert, Create Motion Tween, 81
Insert, Form, 194
Insert, Form Objects, Check Box, 196
Insert, Form Objects, List/Menu, 200, 202
Insert, Form Objects, Radio Button, 199
Insert, Frame, 64
Insert, Hotspot, 359
Insert, Image, 162
Insert, Invisible Tags, Named Anchor, 178
Insert, Keyframe, 65
Insert, Media, Plugin, 170
Insert, New Button, 342
Insert, New Symbol, 88
Insert, Remove Frames, 70
Insert, Table, 182
Modify, Arrange, Bring Forward, 303
Modify, Arrange, Bring to Front, 36, 302
Modify, Arrange, Lock, 35
Modify, Arrange, Send Backward, 303
Modify, Arrange, Send to Back, 36, 302
Modify, Arrange, Unlock, 35
Modify, Break Apart, 87
Modify, Canvas Color, 266
Modify, Canvas Size, 264
Modify, Delete Column, 189
Modify, Frame, 76
Modify, Frameset, Split, 206
Modify, Group, 34, 304
Modify, Image Size, 308
Modify, Layer, 48
Modify, Library, Add Object To Library, 218
Modify, Mask, Group as Mask, 339

Modify, Movie, 62
Modify, Open Linked Page, 173
Modify, Page Properties, 168
Modify, Remove Link, 175, 177
Modify, Shape, 17
Modify, Table, Delete Row, 189
Modify, Table, Insert Column, 188
Modify, Table, Insert Row, 188
Modify, Transform, Distort, 363
Modify, Transform, Edit Center, 33
Modify, Transform, Free Transform, 362
Modify, Transform, Skew, 363
Modify, Trim Canvas, 398, 400
Modify, Ungroup, 304
Site, Define Sites, 250
Site, New Site, Select, 140
Sort by Color, 299
Text, CSS Styles, Edit Style Sheet, 231
Text, CSS Styles, New Style, 230
Text, Font, 43, 158
Transform, Flip Horizontal, 33
Transform, Flip Vertical, 33
Unsharp Mask, 325
View, Bandwidth Profiler, 123
View, Grid, Show Grid, 75, 191
Window, Behaviors, 381
Window, Color Mixer, 300–301
Window, Common Libraries, Buttons, 89
Window, Common Libraries, Sounds, 93, 101
Window, Effect, Bevel and Emboss, Inner Bevel, 326
Window, Effect, Bevel and Emboss, Inset Emboss, 327
Window, Effect, Bevel and Emboss, Outer Bevel, 326
Window, Effect, Bevel and Emboss, Raised Emboss, 327
Window, Effect, Blur, Blur, 328
Window, Effect, Blur, Blur More, 328
Window, Effect, Blur, Gaussian Blur, 328
Window, Effect, Shadow and Glow, Drop Shadow, 330
Window, Effect, Shadow and Glow, Glow, 332
Window, Effect, Shadow and Glow, Inner Glow, 332
Window, Effect, Shadow and Glow, Inner Shadow, 331
Window, Effect, Sharpen, Sharpen More, 329
Window, Effect, Sharpen, Unsharp Mask, 329
Window, Fill, 296
Window, Fill, Effect, 341
Window, Fill, Stroke, 341
Window, Frames, 208
Window, Hide Panels, 136
Window, History, 138
Window, HTML Styles, Apply, 229
Window, Library, 220
Window, Library, Import Symbols, 352
Window, Objects, Select, 137
Window, Optimize, 388, 392
Window, Stroke, Effect, 347
Window, Stroke, Fill, 347
Window, Styles, 336
Window, Swatches, Macintosh System, 298
Window, Swatches, Windows System, 298
Window, Templates, 226
Window, Timelines, Add Object, 242
Window, Timelines, Add Object, Add Keyframe, 246
Window, Timelines, Record Path of Layer, 244
Window, URL, 351
Window/Site, Site, FTP log, 257
Windows, Toolbar, Main, 6
Xtras, Adjust Color, Brightness/Contrast, 320
Xtras, Blur, 322
Xtras, Blur More, 322
Xtras, Blur, Gaussian Blur, 323
Xtras, Sharpen, 324
Xtras, Sharpen, Sharpen More, 324
Xtras, Sharpen, Unsharp Mask, 325
comments
defined, 409
HTML file, 409
connections, remote site, 252–253
contents, opening/closing <body> tag, 148
contrast, image settings, 320–321
copy and paste, HTML code, 402–405
Copy HTML Code dialog box, 402–405
copyrights, heading level guidelines, 155
crop images, 312–313
CSS Style panel, style sheet class editing, 236–237
Ctrl/Cmd key, deleting multiple layers, 47
curve bar, rotating, 18
curved lines
Bezier, 290–291, 293
drawing, 11, 18–19
Custom Modem Settings dialog box, 123

D

Define Sites dialog box, remote site setup, 250–251
descriptive information, opening/closing <head> tags, 148
deselect transparent color, 391
Design view
text-formatting tags, 149
view/edit source code, 150–151
dimensions, movie settings, 62–63
disclaimer information, heading level guidelines, 155
disconnect period, remote site log off time settings, 253
Document window
HTML Styles button, 229
Stop Sign button, 255

documents. *See also* files *and* movies
- canvas colors, 266–267
- canvas sizing, 264–265
- close, 9, 272
- create in Fireworks, 262–263
- import text to Fireworks, 286–287
- move/copy text, 284–285
- naming conventions, 8
- open, 270–271
- paste HTML, 407, 409
- save, 8, 268–269
- start new (blank), 7

Down state, buttons, 90
downloads
- modem tests, 123
- remote site file transfer, 256–257
- streaming sounds, 108

drag-and-drop, sounds, 105
Draw Ellipse tool, Fireworks, 295
Draw Rectangle tool, Fireworks, 295
Draw Shape tool, Fireworks, 294–295
drawing
- Bezier curves, 290–291, 293
- bounding box, 274
- buttons, 90
- circles in Fireworks, 295
- curved lines, 18–19
- freeform lines, Flash, 11
- freeform lines in Fireworks, 289–290
- horizontal lines, 15
- object fills, 24–25
- ovals, 22–23
- rectangles, 22–23
- shapes, 291, 294–295
- squares in Fireworks, 295
- straight lines, Flash, 10
- straight lines in Fireworks, 288–289
- vertical lines, 15

Drawing toolbar, Flash, 4
Dreamweaver
- animation speed settings, 248–249
- background images, 168–169
- create Web page, 144
- create animation by dragging a path, 244–245
- exit properly, 139
- file paths, 305
- Fireworks image map, 400
- flashing animations, 246–247
- font styles, 158–159
- forms, 194–205
- framesets, 206–217
- heading levels, 154–155
- History panel, 138
- HTML styles, 228–237
- HTML tags, 148–149
- hyperlinks, 172–181
- image insertion, 162–163
- indents, 157
- layers, 238–241
- Library items, 218–223
- line breaks, 156
- local site setup, 140–142
- Macintosh startup methods, 135
- most recently used file list, 143
- multimedia insertion, 170–171
- non-HTML text file support, 143
- Objects panel, 137
- open existing Web page, 142–143
- paragraph alignments, 152–153
- remote site setup, 250–257
- save HTML files, 403
- save Web pages, 146–147
- show/hide panels, 136
- single folder site storage advantages, 141, 147
- size images, 166–167
- straight-line animations, 242–243
- tables, 182–193
- templates, 224–227
- text emphasis, 160–161
- text wrapping around images, 164–165
- view/edit source code, 150–151
- Web page title, 145
- Windows PC startup methods, 134

drop shadow, Fireworks effect, 330–331
dwt (template) filename extension, 225

E

Ease control, tween speed settings, 82–83
edges
- bevel, 326–327
- blur, 328–329
- emboss, 327
- sharpen, 329

effects, motion tweens, 80–81
embed `<embed>` tag, Netscape Navigator support, 129
emboss edges, Fireworks images, 327
Enter/Return key, paragraph breaks, 152
Eraser tool, Fireworks, 318–319
error tracking, FTP logs, 257
errors, correcting with History panel, 138
events, 205
Export dialog box, 297, 394, 396
Export preview dialog box, 394

Export Slices option, Export dialog box, 397
export types, selecting, 394–395

F

fields, text, 195
file compression, graphic file formats, 386
file formats
  file compression, 386
  GIF, 163, 387
  graphic quality, 386
  graphics, 386–387
  images, 163
  JPEG, 163, 387
  PNG, 387
  Portable Network Graphic (PNG), 263
File Transfer Protocol (FTP), remote site connection, 252–253
file transfers
  download files, 256–257
  FTP logs, 257
  stop in progress, 255
  upload files, 254–255
file types, select for export, 394–395
filename extensions
  dwt (template), 225
  gif, 162
  htm/html, 216
  jpg, 162
  swf (Flash), 128
files
  close, 9
  download from remote site, 256–257
  frames saved, 399
  hyperlinks, 180–181
  image size considerations, 165
  layers saved, 399
  most recently used list, 6, 143
  naming, 8, 399
  non-HTML text support, 143
  open existing, 6
  organization guidelines, 173
  rename before publishing, 127
  revert to last saved version, 147
  save, 8, 268–269
  save HTML, 403
  start new (blank) document, 7
  stop transfer in progress, 255
  switch between open, 7
  upload to remote site, 254–255
Fill Color button, 17
Fill Color palette, 23, 25
Fill panel, 296–297
fills
  colors, 17
  edge softening, 17
  editing, 16–17
  Fireworks, 296–297
  gradient effects, 25
  objects, 24–25
  reshape, 17
  selection methods, 26, 29
  textures, 297
Fireworks
  2-Up view, 261
  4-Up view, 261
  active area, 349
  Add Text tool, 274
  angled lines, 289
  assign URL to button, 348–351
  behavior assignments, 380–381
  Berber pattern, 297
  bevel edges, 326–327
  Bezier curves, 290–291, 293
  blur edges, 328–329
  blurring an image, 322–323
  bounding box, 274
  brightness/contrast settings, 320–321
  button creation, 342–343
  canvas colors, 266–267
  canvas sizing, 264–265
  circle drawing, 295
  close documents, 272
  color selections, 298–301
  copy and paste HTML code, 402–405
  copy HTML for sliced objects, 406–407
  copy from JavaScript to HTML, 408–409
  copy/paste buttons, 346
  crop images, 312–313
  default effect setting, 334–335
  document creation, 262–263
  Draw Ellipse tool, 295
  Draw Rectangle tool, 295
  Draw Shape tool, 294–295
  drop shadow, 330–331
  edit buttons, 347
  emboss edges, 327
  Eraser tool, 318–319
  erase image pixels, 318–319
  export a polygon slice, 369
  export a slice, 376–377
  export objects, 394–401
  file naming conventions, 268–269
  fills, 296–297

(continued)

Fireworks *(continued)*
folder for saving HTML files, 403
font sizing, 277
font style edits, 278–279
frames export, 398–399
Gaussian blur, 323
glow effects, 332–333
graphic file formats, 386–387
graphics and HTML Editors, 402–409
group/ungroup objects, 304–305
hiding/showing a slice, 370
horizontal lines, 289
Hotspot tool, 358
hotspots, 358–363
image adjustment advantages, 167
image captions, 185
image map export, 400–401
image maps, 364–365
image resolution settings, 310–311
import buttons, 352–353
import objects, 306–307
import text, 286–287
inner glow, 333
inner shadow, 331
Lasso tool, 315
layers exports, 398–399
line (path) edits, 292–293
Line tool, 288–289
Magic Wand tool, 316–317
Marquee tool, 314–315
masked group edits, 340–341
masks, 338–341
Mixer panel, 300–301
move/copy text, 284–285
multiple area selections, 317
name exported files, 399
navigation bars, 177, 354–357
object arrangements, 302–303
object to button conversion, 344–345
onion skinning, 343
open document, 270–271
optimize JPEGs, 392–393
optimizing graphics, 388–391
Original view, 261
paste HTML into folders, 404
Pen tool, 290–291
Pencil tool, 289–290
pixel dimension versus print size, 309
Pointer tool, 314
points measurement, 277
Polygon Slice tool, 368–369
Portable Network Graphic (PNG) file format, 263
preview image changes, 323
Preview view, 261
print size modifications, 309–310
Rectangle Slice tool, 366–367
rollovers, 378–379
save documents, 268–269
select export types, 394–395
select/move image pixels, 314–317
Selection Pointer tool, 292
shadow effects, 330–332
shape drawing, 291, 294–295
sharpen edges, 329
sharpen an image, 324–325
size images, 308–309
slice, 345
slice guide, 367
slice naming conventions, 371
slices exporting, 396–397
square drawing, 295
startup methods, 260
straight lines, 288–289
stroke selections, 295
styles, 336–337
Styles panel, 336–337
Subselection tool, 340–341
supported measurement units, 265
swap images, 382–385
Swatches panel, 298–301
text alignment, 282–283
text attribute editing, 280–281
text colors, 280–281
Text Editor, 275
text entry conventions, 274–275
text orientation, 282–283
text selection methods, 276–277, 279
textures, 297
undo/redo changes, 273
update buttons, 352–353
URL Library panel, 351, 375
URL link to image slice assignment, 374–375
vertical lines, 289
Web-safe colors, 299
Flash
add sound layer, 102–103
add/delete layers, 46–47
assign sound to frames, 104–105
block text box, 41
button creation, 88–99
change unit scale, 109
close open files, 9
copy/paste objects, 30–31

Drawing toolbar, 4
fill editing, 16–17
frame-by-frame animations, 72–75
group/ungroup objects, 34–35
import graphics, 60–61
keyframes, 64–67
label text box, 40
Lasso tool, 28–29
layer properties, 48–49
layer stacking order, 50–51
line segment edits, 14–15
line segment formats, 12–13
Line tool, 10–11
lock/unlock objects, 35
Main (Standard toolbar), 4
Menu bar, 4
most recently used file list, 6
motion tweens, 78–83
mouse navigation techniques, 5
move objects, 30–31
move/copy frames, 68–69
movie properties, 62–63
object alignments, 38–39
object selection methods, 26–29
oval drawings, 22–23
Paint Bucket tool, 24–25
Pen tool, 18–19
Pencil tool, 10–11
publish movies, 126–131
rectangle drawings, 22–23
rotate/flip objects, 32–33
save file before exiting, 9
save files, 8
screen elements, 4
shape tweens, 84–87
sound clips import, 100–101
sounds available, 101
soundtrack layer simulations, 103
stacked objects, 36–37
Stage (Movie) area, 4
streaming sounds, 108–109
switching between open files, 7
symbols, 52–59
text alignments, 44–45
text formats, 42–43
Text tool, 40–41
Timeline, 4
Title bar, 4
work area, 4
Flash Color palette, object fills, 24–25
Flash Editor, stage (movie) display area, 4
Flash Only templates, 129
Flash Player
close a movie, 119
Control menu commands, 119
enable/disable commands, 119
open a movie, 118, 121
play a movie, 118–119, 121
preview movies, 77
test button animations, 94–95
flashing animation, creating, 246–247
flip objects, 32–33
folders
choose destination, 405
file organization guidelines, 173
My Documents, 8
save HTML files, 403
site storage guidelines, 141, 147
template storage, 227
font <font> tag, 149
Font menu, adding fonts, 159
fonts
action list sizing, 115
adding to Font menu, 159
kerning, 45
sans-serif, 159
serif, 159
size, 43, 277
style edits, 43, 158–159
format
line segments, 12–13
paragraph alignments, 152–153
text, 42–43
forms
check boxes, 196–197
labels, 195
lists, 202–203
menus, 200–201
radio buttons, 198–199
text field addition, 195
validate, 204–205
validation triggers, 205
frame actions, versus object actions, 113
Frame Actions dialog box
add actions to frames, 110–111
load movie file into current movie, 116
Stop action assignment, 112–113
Frame by Frame Graph mode, Bandwidth Profiler, 124–125
Frame panel
Ease control, 82–83
property edits, 76
Frame Rate text box, movie settings, 62–63
frame rates
animation guidelines, 249
frames-per-second (fps) measurement, 248–249

INDEX

frame-by-frame animations
- create, 72–75
- gridlines, 75
- in-between frame addition, 73
- object position guidelines, 75
- preview, 77
- versus motion tweens, 79

frames
- action addition, 110–111
- add multiple, 67
- add regular, 64–67
- button Timelines, 88
- content entry conventions, 210–211
- copy, 68–69
- create, 206
- delete, 70–71, 209
- export, 398–399
- hyperlinks, 214–215
- identifying characteristics, 65
- insert external Web-page address, 211
- keyframe conversion, 70–71
- keyframes, 64–67
- move, 68–69
- name conventions, 208
- open existing HTML file, 210–211
- property edits, 76
- save, 216–217
- save to files, 399
- selection methods, 208
- sizing, 67, 212–213
- symbol instance insertion, 54–55

Frames panel
- behavior assignments, 380–381
- frame selection methods, 208
- open existing HTML file, 210–211

frames per second (fps), 62–63
framesets, 207, 217
frames-per-second (fps), animation speed, 248–249
freeform lines
- draw, Flash, 11
- draw in Fireworks, 289–290
- path (line) editing in Fireworks, 292–293

Freeform tool, drawing Bezier curves, 293
FrontPage, open HTML view, 406–407, 409
FTP logs, file transfer errors, 257

G

Garamond, serif font type, 159
Gaussian blur, 323
Get URL action, open a movie in a separate browser window, 117
gif filename extension, 162
GIF images
- versus JPEG images, 162
- graphic file format, 387
- optimizing, 388–391
- preferred format for Web graphic, 388

glows, Fireworks effect, 332–333
gradient effects, object fills, 25
graphic file formats. *See* file formats
graphic quality, graphic file formats, 386
graphics
- change indexed palette, 389
- choose color palette, 389
- copy/paste, 61
- export as HTML and images type, 408
- export, 394–395
- export slices, 396–397
- file formats, 386–387
- import, 60–61
- making canvas transparent, 390
- optimizing, 408
- prepare for export, 402
- select quality, 393
- smoothing, 393
- trimming canvas, 398, 400

Graphics Interchange File (GIF), 387
graphs, Bandwidth Profiler, 124–125
gridlines
- frame-by-frame animation object position, 75
- table cell size, 191

group objects
- lock/unlock, 35
- selection methods, 34–35

guide layers, defined, 49
guided layers, defined, 49

H

handles, bounding box sizing, 285
head <head> tag, 148
heading levels, creating, 154–155
Helvetica, sans-serif font type, 159
History panel, error correction methods, 138
Hit state, buttons, 91
horizontal alignments, Flash objects, 38
horizontal lines
- drawing in Fireworks, 289
- drawing techniques, 15

Hotspot tool, Fireworks, 358
hotspots
- behavior assignments, 380–381

colors, 361
create, 358–359
edits, 360–363
image maps, 364–365
insert, 359
preview, 359
rotate, 362
scaling, 362
shape edits, 361
size, 360
transform, 363
htm/html filename extension, 216
html <html> tag, 148
HTML code
copy to editor, 402
copy for sliced object, 406–407
paste, 404–405
update, 405
view/edit, 150–151
HTML copy code for sliced object, 406–407
HTML documents, open/close <html> tags, 148
HTML editor
open HTML view, 405, 407, 409
reasons for two folders, 405
select for export, 401
HTML files
comments, 409
open in a frame, 210–211
save to folders, 403
select what to copy, 407
HTML format, movie publishing, 128–131
HTML settings, configuring, 403
HTML Setup dialog box, 400–401, 403, 408
HTML styles
apply, 229
edits, 231
HTML tag customization, 230–231
hyperlinks. *See also* links
another page/same site, 172–173
another Web site, 174–175
colors, 173
frames, 214–215
hotspots, 358–363
images, 176–177
navigation bars, 177
other content/same page, 178–179
other files, 180–181
remove, 175, 177
test, 175
URL button assignment, 348–351

I

image <img> tag, supported file formats, 129
image maps
contents of exported, 401
create, 364–365
export to Dreamweaver HTML file format, 400–401
exporting, 400–401
image quality, reducing by optimizing, 392
Image Size dialog box, Fireworks, 308–311
image slice, URL link assignment, 374–375
images. *See also* objects
backgrounds, 168–169
blurs, 322–323
border addition, 163
brightness/contrast settings, 320–321
captions, 185
crop, 312–313
erase individual pixels, 318–319
export, 394–395
file size considerations, 165
Gaussian blur, 323
GIF versus JPEG, 162
hyperlinks, 176–177
insert, 162–163
multiple area selections, 317
pixel color selections, 316–317
pixel dimension versus print size, 309
preview changes, 162, 323
print size modifications, 309–310
resolution settings, 310–311
save exported, 404
select/move pixels, 314–317
sharpening, 324–325
sizing, 166–167, 308–309
slice, 345
supported file formats, 163
swapping, 382–385
table background, 187
text wrapping, 164–165
Import dialog box
described, 60–61, 100
Fireworks, 286–287, 306–307
import
buttons, 90, 352–353
graphics, 60–61
sound clips, 100–101
text to Fireworks, 286–287
inches, Fireworks supported measurement type, 265
indents, creating, 157

index transparency, defined, 391
inner glow, Fireworks effect, 333
inner shadow, Fireworks effect, 331
Insert Named Anchor dialog box, 178
Insert Table dialog box, 182
Instance panel, symbol editing, 58–59
instance reference, symbols, 54–57
Internet service provider (ISP), remote site settings, 251
irregular objects, selection methods, 28–29
italic <i> tag, 149
italic text, 42, 160–161

J

JavaScript, copying to HTML, 408–409
Joint Photographic Experts group (JPEG), 387
JPEG
- graphic file formats, 387
- optimizing, 392–393

JPEG images, versus GIF, 162
jpg filename extension, 162

K

kerning, 45
keyboard shortcuts
- Ctrl+Alt+B (activate button), 91
- Ctrl+Alt+B (Enable Simple Buttons), 97
- Ctrl+down arrow/Cmd+Shift+down (back of layer), 37
- Ctrl+E/Cmd+E (movie-edit mode), 91
- Ctrl+Shift+down arrow/Cmd+Shift+down (back of stack), 37
- Ctrl+Shift+up arrow/Cmd+Shift+up (top of stack), 37
- Ctrl+up arrow/Cmd+up (up one layer), 37
- Flash navigation technique, 5
- Shift+Enter/Shift+Return (Line Break), 156
- stack object arrangements, 37

keyboards, Flash navigation techniques, 5
keyframes
- add, 64–67
- blank versus default, 65
- converting to regular frame, 70–71
- delete, 71
- identify characteristics, 65
- insert sound in frames, 104
- motion tweens, 78–83
- movie loading, 116–117
- Play action assignment, 114–115
- Stop action assignment, 112–113

kilobytes (K), image size, 165

L

label text box, 40
labels
- check boxes, 197
- form lists, 203
- form menus, 201
- form text field, 195
- radio buttons, 199
- versus blocks, 40

Lasso tool
- Fireworks, 315
- object selections, 28–29

Layer Properties dialog box, 48–49
layers
- action organization, 111
- add sound, 102–103
- add/delete, 46–47
- content entry conventions, 239
- copy, 51
- create, 238–239
- create an animation by dragging a path, 244–245
- export, 398–399
- flashing animation, 246–247
- guide, 49
- guided, 49
- importing with objects, 307
- locking, 49
- mask, 49
- names, 106
- naming conventions, 48
- naming sounds, 103
- navigation bar creation, 355–356
- nesting, 239
- normal, 49
- object arrangements, 302–303
- position shuffling, 247
- property settings, 48–49
- repositioning, 240–241
- resizing, 240–241
- saving to files, 399
- sizing, 49
- stacking order, 50–51
- straight-line animation, 242–243
- symbol instance insertion, 54–55
- visibility settings, 241
- Z-index specification, 247

Layers panel
- hide/show a slice, 370
- update a slice, 376

layout table
- create, 190–191
- delete, 193
- rearrange, 192–193

Layout view, layout table creation, 190–191
levels
- headings, 154–155
- stacked objects, 36–37

Library
- imported graphics storage, 61
- symbol shape tweening, 87
- view, 61

Library items
- create, 218–219
- edits, 221–223
- element guidelines, 219
- insert, 220–221
- naming conventions, 219
- site update, 222–223

Library panel
- import buttons, 352–353
- update buttons, 353

Library window
- copy symbols, 53
- preview symbols, 53
- swap symbols, 55
- symbol instance insertion, 54–55

line breaks, inserting, 156
Line Color box, line colors, 13
line numbers, enabling in Code view, 151
line segments
- drawing, 10–11
- edits, 14–15
- format, 12–13
- smoothing, 20–21
- straighten, 20–21

Line tool
- drawing straight lines in Fireworks, 288–289
- horizontal/vertical line drawing, 15
- straight lines, 10

linear gradients, object fills, 25
lines
- angled, 289
- Bezier curves, 290–291, 293
- color settings, 13
- curves, 11, 18–19
- default settings, 12
- drawing, 10–11
- editing, 292–293
- free-form, 11
- freeform, 11, 289–290, 292–293
- horizontal, 289
- reshaping, 14–15
- smoothing, 20–21
- straight, 10, 288–289
- straightening, 20–21
- style settings, 13
- thickness settings, 11–13
- vertical, 289

Link Wizard, URL button assignment, 348–351
linked page, opening, 173
links. *See also* hyperlinks
- hotspots, 358–363
- URL button assignment, 348–351
- URL to image slice assignment, 374–375

lists
- form addition, 202–203
- versus check boxes, 203

Load Movie action, loading movie file into current movie, 116
Local Folder dialog box, 140–141, 147
local sites, setup, 140–142
log off, remote site time settings, 253
logs, FTP, 257
loops, straight-line animation playback, 243

M

Macintosh
- Dreamweaver startup, 135
- open/close windows, 5
- remote site setup, 250–251
- Web-safe colors, 299

Magic Wand tool, Fireworks, 316–317
Main (Standard) toolbar
- Flash element, 4
- hide/display, 6
- open existing files, 6

Marquee tool, Fireworks, 314–315
mask layers, 49
masked groups, edit, 340–341
masks
- create, 338–339
- edit, 340–341

measurements
- centimeters, 265
- Fireworks supported types, 265
- frames per second (fps), 62–63, 248–249
- inches, 265
- kilobytes (K), 165
- pixels, 166, 265
- points, 277

Menu bar, Flash element, 4

menus
- form addition, 200–201
- width determinations, 201

meta <meta> tag, 148
Microsoft Internet Explorer
- <object> tag support, 129
- viewing a Flash movie, 120–121

mistakes
- correct with History panel, 138
- undo, 69, 189
- undo/redo changes, 273

Mixer panel, mix colors, 300–301
modems, speed tests, 123
morphs, shape tweening, 84–87
motion tweens
- create, 78–81
- described, 78
- effects, 80–81
- on-the-fly creation, 81
- speed settings, 82–83
- tests, 81
- versus frame-by-frame animations, 79
- versus shape tweens, 85

mouse
- click-and-drag line edits, 14–15
- click-and-drag object moves, 30
- drawing straight lines, 11
- Flash navigation techniques, 5
- freeform line drawing, 11
- multiple object selections, 27–28
- object selection techniques, 26–29
- reshaping curved lines, 19
- rotate/flip objects, 32–33

Movie Properties dialog box, 62–63
movie-edit mode
- assign sounds to buttons, 107
- previewing buttons, 91

movies. *See also* documents *and* files
- action organization guidelines, 111
- action tests, 113
- alignment edits, 130
- bandwidth tests, 122–125
- button animation, 92–95
- closing, 9
- frame rate guidelines, 62–63
- full-screen playback, 131
- load, 116–117
- load movie file into current movie, 116
- naming conventions, 8
- open in a separate browser window, 117
- Play action assignment, 114–115
- playing in a browser, 120–121
- preview, 77
- property settings, 62–63
- publish, 126–131
- renaming before publishing, 127
- save, 8
- sound layers, 102–103
- start new (blank) document, 7
- Stop action assignment, 112–113
- streaming sounds, 108–109
- test symbols, 59
- view in Flash Player, 118–119

multimedia, Web page insertion, 170–171
My Documents folder, default file save, 8

N

names, add sound library window, open, 106
navigation bar
- create in Fireworks, 354–357
- hyperlinks, 177

nested layers, creating, 239
Netscape Navigator
- <embed> tag support, 129
- view a Flash movie, 120–121

New Document dialog box, 262
New Style dialog box, 230, 336
NFS Server, remote site setup, 250–251
non-HTML text files, Dreamweaver support, 143
Notepad, open HTML file, 408

O

object actions, versus frame actions, 113
Object Actions dialog box, 96–99
object <object> tag, Microsoft Internet Explorer support, 129
objects. *See also* images
- add from Objects panel, 137
- alignments, 38–39
- arrange in Fireworks, 302–303
- bevel edges, 326–327
- blur edges, 328–329
- button conversion, 344–345
- center point settings, 33
- convert to symbols, 52–53
- copy HTML for sliced, 406–407
- copy/paste, 30–31
- drop shadow, 330–331
- emboss edges, 327
- export slices, 406
- fills, 24–25
- flip, 32–33
- frame-by-frame animation positioning, 75

glows, 332–333
group/ungroup, Flash, 34–35
group/ungroup in Fireworks, 304–305
import to Fireworks, 306–307
import with layers, 307
inner glow, 333
inner shadow, 331
irregular selections, 28–29
layer stacking order, 50–51
masks, 338–341
move, 30–31
multiple arrangements, 303
multiple selections, 27–28
overlay-level, 33
rotate, 32–33
selection methods, 26–29
shape tweening, 84–87
sharpen edges, 329
stacked, 36–37
stage-level, 33
straight-line animation, 242–243
style sheet class application, 234–235

Objects panel
add objects, 137
Form button, 194
Insert Check Box button, 196
Insert List/Menu button, 200, 202
Insert Radio Button button, 199
open, 137
slice naming conventions, 371
text slice creation, 372–373
URL link to image slice assignment, 374–375

onion skinning, 343
online images, resolution setting guidelines, 311
Open dialog box
Fireworks document, 270
Flash files, 6
Web page, 142

optimizing graphics, 388–391
orientation, Fireworks text, 282–283
Original view, Fireworks, 261
outdents, creating, 157
ovals, drawing, 22–23
Over state, buttons, 89
overlay-level objects, center point settings, 33

P

Paint Bucket tool, Flash, 24–25
Palatino, serif font type, 159
palettes, Swatches panel, 298
panels, show/hide, 136
paragraph breaks, insert, 152
Paragraph panel, text alignments, 44–45
paragraphs
alignments, 152–153
class application, 235
indents, 157
line breaks, 156
text emphasis, 160–161
width settings, 153

pasting, HTML 402–405
paths. *See* lines
patterns, Berber, 297
Pen tool
Bezier curves, Fireworks, 290–291
curves, Flash, 18–19

Pencil tool
freeform lines, Fireworks, 289–290
freeform lines, Flash, 10–11

pixel dimensions, versus print size, 309
pixels
erase, 318–319
defined, 265
Fireworks supported measurement type, 265
move between documents, 317
resize images, 166–167
select/move, 314–317

Play action, movie assignment, 114–115
plug-ins, multimedia insertion, 170–171
Pointer tool, Fireworks, 314
points, Fireworks measurement unit, 277
Polygon mode, complex shape selections, 29
Polygon Slice tool, Fireworks, 368–369
Portable Network Graphic (PNG) file format
described, 263, 387
graphic file formats, 387
optimize, 388–391

predefined framesets, insert, 207
Preload Images behavior, 384–385
Preview view, Fireworks, 261
previews
animated buttons, 95
animations, 77
buttons, 91
movie before publishing, 127

properties
frames, 76
layers, 48–49
movies, 62–63

Property inspector, text emphasis, 160–161
protections
locked layers, 49
lock/unlock group objects, 35

INDEX

protocols, File Transfer Protocol (FTP), 252–253
publish
  full-screen movie playback, 131
  inserted HTML tags for supported browsers, 129
  movie alignment editing, 130
  movies, 126–127
  playback settings, 130
Publish Settings dialog box
  HTML format, 128–131
  movies, 126–127

Q

QuickTime, frame rate guidelines, 63

R

radial gradients, object fills, 25
radio buttons
  form addition, 198–199
  naming conventions, 199
radius, rectangle corners, 23
Rectangle Settings dialog box, 23
Rectangle Slice tool, Fireworks, 366–367
rectangles, 22–23
redo last action, 273
remote site
  connection methods, 252–253
  download files from, 256–257
  FTP logs, 257
  Internet Service Provider (ISP) settings, 251
  log off time settings, 253
  setup, 250–251
  stop file transfer in progress, 255
  upload files, 254–255
Remove Unused Colors option, graphics optimization, 393
resolutions, image settings, 310–311
Restore Image on MouseOut behavior, 384–385
rollovers
  behavior assignments, 380–381
  creating, 378–379
rotation
  animated GIF, 245
  hotspots, 362
  objects, 32–33
rotation handles, selected objects, 32
rounded corners, rectangle drawing, 23
rows, insert/delete, 188–189

S

same-page hyperlinks, 178–179
sans-serif fonts, 159
Save As dialog box, 8, 146, 268
scripts, button actions, 98, 111
Select File dialog box, multimedia insertion, 170–171
Select Folder dialog box, 404
Select Image Source dialog box, 162, 168
Selection Pointer tool, Fireworks, 292
serif fonts, 159
Set Transparent Index Color button, 390
shadows, drop versus inner, 331
shape tweens, 84–85
shapes
  circles, 295
  create with line tools, 291
  draw with Draw Shape tool, Fireworks, 294–295
  fills, 296–297
  object fills, 24–25
  squares, 295
  tweening effects, 84–87
sharpen images, 324–325
Shift key
  draw lines, Fireworks, 289
  line drawing, 15
  multiple object selections, 27–28
Site Definition dialog box, 140–141
sites
  file organization guidelines, 173
  remote setup, 250–257
  single folder storage advantages, 141, 147
  update, 222–223
size <size> tag, 149
sizing handles, bounding box, 285
Slice Along Guides option, Export dialog box, 397
slice guides, 367
sliced objects, copy HTML code, 406–407
slices
  behavior assignments, 380–381
  defined, 345
  export, 376–377, 396–397
  hide/show, 370
  naming conventions, 371
  polygon, 368–369
  reasons to use, 396
  rectangular, 366–367
  select, 406
  text, 372–373
  update, 376–377
  URL link assignment, 374–375
Smooth mode, 20–21
smoothing, defined, 393
Soften Edges dialog box, 17
sorts, Swatches panel, 299
sound clips, import, 100–101

sound file formats, supported by Flash, 100
sound layers
- add, 102–103
- naming, 103
- place in Timeline, 103

Sound Library, button sounds, 93
sounds
- add to sound layer, 104
- button assignment, 106–107
- button frame addition, 93
- frames assignment, 104–105
- hear sample, 105
- insert keyframe, 104
- select, 101, 105
- streaming sounds, assignment, 108–109

source code, viewing/editing, 150–151
speeds
- animation settings, 248–249
- modem download testing, 123
- motion tweens, 82–83
- movie settings, 62–63

squares, draw, Fireworks, 295
stacked objects, arrange, 36–37
stacking order, layers, 50–51
stage area
- button placement, 91
- line segments, 10–11
- object selection methods, 26–29
- sound addition, 388–391

stage-level objects, center point settings, 33
Standard (Main) toolbar, Flash element, 4
status bar, image size display, 165
Stop action, movie assignment, 112–113
straight lines
- draw, Flash, 10
- draw, Fireworks, 288
- path (line) edits, Fireworks, 292–293

Straighten mode, 20–21
straight-line animation, 242–243
Streaming Graph mode, Bandwidth Profiler, 124
streaming sounds
- assign to movies, 108–109
- cut off problem, 109

strikethrough text, 161
Stroke panel, line thickness slider adjustments, 11, 13
strokes
- color settings, 13
- curves, 18–19
- curvy line drawing, 11
- default settings, 12
- freeform lines, 11
- line thickness slider adjustments, 11
- reshape, 14–15
- shape drawing, 295
- smoothing, 20–21
- straight lines, 10
- straighten, 20–21
- style settings, 13
- thickness settings, 11–13

style sheet class
- apply, 234–235
- described, 232
- edits, 236–237

styles
- Fireworks, 336–337
- font edits, 43, 158–159, 278–279
- HTML, 228–241
- lines, 13
- save, 336
- view, 235

Styles panel, Fireworks, 336–337
Subselection tool, Fireworks, 340–341
subtitles, heading level guidelines, 155
Swap Image dialog box, 384
swap images, 382–385
Swap Symbol dialog box, 55
Swatches panel
- add custom colors, 301
- color sorts, 299
- open a palette, 298

swf (Flash) filename extension, 128
Symbol Properties dialog box
- button creation, 88
- described, 52
- object to button conversion, 345

symbol-edit mode, open button, 106
symbols
- behavior assignment, 53
- buttons, 88–99
- copy, 53
- create, 52–53
- edits, 58–59
- instance editing, 56–57
- instance insertion, 54–55
- motion tweens, 78–83
- naming conventions, 53
- object conversion, 52–53
- preview, 53
- replace, 55
- shape tweening, 87
- tests, 59

INDEX

T

table tags, mark start and end of slices, 407
tables
- alignments, 183
- backgrounds, 186–187
- cell content entry conventions, 184–185
- color background, 186–187
- content edits, 183
- delete rows/columns, 188–189
- enable/disable borders, 183
- Fireworks image captions, 185
- image background, 187
- insert, 182
- insert rows/columns, 188–189
- insert table within, 185
- layout, 190–193

tags
- bold <b>, 149
- body <body>, 148
- embed <embed>, 129
- font <font>, 149
- head <head>, 148
- html <html>, 148
- image <img>, 129
- indicate start and end of slice, 407
- italic <i>, 149
- meta <meta>, 148
- object <object>, 129
- size<size>, 149
- table <table> and </table>, 407
- title <title>, 148

targets, _top, 215
teletype (typewriter style) text, creating, 161
templates
- content guidelines, 225
- create, 224–225
- edit, 226–227
- Flash Only, 129
- folder storage guidelines, 227
- open, 227
- selection methods, 129
- site update, 226–227

Text Editor
- alignments, 282–283
- copy JavaScript, 408
- edit imported text, 287
- Fireworks text entry conventions, 275
- font size, 277
- font style selections, 278–279
- move/copy text, 284–285
- open HTML file, 408
- orientation, 282–283
- select HTML text, 407
- text attribute editing, 280–281
- text colors, 280–281
- text selection methods, 276–277, 279
- view and copy code, 406

text fields, form addition, 195
text format
- alignments, 44–45
- bold text, 160–161
- Character panel, 42–43
- Fireworks entry conventions, 274–275
- font size, 43
- font styles, 43
- italic text, 160–161
- kerning, 45
- strikethrough text, 161
- teletype (typewriter style) text, 161
- underline text, 161

text slice, creating in Fireworks, 372–373
Text tool, Flash, 40–41
text wrapping, around images, 164–165
textures, fills, 297
Timelines
- add layer to button, 106
- add new layers, 102
- add/delete layers, 46–47
- assigning actions to a layer, 111
- button frames, 88
- create an animation by dragging a path, 244–245
- delete frames, 70–71
- Flash element, 4
- flashing animation, 246–247
- frame sizing, 67
- frame-by-frame animations, 72–75
- guide layers, 49
- guided layers, 49
- keyframe deletion, 71
- keyframes, 64–67
- layer position shuffling, 247
- mask layer, 49
- motion tweens, 78–83
- move/copy frames, 68–69
- normal layers, 49
- straight-line animations, 242–243
- symbol-edit mode, 59

Times New Roman, serif font type, 159
title <title> tag, 148
Title bar, Flash element, 4
titles, 145, 155

toolbars
- display/hide, 6
- Drawing, 4
- Standard (Main), 4

_top target, frame hyperlink, 215
transparency, symbol instance, 57
transparent background, 390
transparent colors, 391
triggers, validation, 205
typewriter style (teletype) text, creating, 161

U

underline text, creating, 161
undo last action
- described, 69, 189, 273
- History panel, 138

Uniform Resource Locator (URL)
- button assignments, 348–351
- image slice assignment, 374–375
- open a movie in browser window, 117

unit scales, change, 109
Up state
- buttons, 89
- described, 342

update
- buttons, 352–353
- slices, 376–377

upload files
- remote site, 254–255
- stopping transfer in progress, 255

URL Library panel, 351, 375

V

Validate Form behavior, 204
validation
- browser triggers, 205
- forms, 204–205

values, brightness/contrast, 321
vector graphics, import, 60–61
Verdana, sans-serif font type, 159
vertical alignments, Flash objects, 39
vertical lines
- drawing in Fireworks, 289
- drawing techniques, 15

views, check optimization settings, 388
visibility, layer settings, 241

W

WAV sound file format, 100
waveforms, Flash, 104–105
Web 216, Internet graphics, 389
Web pages
- background color guidelines, 281
- background images, 168–169
- creating, 144
- file organization guidelines, 173
- font style selections, 158–159
- forms, 194–205
- framesets, 206–217
- headings, 154–155
- hyperlinks, 172–181
- image insertion, 162–163
- indents, 157
- line breaks, 156
- multimedia insertion, 170–171
- naming conventions, 145
- navigation bars, 177
- open existing, 142–143
- paragraph alignments, 152–153
- revert to last saved version, 147
- save, 146–147
- size images, 166–167
- split into frames, 206
- tables, 182–193
- text emphasis, 160–161
- text wrapping around images, 164–165
- title creation, 145
- transparency uses, 391

Web servers
- download files from, 256–257
- FTP logs, 257
- log off time settings, 253
- stop file transfer in progress, 255
- upload files, 254–255

Web-safe colors, 299
WebSnap Adaptive, Internet graphic colors, 389
Window menu, switch between open files, 7
windows, open/close, 5
Windows AVI video file, frame rate guidelines, 63
Windows PC
- Dreamweaver startup, 134
- open/close windows, 5
- remote site setup, 250–251
- Web-safe colors, 299

wizards, Link, 348–351
work area, Flash element, 4

Z

Z-indexes, layer position, 247

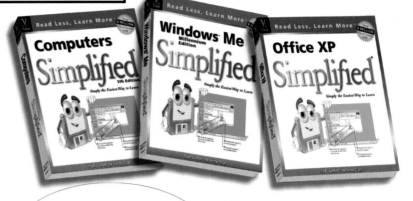

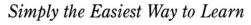